Exposure Therapy

Peter Neudeck • Hans-Ulrich Wittchen
Editors

Exposure Therapy

Rethinking the Model – Refining the Method

Springer

Editors
Peter Neudeck
Praxis für Verhaltenstherapie
Follerstr. 64
50676 Cologne
Germany

Hans-Ulrich Wittchen
Institut für Klinische Psychologie und Psychotherapie
Technische Universität Dresden
Chemnitzer Str. 46
01187 Dresden
Germany

ISBN 978-1-4614-3341-5 e-ISBN 978-1-4614-3342-2
DOI 10.1007/978-1-4614-3342-2
Springer New York Dordrecht Heidelberg London

Library of Congress Control Number: 2012937869

Printed on acid-free paper

Springer is part of Springer Science+Business Media (www.springer.com)

Barbara, Jakob, Johann, and Josef Neudeck
With love and gratefulness

Preface

Exposure therapy is well regarded as a powerful therapeutic agent in the treatment of phobias and anxiety disorders. It is also one of the most empirically supported treatments for anxiety disorders. Over the years, exposure therapy has undergone a number of transformations, from its early form of systematic desensitization, to flooding therapy, to the combination with cognitive therapy. Significant recent advances in the areas of cognition, fear learning, neuroscience, and acceptance based approaches have led to further shifts in the conceptualization and delivery of exposure therapy, as a science-based model of clinical practice. The fundamentals of exposure therapy and the latest science-based developments in its optimization are the topics of this volume. Thus, this volume provides the most up-to-date overview of the mechanisms and implementation of exposure therapy for anxiety and related disorders, proving an invaluable resource to both the researcher and the clinician.

The volume contains four parts. The first part covers the theoretical and formal aspects of exposure therapy, including the ethics of exposure therapy, and the fear learning and neurobiology of extinction and its application to exposure therapy. The second part covers the application of exposure therapy in a number of ways, including in children, the use of interoceptive exposure to feared bodily sensations, and the incorporation of exposure within acceptance-based approaches to behavioral therapy, within schema therapy, and within the cognitive behavioral analysis system of psychotherapy. The third part covers imaginal exposure in terms of the state of the art, the role of anxiety-control strategies, and application to worry and to body image and health-related distress. The fourth part covers cognitive interventions and anxiety-control strategies, including the value of the therapist, the combination of cognitive strategies with exposure, the role of safety behaviors, and the importance of safety when conducting exposure.

Exposure was first formally instituted as a treatment in the context of systematic desensitization. Wolpe (1958) attributed anxiety reduction to counterconditioning or reciprocal inhibition, and thus employed relaxation as a response antagonistic to anxiety in the imagined presence of anxiety-provoking stimuli. At least two developments challenged premises of reciprocal inhibition. First, graduated imaginal exposure was shown to be equally effective whether combined with relaxation training or not (e.g., McGlynn, Solomon, & Barrios, 1979). Also, when relaxation did enhance the efficacy of imaginal systematic desensitization, its effectiveness was attributed to enhanced vividness of imagery, which was associated with *increased* autonomic arousal (e.g., Levin & Gross, 1985). Obviously, the effects were at odds with the intended purpose of relaxation which was to provide a physiological response that was antagonistic to anxious arousal. A second challenge to reciprocal inhibition came from evidence for the efficacy of flooding therapy, involving prolonged and continuous exposure to highly anxiety-provoking stimuli until fear responses decline (e.g., Miller, 2002). Flooding therapy is commonly used in exposure to traumatic images for post-traumatic stress disorder, obsessional content in obsessive-compulsive disorder, and is sometimes used for in-vivo exposure to feared situations for panic disorder and agoraphobia.

Subsequently, habituation was evoked as an explanatory model for systematic desensitization by researchers in the 1960s and 1970s. Habituation seemed appropriate since it refers to reduction in response strength with repeated stimulus presentations, and since self-reported fear and physiological arousal most often decline within and across exposure occasions. The very influential emotional processing theory (Foa & Kozak, 1986; Foa & McNally, 1996) emphasized mechanisms of habituation but not in isolation and rather as a precursor to cognitive correction. That is, habituation was purported to form the basis for long term learning involving changes in "meaning," or lowered probability of harm (i.e., risk) and lessened negativity (i.e., valence) of the stimulus. Emotional processing theory guided clinicians to focus on the initial elevation of fear followed by within- and between-session reductions in fear as signs of treatment success. Although enticing in its face validity, support for the theory has been inconsistent at best (Craske et al., 2008). Rather, the evidence suggests that the amount by which fear habituates from the beginning to the end of an exposure practice (i.e., within-session habituation) is not a good predictor of overall outcomes, and that evidence for between-session habituation is mixed (Craske et al., 2008). An alternative model that derives from cognitive therapy focuses on the cognitive correction component without depending on fear habituation (Salkovskis 1999). Both of these models are reviewed in this volume (Koerner & Fracalanza).

However, the most significant advances of late have derived from the science of extinction-based learning and memory (as covered by Urcelay; Leueken and Maslowski; and Hofmann, Gutner, and Asnaani, in this volume). The evidence from this body of research suggests that the mechanism that is central to extinction learning is inhibitory in nature, at both associative and neurobiological levels. That is, extinction is believed to be mediated by learning an inhibitory set of expectancies regarding the feared stimulus and by enhancing inhibitory neural regulation of excitatory pathways. Thus, the field is shifting toward ways of enhancing inhibitory learning (Craske et al., 2008).

One example of enhancing inhibitory learning is the prevention or removal of "safety signals" or "safety behaviors," as described in this volume (Telch). Common safety signals and behaviors for clients who have an anxiety disorder are the presence of another person, therapists, medications, or food or drink. In the experimental literature, safety signals alleviate distress in the short term, but when they are no longer present, the fear returns, an effect that may derive in part from interference with the development of inhibitory associations. In phobic samples, the availability and use of safety signals and behaviors has been shown to be detrimental to exposure therapy, whereas instructions to refrain from using safety behaviors improved outcomes. However, recent data suggest a benefit to the initial inclusion and then weaning of safety signals to enhance the acceptability of exposure therapy.

Another example derives from evidence for fear extinction to be weakened by antagonists of the glutamate receptors in the amygdala, and evidence for D-*cycloserine to* enhance extinction in animal studies and result in less fear at follow-up, after exposure therapy for specific human fears. This body of research, reviewed by Hofmann, Gutner, and Asnaani in this volume, represents one of the best examples of translational neuroscience. Other examples include the use of propranolol (Kindt, Soeter, & Vervliet, 2009; Soeter & Kindt, 2010; Brunet et al., 2008) and preexposure to the conditional stimulus, prior to or during extinction, to allow memory reconsolidation in order to weaken fear memories (Monfils, Cowansage, Klann, & LeDoux, 2009; Schiller et al., 2010). Each approach, however, has some limitations (Craske, Liao, Brown, & Vervliet, Submitted for publication).

Other strategies that derive from models of inhibitory learning and inhibitory regulation include using multiple contexts throughout exposure therapy to offset context renewal following completion of exposure therapy. This strategy has been shown to reduce the return of fear following completion of exposure therapy. Additional strategies under investigation include retrieval cues to retrieve exposure-based memories, and variability throughout exposure to enhance the storage and retrieval of exposure-based learning (see Craske et al., Submitted for publication).

Aside from the developments deriving from the science of fear learning and memory, other research continues to explore the role of coping skills as augmenters of exposure therapy (as described by Koerner and Fracalanza, Ramnero; and Davlos and Whittal, in this volume). Coping skills traditionally include cognitive restructuring and either breathing retraining and/or relaxation. Presumably, the effects of exposure are augmented by applying the skills (e.g., by disputing the probability of a harmful outcome while being exposed to a feared situation and by regulating dysregulated physiology). However, the evidence for actual augmentation using these coping skills is limited, and what does exist suggests null effects. In other words, recent meta-analyses fail to show differences in effect sizes when exposure therapy is presented primarily in isolation or in combination with coping skills (e.g., Norton & Price, 2007). Furthermore, dismantling studies most often show no difference in outcome from exposure therapy alone or in combination with either cognitive restructuring or somatic coping (see Longmore & Worrell, 2007; Meuret, Wolitzky-Taylor, Twohig, & Craske, in press). Nonetheless, coping skills are typically employed, and are believed to enhance the acceptability of exposure therapy. Chapters in this volume consider the role of anxiety-control strategies (see Koerner & Fracalanza in this volume) and cognitive strategies (see Ramnero; and Davlos & Whittal, in this volume) in the context of exposure.

The role of acceptance-based approaches has begun to be explored (as described by Gloster et al. in this volume) as an alternative to traditional coping skills approaches for exposure therapy. One such approach is Acceptance and Commitment Therapy (ACT) where the goal of behavioral change is to engage in actions that are consistent with life values, which is aided by mindfulness and acceptance, without attempts to reduce fear. The results from randomized controlled trials of ACT are promising (e.g., Forman et al., 2007). Also, evidence already exists showing that brief training in emotional acceptance lowers distress and increases tolerance for experimentally induced anxiety symptoms in individuals with anxiety disorders (Levitt, Brown, Orsillo, & Barlow, 2004). Thus, acceptance may prove particularly useful for enhancing engagement in exposure therapy, especially for patients who do not respond well to traditional coping skills. Moreover, the degree to which exposure is consistent with the Cognitive Behavioral Analysis System of Psychotherapy, another third generation behavior therapy that draws from Skinnerian learning theory, cognitive development and person by environment interactions, is addressed in this volume (see Neudeck and colleagues in this volume). Furthermore, the role of exposure within more psychodynamically oriented treatments such as Schema therapy, where the emphasis is less upon habituation or extinction during exposure therapy, and more upon changing the meaning of emotional triggers through emotional restructuring, is discussed as well (see Jacob, Arntz, and Freidberg in this volume).

Interoceptive exposure, or the exposure to feared bodily sensations, which was originally developed specifically for panic disorder but can be extended to other anxiety disorders also involving fears of bodily sensations (e.g., social anxiety and PTSD) is covered by Gerlach in this volume. Other chapters in this volume address the all important fundamentals of exposure therapy, such as the ethics (Deacon) and safety (Neuner) of exposure therapy, the role of imaginal exposure (Hoyer & Schonfeld, and Hoyer & Beesdo-Baum), the importance of therapist-directed exposure (Lang & Helbig-Lang), exposure therapy for children (Davis, Whiting, and May), the extension of exposure therapy to other disorders, such as hypochondriasis and body dysmorphic disorder (Weck, Ritter, & Stangier), and the dissemination of exposure therapy in practice (Neudeck & Einsle).

In summary, exposure therapy is a highly effective therapeutic tool, and an exemplar of the scientist practitioner model. Advances in the areas of learning, memory, cognition, and neurobiology are continuously applied to improve the outcomes. This volume stands in the tradition of two influential concepts books on exposure therapy published in the 1980s (Hand & Wittchen 1986, 1988; Neudeck & Wittchen, 2004) and represents a scholarly overview of these latest advances along with the most important fundamentals of exposure therapy.

Department of Psychology
Department of Psychiatry and Biobehavioral Sciences
University of California
Los Angeles, CA, USA

Michelle G. Craske

References

Brunet, A., Orr, S. P., Tremblay, J., Robertson, K., Nader, K., & Pitman, R. (2008). Effect of post-retrieval propranolol on psychophysiologic responding during subsequent script-driven traumatic imagery in post-traumatic stress disorder. *Journal of Psychiatric Research, 42*, 503–506.

Craske, M. G., Kircanski, K., Zelikowsky, M., Mystkowski, J., Chowdhury, N., & Baker, A. (2008). Optimizing inhibitory learning during exposure therapy. *Behaviour Research and Therapy, 46*, 5–27.

Craske, M. G., Liao, B., Brown, L. & Vervliet, B. Role of inhibition in exposure therapy. (submitted for publication).

Foa, E. B., & Kozak, M. J. (1986). Emotional processing of fear: exposure to corrective information. *Psychological Bulletin, 99*, 20–35.

Foa, E. B., & McNally, R. J. (1996). Mechanisms of change in exposure therapy. In R. M. Rapee (Ed.), *Current controversies in the anxiety disorders* (pp. 214–227). New York, NY: Guilford Press.

Forman, E. M., Herbert, J. D., Moitra, E., Yeomans, P. D., & Gellar, P. A. (2007). A randomized controlled effectiveness trial of acceptance and commitment therapy and cognitive therapy for anxiety and depression. *Behavior Modification, 31*, 772–799.

Hand, I., & Wittchen, H.-U. (1986). *Panic and Phobias I: Empirical Evidence of Theoretical Models and Long term Effects of Behavioral Treatments*. New York: Springer.

Hand, I., & Wittchen, H.-U. (1988). *Panic and Phobias 2: Treatments and Variables Affecting Course and Outcome*. London: Springer.

Kindt, M., Soeter, M., & Vervliet, B. (2009). Beyond extinction: erasing human fear responses and preventing the return of fear. *Nature Neuroscience, 12*, 256–258.

Levin, R. B., & Gross, A. M. (1985). The role of relaxation in systematic desensitization. *Behaviour Research and Therapy, 23*, 187–196.

Levitt, J. T., Brown, T. A., Orsillo, S. M., & Barlow, D. H. (2004). The effects of acceptance versus suppression of emotion on subjective and psychophysiological response to carbon dioxide challenge in patients with panic disorder. *Behavior Therapy, 35*, 747–766.

Longmore, R. J., & Worrell, M. (2007). Do we need to challenge thoughts in cognitive behavior therapy? *Clinical Psychology Review, 27*, 173–187.

McGlynn, F. D., Solomon, G. S., & Barrios, B. A. (1979). Graded imagination and relaxation as components of experimental desensitization: a psychophysiological evaluation. *Journal of Clinical Psychology, 35*, 542–546.

Meuret, A.-E., Wolitzky-Taylor, K., Twohig, M. P., & Craske, M. G. (in press). Coping skills and exposure therapy in panic disorder and agoraphobia: latest advances and future directions. *Behavior Therapy.* (in press).

Miller, C. (2002). in *Flooding*, ed. by M. Herson, W. Sledge. Encyclopedia of Psychotherapy, vol. 1 (Elsevier Science, New York), pp. 809–813.
Monfils, M. H., Cowansage, K. K., Klann, E., & LeDoux, J. E. (2009). Extinction–reconsolidation boundaries: key to persistent attenuation of fear memories. *Science, 324*, 951–955.
Neudeck, P., & Wittchen, H.-U. (2004). *Konfrontationstherapie bei psychischen Störungen: Theorie und Praxis*. Göttingen: Hogrefe.
Norton, P. J., & Price, E. C. (2007). A meta-analytic review of adult cognitive-behavioral treatment outcome across the anxiety disorders. *Journal of Nervous and Mental Disease, 195*, 521–531.
Salkovskis, P. (1999). Understanding and treating obsessive-compulsive disorder. *Behaviour Research and Therapy, 37*, S29–S52.
Schiller, D., Monfils, M. H., Raio, C. M., Johnson, D. C., LeDoux, J. E., & Phelps, E. A. (2010). Preventing the return of fear in humans using reconsolidation update mechanisms. *Nature, 463*, 49–53.
Soeter, M., & Kindt, M. (2010). Dissociating response systems: erasing fear from memory. *Neurobiology of Learning and Memory, 94*, 30–41.
Wolpe, J. (1958). *Psychotherapy by reciprocal inhibition*. Stanford: Stanford University Press.

Acknowledgments of the Editors

We wish to thank our friends and colleagues who spend their precious time to discuss and suggest ideas to improve the quality of our project. We are grateful to all the authors who contributed their chapters in time. We particularly appreciate the efforts and inspiration of Susanne Knappe (PhD) from the Institute of Clinical Psychology and Psychotherapy of the Technische Universitaet Dresden who helped us completing this edition.

Contents

Chapter 1
Introduction: Rethinking the Model - Refining the Method

Peter Neudeck and Hans-Ulrich Wittchen

Dr. Peter Neudeck is a licensed psychotherapist specialized in cognitive-behavioral therapy. He has been working both in clinical and research positions and has established private practices for psychotherapy in Berlin and Cologne. He is also a lecturer and supervisor for graduate and postgraduate CBT-psychotherapy programs across Germany. He recently received further professional development in CBASP and systemic therapy. His main research activities include psychobiology and psychotherapy of anxiety disorders in exposure based treatments. He has released numerous publications on exposure techniques in mental disorders.

P. Neudeck (✉)
Praxis für Verhaltenstherapie, Follerstr. 64, D-50676 Köln/Cologne, Germany
e-mail: peterneudeck@gmx.de

H.-U. Wittchen
Institute of Clinical Psychology and Psychotherapy, Technische Universitaet Dresden, Chemnitzer Strasse 46, 01187 Dresden, Germany
e-mail: wittchen@psychologie.tu-dresden.de

P. Neudeck and H.-U. Wittchen (eds.), *Exposure Therapy: Rethinking the Model – Refining the Method*, DOI 10.1007/978-1-4614-3342-2_1,

Professor Hans-Ulrich Wittchen is director and CEO of the Institute of Clinical Psychology and Psychotherapy at the Technische Universitaet Dresden, including the Center of Clinical Epidemiology and Longitudinal Studies (CELOS) and the Psychotherapy Outpatient Center. He is and has been principal investigator and co-investigator of many national and international research programs and large-scale epidemiological studies. His work encompasses a wide range of etiological-pathogenetic, family-genetic, experimental, clinical, and epidemiological studies with a focus on prospective-longitudinal studies in addiction, anxiety, mood, and somatic disorders.

1.1 Why a Book on Exposure Therapy?

Exposure therapy is one of the most robust and most effective standard procedures among the behavioral psychotherapy variants. Initially frequently used as a stand-alone treatment particular for anxiety disorders, it is nowadays typically used in the context of a conceptually wider framework of cognitive-behavioral therapies (CBT) in a variety of formats and techniques. Over the past two decades and as a result of the increasing emphasis on cognitive factors, however, exposure therapy and its core principles have also become increasingly diffuse. Being usually embedded in complex CBT procedures, and frequently used interchangeably with the term cognitive-behavior therapy, principles and unique procedures of exposure therapy appear to be more and more confuse, particularly when conceptually important boundaries between cognitive, affective, and behavioral components in the process of intervention have become blurred. We feel that this development is threatening to the integrity of exposure therapy as a scientifically based, highly effective psychological treatment approach. We also see the risk that the apparent lack of attention devoted to exposure therapy and its foundations might result in a deterioration of the effectiveness of behavioral psychotherapies.

The main goal of this book is to stimulate the field to shift attention toward reconsidering the scientific basis of exposure therapy, consolidating the basic models and principles by incorporating novel scientific evidence and to start work into the core questions we need to address, namely "Why does exposure therapy work? Why does cognitive-behavior therapy work?" There have been significant developments in recent years that further endorsed our motivation for this book: First, methods of exposure therapy have been expanded to a wide range of disorders beyond the anxiety spectrum, including body dysmorphic disorder and hypochondriasis. Secondly, exposure techniques also play an important role in the so-called "third wave therapies" (ACT, Schema Therapy, CBASP). Thirdly, a tremendous amount of evidence has been accumulated regarding core aspects of exposure therapies such as ethics, control strategies, and the role of cognitive interventions. And fourth, new data have become available regarding the theoretical foundations and assumed mechanisms of action (i.e., habituation, extinction learning) of exposure therapy.

The aim of this book is to provide practitioners and scientists with a critical review of these developments by state-of-the-art contributions of several outstanding international experts. Given the huge amount of peer-reviewed experimental papers, findings of randomized clinical trials, reviews, and meta-analyses on exposure therapy every year, it was important for us to provide a forum where different approaches (i.e., concerning dissemination in clinical practice, cognitive enhancers, and cognitive interventions, anxiety control strategies) are presented and critically discussed. Although exposure therapy has a long tradition among the behavioral approaches and is considered a "standard procedure," there are many unresolved questions. This book provides an up-to-date appraisal of these issues from various perspectives and highlights the need to rethink the model of exposure therapy.

1.2 The Challenges

A core challenge in exposure therapy and CBT alike refers to the unresolved question, why these therapies work and what are the basic mechanisms of action involved. When we examine highly effective traditional treatment packages like the Panic Control Treatment (PCT) or the Mastery of Your Panic Treatment for anxiety disorders as an example, the dilemma is evident. These packages contain so many elements that it seems a daunting task to find out what actually contributes to successful treatment. The PCT treatment for example combines education, cognitive interventions, relaxation, controlled breathing procedures, and exposure techniques, usually delivered in 11 or 12 weekly sessions. Two techniques are used to change maladaptive fear and anxiety behaviors in particular: The exposure to internal cues (interoceptive exposure) and the exposure to external cues (situational exposure). As Hofmann and Spiegel (1999) pointed out, PCT does not include systematic in situ exposure; for patients with significant situational avoidance a supplement was, however, developed later on. One might ask a whole series of questions, such as: What are the ingredients or core elements of exposure therapy in such complex packages?

What exactly is exposed, how and when? What are the assumed and essential mechanisms of action during in-situ exposure and what makes the difference to interoceptive exposure?

When considering mechanisms of action more closely, it seems to be evident that there are likely many core candidates that we need to look at; and the list of potentially relevant explanatory concepts and models is quite long: From the historically relevant concept of reciprocal inhibition as the working mechanism of systematic desensitization, over Mowrers Two-Factor Theory of Fear Acquisition, Lang's Bioinformational Theory, Rachman's Emotional Processing Theory, Foa and Kozak's Emotional Processing Model, the Cognitive Approach of Perceived Control and Self-Efficacy to more recent neural networking and connectionists models (Tyron, 2005). Each of these theoretical approaches makes contributions to explain changes according to exposure procedures, although the theoretical frameworks of these explanations considerably differ to a substantial amount. It should be noted, however, that most of these models also add more or less to the effects of cognitive interventions in CBT. Thus, these models are not specific and fail to give us a consistent and solid clarification of why exposure therapy works within and outside the context of CBT.

1.3 Purple Hat Therapy

Rosen and Davison (2003) illustrated their listing of empirical supported treatments with an intervention called "Purple Hat Therapy" (PHT). Therein, the patient is asked to wear a purple hat while exposed to a feared stimulus. PHT is more effective then the control treatment due to exposure to the feared situation. The founders and future trainers of the Purple Hat "Therapy", however, will most likely attribute the effectiveness to the purple hat the patient wears during the exposure sessions. Hereafter, special trainings and courses in the PHT and a series of papers about PHT are most likely to be published. Thinking and speculating further, one might assume that the basic mechanism of action of exposure therapy is change of the patients' cognitions. In consequence, the main ingredient of exposure therapy would be that the therapist focuses on the problem-solving skills of the patient, while exposing him to an avoided stimulus. From this context, one might ask: What is the Purple Hat then?

When looking into clinical studies on the effectiveness of exposure therapy in the last decade, methodological problems are evident stressing this issue of the "Purple Hat." For example, Paunovic and Öst (2001) designed a trial to investigate the comparative effectiveness of exposure therapy and CBT in the treatment of posttraumatic stress disorder and found no differences between the treatments on any measure. In the method section of their paper, the procedure of exposure was described as *a graduated confrontation "with anxiety-provoking trauma-related images and situations with the help of the therapist"* (p. 1188). No information is, however, provided about the rationale and context of the procedure. No patient will agree to expose himself/herself to feared stimuli without any prior instruction or the provision of knowledge about the purpose of such a procedure. So is the Purple Hat hiding here? In fact, the CBT procedure in this study was to identify intrusive thoughts and catastrophic interpretations at the first step. The second step was then to recognize faulty thinking and to challenge catastrophic thoughts, followed disputing the thoughts and generating non-catastrophic alternatives (step 3). The final step was to proof the validity of the patient's hypothesis, with "behavioral experiments." After six sessions, the "exposure therapy" started and ran parallel to the cognitive therapy. The authors write: *"Exposure was conducted similarly as described above. The main difference was that there was less time for exposure because cognitive interventions and controlled breathing were also included."* (p. 1189).

So what were the ingredients of the cognitive therapy arm in this study? Problem solving, behavioral experiments, disputing, exposure, and breathing control. In comparison, the ingredients of the exposure therapy condition were imagined and in-vivo exposure.

And what were the *active ingredients* in the two treatment conditions? Did cognitive therapy work through the problem-solving technique or through the behavioral experiments, etc? Did exposure work through controlled breathing? And furthermore: Do behavioral experiments work because they induce a change of beliefs or through exposure?

Hard to say—isn't it? Let us take another example: Investigating the effects of CBT compared with traditional behavior therapy, namely exposure and response prevention (ERP) in group psychotherapy for obsessive–compulsive disorder, McLean et al. (2001) described the CBT condition as follows: *"Behavioral experiments had similar features to ERP; however, the function was different. In ERP, the purpose of repeated exposure was habituation. Behavioral experiments that were completed in the CBT condition were always done to test an appraisal."* (p. 210). One might argue that the difference between the conditions was the introduction; so the core component in both treatments was "exposure." The examples above are representative of methodological problems we find in many clinical treatment studies.

A third example: A recent review of behavioral experiments vs. exposure alone in the treatment of anxiety disorders (McMillan & Lee, 2010) comprised 14 clinical trials. The authors state that they *"found first evidence, that setting up exposure as a cognitive test may be more effective than exposure in which this does not occur"* (p. 474). A notable limitation of the studies reviewed was that the duration of the exposure itself was very short (i.e., 5 min, Kim, 2005; Wells et al., 1995). Only two of the 14 studies used a single duration of more than 30 min for each exposure session (which sounds more reasonable and state of the art to us). The authors concluded: *"There is a need for studies using brief interventions in which differences are limited to the use of exposure as a cognitive test vs. exposure in which that cognitive component is absent, and in which the duration of exposure is substantially longer than that used in the majority of studies reviewed here."* (McMillan & Lee, 2010; p. 475). Furthermore, they suggested variables which need to be changed and tested in future studies, such as the content of the cognitive rationale, or the presence and absence of the therapist and his role for modifying the situation. The authors interpreted their findings as being contrary to Langmore and Worrell's review (Langmore

& Worell, 2007), who concluded that there is no need to challenge thoughts in CBT. McGillan and Lee suggested that exposure might be more effective when there is a challenge in cognitions such as in behavioral experiments.

So here we stand-alone and nude regarding behavioral experiments. How can a method "A" be more effective when adding an ingredient of method "B," albeit not knowing through what method "B" works? And by the way, how do behavioral experiments work if anything: through a change of cognitions or exposure or in some way by both?

Is there a way forward to solve the puzzle and to specifically identify the active ingredients of exposure therapy as well as their role in CBT? One, though imperfect way, has been recently exemplified by a German multicenter study: "Psychological Treatment for Panic Disorder with Agoraphobia: A Randomized Controlled Trial to Examine the Role of Therapist-Guided Exposure in situ in CBT" (Gloster et al., 2011; also see Lang & Helbig-Lang in this book). In this study, two identical treatment packages were compared and only one variable differed between them, namely the absence or presence of the therapist. The introduction of the rational, the frequency of exposure etc was completely equal in both treatment conditions. However, we are aware of putative limits of randomized clinical trials. Albeit thoughtfully developed, they are not really suitable to capture the true complexity of the problem. But at least it is a very first start. Clearly we need to think about novel designs and approaches beyond the traditional study designs, in order to be able to collect data and to develop more specific hypotheses regarding the basic elements, ingredients, and mechanisms of exposure therapy.

This immediately brings up the question how to conceptualize and define exposure therapy. For this book, we suggest the following working definition for exposure: *"Exposure is a component of a treatment package in which the patient is educated about the disorder, prepared and provided with a rationale of the therapeutic change, and exposed to avoided and feared external and internal stimuli."*

The treatment package can be purely behavioral, cognitive–behavioral, rational–emotive, dialectic–behavioral, systemic or interpersonal. Given the conceptual problems discussed above, it makes no sense in our perspective to compare "CBT treatment packages" against "exposure packages." It is like testing apples and oranges. We strongly recommend testing the components of the treatment packages irrespective of their label.

Therefore a standard of components used in such treatment packages is absolutely mandatory. We hypothesize at least the following components to be absolutely necessary:

- Psychoeducation about the disorder
- A patient model of history and maintenance of the disorder
- A cue hierarchy
- A well-described model of how and what kind of rational is provided
- Finally a list of the feared consequences and the avoidance behavior

For the exposure procedure we further need commonly agreed standards of what constitutes exposure, what the therapists is allowed to do (and what not), as well as standards and quality-assured principles of adequate duration, frequency, and application of exposure techniques. Exposure techniques include:

- In-vivo (in-situ) exposure: gradually or massed
- Interoceptive exposure: primary or secondary
- Imaginary exposure: primary, secondary, and preliminary

What about behavioral experiments then? To give a simple answer: a behavioral experiment is not an exposure technique. Studies comparing exposure techniques with behavioral experiments show that there are simply too many confounders, such as the specific instructions to patients, duration, and purpose of exposure or the incorporation of cognitive elements. Because of these many confounders, it is highly questionable whether behavioral experiments could be labeled with sufficient integrity as a form of exposure. Hence, it makes little sense to compare these techniques to each other, but it is of great importance to study them in isolation and separately in order to answer questions like: What works in behavioral experiments and why? Again, it is important to compare different behavioral experiments against each other, instead of comparisons of behavioral experiments with exposure techniques.

Some of the questions raised seem to be very academic, and several seem to move in circles. Past research, for example, was unable to determine what comes first, the cognitive change or the physiological habituation; similarly, studies were also unable to answer the question of what might be the main effect. Maybe it is more important in the future to search for the most effective variant of exposure than to invest to no avail in the search for the "blue flower." For clinical practitioners, it is obvious that a patient habituates during an exposure session and it is no surprise that the patient has changed some of his automatic thoughts or maladaptive appraisals after two or three exposure sessions. In their book "Exposure Therapy for Anxiety" (Abramovitz, Deacon, & Whiteside, 2010) the authors write: *"Specifically therapists are understandably reticent to adopt a treatment plan that deliberately (if only temporally) increases a patient's already distressing anxiety. Consequently, a therapist would only select this treatment if she believed that it was the best method for helping their patients in the long run."* For practitioners, it is more important to get information about what in fact helps the patients. Should they spend a lot of time on explaining the rationale or is there just a little effect? Should they allow anxiety-control strategies such as distraction, or does this reduce the effectiveness? Taking this into account, future investigations on exposure need to search for the important elements of the treatment. In this book, you will hopefully find some of the elements we expect to be confirmed as indispensable for successful exposure.

References

Abramovitz, J. S., Deacon, B. J., & Whiteside, S. P. H. (2010). *Exposure therapy for anxiety: Principles and practice*. New York: Guilford.

Gloster, A. T., Wittchen, H.-U., Einsle, F., Lang, T., Helbig-Lang, S., & Fydrich, T. (2011). Psychological treatment for panic disorder with agoraphobia: A randomized controlled trial to examine the role of therapist-guided exposure in situ in CBT. *Journal of Consulting and Clinical Psychology, 79*(3), 406–420.

Hofmann, S. G., & Spiegel, D. A. (1999). Panic control treatment and its applications. *Journal of Psychotherapy Practice and Research, 8*(1), 3–11.

Kim, E.-J. (2005). The effect of the decreased safety behaviors on anxiety and negative thoughts in social phobics. *Journal of Anxiety Disorders, 19*(1), 69–86.

Langmore, R. J., & Worell, M. (2007). Do we need to challenge thoughts in cognitive behavior therapy? *Clinical Psychology Review, 27*, 173–187.

McLean, P. D., Whittal, M. L., Thordarson, D. S., Taylor, S., Söchting, I., Koch, W. J., et al. (2001). Cognitive versus behavior therapy in the group treatment of obsessive compulsive disorder. *Journal of Consulting and Clinical Psychology, 69*(2), 205–214.

McMillan, D., & Lee, R. (2010). A systematic review of behavioral experiments vs. exposure alone in the treatment of anxiety disorders: A case of exposure while wearing the emperor's new clothes? *Clinical Psychology Review, 330*(5), 467–478.

Paunovic, N., & Öst, L. G. (2001). Cognitive-behavior therapy vs exposure therapy in the treatment of PTSD in refugees. *Behaviour Research and Therapy, 39*, 1183–1197.

Rosen, G. M., & Davison, G. C. (2003). Psychology should list empirically supported principles of change (ESPs) and not credential trademarked therapies or other treatment packages. *Behavior Modification, 27*(3), 300–312.

Tyron, W. W. (2005). Possible mechanisms for why desensitization and exposure therapy work. *Clinical Psychology Review, 25*, 67–95.

Wells, A., Clark, D. M., Salkovskis, P., Ludgate, J., Hackmann, A., & Gelder, M. (1995). Social phobia: The role of in-situation safety behaviors in maintaining anxiety and negative beliefs. *Behavior Therapy, 26*(1), 153–161.

Chapter 2
The Ethics of Exposure Therapy for Anxiety Disorders

Brett Deacon

Brett Deacon is Associate Professor in Psychology at the University of Wyoming, and specializes in the nature and treatment of anxiety disorders.

B. Deacon (✉)
Department of Psychology, University of Wyoming, 1000 E. University Ave., Laramie, WY 82071, USA
e-mail: bdeacon@uwyo.edu

P. Neudeck and H.-U. Wittchen (eds.), *Exposure Therapy: Rethinking the Model – Refining the Method*, DOI 10.1007/978-1-4614-3342-2_2,

2.1 The Ethics of Exposure Therapy

Ethical principles dictate that therapists avoid harming their patients. The admonition against harming patients appears twice in the American Psychological (2002) ethics code, both as a general principle (Principle A: Beneficence and Nonmaleficence; psychologists "take care to do no harm" and "safeguard the welfare and rights" of their patients) and as an ethical standard in human relations (Sect. 3.04; "Psychologists take reasonable steps to avoid harming their patients/clients" and "minimize harm where it is foreseeable and unavoidable"). Despite its safety and tolerability, the unique requirements of exposure therapy sometimes place patients at greater emotional and/or physical risks than many traditional forms of verbal psychotherapy. For example, exposure can involve the remote but real potential for harm when patients handle animals, touch "contaminated" objects such as garbage cans, and vividly recall traumatic memories. Does exposure therapy subject patients to an unacceptably high risk of harm? What are the ethical considerations associated with this treatment?

The effectiveness of exposure-based cognitive-behavioral therapy (CBT) is one of the great success stories in the history of mental health treatment. Hundreds of clinical trials and dozens of meta-analytic reviews have helped establish this treatment as the most empirically supported psychological intervention for the anxiety disorders (Deacon & Abramowitz, 2004; Olatunji, Cisler & Deacon, 2010). Exposure-based CBT approaches are prominently represented on the American Psychological Association's list of "well-established treatments" (Chambless & Ollendick, 2001). Clinical practice guidelines published by the American Psychiatric (2011) and the National Institute for Clinical Excellence (2011) recommend exposure-based CBT approaches as first-line anxiety treatments. An accumulating body of outcome studies suggests that the effectiveness of this approach when applied in community settings with real-world patients is comparable to its efficacy in highly controlled laboratory environments (Stewart & Chambless, 2009). Relative to pharmacotherapy, exposure-based therapy typically produces similar short-term benefit and superior long-term maintenance of treatment gains (e.g., Barlow, Gorman, Shear & Woods, 2000). Exposure therapy is also more cost-effective than pharmacotherapy (Heuzenroeder et al., 2004), more acceptable and preferable to patients and their caregivers (Brown, Deacon, Abramowitz & Whiteside, 2007; Deacon & Abramowitz, 2005), and results in less patient attrition (Huppert, Franklin, Foa & Davidson, 2003). Taken together, these observations make a strong case for exposure-based CBT as the treatment of choice for anxiety disorders. Indeed, this treatment may have more scientific support than any other psychotherapy of any kind, for any problem.

Yet despite its documented effectiveness, exposure therapy techniques are rarely used by practicing clinicians. To illustrate, Foy et al. (1996) reported that exposure therapy was used to treat fewer than 20% of 4,000 veterans with PTSD in the Veteran's Affairs healthcare system, and that it was the primary method of treatment in only 1% of cases. In a sample of over 800 licensed doctoral-level psychologists, Becker, Zayfert and Anderson (2004) found that fewer than 20% of respondents reported using exposure therapy to treat clients with posttraumatic stress disorder (PTSD). Indeed, exposure was not widely utilized even among trauma experts with specialized training in this approach. More broadly, the majority of patients with any anxiety disorder do not receive evidence-based psychotherapy (Stein et al., 2004); indeed, psychodynamic therapy is received as often as CBT (Goisman, Warshaw & Keller, 1999).

How can the widespread failure to disseminate exposure therapy to mental health professionals be explained? Certainly, exposure is hampered by the same set of barriers that obstruct the dissemination of evidence-based psychotherapies more generally. Examples include a lack of training opportunities in graduate and internship programs, a tendency to favor clinical judgment over evidence from randomized controlled trials in identifying effective therapeutic techniques, and the perception that clinical scientists working to disseminate evidence-based treatments have failed to attend to practitioner concerns (Gunter & Whittal, 2010). In addition to these more general reservations about evidence-based treatments, exposure therapy is subject to a potent set of treatment-specific concerns. It is commonplace to encounter therapists who fear that exposure will actively harm their patients, or that subjecting anxious individuals to their feared stimuli is tantamount to torture. As a result of such beliefs, even therapists who are aware of exposure's scientific support may reject it in favor of treatments they deem to be less aversive and more "humane". The all-too-common result of this misplaced compassion is the time, effort, financial expense, and continued emotional suffering associated with receiving inadequate treatment.

2.2 Beliefs About Exposure Therapy

Exposure therapy has a public relations problem with many in the field of psychotherapy (Olatunji, Deacon & Abramowitz, 2009; Richard & Gloster, 2007). Condemnation of exposure often stems from the fact that this intervention evokes distress (albeit temporary), rather than soothes it, as one might intuitively expect a treatment for anxiety to do. A closely-related concern is that through its power to elicit negative effect, exposure has the capacity to actively harm patients. More specific negative beliefs are identified below (Cook, Schnurr & Foa, 2004; Feeney, Hembree & Zoellner, 2003; Gunter & Whittal, 2010; Prochaska & Norcross, 1999; Rosqvist, 2005).

Negative therapist beliefs about exposure therapy for anxiety disorders

- Its ends do not justify its means
- It is rigid and insensitive to the individual needs of the patient
- It interferes with the therapeutic relationship
- It does not work for complex cases
- It is only effective in "ivory tower" research settings and its effects do not generalize to "real-world" clinical settings
- It involves impersonal techniques that are done "to," rather than "with," anxious individuals
- It exacerbates symptoms and causes high rates of attrition
- Patients are better off suffering from their anxiety disorder than undergoing this form of treatment

Given such negative and widespread beliefs about exposure, it is little wonder that this treatment is underutilized, even by practitioners who specialize in the treatment of anxiety (Becker et al., 2004). A more detailed consideration of a number of these negative beliefs about exposure appears below.

2.2.1 *Exposure Will Worsen a Patient's Symptoms*

Another undesirable outcome commonly attributed to exposure therapy is its perceived potential to worsen anxiety symptoms. This concern is sometimes voiced by therapists who believe that; for example, patients with PTSD will be "revictimized" by the process of reliving traumatic memories via imaginal exposure. Foa, Zoellner, Feeny, Hembree and Alvarez-Conrad (2002) directly investigated this issue by examining symptom exacerbation during the course of prolonged exposure. Although the majority of PTSD patients did not experience worsening of their symptoms, a temporary exacerbation following the start of imaginal exposure did occur in a minority of individuals. Importantly, patients whose symptoms initially worsened were not at increased risk of either attrition or failure to improve. Thus, symptom exacerbation during exposure was uncommon, short-lived, and of little prognostic value. Therapists who shun exposure therapy due to concerns about its capacity to make patients feel worse would do well to attend to this finding. The results of Foa et al. (2002) also support the practice of informing patients that exposure is likely to provoke temporary initial distress, but that this experience will eventually prove beneficial following repeated practice.

2.2.2 *Patients Will Drop-Out of Therapy*

Critics of exposure therapy often assume that such a presumably aversive treatment must result in unacceptably high drop-out rates in therapy. This assumption was tested by Hembree et al. (2003), who reviewed studies of prolonged exposure for PTSD (see chapter by Schönfeld & Hoyer in this volume), which is often considered the most difficult-to-tolerate application of exposure therapy. Combined results from 25 clinical trials yielded no significant differences in drop-out rates between prolonged exposure (20.6%), exposure combined with cognitive therapy or anxiety management (26.0%), and Eye Movement Desensitization and Reprocessing (18.9%). Hembree and Cahill (2007) noted that dropout rates for prolonged exposure for PTSD are comparable to those observed in exposure therapy with other anxiety disorders, and are lower than drop-out rates associated with psychotropic medications. Thus, the concern that exposure places patients at higher risk for attrition than other treatment approaches is not supported by the available evidence. The well-established efficacy and acceptability of exposure provides an object lesson in the resilience of anxious individuals, as well as a valuable counterpoint to the perception that patients with anxiety disorders are fragile and unable to cope with the requirements of exposure therapy.

2.2.3 *Patients Will Not Like Exposure Therapy*

Some therapists assume that their patients will dislike exposure therapy, and will instead prefer to undergo treatment that does not entail the distress associated with having to directly confront feared stimuli. This negative perception of exposure appears to pervade public sentiment as well. A study by Richard and Gloster (2007) presented undergraduates and outpatients in a university-based psychotherapy clinic with a series of vignettes describing the application of exposure techniques for different anxiety problems. Some techniques (e.g., interoceptive exposure for panic attacks, exposure and response prevention for OCD, imaginal exposure for PTSD) were perceived as unlikely to be helpful, unacceptable, and even unethical. Others, such as virtual reality exposure therapy for fears of flying, and gradual in-vivo exposure for social phobia, were viewed as more acceptable, helpful, and more ethical.

Fortunately, despite the reservations of some practitioners, exposure therapy appears to be held in generally high esteem by patients. Compared to pharmacotherapy, anxiety patients perceive exposure-based CBT as more credible, acceptable, and more likely to be effective in the long term (Deacon & Abramowitz, 2005; Norton, Allen & Hilton, 1983). The same can be said of parents of clinically anxious children (Brown et al., 2007). Moreover, exposure therapy is rated as at least as acceptable, ethical, and effective as cognitive therapy and relationship-oriented psychotherapy by undergraduate students and agoraphobic patients (Norton et al., 1983). Among patients completing exposure-based CBT for panic disorder, situational and interoceptive exposure are perceived as highly useful despite lower ratings for likeability (Cox, Fergus & Swinson, 1994). These findings suggest that therapist reservations about exposure therapy are not shared by most patients who receive this treatment. Why do therapists seem to overestimate the extent to which their patients will dislike exposure therapy? Richard and Gloster (2007) suggested that anxious patients might be less intimidated by the prospect of experiencing heightened anxiety during exposures because such symptoms are simply temporary exacerbations of familiar and long-standing emotional responses.

2.2.4 *Therapists Might Get Sued if They Use Exposure Techniques*

Clinicians who believe exposure to be inhumane, intolerably aversive, or potentially dangerous may also worry about the legal risks associated with the use of these techniques. They might think it is unwise to leave the office to conduct exposures, and have concerns about the types of exposure tasks patients are asked to complete.

In the author's experience, some supervisors and administrators have voiced such concerns, and in some cases have enforced restrictive policies (e.g., prohibiting clinicians from leaving the clinic with their patients) to minimize perceived legal risks. These reservations are typically based on a misunderstanding of exposure, its efficacy, tolerability, and the manner in which it is ethically and competently conducted. It is useful to consider that exposure merely provokes anxiety, which is no different than what patients are already experiencing, and part of the body's natural defense mechanism (i.e., the *fight or flight* response). In other words, anxiety is not inherently dangerous to the vast majority of people, and those who might be harmed from provoking physiologic arousal (e.g., individuals with severe asthma) are not candidates for exposure (see chapter by Einsle and Neudeck in this volume). As such, this treatment would seem to pose little risk for practicing clinicians.

Richard and Gloster (2007) examined the legal risks associated with exposure therapy by searching the legal record for court cases involving this treatment. Their exhaustive search criteria did not reveal a single instance of litigation related to exposure. Similarly, none of the 84 members of the Anxiety Disorders Association of America surveyed by Richard and Gloster reported knowledge of any legal action or ethics complaints regarding exposure. This survey approach, however, cannot rule out the possibility that relevant complaints have been filed, but dismissed or settled out of court. Yet the available evidence suggests that exposure therapy is acceptably safe and tolerable, and that it carries little risk of actively harming patients (or their therapists).

2.3 Strategies for Minimizing Risk

When conducted properly, exposure therapy is an acceptably safe, tolerable, and effective treatment for anxiety disorders. However, exposure therapy inherently involves more risk than most psychological treatments, and exposure therapists must carefully consider the patient's safety when designing and implementing exposure practices. Under what circumstances does a prospective exposure task involve unacceptable levels of risk? What steps can the therapist take to decrease the probability of psychological and/or physical harm?

2.3.1 Negotiating Informed Consent

Consistent with the ethical imperative to obtain informed consent in psychotherapy (e.g., APA, 2002) exposure therapists must obtain patient consent as soon as possible in treatment. Exposure may be somewhat unique among psychological treatments in that its very nature necessitates constant vigilance to the process of informed consent. Therapists must explain each new exposure practice to the patient, and the patient must agree to proceed before a given task is begun. Informed consent is thus an ongoing process and patients may, and often do, negotiate or even revoke their consent during treatment sessions. Informed consent for a particular exposure task may be discussed at multiple points during therapy sessions. For example, consent for a situational exposure involving conversing with others in a shopping mall may be negotiated in the office while planning the exposure, in the mall prior to initiating conversations, and between conversations while negotiating the next exposure task. To increase the likelihood of patient adherence to anxiety-provoking procedures, treatment manuals (e.g., Abramowitz, Deacon & Whiteside, 2010) often place great emphasis on conveying a clear rationale for exposure and a detailed explanation of its requirements. Because of the unique demands it places on patients and therapists, exposure therapy is likely an exemplar among psychotherapies for satisfying the ethical principle of informed consent.

Informed consent also provides skeptical clinicians with an opportunity to distinguish exposure as a form of therapy from exposure as a form of "torture" (as described in the New York Times; Slater, 2003). The United Nations Convention Against Torture et al. (1987), defines torture as "…any act by which severe pain or suffering, whether physical or mental, is intentionally inflicted on a person for such purposes as obtaining from him or a third person information or a confession, punishing him for an act he committed, or intimidating or coercing him or a third person, or for any reason based on discrimination of any kind, when such pain or suffering is inflicted by or at the instigation of or with the consent or acquiescence of a public official or other person acting in an official capacity" (pp. 197–198). It should be obvious that when provided by a competent practitioner, exposure therapy does not constitute torture. First, the recipient understands the specific procedures to be used and their probable emotional effects. This is akin to informed consent procedures used for medications that includes potential "side effects," including the fact that even if the intervention works properly there may be negative feelings and experiences. Second, the recipient consents to exposure therapy and reserves the right to withdraw this consent at any time. Unlike torture, the patient controls the pace of exposure therapy and coercion is never used to force compliance with treatment.

2.3.2 Determining Acceptable Risk During Exposure Tasks

The probability of patients being harmed in exposure therapy can be reduced by understanding how to determine when a given exposure task entails an unacceptably high level of risk. In certain cases, tasks might be clearly contraindicated, such as intensive hyperventilation for a patient with severe asthma, walking through a dangerous area of town after dark for an assault survivor, and touching bathroom floors for a patient whose immune system is compromised. In the absence of clear-cut risks of harm, the following question may be asked to evaluate whether the risk associated with an exposure is acceptable: *Do at least some people ordinarily confront the situation/stimulus in the course of everyday life without adverse consequences?* The heart-healthy panic disorder patient who fears cardiac arrest may express concern about the safety of briskly walking up and down a stairway for 30 min. However, a trip to the local gym reveals many individuals who engage in this level of vigorous exercise without incident. Someone who has been violently mugged might rebuff the suggestion that she return to using public transportation, yet thousands of other city dwellers use such conveniences on a regular basis.

Regarding contamination-related OCD, many people suffer no ill effects from the routine touching of door handles and trash cans without washing their hands. Some people even occasionally skip showers, fail to wash their hands after using restrooms, and eat finger foods after touching the family pet. Outdoor enthusiasts routinely have close encounters with snakes and spiders without incident, and most everyone has at some point been stuck outside in a thunderstorm without being struck by lightning. An exposure task may be considered to involve acceptable risk if the patient is not at significantly higher risk of experiencing harm than other individuals who engage in the same activity in the course of everyday life largely without incident.

There is no absolute guarantee in exposure therapy, as with life in general, that unanticipated or unwanted outcomes will not occur. Bees sometimes sting. Repeated spinning in a swivel chair may elicit vomiting. If an exposure task could conceivably result in an undesirable but reasonably harmless outcome, the therapist should consider framing it as a test of both the probability and cost of the outcome. In this manner, the unintended occurrence of freezing up during a conversation, being negatively evaluated by strangers, or experiencing a panic attack can provide corrective information regarding the actual badness (or lack thereof) of the outcome. At the same time, it is unethical to conduct an exposure task that the therapist determines to involve an unacceptably high probability of an objectively negative outcome (e.g., serious illness, assault, loss of a valued relationship). Therapists cannot possibly anticipate all conceivable low-probability outcomes in any given situation. It is possible that exposure therapy could result in a claustrophobic patient being stuck in a cramped elevator for days, a driving phobic suffering a fatal car accident, or a flying phobic boarding a plane that subsequently crashes. As in real life, there is no absolute guarantee of safety in exposure therapy. Indeed, one could argue that a primary goal of this treatment is to help patients learn to accept living their lives, and approaching feared situations, in the absence of such a guarantee. The remote possibility of catastrophe should no more preclude a driving exposure than it should prevent the therapist from driving to work.

2.3.3 Time Management During Therapy Sessions

Poor therapist time management during exposure therapy sessions may increase the risk for emotional harm to the patient. Specifically, patients whose high anxiety fails to habituate within the allotted session time during exposure therapy may experience demoralization and express doubts about their ability to benefit from the treatment. To prevent such an occurrence, therapists should schedule longer sessions (e.g., 90–120 min) to account for individual variation in time to habituation. A recent patient whose anxiety took more than 3 h to habituate while holding a spider illustrates that even 2-h sessions may not allow sufficient time for all individuals to show habituation. Framing exposures as "behavioral experiments" designed to test specific anxious predictions may help patients view exposure tasks as useful, even if their anxiety does not habituate. In this context, the failure of habituation to occur may be viewed as a valuable learning experience (e.g., "I was able to tolerate prolonged, high anxiety without losing control or going crazy").

2.3.4 *Therapist Competency*

In addition to the strategies described above, risks can be effectively minimized during exposure therapy by ensuring that exposure therapists are adequately trained (or supervised) and deliver this treatment in a competent manner. Although exposure therapy may seem deceptively straightforward to administer, research indicates that optimal delivery of this treatment requires careful consideration of contexts and other factors that can influence the effectiveness of exposure-based treatment (Powers, Smits, Leyro & Otto, 2007). For example, the mere availability of safety aids (see part four of this volume) during exposure can be highly detrimental to treatment outcome, even if the safety aids are not used (Powers, Smits & Telch, 2004). Therapists interested in using exposure techniques should be adequately trained or supervised by a competent exposure therapist. Castro and Marx (2007) noted that part of protecting client welfare means ensuring that the therapist is both intellectually and emotionally ready to provide adequate and appropriate treatment for each client: "Exposure therapy is not only difficult for the client, it is challenging and strenuous for the therapist. In fact it is not uncommon for the strong emotional responses of the client during exposure therapy to evoke secondary distress in the therapist" (pp. 164–165). This observation indicates that, in addition to skill in implementing exposure methods, competency to conduct exposure therapy requires that therapists have the ability to tolerate the often intense emotional responses of their patients and their own reactions to such responses.

2.3.5 *Therapist Self-Care*

Exposure therapy may pose a risk to the therapist in the form of psychological distress. Such distress is especially likely when conducting imaginal exposure for PTSD, during which the therapist may listen to painfully detailed accounts of truly horrifying trauma narratives. Successfully navigating this demanding work requires exposure therapists to strike a balance between empathy for their patients' pain and maintaining professional distance that allows for therapeutic, professional responses (Foa & Rothbaum, 1998). This balance is difficult to maintain in some instances, as when trauma victims recount particularly terrible experiences during imaginal exposure. However, even the most compassionate therapist must remember that it is his or her job to assist the patient in recovery from clinical anxiety, and losing emotional control is incompatible with this goal. Indeed, patients may draw strength from the therapist's outward expressions of confidence in their ability to tolerate the distress associated with particularly difficult exposures. An important part of one's development as an exposure therapist involves learning to cope with and accept the emotional distress patient's exhibit during particularly challenging exposures. From time to time, unburdening oneself by talking to colleagues, or seeking distraction in the form of other professional or personal activities, is necessary to cope with the unique demands of exposure therapy.

2.4 Maintaining Ethical Boundaries

As described above, some therapists believe that exposure is unethical based on concerns about its aversiveness and presumed capacity to harm patients. However, another source of negative beliefs about the ethics of exposure may reflect concerns about this treatment's potential to create problematic boundary violations and dual relationships. For clinicians whose preferred brand of psychotherapy emphasizes therapist neutrality, passivity, and nondirectiveness, exposure may involve an uncomfortably high level of active engagement with the patient. The idea that such engagement might occur in the context of distinctly unconventional therapeutic activities, such as spinning in a swivel chair or touching objects in public restrooms, likely contributes an additional measure of discomfort. In addition, the practice of leaving the office to conduct exposures may be troubling for therapists who fear that doing so will fundamentally alter the professional nature of the therapeutic relationship. These issues are reviewed below in the context of ethical principles regarding boundaries, and strategies are offered for conducting exposure therapy in an optimally ethical manner.

A *boundary crossing* in psychotherapy refers to a deviation from the typical practice of traditional, strict forms of therapy (Zur, 2005). Therapists have traditionally been encouraged to maintain strict boundaries in order to create a therapeutic context that is in the patient's best interest. Examples of boundaries include time, place, touch, self-disclosure, gifts, and money (Barnett, Lazarus, Vasquez, Moorehead-Slaughter & Johnson, 2007). Among these, the practice of violating the "only in the office" boundary is particularly relevant to exposure therapy. Traditionally, psychotherapy has been conducted without the need to leave the office. Exposure therapy, however, sometimes requires that therapists leave the office with their patients to conduct exposures to feared stimuli that cannot easily be brought into in the office. As a result, exposure therapy for many patients involves at least occasional boundary crossings.

Boundary crossings in the form of out-of-the-office exposures carry the possibility of eroding the strict boundaries inherent in traditional notions of the therapist–patient relationship. Indeed, the conduct of exposure therapy outside the office walls may increase the probability of less-formal interactions, some of which may not be strictly therapeutic. Interactions with patients outside the office have traditionally been considered unadvisable as they are seen as laying the groundwork for dual relationships, including sexual relationships with patients (Barnett et al., 2007). From this viewpoint, exposure field trips may be viewed as a step down a "slippery slope" that may lead to increasingly inappropriate behaviors and ultimately exploitative sexual encounters or other dual relationships. To discourage clinicians from traveling down this slippery slope, the "only in the office" rule has been proposed to ensure that clinicians provide treatment that is in the best interests of their patients (Smith & Fitzpatrick, 1995). Within the context of traditional forms of psychotherapy, the "only in the office" boundary is a logical prescription. However, rigid adherences to this traditional notion of boundaries severely restrict a clinician's ability to practice exposure therapy in an effective manner with many patients. Therapists overly concerned with the ethical "slippery slope" of leaving the office to conduct exposure tasks run the risk of engaging in reductio ad absurdum reasoning (i.e., "if I leave the office with an opposite-sex client, a sexual relationship will inevitably develop"). The effectiveness of exposure therapy provides a powerful demonstration that temporarily crossing boundaries for therapeutic purposes is not necessarily unethical or harmful (Lazarus, 1998). Indeed, the failure to do so may be considered unethical, or at the very least suboptimal, in the exposure-based treatment of some patients with anxiety disorders. Thus, boundary *crossings* do not necessarily lead to boundary *violations*; neither do boundary crossings necessarily place the clinician on a "slippery slope" (e.g., Zur, 2001, 2007).

Crossing some boundaries may be clinically appropriate and even necessary when conducting exposure therapy. Exposure is optimally effective when it is conducted in a therapist-assisted manner (Abramowitz, 1996) and when it occurs in a variety of contexts (Powers et al., 2007). For some patients, exposure outside the office is necessary to ensure that safety learning is not conditional on the presence of specific contexts (e.g., "heart palpitations are not dangerous *as long as I experience them in the hospital where emergency medical attention is available*"). When clinically indicated, exposure therapists may cross additional boundaries associated with traditional therapies by extending the length of sessions beyond 1 h, traveling to the patient's home, or involving strangers in the therapy (e.g., as audience members for a public speaking exposure). Such boundary crossings are not by themselves unethical, nor do they inevitably lead to an increasing series of inappropriate interactions with the patient that ultimately results in an exploitative sexual relationship.

The fact that boundary crossings are not necessarily unethical does not mean that they are always ethical. Likewise, the observation that boundary crossings do not necessarily continue down a slippery slope toward sexual exploitation does not mean that this never occurs. Boundary crossings should only occur when the therapist deems them necessary to assist the patient. If all therapeutic tasks can effectively be conducted inside the office, there is no need to conduct exposures elsewhere. Pope and Keith-Spiegel (2008) outlined a number of steps for practitioners to consider when contemplating a boundary crossing. The most relevant of these is for therapists to imagine the best possible outcome and the worst possible outcome from crossing the boundary and from *not* crossing the boundary. This cost–benefit analysis may be used to determine the overall therapeutic value of engaging in a given boundary crossing during exposure therapy.

2.5 Conclusions

An informed risk–benefit analysis suggests that exposure therapy is generally safe and effective, and is rightfully considered a first-line treatment for anxiety disorders. However, relatively few therapists provide this treatment, and most individuals with anxiety disorders do not receive exposure-based treatment. This chapter reviews a number of negative therapist beliefs about exposure that serve to impede efforts to make this treatment more widely available to patients. Strategies for minimizing the unique risks and ethical challenges associated with exposure therapy are also discussed. It is concluded that therapist beliefs about the intolerable and inhumane nature of exposure therapy, as well as its presumed capacity to harm patients and foster unethical therapist–patient interactions, are not supported by the scientific evidence or the clinical experience of adequately trained exposure therapists. In fact, given well-established effectiveness of exposure therapy, there may be ethical consequences for failing to consider exposure therapy in favor of less effective or unsubstantiated treatments. This is not to say that this treatment is risk-free; indeed, exposure may place patients at greater risk of temporary emotional discomfort than do other forms of psychological treatment. However, by being aware of this possibility and taking steps to manage it, exposure therapists can significantly decrease the risk of harm to their patients while simultaneously providing the most effective psychological treatment available for pathological anxiety.

References

Abramowitz, J. S. (1996). Variants of exposures and response prevention in the treatment of obsessive-compulsive disorder: A meta-analysis. *Behavior Therapy, 27*, 583–600.

Abramowitz, J. S., Deacon, B. J., & Whiteside, S. P. (2010). *Exposure therapy for anxiety: Principles and practice*. New York: Guilford Press.

American Psychiatric Association (2011). American psychiatric association practice guidelines. Accessed 31 Jan 2011 http://www.psychiatryonline.com/pracGuide/pracGuideHome.aspx.

American Psychological Association (2002). Ethical principles of psychologists and code of conduct. Available online http://www.apa.org/ethics/.

Barlow, D. H., Gorman, J. M., Shear, M. K., & Woods, S. W. (2000). Cognitive-behavioral therapy, imipramine, or their combination for panic disorder: A randomized controlled trial. *Journal of the American Medical Association, 283*, 2529–2536.

Barnett, J. E., Lazarus, A. A., Vasquez, M., Moorehead-Slaughter, O., & Johnson, W. B. (2007). Boundary issues and multiple relationships: Fantasy and reality. *Professional Psychology: Research and Practice, 38*, 401–410.

Becker, C., Zayfert, C., & Anderson, E. (2004). A survey of psychologists' attitudes toward utilization of exposure therapy for PTSD. *Behaviour Research and Therapy, 42*, 277–292.

Brown, A., Deacon, B. J., Abramowitz, J. S., & Whiteside, S. P. (2007). Parents' perceptions of pharmacological and cognitive-behavioral treatments for childhood anxiety disorders. *Behaviour Research and Therapy, 45*, 819–828.
Castro, F., & Marx, B. P. (2007). Exposure therapy with adult survivors of childhood sexual assault. In D. C. Richard & D. Lauterbach (Eds.), *Comprehensive handbook of the exposure therapies* (pp. 153–167). New York: Academic.
Chambless, D. L., & Ollendick, T. H. (2001). Empirically supported psychological interventions: Controversies and evidence. *Annual Review of Psychology, 52*, 685–716.
Cook, J. M., Schnurr, P. P., & Foa, E. B. (2004). Bridging the gap between posttraumatic stress disorder research and clinical practice: The example of exposure therapy. *Psychotherapy: Theory, Research, Practice, Training, 41*, 374–387.
Cox, B. J., Fergus, K. D., & Swinson, R. P. (1994). Patient satisfaction with behavioral treatments for panic disorder with agoraphobia. *Journal of Anxiety Disorders, 8*, 193–206.
Deacon, B. J., & Abramowitz, J. S. (2004). Cognitive and behavioral treatment for anxiety disorders: A review of meta-analytic findings. *Journal of Clinical Psychology, 60*, 429–441.
Deacon, B. J., & Abramowitz, J. S. (2005). Patients' perceptions of pharmacological and cognitive-behavioral treatments for anxiety disorders. *Behavior Therapy, 36*, 139–145.
Feeney, N., Hembree, E., & Zoellner, L. (2003). Myths regarding exposure therapy for PTSD. *Cognitive and Behavioral Practice, 10*, 85–90.
Foa, E. B., & Rothbaum, B. O. (1998). *Treating the trauma of rape: Cognitive-behavioral therapy for PTSD*. New York, NY: Guilford Press.
Foa, E. B., Zoellner, L. A., Feeny, N. C., Hembree, E. A., & Alvarez-Conrad, J. (2002). Does imaginal exposure exacerbate PTSD symptoms? *Journal of Consulting and Clinical Psychology, 70*, 1022–1028.
Foy, D. W., Kagan, B., McDermott, C., Leskin, G., Sipprelle, R. C., & Paz, G. (1996). Practical parameters in the use of flooding for treating chronic PTSD. *Clinical Psychology and Psychotherapy, 3*, 169–175.
Goisman, R. M., Warshaw, M. G., & Keller, M. B. (1999). Psychosocial treatment prescriptions for generalized anxiety disorder, panic disorder, and social phobia, 1991–1996. *American Journal of Psychiatry, 156*, 1819–1821.
Gunter, R. W., & Whittal, M. L. (2010). Dissemination of cognitive-behavioral treatments for anxiety disorders: Overcoming barriers and improving patient access. *Clinical Psychology Review, 30*, 194–202.
Hembree, E. A., & Cahill, S. P. (2007). Obstacles to successful implementation of exposure therapy. In D. C. Richard & D. Lauterbach (Eds.), *Comprehensive handbook of the exposure therapies* (pp. 389–408). New York: Academic.
Hembree, E. A., Foa, E. B., Dorfan, N. M., Street, G. P., Kowalski, J., & Tu, X. (2003). Do patients dropout prematurely from exposure therapy for PTSD? *Journal of Traumatic Stress, 16*, 552–562.
Heuzenroeder, L., Donnelly, M., Haby, M. M., Mihalopoulos, C., Rossell, R., Carter, R., et al. (2004). Cost-effectiveness of psychological and pharmacological interventions for generalized anxiety disorder and panic disorder. *Australia and New Zealand Journal of Psychiatry, 38*, 602–612.
Huppert, J. D., Franklin, M. E., Foa, E. B., & Davidson, J. R. (2003). Study refusal and exclusion from a randomized treatment study of generalized social phobia. *Journal of Anxiety Disorders, 17*, 683–693.
Lazarus, A. A. (1998). How do you like these boundaries? *The Clinical Psychologist, 51*, 22–25.
National Institute for Clinical Excellence (2011). Clinical guidelines. Accessed 31 Jan 2011 http://guidance.nice.org.uk/CG.
Norton, G. R., Allen, G. E., & Hilton, J. (1983). The social validity of treatments for agoraphobia. *Behaviour Research and Therapy, 21*, 393–399.
Olatunji, B. O., Cisler, J., & Deacon, B. J. (2010). Efficacy of cognitive behavioral therapy for anxiety disorders: A review of meta-analytic findings. *Psychiatric Clinics of North America, 33*, 557–577.

Olatunji, B. O., Deacon, B. J., & Abramowitz, J. S. (2009). The cruelest cure? Ethical issues in the implementation of exposure-based treatments. *Cognitive and Behavioral Practice, 16*, 172–180.

Pope, K. S., & Keith-Spiegel, P. (2008). A practical approach to boundaries in psychotherapy: making decisions, by passing blunders, and mending fences. *Journal of Clinical Psychology: In Session, 64*, 1–15.

Powers, M. B., Smits, J. A. J., Leyro, T. M., & Otto, M. W. (2007). Translational research perspectives on maximizing the effectiveness of exposure therapy. In D. C. S. Richard & D. L. Lauterbach (Eds.), *Handbook of the exposure therapies* (pp. 109–126). New York: Elsevier.

Powers, M. B., Smits, J. A. J., & Telch, M. J. (2004). Disentangling the effects of safety-behavior utilization and safety-behavior availability during exposure-based treatment: a placebo-controlled trial. *Journal of Consulting and Clinical Psychology, 72*, 448–454.

Prochaska, J., & Norcross, J. (1999). *Systems of psychotherapy: A transtheoretical analysis* (4th ed.). Pacific Grove: Brooks/Cole Publishing.

Richard, D. C. S., & Gloster, A. T. (2007). Exposure therapy has a public relations problem: A dearth of litigation amid a wealth of concern. In D. C. S. Richard & D. Lauterbach (Eds.), *Comprehensive handbook of the exposure therapies* (pp. 409–425). New York: Academic.

Rosqvist, J. (2005). *Exposure treatments for anxiety disorders: A practitioner's guide to concepts, methods, and evidence-based practice*. New York: Routledge.

Slater, L. (2003). The cruelest cure. In New York Times, 3 Nov 2003.

Smith, D., & Fitzpatrick, M. (1995). Patient–therapist boundary issues: An integrative review of theory and research. *Professional Psychology: Research and Practice, 26*, 499–506.

Stein, M. B., Sherbourne, C. D., Craske, M. G., Means-Christensen, A., Bystritsky, A., Katon, W., et al. (2004). Quality of care for primary care patients with anxiety disorders. *American Journal of Psychiatry, 161*, 2230–2237.

Stewart, R. E., & Chambless, D. L. (2009). Cognitive-behavioral therapy for adult anxiety disorders in clinical practice: A meta-analysis of effectiveness studies. *Journal of Consulting and Clinical Psychology, 77*, 595–606.

United Nations Convention Against Torture and Other Cruel, Inhuman or Degrading Treatment or Punishment, GA Res. 39/46, 39 GAOR Supplement (No. 51) at 197, U.N. Document A/39/51, opened for signature 4 February 1985, entered into force 26 June, 1987, Author, New York (1987).

Zur, O. (2001). Out-of-office experience: When crossing office boundaries and engaging in dual relationships are clinically beneficial and ethically sound. *The Independent Practitioner, 21*, 96–98.

Zur, O. (2005). The dumbing down of psychology: Faulty beliefs about boundary crossings and dual relationships. In R. H. Wright & N. A. Cummings (Eds.), *Destructive trends in mental health: The well-intentioned path to harm* (pp. 252–282). New York: Taylor & Francis Group.

Zur, O. (2007). *Boundaries in psychotherapy: Ethical and clinical explorations*. Washington DC: American Psychological Association.

Chapter 3
Dissemination of Exposure Therapy in Clinical Practice: How to Handle the Barriers?

Peter Neudeck and Franziska Einsle

Dr. Peter Neudeck is a licensed psychotherapist specialised in cognitive behavioral therapy. He has been working both in clinical and research positions and has established private practices for psychotherapy in Berlin and Cologne. He is also a lecturer and supervisor for graduate and postgraduate CBT-psychotherapy programmes across Germany. He recently received further professional development in CBASP and systemic therapy. His main research activities include psychobiology and psychotherapy of anxiety disorders in exposure based treatments. He has released numerous publications on exposure techniques in mental disorders.

P. Neudeck (✉)
Praxis für Verhaltenstherapie, Follerstr. 64, D-50676 Köln/Cologne, Germany
e-mail: peterneudeck@gmx.de

F. Einsle
Institute of Clinical Psychology and Psychotherapy, Technische Universitaet Dresden, Chemnitzer Strasse 46, 01187 Dresden, Germany
e-mail: einsle@psychologie.tu-dresden.de

P. Neudeck and H.-U. Wittchen (eds.), *Exposure Therapy: Rethinking the Model – Refining the Method*, DOI 10.1007/978-1-4614-3342-2_3,

Dr. Franziska Einsle works as a scientist at the Institute of Clinical Psychology and Psychotherapy (Technische Universitaet Dresden) and is specialised in exposure therapy. Her main research interests include the implementation of exposure therapy into routine care and the association between anxiety disorders and cardiovascular diseases.

3.1 Exposure-Based Therapy: From RCT to Practical Implementation

Stimulus confrontation (exposure) is a robust and well-established method, which may either be used as a therapy component or module within a broader therapeutic framework, such as in cognitive behavioral therapy, rational emotive therapy, strategic short-term therapy, self-management therapy, or as a stand-alone treatment package, particularly established for the treatment of specific phobias (Neudeck & Wittchen, 2005). Exposure-based therapy requires patients to confront stimuli, either accompanied by the therapist or on their own, without avoidance strategies, sufficiently long and repeated (Hand, 2000). These stimuli may be exteroceptive (e.g., metro, dirt, height and animals) or interoceptive (e.g., bodily symptoms, thoughts, intrusions and worries).

Exposure (or confrontation with feared stimuli) is known to be an effective standard technique in the treatment of anxiety disorders, OCD, PTSD, eating disorders, and addiction. Since the very first publications on exposure in the 1960s and 1970s (Boulougouris & Marks, 1969; Marks, Boulougouris, & Marset, 1971; Meyer, 1966), numerous effectiveness studies have been published internationally (e.g., Abramowitz, 1996; Barlow, 1990; Fedoroff & Taylor, 2001; Foa et al., 2005; Franklin, Abramowitz, Kozak, Levitt, & Foa, 2000; Lindenmeyer, Kolling, & Zimdsars, 2002; Maercker, Zöllner, Rabe, & Karl, 2003).

A meta-analysis of 42 studies on panic disorder with or without agoraphobia showed that exposure-based therapy in combination with relaxation techniques and/or breathing retraining represents the most effective treatment (Sanchez-Meca,

Rosa-Alcazar, Marin-Martinez, & Gomez-Conesa, 2010). Emmelkamp (1994) illustrated long-term effects of exposure-based therapy in agoraphobia: 70–80% of patients showed significant amelioration even years after completion of treatment. Another review proved sustainability as well: follow-up examinations yielded 55–79% responders in OCD patients with a stable reduction of symptoms considering of different definitions of response (Stanley & Turner, 1995). Similarly, a meta-analytic investigation of 19 studies on posttraumatic stress disorder reported effect sizes of 1.13 for the treatment with stimulus exposure (Rosa-Alcázar, Sánchez-Meca, Gómez-Conesa, & Marín-Martínez, 2008).

In summary, there is considerable evidence for a successful stimulus confrontation treatment with positive long-term outcome. Nonetheless, only few studies deal with the challenges of dissemination of exposure-based therapy in routine care (Barlow, Levitt, & Bufka, 1999; Cahill, Foa, Hembree, Marshall, & Nacash, 2006) and reported on putative barriers for the implementation of exposure in the clinical routine.

In those few studies concerning the question, why exposure is often not implemented accurately in clinical practice, notable differences between the attitude of practitioners about the technique ("effective", "stable treatment outcome") versus the frequency at which practitioners use this technique, became obvious. According to a study by Roth, Siegl, Aufdermauer, and Reinecker (2004), about 80% of the therapists use at least one confrontation technique in the treatment of anxiety disorders. While using mostly gradual as well as short-term exposure (≤2 h), the realization of these expositions cannot be classified as correctly. Besides, therapists applying exposure techniques use the same amount of exposure in sensu and in vivo, only one fourth implemented the method in the quotidian environment of the patient. According to this, Freiheit, Vye, Swan, and Cady (2004) reported that only 37% of behavioral therapists use exposure with response prevention in the treatment of OCD, and 26% indicated to use the technique either rarely or not at all. For the treatment of panic disorder, 76% stated to never or rarely conduct interoceptive exposure. These data go along with a study by Goisman et al. (1993) in which only 19% of the interviewed patients reported treatment codable as exposure in vivo during a behaviorally oriented psychotherapy. Böhm, Förstner, Külz, and Voderholzer (2008) asked patients undergoing psychotherapeutic pretreatment about their experiences with exposure treatment in the past therapies. Therein, in the context of behavior therapy in OCD patients, only 27% of treatments included exposure techniques. At the same time, exposure therapy was described as the method of choice in 80% of health insurance applications.

There is no other standard procedure in behavior therapy that has been called into question so frequently, carries such an image problem and has led to such massive technical and personal problems for practitioners. According to this discrepancy between efficacy and use of exposure, this chapter reports on studies about the barriers as well as deduces further research questions below. Empirical results on barriers to implementing exposure in the psychotherapeutic practice are summarised with regard to structural conditions, therapist's attitude as well as fears of practitioners and barriers in regard to content.

3.2 Barriers to the Adequate Implementation of Exposure-Based Techniques

3.2.1 Structural Barriers

Adequate exposure therapy mostly requires leaving the common therapy setting with regard to time and/or place. For example, for successful treatment of OCD it is necessary that the patient confronts with emotional, cognitive as well as physiological aspects of the anxiogenetic situation without using safety behavior (Hand, 1993). Therefore, it may be necessary to accompany a patient with OCD and obsessive cleaning behavior to his flat and confront him in the natural environment. In turn, this forces the therapists to engage in logistic planning and organisational flexibility. When therapists decide to "go outside" with their patients, they should come to agreements on how to react to possible incidents (running into a patient's friend, being asked by passers-by what you are doing here, etc.) beforehand. Furthermore, therapists working outside the office should know the neighborhood well and schedule enough time. The therapist is required to take care of the organisation of exposure so the patient can focus only but entirely on the exposure. To confide in a therapist who gets lost in the woods during an exposure session is difficult. Therefore, the therapist also needs to know, for example, opening times of a museum or the end station of a bus, and to give sensible instructions to the patient how to deal with such situations. When a socially phobic patient is supposed to expose himself to asking strangers in a museum about their opinion on artwork, scheduling the exposure on a day when the museum is actually closed would be very unprofessional. Besides this, the therapist has to organise enough time for exposure giving the patients the feeling that exposure will continue as long as necessary. An exposure session is futile, when it is aborted due to the next patient appointment or closing time.

Hence, one question is whether exposure therapy goes beyond the scope of the psychotherapy out-patient routine by requesting too much planning and preparation. Many colleagues' complaints become obvious here: "Too little time, too much effort".

The point is that exposure therapy requires the patient to confront himself with either a situation or an internal stimulus. This may imply leaving the common therapy setting (with regards to space and time). It requires logistic planning and organisational flexibility, which may represent an obstacle. When interviewed, psychotherapists indicated problems especially with regards to time (40%), insurance and logistics (37%) as the main reasons for not engaging in exposure techniques (Neudeck, 2007). Even without further empirical data, it is obvious that the additional investment in planning and preparation poses a huge obstacle on the implementation of exposure techniques.

3.2.2 *The Therapist's Attitude*

An important barrier to the adequate usage of exposure is given by the basic attitude of psychotherapists regarding confrontation techniques. Typical critical attitudes on exposure are described by Barlow et al. (1999) as well as Feeny, Hembree, and Zoellner (2003): (1) exposure leads to exacerbation of the pathology, patients drop out when they have to decide for this treatment, (2) the patient is passive; during therapy something is happening to him, in which he is not actively involved, (3) exposure is a patronising form of therapy that is not responsive to the individual characteristics rooted in the patient's biography, (4) exposure alone does not suffice for treatment success, the more treatments a patient gets the better will be the outcome, (5) exposure will not prove itself in the clinical routine, since all data from efficacy studies have been collected within a highly structured environment (i.e., artificial, nonrepresentative).

In contrast, therapists regard exposure treatment as a "simple method," a technique, "in which one climbs the tower with a patient until his fear has ceased." These therapists mostly tend to send the patient to expose themselves independently without adequate preparation about dealing with anxiety as well as safety behavior.

Becker, Zayfert, and Anderson (2004) reported that 25% of patients prefer individualised therapy compared to manualised treatments. Of note, Schulte, Künzel, Pepping, and Schulte-Bahrenberg (1991) and van Oppen et al. (2010) pointed out that manuals are more effective at least in phobic patients and in OCD. As Neudeck (2007) reported, students, psychotherapy trainees, and psychotherapeutic practitioners were queried about their opinion on exposure therapy in anxiety disorders. The most frequent barrier to implement exposure in anxiety disorders was "Patients are not convinced by the rationale (78%)". So albeit exposure is regarded as highly effective by practitioners, it is considered as not convincing for patients at the same time. Here, the therapist's attitude is important especially for the effectiveness of psychoeducation as well as cognitive preparation to the motivation of patients. In lieu of this, many therapists point to a lack of training as a reason for not using exposure therapy (Becker et al., 2004; Richard & Gloster, 2007).

3.2.3 *Reservations and Fears of Practitioners*

Another important barrier of the implementation of exposure is rooted in the possibility that this treatment may trigger emotions or behaviors in the patient making the therapist feel helpless. Exposure may cause aggressive, irritated, or offending behavior (i.e., in verbal statements against the therapist). It can also trigger intense sadness. Patients may try to escape from situations whatever it takes. For example, anxiety, helplessness as well as rumination were reported by therapists working with traumatised patients (Traue & Jerg-Bretzke, 2008).

Insecurities may be triggered in therapists, because, for a short period of time during an exposure session, they have to change their compassionate attitude in the patient–therapist relationship to being more directive and active. Therapists also fear irreversible traumata caused by excessive fear (e.g., accidents during motorway exposure). Some therapists indicate that their own fears (spiders, heights, insecure roads) or their own uncertainties ("dissonant relationship," "fear that the patient refuses") play a role in the non-execution of exposure exercises (Neudeck, 2007). Furthermore, due to feared re-traumatization, a too early as well as an exclusive exposure is rejected by therapists in the treatment of PTSD patients (Fischer & Reddemann, 2003). There is evidence that in vivo flooding is an effective treatment in PTSD (Moulds & Nixon, 2006). Also, Neuner (2008; also see chapter in this book) shows that exposure and stabilisation are similarly accepted by patients in terms of increase of symptoms and dropout rates. Data underline that stabilisation is not necessary even in complex traumatised patients (Bichescu, Neuner, Schauer, & Elbert, 2007). In addition, there is a risk that stabilisation methods rather consolidate avoidance behavior in trauma type I as well as in trauma type II, and may hamper successful therapy.

3.2.4 Therapist's Knowledge and Skills

In order to perform exposure effectively, appropriate realization of the methodology is crucial. There is plenty empirical evidence for the application of exposure in vivo in the treatment of phobias (Barlow, Gorman, Shear, & Woods, 2000). Exposure in vivo - either as massed exposure or as exposure accompanied by the therapist - is recommended as method of choice also in the treatment of PTSD and OCD (Abramowitz, 2006; Moulds & Nixon, 2006)

In clinical routine, exposure techniques are often applied methodically inappropriately. Given that massed exposure in vivo in the natural environment is the gold standard of OCD treatment (Abramowitz, 2006), results of a study by Böhm et al. (2008) are impressive: OCD patients report that only one quarter of therapists (23%) chose the massed form of exposure during psychotherapeutic treatment. Additionally, 18% and 23% of confrontations took place in sensu and in the consulting room, respectively. In 18% of treatments, no trainings in self-management had been carried out. On average, only 0.35 exposure exercises took place in the everyday environment of the patient. Further, it is likely that a lot of exposure sessions are not long enough for patients to realise that habituation needs time and repetition of the situations is helpful. Therefore, it is problematic that 71% of patients in the study by Böhm et al. (2008) reported that accompanied exposure sessions did not last longer than 60 minutes. Whether this accounts for the treatment of other disorders as well, needs further evaluation.

Besides maintaining general standards in the implementation of exposure, the therapist first of all has to support the patient in the omission of avoidance and safety behavior. This includes preventing withdrawal from the exposure as well as identifying and preventing the patient from applying safety behaviors and cognitive avoidance. Avoidance and safety behaviors are strategies which help the patient to overcome situations and endure symptoms (Thwaites & Freeston, 2005). Scientists and practitioners agree by no means on the handling of avoidance during exposure exercises. Salkovskis, Clark, Hackman, Wells, and Gelder (1999) distinguished adaptive from maladaptive strategies in their article, with adaptive strategies declared as coping strategies in a positive sense. The results of other studies indicate that maladaptive strategies impair the success of exposure treatment or at least prevent improvement, and should therefore be inhibited (Deacon, Sy, Lickel, & Nelson, 2010; Powers, Smits, & Telch, 2004).

3.3 How to Overcome These Barriers in the Future

The previous paragraph underlined the barriers to the implementation of exposure in clinical routine and showed a complex picture. They all point to the fact that more importance needs to be attached to the communication of knowledge and to skills in exposure techniques. In the following, we describe important problems, whose solutions should improve the use of exposure treatment. Therefore, psychotherapists responsibly working should be experts in the preparation and implementation of this standard technique in its various versions (e.g., massed exposure in vivo, implosion, worry exposure, prolonged exposure in sensu).

3.3.1 The Impact of General Conditions and the Therapist–Patient Relationship

More than one third of the practitioners indicate difficult general conditions as the main reason for not using exposure techniques (Becker et al., 2004). Thus, future studies should involve a detailed analysis on framework conditions (time, manpower, legal and insurance conditions, reimbursement). Hence, the therapist's role poses an important precondition for the success of exposure treatment (Hautzinger, 1997; Margraf & Schneider, 1992). Identification of the concrete steps practitioners undertake to establish a stable and trustworthy working alliance with their patients is of great importance and has not yet been answered sufficiently. Especially the role of cognitive preparation, instructions and coping with avoidance behavior are crucial for the therapist–patient relationship, and also for the motivation with respect to exposure treatment. Another important question refers to whether there is a qualitative change in therapist–patient relationship over the course of exposure therapy.

3.3.2 The Impact of Cognitive Preparation

Hautzinger (1997) stated that no patient experiencing mortal fear will enter an elevator, without a plausible and convincing explanatory model on the reasons to do so.

The relevance of the quality of explanatory models is also described by Frank and Fiegenbaum (2000), as well as Neudeck (2005). More knowledge on the invested amount of time in cognitive preparation and its concrete content is desired. The challenge is to identify and analyse the mechanisms of action in exposure therapy (Marks, 2002). In contrast to numerous discussions on the form and amount of exposure (i.e., Borgeat et al., 2009; Carey, 2011; Gloster et al., 2011), the importance and kind of psychoeducation in the beginning of therapy is still understudied.

Clinical practitioners often reject to apply exposure therapy, because they believe that patients do not understand the rationale behind (Neudeck, 2007). Another unresolved issue concerns possible correlations between the patient's motivations on the one hand and the subjective quality of the therapist's own training in stimulus confrontation techniques on the other hand. In this context, the analysis of duration and frequency as well as concrete contents of vocational training seminars is necessary. In the stage of cognitive preparation, patients compile an individual model of development and maintenance of their disorder. The final step of this therapy stage comprises the deduction of the therapy rationale, which can be achieved in two ways: using thought experiment to discharge the rationale by the patient himself or the therapist, as an "expert" explains the rationale emphasising the high chance of success and praising the method of choice. So far, no empirical data exist concerning the kind of method to deduct the therapy rationale. Similarly, the impact of the cognitive preparation on the patient's motivation for treatment is not known. Future studies should additionally investigate the correlation between special training for therapists (cognitive preparation with deduction of the therapy rationale according to manual) and patient behavior (dropouts, refusing exercises) during therapy.

3.3.3 *The Impact of Instruction*

The transfer from homework and exercises (in self-management and/or computer-assisted) to everyday life is of major importance for the treatment outcome (Marks, Kenwright, McDonough, Whittaker, & Mataix-Cols, 2004; Rosa-Alcázar et al., 2008). It may probably have different consequences for the effect of exposure, when a patient is instructed to deal with his fear or compulsion than if the patient is instructed, to do anything in order to maximise his arousal or fear and to observe any alterations of all modalities (thoughts, feelings and sensations) very closely. When patients are instructed to practice a certain situation, they are likely to conclude afterward, that they overcame "riding the bus," or that they learned "not to control the gas stove." They are, however, often unlikely to conclude that they exposed themselves to the maximum level of arousal or fear without any avoidance behavior. It is well known that there is a difference between the acquisition of fear and the extinction of fear (Bouton, 2007). Conditioned fear is less context specific than learning of extinction. Emphasising the situation and accordingly exercising an everyday situation during exposure, as described by Hoffmann and Hofmann (2004), may cause the patients' difficulties transferring the experience to everyday situations. Studies concerning "the return of the fear" explain why symptoms partially recur in the same way (Rachman, 1979). Instead of making a new experience without using avoiding behavior (thoughts, places, situations), patients practice to cope a single situation. In this context, data from the treatment realisation by practitioners with focus on the role of instructions are missing as well.

3.3.4 The Impact of Dealing with Avoidance Behavior

Due to a certain degree of uncertainty or own phobic parts, therapists may unwittingly calm their patients or are unable to maximise the patient's fear/arousal. A lot of therapists are concerned that exposure situations (i.e., driving on an express-highway; have contact with blood or refuse) are (really) dangerous, probably due to their own experience. They might then end an exposure earlier than appropriate. Albeit, there are no data yet available on the actual behavior of therapists during exposure in vivo, it is important to know whether and how therapists manage to explore subtle avoidance behaviour (e.g., cognitive avoidance) during the preparation of the exposure exercise, and how to inhibit this during exposure. Investigation is needed on whether therapists understand that shifting of attention during the exposure with social-phobic patients is reasonable, whereas it is yet not indicated for agoraphobic and OCD patients, since these patients may use shifted attention as a form of distraction. Furthermore, there are numerous unresolved questions concerning the best re-enforcement of exposure exercises. The impact of unaccompanied vs. accompanied exposure to handle avoidance behavior (Einsle, Lang, Helbig, & Wittchen, 2007), for example, is not much clear. Even though there is slight evidence that therapist-guided exposure is more effective for agoraphobic avoidance and panic attacks than is unaccompanied exposure in the short runs (Gloster et al., 2011), preparation by a therapist directly before exposure is crucial in either condition. Another open question refers to the impact of positive self-instruction as a possible avoidance behavior or guided mastery.

3.4 Conclusion

In summary, a bundle of questions are unanswered concerning the barriers to exposure treatment and the therapists' attitude. Empirical research should gain more information on the formal vocational training and its content, the attitude, and the approach in the preparation and execution of exposure treatment. The only way to promote the high-quality implementation of exposure is that colleagues of in- and out-patient settings are willing to put the transparency, which is characteristic for behavior therapy, into practice and to inform their researching colleagues. In a next step, therapists should give in vivo insight into their work with patients.

References

Abramowitz, J. S. (1996). Variants of exposure and response prevention in the treatment of obsessive-compulsive disorder: A meta-analysis. *Behavior Therapy, 27*(4), 583–600.

Abramowitz, J. S. (2006). The psychological treatment of obsessive-compulsive disorder. *Canada Journal of Psychiatry, 51*(7), 407–416.

Barlow, D. H. (1990). Long-term outcome for patients with panic disorder treated with cognitive therapy. *Journal of Clinical Psychology, 51*(12), 17–23. Suppl A.

Barlow, D. H., Gorman, J. M., Shear, M. K., & Woods, S. W. (2000). Cognitive-behavioral therapy, imipramine, or their combination for panic disorder: A randomized controlled trial. *Journal of the American Medical Association, 283*, 2529–2536.

Barlow, D. H., Levitt, J. T., & Bufka, L. F. (1999). The dissemination of empirically supported treatments: A view to the future. *Behavior Research and Therapy, 37*(Suppl 1), 147–162.

Becker, C. B., Zayfert, C., & Anderson, E. (2004). A survey of psychologists' attitudes towards and utilization of exposure therapy for PTSD. *Behavior Research and Therapy, 42*, 277–292.

Bichescu, D., Neuner, F., Schauer, M., & Elbert, T. (2007). Narrative exposure therapy of imprisonment-related chronic posttraumatic stress disorder and depression. *Behaviour Research and Therapy, 45*, 2212–2220.

Böhm, K., Förstner, U., Külz, A., & Voderholzer, U. (2008). Versorgungsrealität der Zwangsstörungen: Werden Expositionsverfahren eingesetzt? *Verhaltenstherapie, 18*, 18–24.

Borgeat, F., Stankovic, M., Khazaal, Y., Weber Rouget, B., Baumann, M. C., Riquier, F., et al. (2009). Does the form or the amount of exposure make a difference in the Cognitive-Behaviour Therapy treatment of social phobia? *The Journal of Nervous and Mental Disease, 197*(7), 507–513.

Boulougouris, J. C., & Marks, I. M. (1969). Implosion (flooding) – A new treatment for phobias. *British Medicine Journal, 21*, 721–723.

Bouton, M. E. (2007). *Learning and Behavior: A Contemporary Synthesis*. Sunderland, MA: Sinauer Associates Inc.

Cahill, S. P., Foa, E. B., Hembree, E. A., Marshall, R. D., & Nacash, N. (2006). Dissemination of exposure therapy in the treatment of posttraumatic stress disorder. *Journal of Traumatic Stress, 19*(5), 597–610.

Carey, T. A. (2011). Exposure and reorganization: The what and how of effective psychotherapy. *Clinical Psychology Review, 31*, 236–248.

Deacon, B. J., Sy, J. T., Lickel, J. J., & Nelson, E. A. (2010). Does the judicious use of safety behaviors improve the efficacy and acceptability of exposure therapy for claustrophobic fear? *Journal of Behavior Therapy and Experimental Psychiatry, 41*(1), 71–80. Epub 24 Oct 2009.

Einsle, F., Lang, T., Helbig, S., & Wittchen, H. U. (2007). Improving the treatment of panic disorder with agoraphobia: A multicenter randomized controlled therapy study to facilitate understanding the mechanisms of action in exposure therapy. *Anxiety Disorders: A Quarterly Report, 4*(3), 7–8.

Emmelkamp, P. M. G. (1994). Behavior therapy with adults. In S. L. Garfield & A. E. Bergin (Eds.), *Handbook of psychotherapy and behavior change* (4th ed., pp. 379–427). New York: Wiley.

Fedoroff, I. C., & Taylor, S. (2001). Psychological and pharmacological treatments of social phobia: A meta-analysis. *Journal of Clinical Psychopharmacology, 21*(3), 311–324.

Feeny, N. C., Hembree, E. A., & Zoellner, L. A. (2003). Myths regarding exposure therapy for PTSD. *Cognitive and Behavioral Practice, 10*, 85–90.

Fischer, G., & Reddemann, L. (2003). Traumaadaptierte tiefenpsychologische fundierte und analytische Psychotherapie. *Psychotherapie, 48*, 199–209.

Foa, E. B., Hembree, E. A., Cahill, S. P., Rauch, S. A. M., Riggs, D. S., Feeny, N. C., et al. (2005). Randomized trial of prolonged exposure for posttraumatic stress disorder with and without cognitive restructuring: Outcome at academic and community clinics. *Journal of Consulting and Clinical Psychology, 73*(5), 953–964.

Frank, M., & Fiegenbaum, W. (2000). Wer kommt, wer geht, wer profitiert? Wirkfaktoren der kognitiven Vorbereitung auf eine massierte Konfrontationstherapie bei Angstpatienten. *Psychotherapie im Dialog, 3*, 61–66.
Franklin, M. E., Abramowitz, J. S., Kozak, M. J., Levitt, J. T., & Foa, E. B. (2000). Effectiveness of exposure and ritual prevention for obsessive-compulsive disorder: Randomized compared with nonrandomized samples. *Journal of Consulting and Clinical Psychology, 68*, 594–602.
Freiheit, S., Vye, C., Swan, R., & Cady, M. (2004). Cognitive-behavioral therapy for anxiety: Is dissemination working? *The Behavior Therapist, 27*, 25–32.
Gloster, A. T., Wittchen, H. U., Einsle, F., Lang, T., Helbig-Lang, S., Fydrich, T., et al. (2011). Psychological treatment for panic disorder with agoraphobia: A randomized controlled trial to examine the role of therapist-guided exposure in situ in CBT. *Journal of Consulting and Clinical Psychology, 79*(3), 406–420.
Goisman, R. M., Rogers, M. P., Steketee, G. S., Warshaw, M. G., Cuneo, P., & Keller, M. B. (1993). Utilization of behavioral methods in a multicenter anxiety disorders study. *Journal of Clinical Psychiatry, 54*, 213–218.
Hand, I. (1993). Verhaltenstherapie für Zwangskranke und deren Angehörige. In H. J. Möller (Ed.), *Therapie psychotischer Erkrankungen*. Stuttgart: Enke-Verlag.
Hand, I. (2000). Reizkonfrontation. In M. Linden & M. Hautzinger (Eds.), *Verhaltenstherapie, Techniken und Methoden* (pp. 164–174). Berlin: Springer.
Hautzinger, M. (1997). Exposition und Reizkonfrontation. *Psychotherapeut, 42*, 119–125.
Hoffmann, N., & Hofmann, B. (2004). *Expositionen bei Ängsten und Zwängen*. Beltz: Weinheim.
Lindenmeyer, J., Kolling, R., & Zimdsars, P. (2002). Und ewig lockt das Suchtgedächtnis – Expositionsbehandlung bei Alkoholabhängigkeit. In F. Sucht (Ed.), *Die Zukunft der Suchtbehandlung – Trends und Prognosen* (pp. 140–149). Geesthacht: Neuland-Verlag.
Maercker, A., Zöllner, T., Rabe, S., & Karl, A. (2003). Treating PTSD in motor-vehicle accident victims with exposure-plus cognitive reconstructuring: First results of a RCT with psychometric and neurobiological outcomes. *European Psychotherapy, 4*, 112–113. Special Edition.
Margraf, J., & Schneider, S. (1992). Therapeutische Beziehung und Therapieerfolg bei Angststörungen. In J. Magraf & J. C. Brengelmann (Eds.), *Die Therapeut-Patient-Beziehung in der Verhaltenstherapie* (pp. 135–160). München: Röttger.
Marks, I. M. (2002). The maturing of therapy. *British Journal of Psychiatry, 180*, 200–204.
Marks, I. M., Boulougouris, J. C., & Marset, P. (1971). Flooding versus desensitization in the treatment of phobic patients: A crossover study. *British Journal of Psychiatry, 119*, 353–375.
Marks, I. M., Kenwright, M., McDonough, M., Whittaker, M., & Mataix-Cols, D. (2004). Saving clinicians' time by delegating routine aspects of therapy to a computer: A randomized controlled trial in phobia/panic disorder. *Psychological Medicine, 34*(1), 9–17.
Meyer, V. (1966). Modification of expectations in cases with obsessional rituals. *Behavior Research and Therapy, 4*(4), 273–280.
Moulds, M. L., & Nixon, R. D. (2006). In vivo flooding for anxiety disorders: Proposing its utility in the treatment posttraumatic stress disorder. *Journal of Anxiety Disordes, 20*(4), 498–509.
Neudeck, P. (2005). "Bedrohliche Hasen" – Konfrontationstherapie bei Panikstörung. In P. Neudeck & H. U. Wittchen (Eds.), *Konfrontationstherapie bei psychischen Störungen* (pp. 17–46). Göttingen: Hogrefe-Verlag.
Neudeck, P. (2007). Reizkonfrontation in der Praxis. Vortrag bei der Eröffnungsveranstaltung der Verhaltenstherapiewoche in Dresden.
Neudeck, P., & Wittchen, H. U. (2005). *Konfrontationstherapie bei psychischen Störungen*. Göttingen: Hogrefe-Verlag.
Neuner, F. (2008). Stabilisierung vor Konfrontation in der Traumatherapie-Grundregel oder Mythos? *Verhaltenstherapie, 18*, 109–118.
Powers, M. B., Smits, J. A. J., & Telch, M. J. (2004). Disentangling the effects of safety-behavior utilization and safety-behavior availability during exposure-based treatment: A placebo-controlled trial. *Journal of Consulting and Clinical Psychology, 72*(3), 448–454.
Rachman, S. (1979). The return of fear. *Behaviour Research and Therapy, 17*(2), 164–166.

Richard, D. C. S., & Gloster, A. T. (2007). Exposure therapy has a public relations problem: A dearth of litigation amid a wealth of concern. In D. C. S. Richard & D. Lauterbach (Eds.), *Handbook of exposure therapy* (pp. 409–425). Amsterdam: Academic.

Rosa-Alcázar, A. I., Sánchez-Meca, J., Gómez-Conesa, A., & Marín-Martínez, F. (2008). Psychological treatment of obsessive-compulsive disorder: A meta-analysis. *Clinical Psychology Review, 28*(8), 1310–1325.

Roth, C., Siegl, J., Aufdermauer, N., & Reinecker, H. (2004). Therapie von Angst- und Zwangspatienten in der verhaltenstherapeutischen Praxis. *Verhaltenstherapie, 14*, 16–21.

Salkovskis, P. M., Clark, D. M., Hackman, A., Wells, A., & Gelder, M. G. (1999). An experimental investigation of the role of safety behaviours in the maintenance of panic disorder with agoraphobia. *Behaviour Research and Therapy, 37*, 559–574.

Sanchez-Meca, J., Rosa-Alcazar, A. I., Marin-Martinez, F., & Gomez-Conesa, A. (2010). Psychological treatment of panic disorder with or without agoraphobia: A meta-analysis. *Clinical Psychology Review, 30*, 37–50.

Schulte, D., Künzel, R., Pepping, G., & Schulte-Bahrenberg, T. (1991). Maßgeschneiderte Psychotherapie versus Standardtherapie bei der Behandlung von Phobikern. In D. Schulte (Ed.), *Therapeutische Entscheidungen* (pp. 15–42). Göttingen: Hogrefe.

Stanley, M. W., & Turner, S. M. (1995). Current status of pharmacological and behavioral treatment of obsessive-compulsive disorder. *Behavior Therapy, 26*, 163–186.

Thwaites, R., & Freeston, M. H. (2005). Safety-Seeking Behaviours: Fact or Function? How Can We Clinically Differentiate Between Safety Behaviours and Adaptive Coping Strategies Across Anxiety Disorders? *Behavioural and Cognitive Psychotherapy, 33*, 177–188.

Traue, H. C., & Jerg-Bretzke, L. (2008). Wie verarbeiten Therapeuten die traumatischen Erfahrungen ihrer Klienten? *Verhaltenstherapie & Verhaltensmedizin, 29*(2), 171–174.

van Oppen, P., van Balkom, A. J. L. M., Smit, J. H., Schuurmans, J., van Dyck, R., & Emmelkamp, P. M. G. (2010). Does the therapy manual or the therapist matter most in treatment of obsessive-compulsive disorder? A randomized controlled trial of exposure with response or ritual prevention in 118 patients. *Journal of Clinical Psychiatry, 71*(9), 1158–1167.

Chapter 4
Exposure Techniques: The Role of Extinction Learning

Gonzalo P. Urcelay

Gonzalo P. Urcelay is a Teaching Associate at the Department of Experimental Psychology at the University of Cambridge. His research concentrates on learning theories and the neurobiological substrates of acquired behaviour. He is currently conducting studies to assess the involvement of the prefrontal cortex in the transition from goal-directed to habitual behaviors and its relation to preexisting traits such as impulsivity.

G.P. Urcelay (✉)
Department of Experimental Psychology, University of Cambridge,
Downing Street, Cambridge, CB2 3EB, UK
e-mail: gu203@cam.ac.uk

P. Neudeck and H.-U. Wittchen (eds.), *Exposure Therapy: Rethinking the Model – Refining the Method*, DOI 10.1007/978-1-4614-3342-2_4,

4.1 Analogies Between Extinction Learning and Exposure-Based Therapies

There is now considerable agreement that exposure-based therapies represent one of the most effective treatment strategies for psychopathological conditions such as anxiety disorders (Craske et al., 2008; Hofmann, 2007; Hofmann, 2008; McNally, 2007) and drug abuse (Conklin & Tiffany, 2002). The historical roots of exposure-based therapies can be traced back to the studies by Watson and Rayner (1920) found in most textbooks concerning the history of psychology. In short, in their attempt to assess whether emotional responses could be experimentally manipulated in the laboratory, they presented "Little Albert" with a pet rat and allowed the child to play with it. Once Albert was familiar with the pet, they began to present a loud aversive noise each time Albert would reach to touch the rat. The intensity of the noise was high enough to elicit emotional reactions such as crying. After experiencing many rat–noise pairings, the child began to show the emotional reactions that were originally elicited by the loud noise but now to the rat, in the absence of the loud noise. This experiment was important at the time because it provided support for the view that some emotional reactions were learned and could be manipulated in the laboratory, placing psychology among those disciplines that exert experimental control over the phenomena under investigation. In addition, these experiments provided evidence that associative learning mechanisms can be responsible, at least in part, for the changes in behaviour that humans and other animals display in their natural environments. That is, the experience of two contiguous events (stimulus–outcome) results in the establishment of an association between them so that, upon subsequent encounters with one of the events (e.g., the stimulus), subjects will react to it based on the association that was established during those contiguous presentations. In other words, after experiencing two events in close temporal proximity, the stimulus predicts the occurrence of the outcome.

Humans, similar to other animals, are biologically prepared to take advantage of their prior experience to anticipate the occurrence of aversive events that are potentially life threatening (e.g., the appearance of a predator) and also events that promote survival, such as the encounter of food or a mate for reproduction. If the change in behaviour observed upon subsequent encounters with the one event depends on the organism's ability to associate (or link) these two events, experiencing the stimulus event in the absence of the outcome tends to restore the behaviour that was observed before any contiguous presentations was experienced. This change is called extinction (Pavlov, 1927). If one accepts that associations mediate our reactions to the stream of stimulation we experience in our daily lives, it provides a mean by which prior experiences, that evoke reactions of disproportionate magnitude in some anxiety disorders, can be brought under control in the therapist's office.

Exposure-based therapies exploit this idea by having clients experience, under the highly controlled environmental conditions of a therapeutic setting, events that may have been associated with threatening outcomes in the past but that are no longer followed by these outcomes, which is by definition what we referred to as experimental extinction. Exposure therapies attempt to extinguish disproportionate responses that, in some cases, have seriously debilitating consequences in the lives of those who suffer clinical conditions such as anxiety disorders. It should be noted that exposure to stimuli in the absence of the outcome also applies to positive conditioned emotional reactions as is the case with drugs of abuse and palatable foods (i.e., obesity). In fact there is a large literature suggesting that stimuli predictive of drug administration or drug availability elicit cravings, which are a major cause of relapse after prolonged abstinence from drugs (Everitt & Robbins, 2005; Tiffany, 1990). The analogy between exposure therapies and extinction learning is obviously an oversimplification, as there are numerous factors that determine treatment success that go beyond the procedural and behavioural parallels.

Although exposure-based therapies are among the most successful ways to treat anxiety disorders and addiction, they are not immune to relapse, and in fact the conditions under which relapse is often observed strengthens the analogy between these exposure-based approaches and extinction learning. That is, clients relapse after some time has passed since treatment termination, and this obviously occurs outside of the therapist's office. Extinction learning, as it will be described later, is strongly dependent on the environment in which extinction and testing occur, and on the interval between extinction learning and testing. Thus, studies of experimental extinction that use animals in highly controlled settings are devoid of multiple confounds which are unavoidable when studying the effects of exposure in the therapist office such as high attrition rates and interpersonal characteristics of both the therapist and the client. This allows for a precise study of the conditions that increase the extent to which extinction learning will generalise to different environments and tolerate the passage of time, while permitting more secure conclusions and thus allow for theoretical developments.

In this chapter we will describe studies of experimental extinction conducted in human and non human animals, with the intention of highlighting: (1) the conditions under which extinction learning can be enhanced, as a means of translating knowledge obtained in highly controlled experiments to the clinical practise, and (2) some principles that underlie extinction learning and current associative explanations of extinction learning. Because in principle the potential of extinction to reduce the expression of prior experiences applies equally to negative (aversive) and positive (appetitive) outcomes, the studies described here are thought to apply equally to both sources of behavioural change. Although the goal of any psychological theory is to explain and predict the environmental conditions that cause changes in behaviour, one cannot deny the existence of neurobiological processes that underlie these changes. To put it differently, the brain mediates the changes in behaviour which we will assess in light of associative processes, and thus any attempt to separate these two is doomed to failure. Consistent with this rather obvious claim is the fact that exposure-based therapies are often administered in combination with pharmacotherapies (Hofmann, 2007; also see Chap. 6 in this volume).

4.2 Extinction Learning: Does It Erase the Original Memory, or Does It Create a New Memory?

One pressing issue in studies of extinction learning that has important consequences from a translational perspective such as that adopted here is whether extinction learning erases or destroys the original (i.e., excitatory) memory or, instead, results in the learning of a new relation between the stimulus and outcome (Stimulus → noOutcome) that interferes with the original memory (Dickinson, 1980). If extinction learning erases the original memory, successful extinction could remediate the detrimental effects of pervasive memories for ever, a goal that would place psychological therapy at the top of the chart in terms of its effectiveness. However, even in early studies of extinction learning, Pavlov (1927) and his colleagues documented that the change in behaviour brought by extinction learning was vulnerable to the passage of time, a phenomenon which Pavlov named spontaneous recovery. Logically, if recovery from extinction occurs in the absence of additional excitatory training (as is the case in spontaneous recovery), extinction learning cannot be accommodated by an explanation that assumes that it erases the original excitatory memory. That is, if the excitatory memory were to be destroyed by the extinction treatment, no recovery from extinction should be observed. Despite these early observations by Pavlov, some formal theories of learning have assumed that extinction can result in erasure (i.e., unlearning) of the original memory (Rescorla & Wagner, 1972), or at least in partial erasure (Stout & Miller, 2007). In controlled studies using animals, spontaneous recovery has sometimes been observed to be complete (Quirk, 2002). Even if some degree of unlearning occurs during extinction, convergent lines of evidence suggest that most of the original memory is not destroyed and these phenomena will be reviewed in Sect. 4.2.1.

Although in this chapter we will review evidence consistent with the idea that extinction does not result in unlearning or erasure of the original learning (Bouton & Bolles, 1979), erasure is often embraced by researchers interested in the neural and behavioural determinants of extinction learning (Quirk et al., 2010). Still, as noted by many authors (Bouton, Westbrook, Corcoran, & Maren, 2006; Bouton & Woods, 2008; Lovibond, 2004; Rescorla, 2004a), several observations lead to the conclusion that extinction learning does not erase the original learning. Following Bouton and Woods (2008), we will briefly describe six frequently cited recovery effects after extinction. To this list of recovery effects, we will add two more that also suggest that extinction does not erase the original learning (see Fig. 4.1).

4.2.1 Behavioural Phenomena Suggesting New Learning During Extinction

Evidence that extinction recovers with the passage of time, or *spontaneous recovery*, was documented by Pavlov and collaborators in their early studies on extinction

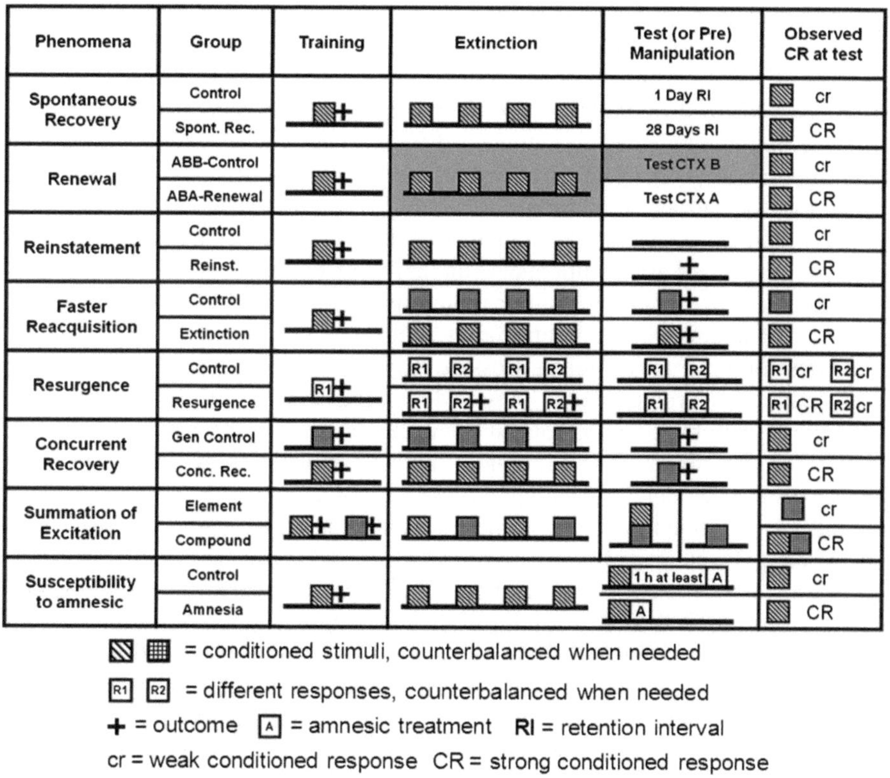

Fig. 4.1 Figure 4.1 depicts eight different phenomena which suggest that extinction does not lead to erasure of an association. See text for details of each procedure as well as sources of evidence. *Shaded boxes* mean that the procedure was conducted in a distinct environment

(Pavlov, 1927). Extinction learning is also vulnerable to changes in the context from where extinction learning occurred, and this has been called *renewal.* Renewal was observed first by Bouton and Bolles (1979), in an experiment in which rats first learned that an auditory stimulus was followed by a brief footshock in one context (A) and then experienced extinction training in which the auditory stimulus was no longer follower by footshock, but in a second context (B). The critical observation was that extinction (i.e., absence of responding) was observed when rats were tested in the extinction context (B) but fear to the auditory stimulus was strong when testing was conducted in the context where the auditory stimulus was followed by footshock (A). Thus, the notation ABA renewal (relative to ABB) will be used here and throughout this chapter to denote the context of training, extinction, and test, respectively. Renewal due to return to the context of original acquisition may be explained by residual excitation to the context summating with fear to the extinguished stimulus; in fact, this is a plausible explanation considering that the critical comparison between ABA and ABB renewal involves comparing stimuli tested in contexts that differ in excitatory strength. However, extinction also recovers, although perhaps not as well, when the context of test is one that has no prior excitatory learning, as it is the case when testing is conducted in a third, neutral context, or in ABC renewal (Urcelay, Lipatova, & Miller, 2009). Thus, extinction learning seems to recover when testing is conducted in a context different than that of extinction learning. A third observation that joins spontaneous recovery and renewal in suggesting that extinction does not erase the original learning is *reinstatement* (Rescorla & Heth, 1975), which is the recovery from extinction learning observed after presenting the outcome alone (the unconditioned stimulus) after extinction and before testing. Reinstatement has important implications for clinical practise as seen in animal models of addiction where relapse after protracted abstinence is speeded with a small dose of the drug (Crombag, Bossert, Koya, & Shaham, 2008). Thus, recovery from extinction learning is better observed after the passage of time (e.g., spontaneous recovery), a change in the context where extinction learning occurred (renewal), or after the administration of a reminder achieved by the presentation of the consequence. Reinstatement is intriguing because it is context specific, when the outcome reminder is presented in a context different from that of testing; the reinstatement effect is largely attenuated.[1]

There are other ways to assess whether extinction erases the excitatory memory trace or instead produces new inhibitory-like learning that interferes with the excitatory content learned during initial acquisition. For example, if extinction erases the excitatory trace, retraining an extinguished memory should result in excitation at least similar to (but clearly never higher) to a second stimulus which has not undergone any prior excitation followed by extinction. In other words, if extinction erased the original memory, reacquisition should be similar for stimuli that have undergone acquisition followed by extinction and for stimuli that have undergone similar exposure but in the absence of excitatory learning (Delamater, 2004). Evidence supporting this prediction has been found in studies by Bouton (1986). The interpretation of these null results in terms of erasure is strengthened by observations that reacquisition after extinction sometimes proceeds slower than in a control group (Calton, Mitchell, & Schachtman, 1996; Denniston & Miller, 2003; Monfils, Cowansage, Klann, & LeDoux, 2009), a finding taken as consistent with a view of extinction that assumes inhibitory learning (Monfils et al., 2009).[2] With this said, the opposite finding has also been reported, namely *faster reacquisition* after extinction, a finding clearly at odds with an interpretation of extinction in terms of erasure (Bouton & Swartzentruber, 1989).

[1] In the drug-addiction literature, the term reinstatement has been adopted to refer to any recovery from extinction achieved by the presentation of an event that was present during drug self-administration, namely the drug itself (proper reinstatement) but also stimuli, contexts, and stress. See Crombag et al. (2008) for a revision of these findings.

[2] Dr MA Wood has made the interesting suggestion (Wood 2011; personal communication Jan 4) that the fact that reacquisition may be slower after extinction cannot be taken as evidence of erasure; because erasure should return the memory to a zero state after which reacquisition should proceed in the same way as a control group.

As noted by Bouton and Woods (2008), *resurgence* and *concurrent recovery* add to the list of phenomena suggesting that extinction memories are better understood in terms of new learning rather than erasure of excitatory traces. Resurgence has been primarily documented in instrumental learning and involves the use of two different levers that allow two different responses (R1 and R2) each followed by a pleasant outcome (i.e., a sweet food pellet). Critical is what happens after acquisition of R1, when this response is undergoing extinction, during which a second lever (R2) is concurrently reinforced (i.e., followed by the consequence). Resurgence, by definition, is the recovery from extinction seen to lever (R1) when the alternative lever (R2) is subsequently subject to extinction treatment (Winterbauer & Bouton, 2010). This phenomenon also has practical interest because often exposure-based therapies are administered concurrently with reinforcement of other behaviours. The effectiveness of the practise then depends, to some extent, on the other behaviours, which if extinguished will result in recovery from extinction in the target behaviour (R1).

Lastly, concurrent recovery refers to the observation that responding to an extinguished stimulus recovers when a second, unrelated stimulus, receives excitatory training (Weidemann & Kehoe, 2004). This is similar to resurgence at first glance, but actually the opposite in manipulation. In resurgence, recovery is observed when the alternative stimulus is undergoing extinction, rather than when the alternative stimulus is reinforced, yet both observations agree with the claim that extinction of the memory did not erase the memory trace.

The phenomena described above have become popular as criteria to determine whether a particular extinction treatment has erased a memory or not (Quirk et al., 2010). It should be noted however, that this interpretation is not impervious to logical problems. For example, evidence that there is no memory does not necessary indicate that the memory is not there. It could simply be the case that the memory is stored but not retrieved (Miller & Matzel, 1988). Thus, demonstrating memory erasure depends on proving the null hypothesis correct, that the erased memory in one group is not different than a group which has no memory (Nader & Hardt, 2009). Because there are ways to circumvent this problem which we will discuss below, it is worth pointing to additional phenomena which also suggest that extinction does not erase the original memory.

One such phenomenon suggesting that extinction leaves some of the original memory available was originally documented by Reberg (1972). In Reberg's study, animals received separate training of two stimuli (i.e., stimuli S1 and S2 which were never presented together) followed by separate extinction of each stimulus. One stimulus (S1) was extinguished to intermediate levels, whereas the remaining stimulus (S2) was extinguished until no conditioned responding was observed during three consecutive extinction trials. After extinction of S2 was complete, subjects received tests with each stimulus alone and with a compound of the two stimuli. If extinction erases the original memory (assuming unlearning is equivalent to erasure), tests with either stimulus alone or a compound should not make any difference. Contrary to this prediction, subjects showed strong conditioned responding when tested with the compound and weak responding when testing was conducted with either stimulus alone. A second group of subjects received similar treatments as mentioned; however, S2 was additionally extinguished during 54 trials, during which no changes in responding were observed (extinction was already complete). During the tests in which S1 and S2 were presented separately, S1 evoked negligible levels of suppression, and S2 evoked behaviour that is consistent with S2 having acquired inhibitory properties during the extinction treatment. This pattern is consistent with the amount of extinction training that these two stimuli received. Still, strong conditioned responding was also observed in the second condition when both stimuli were tested together. This *summation of residual excitation* revealed by the compound test cannot be explained by an explanation that poses that extinction results in memory erasure. These results have been replicated by Rescorla (2006) who exploited this observation to test the predictions of a model that captures extinction as erasure (Rescorla & Wagner, 1972). All in all, the effect documented by Reberg adds to the above-mentioned list in suggesting that extinction, rather than erasing the original excitatory association, establishes new learning which is highly context dependent. Because testing the compound is clearly a different situation from experiencing each stimulus alone, recovery after testing the compound is not surprising.

Finally, another source of evidence for new learning during extinction is revealed by the vulnerability of extinction memories to amnesic treatments. The argument is that, if extinction memories are better captured as new learning, their consolidation ought to follow a similar time course as for other memories. In addition, their expression should be sensitive to reactivation manipulations known to have an effect on excitatory memories. A study by Briggs and Riccio (2007) recently showed that hypothermia-induced amnesia given soon after extinction of an inhibitory avoidance memory, but not 60 min later, attenuates the expression of the extinction memory. But time-dependent gradients should not be a criterion to establish that the memory represents new learning rather than unlearning, after all the process of unlearning could also need some time to get settled. Critically, Experiment 2 in their study showed that the amnestic effect of hypothermia on the extinction memory (which led to high levels of responding) could be alleviated if animals were cooled before testing, presumably because re-cooling them immediately before test reactivated the extinction memory that had presumably undergone amnesia. These experiments demonstrate that extinction memories, like excitatory memories (i.e., reinforcement), are susceptible to retrograde amnesia in a time-dependent fashion. In addition, the amnesic effect is sensitive to reactivation treatments, like new memories which need to undergo consolidation but also seem to recover with the appropriate reminder treatments (Misanin, Miller, & Lewis, 1968).

Despite Pavlov's early observation of spontaneous recovery and the wealth of phenomena suggesting that extinction does not erase the excitatory memory, the argument of memory erasure is frequently made, in particular in the last decade since the possibility of memory disruption after retrieval (i.e., reconsolidation) and new pharmacological treatments (see Chap. 6 by Hofmann et al. this volume) offer promising new avenues for therapists in the clinic whose goal is to relive their clients from the devastating consequences of traumatic events.

4.2.2 Extinction as Context Dependent New Learning

As an alternative to memory erasure of the excitatory association, it has been argued that extinction creates a new memory of the relationship between the Stimulus previously paired with the outcome, and the absence of the Outcome (S–noO), which depends heavily on the context for its expression. The context is defined as a collection of attributes given by distal features of the environment, but following Bouton (1993) this meaning is extended to temporal cues, so that the passage of time is understood as a change in temporal context. Put more precisely, time and space are equivalent and thus both changes of context should result in recovery from extinction. Although spatial and/or temporal contextual attributes modulate the expression of extinction memories, it is not clear which characteristics of extinction make it particularly susceptible to modulation by the context. One possibility, as discussed by Bouton, is that inhibitory S–noO memories are particularly context specific (Bouton, 1993). Alternatively, he also proposed that second learned memories about a particular stimulus are susceptible to modulation by the context. Because an extinction treatment is presumably inhibitory in nature and it is always administered after excitatory treatment, it is not possible to determine from extinction treatments alone which of these two criteria are necessary to observe modulation.

Sissons and Miller (2009) recently conducted experiments that assess these two alternatives. They administered excitatory training of one stimulus followed by inhibitory learning of that same stimulus, while also training a second stimulus that received similar training but in the opposite order. In other words, all subjects received excitatory and inhibitory training of two stimuli in two different stages, but the order was the opposite. They then tested subjects on different stimuli (whichever was trained last), but they did so for different groups at different intervals since the last phase of training. Subjects tested immediately after the end of the second phase of training responded much more to the stimulus that had received excitatory training last, relative to subjects that received inhibitory training last. This is consistent with the view that the second phase of training was dominant when these memories were tested immediately after. However, when different groups of animals were tested after a 21-day retention interval, responding was the opposite of that observed in the immediate test. Subjects responded more to the stimulus which received excitatory training first and inhibitory learning second (in other words, the dominance of inhibitory training seen immediately after the outset of stage 2 training was lost in favour or dominance of the first trained memory), and the opposite was true of subject that received training in the reverse order. These results suggest that there is nothing particularly special about inhibitory memories; it seems to be the case that second learned memories are particularly susceptible to modulation by the context.

Because clinical intervention such as exposure-based therapies are usually administered once the client has already acquired the fearful or appetitive relationship, it may be better to assume that the effects of the treatment, which is always learned in a second stage, will invariably wane with the passage of time. In the next section, I will summarise some variables which, independently of the theoretical framework, enhance extinction learning and reduce recovery from extinction.

4.3 Manipulations that Enhance Extinction Learning

Assuming that extinction learning does not erase the original learning established before extinction takes place, it is worth pointing out variables that reduce recovery from extinction, because in practise these are the variables that may inform the clinician of alternatives to the traditional practise of exposure therapy with the objective of increasing its effectiveness. The summary presented here is not exhaustive and any interested reader may well consult additional literature on this issue (Laborda, McConnell, & Miller, 2011).

4.3.1 Massive Extinction

A strategy to reduce recovery after behavioural extinction has been to administer multiple extinction trials, assuming that more extinction trials will strengthen the extinction memory and alleviate recovery from extinction. For example, Tamai and Nakajima (2000), using fear conditioning in rats, administered training and extinction in the same context but tested in a different context, which should result in recovery from extinction (i.e., AAB renewal). Renewal was indeed observed after rats received 72 extinction trials, but not after 112 extinction trials. However, these parametric differences did not reduce ABA renewal in other groups, which typically results in robust recovery from extinction. These results suggest that extending extinction training does alleviate renewal, but only a weak form of renewal such as AAB renewal. Also using rats and fear conditioning, Denniston, Chang, and Miller (2003) administered 160 or 800 extinction trials. At issue was whether this extreme parametric variation would alleviate ABA renewal, and indeed they found that this was the case. Unfortunately other studies did not succeed in reducing renewal after massive extinction (Rauhut, Thomas, & Ayres, 2001), but this may be due to insufficient extinction given that the maximum number of extinction trials was substantially lower (100 and 144) than those administered by Denniston and colleagues. Further, the length of exposure therapy (i.e., number of sessions) has been directly assessed in several human studies conducted by Foa and colleagues. In general, these studies have found increased efficacy after prolonged exposure therapy relative to adequate controls (Foa et al., 2005). A recent meta-analysis, however, revealed no benefit of prolonged exposure therapy relative to other active treatments (Powers, Halpern, Ferenschak, Gillihan, & Foa, 2010). It is possible that, through different mechanisms, different treatments may achieve similar beneficial outcomes, which should not undermine the potential of prolonged exposure to optimise extinction learning and improve the effectiveness of exposure therapy. Overall, extending exposure seems to be beneficial in reducing recovery, although it is not entirely clear yet how much extinction should be given before treatment is terminated. The answer to this question may well depend on the strength of the fear memory, which makes it difficult but not impossible to determine how much exposure is necessary and sufficient to reduce relapse.

4.3.2 Extinction in the Presence of an Excitor

A candidate manipulation to boost extinction learning and reduce recovery is to increase the amount of fear during extinction trials, although this manipulation may not be the most pleasant for clients. Nevertheless, for extinction of fear to be successful, subjects do need to revaluate the original meaning of the fearful memory, and thus increasing the amount of fear during extinction may facilitate this revaluation. Indeed this outcome is predicted by some theories of learning (Miller & Matzel, 1988; Rescorla & Wagner, 1972), and is consistent with accounts of extinction that suggest that the amount of extinction learning is proportional to the strength of the conditioned response during extinction (Rescorla, 2001). This "rule of thumb" proposed by Rescorla is a powerful principle to anticipate the degree of extinction, and consistent with this idea, several studies have found that conducting extinction learning with two excitatory stimuli presented simultaneously, does alleviate several forms of recovery from extinction (Rescorla, 2000; Rescorla, 2006; Thomas & Ayres, 2004). However, this prediction is not entirely consistent with all theories, since configural models of learning anticipate less extinction when a cue is extinguished in the presence of a second excitatory cue (Pearce, 1987, 1994, 2002). These theories make this prediction because of their emphasis on configural processes occurring when two or more stimuli are presented simultaneously during extinction. Thus, configural theories anticipate recovery from extinction when it is conducted with two stimuli because they posit that during test the presentation of only one stimulus reduces transfer of extinction learning due to the change in stimulation occurring from extinction learning to test, a process that is called generalisation decrement. In fact, studies with pigeons in appetitive preparations have confirmed this prediction, namely that less extinction is sometimes observed when extinction is conducted in the presence of a second excitatory stimulus (Pearce & Wilson, 1991).

Although the reasons for these discrepancies are not entirely clear, these conflicting results may well indicate that multiple processes operate when extinction is conducted in the presence of a second excitatory stimulus. In support of this notion, studies have found no benefit of extinction with a second excitatory cue relative to control animals which received similar amounts of extinction of a cue alone (Urcelay, Lipatova, & Miller, 2009). These studies, in addition, consistently revealed decreased extinction learning in separate groups that received extinction of an excitatory cue but in the presence of a second stimulus which did not undergo excitatory learning (i.e., extinction in the presence of a neutral stimulus). In other words, the mere addition of a second stimulus, independently of its excitatory value, decreased extinction even when testing was conducted in the same context in which extinction took place (ABB), an outcome consistent with configural models (Pearce, 1987, 1994, 2002). Based on these findings, it was hypothesised that extinction in the presence of a second excitor may provide some benefit for extinction learning, but this benefit may be masked by generalisation decrement occurring between extinction and the test. In accordance, Urcelay and colleagues were able to alleviate ABC renewal when they extinguished in compound stimuli of different modalities and durations, which presumably minimised subjects' configuring stimuli during extinction learning and thus facilitated the observation of extinction learning during the test.

Studies using fear conditioning in humans have also failed to support the idea that conducting extinction in the presence of multiple excitatory stimuli facilitates extinction (Lovibond, Davis, & O'Flaherty, 2000; Vervliet, Vansteenwegen, Hermans, & Eelen, 2007), and these failures have also been interpreted in terms of generalisation decrement diminishing any benefits of presenting multiple cues during extinction. An alternative to conducting extinction in the presence of a second excitatory cue is to present the aversive event (i.e., outcome) during extinction, which should increase fear levels to the context during extinction and facilitate extinction learning. A study in humans (Vervliet, Vansteenwegen, & Hermans, 2010) and one employing rats in a fear-conditioning preparation both showed attenuated renewal by presenting during extinction unsignalled presentations of the footshock outcome interspersed with extinction trials (Rauhut et al., 2001). Although this alternative has implications for theories of extinction, it is difficult to see in practise how this would be implemented in a therapeutic situation without raising ethical concerns (see Chap. 2 by Deacon in this volume).

4.3.3 Use of Retrieval Cues Associated with Extinction

One technique to reduce relapse after exposure-based therapies is provided by the use of different stimuli, or objects, that clients will associate with the calmness and interpersonal support of the therapeutic setting, which they can then take with themselves to aid the retrieval of the support and calmness that surrounds the therapeutic environment. In other words, introducing novel stimuli to the extinction session, as long as they do not provoke any unconditioned effects, may be beneficial because of the potential that these stimuli will have, outside of the therapist's office, to reduce fear in a novel situation. In fact some interventions make use of safety objects to aid long-term effectiveness of therapeutic programmes while at the same time reducing relapse.

Whether these cues provide any benefit can be studied under controlled laboratory situations. For example, Brooks and Bouton (1993) used an appetitive preparation in which rats responded to the illumination of a food-predictive light by nose poking in the food magazine situated inside the conditioning box. Once training was stable, all animals were shifted to extinction. During extinction, some animals were presented with a stimulus four times at the beginning of each extinction session and on 75% of the extinction trials immediately before the cue. Thus, the stimulus clearly came to signal the extinction session and the extinction trials, perhaps functioning as an occasion setter (Holland, 1992), as the stimulus added during the extinction session did not have any excitatory or inhibitory properties on its own. Critically, when subjects were given a test six days later, those that had this neutral stimulus presented before the first test trial showed less spontaneous recovery. Presumably, the stimulus was capable of facilitating retrieval of the extinction session and consequently attenuated responding during a delayed test. These findings were soon replicated but in a counterconditioning design that differs from extinction in that during the second phase subjects are usually presented with the same stimulus they experienced during the original training, but now paired with a different consequence (Brooks & Bouton, 1994). Similar findings have been reported in humans. For example, Vervliet et al. (2007) administered electrodermal conditioning to a stimulus in humans, which then was followed by extinction training. However, before conditioning and extinction began, each phase was associated with a particular cue which signalled that the acquisition or extinction session had begun. When subjects were presented with the retrieval cues immediately before the test, they showed substantially more recovery from extinction when tested in the presence of the acquisition retrieval cue, although the extinction retrieval cue was not able to alleviate recovery from extinction.

Taken together, these findings in rats and humans suggest that retrieval cues present during acquisition or the extinction treatment can modulate the amount of recovery from extinction, and thus are critical when considering relapse. They do so, presumably, by virtue of their capacity to facilitate retrieval of memory of the extinction session which makes extinction (and counterconditioning) less vulnerable to the multiple sources of relapse that may be encountered on a day in the life of a patient.

4.3.4 Extinction in Multiple Contexts

Memories of extinction are best characterised as being highly context dependent and to transfer poorly to novel situations, and we just saw that stimuli that are associated with extinction can act like contexts and facilitate transfer of extinction between contexts. Similarly, it could be speculated that conducting extinction in multiple contexts will prevent the context specificity of extinction and facilitate its retrieval in new situations (Bouton, 1991). This prediction has important implications as many exposure-based treatments include exposure in situ and also in novel situations. Gunther, Denniston, and Miller (1998) conducted an experiment in which different groups of rats experienced fear conditioning followed by extinction either in a single context or in three different contexts. The results indicated that extinction in multiple contexts did strengthen the extinction memory, as evidenced by less ABC renewal. However, a follow-up experiment suggested that this benefit was not observed if the excitatory memory was trained in multiple contexts, suggesting that subjects experiencing traumatic events in multiple locations would not benefit from extinction in multiple contexts.

In addition, other studies have suggested that the effect of extinction in multiple contexts is constrained by other experimental variables; thus, not all studies have replicated the original findings by Gunther and colleagues (Bouton, García-Gutiérrez, Zilski, & Moody, 2006; Neumann, Lipp, & Cory, 2007). Nevertheless, the beneficial effects of extinction in multiple contexts has been replicated in fear conditioning (Thomas, Vurbic, & Novak, 2009), in studies involving taste aversions (Chelonis, Calton, Hart, & Schachtman, 1999), and in humans (Neumann, 2008). Importantly, the benefits of extinction in multiple contexts upon recovery from extinction has been observed in spider-fearful participants, a finding in a critical population which suggests that this manipulation should be taken seriously due to its potential to alleviate return of fear and subsequent relapse (Rowe & Craske, 1998; Vansteenwegen et al., 2007).

4.3.5 Interval Between Acquisition and Extinction

Several studies have assessed whether extinction learning immediately after acquisition alleviates recovery from extinction. This variable is important because interventions such as immediate debriefing have been adopted as a strategy for dealing with traumatic events (Campfield & Hills, 2001), although the success of these manipulations has been questioned in a meta-analysis (van Emmerik, Kamphuis, Hulsbosch, & Emmelkamp, 2002). Studies in the laboratory using rats and pigeons in appetitive Pavlovian or instrumental preparations have found that when the interval between acquisition and extinction is lengthened, extinction is less (as opposed to more) vulnerable to different manipulations that induce recovery (Rescorla, 2004b). For example, rats received training in which two different cues were each followed by food pellets before one of them was extinguished completely. At the end of extinction of the first cue, all subjects experienced extinction of the alternative stimulus. This and other experiments consistently demonstrated that delayed extinction was resistant to spontaneous recovery assessed five days later, suggesting that delayed, rather than immediate extinction, is beneficial for extinction as it decreased its recovery. However, studies in rats using fear conditioning have observed that extinction given ten minutes after fear acquisition can alleviate recovery assessed through renewal, spontaneous recovery, and reinstatement (Myers, Ressler, & Davis, 2006). It should be noted that the data do not seem to reveal a large behavioural effect of immediate extinction, as if immediate exposure may only slightly dampen fear which does not show recovery. This becomes evident when immediate extinction is compared with delayed exposure which substantially decreases fear but shows recovery given the appropriate treatment (Myers et al., 2006).

The reasons for these discrepancies are not clear, although soon after the publication of these latter findings, experiments run in several laboratories using rats and fear conditioning followed by extinction showed no benefit of immediate extinction when given up to 6 h after fear acquisition, compared with extinction given a day after fear acquisition (Archbold, Bouton, & Nader, 2010; Chang & Maren, 2009; Maren, Chang, & Thompson, 2006; Woods & Bouton, 2008). Although some studies have replicated the basic finding by Myers et al. (2006), the benefit of the immediate extinction treatment was better observed when testing was delayed rather than soon after extinction treatment (Johnson, Escobar, & Kimble, 2010). In general, fear-conditioning studies in humans have failed to observe benefits from immediate extinction (Alvarez, Johnson, & Grillon, 2007; Huff, Hernandez, Blanding, & LaBar, 2009; Schiller et al., 2008), although other studies have been able to replicate the immediate extinction effect but under select circumstances (Norrholm et al., 2008).

Lopez and colleagues (Lopez, de Vasconcelos, & Cassel, 2008) trained rats in a water maze (i.e., spatial memories) and administered extinction at much longer intervals after acquisition (5 days vs. 25 days). They found that delayed extinction treatment does not result in appreciable extinction when given on separate days. In fact, 25 days after acquisition, three exposure sessions given on three consecutive days resulted in a progressive improvement in spatial memory (Lopez et al., 2008; also see Rohrbaugh & Riccio, 1970). This difference presumably results from the use of spaced extinction sessions given on separate days, perhaps because (relatively few) spaced exposure given 25 days after acquisition, when the memory has been consolidated, may act as reminders rather than effectively extinguish the original memory. This is not surprising, as seen below; protocols employing largely spaced extinction trials may sometimes act as reminders rather than trigger behavioural extinction (Cain, Blouin, & Barad, 2003). Indeed, a follow-up study in which immediate (5 day) and delayed (25 day) extinction was given on three consecutive trials, but all in one day, found no differences between 5- or 25-day-old memories, presumably because the consecutive extinction trials prevented the repeated reactivation of the excitatory memory that competes with the establishment of extinction memory. Similar findings were observed when the physical salience of the cue was increased; suggesting that exposure to strong memory cues facilitated extinction learning in detriment of memory reactivation. Thus, these experiments in spatial learning suggest that the effectiveness of immediate vs. delayed extinction depends, at least in part, on the strength of the memory and the induction of behavioural extinction. When old memories are given a widely spaced extinction regimen, exposure increases the strength of the memories instead of behavioural extinction, a finding that has recently received support using fear preparations (Inda, Muravieva, & Alberini, 2011; Rohrbaugh & Riccio, 1970). These results highlight the complex nature of exposure treatments which not always result in behavioural extinction, in particular when given long after the memory has been acquired and with a widely spaced exposure regimen.

4.3.6 The Spacing of Extinction Trials

It is widely acknowledged that spaced acquisition is beneficial for memory retention (Barela, 1999). In the clinic, the amount of time between sessions may be an important variable and there is a large variability in the spacing of sessions between treatments. For example, some treatments involve massed exposure limited to a week or so, whereas conventional treatments are administered weekly over a period of several months. In addition, some have distinguished within-session reduction in fear from between-session reductions in fear (Craske et al., 2008). In the laboratory, the spacing of extinction trials has received a great deal of attention, but unfortunately it is not yet entirely clear which alternative (e.g., massed vs. spaced) is better. In some studies, massed extinction has been observed to enhance extinction (Cain et al., 2003; Rescorla & Durlach, 1987), the opposite finding has, however, also been observed (e.g., Urcelay, Wheeler, & Miller, 2009).

One explanation for these contradictory findings is revealed by the distinction made above between memory reactivation and successful extinction (Leet, Milton & Everitt, 2006). Extinction learning involves multiple presentations of the stimulus alone, which presumably activates a representation of the consequence and allows for an update of that memory representation, so that future encounters with the stimulus will be less likely to evoke a memory representation of the [aversive] outcome. If the memory is reactivated but not updated, the representation of the consequence evoked by the stimulus may actually be strengthened, as if the original relationship were being rehearsed and strengthened rather than learning a new relationship. Support for this speculation was found in a study by Lee and colleagues (Lee et al. 2006). Rats received fear conditioning training in which an auditory cue was consistently followed by a brief footshock. The following day, some animals experienced one presentation of the cue alone. One presentation of the stimulus was not sufficient to induce extinction, as evidenced by freezing to the stimulus tested on the day after the single presentation. However, it did seem to reactivate the memory making it vulnerable to disruption by an amnesic agent (Misanin et al., 1968). The implications for the spacing of extinction trials are that, when extinction trials are widely spaced, it is possible that each presentation of the stimulus reactivates a memory representation of the outcome without resulting in the formation of a new memory. Some empirical findings agree with this observation. In the studies by Cain et al. (2003) in which massed extinction was superior to spaced extinction in terms of diminished recovery, the subjects that received the spaced treatment did not stop freezing during the extinction session. In other words, these subjects never showed any extinction learning. It is not surprising then that these subjects showed strong fear during the delayed test (i.e., spontaneous recovery) or when tested in a different context (i.e., renewal). A somewhat similar distinction is that between the decrease in fear observed within a session and that observed between sessions (Craske et al., 2008; Davis, Ressler, Rothbaum, & Richardson, 2006; Drew, Yang, Ohyama, & Balsam, 2004). Within-session extinction reflects the update that occurs on a given trial as a consequence of the learning that occurred on the trial immediately preceding that trial, whereas between session extinction (or transfer) reflects long-term changes as a consequence of prior learning. Moreover, the intervals between extinction trials (hereafter, intertrial interval [ITI]) within a session are spent in the same context, whereas the interval between sessions is spent on the home cages. This distinction is important in the context of the present discussion because rapid changes which are typically observed during the course of extinction may not necessary result in the enduring changes which are the main objective of therapy.

One candidate explanation for the discrepant findings observed in both humans and other animals is that massed extinction trials may increase within-session extinction, but this learning may transfer poorly to future encounters with the fearful stimulus. This conclusion is well captured by a human contingency learning study in which the ITI was manipulated in different groups of subjects (Orinstein, Urcelay, & Miller, 2010). After acquisition, subjects were assigned to one of three conditions. The Control condition received no extinction trials. A second condition named Spaced did experience extinction trials which were evenly distributed among presentations of several other stimuli that in this study acted as filler cues. A third Group, named Expanding (Bjork & Bjork, 2006), received extinction treatment similar in the number of trials to that received by Group Spaced, but in this group the distribution of extinction trials started being relatively massed and progressively became more spaced, resulting in longer intervals between extinction trials as extinction learning progressed. Stimuli were different foods that a fictitious character had eaten at a particular restaurant (i.e., the restaurant acted as a contextual stimulus), and the outcome was represented by adverse consequences of the food consumption (i.e., diarrhoea). Participants were required to rate each cue on each trial as it was presented, which allowed for the collection of data during extinction trials, and ultimately assess the effect of holding the ITI during extinction constant vs. increasing it as the extinction treatment progressed. To put it differently, subjects which received the extinction treatment with the expanding ITI started extinction with short intervals between extinction trials and progressively shifted towards longer ITI between extinction trials.

As predicted, subjects in the expanding condition showed a faster drop of their ratings than those receiving extinction trials with a constant ITI between extinction trials. The early benefit of massed extinction trials was eventually compensated by the amount of exposure, so that both groups ended the extinction session rating the target stimulus similarly. Intriguingly, a test of ABA renewal revealed no benefit of Expanding vs. Constant ITIs. Thus, the sharp decrease in ratings observed early during extinction did not attenuate recovery from extinction, consistent with the above-mentioned reviews highlighting the differences between what is observed during extinction, and transfers to situations outside the extinction setting. In fact, if one were to learn a lesson from these experiments and try to translate to the clinic, it would be that therapists should rely little on the fear assessments obtained in the therapist's office, as it may well give them a picture that changes drastically once the client has left the office. Fortunately, multiple assessments over time, and in different scenarios, are already standard in clinical practise.

The effect of spacing or massing extinction trials thus may differ depending on whether one looks at what happens during extinction and what happens on a subsequent test. There are various studies in which the spacing of extinction trials was systematically manipulated and then tested outside of the extinction session. As stated, these results are inconsistent and no clear picture has emerged. I will argue here that this possibly results from the use of different intervals during extinction, which may comprise more than one process. The relationship between increasing the ITI during extinction and the degree to which extinction learning is resistant to recovery is not linear, so that increasing the ITI during extinction (i.e., spacing extinction trials) may optimise extinction learning and alleviate recovery from extinction, but not when extinction trials are too spaced. When extinction is conducted with parameters that do indeed lead to extinction, an extinction trial n capitalises on the previous extinction trial $n-1$. However, if trial n is too far removed in time from the previous trial (i.e., presented a day later), it no longer benefits from the extinction that occurred on $n-1$, and thus is less effective in producing extinction learning. For example, it has been observed that a single presentation of a previously trained stimulus will elicit conditioned responding, presumably because it brings the memory into an active state. But one trial alone does not necessary produce extinction learning; in fact a single presentation may reactivate the memory and strengthen it (Inda et al., 2011; Pavlov, 1927; Rohrbaugh & Riccio, 1970). If trial n–1 occurs long before trial n, trial n will be experienced as a reactivation trial, a reminder of the aversive situation.

Recent neurobiological evidence suggests that one single presentation of a cue starts a cascade of molecular events that are different from those observed after ten presentations of a similarly trained stimulus (Lee et al., 2006). In fact, some have argued that the molecular cascade responsible for extinction learning is not initiated until the presentation of the stimulus itself has ended (Pedreira, Pérez-Cuesta, & Maldonado, 2004). This is consistent with the conflicting results discussed above. In the report by Cain et al. (2003), rats that received the spaced extinction protocol did not decrease freezing during the extinction session; in other words, the behaviour in these animals never seemed to extinguish. The fact that these animals responded more during the tests of recovery from extinction than animals trained with massed extinction trials does not suggest that extinction is more effective with massed extinction training because, in the groups extinguished with spaced trials, extinction never happened in first place. Obviously the optimal interval between extinction trials will vary depending on the task being used, the response under consideration, and a myriad of different conditions such as the strength of the original memory, and the depth of processing during extinction. One principle seems to emerge from this discussion though. Spacing extinction trials strengthens extinction learning, but only to a certain extent, when extinction trials are too spaced, extinction learning no longer takes place. The argument is that spaced presentations of the stimulus no longer benefit from the immediately preceding trial.

4.3.7 Pre-Extinction Retrieval

Traditionally, memories have been thought to necessitate a period of time (at least 6 h) after training for them to become consolidated and permanently stored in the brain (McGaugh, 1966, 2000). If an amnestic treatment is given within this critical window, it will weaken the memory being stored. Although appealing due to its simplicity, this idea was challenged by experiments in which the amnestic treatment was given postmemory reactivation a day later, a long time after the putative critical window of consolidation (Misanin et al., 1968). According to consolidation theory (McGaugh, 1966), once a memory is stabilized it should no longer be vulnerable to the effect of the amnestic treatment. In the experiment by Misanin et al. (1968), the amnestic treatment was equally effective when given after memory reactivation, suggesting that reactivated memories could also be affected by the amnesic treatment. The idea that reactivated memories can undergo a second "round" of consolidation, or reconsolidation, regained popularity recently after studies in fear conditioning replicated these findings with a high degree of specificity in the neural substrates underlying the behavioural observation (Nader & Hardt, 2009; Nader, Schafe, & Le Doux, 2000).

The idea that once active, memories can be modified is not new (Lewis, 1979; Bjork, 1975). Nevertheless, the last decade has seen a vigorous re-emergence of studies investigating the mechanisms and neurobiological processes underlying consolidation and reconsolidation, as these treatments could potentially act in a similar way as extinction-like treatments, in the sense that they may allow targeting specific memories, reactivating them, and then attempting to decrease the strength of the memory traces. The administration of amnesic treatments ordinarily involves potentially toxic drugs which may have undesirable effects due to a lack of specificity; therefore, this is not currently a standard practise. Alternatively, after memory reactivation one could administer extinction treatment when the memory is active and hence hyper vulnerable to the effects of extinction, while at the same time controlling to some extent for specificity in terms of the content of the memory. If, after reactivation, the memory is in a labile state, then following reactivation with a robust extinction treatment may enhance extinction and alleviate recovery from extinction. This was the rationale used by Monfils and colleagues in a series of studies in rats using fear conditioning (Monfils et al., 2009). They trained rats in a fear-conditioning preparation and a day after they gave them a single extinction session with 20 extinction trials. All groups received extinction, but they differed in the length of the interval between the first extinction trial (which acts as a reminder and produces memory reactivation) and the rest of the extinction regimen. That is, different groups received extinction training 10 min, 1, 6, or 24 h after the first presentation, which presumably produced memory reactivation. Subjects that experienced extinction treatment within an hour after reactivation, but not 6 or 24 h after reactivation (or no reactivation, with an ITI of 3 min between extinction trials), showed attenuated renewal, spontaneous recovery, and reinstatement. In addition, these subjects were slower to reacquire a fear response to the extinguished cue.

The mechanism by which this occurs is far from fully understood in that the critical difference between subjects which received extinction 10 min after reactivation and those who did not, was that the first ITI between extinction trials 1 and 2 was only 7 min longer (the ITI during extinction was 3 min). This finding was soon replicated in human fear conditioning (Schiller et al., 2010), using similar parameters to those used with rats, and with the addition of a within-subjects design, thereby suggesting some generality to this finding. Moreover, in humans, the benefit of retrieval prior to extinction was observed in a test conducted 12 months after acquisition and extinction. Unfortunately, replications from other laboratories have not always been successful (Chan, Leung, Westbrook, & McNally, 2010; Soeter & Kindt, 2011). For example, Chan et al. (2010) found in six experiments that, if anything, the reactivation trial increased renewal and reinstatement. They observed that the similarity between the context of training and the context where retrieval was administered may have been one reason for the lack of replication (also see, Soeter & Kindt, 2011).

Whether reactivation (which is equivalent to a single extinction trial) prior to extinction truly facilitates unlearning-like learning (in contrast to an interfering inhibitory-like memory) may require the test of time and replication. In studies conducted in the Psychological Laboratory at the University of Cambridge (Wood, 2010), the effect has been observed consistently in rats. Thus, Wood asked, for example, whether reactivation prior to extinction results in inhibitory memories that pass summation and retardation tests of inhibition, two canonical tests of conditioned inhibition[3] (Rescorla, 1969). Although memories that underwent reactivation prior to extinction were slower to reacquire excitatory properties (retardation test), they did not seem to pass a summation test for inhibition (Wood, 2010). In addition, Wood also assessed the specificity of reactivation prior to extinction, by conducting the mentioned protocol but in addition assessing the impact on acquisition of fear to a novel stimulus, which had not undergone any previous training. Surprisingly, she observed that administering reactivation followed by extinction rendered a (i.e., different) novel cue retarded in acquisition with the same outcome, suggesting that reactivation prior to extinction of the cue may produce some of its effects by changing the properties of the footshock representation (i.e., the outcome). This may explain why training of a novel cue was also retarded. In addition, for reactivation prior to extinction to be effective, subjects need to be removed from the context during the interval between reactivation and the subsequent extinction trials, otherwise the benefit of reactivation was no longer observed. In other words, the effect of reactivation prior to extinction depended on subjects being removed from the experimental setting, presumably because the reactivated memory needs to be updated and this is prevented if subjects remain in the context where retrieval occurred (Wood, 2010).

[3] In the associative-learning literature, inhibition refers to the explicit preventative relation between a stimulus and the outcome, which is inferred when the putative inhibitor attenuates the response elicited by an excitatory cue that has been trained separately (summation test), in addition to the putative inhibitor showing retarded emergence of excitatory learning (retardation test).

One pressing question for an explanation in terms of reconsolidation relates to the specification of the mechanism underlying the phenomenon. For example, given acquisition and reactivation prior to extinction treatment, one could speculate that a new instance of reactivation should destabilize the extinction memory and facilitate acquisition of fear, since the second reactivation after extinction should retrieve the extinguished (dominant) memory and allow for faster reacquisition. This outcome was not observed in Woods' experiments, but she observed that when the second reactivation was followed by reinforcement (i.e., the outcome) it reinstated the excitatory properties of the stimulus, which is consistent with the idea that for reconsolidation to occur the reactivated memory needs to be updated, as proposed by Lee (2009). Finally, another report that replicated the effect using tests of spontaneous recovery and renewal, also showed that if extinction (with and without prior reactivation) is conducted seven days after acquisition, there is no effect or reactivation prior to retrieval (Clem & Huganir, 2010). Overall, the available data so far suggests that there may be instances in which reactivation prior to extinction does facilitate extinction and alleviate recovery, but many boundary conditions apply, which makes it, to date, difficult to translate these findings directly into a clinical setting.

4.4 Theoretical Implications

In order to facilitate a brief summary of the findings reviewed in this chapter, we will describe two general theoretical approaches aimed to address the characteristics of extinction memories. One, which we will refer to as "associative," focuses on quantifying the strength of the connection between a stimulus and the outcome and is less concerned with temporal variables such as the interval between training and extinction, the benefit of conducting extinction in multiple contexts, or the effect of reactivating the excitatory memory before extinction. A second family of theories, which we will call "mnemonic" is less explicit about the strength of the connection between stimulus and outcome (and also S–noO), and focus on the conditions that constrain or enhance the expression of that learning. This distinction is rather general and made for the purpose of clarifying the emphasis of one or the other explanatory constructs. Ultimately, it may well be the case that a theory that is intended to account for the full range of phenomena will necessitate both approaches (i.e., hybrid).

4.4.1 Associative Theories

Associative theories of learning provide a quantitative measure of the strength of the connection between stimulus and outcome, but assume different factors to be critical in the update of these connections. For example, the Rescorla–Wagner model poses that during extinction learning, the excitatory connection between the stimulus and the outcome that was formed during acquisition will decrease until it reaches a value close to zero. Thus, extinction is reflected by a loss in associative strength between the stimulus and the outcome, which is equivalent to assuming memory erasure. Despite this failure of the theory to account for a key signature of extinction learning such as its recovery, the model has been an invaluable source of predictions concerning other phenomena, many of which have successfully been tested in the laboratory (Rescorla, 2000). Models conceived soon after the R–W model have avoided this shortcoming by assuming that, during extinction training, subjects form a new S–NoO association which influences behaviour in a way opposite to the influence of excitatory associations formed during training (Konorski, 1967; Pearce & Hall, 1980). Although these models do not fare any better than R–W when explaining recovery from extinction (i.e., in principle they do not anticipate recovery from extinction), by assuming that inhibitory S–noO associations generalise less easily to new situations than excitatory associations do (Spence, 1936), these models are able to account for some forms of recovery from extinction. Variations of these models have proliferated in the literature in the last decades, perhaps due to the interest on extinction itself, in addition to the potential of extinction to inform which variables may turn out to be critical in the clinic (Gershman, Blei, & Niv, 2010; Redish, Jensen, Johnson, & Kurth-Nelson, 2007).

Associative models, although not fully accurate when it comes to anticipating recovery from extinction, do make specific predictions when during extinction the stimulus being extinguished interacts with other stimuli, as it is the case when extinction is conducted in the presence of a second excitor, or even a conditioned inhibitor (Lovibond et al. 2009). One possible reason why these theories fare well in these scenarios is that most of these models were designed to account for interactions between stimuli, like, for example, overshadowing or blocking. Because these models were designed with these phenomena in mind, they do not anticipate that extinction will recover, but they correctly predict what the net result will be of extinguishing a stimulus in compound with other stimuli. In addition, these models make some specific assumptions about the role played by contextual stimuli. Importantly, they treat the context like any other discrete stimulus, so that the context can enter in competition with the stimulus being extinguished, rather than modulating the expression of extinction which is what can be safely concluded to be at least one putative role of the context from the evidence reviewed above. Consistent with this assumption about the context are data supporting specific predictions made by these models but only when extinction is conducted with massed trials, a situation that leaves little room for context-alone exposure and thus is more likely to engage the context as a competing stimulus (Urcelay & Miller, 2010; Urcelay, Witnauer, & Miller, in press). Thus, associative models accurately predict interactions between stimuli during extinction, but fail to explain recovery from extinction, a characteristic that, for the sake of any translational effort, is critical since the analogy between extinction and exposure-based therapies is mostly based on the fact that behaviour recovers when some aspect of the situation change between extinction and test. That is, clients that receive exposure-based therapies relapse when they leave the therapist office (a situation analogous to renewal) or with the passage of time, a situation analogous to spontaneous recovery (Orinstein et al., 2010).

4.4.2 Mnemonic Theories

The second family of models that we described above, the mnemonic theories, do not always specify the quantitative aspects of the change in behaviour, but they make more accurate predictions regarding the conditions that ensure the expression (or its absence) in similar or novel environments (i.e., contexts). The root of these theories can be found in verbal learning experiments conducted in the middle of the last century, which gave rise to numerous models of memory interference (Spear, 1978). An important point should be noted here: extinction itself is a form of interference in which a stimulus, during an initial phase, has an excitatory relationship with the outcome (S–O), but when extinction learning begins, that relationship changes because the stimulus no longer is followed by the outcome (S–noO), which is essentially a two-phase memory interference design. The model proposed by Bouton (1993) explains very well some characteristics of latent inhibition, which is similar to extinction but with the order of the treatments reversed (S–noO first followed by S–O in a second phase). A similar important aspect of this model is the treatment of contextual information (also see; Spear, 1978). Mnemonic models assume that the context functions like facilitator of retrieval for extinction, and this is why they are so successful in anticipating the difficulties observed in the laboratory and in the clinic for exposure (i.e., extinction) to transfer to situations outside the context where extinction occurs. These models assume that the context modulates the expression of extinction, presumably because second learned information, which produces interference, is highly context dependent (Sissons & Miller, 2009). Phenomena like the benefit of reactivating memories before extinction (Monfils et al., 2009; Wood, 2010) are closer in spirit to these models than to associative models. The reason for this is that the phenomenon of reconsolidation is indeed related to interference much more than it relates with competition between different sources of information, in the sense that memories are assumed to be in different states, although there is little specification of the quantitative attributes of these memories. Rather, explanatory constructs such as reconsolidation provide descriptions of the underlying processes responsible for the phenomena under question (i.e., memory reactivation, which then becomes context dependent (DeVietti & Holliday, 1972) just like extinction treatments and exposure-based therapies).

Taken all together, associative and mnemonic theories of extinction seem to emphasise different aspects of extinction learning. Whereas associative models concentrate on what occurs during extinction learning (hence their accurate predictions regarding interactions between stimuli during extinction), mnemonic models fare much better with the expression of extinction, a stage relatively isolated from the process of extinction on itself (Urcelay & Miller, 2008). Whether the critical differences between these families of theories arise from their differential treatment of contextual information is not entirely clear, although recent fear-conditioning experiments conducted in rats suggest that seemingly trivial parametric variations may result in contexts playing largely different roles in information processing (Urcelay & Miller, 2010; Urcelay et al., in press). This may give some insight concerning the successes and failures of these models, as they make largely different assumptions about the function played by contexts. A challenging possibility is to incorporate these different functions of contextual information into one parsimonious model. These two functions, it should be noted, are not mutually exclusive; it is likely that contexts can play both roles at once. If this is done properly, then a theory that can specify the circumstances under which contexts will behave like any other stimulus or instead modulate the expression of stimuli trained inside them will likely provide a full account of the phenomena related to extinction learning, and perhaps better approximate the needs of those working in the clinical setting.

Overall, in this chapter we have characterised current understanding of extinction learning, which seems to be best captured as new learning of the relationship between stimuli and outcomes (indeed S–noO), rather than erasure of previously learned relationships. We further described several strategies that have been developed in the laboratory with the intention of overcoming what seems to be a critical characteristic of extinction learning, which is its recovery. Of course, these strategies are not recipes but rather, as should be obvious to the reader, avenues that are being explored in the laboratory and are still subject to much heated debate. Finally, we have outlined some of the conflicts between families of models aimed at explaining extinction learning, with the intention of highlighting those areas in which integration is needed. Together with pharmacotherapies, behavioural approximations to anxiety disorders and addiction currently represent the first line of treatment, and extinction processes seem to have an important role in their effectiveness. A challenge for the future is to better understand these, and perhaps their interaction (see Chap. 6 by Hofmann et al. this volume), to better achieve the desired clinical outcome that ultimately will lead to maximal success.

Acknowledgments GPU was supported by a Marie Curie Intra-European Fellowship (PIEF-GA-2009-237608) awarded by the European Commission. This review reflects only the authors' views and the European Community is not liable for any use that may be made of the information contained therein. The author wishes to thank Anthony Dickinson, Anushka B. P. Fernando, Ralph R. Miller, Melissa A. Wood and the editors of this volume for invaluable comments concerning this chapter.

References

Alvarez, R. P., Johnson, L., & Grillon, C. (2007). Contextual-specificity of short-delay extinction in humans: Renewal of fear-potentiated startle in a virtual environment. *Learning and Memory, 14*(4), 247–253.

Archbold, G. E. B., Bouton, M. E., & Nader, K. (2010). Evidence for the persistence of contextual fear memories following immediate extinction. *European Journal of Neuroscience, 31*, 1303–1311.

Barela, P. B. (1999). Theoretical mechanisms underlying the trial-spacing effect in Pavlovian fear conditioning. *Journal of Experimental Psychology: Animal Behavior Processes, 25*(2), 177–193.

Bjork, R. A. (1975). Retrieval as a memory modifier: An interpretation of negative recency and related phenomena. In R. Solso (Ed.), *Information processing and cognition: The Loyola Symposium* (pp. 123–144). Hillsdale, NJ: Lawrence Erlbaum Associates.

Bjork, R. A., & Bjork, E. L. (2006). Optimizing treatment and instruction: Implications of a new theory of disuse. In L. Nilsson, N. Ohta, L. Nilsson, & N. Ohta (Eds.), *Memory and society: Psychological perspectives* (pp. 116–140). New York: Psychology Press.

Bouton, M. E. (1986). Slow reacquisition following the extinction of conditioned suppression. *Learning and Motivation, 17*, 1–15.

Bouton, M. E. (1991). A contextual analysis of fear extinction. In P. R. Martin (Ed.), *Handbook of behavior therapy and psychological science: An integrative approach* (Pergamon general psychology series, Vol. 164, pp. 435–453). Elmsford, NY: Pergamon Press.

Bouton, M. E. (1993). Context, time, and memory retrieval in the interference paradigms of Pavlovian learning. *Psychological Bulletin, 114*(1), 80–99.

Bouton, M. E., & Bolles, R. C. (1979). Role of conditioned contextual stimuli in reinstatement of extinguished fear. *Journal of Experimental Psychology-Animal Behavior Processes, 5*, 368–378.

Bouton, M. E., García-Gutiérrez, A., Zilski, J., & Moody, E. W. (2006). Extinction in multiple contexts does not necessarily make extinction less vulnerable to relapse. *Behaviour Research and Therapy, 44*, 983–994.

Bouton, M. E., & Swartzentruber, D. (1989). Slow reacquisition following extinction: Context, encoding, and retrieval mechanisms. *Journal of Experimental Psychology: Animal Behavior Processes, 15*, 43–53.

Bouton, M. E., Westbrook, R. F., Corcoran, K. A., & Maren, S. (2006). Contextual and temporal modulation of extinction: Behavioral and biological mechanisms. *Biological Psychiatry, 60*, 352–360.

Bouton, M. E., & Woods, A. M. (2008). Extinction: Behavioral mechanisms and their implications. In J. H. Byrne (Ed.), *Learning and memory: A comprehensive reference* (pp. 151–171). Oxford: Academic.

Briggs, J. F., & Riccio, D. C. (2007). Retrograde amnesia for extinction: Similarities with amnesia for original acquisition memories. *Learning & Behavior, 35*(3), 131–140.

Brooks, D. C., & Bouton, M. E. (1993). A retrieval cue for extinction attenuates spontaneous recovery. *Journal of Experimental Psychology: Animal Behavior Processes, 19*, 77–89.

Brooks, D. C., & Bouton, M. E. (1994). A retrieval cue for extinction attenuates response recovery (renewal) caused by a return to the conditioning context. *Journal of Experimental Psychology: Animal Behavior Processes, 20*(4), 366–379.

Cain, C. K., Blouin, A. M., & Barad, M. (2003). Temporally massed CS presentations generate more fear extinction than spaced presentations. *Journal of Experimental Psychology: Animal Behavior Processes, 29*, 323–333.

Calton, J. L., Mitchell, K. G., & Schachtman, T. R. (1996). Conditioned inhibition produced by extinction of a conditioned stimulus. *Learning and Motivation, 27*, 335–361.

Campfield, K. M., & Hills, A. M. (2001). Effect of timing of critical incident stress debriefing (CISD) on posttraumatic symptoms. *Journal of Traumatic Stress, 14*, 327–340.

Chan, W. Y. M., Leung, H. T., Westbrook, R. F., & McNally, G. P. (2010). Effects of recent exposure to a conditioned stimulus on extinction of Pavlovian fear conditioning. *Learning and Memory, 17*, 512–521.

Chang, C., & Maren, S. (2009). Early extinction after fear conditioning yields a context-independent and short-term suppression of conditional freezing in rats. *Learning and Memory, 16*, 62–68.

Chelonis, J. J., Calton, J. L., Hart, J. A., & Schachtman, T. R. (1999). Attenuation of the renewal effect by extinction in multiple contexts. *Learning and Motivation, 30*, 1–14.

Clem, R. L., & Huganir, R. L. (2010). Calcium-permeable AMPA receptor dynamics mediate fear memory erasure. *Science, 330*(6007), 1108–1012.

Conklin, C. A., & Tiffany, S. T. (2002). Applying extinction research and theory to cue-exposure addiction treatments. *Addiction, 97*, 155–167.

Craske, M. G., Kircanski, K., Zelikowsky, M., Mystkowski, J., Chowdhury, N., & Baker, A. (2008). Optimizing inhibitory learning during exposure therapy. *Behaviour Research and Therapy, 46*, 5–27.

Crombag, H. S., Bossert, J. M., Koya, E., & Shaham, Y. (2008). Context-induced relapse to drug seeking: A review. *Philosophical Transactions of the Royal Society of London B Biological Sciences, 363*, 3233–3243.

Davis, M., Ressler, K., Rothbaum, B. O., & Richardson, R. (2006). Effects of D-cycloserine on extinction: Translation from preclinical to clinical work. *Biological Psychiatry, 60*, 369–375.

Delamater, A. R. (2004). Experimental extinction in Pavlovian conditioning: Behavioural and neuroscience perspectives. *Quarterly Journal of Experimental Psychology B, 57*, 97–132.

Denniston, J. C., Chang, R. C., & Miller, R. R. (2003). Massive extinction treatment attenuates the renewal effect. *Learning and Motivation, 34*(1), 68–86.

Denniston, J. C., & Miller, R. R. (2003). The role of temporal variables in inhibition produced through extinction. *Learning & Behavior, 31*, 35–48.

DeVietti, T. L., & Holliday, J. H. (1972). Retrograde amnesia produced by electroconvulsive shock after reactivation of a consolidated memory trace: A replication. *Psychonomic Science, 29*, 137–138.

Dickinson, A. (1980). *Contemporary animal learning theory*. Cambridge UK: Cambridge University Press.

Drew, M. R., Yang, C., Ohyama, T., & Balsam, P. D. (2004). Temporal specificity of extinction in autoshaping. *Journal of Experimental Psychology-Animal Behavior Processes, 30*, 163–176.

Everitt, B. J., & Robbins, T. W. (2005). Neural systems of reinforcement for drug addiction: From actions to habits to compulsion. *Nature Neuroscience, 8*(11), 1481–1489.

Foa, E. B., Hembree, E. A., Cahill, S. P., Rauch, S. A. M., Riggs, D. S., Feeny, N. C., et al. (2005). Randomized trial of prolonged exposure for posttraumatic stress disorder with and without cognitive restructuring: Outcome at academic and community clinics. *Journal of Consulting and Clinical Psychology, 73*, 953–964.

Gershman, S. J., Blei, D. M., & Niv, Y. (2010). Context, learning, and extinction. *Psychological Review, 117*(1), 197–209.

Gunther, L. M., Denniston, J. C., & Miller, R. R. (1998). Conducting exposure treatment in multiple contexts can prevent relapse. *Behaviour Research and Therapy, 36*, 75–91.

Hofmann, S. G. (2007). Enhancing exposure-based therapy from a translational research perspective. *Behaviour Research and Therapy, 45*, 1987–2001.

Hofmann, S. G. (2008). Cognitive processes during fear acquisition and extinction in animals and humans: Implications for exposure therapy of anxiety disorders. *Clinical Psychology Review, 28*, 199–210.

Holland, P. C. (1992). Occasion setting in Pavlovian conditioning. *The Psychology of Learning and Motivation: Advances in Research and Theory, 28*, 69–125.

Huff, N. C., Hernandez, J. A., Blanding, N. Q., & LaBar, K. S. (2009). Delayed extinction attenuates conditioned fear renewal and spontaneous recovery in humans. *Behavioral Neuroscience, 123*, 834–843.

Inda, M. C., Muravieva, E. V., & Alberini, C. M. (2011). Memory retrieval and the passage of time: From reconsolidation and strengthening to extinction. *Journal of Neuroscience, 31*, 1635–1643.

Johnson, J. S., Escobar, M., & Kimble, W. L. (2010). Long term maintenance of immediate or delayed extinction is determined by the extinction-test interval. *Learning and Memory, 17*, 639–644.

Konorski, J. J. (1967). *Integrative activity of the brain*. Chicago: University of Chicago Press.

Laborda, M. A., McConnell, B. L., & Miller, R. R. (2011). Behavioral techniques to reduce relapse after exposure therapy. *Associative Learning and Conditioning Theory, 1*, 79–104.

Lee, J. L. C. (2009). Reconsolidation: Maintaining memory relevance. *Trends in Neuroscience, 32*, 413–420.

Lee, J. L. C., Milton, A. L., & Everitt, B. J. (2006). Reconsolidation and extinction of conditioned fear: Inhibition and potentiation. *The Journal of Neuroscience, 26*(39), 10051–10056.
Lewis, D. J. (1979). Psychobiology of active and inactive memory. *Psychological Bulletin, 86*, 1054–1083.
Lopez, J., de Vasconcelos, A. P., & Cassel, J.-C. (2008). Differential sensitivity of recent vs. remote memory traces to extinction in a water-maze task in rats. *Neurobiology of Learning and Memory, 90*, 460–466.
Lovibond, P. F. (2004). Cognitive processes in extinction. *Learning and Memory, 11*, 495–500.
Lovibond, P. F., Davis, N. R., & O'Flaherty, A. S. (2000). Protection from extinction in human fear conditioning. *Behavior Research & Therapy, 38*(10), 967–983.
Lovibond, P. F., Mitchell, C. J., Minard, E., Brady, A., & Menzies, R. G. (2009). Safety behaviours preserve threat beliefs: Protection from extinction of human fear conditioning by an avoidance response. *Behavior Research & Therapy, 47*, 716–720.
Maren, S., Chang, C., & Thompson, R. F. (2006). Recent fear is resistant to extinction. *PNAS Proceedings of the National Academy of Sciences of the United States of America, 103*, 18020–18025.
McGaugh, J. L. (1966). Time-dependent processes in memory storage. *Science, 153*, 1351–1358.
McGaugh, J. L. (2000). Memory–a century of consolidation. *Science, 287*, 248–251.
McNally, R. J. (2007). Mechanisms of exposure therapy: How neuroscience can improve psychological treatments for anxiety disorders. *Clinical Psychology Review, 27*, 750–759.
Miller, R. R., & Matzel, L. D. (1988). The comparator hypothesis: A response rule for the expression of associations. In G. H. Bower (Ed.), *The psychology of learning and motivation: Advances in research and theory* (Vol. 22, pp. 51–92). San Diego, CA: Academic.
Misanin, J. R., Miller, R. R., & Lewis, D. J. (1968). Retrograde amnesia produced by electroconvulsive shock after reactivation of a consolidated memory trace. *Science, 160*, 554–555.
Monfils, M. H., Cowansage, K. K., Klann, E., & LeDoux, J. E. (2009). Extinction-reconsolidation boundaries: Key to persistent attenuation of fear memories. *Science, 324*, 951–955.
Myers, K. M., Ressler, K. J., & Davis, M. (2006). Different mechanisms of fear extinction dependent on length of time since fear acquisition. *Learning & Memory, 13*, 216–223.
Nader, K., & Hardt, O. (2009). A single standard for memory: The case for reconsolidation. *Nature Reviews Neuroscience, 10*, 224–234.
Nader, K., Schafe, G. E., & Le Doux, J. E. (2000). Fear memories require protein synthesis in the amygdala for reconsolidation after retrieval. *Nature, 406*, 722–726.
Neumann, D. L. (2008). The effects of context changes on the reinstatement of extinguished conditioned behavior in a conditioned suppression task with humans. *Learning and Motivation, 39*, 114–135.
Neumann, D. L., Lipp, O. V., & Cory, S. E. (2007). Conducting extinction in multiple contexts does not necessarily attenuate the renewal of shock expectancy in a fear-conditioning procedure with humans. *Behaviour Research and Therapy, 45*, 385–394.
Norrholm, S. D., Vervliet, B., Jovanovic, T., Boshoven, W., Myers, K. M., Davis, M., et al. (2008). Timing of extinction relative to acquisition: A parametric analysis of fear extinction in humans. *Behavioral Neuroscience, 122*(5), 1016–1030.
Orinstein, A. J., Urcelay, G. P., & Miller, R. R. (2010). Expanding the intertrial interval during extinction: Response cessation and recovery. *Behavior Therapy, 41*, 14–29.
Pavlov, I. P. (1927). *Conditioned reflexes: An investigation of the physiological activity of the cerebral cortex*. Oxford, UK: Oxford University Press.
Pearce, J. M. (1987). A model for stimulus generalization in Pavlovian conditioning. *Psychological Review, 94*, 61–73.
Pearce, J. M. (1994). Similarity and discrimination: A selective review and a connectionist model. *Psychological Review, 101*, 587–607.
Pearce, J. M. (2002). Evaluation and development of a connectionist theory of configural learning. *Animal Learning & Behavior, 30*, 73–95.
Pearce, J. M., & Hall, G. (1980). A model for Pavlovian learning: Variations in the effectiveness of conditioned but not of unconditioned stimuli. *Psychological Review, 87*(6), 532–552.

Pearce, J. M., & Wilson, P. N. (1991). Effects of extinction with a compound conditioned stimulus. *Journal of Experimental Psychology: Animal Behavior Processes, 17*, 151–162.
Pedreira, M. E., Pérez-Cuesta, L. M., & Maldonado, H. (2004). Mismatch between what is expected and what actually occurs triggers memory reconsolidation or extinction. *Learning and Memory, 11*, 579–585.
Powers, M. B., Halpern, J. M., Ferenschak, M. P., Gillihan, S. J., & Foa, E. B. (2010). A meta-analytic review of prolonged exposure for posttraumatic stress disorder. *Clinical Psychology Review, 30*(6), 635–641.
Quirk, G. J. (2002). Memory for extinction of conditioned fear is long-lasting and persists following spontaneous recovery. *Learning and Memory, 9*, 402–407.
Quirk, G. J., Paré, D., Richardson, R., Herry, C., Monfils, M. H., Schiller, D., et al. (2010). Erasing fear memories with extinction training. *The Journal of Neuroscience, 30*, 14993–14997.
Rauhut, A. S., Thomas, B. L., & Ayres, J. J. B. (2001). Treatments that weaken Pavlovian conditioned fear and thwart its renewal in rats: Implications for treating human phobias. *Journal of Experimental Psychology: Animal Behavior Processes, 27*, 99–114.
Reberg, D. (1972). Compound tests for excitation in early acquisition and after prolonged extinction of conditioned suppression. *Learning and Motivation, 3*, 246–258.
Redish, A., Jensen, S., Johnson, A., & Kurth-Nelson, Z. (2007). Reconciling reinforcement learning models with behavioral extinction and renewal: Implications for addiction, relapse, and problem gambling. *Psychological Review, 114*(3), 784–805.
Rescorla, R. A. (1969). Pavlovian conditioned inhibition. *Psychological Bulletin, 72*, 77–94.
Rescorla, R. A. (2000). Extinction can be enhanced by a concurrent excitor. *Journal of Experimental Psychology: Animal Behavior Processes, 26*, 251–260.
Rescorla, R. A. (2001). Experimental extinction. In R. R. Mowrer & S. B. Klein (Eds.), *Handbook of contemporary learning theories* (pp. 119–154). Mahwah, NJ: Lawrence Erlbaum Associates Publishers.
Rescorla, R. A. (2004a). Spontaneous recovery. *Learning & Memory, 11*, 501–509.
Rescorla, R. A. (2004b). Spontaneous recovery varies inversely with the training-extinction interval. *Learning and Behavior, 32*, 401–408.
Rescorla, R. A. (2006). Deepened extinction from compound stimulus presentation. *Journal of Experimental Psychology: Animal Behavior Processes, 32*, 135–144.
Rescorla, R. A., & Durlach, P. J. (1987). The role of context in intertrial interval effects in autoshaping. *The Quarterly Journal of Experimental Psychology B: Comparative and Physiological Psychology, 39B*, 35–48.
Rescorla, R. A., & Heth, C. (1975). Reinstatement of fear to an extinguished conditioned stimulus. *Journal of Experimental Psychology: Animal Behavior Processes, 1*(1), 88–96.
Rescorla, R. A., & Wagner, A. R. (1972). A theory of Pavlovian conditioning: variations in the effectiveness of reinforcement and nonreinforcement. In A. H. Black & W. F. Prokasy (Eds.), *Classical conditioning II: Current research and theory* (pp. 64–99). New York: Appleton-Century-Crofts.
Rohrbaugh, M., & Riccio, D. C. (1970). Paradoxical enhancement of learned fear. *Journal of Abnormal Psychology, 75*(2), 210–216.
Rowe, M. K., & Craske, M. G. (1998). Effects of varied-stimulus exposure training on fear reduction and return of fear. *Behaviour Research and Therapy, 36*, 719–734.
Schiller, D., Cain, C. K., Curley, N. G., Schwartz, J. S., Stern, S. A., Ledoux, J. E., et al. (2008). Evidence for recovery of fear following immediate extinction in rats and humans. *Learning & Memory, 15*, 394–402.
Schiller, D., Monfils, M. H., Raio, C. M., Johnson, D. C., LeDoux, J. E., & Phelps, E. A. (2010). Preventing the return of fear in humans using reconsolidation update mechanisms. *Nature, 463*, 49–53.
Sissons, H. T., & Miller, R. R. (2009). Spontaneous recovery of excitation and inhibition. *Journal of Experimental Psychology-Animal Behavior Processes, 35*, 419–426.
Soeter, M., & Kindt, M. (2011). Disrupting reconsolidation: Pharmacological and behavioral manipulations. *Learning & Memory, 18*, 357–366.

Spear, N. E. (1978). *The processing of memories: Forgetting and retention*. New Jersey: Lawrence Erlbaum.
Spence, K. W. (1936). The nature of discrimination learning in animals. *Psychological Review, 43*, 427–449.
Stout, S. C., & Miller, R. R. (2007). Sometimes-competing retrieval (SOCR): A formalization of the comparator hypothesis. *Psychological Review, 114*, 759–783.
Tamai, N., & Nakajima, S. (2000). Renewal of formerly conditioned fear in rats after extensive extinction training. *International Journal of comparative Psychology, 13*(3), 137–147.
Thomas, B. L., & Ayres, J. J. B. (2004). Use of the ABA fear renewal paradigm to assess the effects of extinction with co-present fear inhibitors or excitors: Implications for theories of extinction and for treating human fears and phobias. *Learning and Motivation, 35*, 22–52.
Thomas, B. L., Vurbic, D., & Novak, C. (2009). Extensive extinction in multiple contexts eliminates the renewal of conditioned fear in rats. *Learning and Motivation, 40*, 147–159.
Tiffany, S. T. (1990). A cognitive model of drug urges and drug-use behavior: Role of automatic and nonautomatic processes. *Psychological Review, 97*, 147–168.
Urcelay, G. P., Witnauer, J. E., & Miller, R. R. (in press). The dual role of the context in postpeak performance decrements resulting from extended training. *Learning and Behavior*.
Urcelay, G. P., Lipatova, O., & Miller, R. R. (2009). Constraints on enhanced extinction resulting from extinction treatment in the presence of an added excitor. *Learning and Motivation, 40*, 343–363.
Urcelay, G. P., & Miller, R. R. (2008). Retrieval from memory. In J. H. Byrne (Ed.), *Learning and memory: A comprehensive reference* (pp. 53–73). Oxford: Academic.
Urcelay, G. P., & Miller, R. R. (2010). Two roles of the context in Pavlovian fear conditioning. *Journal of Experimental Psychology: Animal Behavior Processes, 36*(2), 268–280.
Urcelay, G. P., Wheeler, D. S., & Miller, R. R. (2009). Spacing extinction trials alleviates renewal and spontaneous recovery. *Learning and Behavior, 37*, 60–73.
van Emmerik, A. P., Kamphuis, J. H., Hulsbosch, A. M., & Emmelkamp, P. G. (2002). Single session debriefing after psychological trauma: A meta-analysis. *The Lancet, 360*(9335), 766–771.
Vansteenwegen, D., Vervliet, B., Iberico, C., Baeyens, F., Van den Bergh, O., & Hermans, D. (2007). The repeated confrontation with videotapes of spiders in multiple contexts attenuates renewal of fear in spider-anxious students. *Behaviour Research and Therapy, 45*, 1169–1179.
Vervliet, B., Vansteenwegen, D., & Hermans, D. (2010). Unpaired shocks during extinction weaken the contextual renewal of a conditioned discrimination. *Learning and Motivation, 41*(1), 22–31.
Vervliet, B., Vansteenwegen, D., Hermans, D., & Eelen, P. (2007). Concurrent excitors limit the extinction of conditioned fear in humans. *Behaviour Research and Therapy, 45*, 375–383.
Watson, J. B., & Rayner, R. (1920). Conditioned emotional reactions. *Journal of Experimental Psychology, 3*, 1–14.
Weidemann, G., & Kehoe, E. (2004). Recovery of the rabbit's conditioned nictitating membrane response without direct reinforcement after extinction. *Learning and Behavior, 32*(4), 409–426 [Serial online].
Winterbauer, N. E., & Bouton, M. E. (2010). Mechanisms of resurgence of an extinguished instrumental behavior. *Journal of Experimental Psychology: Animal Behavior Processes, 36*, 343–353.
Wood, M. A. (2010). *A psychological analysis of the effects of memory retrieval prior to extinction on the reacquisition of a conditioned fear association*. Dissertation submitted to the University of Cambridge.
Woods, A. M., & Bouton, M. E. (2008). Immediate extinction causes a less durable loss of performance than delayed extinction following either fear or appetitive conditioning. *Learning and Memory, 15*, 909–920.

Chapter 5
The Neural Substrates of Fear Extinction

Ulrike Lueken and Nina Isabel Maslowski

Dr. Ulrike Lueken works as a researcher at the Institute of Clinical Psychology and Psychotherapy, Technische Universitaet Dresden (Germany), and as a therapist at the institute's outpatient center. She is doing fMRI research on fear and anxiety disorders and their neural mechanisms of change during CBT treatment.

U. Lueken (✉) • N.I. Maslowski
Institute of Clinical Psychology and Psychotherapy, Technische Universitaet Dresden, Chemnitzer Strasse 46, D-01187 Dresden, Germany

Neuroimaging Center, Department of Psychology, Technische Universitaet Dresden, Dresden, Germany
e-mail: lueken@psychologie.tu-dresden.de; maslowski@psychologie.tu-dresden.de

P. Neudeck and H.-U. Wittchen (eds.), *Exposure Therapy: Rethinking the Model – Refining the Method*, DOI 10.1007/978-1-4614-3342-2_5,

Nina I. Maslowski is a doctoral student at the Institute of Clinical Psychology and Psychotherapy, Technische Universitaet Dresden (Germany), and currently enrolled in a cognitive behavioral psychotherapy training program.

5.1 From Fear Learning to the Unlearning of Fear: A Translational Research Perspective

Within the last two decades, extensive knowledge about the neural mechanisms of fear conditioning could be obtained from both animal and human research (Bechara et al., 1995; LaBar, LeDoux, Spencer, & Phelps, 1995; LaBar, Gatenby, Gore, LeDoux, & Phelps, 1998; LeDoux, 1996). The groundbreaking studies by Joseph LeDoux (1996) have provided important insights into the functional relevance of the amygdala as part of a system for the early detection of biologically significant stimuli. Fear learning holds an evolutionary benefit in preventing the organism from danger; fear "unlearning" or fear-inhibitory learning, however, allows for a flexible adjustment of fear-related associations in a changing environment. It is thus plausible to assume that a failure in readjusting these associations might constitute a predisposing factor for the development and maintenance of anxiety disorders. Behavioral exposure as a key component of cognitive behavioral therapy (CBT) bears procedural similarities to extinction of conditioned fear in animal models (Craske et al., 2008). When applying a translational perspective, knowledge about neural mechanisms of fear extinction learning and recall may have the potential to directly improve exposure-based therapies (see Urcelay in this book). Consistent with this view, neuroscience research has begun to shift attention from mechanisms of learning to those involved in the unlearning of fear, thereby providing important insights into those brain systems potentially involved in the pathogenesis of, and recovery from, fear (Delgado, Olsson, & Phelps, 2006; Myers & Davis, 2002; Quirk, 2006).

When a conditioned stimulus (CS) is repeatedly presented in the absence of the unconditioned, aversive stimulus (US), the conditioned response (CR) will gradually diminish. This phenomenon is being referred to as "extinction" and can clearly be

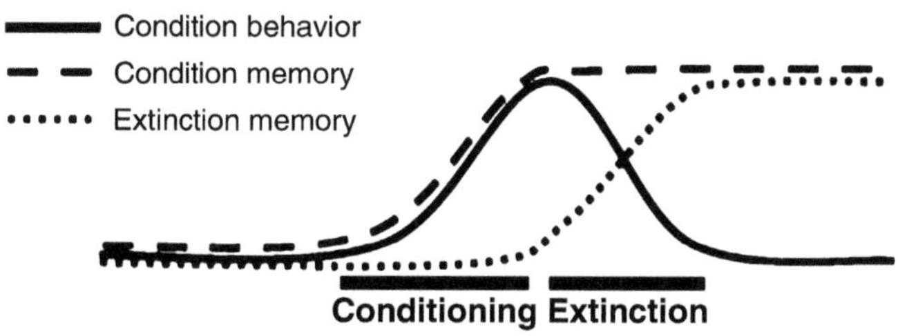

Fig. 5.1 Relationship of fear conditioning and extinction memory traces. The strength of these two memory traces determinates the magnitude of a conditioned fear response (adopted from Quirk et al., 2006)

described on a behavioral level. Since the initial work of Pavlov (1927), the underlying processes, however, have been interpreted in many different ways (Rescorla, 1988). Emerging evidence from brain research now offers unique insights into how the brain mediates extinction and this also contributes to our understanding of the actual "nature" of extinction, and, eventually, the processes that underlie exposure therapy. As being already noted by Pavlov (1927) and later by Konorski (1967), extinction training does not result in an irreversible erasure of the conditioned fear association (CS/US+). Instead, it induces the forming of an alternative memory trace, that is, an inhibitory CS/no US (CS/US-) association.

On a behavioral level, the strength of the respective memory trace finally determinates the magnitude of the CR (Quirk, Garcia, & Gonzalez-Lima, 2006; Fig. 5.1). Behavioral phenomena such as spontaneous recovery of fear, fear renewal, and the context dependency of fear extinction confirm that even after the extinction training has been successfully accomplished, the CR can be recalled again, thus proving its permanent existence (Bouton, 2002). Recent evidence, however, challenges this view of extinction being solely new, inhibitory learning. Instead, fear memories appear to be subject to erasure-like mechanisms, at least under certain circumstances (for reviews see Maren, 2011; Quirk et al., 2010).

Several lines of animal and human research have recently been incorporated into a first working model of those brain systems mediating fear extinction processes (Sotres-Bayon, Cain, & LeDoux, 2006). The amygdala, the ventro-medial prefrontal cortex (vmPFC), and the hippocampus are suggested to be potential core structures of the so-called extinction circuitry, each subserving distinct functional aspects in the process of extinction learning and recall. Specifically, the vmPFC seems to be a crucial structure for extinction recall, signaling a shift from fear expression to fear inhibition (Milad & Quirk, 2002). Fear conditioning is furthermore modulated by genetic polymorphisms of the serotonergic and dopaminergic systems (Garpenstrand, Annas, Ekblom, Oreland, & Fredrikson, 2001; Holmes, Yang, Lesch, Crawley, & Murphy, 2003; Lonsdorf et al., 2009). A functional variant in the promoter region of the serotonin transporter gene (5-HTTLPR) is related to altered fear conditioning with subjects carrying the short (s) risk allele showing enhanced CRs.

Fear extinction, on the other hand, has been reported to be modulated by dopaminergic tone as reflected by the *COMT* Val^{158}Met polymorphism with val allele carriers showing more efficient extinction learning. (Garpenstrand et al., 2001; Lonsdorf et al., 2009).

Evidence is also accumulating that extinction learning in animals and exposure-based treatment can be modulated by pharmacological agents such as D-Cycloserine (DCS), a partial N-methyl-D-aspartate (NMDA) agonist (see Hofmann et al. in this book). Recent animal and clinical human studies highlight the potential of DCS to facilitate the effects of extinction and exposure-based therapy in several anxiety disorders by enhancing NMDA-gated neuronal plasticity of glutamate receptors (Hofmann et al., 2006; Kushner et al., 2007; Otto et al., 2010; Ressler et al., 2004; Walker, Ressler, Lu, & Davis, 2002; Wilhelm et al., 2008). Ressler et al. (2004) hypothesize that DCS in specific phobia primarily enhances the associative component of extinction learning during exposure therapy. They also found increased self-exposure in the early and late postassessment periods in the DCS groups compared to the placebo group. This finding seems to support the idea that DCS treatment prior to exposure enhances extinction so that subjects were less fearful in the real world and less likely to avoid the feared stimulus. In a recent meta-analysis an overall large effect size of DCS treatment was reported for animal and human studies combined (Norberg, Krystal, & Tolin, 2008).

Although the rapid development in the field of extinction research and pharmacological enhancement (see Hofmann et al. in this book) of emotional-associative learning yields promising results, several basic questions about the neural underpinnings and mechanisms of action, particularly in patients, still remain speculative. Recent research activities have only begun to decode the neural basis of the extinction circuit in humans and to study the precise mechanisms and neural target sites of DCS-facilitated learning in the human brain (Kalisch et al., 2009; Onur et al., 2010). In this regard, pharmacological approaches to treat anxiety disorders may change from mere symptom reduction to enhancing CBT-induced new learning, thus offering exciting perspectives for synergies between pharmacological and psychological treatments.

5.2 Fear Extinction Induces New Memory Formation: Implications for Experimental Designs

It is important to note that the term "extinction" can be used in at least three different ways. A more sophisticated terminology may help to describe related, but differing aspects of extinction more precisely. As outlined by Myers and Davis (2002), extinction refers to the experimental procedure, that is, the repeated presentation of the CS alone following the conditioning procedure. In accordance with current research about extinction, this aspect is called *extinction training* in order to disentangle it from other phenomena associated with the term extinction. Second, extinction also describes the behavioral effect, that is, changes in the amplitude of the CR. In general, extinction training results in gradually decreasing amplitudes of the CR. Depending on the timeframe, two different phenomena can be studied. Changes in the CR during extinction training are called *within-session extinction*, while recall and expression of the CR after the extinction training has been accomplished is described by the term *extinction retention* or *recall*. Third, the neurochemical and molecular processes induced by the extinction training that underlie the behavioral effects on a neuronal level can be described by the term *extinction* itself.

Fear learning and unlearning can be subsumed under the implicit (i.e., nonconscious) memory system. Learning induces neuronal plasticity, meaning that new experiences (such as a traumatic event or subsequent treatment-related exposure) are able to alter neuronal functionality. In that sense, learning can be conceptualized as an activity-dependent reshaping of our brains, or, as already pointed out by the famous psychologist Hebb (1949): "what fires together wires together." The cellular and molecular basis of neuroplasticity has been decoded in detail (Kandel, 2001), and we will shortly exemplify these signal transduction pathways for the amygdaloid complex (LeDoux, 2007; Sah, Faber, Lopez, & Power, 2003). In the lateral amygdala, glutamate is our neurotransmitter of interest. When being released to the postsynaptic cleft, glutamate binds to several receptors, among them α-amino-3-hydroxy-5-methyl-4-isoxazolepropionic acid (AMPA) and NMDA receptors. While AMPA receptors immediately get activated by glutamate and transfer the postsynaptic excitatory potentials, NMDA receptor channels remain blocked by magnesium ions. It requires a simultaneous, co-occurring potential (for example, the convergence of CS and US information) to activate NMDA receptors, allow for calcium inflow, and to induce long-term potentiation (LTP). Calcium signaling in turn initiates a complex cascade including the phosphorylation and activation of different kinases, transcription factors, and, eventually, gene expression and protein synthesis. These are the tools enabling the growth of new synaptic connections. The stabilization of memory via protein synthesis after learning has occurred is called consolidation. It lasts for several hours and is enhanced during sleep (Gais & Born, 2004; Spoormaker et al., 2010). The process of memory formation and recall undergoes a distinct temporal sequence. During the encoding phase, new associations are established. During memory consolidation, these temporarily instable associations are conveyed into enduring memory traces that can later on again become accessible during memory recall. Under experimental conditions the task design should account for these different processes and tailor appropriate time windows for tracking the acquisition, consolidation, and recall of emotional-associative memories. Indeed, conventional fear-conditioning paradigms are often of limited use for the analysis of fear extinction with regard to the following aspects. Classical fear conditioning paradigms typically consist of a habituation phase, a fear acquisition phase where the CS is repeatedly followed by the US, and a successive extinction training phase, where the CS is presented alone again. First, although this set-up allows for the recall of the CR during the extinction training, it is lacking an extinction recall phase. Experiments focusing on extinction processes thus should include an additional experimental phase (usually after 24 h to allow for sufficient consolidation) to assess

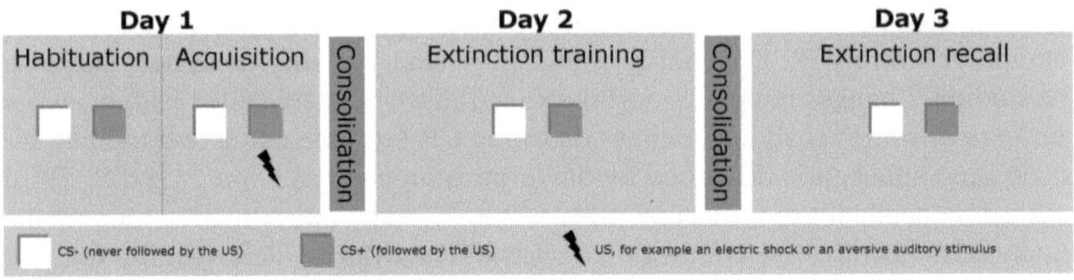

Fig. 5.2 Delayed fear extinction task. This task design allows for a separate induction and analysis of fear conditioning, extinction training, and extinction recall processes. Stages of emotional-associative learning are separated by distinct consolidation phases

the amount of extinction recall. Second, extinction training in conventional paradigms is confounded by two processes: on the one hand, the CR is recalled, but, at the same time, new learning about the inhibitory CS/US- association (within-session extinction) is induced. Thus, the magnitude of the CR represents the combined effect of both processes. In relation to the latter problem, conventional tasks do not allow for sufficient consolidation of the fear association (CS/US+). Delayed fear extinction tasks (see Fig. 5.2) are a valuable alternative where extinction training is scheduled after 24 h following fear acquisition (and then complemented by an extinction recall phase after another 24 h). In general, the investigation of fear extinction processes requires specific task designs that adequately account for the different learning and memory formation processes that occur during emotional-associative learning. In particular, fear extinction designs necessarily include testing on several days and are thus only partly comparable to classical fear-conditioning paradigms.

5.3 The Neural Basis of Fear Extinction

5.3.1 The Amygdala, Part I: Acquisition and Expression of Conditioned Fear

Before taking a closer look at the neural underpinnings of extinction learning and recall, we will start with a short summary of those mechanisms involved in the acquisition and expression of conditioned fear, focusing on the amygdala as our key region of interest. As part of the limbic system, the amygdala is localized in the diencephalon, medial to the anterior portion of the temporal lobe. There is extensive and elegant animal literature on the neuroanatomy and physiology of this structure (Amaral, Price, Pitkänen, & Carmichael, 1992; LeDoux, 2007; Pape & Pare, 2010). The amygdala can be divided into several subnuclei, among them the basolateral region, consisting of the lateral, basal, and accessory basal nuclei. The basolateral amygdala (BLA) can be viewed as the main input station as it receives extensive afferent information from virtually all sensory senses. Information is relayed via multiple routes, including subcortical ("low road") and cortical ("high road") afferents (LeDoux, Iwata, Cicchetti, & Reis, 1988). Via the thalamo-amygdaloid pathway, sensory information can be directly projected from the thalamus to the BLA, thus bypassing cortical higher-order processing. Fear reactions can be initiated almost exclusively by this "low road," thus enabling the organism to react immediately, but by the expense of an elaborate cortical analysis. The latter can be provided by the "high road" feeding neocortical sensory information back to the BLA. Transmission within the "high road" is however slower, since more synaptic connections are involved. Further, feedback from the amygdala is relayed back to the primary and secondary sensory association cortices, allowing for a modulation of cortical processing (Amaral et al., 1992). As information from different sensory channels coincides in the BLA, the association of the CS and US most likely takes place here (Romanski, Clugnet, Bordi, & LeDoux, 1993). In terms of neuronal plasticity, the coincidence of these stimuli triggers depolarization of NMDA receptors, followed by neuronal plasticity as outlined above. Fear learning is thus closely connected to the BLA. In contrast, the central nucleus (CA) sends multiple ascending and descending projections to the PFC, but also to major downstream autonomic and neuroendocrine control centers (Amaral et al., 1992). We can conceptualize the CA as the main output station of the amygdala which is essential for the expression of physiological fear components. Information from the BLA to CA flows via multiple connections, involving the so-called intercalated cell masses (ITC) that function as a relay node between BLA and CA (Pare & Smith, 1993). ITC are important for inhibitory feedback control which can explain why the amygdala shows a fast habituation profile; moreover, ITC are associated with inhibitory PFC modulation of the amygdala during extinction recall (Royer & Pare, 2002).

Human studies corroborate the relevance of the amygdala for fear learning as well, although, due to the limited resolution of lesion and neuroimaging studies, findings mainly relate to the amygdala as a whole rather than to its subnuclei. Evidence is provided from single case (Bechara et al., 1995) and group lesion studies (LaBar et al., 1995; Peper, Karcher, Wohlfarth, Reinshagen, & LeDoux, 2001) that the amygdala is crucial for fear conditioning. Patients with focal lesions of medial temporal lobe structures, including the amygdala, exhibit impaired CRs. A double dissociation between declarative and emotional memory components was reported by Bechara et al. (1995) for two patients with hippocampal vs. amygdalar lesions: While the former patient showed enhanced skin conductance reactions toward the CS+, but no declarative memory about stimulus contingencies, the latter patient could recall stimulus contingencies, but was unable to develop a CR. Studies using functional magnetic resonance imaging (fMRI) further support the role of the amygdala for fear conditioning in non-brain-damaged humans (Büchel et al., 1998; Sehlmeyer et al., 2009). These converging lines of evidence emphasize that the amygdala is a central component of the fear circuitry, including the encoding and expression of conditioned fear responses. However, recent extinction studies suggest a broader concept of the amygdala being also involved in unlearning the fear response (Barad, Gean, & Lutz, 2006). Caution is, however, warranted for an exclusively amygdalocentric view on fear conditioning: although many animal studies emphasize the central role of the amygdala, human neuroimaging studies show that a widespread fronto-limbic network is activated by fear conditioning, including the anterior cingulate cortex, insula, hippocampus, striatum, thalamus, frontal cortex, and sensorimotor cortex (for a review see Sehlmeyer et al., 2009). These findings indicate that phylogenetic differences between rodents and humans should be acknowledged, with higher cortical, particularly prefrontal areas playing an increasingly important role in emotional processing and regulation in humans.

5.3.2 The Amygdala, Part II: Updating of CS/US Contingencies During Extinction Training

Evidence from animal and human studies is accumulating that the amygdala is not only crucial for the acquisition and expression of a conditioned fear response, but is also involved in the extinction process, presumably in the updating of CS/US contingencies during extinction training. For example, electrophysiological studies showed that cell activity in the lateral amygdala (LA) of rats increased during fear conditioning and decreased in the extinction training phase (Quirk, Repa, & LeDoux, 1995). Activity in the (B) LA, the proposed site of sensory convergence of the US and CS, was likely modulated by changing contingencies from acquisition to extinction training. Other lines of evidence used pharmacological modulation of NMDA receptors within the BLA. Injection of NMDA antagonists (Falls, Miserendino, & Davis, 1992) or agonists like DCS (Walker et al., 2002) prior to the extinction training modulated the extinction success in a dose-dependent manner in the rodent brain.

Human neuroimaging studies further support the view that the amygdala is involved in the process of extinction learning. Using fMRI, LaBar et al. (1998) showed a temporally graded amygdala response during extinction learning, thus supplementing electrophysiological findings from animal research (Quirk, Armony, & LeDoux, 1997). In another fMRI study, alteration of contingencies was followed by increased amygdala activation, suggesting that this region is involved in processing environmental changes in biologically relevant (e.g., aversive) stimuli (Knight, Cheng, Smith, Stein, & Helmstetter, 2004). Using an extinction recall design, Phelps, Delgado, Nearing, & LeDoux (2004) also found increased amygdala activation during both the acquisition and extinction training phases, but not for the expression of extinction during recall after a one-day delay. Moreover, amygdala activation toward the CS+ reversed from acquisition to extinction with an increased blood-oxygene-level dependent (BOLD) signal during the acquisition phase, but a decrease in the BOLD response during the extinction training. Using a fear-conditioning reversal paradigm, Schiller, Levy, Niv, LeDoux, & Phelps (2008) were moreover able to show that amygdala and striatal responses tracked the fear-predictive stimuli, flexibly flipping their responses from one predictive stimulus to another, thus corroborating the notion that the amygdala updates CS/US contingencies.

In summary, the amygdala likely serves as a change detector for stimulus associations in classical conditioning and extinction, thus signaling the modulation of associative memory traces, which, in turn, might activate additional structures also involved in the extinction process.

5.3.3 The vmPFC: Recall of Extinction Memories

First insights into the unique contribution of the vmPFC during extinction were provided by experimental lesion studies on rodents. In one of these studies, Morgan & LeDoux (1995) reported prolonged within-session extinction in rats with vmPFC lesions when compared to sham-lesioned rats. In a series of influential experiments, Quirk, Russo, Barron, & Lebron (2000) and Milad & Quirk (2002) further provided substantial evidence for vmPFC functions during the process of extinction. First, they showed that infralimbic cortex lesions (IL; the rat homologous region to the human vmPFC), did not affect conditioning or initial extinction learning, but prevented the recall of extinction on the next day, indicating that the vmPFC is a potential site for the long-term storage of extinction memory. Second, these findings were paralleled by single-unit recordings from cells within the IL that displayed characteristic response patterns only during the recall of extinction. These activation patterns were correlated with the magnitude of the CR. Third, pairing brief electrical stimulation of the IL with the CS- reduced freezing behavior in nonextinguished rats, thus simulating extinction memory. Pharmacological modulation of molecular processes during consolidation in the vmPFC after extinction training can also block long-term extinction memory (Santini, Ge, Ren, Pena, & Quirk, 2004).

In humans, neuroimaging studies have affirmed the relevance of the vmPFC and OFC for extinction recall as well (Gottfried & Dolan, 2004; Milad et al., 2007; Phelps et al., 2004). Moreover, hippocampal activation has frequently been observed during extinction recall, indicating that contextual influences are important during the recall of extinction memories (Kalisch et al., 2006; Milad et al., 2007). Results are, however, not always that clear-cut. For example, Phelps et al. (2004) reported different regions within the vmPFC to be associated with fear conditioning and extinction during all experimental phases, including the extinction recall on day two. In particular, a relative increase as represented by less decreased activity was observed in the vmPFC from extinction training to recall on day two. Although extinction success within the training phase predicted activation of the vmPFC during the extinction recall, it needs to be clarified how decreases in BOLD activity can be adequately interpreted. In accordance, Milad et al. (2005) reported the cortical thickness of the vmPFC to be associated with performance on extinction recall. Interestingly, the locus reported by Milad et al. was closely mapped to the peak voxel of activation during extinction recall from the Phelps et al. study.

The vmPFC and OFC may also hold a core function in mediating fear reactions beyond the paradigm of fear extinction. It should be noted that fear extinction represents only one procedure among others to modify fear reactions. Schiller and Delgado (2010) recently reported overlapping functional activation patterns in a brain circuit involved in the flexible control during three different experimental approaches (fear extinction, fear reversal learning, and cognitive reappraisal of CS/US contingencies). While the amygdala and the striatum tracked the strength of the conditioned fear signal, vmPFC activity increased either during fear extinction, reversal, or cognitive reappraisal. The latter was additionally associated with activation of the dorsolateral (dl) PFC, suggesting indirect top–down modulation via the vmPFC of the amygdala by this region when cognitive strategies are used. Other authors suggest that the OFC is involved in operant extinction learning (Finger, Mitchell, Jones, & Blair, 2008), further underlining the role of the vmPFC and OFC in regulating learned fear, and that fear extinction only represents one among different approaches on how to modify fear.

5.3.4 The Hippocampus: Contextual Modulation of Extinction Recall

Behavioral experiments provide evidence that the recall of extinction is highly context dependent (Bouton, Westbrook, Corcoran, & Maren, 2006). Several lines from animal and human research suggest that the hippocampus might be a potential neurobiological substrate of context dependency within associative learning (Corcoran & Maren, 2001; Kalisch et al., 2006; Lang et al., 2009). Animal studies show that neurotoxic lesions of the hippocampus do not affect fear conditioning per se (Frohardt, Guarraci, & Bouton, 2000). This finding is paralleled by clinical observations about a double dissociation of conditioning and declarative knowledge relative to amygdala- or hippocampus-based brain lesions in humans (Bechara et al., 1995), where fear conditioning was unimpaired in a patient with selected lesions of the hippocampus. Using functional inactivation of the hippocampus during extinction recall by infusions of muscimol (a Gamma-aminobutyric acid (GABA) receptor agonist), Corcoran and Maren (2001) showed a selective impairment in the context-specific expression of extinction: while saline-treated rats clearly differentiated between a context where extinction training had taken place (reduced freezing) and a new context (enhanced freezing), muscimol-treated rats showed comparable rates of freezing in both contexts, being in the midrange of those from the control group. Using fMRI, hippocampal involvement during the context dependent recall of extinction has been demonstrated (Kalisch et al., 2006; Lang et al., 2009). The vmPFC and the hippocampus were both activated during extinction with the positive correlation between the activation magnitude depending on the context of extinction recall. These findings are consistent with the view that the hippocampus confers context dependence on the vmPFC and exerts a modulatory gating control on the expression of extinction memory (Sotres-Bayon et al., 2006).

5.3.5 New Perspectives on Fear Extinction: Erasure or Inhibition?

The common view on fear extinction holds that the original fear memory is not affected; instead, a new, inhibitory CS/US- memory trace will be established. Consequently, return of fear is commonly observed and manifests in behavioral phenomena such as spontaneous recovery, reinstatement, or context dependent reactivation of conditioned fear. New lines of evidence do however challenge this traditional view, indicating that fear memories can indeed be erased by extinction training under certain circumstances. Depending on the time window, different extinction mechanisms may be recruited, ranging from new memory formation to erasure-like mechanisms. We will shortly outline the rationale behind and describe those circumstances that might lead to erasure, rather than new inhibitory learning during extinction training. Starting on the molecular level, depotentiation can reverse LTP by administering low-frequency stimulation to the same synapse after LTP has been induced. Extinction training can induce depotentiation in the LA and results in removal of AMPA receptors that have previously been created as a result of neuronal plasticity (Kim et al., 2007; Lin, Yeh, Lu, & Gean, 2003; Lin, Wang, Tai, & Tsai, 2010). Of note, these processes are critically dependent on the time window where memory traces are a transient shape, and thus unstable and susceptible to disruption for depotentiation to take place.

There are three time windows of interest: The first one is the time interval immediately after fear conditioning has been induced and consolidation is being initiated. As has been shown in a remarkable animal study by Myers, Ressler, & Davis (2006), induction of immediate extinction training about 10 min after fear conditioning precluded a CR to be reinstated, or re-evoked in a different context. In contrast, delayed extinction (24–72 h) resulted in reinstatement, renewal, and spontaneous recovery of extinguished fear, indicating that the fear memory was still in place. Other researchers were, however, not always able to replicate these initial findings (Maren & Chang, 2006; Schiller et al., 2008), and the predictive value of the initial extinction interval determining the particular extinction mechanism remains to be evaluated. If replicated, findings could indicate a two-stage model of extinction, where immediate extinction might result in (partly) erasure by directly recoding CS/US contingencies in the amygdala even before consolidation of the fear memory has been accomplished, while delayed extinction might recruit additional mechanisms by establishing a new memory trace in conjunction with the PFC.

The second time window relates to the retrieval phase of memory. As has been shown by Nader, Schafe, & Le Doux (2000), memory retrieval is an active process rendering the memory trace temporarily labile and in a destabilized state, requiring protein-dependent reconsolidation. In other words, retrieving a particular memory likely changes the memory itself. Interfering with this memory trace during retrieval enhances the likelihood of memory loss. In line with this it has been shown that reactivation of a CR immediately before extinction training abolished return of fear not only in animals (Monfils, Cowansage, Klann, & LeDoux, 2009), but also in humans with long-lasting effects over one year (Schiller et al., 2010). In contrast to immediate extinction designs, interference with existing fear memories during reconsolidation offers unique possibilities for therapeutic approaches. It remains to be evaluated yet if these basic experimental findings can improve exposure techniques for treating pathological anxiety. Unlike experimentally induced conditioned fear, traumatic fear memories are much more complex and the question if these memories can be truly erased may depend on the degree to which the entire memory structure can get reactivated and targeted during exposure.

A third time window relates to the developmental stage of an organism (Kim, Li, & Richardson, 2011; Kim & Richardson, 2010). Recent findings support the view of a developmental switch in extinction mechanisms (Gogolla, Caroni, Luthi, & Herry, 2009; Herry et al., 2010). It is well known that the development and shaping of brain circuits underlies so-called "critical periods" during which particular neuroplastic changes can take place (e.g., binocular vision; see Hensch, 2005 for a review). Similar critical periods for erasure-like mechanisms in fear extinction have recently been detected in the rodent brain. Fear extinction in postweaning rats (24 days old) was associated with hallmark recovery of fear phenomena and involved NMDA receptors as well as medial PFC activity, suggesting an inhibitory fear learning mechanism taking place in this particular stage. In contrast, juvenile preweaning rats (17 days old) did neither show return of fear, nor involvement of prefrontal or NMDA-gated activity. This developmental switch in fear-extinction mechanisms was paralleled by the advent of perineural nets (PNN) (Gogolla et al., 2009). Further, degrading the PNN in adult rats resulted in a reversal of fear extinction mechanisms back to erasure. Findings indicate that PNN's are necessary to prevent fear memories from destabilization via LTP and that until these networks are established fear erasure still can take place (Gogolla et al., 2009). As pointed out by Herry (p. 606; Herry et al., 2010) "the developmental regulation of amygdala circuit function underlying extinction-induced memory erasure enables juvenile animals to adhere to the most recently learned information, a strategy that might increase chances of survival," thus pointing toward the adaptive value of this early extinction mechanism.

In summary, this body of evidence suggests that multiple pathways for changing fear memories do exist which could in turn trigger novel approaches toward the treatment of pathological fear. From a translational perspective, the identification of those time windows under which erasure-like mechanisms take place could hold important implications for clinical interventions in improving durable extinction of traumatic events.

5.4 Altered-Fear Conditioning and Extinction in the Anxiety Disorders

Models based on learning theories have emphasized dysfunctional alterations in emotional-associative learning (i.e., fear conditioning and extinction) as putative pathogenetic mechanisms promoting the development and maintenance of pathological fear and anxiety (Craske et al., 2008). Since conditioning processes are discussed to constitute a key mechanism underlying fear and anxiety, it seems plausible to search for anxiety-specific changes in fear conditioning and extinction, including its neural substrates. Specifically, it has been hypothesized that anxiety patients display an increased resistance to the extinction of pathological fear memories, and several studies, albeit predominantly using psychophysiological, but not neuroimaging outcome measures, are available that reliably underline this assumption (Blechert, Michael, Vriends, Margraf, & Wilhelm, 2007; Hermann, Ziegler, Birbaumer, & Flor, 2002; Milad et al., 2009; Orr et al., 2000; Rougemont-Bucking et al., 2011; Wessa & Flor, 2007). To better understand the active components of and, eventually, to optimize exposure therapy, it is necessary to investigate the neurobiological basis of emotional-associative learning in general as well as specific alterations observable in patients suffering from anxiety disorders. By applying fear conditioning and extinction paradigms in experimentally controlled settings, disorder-specific alterations could be elucidated, thus further bridging the gap between basic and applied research.

When searching for dysfunctional fear conditioning and extinction circuits related to pathological fear, two questions are of particular interest: First, what is the actual nature of deficit: can we observe enhanced acquisition of fear memories, deficient extinction learning, attenuated extinction recall, or other processes such as overgeneralization of fear or deficient context sensitivity? Second, do all patients show the same alterations, or are there disorder-specific deficits? Comparative studies with appropriate experimental designs are in charge for answering these questions (see Craske et al., 2009 for a comprehensive discussion). It has, however, to be stated that in contrast to the extensive body of literature from animal research, the majority of translational studies on anxiety disorders is lacking a comparative approach or complex paradigms that allow for the differentiation of fear conditioning, extinction learning, and recall. It is beyond the scope of this chapter to fully review all psychophysiological studies conducted on fear conditioning in different types of anxiety disorders in detail. A quantitative meta-analysis by Lissek et al. (2005), accounting for 20 studies applying classical fear-conditioning paradigms with psychophysiological outcome measures to patients with anxiety disorders (including post-traumatic stress disorder (PTSD), panic disorder (PD), generalized anxiety disorder (GAD), social anxiety disorder (SAD), and "neurotic" patients) gives first evidence for anxiety-specific alterations: overall, anxiety patients showed enhanced fear-conditioned responses during acquisition and extinction, but aggregated effect sizes for patient-control differences were relatively small and higher in studies that applied simple conditioning vs. discrimination-learning paradigms. Patient-control differences in conditioning were attributed to enhanced excitatory conditioning to the paired conditioned stimulus (CS+; "danger cues") and impaired inhibitory conditioning (impairment in inhibitory fear processing) to the unpaired conditioned stimulus (CS-; "safety cue") in patients. The latter observation could account for the smaller effect sizes found in differential fear-conditioning tasks where overgeneralization of fear toward the CS- masks the differential fear response. It could be assumed that altered emotional-associative learning is not restricted to enhanced fear conditioning per se, but may also encompass other deficits such as overgeneralization of fear toward safe conditions in some, but not all anxiety disorders. Unfortunately, due to the heterogeneous patient population and insufficient sample sizes for disorder-specific reanalyses, findings are inconclusive regarding differences in emotional-associative learning between the anxiety disorders, which remain to be examined (Craske et al., 2009).

Recent research concentrates on the neurobiological substrates of PTSD as a model disorder for impaired fear extinction. The following paragraphs provide a summary of studies on fear extinction in experimentally controlled settings, including measurements of physiological and neural activity. We will start with studies on PTSD patients and then continue with a relative compact section on other anxiety disorders.

5.4.1 Fear Extinction in Post-Traumatic Stress Disorder

Several studies have investigated fear conditioning and extinction in PTSD patients (including psychophysiological and neuroimaging approaches) and, albeit some heterogeneity, generally point toward deficiencies in fear extinction and discrimination learning that may provide a basis for the characteristic re-experiencing of trauma-related symptoms, avoidance, and hypervigilance in those patients (Blechert et al., 2007; Lissek et al., 2005; Milad et al., 2009; Orr et al., 2000). An experiment by Blechert et al. (2007), comprising a one-day differential fear-conditioning paradigm with habituation, acquisition, and extinction training phases, provided evidence for enhanced differential conditioning in the late acquisition phase and, more importantly, attenuated extinction learning in psychophysiological fear indicators responding to the CS+ in the patient group compared to healthy controls. Also, an US expectancy bias was found during extinction in the PTSD group, that is, patients overestimated the probability of the US administration after the CS+ had been presented. Further, deficits in verbal discriminative fear learning were identified, since one third of the PTSD patients displayed differential conditioning (as measured by electrodermal activity and subjective valence ratings) without being aware of the CS/US contingency. In a postexperimental behavioral test, the patient group displayed higher avoidance of the CS+ as indicated by the selection of a chocolate bar depicting the CS- instead of the CS+ picture. Interestingly, when contrasting PTSD patients with individuals that had experienced a traumatic event without developing PTSD, no significant differences were observed, except for enhanced skin conductance responses (SCR) to the CS+ and the CS- during the second part of the extinction phase in the patient group. In a similar vein, Wessa and Flor (2007) observed successful conditioning as indicated by psychophysiological measures in response to a trauma-related US only in trauma-exposed subjects with and without PTSD, but not in healthy controls. Further, attenuated extinction training was reported for PTSD subjects. Altered fear conditioning and attenuated extinction learning in PTSD patients when compared to trauma-exposed healthy controls has also been reported by Orr et al. (2000), thus confirming changes in emotional-associative learning for this patient group.

Considering the neurobiological substrates of the above-mentioned deficits in emotional-associative learning, some studies applying neuroimaging techniques have specified brain structures and networks which appear to mediate dysfunctional fear extinction in PTSD populations (Bremner et al., 2005; Milad et al., 2009; Rougemont-Bucking et al., 2011). Bremner et al. (2005) examined female PTSD patients that had experienced early childhood sexual abuse using positron emission tomography in a one-day fear conditioning and extinction training paradigm. Compared to healthy controls, patients showed, among others, enhanced left amygdala activation during fear acquisition and less activation in orbitofrontal and medial prefrontal areas, including the anterior cingulate cortex (ACC), during extinction learning. By employing a two-day fear conditioning and extinction paradigm (extinction recall was conducted on day two), Milad et al. (2009) identified an impaired extinction recall, that is, deficient retrieval and behavioral expression of the extinction memory, in PTSD patients when compared to trauma-exposed, but mentally healthy control subjects as indicated by psychophysiological measures. According to the authors, these impairments were associated with decreased activation in the vmPFC and hippocampus as well as higher activation in the dorsal ACC (dACC) during extinction recall as was observed in the patient group. Although no significant between-group differences were found on day one as measured by SCR, fMRI data revealed enhanced amygdala activation and decreased activation in the vmPFC during extinction training in PTSD patients. The authors argue that this patient-specific brain activation in the extinction training phase could be related to a deficient consolidation of the extinction memory. Altogether, Milad et al. provided further evidence for PTSD-related impairments in extinction memory consolidation and extinction recall, with simultaneously specifying the underlying neurobiological mechanisms. A reanalysis of the data set used by Milad et al. was conducted by Rougemont-Bucking et al. (2011), with a slightly different sample composition, focusing on SCR and fMRI responses toward the presentation of the context, but not the CS stimulus, displayed during conditioning vs. extinction training and recall.[1] Moreover, by splitting the experimental phases into two parts for the purpose of data analysis, the reanalysis enabled an inspection of temporal dynamics in fear extinction (e.g., early vs. late extinction recall). Mostly in line with the previous findings, the reanalysis also revealed decreased vmPFC activation and increased dACC activation in response to the presentation of the different context during extinction recall in PTSD patients. Interestingly, no between-group differences regarding psychophysiological measures were observable in neither phase of the two-day experimental design, implying that there was no actual fear response to the contextual cues. Nevertheless and in contrast to Milad et al. (2009), the authors found altered

[1] *Note*: In this protocol, the CS was presented within a context image in a counterbalanced manner, that is, in context A during conditioning and in context B during extinction training and recall, respectively. In each trial, the context image was presented alone prior to its combination with the CS.

neural activation in the patient group already during late conditioning with patients exhibiting a stronger activation of the dACC toward the context cues in the second half of acquisition. Further, with respect to the extinction training phase, a greater dACC activation in the first half and decreased vmPFC activation in the second half were revealed in PTSD patients. Rougemont-Bücking et al. suggest that these findings support the hypothesis that processing of contextual information is altered in PTSD: The vmPFC appears to be involved not only in controlling the fear response by inhibition of the amygdala but also in memorizing and recognizing a "safe" context where no negative consequences (i.e., the US in this experimental context) occur. In addition to this potential vmPFC-related failure to process safety information during extinction training and recall, the hyperactivation of the dACC might be related to inadequate, excessive signaling of danger-related information.

Based upon neuroimaging studies, a neurocircuitry of PTSD (Rauch, Shin, & Phelps, 2006) has been proposed, with the amygdala, the vmPFC, and the hippocampus representing the brain structures of particular interest. A hypersensitivity of the amygdala, manifest in enhanced fear-conditioned responses, has been hypothesized, altogether with a dysfunctional vmPFC-modulation of the amygdala (being associated with impaired extinction) and deficits in hippocampal function which result in impaired discrimination learning (regarding the distinction of "safe" vs. "dangerous" contexts) and altered contingency awareness.

In summary, neuroimaging studies on fear extinction in PTSD patients indicate abnormalities in frontolimbic networks which are very likely involved in fear extinction, including the amygdala and the vmPFC, in line with the hypothesized neurocircuitry of PTSD. To our knowledge, investigations of treatment effects, particularly exposure-related functional changes of neural activation patterns specifically associated with fear extinction, are not available yet. Nevertheless, promising results emerged from longitudinal fMRI studies employing other experimental approaches than fear extinction (e.g., emotional face memory-encoding task): Poor treatment outcome following a CBT intervention was associated with higher bilateral amygdala and ventral ACC activation toward fear-eliciting stimuli prior to treatment (Bryant et al., 2008); functional changes in the hippocampus and subgenual ACC might be related to recovery or, at least, PTSD symptom improvement (Dickie, Brunet, Akerib, & Armony, 2011). Since the aforementioned brain regions belong to the neurocircuitry of fear conditioning and extinction, it could be assumed that behavioral changes during psychological treatment may also be associated with functional brain changes as measurable by fear extinction paradigms.

5.4.2 Fear Conditioning and Extinction in Other Anxiety Disorders

Fear conditioning studies on PD suggest alterations in emotional-associative learning, namely reduced extinction learning (Michael, Blechert, Vriends, Margraf, & Wilhelm, 2007) and impaired discriminative learning (Lissek et al., 2009, 2010) in psychophysiological reactivity and subjective stimulus evaluations. Corroborating previous findings on impaired discriminative learning, Tuescher et al. (2011) reported enhanced neural activation toward the "safe" cue in the subgenual cingulate, ventral striatum, and extended amygdala in PD patients as investigated by an instructed fear conditioning paradigm, but not in healthy control subjects or PTSD patients. PTSD patients, on the other hand, did not show the temporal pattern of activity decrease found in control subjects during the threat condition, pointing toward deficits in habituation processes. It can furthermore be hypothesized that while extinction learning deficits can be detected in different anxiety disorders such as PD and PTSD, deficits in discriminatory learning as evidenced by enhanced responding toward safety cues such as the CS- appears to be specific for PD in this study. From a transdiagnostic perspective, comparative approaches such as employed by Tuescher et al. (2011) may support the development of more differentiated pathophysiological models of anxiety disorders, including their neurobiological foundations.

Our literature review revealed only a few studies explicitly examining neural correlates of fear conditioning and extinction in other anxiety disorders, for example, SAD or specific phobia (Hermann et al., 2002; Lissek et al., 2008; Schweckendiek et al., 2011). Regarding SAD, no enhanced fear acquisition, but exaggerated unconditioned stimulus expectancy and overall elevated autonomic arousal, as well as delayed extinction training has been reported (Hermann et al., 2002). Testing the hypothesis of enhanced general vs. phobia-specific conditionability in SAD, Lissek et al. (2008) employed socially relevant (e.g., facial expressions) stimuli, but no disorder-unrelated aversive US. In contrast to healthy controls that did not show any conditioning at all, only SAD patients developed a CR in this particular task. Findings support the notion that these patients are particularly vulnerable toward disorder-specific aversive cues that facilitate fear conditioning in this group. In line with these findings, an fMRI study by Schweckendiek et al. (2011) revealed enhanced activation toward a phobia-specific CS in fear network-associated brain structures, for example, the amygdala, the ACC, and medial prefrontal cortex, in patients only.

5.5 Summary and Conclusions

Based on very ancient, that is, evolutionary roots, fear conditioning and extinction represent one of the most fundamental learning mechanisms enabling the organism to constantly adapt to changing environmental challenges in order to successfully avoid dangerous contexts and maximize survival. Altered emotional-associative learning such as enhanced fear conditioning or attenuated extinction learning could severely impair the individual's ability to flexibly readjust behavior in response to environmental changes, resulting in exaggerated and inadequate fear, as present in the anxiety disorders.

A large amount of preclinical research has contributed to unravel the neurobiological basis of fear conditioning and extinction. Across different levels of analysis, findings from molecular, cellular, and systems mechanisms subserve to outline a first working model of the fear extinction circuit. In this model, the amygdala represents a proximal control for the modulation and expression of behavioral components of CS/US mediated associations. Within this local circuit, changes in contingencies can be directly detected and processed as deviants from expected associations. During extinction training, the formerly acquired CS/US association is gradually modulated with repeated presentations of the CS without the US toward a CS/no US association. This extinction memory trace is then consolidated and stored in conjunction with the vmPFC. Being confronted with the CS again, this memory trace gets activated, followed by the inhibition of a fear response via prefrontal projections to ITC within the amygdala. However, when the extinguished CS is presented outside the appropriate context, hippocampal input might act as a gate control which in turn inhibits vmPFC outputs to the amygdala, thus resulting again in an increase of the CR in a different context. Very recent findings expand and differentiate this working model of the extinction circuit, among them studies evidencing alternative mechanisms of erasure-like extinction, or pharmacological approaches trying to enhance extinction memory formation. Although the precise mechanisms are still not entirely uncovered, these preclinical studies hold a direct appeal for translational approaches on how to improve CBT tratments.

In contrast to this large body of preclinical investigations, research on neural substrates of fear conditioning and extinction in relation to anxiety disorders has only begun to adopt findings from basic research to clinical conditions. Although promising results have been obtained for a better understanding of the neurocircuitry of PTSD within the terminology of emotional-associative learning, less is known about other disorders, for example PD, SAD, specific phobia, or generalized anxiety disorder. Changes in fear conditioning and extinction have been proposed to constitute a key pathological mechanism in the development and maintenance of anxiety disorders by many researchers, yet data on the precise neural substrate of the underlying deficit, specificity of neurocircuits for different anxiety disorders, or their predictive value for treatment approaches are, however, largely missing. Although the implicated neurocircuitry so far provides a heuristic model for the next step of research, there is a clear need for more comparative research. Future studies should stronger employ transdiagnostic approaches and comprehensive paradigms that do allow for the simultaneous investigation of fear conditioning, extinction learning, as well as recall deficits. Employing intermediate phenotypes such as highly trait anxious or anxiety-sensitive subjects could be a valuable approach to study the neural mechanisms underlying altered fear conditioning and extinction, supplemented by studies on high-risk populations with prospective longitudinal designs that could further help to disentangle causes from consequences in relation to altered mechanisms of fear learning and unlearning.

Another central challenge for testing pathophysiological models based on learning theories remains: Assuming that fear extinction underlies psychological treatments such as exposure therapy, can we detect neuroplasticity in brain circuits mediating fear extinction that covariates with behavioral changes? Although direct approaches experimentally manipulating changes in emotional-associative learning before and after psychological treatment are still lacking, treatment response has been reported to be associated with changes in fear circuitry structures such as the amygdala, insula, ACC, and hippocampus (Bryant et al., 2008; Dickie et al., 2011; Goossens, Sunaert, Peeters, Griez, & Schruers, 2007). It remains to be evaluated if these findings are also indicative for changes in fear conditioning and extinction.

Focusing on mindfulness and acceptance-based approaches in the treatment of anxiety disorders (see Gloster et al. in this book), these are also hypothesized to strengthen extinction learning during exposure procedures (Treanor, 2011). Enhanced activity in prefrontal regions such as the mPFC has been proposed as one potential pathway mediating these effects. Interestingly, this region has not only been associated with the processing of contextual information and the behavioral expression of fear after extinction alongside with the hippocampus (Maren, 2011), but has also been implicated in meditation activities and trait mindfulness (Creswell, Way, Eisenberger, & Lieberman, 2007; Holzel et al., 2007). It could indeed be hypothesized that the different approaches to treat pathological fear and anxiety may converge upon similar brain circuits subserving emotional regulation in a broader sense. Differentiating the precise neurobiological mechanisms of action behind these interventions represents one of the major challenges for future endeavors in clinical research.

References

Amaral, D. G., Price, J. C., Pitkänen, A., & Carmichael, S. T. (1992). Anatomical organisation of the primate amygdaloid complex. In J. P. Aggleton (Ed.), *The amygdala: Neurobiological aspects of emotion, memory, and mental dysfunction* (pp. 1–66). New York: Wiley.

Barad, M., Gean, P. W., & Lutz, B. (2006). The role of the amygdala in the extinction of conditioned fear. *Biological Psychiatry, 60*, 322–328.

Bechara, A., Tranel, D., Damasio, H., Adolphs, R., Rockland, C., & Damasio, A. R. (1995). Double dissociation of conditioning and declarative knowledge relative to the amygdala and hippocampus in humans. *Science, 269*, 1115–1118.

Blechert, J., Michael, T., Vriends, N., Margraf, J., & Wilhelm, F. H. (2007). Fear conditioning in posttraumatic stress disorder: Evidence for delayed extinction of autonomic, experiential, and behavioural responses. *Behaviour Research and Therapy, 45*, 2019–2033.

Bouton, M. E. (2002). Context, ambiguity, and unlearning: Sources of relapse after behavioral extinction. *Biological Psychiatry, 52*, 976–986.

Bouton, M. E., Westbrook, R. F., Corcoran, K. A., & Maren, S. (2006). Contextual and Temporal Modulation of Extinction: Behavioral and Biological Mechanisms. *Biological Psychiatry, 60*, 352–360.

Bremner, J. D., Vermetten, E., Schmahl, C., Vaccarino, V., Vythilingam, M., Afzal, N., et al. (2005). Positron emission tomographic imaging of neural correlates of a fear acquisition and extinction paradigm in women with childhood sexual-abuse-related post-traumatic stress disorder. *Psychological Medicine, 35*, 791–806.

Bryant, R. A., Felmingham, K., Kemp, A., Das, P., Hughes, G., Peduto, A., et al. (2008). Amygdala and ventral anterior cingulate activation predicts treatment response to cognitive behaviour therapy for post-traumatic stress disorder. *Psychological Medicine, 38*, 555–561.

Büchel, C., Morris, J., Dolan, R. J., & Friston, K. J. (1998). Brain systems mediating aversive conditioning: An event-related fMRI study. *Neuron, 20*, 947–957.

Corcoran, K. A., & Maren, S. (2001). Hippocampal inactivation disrupts contextual retrieval of fear memory after extinction. *Journal of Neuroscience, 21*, 1720–1726.
Craske, M. G., Kircanski, K., Zelikowsky, M., Mystkowski, J., Chowdhury, N., & Baker, A. (2008). Optimizing inhibitory learning during exposure therapy. *Behaviour Research and Therapy, 46*, 5–27.
Craske, M. G., Rauch, S. L., Ursano, R., Prenoveau, J., Pine, D. S., & Zinbarg, R. E. (2009). What is an anxiety disorder? *Depression and Anxiety, 26*, 1066–1085.
Creswell, J. D., Way, B. M., Eisenberger, N. I., & Lieberman, M. D. (2007). Neural correlates of dispositional mindfulness during affect labeling. *Psychosomatic Medicine, 69*, 560–565.
Delgado, M. R., Olsson, A., & Phelps, E. A. (2006). Extending animal models of fear conditioning to humans. *Biological Psychology, 73*, 39–48.
Dickie, E. W., Brunet, A., Akerib, V., & Armony, J. L. (2011). Neural correlates of recovery from post-traumatic stress disorder: A longitudinal fMRI investigation of memory encoding. *Neuropsychologia, 49*, 1771–1778.
Falls, W. A., Miserendino, M. J. D., & Davis, M. (1992). Extinction of fear-potentiated startle – blockade by infusion of an Nmda antagonist into the amygdala. *Journal of Neuroscience, 12*, 854–863.
Finger, E. C., Mitchell, D. G. V., Jones, M., & Blair, R. J. R. (2008). Dissociable roles of medial orbitofrontal cortex in human operant extinction learning. *Neuroimage, 43*, 748–755.
Frohardt, R. J., Guarraci, F. A., & Bouton, M. E. (2000). The effects of neurotoxic hippocampal lesions on two effects of context after fear extinction. *Behavioral Neuroscience, 114*, 227–240.
Gais, S., & Born, J. (2004). Declarative memory consolidation: Mechanisms acting during human sleep. *Learning & Memory, 11*, 679–685.
Garpenstrand, H., Annas, P., Ekblom, J., Oreland, L., & Fredrikson, M. (2001). Human fear conditioning is related to dopaminergic and serotonergic biological markers. *Behavioral Neuroscience, 115*, 358–364.
Gogolla, N., Caroni, P., Luthi, A., & Herry, C. (2009). Perineuronal nets protect fear memories from erasure. *Science, 325*, 1258–1261.
Goossens, L., Sunaert, S., Peeters, R., Griez, E. J. L., & Schruers, K. R. J. (2007). Amygdala hyperfunction in phobic fear normalizes after exposure. *Biological Psychiatry, 62*, 1119–1125.
Gottfried, J. A., & Dolan, R. J. (2004). Human orbitofrontal cortex mediates extinction learning while accessing conditioned representations of value. *Nature Neuroscience, 7*, 1145–1153.
Hebb, D. O. (1949). *The Organization of Behavior*. New York: Wiley.
Hensch, T. K. (2005). Critical period plasticity in local cortical circuits. *Nature Reviews Neuroscience, 6*, 877–888.
Hermann, C., Ziegler, S., Birbaumer, N., & Flor, H. (2002). Psychophysiological and subjective indicators of aversive Pavlovian conditioning in generalized social phobia. *Biological Psychiatry, 52*, 328–337.
Herry, C., Ferraguti, F., Singewald, N., Letzkus, J. J., Ehrlich, I., & Luthi, A. (2010). Neuronal circuits of fear extinction. *European Journal of Neuroscience, 31*, 599–612.
Hofmann, S. G., Meuret, A. E., Smith, J. A., Simon, N. M., Pollack, M. H., Eisenmenger, K., et al. (2006). Augmentation of exposure therapy for social anxiety disorder with D-Cycloserine. *Archives of General Psychiatry, 63*, 298–304.
Holmes, A., Yang, R. J., Lesch, K. P., Crawley, J. N., & Murphy, D. L. (2003). Mice lacking the serotonin transporter exhibit 5-HT(1A) receptor-mediated abnormalities in tests for anxiety-like behavior. *Neuropsychopharmacology, 28*, 2077–2088.
Holzel, B. K., Ott, U., Hempel, H., Hackl, A., Wolf, K., Stark, R., et al. (2007). Differential engagement of anterior cingulate and adjacent medial frontal cortex in adept meditators and non-meditators. *Neuroscience Letters, 421*, 16–21.
Kalisch, R., Holt, B., Petrovic, P., De Martino, B., Kloppel, S., Buchel, C., et al. (2009). The NMDA agonist D-cycloserine facilitates fear memory consolidation in humans. *Cerebral Cortex, 19*, 187–196.

Kalisch, R., Korenfeld, E., Stephan, K. E., Weiskopf, N., Seymour, B., & Dolan, R. J. (2006). Context-dependent human extinction memory is mediated by a ventromedial prefrontal and hippocampal network. *Journal of Neuroscience, 26*, 9503–9511.

Kandel, E. R. (2001). The molecular biology of memory storage: A dialogue between genes and synapses. *Science, 294*, 1030–1038.

Kim, J., Lee, S., Park, K., Hong, I., Song, B., Son, G., et al. (2007). Amygdala depotentiation and fear extinction. *Proceedings of the National Academy of Sciences of the United States of America, 104*, 20955–20960.

Kim, J. H., Li, S., & Richardson, R. (2011). Immunohistochemical analyses of long-term extinction of conditioned fear in adolescent rats. *Cerebral Cortex, 21*, 530–538.

Kim, J. H., & Richardson, R. (2010). New findings on extinction of conditioned fear early in development: Theoretical and clinical implications. *Biological Psychiatry, 67*, 297–303.

Knight, D. C., Cheng, D. T., Smith, C. N., Stein, E. A., & Helmstetter, F. J. (2004). Neural substrates mediating human delay and trace fear conditioning. *Journal of Neuroscience, 24*, 218–228.

Konorski, J. (1967). *Integrative Activity of the Brain*. Chicago: University Chicago Press.

Kushner, M. G., Kim, S. W., Donahue, C., Thuras, P., Adson, D., Kotlyar, M., et al. (2007). D-cycloserine augmented exposure therapy for obsessive-compulsive disorder. *Biological Psychiatry, 62*, 835–838.

LaBar, K. S., Gatenby, J. C., Gore, J. C., LeDoux, J. E., & Phelps, E. A. (1998). Human amygdala activation during conditioned fear acquisition and extinction: A mixed-trial fMRI study. *Neuron, 20*, 937–945.

LaBar, K. S., LeDoux, J. E., Spencer, D. D., & Phelps, E. A. (1995). Impaired fear conditioning following unilateral temporal lobectomy in humans. *Journal of Neurocience, 15*, 6846–6855.

Lang, S., Kroll, A., Lipinski, S. J., Wessa, M., Ridder, S., Christmann, C., et al. (2009). Context conditioning and extinction in humans: Differential contribution of the hippocampus, amygdala and prefrontal cortex. *European Journal of Neuroscience, 29*, 823–832.

LeDoux, J. (1996). *The emotional brain*. New York: Simon and Schuster.

LeDoux, J. (2007). The amygdala. *Current Biology, 17*, R868–R874.

LeDoux, J. E., Iwata, J., Cicchetti, P., & Reis, D. J. (1988). Different projections of the central amygdaloid nucleus mediate autonomic and behavioral correlates of conditioned fear. *Journal of Neurosience, 8*, 2517–2529.

Lin, P., Wang, S., Tai, M., & Tsai, Y. (2010). Differential involvement of medial prefrontal cortex and basolateral amygdala extracellular signal-regulated kinase in extinction of conditioned taste aversion is dependent on different intervals of extinction following conditioning. *Neuroscience, 171*, 125–133.

Lin, C. H., Yeh, S. H., Lu, H. Y., & Gean, P. W. (2003). The similarities and diversities of signal pathways leading to consolidation of conditioning and consolidation of extinction of fear memory. *Journal of Neuroscience, 23*, 8310–8317.

Lissek, S., Levenson, J., Biggs, A. L., Johnson, L. L., Arneli, R., Pine, D. S., et al. (2008). Elevated fear conditioning to socially relevant unconditioned stimuli in social anxiety disorder. *American Journal of Psychiatry, 165*, 124–132.

Lissek, S., Powers, A. S., McClure, E. B., Phelps, E. A., Woldehawariat, G., Grillon, C., et al. (2005). Classical fear conditioning in the anxiety disorders: A meta-analysis. *Behaviour Research and Therapy, 43*, 1391–1424.

Lissek, S., Rabin, S., Heller, R. E., Lukenbaugh, D., Geraci, M., Pine, D. S., et al. (2010). Overgeneralization of conditioned fear as a pathogenic marker of panic disorder. *American Journal of Psychiatry, 167*, 47–55.

Lissek, S., Rabin, S. J., McDowell, D. J., Dvir, S., Bradford, D. E., Geraci, M., et al. (2009). Impaired discriminative fear-conditioning resulting from elevated fear responding to learned safety cues among individuals with panic disorder. *Behavior Research and Therapy, 47*, 111–118.

Lonsdorf, T. B., Weike, A. I., Nikamo, P., Schalling, M., Hamm, A. O., & Ohman, A. (2009). Genetic gating of human fear learning and extinction: Possible implications for gene-environment interaction in anxiety disorder. *Psychological Science, 20*, 198–206.

Maren, S. (2011). Seeking a spotless mind: Extinction, deconsolidation, and erasure of fear memory. *Neuron, 70*, 830–845.
Maren, S., & Chang, C. H. (2006). Recent fear is resistant to extinction. *Proceedings of the National Academy of Sciences of the United States of America, 103*, 18020–18025.
Michael, T., Blechert, J., Vriends, N., Margraf, J., & Wilhelm, F. H. (2007). Fear conditioning in panic disorder: Enhanced resistance to extinction. *Journal of Abnormal Psychology, 116*, 612–617.
Milad, M. R., Pitman, R. K., Ellis, C. B., Gold, A. L., Shin, L. M., Lasko, N. B., et al. (2009). Neurobiological basis of failure to recall extinction memory in posttraumatic stress disorder. *Biological Psychiatry, 66*, 1075–1082.
Milad, M. R., Quinn, B. T., Pitman, R. K., Orr, S. P., Fischl, B., & Rauch, S. L. (2005). Thickness of ventromedial prefrontal cortex in humans is correlated with extinction memory. *Proceedings of the National Academy of Sciences of the United States of America, 102*, 10706–10711.
Milad, M. R., & Quirk, G. J. (2002). Neurons in medial prefrontal cortex signal memory for fear extinction. *Nature, 420*, 70–74.
Milad, M. R., Wright, C. I., Orr, S. P., Pitman, R. K., Quirk, G. J., & Rauch, S. L. (2007). Recall of fear extinction in humans activates the ventromedial prefrontal cortex and hippocampus in concert. *Biological Psychiatry, 62*, 446–454.
Monfils, M. H., Cowansage, K. K., Klann, E., & LeDoux, J. E. (2009). Extinction-reconsolidation boundaries: Key to persistent attenuation of fear memories. *Science, 324*, 951–955.
Morgan, M. A., & LeDoux, J. E. (1995). Differential contribution of dorsal and ventral medial prefrontal cortex to the acquisition and extinction of conditioned fear in rats. *Behavioral Neuroscience, 109*, 681–688.
Myers, K. M., & Davis, M. (2002). Behavioral and neural analysis of extinction. *Neuron, 36*, 567–584.
Myers, K. M., Ressler, K. J., & Davis, M. (2006). Different mechanisms of fear extinction dependent on length of time since fear acquisition. *Learning and Memory, 13*, 216–223.
Nader, K., Schafe, G. E., & Le Doux, J. E. (2000). Fear memories require protein synthesis in the amygdala for reconsolidation after retrieval. *Nature, 406*, 722–726.
Norberg, M. M., Krystal, J. H., & Tolin, D. F. (2008). A meta-analysis of D-cycloserine and the facilitation of fear extinction and exposure therapy. *Biological Psychiatry, 63*, 1118–1126.
Onur, O. A., Schlaepfer, T. E., Kukolja, J., Bauer, A., Jeung, H., Patin, A., et al. (2010). The N-Methyl-D-Aspartate Receptor Co-agonist D-Cycloserine facilitates declarative learning and hippocampal activity in humans. *Biological Psychiatry, 67*, 1205–1211.
Orr, S. P., Metzger, L. J., Lasko, N. B., Macklin, M. L., Peri, T., & Pitman, R. K. (2000). De novo conditioning in trauma-exposed individuals with and without posttraumatic stress disorder. *Journal of Abnormal Psychology, 109*, 290–298.
Otto, M. W., Tolin, D. F., Simon, N. M., Pearlson, G. D., Basden, S., Meunier, S. A., et al. (2010). Efficacy of D-cycloserine for enhancing response to cognitive-behavior therapy for panic disorder. *Biological Psychiatry, 67*, 365–370.
Pape, H. C., & Pare, D. (2010). Plastic synaptic networks of the amygdala for the acquisition, expression, and extinction of conditioned fear. *Physiological Reviews, 90*, 419–463.
Pare, D., & Smith, Y. (1993). The intercalated cell masses project to the central and medial nuclei of the amygdala in cats. *Neuroscience, 57*, 1077–1090.
Pavlov, I. P. (1927). *Conditioned reflexes*. New York: Dover.
Peper, M., Karcher, S., Wohlfarth, R., Reinshagen, G., & LeDoux, J. E. (2001). Aversive learning in patients with unilateral lesions of the amygdala and hippocampus. *Biological Psychology, 58*, 1–23.
Phelps, E. A., Delgado, M. R., Nearing, K. I., & LeDoux, J. E. (2004). Extinction learning in humans: Role of the amygdala and vmPFC. *Neuron, 43*, 897–905.
Quirk, G. J. et al. (2006). Prefrontal mechanisms in extinction of conditioned frear. *Biol Psychiatry, 60*, 337-343. Page 338, Figure 1.
Quirk, G. J., Armony, J. L., & LeDoux, J. E. (1997). Fear conditioning enhances different temporal components of tone-evoked spike trains in auditory cortex and lateral amygdala. *Neuron, 19*, 613–624.

Quirk, G. J., Garcia, R., & Gonzalez-Lima, F. (2006). Prefrontal mechanisms in extinction of conditioned fear. *Biological Psychiatry, 60*, 337–343.

Quirk, G. J., Pare, D., Richardson, R., Herry, C., Monfils, M. H., Schiller, D., et al. (2010). Erasing fear memories with extinction training. *Journal of Neuroscience, 30*, 14993–14997.

Quirk, G. J., Repa, C., & LeDoux, J. E. (1995). Fear conditioning enhances short-latency auditory responses of lateral amygdala neurons: Parallel recordings in the freely behaving rat. *Neuron, 15*, 1029–1039.

Quirk, G. J., Russo, G. K., Barron, J. L., & Lebron, K. (2000). The role of ventromedial prefrontal cortex in the recovery of extinguished fear. *Journal of Neuroscience, 20*, 6225–6231.

Rauch, S. L., Shin, L. M., & Phelps, E. A. (2006). Neurocircuitry models of posttraumatic stress disorder and extinction: Human neuroimaging research – Past, present, and future. *Biological Psychiatry, 60*, 376–382.

Rescorla, R. A. (1988). Pavlovian conditioning. It's not what you think it is. *The American Psychologist, 43*, 151–160.

Ressler, K. J., Rothbaum, B. O., Tannenbaum, L., Anderson, P., Graap, K., Zimand, E., et al. (2004). Cognitive enhancers as adjuncts to psychotherapy – Use of D-cycloserine in phobic individuals to facilitate extinction of fear. *Archives of General Psychiatry, 61*, 1136–1144.

Romanski, L. M., Clugnet, M. C., Bordi, F., & LeDoux, J. E. (1993). Somatosensory and auditory convergence in the lateral nucleus of the amygdala. *Behavioral Neuroscience, 107*, 444–450.

Rougemont-Bucking, A., Linnman, C., Zeffiro, T. A., Zeidan, M. A., Lebron-Milad, K., Rodriguez-Romaguera, J., et al. (2011). Altered Processing of Contextual Information during Fear Extinction in PTSD: An fMRI Study. *CNS Neuroscience & Therapeutics, 17*, 227–236.

Royer, S., & Pare, D. (2002). Bidirectional synaptic plasticity in intercalated amygdala neurons and the extinction of conditioned fear responses. *Neuroscience, 115*, 455–462.

Sah, P., Faber, E. S., Lopez, D. A., & Power, J. (2003). The amygdaloid complex: Anatomy and physiology. *Physiological Reviews, 83*, 803–834.

Santini, E., Ge, H., Ren, K., Pena, D. O., & Quirk, G. J. (2004). Consolidation of fear extinction requires protein synthesis in the medial prefrontal cortex. *Journal of Neuroscience, 24*, 5704–5710.

Schiller, D., & Delgado, M. R. (2010). Overlapping neural systems mediating extinction, reversal and regulation of fear. *Trends in Cognitive Sciences, 14*, 268–276.

Schiller, D., Levy, I., Niv, Y., LeDoux, J. E., & Phelps, E. A. (2008). From fear to safety and back: Reversal of fear in the human brain. *Journal of Neuroscience, 28*, 11517–11525.

Schiller, D., Monfils, M. H., Raio, C. M., Johnson, D. C., LeDoux, J. E., & Phelps, E. A. (2010). Preventing the return of fear in humans using reconsolidation update mechanisms. *Nature, 463*, 49–U51.

Schweckendiek, J., Klucken, T., Merz, C. J., Tabbert, K., Walter, B., Ambach, W., et al. (2011). Weaving the (neuronal) web: Fear learning in spider phobia. *Neuroimage, 54*, 681–688.

Sehlmeyer, C., Schoning, S., Zwitserlood, P., Pfleiderer, B., Kircher, T., Arolt, V., et al. (2009). Human fear conditioning and extinction in neuroimaging: A systematic review. *PLoS One, 4*, e5865.

Sotres-Bayon, F., Cain, C. K., & LeDoux, J. E. (2006). Brain mechanisms of fear extinction: Historical perspectives on the contribution of prefrontal cortex. *Biological Psychiatry, 60*, 329–336.

Spoormaker, V. I., Sturm, A., Andrade, K. C., Schroter, M. S., Goya-Maldonado, R., Holsboer, F., et al. (2010). The neural correlates and temporal sequence of the relationship between shock exposure, disturbed sleep and impaired consolidation of fear extinction. *Journal of Psychiatric Research, 44*, 1121–1128.

Treanor, M. (2011). The potential impact of mindfulness on exposure and extinction learning in anxiety disorders. *Clinical Psychology Review, 31*, 617–625.

Tuescher, O., Protopopescu, X., Pan, H., Cloitre, M., Butler, T., Goldstein, M., et al. (2011). Differential activity of subgenual cingulate and brainstem in panic disorder and PTSD. *Journal of Anxiety Disorders, 25*, 251–257.

Walker, D. L., Ressler, K. J., Lu, K. T., & Davis, M. (2002). Facilitation of conditioned fear extinction by systemic administration or intra-amygdala infusions of D-cycloserine as assessed with fear-potentiated startle in rats. *Journal of Neuroscience, 22*, 2343–2351.

Wessa, M., & Flor, H. (2007). Failure of extinction of fear responses in posttraumatic stress disorder: Evidence from second-order conditioning. *American Journal of Psychiatry, 164*, 1684–1692.

Wilhelm, S., Buhlmann, U., Tolin, D. F., Meunier, S. A., Pearlson, G. D., Reese, H. E., et al. (2008). Augmentation of behavior therapy with D-cycloserine for obsessive-compulsive disorder. *American Journal of Psychiatry, 165*, 335–341.

Chapter 6
Cognitive Enhancers in Exposure Therapy for Anxiety and Related Disorders

Stefan G. Hofmann, Cassidy A. Gutner, and Anu Asnaani

Dr. Stefan G. Hofmann is a Professor in the Clinical Psychology Program at Boston University, where he directs the Social Anxiety Program at the Center for Anxiety & Related Disorders.

S.G. Hofmann (✉) • C.A. Gutner • A. Asnaani
Psychotherapy and Emotion Research Laboratory, Department of Psychology, Boston University, 648 Beacon Street, 6th floor, Boston, MA 02215, USA
e-mail: shofmann@bu.edu; cgutner@bu.edu; aasnaani@bu.edu

P. Neudeck and H.-U. Wittchen (eds.), *Exposure Therapy: Rethinking the Model – Refining the Method*, DOI 10.1007/978-1-4614-3342-2_6,

Cassidy is in the final year of her doctoral degree in Clinical Psychology, and is currently completing her clinical internship at the San Diego VA.

Anu is an advanced doctoral student in the Clinical Psychology program at Boston University, who will be starting her clinical internship at Brown Medical School in July 2012.

6.1 Introduction

Cognitive-behavioral therapy (CBT) is grounded in a model based on the hypothesis that dysfunctional cognitions are causally linked to emotional distress. As a result, restructuring these dysfunctional cognitions leads to improvements in both emotional distress and nonadaptive behaviors. CBT is one of the most effective treatments for anxiety and related disorders and is typically a short-term treatment that takes place in weekly 1-h sessions and lasts for 12–15 sessions (e.g., Cape, Whittington, Buszewicz, Wallace, & Underwood, 2010; Gould, Otto, & Pollack, 1995; Hofmann & Smits, 2008; Stewart & Chambless, 2009). CBT is comprised of precise and unique components that work synergistically to introduce the exposure rationale and concepts of cognitive restructuring. With respect to cognitive restructuring, individuals are taught to identify maladaptive automatic thoughts to examine thinking errors, highlight the link between anxious mood states and automatic thoughts, and ultimately, generate rational responses to their maladaptive automatic thoughts. The behavioral component of CBT is targeted by asking patients to identify avoidance strategies that are ideally required to be eliminated during exposure to the feared stimuli. When the patient approaches the feared situation in a hierarchical manner, cognitive restructuring techniques are employed and avoidance strategies are eliminated. Behavioral experiments as part of exposures are designed to test the quality/realistic nature of the previously held maladaptive thoughts.

Alternative therapies, such as pharmacotherapy, are not as durable at follow-up as compared to CBT (e.g., Barlow, Gorman, Shear, & Woods, 2000) despite their ability to produce symptom reduction at post-treatment and during medication maintenance (see Baldwin et al., 2005). Although there is support for both modalities, there continues to be room for improvement in these efficacious treatments (Hofmann & Smits, 2008). Controlled CBT trials produce an average treatment effect size of 0.73, demonstrating a significant area to target with respect to treatment improvement (Hofmann & Smits, 2008). However, these results are from brief treatments that target anxiety disorders with significant chronicity, demonstrating the utility of psychoeducation, cognitive restructuring and extinction-based learning that results from exposures in CBT treatment. Furthermore, these results demonstrate learning in the face of memory deficits that can be associated with anxiety disorders (Airaksinen, Larsson, & Forsell, 2005; Asmundson, Stein, Larsen, & Walker, 1994). With respect to pharmacotherapy studies, similar results have been demonstrated (Roy-Byrne & Cowley, 2002). However, partial or nonresponse to treatment is present in over half of patients failing to respond to first line CBT or pharmacotherapy (Pollack et al., 2008), leaving room for improvement.

Combination treatment has been studied extensively to further examine the enhanced efficacy of these treatment modalities in conjunction with one another (e.g., CBT plus anxiolytic medication). Nonetheless, a recent meta-analysis investigating the comparison of combination strategies with CBT plus placebo demonstrates the modest benefit to combination therapy immediately following treatment (effect size = 0.59) and no added benefit at 6-month follow-up (Hofmann, Sawyer, Korte, & Smits, 2009). As a result of the less than ideal effect of these treatment modalities, more recent research has focused on using pharmacotherapy as a means of augmenting core learning processes of CBT rather than as a stand-alone anxiolytic (Davis, Barad, Otto, & Southwick, 2006; Hofmann, 2007). The goal of this chapter is to provide a review of cognitive enhancers as augmentation agents to the treatment of anxiety and related disorders with respect to exposure-based therapy (for a recent comprehensive review, see also Hofmann, Smits, Asnaani, Gutner, & Otto, 2011).

6.2 D-Cycloserine

One of the most promising augmentation strategies with CBT is the use of D-cycloserine (DCS; Hofmann, 2007; Norberg, Krystal, & Tolin, 2008) that resulted from animal research investigating the role of extinction learning and its primary brain circuits (see Davis, Ressler, Rothbaum, & Richardson, 2006). This line of research has focused on the glutamatergic N-Methyl-D-Aspartate (NMDA) receptor in the amygdala, which is the same area believed to modulate extinction-based learning utilized in exposure-based therapy. Agonists that inhibit NMDA receptors block the retention of extinction learning (Falls, Miserendino, & Davis, 1992), while partial agonists, including DCS, enhance the consolidation of new learning during the extinction process (Walker, Ressler, Lu, & Davis, 2002). Moreover, the augmentation effects of DCS persist for several hours after the administration (see Richardson, Ledgerwood, & Cranney, 2004), suggesting a significant role of DCS in the consolidation of memory during extinction learning. Animal research has outlined that extinction learning is necessary during extinction training to see the resulting benefits of DCS enhancement on succeeding trials (Bouton, Vurbic, & Woods, 2008).

Research on DCS in humans has been studied in placebo-controlled trials pairing DCS with exposure sessions to treat fear-based disorders. Ressler et al. (2004) used DCS with height phobic patients in virtual reality exposures and after two exposures with DCS the enhancement of treatment was observed in individuals receiving the DCS versus placebo. The DCS group in this study demonstrated significantly enhanced extinction learning at 1–2 weeks and 3-months post-treatment, as well as more exposure to heights in real life. These results suggest that the enhancement effect of DCS was observed even when an inadequate number of extinction sessions were given (see Walker et al., 2002), DCS may enhance exposure using virtual reality equipment, and it may influence willingness to continue exposures after treatment has ended.

Subsequent studies have applied DCS augmentation treatment to clinical trials. In a study investigating the effects on a group on individuals with social anxiety disorder, 27 patients were randomized to 50 mg of DCS or placebo (Hofmann et al., 2006a; Hofmann, Pollack, & Otto, 2006b). The pill was administered 1-h prior to exposures in the last four sessions (all of which involved social exposures) of a five-session protocol of weekly treatment. Social phobia patients in the DCS group demonstrated significantly greater improvements at post-treatment and 1-month follow-up. These results were later replicated in a larger social anxiety sample (Guastella et al., 2008) and in panic disorder (Otto et al., 2009). The panic trial consisted of 31 patients with panic disorder in a five-session treatment. Exposures occurred during the final three-sessions and relied on exposures to feared internal sensations. Although the majority of these patients failed to respond to prior pharmacotherapy (87%), there was a large effect of DCS relative to the placebo group.

Although DCS augmentation strategies have been an effective tool for exposure-based treatments in social anxiety disorder and panic disorder, there has been less success with obsessive–compulsive disorder (OCD; Kushner et al., 2007; Storch et al., 2010; Wilhelm et al., 2008). These studies utilized slightly different procedures

Table 6.1 Summary of empirically supported effects of cognitive enhancers in clinical populations

Authors (year)	Cognitive enhancer	Disorder	Results
Ressler et al. (2004)	DCS	Height phobia	Positive effect on exposure as compared to placebo-augmented exposure
Hofmann et al. (2006a, 2006b)	DCS	SAD	Positive effect on exposure as compared to placebo-augmented exposure
Guastella et al. (2008)	DCS	SAD	Positive effect on exposure as compared to placebo-augmented exposure
Otto et al. (2009)	DCS	Panic disorder	Positive effect on exposure as compared to placebo-augmented exposure
Kushner et al. (2007)	DCS	OCD	Positive effect on exposure as compared to placebo-augmented exposure by mid-treatment. Weakened effect with continuous drug administration
Wilhelm et al. (2008)	DCS	OCD	Positive effect on exposure as compared to placebo-augmented exposure by mid-treatment. Weakened effect with continuous drug administration
Storch et al. (2010)	DCS	OCD	No effect as compared to placebo at posttreatment
Powers et al. (2009)	Yohimbine	Claustrophobia	Greater gains than placebo-augmented exposure sessions
Soravia et al. (2006)	Cortisol	Spider phobia	Greater fear reduction than after placebo-augmented exposure sessions
Mystkowski et al. (2003)	Caffeine	Spider phobia	Limited evidence for significant fear reduction versus placebo

Note: *DCS* D-cycloserine, *SAD* Social Anxiety Disorder, *OCD* Obsessive-Compulsive Disorder

than the previously mentioned trials in that they used twice weekly exposure sessions and/or DCS was given more frequently across treatment. This design is less ideal as efficacy of DCS augmentation decreases with successive administration (Kushner et al., 2007; Wilhelm et al., 2008), thus suggesting a potential role of DCS in enhancing the speed at which one recovers during acutely administered DCS. However, DCS did not demonstrate an effect in the study conducted by Storch et al. (2010) that investigated the effect of 250 mg of DCS 4 h prior to 12 CBT sessions on youth with OCD. Notably, the design of this study is significantly different than the other DCS trials, suggesting the importance of frequency, dose, and dosing schedule on outcomes. Similar DCS studies are underway investigating the effects on exposure therapy for post-traumatic stress disorder (Table 6.1).

There are several limitations of DCS augmentation with respect to both dosing and learning that must be discussed. To begin with, there has yet to be a study investigating the optimal dose of DCS for extinction learning. However, several studies have investigated various dosing increments that have guided current research. For example, Ressler et al. (2004) used a single dose of 50 mg or 500 mg of DCS and found no significant difference between them. More recent studies have investigated a variety of doses ranging from 50 mg to 125 mg and have all been found to be adequate for the enhancement of exposure therapy (e.g., Guastella et al., 2008; Hofmann et al., 2006a, 2006b; Kushner et al., 2007; Otto, Tolin, Simon, et al., 2010; Wilhelm et al., 2008). However, it should be noted that use of a higher dose appears to increase the chances of producing side effects as well as tolerance to the medication. Animal studies have suggested that tolerance to DCS may be reached fairly quickly as a result of repeated dosing (see Hofmann, Pollack, & Otto, 2006b for review). Although the studies on DCS have ranged in design, it is possible that one of the variables responsible for weaker results is the frequency (e.g., twice a week) and amount (e.g. large amounts of DCS) of dosing as seen in studies with weaker results (e.g., Kushner et al., 2007; Storch et al., 2010). It should be noted that all of the studies demonstrating an effect of DCS were double-blind randomized placebo-controlled studies (i.e., DCS plus exposure therapy was superior to placebo plus exposure therapy).

6.3 Methylene Blue

Animal and human studies have demonstrated the importance of activation in the medial prefrontal cortex (mPFC) in extinction recall as well as extinction retention in animals (e.g., Barrett, Shumake, Jones, & Gonzalez-Lima, 2003; Herry & Garcia, 2002; Milad & Quirk, 2002; Milad, Vidal-Gonzalez, & Quirk, 2004). The mPFC appears to be a critical component of consolidation of extinction memory (Quirk, Garcia, & González-Lima, 2006), highlighted by the research demonstrating that lesions in the ventral mPFC impair extinction retention but not necessarily extinction learning (Lebrón, Milad, & Quirk, 2004; Morgan, Romanski, & LeDoux, 1993; Quirk, Russo, Barron, & Lebron, 2000). As a result of this line of research, developing augmentation strategies to target the mPFC in fear extinction paradigms may be beneficial.

Methylene blue (MB) has been the focus of such research and has initial empirical support for stimulation of the mPFC (Gonzalez-Lima & Bruchey, 2004). MB is different than DCS in that it does not target a specific neurotransmitter system, but rather has a more nonspecific action that activates the mPFC area by effecting brain cytochrome oxidase activity. The increase of brain cytochrome oxidase activity caused by MB enhances oxidative energy metabolism, which consequently supplies energy to the synapses involved in extinction memory consolidation (Gonzalez-Lima & Bruchey, 2004). Furthermore, animal studies have demonstrated that administration of MB postextinction yields greater extinction retention and brain cytochrome oxidase activity, especially in the prefrontal cortex (Gonzalez-Lima & Bruchey, 2004). To date there are no studies of MB in humans although trials are currently underway. The possible clinical implications of these findings could be that MB might prevent relapse after exposure therapy.

6.4 Dopamine

Another cognitive enhancer that has gained momentum from animal research is dopamine. This line of research stems from work on nonhuman primates which demonstrates that catecholamine modulation involving dopamine in prefrontal cortex is involved in higher-level cognition, specifically working memory. More specifically, the D1 receptor in the dorsolateral prefrontal cortex is crucial to spatial working memory in monkeys (Sawaguchi & Goldman-Rakic, 1991). The D1 receptors, which largely exist on the pyramidal cells, activate the pyramidal neurons and enhance responsiveness of postsynaptic NMDA receptors on the pyramidal cells (Seamans & Yang, 2004). With respect to mechanisms of action, the D1 receptors attenuate recurrent excitation, likely through presynaptic inhibition of glutamate release (see Seamans & Yang, 2004), which likely constrains local activation during cognitive processes. As a result, the D1 receptor-mediated action in the PFC decreases responsiveness of surrounding circuitry that typically activates the circuit by potentiating intense focal activity (Goldman-Rakic, Castner, Svensson, Siever, & Williams, 2004). Moreover, activation of the D1 receptor manipulates the strength of the representation of glutamate-encoded information in the PFC, including a decrease of background PFC activity (Seamans & Yang, 2004). As a result, there is self-sustained activity to both noise and distractors (Durstewitz & Seamans, 2002).

Notably, dopamine has also demonstrated a clear role in motivation and reward seeking, which has further implications for anxiety disorders. Specifically, in these disorders there is an inhibitory effect on dopaminergic activity, which is a direct response to GABA and serotonin neurotransmitters. GABA or serotonin levels are often low in anxiety disorders and as a result, overactivity of dopamine in the brain regions specific to anxiety pathology is seen (Nikolaus, Antke, Beu, & Müller, 2010). Furthermore, evidence from neuroimaging and lesion studies demonstrate a higher binding potential at the dopamine receptors in the mesolimbic and striatal brain regions, which may be related to more anxiety and compulsion-related disorders (de la Mora, Gallegos-Cari, Arizmendi-García, Marcellino, & Fuxe, 2010; Olver et al., 2009; Stein & Ludik, 2000), as well as similar patterns in people reporting symptoms of generalized social anxiety (Furmark, 2009; Sareen et al., 2007; van der Wee et al., 2008).

The relationship between dopamine and anxiety symptoms has paved the way to research investigating direct and indirect methods of manipulating dopamine levels in applicable brain areas. Direct methods targeting the blockage of dopamine receptor by dopamine antagonists, which would in turn produce anxiolytic effects, could serve as a promising direct method of action. Such a method would be ideal for reducing symptoms in disorders such as OCD and generalized social anxiety where dopamine is implicated. Although preclinical research suggests that these antagonists may reduce dopamine activity, clinical studies are necessary to determine whether such results translate into an observable decline in anxiety symptoms. The more indirect methods typically involve serotonin-reuptake inhibitors for disorders like OCD. Such methodology increases synaptic serotonin, resulting in an inhibition in dopamine release. Unfortunately, serotonin-reuptake inhibitors have not been found to be effective on their own (Koo, Kim, Roh, & Kim, 2010).

6.5 Norepinephrine

Another agent implicated in PFC-dependent cognitive functioning besides MB and dopamine is the neurotransmitter norepinephrine. Animal research has demonstrated that α_2 receptors, likely on post-synaptic sites, impact working memory performance (Arnsten & Goldman-Rakic, 1985). It is possible that α_2 agonists such as norepinephrine may manipulate the balance of locus coeruleus activity in a way that may optimize decision-making performance or it may enhance sustained PFC activity (Arnsten, 2004).

6.6 Yohimbine

Another augmentation agent implicated in stimulating the mPFC is yohimbine hydrochloride, which is categorized as a selective competitive α_2-adrenergic receptor antagonist. Yohimbine blocks autoreceptor inhibition of norepinephrine release, which increases the extracellular levels in the mPFC (see Holmes & Quirk, 2010). Research on yohimbine initially produced varying results with respect to its effect on extinction learning. However, animal studies utilizing a systemic administration have increased the rate of extinction learning during massed exposures as well as yielded significant effects on fear extinction with spaced trials (Cain, Blouin, & Barad, 2004). Such results are promising as they typically result in minimal extinction learning in comparison to massed trials.

In a recent study on humans, evidence has been found supporting use of yohimbine hydrocholorine in augmenting exposure-based treatments (Powers, Smits, Otto, Sanders, & Emmelkamp, 2009). The randomized study provided adults with claustrophobic fear with two-exposure treatment session after administration of yohimbine hydrochloride (10.8 mg) or a pill placebo. Individuals in the yohimbine augmentation exposure group demonstrated better outcomes compared to those in the pill placebo-augmented exposure group. Furthermore, in this study yohimbine hydrochloride was well tolerated by individuals. It is important to note that a recent review demonstrates that these findings are inconsistent with animal research. In fact, some studies have found that yohimbine augmentation impairs extinction learning (Holmes & Quirk, 2010).

The mixed results produced by yohimbine augmentation led Holmes and Quirk to question whether the potential beneficial effects of yohimbine augmentation occur through noradrenergic stimulation (α_2-adrenoreceptor) versus alternative mechanisms (5-HT1a or D2). Another limitation of yohimbine may be related to how well it is tolerated. In a recent study, adverse effects were not encountered, and results propose that yohimbine has the potential to be panicogenic when given at doses above 10.8 mg, and further, this is elevated in individuals who fear physiologic arousal (Charney, Heninger, & Breier, 1984; Charney, Woods, Goodman, & Heninger, 1987). Although this may be viewed as a side effect, others may view this as an added benefit as repeated exposure to feared physiological reactions of the body (e.g., increased heart rate, tightness in the chest, lightheadedness) have been shown to be efficacious in the treatment of panic and other related disorders, which is thought to be a result of fear extinction (Hofmann & Smits, 2008). Lastly, the differential results of yohimbine augmentation have been attributed to differences that may be related to mouse strain-related discrepancies in the alacrity of extinction learning, the paradigm used in the study to assess the extinction learning, as well as sensitivity to context dependence versus cue-focused aspects of fear stimuli (Morris & Bouton, 2007). Although yohimbine has demonstrated potentially promising results (Powers et al., 2009), more research is necessary to investigate the mechanisms of action as well as the reliability of findings.

6.7 Endocannabinoids

It has been observed that there is a large presence of CB1 receptors in brain regions (e.g., amygdala and hippocampus) associated with anxiety and emotional learning more generally. Thus, another novel therapeutic approach for anxiety and related disorders has focused on this endogenous cannabinoid (also called the endocannabinoid) system (Porter & Felder, 2001). There are two types of cannabinoid receptors: CB1, which is most populous in the peripheral and central nervous system, and CB2, which is more often involved in the immune and enteric nervous system, along with the glial cells in the central nervous system. Animal and clinical studies have provided evidence for a dose-dependent relationship between cannabinoid agonists and anxiolytic effects of these drugs; that is, lower doses appear to produce an anxiolytic effect in animals while higher doses produce an anxiogenic effect (Pacher, Bátkai, & Kunos, 2006; Viveros, Llorente, Moreno, & Marco, 2005). In human studies of depression (which is highly comorbid with anxiety), CB1 receptors seem to be implicated (Vinod & Hungund, 2006), and as a result, these receptors sites are being explored as possible target sites for treatment of depression (Stein, Ipser, & Seedat, 2006). Further, there appears to be a modulation of basal anxiety by the cannabinoid system, along with an interaction with the acquisition of conditioned fear, as seen in disorders such as PTSD and the specific phobias. Indeed, studies have found that CB1 antagonists decrease acquisition of contextual fear conditioning involving the amygdala and hippocampus (Arenos, Musty, & Bucci, 2006), along with the overall acquisition and expression of fear conditioning (Haller, Bakos, Szirmay, Ledent, & Freund, 2002).

As discussed previously, extinction learning serves as the foundation for most empirically supported treatment for anxiety disorders, and the endocannabinoid system has been linked to such extinction learning in animal models (e.g., Chhatwal et al., 2009; Marsicano, Moosmann, Hermann, Lutz, & Behl, 2002). Specifically, the CB1 antagonists cause significant deficits in extinction learning; this would suggest that CB1 activation plays a key role in such learning, and therefore CB1 agonists provide an opportune avenue for exploration of a novel augmentation treatment for anxiety (Chhatwal, Davis, Maguschak, & Ressler, 2005).

6.8 Cortisol

Chronic elevations in glucocorticoids have been typically associated with deficits in memory functioning. However, there has recently been a shift to a modified conceptualization of cortisol's effects on memory, given growing evidence in human and animal samples that acute increases in glucocorticoids can actually enhance emotional memory consolidation and extinction-based learning (for a review see Lupien et al., 2005; Otto, McHugh, & Kantak, 2010). Specifically, cortisol activation has been implicated in the promotion of new learning in animals (Barreto, Volpato, & Pottinger, 2006; Yang, Chao, Ro, Wo, & Lu, 2007), while acute corticosterone increases seem to impair the reconsolidation of existing memories (Cai, Blundell, Han, Greene, & Powell, 2006; Pakdel & Rashidy-Pour, 2007). Such findings provide information about various mechanisms through which clinical interventions may be able to target creation of adaptive memories.

In humans, the memory-enhancing effects of cortisol have also been investigated (e.g., Beckner, Tucker, Delville, & Mohr, 2006; Cahill, Gorski, & Le, 2003), particularly around presentation of emotional stimuli (Abercrombie, Speck, & Monticelli, 2006; Buchanan & Lovallo, 2001; Putman, Van Honk, Kessels, Mulder, & Koppeschaar, 2004). In addition, cortisol has also been linked to augmentation of extinction learning in humans. For instance, Soravia et al. (2006) studied the relative effects of 10 mg of oral cortisol as compared to placebo on exposure to spider pictures. Study pills were administered to all participants an hour before the exposure exercise, for a total number of six-sessions occurring over 2 weeks, to reveal a significantly greater fear reduction in those patients in the cortisol condition. Also, cortisol levels have been found to be associated with clinical outcomes in patients, and while these findings are at a preliminary stage, they all point to a fascinating potential for cortisol-aided extinction learning. Of note, Junghanns et al. (2005) showed that individuals with alcohol dependence experiencing greater cortisol reactivity during 60-min cue exposures showed lower relapse rates at 6 weeks post-treatment. Similarly, cortisol levels (although not cortisol reactivity in this case) predicted the clinical outcomes following in vivo exposure sessions in patients diagnosed with panic disorder and agoraphobia (Siegmund et al., 2011). Furthermore, rape victims undergoing successful exposure-based treatment for their symptoms of post-traumatic stress disorder showed a decrease in their salivary cortisol levels after treatment.

Despite this tentative evidence for a beneficial effect of heightened cortisol levels, the majority of anxiolytic medications (both benzodiazepines and antidepressants) actually result in the suppression of cortisol reactivity (e.g., Curtis, Abelson, & Gold, 1997; Fries, Hellhammer, & Hellhammer, 2006; Pomara, Willoughby, Sidtis, Cooper, & Greenblatt, 2005; Rohrer, von Richthofen, Schulz, Beyer, & Lehnert, 1994). Thus, after reviewing the body of evidence for a facilitation effect of cortisol on extinction memory, Otto et al. (2010) argued that anxioloytic medications may be interfering with extinction learning in exposure-based CBT, thereby hampering the benefits of combination treatment of CBT and simultaneous medication treatment for anxiety. If such information is more routinely taken into consideration, it may help clinicians to more knowledgably recommend the use of combination treatments depending on the treatment profile of patients seeking treatment.

6.9 Nutrients and Botanicals

One other avenue of potential augmentation agents lies in the naturally occurring and other widely used compounds such as omega-3 fatty acids, caffeine, and nicotine. A brief review of the body of evidence on the effects of these substances on the fear and alarm system activated in the anxiety disorders is provided below.

6.9.1 Caffeine

Caffeine, a psychostimulant that is part of the larger family of methylxanthine compounds, is one of the most widely consumed substances. Caffeine has been shown to modulate brain activity and cerebral blood flow (Chen & Parrish, 2009), with the primary site of action of the substance at the adenosine receptors. In addition, while low to moderate consumption of caffeine has been linked to increased alertness and mental focus, higher intake patterns have been associated with the exacerbation of negative feelings such as insomnia and anxiety (Yun, Doux & Daniel, 2007). Furthermore, individuals with a history of panic attacks show a heightened sensitivity and reactivity to caffeine than their nonanxious counterparts (Boulenger, Uhde, Wolff, & Post, 1984). Indeed, patients diagnosed with panic disorder or agoraphobia reported greater frequency and intensity of fear and physical symptoms (e.g., trembling, palpitations, nausea, and tremors) when they ingested equal doses of caffeine as a control group, and these symptom reports were significantly correlated to plasma caffeine levels (Charney, Heninger, & Jatlow, 1985). Similar results were observed in samples of social phobics with a fear of public performance

(Nardi et al., 2008; Aouizerate, Martin-Guehl, & Tignol, 2004), although there were mixed findings for more generalized cases of social anxiety. Overall, this and other studies directly measuring of the effects of caffeine administration on adenosine receptivity suggest an association between caffeine-induced neural activity at adenosine receptor sites and a fear of physical symptoms (DeMet et al., 1989; Nardi et al., 2008).

To develop a better understanding of how caffeine impacts the fear and alarm circuitry, several researchers have employed the use of caffeine challenge tasks with patients diagnosed with panic disorder. Such paradigms have largely involved the administration of various doses of caffeine (e.g., 200–400 mg), followed by performance on tasks that induce typical symptoms of panic attacks, such as breath holding, CO_2 inhalation, and hyperventilation. Such studies have shown that individuals with panic disorder demonstrate a reduced capacity to tolerate unpleasant physical symptoms experienced in such tasks after consuming caffeine, while caffeine intake is unrelated to tolerance of unpleasant physical symptoms in nonanxious controls (Masdrakis, Markianos, Vaidakis, Papakostas, & Oulis, 2009). So far there has been only limited evidence for a beneficial application of caffeine in the treatment of anxiety. Specifically, Mystkowski, Mineka, Vernon, and Zinbarg (2003) delivered caffeine or placebo at the time of an exposure session for spider phobia, and once more at a follow-up visit a week later, when participants were assessed for a return of fear. The results pointed to a beneficial effect on reduction of fear in individuals experiencing congruent drug states (i.e., ingestion of caffeine at both test and follow-up time-points) than those in incongruent drug states (Mystkowski et al., 2003). These results must be interpreted with caution, however, because a similar pattern was observed in those individuals receiving placebo at both test and follow-up. This would indicate the benefits of a more general state-dependent learning in extinction of fear, and not a specific additive augmentation with caffeine.

6.9.2 Omega-3 Fatty Acids

Combinations of saturated, monosaturated, and polyunsaturated fatty acids combine to form lipids, which are the major constituent of brain tissue; therefore, these substances are important and abundant in mammals. Several foods (e.g., flaxseed, canola, and soy) are rich sources of several key omega-3 fatty acids, namely a-linolenic (or ALA) and linoleic acid, and allow for unencumbered synthesis of these constituents. Other important fatty acids, such as docosahexaenoic acid (or DHA), which makes up some 10–20% of brain fatty tissue, are not as easily synthesized from dietary sources, and are instead derived from preformed sources such as fatty fish (e.g., tuna and salmon) (McNamara & Carlson, 2006). Deficiencies in fatty acids have been implicated in the presence of neurocognitive deficits, elevated aggression, anxiety, and depression, along with hindered dopamine and serotonin transmission in animals.

The effects of an omega-3 fatty acid deficiency look a little different in humans. In particular, deficits (as seen most frequently in preterm babies) have been linked to an increased risk for attention-based pathology such as attention deficit/hyperactivity disorder (ADHD), other psychopathology such as schizophrenia, and in delays in maturation of cortical gray matter. For the most part, the research on the effects of omega-3 fatty acid supplements on humans has been pretty limited, but animal studies indicate that a deficit in these brain matter constituents may be implicated in higher rates of depression (Klokk, Gotestam & Mykletun, 2010; Timonen et al., 2004). The few correlational studies of these compounds have not found a clear positive association of baseline omega-3 levels on responsiveness to traditional SSRIs in the treatment of depression (Fiedorowicz, Hale, Spector, & Coryell, 2010). Yet, there remains much room for exploration of this compound as a potential augmentation agent for the treatment of anxiety, particularly because there is a relatively supported linkage between omega-3 deficiency and anxiety in animals.

6.9.3 Nicotine

There has been a widespread understanding that nicotine use is commonly present in individuals suffering from psychiatric illnesses such as schizophrenia, depression, and certain anxiety disorders. In particular, a higher proportion of smokers have been observed in samples of patients with panic disorder (Breslau & Klein, 1999). In contrast, there is a lower incidence of nicotine dependence in individuals meeting criteria for OCD, therefore, creating a mixed message of how nicotine precisely affects the fear and alarm system. In animals, there appears to be a dose-dependent relationship of nicotine to anxiety, such that low doses of the substance are linked to anxiolytic effects, and higher doses are linked to anxiogenic effects in nonhuman subjects (Brioni, O'Neill, Kim, & Decker, 1993; File, Kenny, & Ouagazzal, 1998). Other researchers have hypothesized that it is particular types of anxiety that determine a beneficial or harmful change in anxiety levels as a result of nicotine use, which may be more consistent with the human association studies. Specifically, administration of nicotine in animals undergoing the elevated plus maze (a model for specific phobia) produces anxiolytic effects, as compared to the anxiogenic effects of nicotine observed in social interaction tasks (File, Cheeta, & Kenny, 2000).

Such preclinical findings can direct researchers to conceptualizing nicotine's effects as disorder-specific, therefore explaining some of the differential rates of use across the anxiety disorders. Several human studies utilized similar paradigms as described with animals above. Of note, one study delivered small doses of nicotine transdermally (via a patch) to nonsmoking subjects just before they engaged in a CO_2 inhalation task (Cosci, Abrams, Schruers, Rickelt, & Griez, 2006). The study showed that while nicotine increased physiological arousal (as measured by blood pressure and heart rate), it did not cause panic symptoms in control subjects. On the other hand, smaller studies utilizing clinical populations diagnosed with OCD have found a beneficial reduction in the compulsive symptoms of the disorder due to transdermal administration of nicotine (Salín-Pascual & Basañez-Villa, 2003). Overall, there remains a need for more systematic examination of the effects of nicotine in healthy and clinical populations to determine whether this agent is actually beneficial in reducing the fear response in anxiety patients.

6.10 Genetic Modulation

Alterations in gene expression have become a recent useful lens through which to better understand the learning processes present in memory formation and consolidation. Two biomarkers garnering increasing interest have been the brain-derived neurotrophic factor (BDNF) and KIBRA, both of which have been highlighted for their roles in learning and memory. While neither has been directly manipulated so far, both of these biomarkers are discussed briefly below in the context of raising awareness of other potentially useful sites of action for development of future cognitive enhancers.

6.10.1 BDNF

BDNF is part of the neurotrophin family of growth factors, and affects the synaptic plasticity of neurons within the adult central nervous system, particularly those involved in learning and memory (Egan et al., 2003; Hariri et al., 2003). BDNF serves a primary role in the biological substrates of psychological disorders, and is involved in the acquisition and extinction of fear learning (Charney & Manji, 2004; Nestler et al., 2002). As mentioned earlier, in the anxiety disorders there is impairment in the ability to recognize and remember safety and threat cues during a fearful experience, in order to most effectively achieve extinction learning (e.g., Lissek et al., 2005; Rauch, Shin, & Phelps, 2006). Animal research indicates that genetic and pharmacological inhibition of BDNF signaling leads to significant memory impairments across different types of memory tasks (see Yu et al., 2009) as a result of a decrease in long-term potentiation. In addition, it has been demonstrated that BDNF mediates extinction memory consolidation within the intralimbic medial prefrontal cortex (IL mPFC).

Given these observable mechanisms in animal models, attention is being paid to the functioning of this biomarker within human subjects. A sample of 42 outpatients with panic disorder were treated with manualized cognitive-behavioral treatment (CBT), and it was found that those individuals responding poorly to CBT evidenced significantly lower serum BDNF levels (25.9 ng/ml [S.D. 8.7]) relative to patients showing a good response to the psychological treatment (33.7 ng/ml [S.D. 7.5]) (Kobayashi et al., 2005). Thus, a pharmacological agent that can directly increase concentrations of hippocampal BDNF may provide a fruitful avenue through which to increase responsivity to otherwise efficacious treatments such as CBT. Alternatively, there is growing evidence favoring the use of aerobic exercise as a nonpharmacological means through which to modify hippocampal BDNF (Berchtold, Castello, & Cotman, 2010; Cotman & Berchtold, 2002). Indeed, 30-min bouts of moderate-intensity exercise have been shown to restore the reduced BDNF concentrations observed in patients with panic disorder (Ströhle et al., 2010), and provide a meaningful direction to pursue in currently ongoing studies as a potential cognitive enhancer of exposure-based treatments for anxiety.

Human research has illuminated one single nucleotide polymorphism, the human specific BDNF nucleotide ($BDNF_{Met}$), in the BDNF gene (Val66Met) that has been linked to hippocampal volume and hippocampal-dependent memory (Bueller et al., 2006; Egan et al., 2003; Hariri et al., 2003), as well the role it has been shown to play in individual vulnerability to anxiety and depression (Momose et al., 2002; Sen et al., 2003; Sklar et al., 2002; Ventriglia et al., 2002). In particular, extinction learning appears to be impaired in human subjects carrying the $BDNF_{Met}$ allele, and imaging research has indicated less ventromedial prefrontal cortical activity and greater amygdala activation in these carriers (Soliman et al., 2010). This would suggest that there exists a hyporesponsiveness in brain regions that are crucial for extinction learning in these allele carriers. In sum, understanding the effect of the $BDNF_{Met}$ allele on extinction learning could lead to a clearer conceptualization of how to most effectively enhance treatment for anxiety, particularly given the dysregulation of BDNF in the anxiety disorders (Kaplan, Vasterling, & Vedak, 2010).

6.10.2 KIBRA

KIBRA (also known as WWC1) is a molecule that is involved with the post-synaptic protein dendrin, and was first discussed by Kremerskothen et al. (2003). KIBRA has demonstrated a key genetic role in memory and cognition (Papassotiropoulos et al., 2006), and is most commonly expressed in the kidney and brain in adults. Further, KIBRA is prominent in structures implicated in memory such as the hippocampus, cortex, cerebellum, and the hypothalamus (Johannsen, Duning, Pavenstädt, Kremerskothen, & Boeckers, 2008). In the case of this particular biomarker, carriers of certain KIBRA T-alleles (e.g., rs17070145, rs6439886) have shown significantly better performance on episodic memory tasks compared to subjects who are homozygous for the C allele at either polymorphism (see Schneider et al., 2010 for a review). Imaging studies have revealed greater brain activation in areas implicated in memory retrieval for those individuals with WWC1 (rs1707145) T-allele noncarriers as compared to the T-allele carriers during an episodic memory task. The research thus far on KIBRA, however, has involved healthy controls or individuals with dementia, and has therefore not yet focused on anxiety symptoms. This still remains an important area to explore further as KIBRA may serve to ameliorate the memory impairments often seen in patients with anxiety disorders, which can prevent them from effectively engaging in otherwise efficacious psychological treatments.

6.11 Conclusion

CBT is an empirically supported treatment for anxiety and related disorders that is rooted in exposure therapy and has demonstrated promise in significantly decreasing, and often times eliminating, symptoms. The current chapter offers an overview of a range of potential cognitive enhancers that may offer further enhancement of traditional CBT. To date, DCS has demonstrated the greatest promise and potential in further enhancing CBT across several anxiety disorders. More specifically, the NMDA receptor may be a promising focus when investigating new cognitive enhancers for CBT. Furthermore, the role of biological markers is important. BDNF and KIBRA are important to biological markers with respect to genetic modulators, as well as treatment efficacy.

The advancement in cognitive enhancers sheds further light on the disappointing results of using combination treatments (e.g., CBT plus pharmacotherapy). Combining CBT with anxiolytic agents such as SSRIs have not been shown to be more effective than monotherapies (Hofmann et al., 2009). The combination of CBT with cognitive enhancers is a more recent approach that is founded in neuroscience and has taken basic science and translated it into clinical practice. This new approach is advantageous in numerous ways, including the fact that such cognitive enhancers target a specific mechanism of treatment process and are not delivered in a chronic dosing that is typical of traditional pharmacotherapy. Furthermore, the increased investigation into cognitive enhancers may lead to further understanding about the specific mechanisms of action responsible for treatment change in exposure-based therapies for the anxiety disorders.

References

Abercrombie, H. C., Speck, N. S., & Monticelli, R. M. (2006). Endogenous cortisol elevations are related to memory facilitation only in individuals who are emotionally aroused. *Psychoneuroendocrinology, 31*, 187–196.

Airaksinen, E., Larsson, M., & Forsell, Y. (2005). Neuropsychologcial functions in anxiety disorders in population-based samples; Evidence of episodic memory dysfunction. *Journal of Psychiatric Research, 39*, 207–214.

Aouizerate, B., Martin-Guehl, C., & Tignol, J. (2004). Neurobiology and pharmacotherapy of social phobia. *Encephale, 30*, 301–313.

Arenos, J. D., Musty, R. E., & Bucci, D. J. (2006). Blockade of cannabinoid CB1 receptors alters contextual learning and memory. *European Journal of Pharmacology, 539*, 177–183.

Arnsten, A. F. (2004). Adrenergic targets for the treatment of cognitive deficits in schizophrenia. *Psychopharmacology, 174*, 25–31.

Arnsten, A. F., & Goldman-Rakic, P. S. (1985). Alpha 2-adrenergic mechanisms in prefrontal cortex associated with cognitive decline in aged nonhuman primates. *Science, 230*, 1273–1276.

Asmundson, G. J., Stein, M. B., Larsen, D. K., & Walker, J. R. (1994). Neurocognitive function in panic disorder and social phobia patients. *Anxiety, 1*, 201–207.

Baldwin, D. S., Anderson, I. M., Nutt, D. J., Bandelow, B., Bon, A., Davidson, J. R., et al. (2005). British Association for Psychopharmacology: Evidence-based guidelines for the

pharmacological treatment of anxiety disorders: Recommendations from the British Association for Psychopharmacology. *Journal of Psychopharmacology, 19*, 567–596.
Barlow, D. H., Gorman, J. M., Shear, M. K., & Woods, S. W. (2000). Cognitive-behavioral therapy, imipramine or their combination for panic disorder: A randomized controlled trial. *Journal of the American Medical Association, 283*, 2529–2536.
Barreto, R. E., Volpato, G. L., & Pottinger, T. G. (2006). The effect of elevated blood cortisol levels on the extinction of a conditioned stress response in rainbow trout. *Hormones and Behavior, 50*, 484–488.
Barrett, D., Shumake, J., Jones, D., & Gonzalez-Lima, F. (2003). Metabolic mapping of mouse brain activity after extinction of a conditioned emotional response. *Journal of Neuroscience, 23*, 5740–5749.
Beckner, V. E., Tucker, D. M., Delville, Y., & Mohr, D. C. (2006). Stress facilitates consolidation of verbal memory for a film but does not affect retrieval. *Behavioral Neuroscience, 120*, 518–527.
Berchtold, N. C., Castello, N., & Cotman, C. W. (2010). Exercise and time-dependent benefits to learning and memory. *Neuroscience, 167*, 588–597.
Boulenger, J. P., Uhde, T. W., Wolff, E. A., IIIrd, & Post, R. M. (1984). Increased sensitivity to caffeine in patients with panic disorders: Preliminary evidence. *Archives of General Psychiatry, 41*, 1067–1071.
Bouton, M. E., Vurbic, D., & Woods, A. M. (2008). D-cycloserine facilitates context-specific fear extinction learning. *Neurobiology of Learning & Memory, 90*, 504–510.
Breslau, N., & Klein, D. F. (1999). Smoking and panic attacks: An epidemiologic investigation. *Archives of General Psychiatry, 56*, 1141–1147.
Brioni, J. D., O'Neill, A. B., Kim, D. J., & Decker, M. W. (1993). Nicotinic receptor agonists exhibit anxiolytic like effects on the elevated plus-maze test. *European Journal of Pharmacology, 238*, 1–8.
Buchanan, T. W., & Lovallo, W. R. (2001). Enhanced memory for emotional material following stress-level cortisol treatment in humans. *Psychoneuroendocrinology, 26*, 307–317.
Bueller, J. A., Aftab, M., Sen, S., Gomez-Hassan, D., Burmeister, M., & Zubieta, J. K. (2006). BDNF Val66Met allele is associated with reduced hippocampal volume in healthy subjects. *Biological Psychiatry, 599*, 812–815.
Cahill, L., Gorski, L., & Le, K. (2003). Enhanced human memory consolidation with post-learning stress: Interaction with the degree of arousal at encoding. *Learning & Memory, 10*, 270–274.
Cai, W. H., Blundell, J., Han, J., Greene, R. W., & Powell, C. M. (2006). Postreactivation glucocorticoids impair recall of established fear memory. *Journal of Neuroscience, 26*, 9560–9566.
Cain, C. K., Blouin, A. M., & Barad, M. (2004). Adrenergic transmission facilitates extinction of conditional fear in mice. *Learning & Memory, 11*, 1791–87.
Cape, J., Whittington, C., Buszewicz, M., Wallace, P., & Underwood, L. (2010). Brief psychological therapies for anxiety and depression in primary care: Meta-analysis and meta-regression. *BMC Medical Ethics, 25*, 38.
Charney, D. S., Heninger, G. R., & Breier, A. (1984). Noradrenergic function in panic anxiety. *Effects of yohimbine in healthy subjects and patients with agoraphobia and panic disorder. Archives of General Psychiatry, 41*, 751–763.
Charney, D. S., Heninger, G. R., & Jatlow, P. I. (1985). Increased anxiogenic effects of caffeine in panic disorders. *Archives of General Psychiatry, 42*, 233–243.
Charney, D. S., & Manji, H. K. (2004). Life stress, genes, and depression: Multiple pathways lead to increased risk and new opportunities for intervention. *Science's STKE Signal Transduction Knowledge Environment, 2004*(225), r5.
Charney, D. S., Woods, S. W., Goodman, W. K., & Heninger, G. R. (1987). Neurobiological mechanisms of panic anxiety: Biochemical and behavioral correlates of yohimbine-induced panic attacks. *American Journal of Psychiatry, 144*, 1030–1036.
Chen, Y., & Parrish, T. B. (2009). Caffeine dose effect on activation-induced BOLD and CBF responses. *Neuroimage, 46*, 577–583.

Chhatwal, J. P., Davis, M., Maguschak, K. A., & Ressler, K. J. (2005). Enhancing cannabinoid neurotransmission augments the extinction of conditioned fear. *Neuropsychopharmacology, 30*, 516–524.

Chhatwal, J. P., Gutman, A. R., Maguschak, K. A., Bowser, M. E., Yang, Y., Davis, M., et al. (2009). Functional interactions between endocannabinoid and CCK neurotransmitter systems may be critical for extinction learning. *Neuropsychopharmacology, 34*, 509–521.

Cosci, F., Abrams, K., Schruers, K. R., Rickelt, J., & Griez, E. J. (2006). Effect of nicotine on 35% CO_2-induced anxiety: A study in healthy volunteers. *Nicotine & Tobacco Research, 8*, 511–517.

Cotman, C. W., & Berchtold, N. C. (2002). Exercise: A behavioral intervention to enhance brain health and plasticity. *Trends in Neuroscience, 25*, 295–301.

Curtis, G. C., Abelson, J. L., & Gold, P. W. (1997). Adrenocorticotropic hormone and cortisol responses to corticotropin-releasing hormone: Changes in panic disorder and effects of alprazolam treatment. *Biological Psychiatry, 41*, 76–85.

Davis, M., Barad, M., Otto, M. W., & Southwick, S. (2006). Combining pharmacotherapy with cognitive behavior therapy: Traditional and new approaches. *Journal of Traumatic Stress, 19*, 571–581.

Davis, M., Ressler, K., Rothbaum, B. O., & Richardson, R. (2006). Effects of D-cycloserine on extinction: Translation from preclinical to clinical work. *Biological Psychiatry, 60*, 369–375.

de la Mora, M. P., Gallegos-Cari, A., Arizmendi-García, Y., Marcellino, D., & Fuxe, K. (2010). Role of dopamine receptor mechanisms in the amygdaloid modulation of fear and anxiety: Structural and functional analysis. *Progress in Neurobiology, 90*, 198–216.

DeMet, E., Stein, M. K., Tran, C., Chicz-DeMet, A., Sangdahl, C., & Nelsons, J. (1989). Caffeine taste test for panic disorder: Adenosine receptor supersensitivity. *Psychiatric Research, 30*, 231–242.

Durstewitz, D., & Seamans, J. K. (2002). The computational role of dopamine D1 receptors in working memory. *Neural Network, 15*, 561–572.

Egan, M. F., Kojima, M., Callicott, J. H., Goldberg, T. E., Kolachana, B. S., Bertolino, A., et al. (2003). The BDNF val66met polymorphism affects activity-dependent secretion of BDNF and human memory and hippocampal function. *Cell, 112*, 257–269.

Falls, W. A., Miserendino, M. J., & Davis, M. (1992). Extinction of fear-potentiated startle: Blockade by infusion of an NMDA antagonist into the amygdala. *Journal of Neuroscience, 12*, 854–863.

Fiedorowicz, J. G., Hale, N., Spector, A. A., & Coryell, W. H. (2010). Neuroticism but not omega-3 fatty acid levels correlate with early responsiveness to escitalopram. *Annals of Clinical Psychiatry, 22*, 157–163.

File, S. E., Cheeta, S., & Kenny, P. J. (2000). Neurobiological mechanisms by which nicotine mediates different types of anxiety. *European Journal of Pharmacology, 393*(1–3), 231–236.

File, S. E., Kenny, P. J., & Ouagazzal, A. M. (1998). Bimodal modulation by nicotine of anxiety in the social interaction test: Role of the dorsal hippocampus. *Behavioral Neuroscience, 112*, 1423–1429.

Fries, E., Hellhammer, D. H., & Hellhammer, J. (2006). Attenuation of the hypothalamic–pituitary–adrenal axis responsivity to the Trier Social Stress Test by the benzodiazepine alprazolam. *Psychoneuroendocrinology, 31*, 1278–1288.

Furmark, T. (2009). Neurobiological aspects of social anxiety disorder. *Journal of Psychiatry and Related Sciences, 46*, 5–12.

Goldman-Rakic, P. S., Castner, S. A., Svensson, T. H., Siever, L. J., & Williams, G. V. (2004). Targeting the dopamine D1 receptor in schizophrenia: Insights for cognitive dysfunction. *Psychopharmacology, 174*, 3–16.

Gonzalez-Lima, F., & Bruchey, A. K. (2004). Extinction memory improvement by the metabolic enhancer methylene blue. *Learning & Memory, 11*, 633–640.

Gould, R. A., Otto, M. W., & Pollack, M. H. (1995). A meta-analysis of treatment outcome for panic disorder. *Clinical Psychology Review, 15*, 819–844.

Guastella, A. J., Richardson, R., Lovibond, P. F., Rapee, R. M., Gaston, J. E., Mitchell, P., et al. (2008). A randomized controlled trial of D-cycloserine enhancement of exposure therapy for social anxiety disorder. *Biological Psychiatry, 63*, 544–549.

Haller, J., Bakos, N., Szirmay, M., Ledent, C., & Freund, T. F. (2002). The effects of genetic and pharmacological blockade of the CB1 cannabinoid receptor on anxiety. *European Journal of Neuroscience, 16*, 1395–1398.

Hariri, A. R., Goldberg, T. E., Mattay, V. S., Kolachana, B. S., Callicott, J. H., Egan, M. F., et al. (2003). Brain-derived neurotrophic factor val66met polymorphism affects human memory-related hippocampal activity and predicts memory performance. *Journal of Neuroscience, 23*, 6690–6694.

Herry, C., & Garcia, R. (2002). Prefrontal cortex long-term potentiation, but not long-term depression, is associated with the maintenance of extinction of learned fear in mice. *Journal of Neuroscience, 22*, 577–583.

Hofmann, S. G. (2007). Enhancing exposure-based therapy from a translational research perspective. *Behaviour Research & Therapy, 45*, 1987–2001.

Hofmann, S. G., Meuret, A. E., Smits, J. A. J., Simon, N. M., Pollack, M. H., Eisenmenger, K. C., et al. (2006). Augmentation of exposure therapy for social anxiety disorder with D-Cycloserine. *Archives of General Psychiatry, 63*, 298–304.

Hofmann, S. G., Pollack, M. H., & Otto, M. W. (2006). Augmentation treatment of psychotherapy for anxiety disorders with D-cycloserine. *CNS Drug Review, 12*, 208–217.

Hofmann, S. G., Sawyer, A. T., Korte, K. J., & Smits, J. A. J. (2009). Is it beneficial to add pharmacotherapy to cognitive-behavioral therapy when treating anxiety disorders? A meta-analytic review. *International Journal of Cognitive Therapy, 2*, 160–175.

Hofmann, S. G., & Smits, J. A. J. (2008). Cognitive-behavioral therapy for adult anxiety disorders: A meta-analysis of randomized placebo-controlled trials. *Journal of Clinical Psychiatry, 69*, 621–632.

Hofmann, S. G., Smits, J. A. J., Asnaani, A., Gutner, C. A., & Otto, M. W. (2011). Cognitive enhancers for anxiety disorders. *Pharmacology Biochemistry and Behavior, 99*, 275–284.

Holmes, A., & Quirk, G. J. (2010). Pharmacological facilitation of fear extinction and the search for adjunct treatments for anxiety disorders–the case of yohimbine. *Trends in Pharmacological Science, 31*, 2–7.

Johannsen, S., Duning, K., Pavenstädt, H., Kremerskothen, J., & Boeckers, T. M. (2008). Temporal-spatial expression and novel biochemical properties of the memory-related protein KIBRA. *Neuroscience, 155*, 1165–1173.

Junghanns, K., Tietz, U., Dibbelt, L., Kuether, M., Jurth, R., Ehrenthal, D., et al. (2005). Attenuated salivary cortisol secretion under cue exposure is associated with early relapse. *Alcohol & Alcoholism, 40*, 80–85.

Kaplan, G. B., Vasterling, J. J., & Vedak, P. C. (2010). Brain-derived neurotrophic factor in traumatic brain injury, post-traumatic stress disorder, and their comorbid conditions: Role in pathogenesis and treatment. *Behavioral Pharmacology, 21*, 427–437.

Klokk, M., Gotestam, K. G., & Mykletun, A. (2010). Factors accounting for the association between anxiety and depression, and eczema: The Hordaland health study (HUSK). *BMC Dermatology, 10*, 3.

Kobayashi, K., Shimizu, E., Hashimoto, K., Mitsumori, M., Koike, K., Okamura, N., et al. (2005). Serum brain-derived neurotrophic factor (BDNF) levels in patients with panic disorder: As a biological predictor of response to group cognitive behavioral therapy. *Progress in Neuro-Psychopharmacology and Biological Psychiatry, 29*, 658–663.

Koo, M. S., Kim, E. J., Roh, D., & Kim, C. H. (2010). Role of dopamine in the pathophysiology and treatment of obsessive-compulsive disorder. *Expert Review of Neurotherapeutics, 10*, 275–290.

Kremerskothen, J., Plaas, C., Büther, K., Finger, I., Veltel, S., Matanis, T., et al. (2003). Characterization of KIBRA, a novel WW domain-containing protein. *Biochemical and Biophysical Research Communications, 300*, 862–867.

Kushner, M. G., Kim, S. W., Donahue, C., Thuras, P., Adson, D., Kotlyar, M., et al. (2007). D-cycloserine augmented exposure therapy for obsessive-compulsive disorder. *Biological Psychiatry, 62*, 835–838.

Lebrón, K., Milad, M. R., & Quirk, G. J. (2004). Delayed recall of fear extinction in rats with lesions of ventral medial prefrontal cortex. *Learning & Memory, 11*, 544–548.

Lissek, S., Powers, A. S., McClure, E. B., Phelps, E. A., Woldehawariat, G., Grillon, C., et al. (2005). Classical fear conditioning in the anxiety disorders: A meta-analysis. *Behaviour Research & Therapy, 43*, 1391–424.

Lupien, S. J., Friocco, A., Wan, N., Maheu, F., Lord, C., Schramek, T., et al. (2005). Stress hormones and human memory function across the lifespan. *Psychoneuroendocrinology, 30*, 225–242.

Marsicano, G., Moosmann, B., Hermann, H., Lutz, B., & Behl, C. (2002). Neuroprotective properties of cannabinoids against oxidative stress: role of the cannabinoid receptor CB1. *Journal of Neurochemistry, 80*(3), 448–456.

Masdrakis, V. G., Markianos, M., Vaidakis, N., Papakostas, Y. G., & Oulis, P. (2009). Caffeine challenge and breath-holding duration in patients with panic disorder. *Progress in Neuro-Psychopharmacology and Biological Psychiatry, 33*, 41–44.

McNamara, R. K., & Carlson, S. E. (2006). Role of omega-3 fatty acids in brain development and function: Potential implications for the pathogenesis and prevention of psychopathology. *Prostaglandins, Leukotrienes and Essential Fatty Acids, 75*, 329–349.

Milad, M. R., & Quirk, G. J. (2002). Neurons in medial prefrontal cortex signal memory for fear extinction. *Nature, 420*, 70–74.

Milad, M. R., Vidal-Gonzalez, I., & Quirk, G. J. (2004). Electrical stimulation of medial prefrontal cortex reduces conditioned fear in a temporally specific manner. *Behavioral Neuroscience, 118*, 389–394.

Momose, Y., Murata, M., Kobayashi, K., Tachikawa, M., Nakabayashi, Y., Kanazawa, I., et al. (2002). Association studies of multiple candidate genes for Parkinson's disease using single nucleotide polymorphisms. *Annals of Neurology, 51*, 133–136.

Morgan, M. A., Romanski, L. M., & LeDoux, J. E. (1993). Extinction of emotional learning: Contribution of medial prefrontal cortex. *Neuroscience Letters, 163*, 109–113.

Morris, R. W., & Bouton, M. E. (2007). The effect of yohimbine on the extinction of conditioned fear: A role for context. *Behavioral Neuroscience, 121*, 501–14.

Mystkowski, J. L., Mineka, S., Vernon, L. L., & Zinbarg, R. E. (2003). Changes in caffeine states enhance return of fear in spider phobia. *Journal of Consulting and Clinical Psychology, 71*, 243–50.

Nardi, A. E., Valença, A. M., Nascimento, I., Freire, R. C., Veras, A. B., de-Melo-Neto, V. L., et al. (2008). A caffeine challenge test in panic disorder patients, their healthy first-degree relatives, and healthy controls. *Depression and Anxiety, 25*, 847–853.

Nestler, E. J., Barrot, M., DiLeone, R. J., Eisch, A. J., Gold, S. J., & Monteggia, L. M. (2002). Neurobiology of Depression. *Neuron, 34*, 13–25.

Nikolaus, S., Antke, C., Beu, M., & Müller, H. W. (2010). Cortical GABA, striatal dopamine and midbrain serotonin as the key players in compulsive and anxiety disorders–results from in vivo imaging studies. *Reviews in the Neurosciences, 21*, 119–139.

Norberg, M. M., Krystal, J. H., & Tolin, D. F. (2008). A meta-analysis of D-cycloserine and the facilitation of fear extinction and exposure therapy. *Biological Psychiatry, 63*, 1118–1126.

Olver, J. S., O'Keefe, G., Jones, G. R., Burrows, G. D., Tochon-Danguy, H. J., Ackermann, U., et al. (2009). Dopamine D1 receptor binding in the striatum of patients with obsessive-compulsive disorder. *Journal of Affective Disorders, 114*, 321–326.

Otto, M. W., Basden, S. L., McHugh, R. K., Kantak, K. M., Deckersbach, T., Cather, C., et al. (2009). Effects of D-cycloserine administration on weekly non-emotional memory tasks in healthy participants. *Psychotherapy & Psychosomatics, 78*, 49–54.

Otto, M. W., McHugh, R. K., & Kantak, K. M. (2010). Combined pharmacotherapy and cognitive-behavioral therapy for anxiety disorders: Medication effects, glucocorticoids, and attenuated outcomes. *Clinical Psychology: Science and Practice, 37*, 91–103.

Otto, M. W., Tolin, D. F., Simon, N. M., Pearlson, G. D., Basden, S., Meunier, S. A., et al. (2010). Efficacy of D-cycloserine for enhancing response to cognitive behavioral therapy for panic disorder. *Biological Psychiatry, 67*, 365–370.

Pacher, P., Bátkai, S., & Kunos, G. (2006). The endocannabinoid system as an emerging target of pharmacotherapy. *Pharmacology Review, 58*, 389–462.

Pakdel, R., & Rashidy-Pour, A. (2007). Microinjections of the dopamine D2 receptor antagonist sulpiride into the medial prefrontal cortex attenuate glucocorticoid-induced impairment of long-term memory retrieval in rats. *Neurobiology of Learning and Memory, 37*, 385–390.

Papassotiropoulos, A., Stephan, D. A., Huentelman, M. J., Hoerndli, F. J., Craig, D. W., Pearson, J. V., et al. (2006). Common Kibra alleles are associated with human memory performance. *Science, 314*, 475–458.

Pollack, M. H., Otto, M. W., Roy-Byrne, P. P., Coplan, J. D., Rothbaum, B. O., Simon, N. M., et al. (2008). Novel treatment approaches for refractory anxiety disorders. *Depression & Anxiety, 25*, 467–476.

Pomara, N., Willoughby, L. M., Sidtis, J. J., Cooper, T. B., & Greenblatt, D. J. (2005). Cortisol response to diazepam: Its relationship to age, dose, duration of treatment, and presence of generalized anxiety disorder. *Psychopharmacology, 178*, 1–8.

Porter, A. C., & Felder, C. C. (2001). The endocannabinoid nervous system: Unique opportunities for therapeutic intervention. *Pharmacology & Therapeutics, 901*, 45–60.

Powers, M. B., Smits, J. A., Otto, M. W., Sanders, C., & Emmelkamp, P. M. (2009). Facilitation of fear extinction in phobic participants with a novel cognitive enhancer: A randomizedplacebo controlled trial of yohimbine augmentation. *Journal of Anxiety Disorders, 23*, 350–356.

Putman, P., Van Honk, J., Kessels, R. P., Mulder, M., & Koppeschaar, H. P. (2004). Salivary cortisol and short and long-term memory for emotional faces in healthy young women. *Psychoneuroendocrinology, 29*, 953–60.

Quirk, G. J., Garcia, R., & González-Lima, F. (2006). Prefrontal mechanisms in extinction of conditioned fear. *Biological Psychiatry, 60*, 337–343.

Quirk, G. J., Russo, G. K., Barron, J. L., & Lebron, K. (2000). The role of ventromedial prefrontal cortex in the recovery of extinguished fear. *Journal of Neuroscience, 20*, 6225–6231.

Rauch, S. L., Shin, L. M., & Phelps, E. A. (2006). Neurocircuitry models of posttraumatic stress disorder and extinction: Human neuroimaging research—past, present, and future. *Biological Psychiatry, 60*, 376–382.

Ressler, K. J., Rothbaum, B. O., Tannenbaum, L., Anderson, P., Graap, K., Zimand, E., et al. (2004). Cognitive enhancers as adjuncts to psychotherapy: Use of D-cycloserine in phobic individuals to facilitate extinction of fear. *Archives of General Psychiatry, 61*, 1136–1144.

Richardson, R., Ledgerwood, L., & Cranney, J. (2004). Facilitation of fear extinction by D-cycloserine: Theoretical and clinical implications. *Learning & Memory, 11*, 510–516.

Rohrer, T., von Richthofen, V., Schulz, C., Beyer, J., & Lehnert, H. (1994). The stress-, but not corticotropin-releasing hormone-induced activation of the pituitary–adrenal axis in man is blocked by alprazolam. *Hormone and Metabolic Research, 26*, 200–206.

Roy-Byrne, P. P., & Cowley, D. S. (2002). Pharmacological treatments for panic disorder, generalized anxiety disorder, specific phobia, and social anxiety disorder. In P. E. Nathan & J. M. Gorman (Eds.), *A Guide to Treatments That Work* (2nd ed., pp. 337–365). New York, NY: Oxford University Press.

Salín-Pascual, R. J., & Basañez-Villa, E. (2003). Changes in compulsion and anxiety symptoms with nicotine transdermal patches in non-smoking obsessive-compulsive disorder patients. *Revista de Investigacion Clinica, 55*, 650–654.

Sareen, J., Campbell, D. W., Leslie, W. D., Malisza, K. L., Stein, M. B., Paulus, M. P., et al. (2007). Striatal function in generalized social phobia: A functional magnetic resonance imaging study. *Biological Psychiatry, 61*, 396–404.

Sawaguchi, T., & Goldman-Rakic, P. S. (1991). D1 dopamine receptors in prefrontal cortex: Involvement in working memory. *Science, 251*, 947–950.

Schneider, A., Huentelman, M. J., Kremerskothen, J., Duning, K., Spoelgen, R., & Nikolich, K. (2010). KIBRA: A New Gateway to Learning and Memory? *Frontiers in Aging & Neuroscience, 2*, 4.

Seamans, J. K., & Yang, C. R. (2004). The principal features and mechanisms of dopamine modulation in the prefrontal cortex. *Progress in Neurobiology, 74*, 1–58.

Sen, S., Nesse, R. M., Stoltenberg, S. F., Li, S., Gleiberman, L., Chakravarti, A., et al. (2003). BDNF coding variant is associated with the NEO personality inventory domain neuroticism, a risk factor for depression. *Neuropsychopharmacology, 28*, 397–401.

Siegmund, A., Köster, L., Meves, A. M., Plag, J., Stoy, M., & Ströhle, A. (2011). Stress hormones during flooding therapy and their relationship to therapy outcome in patients with panic disorder and agoraphobia. *Journal of Psychiatric Research, 45*, 339–346.

Sklar, P., Gabriel, S. B., McInnis, M. G., Bennett, P., Lim, Y. M., Tsan, G., et al. (2002). Family-based association study of 76 candidate genes in bipolar disorder: BDNF is a potential risk locus. Brain-derived neutrophic factor. *Molecular Psychiatry, 76*, 579–593.
Soliman, F., Glatt, C. E., Bath, K. G., Levita, L., Jones, R. M., Pattwell, S. S., et al. (2010). A genetic variant BDNF polymorphism alters extinction learning in both mouse and human. *Science, 327*, 863–866.
Soravia, L. M., Heinrichs, M., Aerni, A., Maroni, C., Schelling, G., Ehlert, U., et al. (2006). Glucocorticoids reduce phobic fear in humans. *Proceedings of the National Academy of Sciences of the United States of America, 103*, 5585–5590.
Stein, D. J., Ipser, J. C., & Seedat, S. (2006). Pharmacotherapy for post traumatic stress disorder (PTSD). *Cochrane Database System Review, 25*, CD002795.
Stein, D. J., & Ludik, J. (2000). A neural network of obsessive-compulsive disorder: Modelling cognitive disinhibition and neurotransmitter dysfunction. *Medical Hypotheses, 55*, 168–176.
Stewart, R. E., & Chambless, D. L. (2009). Cognitive-behavioral therapy for adult anxiety disorders in clinical practice: A meta-analysis of effectiveness studies. *Journal of Consulting & Clinical Psychology, 77*, 595–606.
Storch, E. A., Murphy, T. K., Goodman, W. K., Geffken, G. R., Lewin, A. B., Henin, A., et al. (2010). A preliminary study of D-cycloserine augmentation of cognitive-behavioral therapy in pediatric obsessive-compulsive disorder. *Biological Psychiatry, 68*, 1073–1076.
Ströhle, A., Stoy, M., Graetz, B., Scheel, M., Wittmann, A., Gallinat, J., et al. (2010). Acute exercise ameliorates reduced brain-derived neurotrophic factor in patients with panic disorder. *Psychoneuroendocrinology, 35*, 364–368.
Timonen, M., Horrobin, D., Jokelainen, J., Laitinen, J., Herva, A., & Räsänen, P. (2004). Fish consumption and depression: The Northern Finland 1966 birth cohort study. *Journal of Affective Disorders, 82*, 447–452.
van der Wee, N. J., van Veen, J. F., Stevens, H., van Vliet, I. M., van Rijk, P. P., & Westenberg, H. G. (2008). Increased serotonin and dopamine transporter binding in psychotropic medication-naive patients with generalized social anxiety disorder shown by 123I-beta-(4-iodophenyl)-tropane SPECT. *Journal of Nuclear Medicine, 49*, 757–763.
Ventriglia, M., Bocchio Chiavetto, L., Benussi, L., Binetti, G., Zanetti, O., Riva, M. A., et al. (2002). Association between the BDNF 196 A/G polymorphism and sporadic Alzheimer's disease. *Molecular Psychiatry, 7*, 136–137.
Vinod, K. Y., & Hungund, B. L. (2006). Role of the endocannabinoid system in depression and suicide. *Trends in Pharmacological Sciences, 27*, 539–545.
Viveros, M. P., Llorente, R., Moreno, E., & Marco, E. M. (2005). Behavioural and neuroendocrine effects of cannabinoids in critical developmental periods. *Behavioural Pharmacology, 16*, 353–362.
Walker, D. L., Ressler, K. J., Lu, K. T., & Davis, M. (2002). Facilitation of conditioned fear extinction by systemic administration or intra-amygdala infusions of D-cycloserine as assessed with fear-potentiated startle in rats. *Journal of Neuroscience, 22*, 2343–2351.
Wilhelm, S., Buhlmann, U., Tolin, D. F., Meunier, S. A., Pearlson, G. D., Reese, H. E., et al. (2008). Augmentation of behavior therapy with D-cycloserine for obsessive-compulsive disorder. *American Journal of Psychiatry, 165*, 335–341.
Yang, Y. L., Chao, P. K., Ro, L. S., Wo, Y. Y., & Lu, K. T. (2007). Glutamate NMDA receptors within the amygdala participate in the modulatory effect of glucocorticoids on extinction of conditioned fear in rats. *Neuropsychopharmacology, 32*, 1042–1051.
Yu, H., Wang, Y., Pattwell, S., Jing, D., Liu, T., Zhang, Y., et al. (2009). Variant BDNF Val66Met polymorphism affects extinction of conditioned aversive memory. *Journal of Neuroscience, 29*, 4056–4064.
Yun, A. J., Doux, J. D., & Daniel, S. M. (2007). Brewing controversies: Darwinian perspective on the adaptive and maladaptive effects of caffeine and ethanol as dietary autonomic modulators. *Medical Hypotheses, 68*, 31–36.

Chapter 7
Exposure Therapy for Anxiety Disorders in Children

Thompson E. Davis III, Sara E. Whiting, and Anna C. May

Thompson E. Davis III, Ph.D., is an Associate Professor of Clinical Psychology at Louisiana State University in Baton Rouge, LA, and is Founder/Director of the Laboratory for Anxiety, Phobia, and Internalizing Disorder Studies (LAPIS). He has been researching and conducting exposure therapies with children and adults for over 10 years and is the (co)author of over 40 publications, with several on child anxiety treatment and exposure therapies. His research and clinical interests focus on anxiety disorders, particularly the assessment and treatment of specific phobias in children and adults.

T.E. Davis III (✉) • S.E. Whiting • A.C. May
Laboratory for Anxiety, Phobia, & Internalizing Disorder Studies (LAPIS), Department of Psychology, Louisiana State University, 236 Audubon Hall, Baton Rouge, LA 70803, USA
e-mail: ted@lsu.edu

P. Neudeck and H.-U. Wittchen (eds.), *Exposure Therapy: Rethinking the Model – Refining the Method*, DOI 10.1007/978-1-4614-3342-2_7,

Sara E. Whiting, M.A., is a doctoral student in Clinical Psychology at Louisiana State University in Baton Rouge, LA, under the mentorship of Thompson E. Davis III, Ph.D. She received her Master of Arts in Clinical Psychology from Louisiana State University and her Bachelor of Arts in Psychology from Smith College in Northampton, MA. She also trained as a clinical research assistant at the Anxiety Disorders Center at the Institute of Living/Hartford Hospital in Hartford, CT. Her research and clinical interests include anxiety and obsessive–compulsive spectrum disorders in children and adolescents, development and use of evidence-based assessments, and exposure therapies for children, adolescents, and adults.

Anna C. May, M.A., is a doctoral student in the Clinical Psychology Program at Louisiana State University in Baton Rouge, LA, under the mentorship of Thompson E. Davis III, Ph.D. She received her Masters of Arts in Psychology from New York University and her Bachelor of Science in Psychology from the University of Florida. She was a research assistant at the New York University Child Study Center helping with research on treating children with anxiety disorders and somatic symptoms. Her research and clinical interests include the somatization of anxiety, chronic illness and anxiety, and the dissemination of evidence-based treatments in the community.

7.1 Introduction

Anxiety disorders in children are particularly problematic, debilitating, and, unfortunately, common (Davis, 2009). Estimates of anxiety disorders have placed the rates in preadolescent children between 2.4% and 23.9% (Cartwright-Hatton, McNicol, & Doubleday, 2006); while at least one study has suggested almost 10% of children will meet criteria for at least one anxiety disorder by 16 years of age (Costello, Mustillo, Erkanli, Keeler, & Angold, 2003). Further, childhood anxiety disorders have been associated with academic problems (Last, Hansen, & Franco, 1997), impaired intellectual ability (i.e., IQ; Davis, Ollendick, & Nebel-Schwalm, 2008), and social and emotional difficulties (Grills & Ollendick, 2002; Kovacs, Gatsonis, Paulauskas, & Richards, 1989; McGee, Feehan, Williams, & Anderson, 1992). Worse yet, the detrimental effects of childhood anxiety have been found to be associated with increased risks for psychopathology and educational problems in young adulthood (Cantwell & Baker, 1989; Seligman & Ollendick, 1999; Woodward & Fergusson, 2001). As a result, an important area of research over the past several decades has been the development, evaluation, and dissemination of efficacious treatments for these disorders. The following chapter will briefly review the outcome of these efforts, including important topics in the assessment and treatment of childhood anxiety disorders and the current evidence in support of certain treatments.

7.2 Evidence-Based Assessment

Before initiating therapy, it is important to properly assess the child's presenting problems to determine the extent of the difficulty and consider the most appropriate course of treatment. It is also important to continue to assess the child throughout treatment to evaluate progress and to make changes accordingly. Silverman and Ollendick (2005) have developed guidelines for comprehensive evidence-based anxiety assessments in children. First, to determine the presence of a clinically significant anxiety disorder, a structured or semi-structured diagnostic interview should be given. The use of rating scale information to determine the type and severity of symptoms is also useful in supplementing information provided during interviews. Furthermore, this assessment package should be administered to multiple informants that have interacted with the child across several settings (e.g., home and school). In addition, behavioral avoidance tasks (BATs) are useful tools for the clinician to observe the child's behavior when interacting with a feared stimulus. Such tasks may give the clinician additional information that can help with diagnosis as well as inform treatment planning, especially when exposure techniques are to be utilized.

Evidence-based assessment	
Component	Purpose
Structured/ semi-structured diagnostic interview	Clarify diagnostic criteria and symptom presentation
Rating scales	Assess symptom severity and associated features
Multiple informants	Assess symptoms and behavior across several settings
Behavioral avoidance tasks	Directly observe behavior and symptoms when child interacts with a feared situation

There are many published and widely used assessment instruments for children with anxiety disorders. Widely recommended instruments include the Anxiety Disorders Interview Schedule for Children for DSM-IV (ADIS-C/P; Silverman & Albano, 1996), the Child Behavior Checklist and other Achenbach forms (CBCL; Achenbach & Rescorl'a, 2001), the Multidimensional Anxiety Scale for Children (MASC; March, Parker, Sullivan, Stallings, & Conners, 1997), and the Revised Children's Manifest Anxiety Scale (RCMAS; Reynolds & Richmond, 1978—Recently updated to the second edition).

When performing an assessment, it is important to gain information from multiple informants who can report on the child's behavior in several environments even though disagreement between informants about symptoms, disorders, and severity are common (Grills & Ollendick, 2002; Jenson et al., 1999; Silverman & Ollendick, 2005). For example, the parent might be more accurate in reporting some internalizing symptoms, while the child might be more accurate in reporting others; however, one is not usually better than another. When discrepancies arise, clinician verification has shown, in roughly 60% of cases, parents and children are equal at identifying an anxiety disorder (Jenson et al., 1999). Parental reports often differ from each other as well as teacher reports for reasons still being investigated (for further review, see De Los Reyes & Kazdin, 2005; Grills & Ollendick, 2003; and Silverman & Ollendick, 2005). Due to these issues, it is necessary to have reports from multiple informants in order to inform the clinician's diagnosis.

It is also important to conduct evidence-based assessments even if a clinician is planning to use an empirically supported treatment. If the child is not assessed properly, the treatment may not be as effective because it may not address the correct problem (Davis, 2009). Due to the varying ways any one disorder can manifest, symptoms often overlap between disorders, and co-morbidity is common. For these reasons, properly diagnosing and examining differential diagnoses is extremely important.

A functional assessment may also be helpful, especially for determining target areas for therapeutic interventions. A functional assessment based on the cognitive-behavioral model includes six components: identifying factors that might have led to the development of the anxiety disorder, determining the cognitive distortions that arise when the child comes into contact with the feared stimulus, observing the behavioral reactions when exposed to the feared stimulus, determining the physiological symptoms that arise when exposed to the stimulus, observing the environmental factors that are contributing to the maintenance of the fear, and, finally, creating a fear hierarchy for planning exposures to the feared stimulus (Ollendick, Davis, & Muris, 2004).

Example functional assessment	
1. Development factors	Saw a friend bitten by a dog; brother is afraid of dogs (modeling)
2. Cognitive distortions	"The dog will bite me"; "All dogs are mean"
3. Behavioral reactions	Ran away from dog; Cried when saw dog
4. Physiological response	Breathing increased; Felt nauseous
5. Environmental factors	Receives attention when afraid of dogs
6. Fear hierarchy (0–8 fear rating)	Watch dog through a window (2)
	Stand in room with caged dog (3)
	Stand across from leashed dog (4)
	Stand next to leashed dog (5)
	Be in room with dog off leash (6)
	Pet leashed dog (7)
	Play ball with dog off leash (8)

7.2.1 *Behavioral and Cognitive-Behavioral Treatments for Childhood Anxiety Disorders*

Today, there are several treatments available to clinicians treating children with anxiety disorders. What follows is a brief description of many of those treatments that have shown promise for reducing children's anxiety symptoms. In particular, a focus will be on evidence-based treatments for childhood anxiety disorders and, especially, those treatments meeting empirically supported treatment criteria—mainly exposure-based treatments (see Davis, 2009 for a more detailed review).

7.2.1.1 Behavior Therapy

Behavior therapy is often one of the most effective treatments, especially when working with younger children who are unable to understand the cognitive components of other therapies. Behavior therapy is based on learning theory, using both classical and operant conditioning principles (Davis & Ollendick, 2005), to increase desired behavior and extinguish undesired behavior. Three specific techniques that are often used are systematic desensitization, reinforced practice, and participant modeling (note: these techniques have been used as stand-alone treatments; however, more recently they have typically been used in varying combinations as part of larger treatment packages).

Systematic Desensitization

Wolpe (1958) combined conditioning research with the relaxation research of Jacobson (1938) to develop systematic desensitization. Systematic desensitization is based on classical conditioning theory in which fear is seen as a conditioned response. To combat fear, a child is instructed in performing an emotionally incompatible response during exposure (e.g., relaxation). Through the association of an incompatible response to the fear-evoking stimulus, it was originally thought that counterconditioning was taking place. More recent evidence, however, points to competing, context-specific learning as the primary mechanism of change (see Bouton, 2004 for a review). Overall, the goal of systematic desensitization is to have the child feel relaxed when encountering the feared stimulus gradually (i.e., if the child feels afraid then treatment is progressing incorrectly or too fast). While systematic desensitization is typically achieved through relaxation training, theoretically, other counter anxiety responses can be utilized such as humor or eating (Wolpe, 1958).

Reinforced Practice

Reinforced practice was developed primarily as a treatment for specific phobias in the 1960s. Reinforced practice combines the principles of reinforcement, in vivo exposure, and therapist instruction and feedback to guide the participant to gradually encounter the feared stimulus (Davis & Ollendick, 2005). Through the use of reinforcement, a child is kept in the fearful situation until the anxiety subsides and the child learns to no longer fear the situation, thus eliminating avoidant behavior. This technique is useful with children because it does not rely on an explicit cognitive component, which may not be developmentally appropriate for children. Through successive reinforced behavioral experiments, reinforced practice keeps the child in the feared situation and provides additional incentive for children to progress up their fear hierarchies (Davis & Ollendick, 2005).

Participant Modeling

Participant modeling, originally called contact desensitization, was developed by Ritter (1965, 1968) and based on social-learning theory. Bandura (1969) demonstrated that many behaviors are learned through observation and the therapeutic application of those observations formed the basis of participant modeling. At its essence, participant modeling makes use of social models as a means to change behavior. The child observes a model interacting with a feared stimulus in a positive manner, and this positive interaction teaches the child that the stimulus is not something to be feared or avoided. Participant modeling goes a step further by incorporating verbal and behavioral therapist instruction in the child's presence to facilitate vicarious extinction (Davis & Ollendick, 2005). While the child does not directly interact with the feared stimulus in participant modeling, a fear response is often elicited in children who are merely observing the stimulus; extinction of the fear response is learned through sustained observation. Therefore, participant modeling can be considered a form of exposure therapy despite the lack of direct contact with the feared stimulus.

Cognitive-Behavioral Therapy

Cognitive-behavioral therapy (CBT) combines theories and techniques of both cognitive therapy and behavioral therapy. Some of the behavioral techniques used include modeling, reinforcement, and exposure. Cognitive distortions are also addressed before, during, and after these behavioral techniques to target the role cognitions play in maintaining fearful behavior. These faulty cognitions create a bias in information processing and, in turn, schemas, which form a reciprocal link with behavior (Beck, 1993). The cognitive aspect of treatment involves challenging the distorted cognitions and replacing distorted schemas with new ways to interpret the situation or stimulus (Kendall, 1993). CBT also creates a situation in which distorted cognitions can be tested and shown to be false or greatly exaggerated. The strength of an exposure not only lies in the reduction of anxiety due to the duration of the contact with the stimulus, but often in showing the child that the feared response is unlikely to happen. If, for example, the child is afraid of a dog and the feared response is that the dog will bite him, exposure to a nonaggressive dog will show the child that the dog will not bite him. This encounter will hopefully generalize to the understanding that most dogs will not bite aggressively. Thus, the clinician and child "test" the theory that dogs will bite and "prove" that theory wrong, hopefully altering the child's schema. CBT utilizes the strengths of both techniques and capitalizes on the reciprocal nature of cognitions and behavior in maintaining a fear as well as the reduction in the physiological response achieved by exposure and habituation. Thus, CBT targets all three aspects of the anxious response (i.e., cognition, behavior, and physiology; Davis & Ollendick, 2005).

7.2.1.2 Exposure

Exposure is one of the most important and central treatment techniques utilized for anxiety disorders. An exposure is simply encountering, experiencing, or interacting with a feared stimulus purposefully and without escaping, until the fear response has diminished. Typically, exposures involve first creating a fear hierarchy of increasingly fear- or anxiety-provoking experiences. Exposure is then typically conducted by working with the child to gradually encounter these hierarchical steps in a supportive and controlled manner. There are at least two kinds of exposures, in vivo and imaginal. In vivo exposures involve the child actually coming into contact with or experiencing the feared stimulus, whereas imaginal exposure has the child imagine, in detail, an encounter with the stimulus. Bioinformational and emotional processing theories suggest that in-vivo exposures would be more effective because the emotional network likely has greater activation when a child physically comes into contact with the feared stimulus rather than merely thinking about it (Davis, 2009). Also, children may be limited by their developmental capacities and have greater difficulty with imaginal exposures (Davis & Ollendick, 2005). Overall, it is thought that when the emotional network is activated the child habituates to the emotional response over the course of the exposure and eventually the physiological arousal subsides. A person cannot stay in a state of perpetual physiological arousal and this is the basis of exposure therapy. Imaginal exposure is generally used when it is dangerous or inappropriate, due to fear level, for the child to encounter a certain stimulus or when access to a stimulus is impractical.

7.2.2 *Empirical Status of Exposure-Based Treatments for Child Anxiety*

The Task Force on Promotion and Dissemination of Psychological Procedures (Task Force on Promotion and Dissemination of Psychological Procedures, 1995) has outlined guidelines with which to evaluate the efficacy of psychological treatments based upon empirical findings. According to these guidelines, well-established treatments are those that have been found to be equivalent to other established treatments, superior to treatments with less empirical support, or superior to placebo conditions in at least two independently conducted, randomized controlled trials. Probably efficacious treatments are those that have been shown to be superior to a wait-list control group in at least two trials or have met all criteria for well-established treatments with the exception of replication by independently conducted investigations. Experimental treatments do not meet the requirements to be considered probably efficacious or have yet to be empirically investigated. Many early treatment studies exist that focus solely on behavior therapies for children; however, due to methodological limitations, only a subset of these investigations meet the Task Force criteria for evaluating treatment effectiveness. What follows is the current empirical classification of exposure-based treatments for childhood anxiety disorders based upon these Task Force criteria (for more detailed reviews, see Davis, 2009 and Davis, May, & Whiting, 2011).

7.2.2.1 Specific Phobia

For treating children with specific phobias, two therapies are recommended given the extant empirical support. Systematic desensitization (SD) has been shown to be superior to a wait-list control condition in only one study (Cornwall, Spence, & Schotte, 1996), and therefore is considered an experimental treatment. A more recent empirical focus has been CBT for phobic children, in the form of one-session treatment (OST; Davis, Ollendick, & Öst, 2009; Zlomke & Davis, 2008). Two trials by Muris and colleagues have found OST to be superior to eye-movement desensitization and repossessing therapy (Muris, Merckelbach, Holdrinet, & Sijsenaar, 1998; Muris, Merckelbach, Van Haaften, & Mayer, 1997). Similarly, OST was found to be superior to a psychological placebo (Ollendick, Davis, & Sirbu, 2009) as well as to wait-list control groups (Ollendick et al., 2009; Öst, Svensson, Hellstrom, & Lindwall, 2001). Due to these widely replicated results, OST for specific phobia in children merits well-established status according to the Task Force criteria (Davis et al., 2011).

7.2.2.2 Social Phobia

Behavior therapy, including social skills training and exposure, for childhood social phobia, has been found to be superior to a psychological placebo condition (Beidel, Turner, & Morris, 2000). To date, however, no published study has attempted to replicate these findings. Therefore, behavior therapy must currently be considered a probably efficacious treatment for social phobia in children. Group format CBT has also been examined as a treatment for children's social anxiety. Two independently conducted trials have found group CBT to be superior to wait-list control groups for reducing social phobia symptoms in children (Gallagher, Rabian, & McCloskey, 2004; Spence, Donovan, & Brechman-Toussaint, 2000). Based upon the current literature, group CBT can also be considered probably efficacious for treating social phobia in children.

7.2.2.3 Obsessive–Compulsive Disorder

CBT, including exposure with response prevention techniques, for childhood obsessive–compulsive disorder (OCD) has been the predominantly studied treatment in the literature to date. Individual CBT for pediatric OCD has been found to be superior to a wait-list control condition (Barrett, Healy-Farrell, & March, 2004) as well as pill–placebo (POTS, 2004), and clomipramine pharmacological treatment (de Haan, Hoogduin, Buitelaar, & Keijsers, 1998). Similarly, group CBT has been found to be superior to a wait-list control group and equivalent to individual CBT for significantly reducing childhood OCD symptomatology (Barrett et al., 2004). Therefore, individual CBT meets criteria for a well-established treatment for OCD in children. However, group CBT has yet to be replicated empirically and therefore must still be considered experimental.

7.2.2.4 Posttraumatic Stress Disorder

Individual CBT has been shown to be superior to a wait-list control condition for reducing children's posttraumatic stress disorder (PTSD) symptomatology (King et al., 2000). Group CBT has also demonstrated significant reductions in children's

PTSD symptomatology over a wait-list condition (Stein et al., 2003). Additionally, Deblinger, Lippmann, and Steer (1996) have demonstrated significantly greater treatment response from individual CBT as opposed to typical community care and CBT with parents only. Lastly, individual CBT has been shown to be superior to child-centered therapy (Cohen, Deblinger, Mannarino, & Steer, 2004). Taken together, these studies show that individual CBT for childhood PTSD is a well-established treatment. However, group CBT for children with PTSD remains experimental, as the results from Stein et al. have yet to be replicated.

7.2.2.5 Transdiagnostic Trials

As a field, researchers have commonly grouped several anxiety disorders together to form transdiagnostic samples of anxious children (e.g., sampling from populations of children with social phobia, separation anxiety disorder, generalized anxiety disorder, etc. for a single trial). While this makes interpretation of treatment efficacy for individual disorders less exact, it allows researchers and clinicians to make broad conclusions regarding treatment effects. Additionally, by using such combined samples, results can be suggestive (though not conclusive) that some effective therapeutic techniques are universal to anxiety disorders in children.

Overall, ten trials have demonstrated that individual or group CBT significantly reduces anxiety symptomatology in children above wait-list control conditions (Barrett, 1998; Barrett, Dadds, & Rapee, 1996; Flannery-Schroeder & Kendall, 2000; Kendall, 1994; Kendall et al., 1997; King et al., 1998; Nauta, Scholing, Emmelkamp, & Minderaa, 2003; Shortt, Barrett & Fox, 2001; Silverman et al., 1999; Spence, Holmes, March, & Lipp, 2006). Additionally, group CBT has been found to be superior to two psychological placebo conditions (Ginsburg & Drake, 2002; Muris, Meesters, & van Melick, 2002). To date, only one trial has found individual CBT to be superior to a pharmacological placebo condition and equivalent to sertraline pharmacological treatment (Walkup et al., 2008). Based on these findings, individual CBT can be considered a probably efficacious treatment, as it has yet to be replicated. Group CBT can be considered a well-established treatment for reducing childhood anxiety symptomatology broadly.

Due to an increasing need for dissemination of efficacious treatments, bibliotherapies have recently been investigated as a method for providing services to rural or underserviced populations. Two studies have shown CBT, given in bibliotherapy format, to be superior to wait-list control conditions (Lyneham & Rapee, 2006; Rapee, Abbott, & Lyneham, 2006). However, in one trial, group administered CBT was shown to be superior to CBT given in bibliotherapy format (Rapee et al., 2006). Further study is needed to clarify the effectiveness of CBT bibliotherapy as well as the specific diagnostic qualities for which the treatment will be appropriate. Nevertheless, CBT delivered in bibliotherapy format meets criteria for a probably efficacious treatment for clinically anxious children.

7.2.2.6 Combination Treatments

A more recent investigation has been the addition of pharmacological treatment to established therapeutic treatments in an effort to improve effectiveness. Combination sertraline pharmacotherapy with individual CBT for pediatric OCD has demonstrated significantly greater treatment responses than unimodal pharmacological or individual CBT treatments as well as a pill–placebo condition (POTS, 2004). Despite these encouraging findings, combination treatment for pediatric OCD remains probably efficacious, as no study has yet replicated these results.

With the exception of pediatric OCD, combining pharmacotherapy with exposure therapies has not yet been investigated among individual childhood anxiety disorders. However, investigators have examined combination sertraline pharmacotherapy with individual CBT in a transdiagnostic sample of anxious children (Walkup et al., 2008). As compared to pill–placebo and unimodal individual CBT or sertraline only treatments, combination treatment was found to be superior to either unimodal treatment as well as the pill–placebo. Therefore, combination treatment for childhood anxiety disorders remains probably efficacious. While these findings are suggestive that combination treatment for childhood anxiety disorders may be effective, further clarification of treatment efficacy and diagnosis-specific effects is needed before such determinations can be made conclusively.

7.3 Limitations and Barriers to Treatment Response

Despite the development of rigorously tested, efficacious treatments for childhood anxiety disorders, relapse and incomplete response to exposure-based treatment occurs. Two of the more commonly cited barriers to treatment response are familial factors (e.g., family dysfunction, interfering parental psychopathology, etc.) and patient factors (e.g., symptom severity, comorbidity, etc.; Berman, Weems, Silverman, & Kutines, 2000; Crawford & Manassis, 2001; Southam-Gerow, Kendall, & Weersing, 2001). Likewise, exposure-based techniques, while helpful for many children, are not always appropriate for atypically developing populations such as children with cognitive, intellectual, or developmental disabilities. In such difficult to treat cases, modifications to established therapies are indicated. For children with familial treatment barriers, the inclusion of parents in the child's treatment and/or the use of family therapy techniques may be indicated. Likewise, for severe cases or cases with comorbid conditions, the addition of alternate therapies such as combination therapy or therapies to address interfering comorbid conditions may prove more effective than standard exposure-based therapies alone. For atypically developing children, additional language, behavioral, or other modification may help the child to better engage in the therapeutic process (for an extensive review of treatment modifications for this population, please see Moree & Davis, 2010).

Regardless of the barriers to treatment response, a four-stage process for therapeutic intervention is recommended (Ollendick et al., 2009). First, the child should be thoroughly assessed using evidence-based assessment practices and, based upon the clinician's case conceptualization, an evidence-based treatment should be implemented by a clinician trained in the chosen technique(s). If the child's symptoms do not respond to a sufficient trial, the clinician should begin a second stage in which one or more of the following are added to supplement the chosen therapy: increasing treatment frequency or intensity, treating or eliminating specific treatment obstacles, changing the focus of treatment to an interfering comorbid condition, and/or reevaluating the initial diagnoses or case conceptualization. If these treatment modifications remain unsuccessful, the clinician should then implement another evidence-based treatment, which can include other therapies, pharmacological treatment, or the combination of the two. Finally, if a significant response to treatment is observed, skills for maintaining and generalizing treatment gains should be administered.

References

Achenbach, T. M., & Rescorla, L. A. (2001). *Manual for the ASEBA school-age forms & profiles*. Burlington: University of Vermont.

Bandura, A. (1969). *Principles of behavior modification*. New York: Holt, Rinehart, & Winston.

Barrett, P. (1998). Evaluation of cognitive-behavioral group treatments for childhood anxiety disorders. *Journal of Clinical Child Psychology, 27*, 459–468.

Barrett, P., Dadds, M., & Rapee, R. (1996). Family treatment of childhood anxiety: A controlled trial. *Journal of Consulting and Clinical Psychology, 64*, 333–342.

Barrett, P., Healy-Farrell, L., & March, J. (2004). Cognitive-behavioral family treatment of childhood obsessive-compulsive disorder: A controlled trial. *Journal of the American Academy of Child and Adolescent Psychiatry, 43*, 46–62.

Beck, A. T. (1993). Cognitive therapy: Past, present, and future. *Journal of Consulting and Clinical Psychology, 61*, 194–198.

Beidel, D., Turner, S., & Morris, T. (2000). Behavioral treatment of childhood social phobia. *Journal of Consulting and Clinical Psychology, 68*, 1072–1080.

Berman, S. L., Weems, C. F., Silverman, W. K., & Kutines, W. M. (2000). Predictors of outcome in exposure-based cognitive and behavioral treatments for phobic and anxiety disorders in children. *Behavior Therapy, 31*, 713–731.

Bouton, M. (2004). Context and behavioral processes in extinction. *Learning and Memory, 11*, 485–494.

Cantwell, D., & Baker, L. (1989). Stability and natural history of DSM-III childhood diagnoses. *Journal of the American Academy of Child and Adolescent Psychiatry, 28*, 691–700.

Cartwright-Hatton, S., McNicol, K., & Doubleday, E. (2006). Anxiety in a neglected population: Prevalence of anxiety disorders in pre-adolescent children. *Clinical Psychology Review, 26*, 817–833.

Cohen, J., Deblinger, E., Mannarino, A., & Steer, R. (2004). A multisite, randomized controlled trial for children with sexual abuse-related PTSD symptoms. *Journal of the American Academy of Child and Adolescent Psychiatry, 43*, 393–402.

Cornwall, E., Spence, S., & Schotte, D. (1996). The effectiveness of emotive imagery in the treatment of darkness phobia in children. *Behaviour Change, 13*, 223–229.

Costello, E. J., Mustillo, S., Erkanli, A., Keeler, G., & Angold, A. (2003). Prevalence and development of psychiatric disorders in childhood and adolescence. *Archives of General Psychiatry, 60*, 837–844.
Crawford, A. M., & Manassis, K. (2001). Familial predictors of treatment outcome in childhood anxiety disorders. *Journal of the American Academy of Child and Adolescent Psychiatry, 40*, 1182–1189.
Davis, T. E., III. (2009). PTSD, anxiety, and phobias. In J. Matson, F. Andrasik, & M. Matson (Eds.), *Treating childhood psychopathology and developmental disorders* (pp. 183–220). New York: Springer.
Davis, T. E., III, May, A. C., & Whiting, S. E. (2011). Evidence-based treatment of anxiety and phobia in children and adolescents: Current status and effects on the emotional response. *Clinical Psychology Review, 31*, 592–602.
Davis, T. E., III, & Ollendick, T. H. (2005). A critical review of empirically supported treatments for specific phobia in children: Do efficacious treatments address the components of a phobic response? *Clinical Psychology: Science and Practice, 12*, 144–160.
Davis, T. E., III, Ollendick, T. H., & Nebel-Schwalm, M. (2008). Intellectual ability and achievement in anxiety-disordered children: A clarification and extension of the literature. *Journal of Psychopathology and Behavioral Assessment, 30*, 43–51.
Davis, T. E., III, Ollendick, T. H., & Öst, L. G. (2009). Intensive treatment of specific phobias in children and adolescents. *Cognitive and Behavioral Practice, 16*, 294–303.
Deblinger, E., Lippmann, J., & Steer, R. (1996). Sexually abused children suffering posttraumatic stress symptoms: Initial treatment outcome findings. *Child Maltreatment, 1*, 310–321.
de Haan, E., Hoogduin, K., Buitelaar, J., & Keijsers, G. (1998). Behavior therapy versus clomipramine for the treatment of obsessive-compulsive disorder in children and adolescents. *Journal of the American Academy of Child and Adolescent Psychiatry, 37*, 1022–1029.
De Los Reyes, A., & Kazdin, A. (2005). Informant discrepancies in the assessment of childhood psychopathology: A critical review, theoretical framework, and recommendations for further study. *Psychological Bulletin, 131*, 483–509.
Flannery-Schroeder, E., & Kendall, P. (2000). Group and individual cognitive-behavioral treatments for youth with anxiety disorders: A randomized clinical trial. *Cognitive Therapy and Research, 24*, 251–278.
Gallagher, H., Rabian, B., & McCloskey, M. (2004). A brief cognitive-behavioral intervention for social phobia in childhood. *Journal of Anxiety Disorders, 18*, 459–479.
Ginsburg, G. S., & Drake, K. L. (2002). School-based treatment for anxious African–American adolescents: A controlled pilot study. *Journal of the American Academy of Child and Adolescent Psychiatry, 41*, 768–775.
Grills, A., & Ollendick, T. H. (2002). Peer victimization, global self-worth, and anxiety in middle-school children. *Journal of Clinical Child and Adolescent Psychology, 31*, 59–68.
Grills, A., & Ollendick, T. H. (2003). Multiple informant agreement and the anxiety disorders interview schedule for parents and children. *Journal of the American Academy of Child and Adolescent Psychiatry, 42*, 30–40.
Jacobson, E. (1938). *Progressive relaxation*. Chicago: University of Chicago Press.
Jenson, P. S., Rubio-Stipec, M., Canino, G., Bird, H. R., Dulcan, M. K., Schwab-Stone, M. E., et al. (1999). Parent and child contributions to diagnosis of mental disorder: Are both informants always necessary? *Journal of the American Academy of Child and Adolescent Psychiatry, 38*, 1569–1579.
Kendall, P. C. (1993). Cognitive-behavioral therapies with youth: Guiding theory, current status, and emerging developments. *Journal of Consulting and Clinical Psychology, 61*, 235–247.
Kendall, P. (1994). Treating anxiety disorders in children: Results of a randomized clinical trial. *Journal of Consulting and Clinical Psychology, 62*, 100–110.
Kendall, P., Flannery-Schroeder, E., Panichelli-Mindel, S., Southam-Gerow, M., Henin, A., & Warman, M. (1997). Therapy for youths with anxiety disorders: A second randomized clinical trial. *Journal of Consulting and Clinical Psychology, 65*, 366–380.

King, N., Tonge, B., Heyne, D., Pritchard, M., Rollings, S., Young, D., et al. (1998). Cognitive-behavioral treatment of school-refusing children: A controlled evaluation. *Journal of the American Academy of Child and Adolescent Psychiatry, 37*, 395–403.

King, N., Tonge, B., Mullen, P., Myerson, N., Heyne, D., Rollings, S., et al. (2000). Treating sexually abuse children with posttraumatic stress symptoms: A randomized clinical trial. *Journal of the American Academy of Child and Adolescent Psychiatry, 39*, 1347–1355.

Kovacs, M., Gatsonis, C., Paulauskas, S., & Richards, C. (1989). Depressive disorders in childhood: IV. A longitudinal study of comorbidity with and risk for anxiety disorders. *Archives of General Psychiatry, 46*, 776–782.

Last, C., Hansen, C., & Franco, N. (1997). Anxious children in adulthood: A prospective study of adjustment. *Journal of the American Academy of Child and Adolescent Psychiatry, 36*, 645–652.

Lyneham, H. J., & Rapee, R. M. (2006). Evaluation of therapist-supported parent-implemented CBT for anxiety disorders in rural children. *Behaviour Research and Therapy, 44*, 1287–1300.

March, J., Parker, J., Sullivan, K., Stallings, P., & Conners, C. K. (1997). The multidimensional anxiety scale for children (MASC): Factor structure, reliability, and validity. *Journal of the American Academy of Child and Adolescent Psychiatry, 36*, 554–565.

McGee, R., Feehan, M., Williams, S., & Anderson, J. (1992). DSM-III disorders from age 11 to 15 years. *Journal of the American Academy of Child and Adolescent Psychiatry, 31*, 50–59.

Moree, B., & Davis, T. E., III. (2010). Cognitive-behavioral therapy for anxiety in children diagnosed with autism spectrum disorders: Modification trends. *Research in Autism Spectrum Disorders, 4*, 346–354.

Muris, P., Merckelbach, H., Holdrinet, I., & Sijsenaar, M. (1998). Treating phobic children: Effects of EMDR versus exposure. *Journal of Consulting and Clinical Psychology, 66*, 193–198.

Muris, P., Merckelbach, H., Van Haaften, H., & Mayer, B. (1997). Eye movement desensitisation and reprocessing versus exposure in vivo: A single-session crossover study of spider-phobic children. *British Journal of Psychiatry, 171*, 82–86.

Muris, P., Meesters, C., & van Melick, M. (2002). Treatment of childhood anxiety disorders: A preliminary comparison between cognitive-behavioral group therapy and a psychological placebo intervention. *Journal of Behavior Therapy and Experimental Psychiatry, 33*, 143–158.

Nauta, M., Scholing, A., Emmelkamp, P., & Minderaa, R. (2003). Cognitive-behavioral therapy for children with anxiety disorders in a clinical setting: No additional effect of a cognitive parent training. *Journal of the American Academy of Child and Adolescent Psychiatry, 42*, 1270–1278.

Ollendick, T. H., Davis, T. E., III, & Muris, P. (2004). Treatment of specific phobia in children and adolescents. In P. Barrett & T. H. Ollendick (Eds.), *The handbook of interventions that work with children and adolescents—From prevention to treatment* (pp. 273–299). West Sussex, England: Wiley.

Ollendick, T. H., Davis, T. E., III, & Sirbu, C. V. (2009). Phobias. In D. McKay & E. Storch (Eds.), *Cognitive behavior therapy for children: Treating complex and refractory case* (pp. 171–200). New York: Springer.

Öst, L. G., Svensson, L., Hellstrom, K., & Lindwall, R. (2001). One-session treatment of specific phobias in youths: A randomized clinical trial. *Journal of Consulting and Clinical Psychology, 69*, 814–824.

Pediatric OCD treatment study (POTS) team. (2004). Cognitive-behavior therapy, sertraline, and their combination for children and adolescents with obsessive-compulsive disorder: The pediatric OCD treatment study (POTS) randomized controlled trial. *Journal of the American Medical Association, 292*, 1969–1976.

Rapee, R. M., Abbott, M. J., & Lyneham, H. J. (2006). Bibliotherapy for children with anxiety disorders using written materials for parents: A randomized control trial. *Journal of Consulting and Clinical Psychology, 74*, 436–444.

Reynolds, C. R., & Richmond, B. O. (1978). What I think and feel: A revised measure of children's manifest anxiety. *Journal of Abnormal Child Psychiatry, 6*, 271–290.

Ritter, B. (1965). The treatment of a dissection phobia. Unpublished manuscript, Queens College.
Ritter, B. (1968). The group desensitization of children's snake phobias using vicarious and contact desensitization procedures. *Behaviour Research and Therapy, 6*, 1–6.
Seligman, L., & Ollendick, T. H. (1999). Anxiety disorders. In H. C. Steinhauser & F. Verhulst (Eds.), *Risks and outcomes in developmental psychopathology* (pp. 103–120). New York: Oxford University Press.
Shortt, A., Barrett, P., & Fox, T. (2001). Evaluating the FRIENDS program: A cognitive-behavioral group treatment for anxious children and their parents. *Journal of Clinical Child Psychology, 30*, 525–535.
Silverman, W. K., & Albano, A. M. (1996). *Anxiety disorders interview schedule for dsm-IV, child and parent versions*. San Antonio: Psychological Corporation.
Silverman, W., Kurtines, W., Ginsburg, G., Weems, C., Lumpkin, P., & Carmichael, D. (1999). Treating anxiety disorders in children with group cognitive-behavioral therapy: A randomized clinical trial. *Journal of Consulting and Clinical Psychology, 67*, 995–1003.
Silverman, W., & Ollendick, T. H. (2005). Evidence-based assessment of anxiety and its disorders in children and adolescents. *Journal of Clinical Child and Adolescent Psychology, 34*, 380–411.
Southam-Gerow, M. A., Kendall, P. C., & Weersing, V. R. (2001). Examining outcome variability: Correlates of treatment response in a child and adolescent anxiety clinic. *Journal of Clinical Child Psychology, 30*, 422–436.
Spence, S., Donovan, C., & Brechman-Toussaint, M. (2000). The treatment of childhood social phobia: The effectiveness of a social skills training-based, cognitive-behavioural intervention, with and without parental involvement. *Journal of Child Psychology and Psychiatry and Allied Disciplines, 41*, 713–726.
Spence, S., Holmes, J., March, S., & Lipp, O. (2006). The feasibility and outcome of clinic plus internet delivery of cognitive-behavior therapy for childhood anxiety. *Journal of Consulting and Clinical Psychology, 74*, 614–621.
Stein, B., Jaycox, L., Kataoka, S., Wong, M., Tu, W., Elliot, M., & Fink, A. (2003). A mental health intervention for schoolchildren exposed to violence: A randomized controlled trial. *Journal of the American Medical Association, 290*, 603–611.
Task Force on Promotion and Dissemination of Psychological Procedures. (1995). Training in and dissemination of empirically validated psychological treatments: Report and recommendations. *The Clinical Psychologist, 48*, 3–23.
Walkup, J. T., Albano, A. M., Piacentini, J., Birmaher, B., Compton, S. N., Sherrill, J. T., et al. (2008). Cognitive behavioral therapy, sertraline, or a combination in childhood anxiety. *The New England Journal of Medicine, 359*, 2753–2766.
Wolpe, J. (1958). *Psychotherapy by reciprocal inhibition*. Stanford: Stanford University Press.
Woodward, L., & Fergusson, D. (2001). Life course outcomes of young people with anxiety disorders in adolescence. *Journal of the American Academy of Child and Adolescent Psychiatry, 40*, 1086–1093.
Zlomke, K., & Davis, T. E., III. (2008). One-session treatment of specific phobias: A detailed description and review of treatment efficacy. *Behavior Therapy, 39*, 207–223.

Chapter 8
Aspects of Exposure Therapy in Acceptance and Commitment Therapy

A.T. Gloster, K.V. Hummel, I. Lyudmirskaya, C. Hauke, and R.F. Sonntag

Andrew Gloster

Rainer Sonntag

A.T. Gloster (✉)
University of Basel, Institute for Psychology, Clinical Psychology, and Psychotherapy, Missionsstrasse 62A, 4055 Basel, Switzerland
e-mail: andrew.gloster@unibas.ch

K.V. Hummel • I. Lyudmirskaya • C. Hauke
Technische Universität Dresden, Institute of Clinical Psychology and Psychotherapy, Chemnitzer Str. 46, D-01187 Dresden, Germany
e-mail: hummel@psychologie.tu-dresden.de; il@psychologie.tu-dresden.de; hauke@psychologie.tu-dresden.de

R.F. Sonntag
FA für Psychiatrie & Psychotherapie; FA Psychotherapeutische Medizin, In der Wüste 18, D-57462 Olpe Germany
e-mail: Raisonn@aol.com

P. Neudeck and H.-U. Wittchen (eds.), *Exposure Therapy: Rethinking the Model – Refining the Method*, DOI 10.1007/978-1-4614-3342-2_8,

Andrew Gloster was an assistant professor at the Technische Universität Dresden, where this work was completed. Dr. Gloster specializes in the nature, treatment, and process of anxiety and affective disorders, with an emphasis on behavioral and ACT approaches. Dr. Gloster is now an assistant professor at the University of Basel.

Rainer Sonntag is in private practice in Olpe, Germany. Dr. Sonntag specializes in behavioral and ACT approaches to treatment and is a peer-reviewed ACT trainer.

Katrin Hummel

Irina Lyudmirskaya

Christina Hauke

Katrin Hummel is currently a graduate student at the Technische Universität Dresden.

Irina Lyudmirskaya is currently a graduate student at the Technische Universität Dresden.

Christina Hauke is currently a graduate student at the Technische Universität Dresden.

8.1 Aspects of Exposure Therapy in Acceptance and Commitment Therapy

Acceptance and Commitment Therapy (ACT), a behavioral and cognitive therapy with strong behavior analytic roots, aims to promote psychological flexibility. That is, the ability to contact the present moment fully as a conscious human being, and to change or persist in behavior when doing so serves valued ends (Hayes, Luoma, Bond, Masuda, & Lillis, 2006). Toward this end, patients are, among other things, encouraged to experience and engage with that which has been avoided when it is useful to do so. In this context, avoidance is broadly understood as the unwillingness to contact negative psychological content such as emotions, thoughts, memories, or bodily sensations and the attempt to alter the form, frequency, or situations that elicit these experiences and is called *experiential avoidance* (Hayes, Strosahl, & Wilson, 1999). To the degree that systematically engaging with hitherto avoided experience constitutes exposure, then the procedural element of exposure is an important element within ACT. As we will examine in this chapter, however, exposure within ACT occurs in a different context than in traditional CBT and with different aims (Hayes, 1999; Wilson, 2008). We undertake this examination with two goals in mind. First, we wish to elucidate possible mechanisms of action that are at play in traditional exposure procedures and exposure within ACT. The understanding of such mechanisms is crucial, if also notoriously difficult to pinpoint (Wittchen & Gloster, 2009). Second, we will use this information to highlight potential possibilities to improve treatment.

We state these goals while simultaneously acknowledging the complicated and sometimes contrived nature of such comparisons. Whether two things are deemed similar or different often depends on definitions, one's vantage point, and assumptions. For example, topographical similarity, function similarity, and procedural similarity have all been cited as key metrics in determining such issues (Tolin, 2009; Wilson, 1997). Furthermore, examination of these issues necessitates an abstraction of treatment components. Exposure itself is difficult to define (Hayes, 2008) and procedures are nearly always used in combination with other elements (e.g., psychoeducation). Similarly, processes believed to exist within ACT are interconnected; a fact that renders examinations of its elements in isolation somewhat artificial. With these caveats in mind, we will examine current theory and select empirical studies to shed light on these issues (Arch & Craske, 2008; Hayes, 2008; Heimberg & Ritter, 2008).

8.2 Exposure: Established Use and Theory

Our starting point for comparing exposure procedures in traditional CBT and ACT requires a brief examination of what is meant by exposure in general and what are the currently accepted goals and mechanisms of action associated with its use. Exposure has been defined in various ways, yet most authors highlight the fact that it involves deliberate, planned, systematic, often repeated, and sometimes prolonged exposure to a feared, negatively arousing, or avoided stimulus (Moscovitch, Antony, & Swinson, 2009; Richard, Lauterbach, & Gloster, 2007). For example, anxiety-evoking stimuli include various external (e.g., spider, bus, public speaking, germs) or internal (e.g., heartbeat, sweat, thoughts, memories) experiences that individuals typically avoid or try to escape from. Exposure therapy involves systematically contacting these feared and avoided stimuli, an experience that has previously been hindered by avoidance and escape behaviors.

We believe that it is generally agreed upon that exposure procedures utilized in traditional CBT are implemented with the goal of fear reduction. Simultaneously, we acknowledge positive effects of exposure-based CBT on broader outcomes such as physical health or social functioning (e.g., Telch, Schmidt, Jaimez, Jaquin, & Harrington, 1995). Accordingly, the implicit assumption of traditional exposure-based CBT procedures seems to be: reduce fear and anxiety associated with avoided stimuli and the other components of one's life will be able to fall into place.

As such, exposure-based procedures have traditionally been used as a symptom-reducing approach aiming to decouple the learned fearful responses maintained by overt or covert avoidance behavior.

In order to provide a clear comparison to ACT below, we now briefly review the two most prominent theories about the mechanisms of action in traditional exposure: habituation and extinction. Identification of these mechanisms not only informs our understanding of this important component of CBT, but also suggests why some patients relapse after treatment or do not benefit from treatment at all. It is important to note that the exploration of possible mechanisms of action is strongly tied to the goal of treatment itself. This is but one of many reasons for the existence of varying accounts of the mechanisms of action.

The concept of *habituation* (Groves & Thompson, 1970) describes the diminished response (usually described at the physiological level, but sometimes at the psychological level) to repeated stimulation. Habituation has been heavily discussed as a necessary component of fear reduction in exposure-based CBT and is commonly misused as a synonymous term with fear reduction (Moscovitch et al., 2009). However, assumptions of the habituation concept have been widely criticized due to inconsistent and incompatible empirical support (for complete summary, see Moscovitch et al., 2009; Tyron, 2005). Most importantly, theoretical and practical implications of habituation are largely incompatible with the assumption that new learning occurs during exposure. As reviewed below, current theories on the mechanisms of action of exposure point to new learning.

Extinction is arguably the most accepted behavioral learning principle thought to drive fear reduction during exposure therapy. Extinction learning, as understood in Pavlovian conditioning models, occurs if an individual is repeatedly confronted with a CS (e.g., bus, elevated heart rate) without the presence of the feared consequences (US; e.g., accident, heart attack) thereby diminishing the conditioned fear response (CR; e.g., panic attack). The principle of exposure is hereby to decouple the original association of the CS with the US, thus diminishing the CR.

In contrary to early assumptions of "unlearning the CS-US association" as the major principle underlying extinction, current theory (e.g., Craske et al., 2008; Otto, Smits, & Reese, 2005) suggests that fear reduction occurs as the result of learning new CS–US associations. In this sense, the CS becomes associated with a new "safe" meaning (safety learning; e.g., Otto et al., 2005) and no longer only with harm and fear. Thus, as a result of safety learning, newly established safety associations compete with former fear associations; the association recalled at a particular moment depends on factors such as the strength of the learned safety associations and the temporal and contextual features of the recall environment. When anxiety diminishes, the safety-oriented associations successfully inhibit the older, danger-laden associations, a process termed "inhibitory learning" by Craske et al., representing the most up-to-date view on extinction learning consistent with current empirical evidence. One major implication for successful fear reduction within an account of inhibitory learning is the importance of eliminating safety signals or safety behavior (e.g., carrying a talisman, having company) onto which the nonoccurrence of the feared consequences and the fear reduction during exposure could be alternatively attributed (Barlow, 1988).

In summary, formal exposure therapies imply systematic and often repeated confrontation to fearful stimuli and simultaneous prevention from safety behaviors with the goal of fear reduction and subsequent change in behavior and cognition. While to which degree and in which form habituation and extinction learning take place during exposure remains a matter of debate, there is considerable evidence that exposure therapy implies "new inhibitory learning."

8.3 Exposure Elements Within ACT

8.3.1 Brief Description of ACT

In order to characterize exposure elements within ACT, it is necessary to briefly describe ACT in general. In the service of examining the relationship between exposure and ACT, we will concentrate on the salient factors necessary for the comparison. This will necessarily exclude some elements, as an exhaustive description of these processes exceeds the scope of this chapter (interested readers can consult several sources: Hayes et al., 1999; Hayes et al., 2006; Luoma, Hayes, & Walser, 2007; Wilson, 2008).

Six core processes have been postulated to underlie ACT interventions: acceptance, cognitive defusion, values, present moment awareness, self-as-context, and commitment (Hayes et al., 2006). These processes are depicted in Fig. 8.1. From the perspective of the client, these processes can also be conceived as skills training of interdependent processes/skills that promote psychological flexibility with the goal of (1) learning that their attempts to control their feelings and sensations have been largely unsuccessful and may have exacerbated the problem, (2) discovering that acceptance is an alternative to struggling with feared/uncomfortable symptoms, (3) experiencing the whole range of emotions, sensations, and thoughts here and now for what they are (and not what the patient fears or believes them to be), and (4) cultivating and concentrating on living their lives according to their personal values (as opposed to trying to avoid negative feelings) (Luoma et al., 2007).

Exposure elements relate to these goals in several ways. When salient psychological stimuli (i.e., thoughts, memories, emotions, visualization, bodily sensations) stand between the patient and that which is vital for the patient, it becomes a central theme in the patient's life and the work in therapy. Within ACT, avoided emotional content is purposely and systematically brought forth through various means, in a manner reminiscent of traditional exposure procedures. The processes and techniques of ACT are tools used in order to learn to interact differently with the content. In this respect, ACT is consistent with newest theories of mechanisms of action of exposure based on inhibitory learning (Craske et al., 2008; Otto et al., 2005).

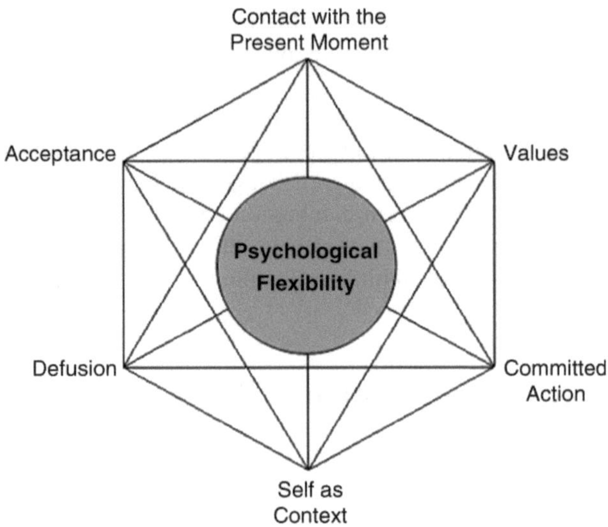

Fig. 8.1 The facets of psychological flexibility according to the model of change underlying ACT (In Hayes, Strosahl, Bunting, Twohig & Wilson, 2004, p.7)

Parenthetically, our discussion is complicated by the lack of precision in some terminology—a fact that has led to calls for more precision in scientific discourse (Friman, Hayes, & Wilson, 1998; Hayes, 2008; Hayes & Plumb, 2007). Psychological content can be understood from an ACT perspective as the present moment experience of past events, verbal and nonverbal, that have been framed into verbal constructs which now are referred to in a context-dependent way and thereby occasion specific behaviors. For example, a dangerous event or the verbal construct of a dangerous event is referred to in a current situation; this "reference" then transforms a safe situation (e.g., standing in a supermarket) into a dangerous one and elicits a respondent-like avoidance move. The same could happen with a "safe" physiological response like heartbeat. The response itself is relationally framed as dangerous and thereby transformed into a dangerous event. Escape or avoidance, then, consists of a change of behaviors, i.e., alternative behaviors that are chosen which are not aversive. Of course, there is a high probability that the newly chosen avoidance behaviors again are framed relationally and transformed to become aversive, which may explain why avoidance tends to escalate.

Relational Frame Theory

Relational frame theory (RFT) is a coherent set of principles providing a basis from which to study how the cognitive and language abilities of humans influence conditioning processes. Beyond mere linear, unidirectional, and hypothetical associations, this pragmatic approach has begun to show how

(continued)

(continued)

verbal cues can occasion a host of arbitrary relational responses, i.e., responses where, for example, one stimulus is responded to in terms of another stimulus without any direct training of both stimuli. Such responses to indirect stimulus relations are said to be derived and depend on cues that specify the relational response.

For example, a person responds to an electric shock with an escape movement. Then the electric shock is directly related to a symbol like § (classical conditioning), which acquires some of the stimulus functions of the electric shock and therefore is avoided. In the next step, § is directly related to another symbol #. Although # has never been directly related to the electric shock, it may now also occasion an escape response. With some previous training on relational cues, # may even occasion a stronger response than § if it has been related to # with a cue denoting that # is bigger than §.

There is evidence that different kinds of relational responses are learned early in life. Because they are arbitrarily applicable (if not always arbitrarily applied) and in a sense "frame" subsequent responses, they are called "relational frames." Reference to relational frames as nouns is done out of convenience, but it is more accurate to think of these processes as verbs: "relationally framing." Some relational frames that have been investigated intensely so far are equivalence or coordination, comparison (smaller, larger), and hierarchy.

As mentioned above, some ACT tools are designed to augment the process of learning to interact in a new way with one's psychological content. For example, values, among other things, explicitly give the patient a clear reason for engaging with the hitherto avoided psychological content that does not rely on anxiety/emotional reduction. As such, values function as self-chosen, intrinsic reinforces that are made psychologically salient during the therapy. It is likely that therapists using traditional exposure would also endorse the fact that fear reduction facilitates important changes in the rest of the patient's life (see Telch et al., 1995). Nevertheless, explicit discussions of such processes are, to our knowledge, not standard within CBT exposure protocols.

8.3.2 ACT Processes

We now turn to the six interconnected processes commonly used to view behavioral patterns within ACT (Hayes et al., 2006; Wilson, Bordieri, Flynn, Lucas, & Slater, 2010). In addition to describing the theoretical and procedural link between ACT interventions and exposure, we will present selected empirical findings that inform this examination. We selected studies that utilized exposure analogue paradigms (i.e., presenting participants with aversive stimuli) in order to better isolate potential mechanisms of action associated with individual ACT processes (see Table 8.1). Each of these studies targeted one or more components of ACT with the goal of experimental precision and we will concentrate on these highlighted aspects. We acknowledge once again, however, that such an examination of interconnected processes is somewhat of a simplification. Due to the specific goals of this chapter and space limitations, we excluded ACT-related therapy outcome trials even though this literature is important, promising, and growing (Forman, Herbert, Moitra, Yeomans, & Geller, 2007; Roemer, Orsillo, & Salters-Pedneault, 2008; Twohig et al., 2010; Wicksell, Ahlqvist, Bring, Melin, & Olsson, 2008).

8.3.2.1 Acceptance

Acceptance has been defined as the process of "…experiencing events fully and without defense…and making contact with the automatic and direct stimulus functions of events, without acting to reduce or manipulate those functions, and without acting on the basis solely of their derived verbal functions" (Hayes, 1994, p.30). Acceptance therefore involves taking a nonevaluative stance toward that which occurs psychologically. This process has been characterized as one involving compassion, kindness, openness, present-centeredness, and willingness. Applied to anxiety disorders, acceptance means letting go of one's fight with fear and anxiety by developing the willingness to experience anxious thoughts, memories, sensations, and feelings as they are, without acting to avoid or to escape (Eifert & Forsyth, 2005).

The goal of exercises that deal with acceptance is to enable new experiences that help patients to develop flexible behavioral repertoires (Hayes, 2004). Therapists work with patients to decrease experiential avoidance by increasing their willingness to experience uncomfortable and feared stimuli. In appropriately designed exercises, a patient will literally practice cultivating willingness (via an accepting stance to the negative emotions). Willingness may be one way in which the mechanisms of action in ACT and traditional exposure differ. Within ACT, a patient would be encouraged to sit with an emotion, to truly experience it without doing anything to change it, and to make psychological space for the emotions and associated thoughts and memories. Patients are encouraged to experience such emotions for the purpose of *practicing having the emotions* without avoiding and so that they are able to pursue their values in the face of such aversive psychological content when encountered in the future. They are not, however, supported in experiencing anxiety or other emotions *so that it will ultimately go away* (i.e., habituation rationale). Within ACT, such a stance would be seen as bolstering an experiential avoidance agenda rather than acceptance. That said, some patients undergoing traditional CBT exposure may naturally react to the procedures by increasing their willingness to experience such emotions.

Application of acceptance strategies in the face of aversive stimuli such as panic-provoking stimuli, pain, cravings, and negative mood inductions have been

Table 8.1 Effect of ACT process in laboratory studies using analogue exposure paradigms

Component	Citation	Sample	Procedure/method	Outcome
Acceptance	Campbell-Sills et al., 2006	$n=60$, diagnosed with anxiety and mood disorders	– Patients were randomized to two conditions (listen to a suppression vs. an acceptance rational) – All patients watched an emotion-provoking movie – Pre-, intermediate and postassessment of subjective distress, skin-conductance level, respiratory sinus arrhythmia and heart rate	– No differences in skin conductance or respiratory sinus arrhythmia in respond to the movie across conditions – Less negative affect in the acceptance condition during the postmovie recovery period – Increased heart rate in the suppression condition and decreased heart rate in the acceptance condition in response to the movie
	Eifert & Heffner, 2003	$n=66$ anxiety sensitive females	– Participants were trained in three different procedures: acceptance context (mindfully notice their symptoms), control context (dominate symptoms using diaphragmatic breathing), and no instructions for dealing with symptoms – All participants were exposed to two periods of 10% carbon enriched air – Behavioral measures of *latency, willingness to return, and drop-outs*; self-reported measures of level of discomfort in front of and during the exposure (SUDS), of psychological reactivity to the inhalation (DSQ) and of emotional avoidance (AAQ); psychological measures (heart rate and skin conductance)	– Less intensive cognitive symptoms and less experienced fear in acceptance group – Not less pronounced physiological symptoms in acceptance group – Less catastrophic thoughts and more willingness to repeat the trial in acceptance condition
	Feldner et al., 2003	$n=48$ participants high or low in emotional avoidance	– One half of the participants were assigned to inhibit the negative experiences induced by the challenge (suppression condition), whereas the other half used to observe their emotional reactions (observation condition) – All participants were exposed to 20% carbon dioxide-enriched air – Measures of emotional avoidance (AAQ); subjective units of distress (SUDs); measures of emotional response before and after the CO_2 inhalations (SAM), perceived efficacy in adjusting of emotional response during the exposure to CO_2; attempts to regulate the emotional reaction during the challenge; physiological measurement of heart rate	– Participants with scored high in emotional avoidance reported less efficacy in regulation of their emotional reactions during the challenge, and greater levels of displeasure as the participants low in emotional avoidance – Persons scored high in emotional avoidance reported greater anxiety in the suppression condition than participants of the observation condition

(continued)

Table 8.1 (continued)

Component	Citation	Sample	Procedure/method	Outcome
	Forman et al., 2007	$n=98$ undergraduate students	– Assessment of personal differences in the psychological impact of the viand surrounding (PFS) – Assessment of food craving (FCQ-S) – All participants were randomly assigned to one of three conditions: control condition, acceptance condition, and no intervention group and gave transparent boxes of chocolate	– Significant benefit of acceptance strategies in controlling of craving and supporting abstinence in participants reporting high liability to the presence of food
	Hayes, Bisset et al., 1999	$n=32$; university students	– Participants were randomized to one of three rationales (acceptance-based vs. control-based vs. attention placebo) – All participants completed a cold pressure task with ice water – Pre- and postassessment of tolerance to pain, self-reported pain, unpleasantness, and sensation; believability of thoughts and feelings as reasons for stopping the task	– Significantly greater pain tolerance in the acceptance condition compared to control and placebo condition – No significant group differences in self-reported pain, unpleasantness, and sensation – Significant group differences in believability with least believability in the acceptance condition
	Keogh et al., 2005	$n=62$ students	– Participants were randomized to two different instructions: acceptance and control – All individuals were exposed to cold pressor two times – Assessment of individual pain tolerance (SF-MPQ)	– Reduction of reported subjective pain under acceptance condition compared to another condition – Significant gender differences in pain tolerance: women reported less pain tolerance than men – Acceptance-based strategies liked to be more useful for women while dealing with pain
	Levitt et al., 2004	$n=60$; diagnosed with panic disorder	– All patients were randomized to three conditions: acceptance, suppression, and control – All participants were exposed to 15-minute 5.5% carbon dioxide challenge – Laboratory measures (rating of anxiety throughout CO_2 inhalation and during the last 5 minutes after the challenge), autonomic arousal due to inhalation (MASQ-AA); psychophysiological measures (heart rate and skin temperature); avoidance measures (willingness to participate)	– The participants of acceptance condition reported less subjective anxiety and more willingness to participate in the second challenge as the individuals assigned to another two conditions – No significant group differences of self-report panic symptoms and physiological response
	Liverant et al., 2008	$n=60$; diagnosed with unipolar depression	– All participants received a mood induction via film eliciting sadness. In a first step, no coping instruction was given, in a second step participants were randomized to an acceptance vs. suppression condition involving audiotaped coping instructions – Several assessment of subjective emotional experience in response to the mood induction and use of coping strategies	– The suppression group showed reduced increase in sadness in response to the mood induction relative to the acceptance group, yet the higher initial sadness levels in the acceptance group decreased more steeply – Anxiety about the experience of depressed mood moderated the relationship of coping strategy and sadness. At lower levels of anxiety the suppression group showed less sadness relative to the

Luciano et al., 2010	$n=38$; university students	– Participants were randomly assigned to one of four conditions: (1) ACT protocol with coherent acceptance task followed by experiential avoidance protocol with a coherent suppression task, (2) protocols in reversed order, (3) and (4) serve as control conditions with tasks but no protocol – Computerized (acceptance and suppression) tasks with intermittently presented aversive noise through headphones – Assessment of level of discomfort at different points during the procedure	– Participants receiving the ACT protocol and ACT-consistent task in the first place before experiencing to control discomfort (Avoidance protocol and task) reported significantly lower levels of discomfort in response to aversive noise relative to the four other conditions
Masedo & Esteve, 2007	$n=219$ undergraduate students	– All participants were assigned to three conditions: acceptance, suppression, and spontaneous coping – All individuals were exposed to a cold pressor – Assessment of subjective pain; assessment of subjective distress; ratings of pain recovery and distress recovery	– Significant group differences in tolerance of pain: tolerance time of acceptance group was significant longer in comparison to other two groups – Significant group differences in pain ratings: in acceptance group significant lower pain ratings – Significant group differences in subjective distress: acceptance group rated distress significant lower – Pain recovery ratings in acceptance group are significant lower – Distress recovery ratings were significant lower in the acceptance group
McMullen et al., 2008	$n=80$, university students and ex-students	– Participants were randomized to five coping conditions (full-acceptance vs. full-distraction vs. instruction-based-acceptance vs. instruction-based distraction vs. no-instruction). The two full coping conditions included instructions, an experiential exercise and a metaphor. The two instruction-based groups included a brief instruction – Participants completed two trials of a number matching task (pre- and post- to introduction of coping conditions) with an intermittently given choice to either continue and receive a shock or to stop the task (shock tolerance). When receiving the shock they rated the painfulness. Believability was assessed as the relationship between subjective painfulness and shock tolerance	– The full-acceptance conditions showed the strongest shock tolerance compared to other groups and the instruction-distraction showed the weakest shock tolerance – All five groups did not differ in the subjective painfulness – Believability was lower is both acceptance conditions compared to other conditions

(continued)

Table 8.1 (continued)

Component	Citation	Sample	Procedure/method	Outcome
	Roche et al., 2007	$n=20$ undergraduate volunteers	– All participants were randomized to one of the four conditions: acceptance and control under high demand (the experimenter sat about one meter away from the participant and got an eye contact requiring the participant to do his best for the experimenter), and under low demand (about 2.4 m away from the participants, minimal eye contact, and no requests) – All participants were exposed to a cold pressor before, immediately after, and 10 minutes after one of the two intervention – Assessment of trait and state levels of anxiety (STAS-S-T); assessment of self-reported or felt pain – Unpleasantness and sensation referred to challenge	– Demand characteristics influence pain behavior significantly – acceptance-based strategy used to be more the motion of demand as the control-based strategy – Demand characteristics had no influence on ratings of pain
	Vowles et al., 2007	$n=74$; diagnosed with chronic low back pain	– All participants were assigned to three different conditions related to pain: Pain acceptance, pain control, and continued practice – Measures of depression (BDI), pain-related anxiety , pain-related acceptance; assessment of physical impairment (PII); verbal ratings of physical impairment; follow-up questionnaire	– Acceptance group showed significant higher overall functioning on a set of standardized physical tasks in comparison to other groups – The acceptance group showed a 16.3% improvement in impairment, whereas the control group declined by 8.3% and the continued practice group mended by 2.5%
Defusion	Gutiérrez et al., 2004	$n=40$ nonclinical students	– All participants were randomized to an acceptance condition (disconnection of pain-related thoughts and feelings from the action) or control condition (altering and controlling pain-related experiences) – All participants were exposed to increasing painful shocks and performed the task twice, before and after becoming the experimental protocol – The task in both conditions consisted of value-oriented context that assisted the participants to go on with the task in spite of pain – Participants had a choice to participate in the next task and be shocked or to quit the challenge, whereas each choice had its costs and profits – Obtained measures of pain tolerance and self-reports of pain were gained at pre- and postintervention	– The participants of acceptance condition exhibited significantly more tolerance to pain, especially during exposure to highly painful shocks and lower believability of painful experience compared to the participants of the control condition

Masuda et al., 2004	$n=8$ undergraduate female	– Comparison of defusion technique to a distraction task and to a thought control task – All participants used to generate self-relevant negative thought and restate it in one word – Assessment of degree of discomfort and the believability of that thought	– Significant reduction in discomfort related to the negative thoughts and in believability of these thoughts in defusion group
Masuda et al., 2009	Experiment 1 $n=75$ undergraduate students	– All participants used to generate one self-related disturbing and believable negative thought and restate that thought in one word – Assessment of degree of discomfort and the believability of that thought – All participants were randomized to one of three conditions: (1) only defusion rationale and training, (2) defusion rationale and training plus 3 seconds repetition of negative thought, (3) and defusion rationale and training plus 20 seconds repetition of a negative thought	– Significant smaller reduction of discomfort and believability in the rationale condition only compared to rationale plus 3 seconds or 20 seconds repetition – Reduced believability of negative thoughts under the condition 3 compared to condition 2
	Experiment 2 $n=67$ undergraduate students	– Conditions identical to the first experiment – All participants were randomized to three different repetition durations of self-relevant negative thought: 1 second, 10 or 30 seconds	– Significant lower reduction in emotional discomfort and believability in 1-second condition compared to 10 and 30 seconds conditions
Masuda et al., 2010	$n=132$ undergraduate students	– All participants used to generate one self-related disturbing and believable negative thought and restate that thought in one word – Assessment of degree of discomfort and the believability of that thought – Participants were randomized to three conditions: cognitive defusion (defusion rationale, defusion training and 30 seconds repetition of self- relevant negative word), thought distraction (thought distraction rationale, distraction training, and attempt to distract from the negative word), and distraction-based experimental tasks (reading a neutral text about Japan)	– Significant lower levels of emotional discomfort and believability of the self-related negative thought under the defusion condition compared to another two conditions – Additional: beneficial results for the cognitive defusion for participants with increased depressive ratings

(continued)

Table 8.1 (continued)

Component	Citation	Sample	Procedure/method	Outcome
Present moment	Arch & Craske, 2006	$n=60$ undergraduate and graduate students	– Assessment of social desirability; assessment of emotional responding; behavioral measures as an account of slides participants agreed to view; heart rate measure – Participants were randomized to one of three instructions: focused breathing (mindfulness mediation exercise), worry, and unfocused attention (request to think about anything) – Three measurement periods of reaction to viewed slides: T1 (before the induction), T2 and T3 (after instruction) – Three block of slides (positive, neutral, and negative) to each time	– Lower negative emotion and overall emotional fugacity in reaction to the after-induction slides in the focused breathing compared to worry condition – Increased willingness to view negative slides under focused breathing condition compared to unfocused attention condition – Positive reactions to the neutral slides before and after induction under focused breathing condition in comparison to another two conditions whose participants responded significantly more negative to neutral slides over time
	Arch & Craske, 2010	$n=90$ participants with anxiety disorder and nonanxious individuals	– Assessment of trait mindfulness – Participants were assigned to hyperventilation tasks and relaxation tasks in order assess anxiety-related experiences and willingness to experience the sensations	– Less negative affect related to trait mindfulness among high-anxiety individuals – Longer duration of hyperventilation and less fear of relaxation were associated with trait mindfulness
	Broderick, 2005	$n=177$ undergraduate students	– Assessment of positive and negative mood at three times (PANAS1-3) – Negative mood induction by listening and reading of sad segments – Randomization to three conditions: rumination, distraction, and mindfulness mediation	– Less dysphoric mood after dealing with provoking stimuli under mindfulness condition
Values	Creswell et al., 2005	$n=85$, university students	– Participants were randomly assigned to one of two conditions (value-affirmation condition vs. control condition) – Affirmation of values was manipulated by answering questions regarding individual top-rated values, control participants answered questions relating low rated personal values. Stress response was induced employing the Trier Social Stress Test – Assessment of self-resources and personal values prior to procedure. Saliva samples for analyzing cortisol levels at baseline and following the stress test	– Participants in the value-affirmation condition showed significantly lower overall cortisol response and lower increase in cortisol response from baseline to poststress-onset compared to control participants – The two groups did neither differ in their cardiovascular stress response nor in their perception of stress – Self-resources (e.g., self-esteem) moderated the effect of value affirmation on perceived stress with lower stress perceptions in the value-affirmation condition compared to the control condition for individuals with increased self-resources

Páez-Blarrina et al., 2008	$n=30$ undergraduate students	– All participants were randomized to one of three conditions: acceptance (ACT), control (CONT), and untrained condition – Participants got ACT-focused protocol, the CONT values protocol or the untrained condition – After that all individuals were exposed to the first pain challenge (Test 1) – Participants who achieved the highest amount of shocks (15) were deposed, whereas the other got coping protocol (either ACT defusion or CONT suppression) and went the second pain challenge (Test 2)	– Test 1: Participants of ACT condition showed greater pain tolerance and less pain believability compared to participants of another two conditions – Test 2: replication of benefit of the ACT protocol

extensively subjected to empirical scrutiny in laboratory analogue studies (Campbell-Sills, Barlow, Brown, & Hofmann, 2006; Eifert & Heffner, 2003; Feldner, Zvolensky, Eifert, & Spira, 2003; Forman et al., 2007; Keogh, Bond, Hanmer, & Tilston, 2005; Levitt, Brown, Orsillo, & Barlow, 2004; Liverant, Brown, Barlow, & Roemer, 2008; Luciano et al., 2010). For example, Eifert and Heffner (2003) exposed participants to several trials in which they inhaled 10% carbon dioxide-enriched air, a procedure known to induce anxiety. Prior to the inhalation procedure, participants were either trained in an ACT-based acceptance strategy or in a control strategy that included diaphragmatic breathing. Results showed that participants in the acceptance condition were less avoidant and more willing to repeat the CO_2 session and reported fewer and less-intense cognitive and fear symptoms during inhalations. Acceptance strategies have also been examined with stimuli of emotional and sensory pain (e.g., Gutiérrez, Luciano, Rodríguez, & Fink, 2004; Hayes, Bisset et al., 1999; Keogh et al., 2005; Masedo & Esteve, 2007, McMullen et al., 2008; Roche, Forsyth, & Maher, 2007; Vowles et al., 2007). For example, McMullen et al. (2008) compared the impact of acceptance versus distraction strategies on the tolerance of pain and examined additionally how the way in which the two coping strategies were delivered (instruction only versus instruction combined with an exercise and metaphor) effects tolerance of pain. Participants in the acceptance condition involving experiential exercises and metaphors showed the highest behavioral willingness (i.e., the highest willingness to experience the most pain, but no differences in subjective reports of pain) compared to participants who received coping instructions only or no instruction at all. In contrast, the different instructions did not differentially impact self-reported pain over the course of the experiment.

Taken together, these studies suggest that acceptance strategies are associated with the willingness to continue interacting with aversive stimuli. Assuming that anxiety, pain, negative thoughts, and emotions may return in one's life, the cultivation of willingness via acceptance is a crucial skill. At the same time, the experiential and metaphor-based manner in which ACT acceptance strategies are delivered may be a critical and important aspect of their effectiveness.

8.3.2.2 Defusion

Defusion refers to altering the *function* of thoughts and cognitions, thereby changing the way one interacts with them. Defusion is achieved by promoting contexts in which unhelpful functions of thoughts and cognitions are diminished (Hayes et al., 2006). Successful defusion will support patients in differentiating themselves from their thoughts by no longer taking them for what they think they are (e.g., taking the content of the thoughts to be 1:1 with reality), but instead to understand them simply as thoughts.

Numerous techniques ranging from formal to informal are used to promote defusion. In several techniques, exposure procedures are of little relevance. For example, metaphors (i.e., the mind as a chess or volleyball game) and unconventional use of language (i.e., "thank your mind for that thought") are used to promote defusion.

In other techniques, the negative content is brought forth and played with. In such circumstances, exposure does indeed play a role, although it may lack some of the formal characteristics. For example, in the so-called MILK exercise patients repeat the word milk (and other words) for at least a minute until the stimulus aspects of the word milk start to change. One goal of this exercise is to sensitize the patient for the difference of how a word is experienced psychologically when taken literarily versus when not. Then, by the way of comparison, a patient is often asked to take emotionally difficult cognitive content and repeat the procedure. For example, "I can't handle this," "I'm a loser," etc. As this content is repeated for a minute, the patient is indeed coming in contact with the feared stimuli/ negative cognitions in a new way. As stated previously, such an exercise entails some of the former characteristics of exposure (i.e., systematic, repeated presentation of a feared, negatively arousing, or avoided stimulus), but with the key difference that changing thought content (i.e., diminishing the frequency of thinking "I'm a loser") and reducing anxiety/ emotion are not the primary goals. The science behind defusion, that is, RFT, presents tantalizing hypotheses as to what must occur within an exposure procedure for its positive effects to unfold. For example, if the stimulus control of a negative internal cognition begins to weaken within one minute using defusion, perhaps behavioral exposure procedures could be facilitated by incorporating purposeful cognitive defusion. Theoretical and empirical work is needed to determine whether theories of verbal relations that support defusion are compatible or even synergistic with theories of inhibitory learning (Craske et al., 2008).

In order to examine the effects of defusion, several empirical studies have utilized paradigms that expose participants to aversive self-referential thoughts (Masuda et al., 2009; Masuda et al., 2010; Masuda, Hayes, Sackett, & Twohig, 2004). The authors demonstrate that a commonly used defusion exercise implying rapid repetition of a negative self-referring word reduced associated discomfort and believability of that thought more than distraction or thought control strategies (Masuda et al., 2004; Masuda et al., 2010). Further, the effects of word repetition on discomfort and believability are thought to be differentially related to the duration of word repetition, with greater effects only on believability in the prolonged repetition (20 s) condition compared to shorter repetitions (3 s) (Masuda et al., 2009).

Other research groups investigated defusion processes by exposing participants to increasing painful shocks (Gutiérrez et al., 2004; Páez-Blarrina et al., 2008). In one such study, higher pain tolerance and lower believability of subjective discomfort was observed in participants instructed to disconnect pain-related thoughts and feelings from actions in comparison to participants who were instructed to modify or control pain-related thoughts and feelings (Gutiérrez et al., 2004).

Taken together, these studies suggest that cognitive defusion reliably reduces the believability of thoughts and associated emotional discomfort, at least over the short term in controlled laboratory environments. Reduction in the believability of thoughts may be an important precursor to more traditional exposure procedures, as the reduction in this barrier may allow the patient to more fully engage with the stimuli. This, in turn, likely facilitates new inhibitory learning.

8.3.2.3 Present Moment Focus

This process refers to the process of contacting what is occurring here and now in internal experience and the environment and cultivating a nonjudgmental, open, and curious manner toward whatever is present at a given moment (Hayes et al., 2006). Cultivation of present moment awareness—often referred to as mindfulness (Brown & Ryan, 2003)—aims to help the patient develop a new relationship to internal experience and to experience the world more directly in the service of psychological flexibility (Fletcher & Hayes, 2005; Hayes & Plumb, 2007).

Present moment focus and exposure procedures share an explicitly nonavoidance stance toward internal and external experience. Unlike acceptance and some defusion exercises, the procedure of exposure cannot be easily mapped onto any one mindfulness exercise, however. Instead, it is likely that present moment focus is a quality achieved in exposure done well. That is, systematic engagement with stimuli without avoiding even in subtle ways. This is not easy (Olatunji, Deacon, & Abramowitz, 2009). Yet, when a patient is able to undergo exposure without engaging in any subtle forms of avoidance (experiential or otherwise), present moment awareness likely results even when it is not directly targeted. That is, patients who truly engage with the feared symptoms, thoughts, or images—and not interacting with them so they will subside—are likely cultivating a present moment stance. Indeed, it has been observed that experiential avoidance is difficult to maintain while focusing on the present moment (Wilson, 2008). Once again, this hypothesis is both interesting and underexamined. In fact, only a couple of analogue studies attempted to directly isolate the effects of present moment awareness in exposure-like paradigms (although present moment awareness elements were necessarily present in the previous studies discussed). In one study, Arch and Craske (2006) exposed participants to positive, neutral, and negative slides in combination after inducing mindful focused breathing, worrying, or unfocused attention. Results indicated that 15 min of focused mindful breathing lead to reduced negative affect compared to worrying and increased willingness to view additional negative slides compared to unfocused attention. In another study, Broderick (2005) induced sad moods followed by randomization to rumination, distraction, or mindfulness meditation. Less dysphoric mood was observed in the mindfulness meditation in comparison to the other two conditions.

In a subsequent study, Arch and Craske (2010) did not directly manipulate mindfulness, but rather examined the effect of trait levels of mindfulness (as measured by questionnaire) in participants with anxiety disorder and nonanxious individuals in response to hyperventilation and relaxation stressors. Results indicated that higher trait levels of mindfulness were associated with dampened subjective anxiety and behavioral avoidance responses, particularly among the anxiety disorder participants.

Results of these studies suggest that present moment awareness can be experimentally increased and that such interventions—similar to those utilized in ACT—increase the willingness to behaviorally stay in contact with even negative psychological content and can reduce acute negative affect. It also appears as if even trait levels of mindfulness are associated with positive effect.

In summary, present moment focus is inherent in both traditional exposure and ACT. In ACT, present moment focus can be considered a process and a means to an end. Although speculative, some form of present moment awareness likely manifests within or results from traditional exposure procedures as well.

8.3.2.4 Values

In ACT, values are defined as "…freely chosen, verbally constructed consequences of ongoing, dynamic, evolving patterns of activity, which establish predominant reinforcers for that activity that are intrinsic in engagement in the valued behavioral pattern itself." (Wilson, 2008, p. 64). As previously indicated, values in ACT are linked to other processes such as acceptance, mindfulness, defusion, and self-as-context. Stated simply, values reinforce the hard work of cultivating willingness, defusion, and contact with the present moment (Hayes et al., in press).

The relationship between deliberately engaging in previously avoided behaviors, a type of exposure in ACT, and values is likely bidirectional. The reinforcing aspect of values provides the framework and justification for engaging in previously avoided behaviors when necessary to move forward in valued life directions. By providing a salient explicit reason for doing the hard work, patients may be more likely to do the work. For example, a patient may avoid plane flights for decades due to panic attacks and associated feelings of impending death. This may be justified with statements such as, "I can drive and don't need to fly." This may be maintained even in the face of suffering (e.g., complaints from the family, inability to advance at work). However, if the patients' value of being a good father comes into focus (e.g., his daughter moved to Japan and he must fly to visit and support her), the verbally established reinforcer is now in place to aid the patient in engaging in necessary behavioral patterns.

Empirically, the role of values as reinforcers has been demonstrated in terms of increasing the willingness to continue pain challenges. For example, Páez-Blarrina et al. (2008) carefully manipulated values in three steps. First, participants were given an example of people continuing doing things despite severe discomfort (i.e., going to work despite pain in order to feed their family). Second, they were asked to generate examples from their own lives when they continued to do something despite discomfort. This step was undertaken in order to establish and accentuate the relation between valued actions and private events. Finally, the relationship between accepting and continuing the forthcoming task (receiving shocks) despite discomfort and helping to improve the lives of others based on the knowledge gained from the experiment was explicitly linked. This was done in order to create a functional equivalence between their discomfort and values. The control group underwent three parallel steps in which functional equivalence was established between the task and values. However, the general and personal examples were about situations where someone stopped performing a task because it was too painful. Results indicated longer duration of continuation and higher rates of continuation despite high levels of discomfort in the group that generated personal examples of continuing a task versus those whose examples highlighted discontinuing.

Although not directly linked to an ACT protocol, the impact of personal values has also been observed on the level of neuroendocrine reactivity to stress (Creswell et al., 2005). Specifically, affirmation of personal values reduced cortisol responses to a social stress test direct after the task and also 45 minutes later.

Taken together, these studies suggest that activating awareness of personal values are advantageous and perhaps even protective in the face of stressful or even painful experiences. Values likely help participants orient themselves to a larger reason to engage in aversive tasks and aid them in not giving up.

8.3.2.5 Committed Action

"Commitments in ACT involve defining goals in specific areas along one's valued path, then acting on these goals while anticipating and making room for psychological barriers." (Hayes, Strosahl, Bunting, Twohig, & Wilson, 2004, p.3) Thus, in one sense practicing willingness to experience negative emotions is synonymous with committed action. That is, the patient commits in the present moment to encountering difficult psychological material. Any step in this direction is interpreted as fulfilling the commitment of acting consistent with a value. This holds true even if the patient engages in avoidance or otherwise breaks off the exposure procedure. Because commitment is always (and ever repeatedly) occurring in the present, utilization of experiential avoidance or other safety behaviors (which is inconsistent with acceptance, willingness, and present moment awareness) is followed by a new commitment in this moment to experience negative cognitions and emotions associated with the committed behavior in the service of a value. We are unaware of any empirical studies that have directly isolated and tested committed action in an analogue study. This is likely due to the nature of committed action: in some sense, practicing willingness to experience negative emotion is committed action in its own right.

8.3.2.6 Self-as-context

Self as context is a sense of self that refers to a person's behavior of perspective-taking. It is a skill that builds if environmental and private stimuli are repeatedly contacted or observed with an awareness of the distinction between the stimuli observed and the observer. For example, if a father says to his child "this behavior is bad" instead of "you are bad," the child is implicitly taught to make a distinction between himself and his behavior. In other words, self-as-context refers to a sense of perspective which is inherent in any mindful experience (in our example, the father's remark helped the child observe and become aware of his behavior). Self-as-context is the behavior of taking the perspective of I-here-now. Self-as-context refers to the experience that the "notion of self" is no more or less than the constant stream of experience that flows through us at each moment—that the self is simply the context in which experience occurs, rather than a fixed entity. Skillful performance of self-as-context (or perspective taking for that matter) is accompanied by an experience of inner stability and calmness. This refers to its transcendent quality: "No matter what happens, this experiential core of I-here-now will always be there as long as I live." There is a sense of freedom and boundlessness that comes with this kind of self-experience. It is often said that "human beings are the only species … that has the ability to reflect on itself" (Wilson, 2009, p. 387). In any individual case, who is it who reflects? Self-as-context is the answer to this peculiar question.

Clinically, self-as-context work is indicated when a client strongly identifies with certain experiences, habitual activities, or cognitions. Rather than discussing core beliefs, for example, in self-as-context training the psychological content is acknowledged and exercises are performed so that the client can experience the difference between himself as a whole person and the diverse psychological content. From the perspective of I-here-now it becomes easier to accept painful experiences that show up during exposure and to behave in ways that neither follow nor fight core beliefs.

Colloquially, self-as-context experientially provides a firm (psychological) ground from which difficult exposure work can be done. The ground is firm exactly because it is contentless. What does this mean? Everything we see, hear, touch etc., our interoceptive sensations, our emotions, and what we think, including what we think about ourselves, is subject to change. If, however, our experience of self and identity depends too heavily on the changing content of our experience, then we tend to experience ourselves as instable (as, for example, in Borderline Personality Disorder) or we will have to make great efforts to keep our experiential content constant (as, for example, in Obsessive Personality Disorder and many other clinical conditions where experiential avoidance is employed to protect a content-dependent, conceptual self from threatening experiences like panic). If we learn, however, to experientially contact the locus (I-here-now) or the "space" (pure consciousness or the "Global Workspace," [Edelman, Gally, & Baars, 2011]) that these ever changing contents are connected to or entailed, we may be able to advance a stable and continuing self-experience that transcends any necessarily reductive content-dependent identity. As an aside, paradoxically it is exactly this content-free stance that paves the way for truly personal choices of values that are less dependent on social conformity and expectations from others because personal choice is less constrained by prejudice, narrow rational concepts, or informational limitedness. The main point here is that self-as-context supports acceptance of personal values and choice in an important way (Hayes & Gregg, 2000).

Methodologically it seems (to us at least) quite difficult to experimentally isolate the process of self-as-context. Because the development of this sense of self is intricately related to other behavioral concepts like acceptance, defusion, emotional, and self-regulation, major efforts will be necessary to get around these potential confounding variables. Indirect support of its importance, however, may be gained from the large literature on the self (e.g., Swann & Bosson, 2010). To the best of our knowledge so far no published studies have specifically addressed the clinical impact of self-as-context interventions in relation to exposure procedures.

Nevertheless, self-as-context is considered important from an ACT perspective and "…fostered in ACT by mindfulness exercises, metaphors, and experiential processes." (Hayes et al., in press, p.13).

8.4 Conclusion

The six components—acceptance, defusion, present moment awareness, self as a context, values and committed action—can be organized the following way. The first four relate to acceptance and mindfulness process; the last four are commitment and behavior change processes (present moment awareness and self-as-context are in both groupings). Hence, we can define ACT as a behavioral and cognitive intervention that utilizes acceptance and mindfulness processes, and commitment and behavior-change processes, to produce psychological flexibility (Gloster, Klotsche, Chaker, Hummel, & Hoyer, 2011; Kashdan & Rottenberg, 2010). Therapy emphasizes the acceptance and mindfulness processes that reduce excessive literality and create a more conscious, present, flexible approach to psychological experiences. ACT also aims to reinforce the commitment and behavior change that increase values-based action (Hayes et al., in press).

The empirical evidence surrounding ACT procedures in component studies that utilize exposure analogue paradigms is promising. All the studies reviewed underline the benefit of acceptance-based approach in increasing tolerance of negative sensations and feelings and decreasing inflexible reactions to these negative stimuli. Based on these empirical studies, we feel that ACT-related processes allow individuals to learn adaptive behavioral repertoires in the face of aversive stimuli. Thus, appropriately applied, exposure procedures can be a significant part of ACT.

An equally interesting question, however, is whether ACT components can help to improve traditional exposure therapy—one of the most efficacious therapeutic procedures in the psychological literature. Despite the efficacy of exposure, it remains underutilized, in part because of concerns of therapists and the aversiveness experienced by patients (Olatunji et al., 2009; Richard & Gloster, 2007). It remains an important empirical question whether ACT components can improve the dissemination, receptiveness, and effectiveness of this procedure. The evidence reviewed in this chapter suggests that there are promising areas for cross-fertilization in both research and therapeutic contexts.

In our opinion, further clarification and specification of the mechanisms of action of exposure procedures in both traditional exposure and as utilized within ACT are strongly advocated. Toward this end, analytic, theoretical, empirical, and perhaps even philosophical assumptions will need to be explicated and sharpened through iterative discourse. Indeed, thoughtful work in this area has begun (Arch & Craske, 2008; Hayes, 2008; Hofmann & Asmundson, 2011; Roemer, Erisman, & Orsillo, 2009). Clarification of these issues promises to improve our ability to help patients yet will simultaneously challenge us with further specifications in assumptions and terminology.

Acknowledgments Preparation of this manuscript was supported in part from the German Federal Ministry of Education and Research Grant BMBF (Project 01GV0615). We wish to thank Joanna Arch for her helpful comments on a previous draft of this chapter.

References

Arch, J. J., & Craske, M. G. (2006). Mechanisms of mindfulness: Emotion regulation following a focused breathing induction. *Behaviour Research and Therapy, 44*, 1849–1858.

Arch, J. J., & Craske, M. G. (2008). Acceptance and commitment therapy and cognitive behavioral therapy for anxiety disorders: Different treatments, similar mechanisms? *Clinical Psychology, Science and Practice, 15*, 263–279.

Arch, J. J., & Craske, M. G. (2010). Laboratory stressors in clinically anxious and non-anxious individuals: The moderating role of mindfulness. *Behaviour Research and Therapy, 48*, 495–505.

Barlow, D. (1988). *Anxiety and its disorders: The nature and treatment of anxiety and panic*. New York: Guilford Press.

Broderick, P. C. (2005). Mindfulness and coping with dysphoric mood: Contrasts with rumination and distraction. *Cognitive Therapy and Research, 29*, 501–510.

Brown, K. W., & Ryan R. M. (2003). The benefits of being present: Mindfulness and its role in psychological well-being. *Journal of Personality and Social Psychology, 84*(4), 822–848.

Campbell-Sills, L., Barlow, D. H., Brown, T. A., & Hofmann, S. G. (2006). Effects of supression and acceptance on emotional responses of individuals with anxiety and mood disorder. *Behavior Research and Therapy, 44*, 1251–1263.

Craske, M., Kircanski, K., Zelikowsky, M., Mystkowski, J., Chowdhury, N., & Baker, A. (2008). Optimizing inhibitory learning during exposure therapy. *Behaviour Research and Therapy, 46*, 5–27.

Creswell, J. D., Welch, W. T., Taylor, S. E., Sherman, D. K., Gruenewald, T. L., & Mann, T. (2005). Affirmation of personal values buffers neuroendocrine and psychological stress responses. *Psychological Science, 16*(11), 846–851.

Edelman, G. M., Gally, J. A., & Baars, B. J. (2011). Biology of consciousness. *Frontiers in Psychology, 2*, 1–7.

Eifert, G. H., & Forsyth, J. P. (2005). *Acceptance & commitment therapy for anxiety disorders: A practitioner's treatment guide to using mindfulness, acceptance, and values-based behavior change strategies*. Oakland: New Harbinger Publications.

Eifert, G. H., & Heffner, M. (2003). The effects of acceptance versus control contexts on avoidance of panic-related symptoms. *Journal of Behavior Therapy, 34*, 239–312.

Feldner, M. T., Zvolensky, M. J., Eifert, G. H., & Spira, A. P. (2003). Emotional avoidance: An experimental test of individual differences and response suppression using biological challenge. *Behavior Research and Therapy, 41*, 403–411.

Fletcher, L., & Hayes, S. C. (2005). Relational frame theory, acceptance and commitment therapy, and a functional analytic definition of mindfulness. *Journal of Rational-Emotive and Cognitive-Behavioral Therapy, 23*(4), 315–336.

Forman, E. M., Herbert, J. D., Moitra, E., Yeomans, P. D., & Geller, P. A. (2007). A randomized controlled effectiveness trial of acceptance and commitment therapy and cognitive therapy of anxiety and depression. *Behavior Modification, 31*(6), 772–799.

Friman, P. C., Hayes, S. C., & Wilson, K. G. (1998). Why behavior analysts should study emotion: The example of anxiety. *Journal of Applied Behavior, 31*(1), 137–156.

Gloster, A. T., Klotsche, J., Chaker, S., Hummel, K. V., & Hoyer, J. (2011). Assessing psychological flexibility: What does it add above and beyond existing constructs. *Psychological Assessment, 23*(4), 970–982. doi:10.1037/a0024135.

Groves, P. M., & Thompson, R. F. (1970). Habituation: A dual-process theory. *Psychological Review, 77*, 419–450.
Gutiérrez, O., Luciano, C., Rodríguez, M., & Fink, B. C. (2004). Comparisson between an acceptance-based and a cognitive-control-based protocol for coping with pain. *Behavior Therapy, 35*, 767–783.
Hayes, S. C. (1994). Content, context, and the types of psychological acceptance. In S. C. Hayes, N. S. Jacobson, V. M. Follette, & M. J. Dougher (Eds.), *Acceptance and change: Content and context in psychotherapy* (pp. 13–32). Reno: Context Press.
Hayes, S. C. (1999). Science and the success of behavioral healthcare. *Behavioral Healthcare Tomorrow, 8*(3), 54–56.
Hayes, S. C. (2004). Acceptance and commitment therapy, relational frame theory, and the third wave of behavioral and cognitive therapies. *Behavior Therapy, 35*, 639–665.
Hayes, S. C. (2008). Climbing our hills: A beginning conversation on the comparison of acceptance and commitment therapy and traditional cognitive behavioral therapy. *Clinical Psychology: Science & Practice, 5*, 286–295.
Hayes, S. C., Bisset, R. T., Korn, Z., Zettle, R. D., Rosenfarb, I. S., Cooper, L. D., et al. (1999). The impact of acceptance versus control rationales on pain tolerance. *Psychological Record, 49*(1), 33–47.
Hayes, S. C., & Gregg, J. (2000). Functional contextualism and the self. In C. Muran (Ed.), *Self-relations in the psychotherapy process* (pp. 291–307). Washington: American Psychological Association.
Hayes, S. C., Levin, M., Plumb, J., Boulanger, J., & Pistorello, J. Acceptance and commitment therapy and contextual behavioral science: Examining the progress of a distinctive model of behavioral and cognitive therapy. *Behavior Therapy* (in press, pp. 1–29).
Hayes, S. C., Luoma, J., Bond, F., Masuda, A., & Lillis, J. (2006). Acceptance and commitment therapy: Model, processes, and outcomes. *Behaviour Research and Therapy, 44*, 1–25.
Hayes, S. C., & Plumb, J. C. (2007). Mindfulness from the bottom up: Providing an inductive framework for understanding mindfulness processes and their application to human suffering. *Psychological Inquiry, 18*(4), 242–248.
Hayes, S. C., Strosahl, K. D., Bunting, K., Twohig, M., & Wilson, K. G. (2004). What is acceptance and commitment therapy? In S. C. Hayes & K. D. Strosahl (Eds.), *A practical guide to acceptance and commitment therapy*. New York: Springer.
Hayes, S. C., Strosahl, K., & Wilson, K. (1999). *Acceptance and commitment therapy: An experiential approach to behavior change*. New York: Guilford Press.
Heimberg, R. G., & Ritter, M. R. (2008). Cognitive behavioral therapy and acceptance and commitment therapy for the anxiety disorders: Two approaches with much to offer. *Clinical Psychology: Science & Practice, 5*, 296–298.
Hofmann, S. G., & Asmundson, G. J. G. (2011). The science of cognitive behavioral therapy. *Behavior Therapy*. doi:10.1016/j.beth.2009.01.007.
Keogh, E., Bond, F. W., Hanmer, R., & Tilston, J. (2005). Comparing acceptance- and control-based coping instructions on the cold-pressor pain experiences of healthy men and women. *European Journal of Pain, 9*, 591–598.
Kashdan, T. B., & Rottenberg, J. (2010). Psychological flexibility as a fundamental aspect of health. *Clinical Psychology Review, 30*, 865–878. doi:10.1016/j.cpr.2010.03.001.
Levitt, J. T., Brown, T. A., Orsillo, S. M., & Barlow, D. H. (2004). The effects of acceptance versus supression fo emotion on subjective and psychophysiological response to carbon dioxide challenge in patients with panic disorder. *Behavior Therapy, 35*, 747–766.
Liverant, G. I., Brown, T. A., Barlow, D. H., & Roemer, L. (2008). Emotion regulation in unipolar depression: The effects of acceptance and suppression of subjective emotional experience on the intensity and duration of sadness and negative affect. *Behavior Research and Therapy, 46*(11), 1201–1209.
Luciano, C., Molina, F., Gutierrez-Martinez, O., Barnes-Holmes, D., Valdivia-Salas, S., Cabello, F., et al. (2010). The impact of acceptance-based versus avoidance-based protocols on discomfort. *Behavior Modification, 34*, 94–119.

Luoma, J. B., Hayes, S. C., & Walser, R. D. (2007). *Learning ACT: An acceptance & commitment therapy skills-training manual for therapists. ACT-Training. Acceptance and commitment therapy: Ein Handbuch*. Oakland: New Harbinger.

Masedo, A. I., & Esteve, M. R. (2007). Effects of suppression, acceptance and spontaneous coping on pain tolerance, pain intensity and distress. *Behavior Research and Therapy, 45*, 199–209.

Masuda, A., Hayes, S. C., Sackett, C. F., & Twohig, M. P. (2004). Cognitive defusion and self-relevant negative thoughts: Examining the impact of a ninety year old technique. *Behavior Research and Therapy, 42*, 477–485.

Masuda, A., Hayes, S. C., Twohig, M. P., Drossel, C., Lillis, J., & Washio, Y. (2009). A parametric study of cognitive defusion and the believability and discomfort of negative self-relevant thoughts. *Behavior Modification, 33*(2), 250–262.

Masuda, A., Twohig, M. P., Stormo, A. R., Feinstein, A. B., Chou, Y., & Wendell, J. W. (2010). The effects of cognitive defusion and thought distraction onemotional discomfort and believability of negative self-referential thoughts. *Journal of Behavior Therapy and Experimental Psychiatry, 41*, 11–17.

McMullen, J., Barnes-Holmes, D., Barnes-Holmes, Y., Stewart, I., Luciano, C., & Cochrane, A. (2008). Acceptance versus distraction: Brief instructions, metaphors and exercises in increasing tolerance for self-delivered electric shocks. *Behavior Research and Therapy, 46*(1), 122–129.

Moscovitch, D., Antony, M., & Swinson, R. (2009). Exposure-based treatments for anxiety disorders: theory and process. In M. Antony & M. Stein (Eds.), *Oxford handbook of anxiety and related disorders* (pp. 461–475). New York: Oxford University Press.

Olatunji, B. O., Deacon, B. J., & Abramowitz, J. S. (2009). The cruelest cure? Ethical issues in the implementation of exposure-based treatments. *Cognitive and Behavioral Practice, 16*(2), 172–180.

Otto, M., Smits, J., & Reese, H. (2005). Combined psychotherapy and pharmacotherapy for mood and anxiety disorders in adults: Review and analysis. *Clinical Psychology-Science and Practice, 12*, 72–86.

Páez-Blarrina, M., Luciano, C., Gutiérrez-Martínez, O., Valdivia, S., Ortega, J., & Rodríguez-Valverde, M. (2008). The role of values with personal examples in altering the function of pain: Comparison between acceptance-based and cognitive-control-based protocols. *Behaviour Research and Therapy, 46*, 84–97.

Richard, D. C., & Gloster, A. T. (2007). Exposure therapy has a public relation problem: A dearth of litigation amid a wealth of concern. In D. C. Richard & D. Lauterbach (Eds.), *Handbook of exposure therapies*. Amsterdam: Elsevier.

Richard, D. C., Lauterbach, D., & Gloster, A. T. (2007). Description, mechanisms of action, and assessment. In D. C. Richard & D. Lauterbach (Eds.), *Handbook of exposure therapies*. Amsterdam: Elsevier.

Roche, B., Forsyth, J. P., & Maher, E. (2007). The impact of demand characteristics on brief acceptance- and control-based interventions for pain tolerance. *Cognitive and Behavioral Practice, 14*(4), 381–393.

Roemer, L., Erisman, S. M., & Orsillo, S. M. (2009). Mindfulness and acceptance-based treatments for anxiety disorders. In M. M. Antony & M. B. Stein (Eds.), *Oxford handbook of anxiety and related disorders*. Oxford: Oxford University Press.

Roemer, L., Orsillo, S. M., & Salters-Pedneault, K. (2008). Efficacy of an acceptance-based behavior therapy for generalized anxiety disorder: Evaluation in a randomized controlled trial. *Journal of Consulting and Clinical Psychology, 76*(6), 1083–1089.

Swann, W. B., Jr., & Bosson, J. (2010). Self and Identity. In S. T. Fiske, D. T. Gilbert, & G. Lindzey (Eds.), *Handbook of social psychology* (5th ed., pp. 589–628). New York: McGraw-Hill.

Telch, M., Schmidt, N., Jaimez, T., Jaquin, K., & Harrington, P. (1995). Impact of cognitive-behavioral treatment on quality-of-life in panic disorder patients. *Journal of Consulting and Clinical Psychology, 63*, 823–830.

Tolin, D. F. (2009). Alphabet soup: ERP, CT, and ACT for OCD. *Cognitive and Behavioral Practice, 16*, 40–48.

Twohig, M. P., Hayes, S. C., Plumb, J. C., Pruitt, L. D., Collins, A. B., Hazlett-Stevens, H., et al. (2010). A randomized clinical trial of acceptance and commitment therapy versus progressive relaxation training for obsessive-compulsive disorder. *Journal of Consulting and Clinical Psychology, 78*, 705–716.

Tyron, W. (2005). Possible mechanisms for why desensitization and exposure therapy work. *Clinical Psychology Review, 25*, 67–95.

Vowles, K. E., McNeil, D. W., Gross, R. T., McDaniel, M., Mouse, A., Bates, M., Gallimore, P., et al. (2007). Effects of pain acceptance and pain control strategies on physical impairment in individuals with chronic low back pain. *Behavior Therapy, 38*, 412–425.

Wicksell, R. K., Ahlqvist, J., Bring, A., Melin, L., & Olsson, G. L. (2008). Can exposure and acceptance strategies improve functioning and life satisfaction in people with chronic pain and whiplash-associated disorders (WAD)? A randomized controlled trial. *Cognitive Behavior Therapy, 37*(3), 1–14.

Wilson, K. G. (1997). Science and treatment development: Lessons from the history of behavior therapy. *Behavior Therapy, 28*, 547–558.

Wilson, K. G. (2008). *Mindfulness for two: An acceptance and commitment therapy approach to mindfulness in psychotherapy*. Oakland: New Harbinger Publications, Inc.

Wilson, K. G., Bordieri, M., Flynn, M. K., Lucas, N., & Slater, R. (2010). Understanding Acceptance and Commitment Therapy in context: A history of similarities and differences with other cognitive behavior therapies. In J. Herbert & E. Forman (Eds.), *Acceptance and mindulness in cognitive behavior therapy*. Haboken: Wiley.

Wilson, T. D. (2009). Know thyself. *Perspectives on Psychological Science, 4*(4), 384–389.

Wittchen, H. U., & Gloster, A. (2009). Developments in the treatment and diagnosis of anxiety disorders. *Psychiatric Clinics of North America, 32,* xii–xix.

Chapter 9
Exposure Aspects of the Interpersonal Discrimination Exercise (IDE) and the Situational Analysis (SA) in Cognitive Behavioral Analysis System of Psychotherapy (CBASP)

P. Neudeck, H. Walter, and D. Schoepf

Dr. Peter Neudeck is a licensed psychotherapist specialized in cognitive behavioral therapy. He has been working both in clinical and research positions and has established private practices for psychotherapy in Berlin and Cologne. He is also a lecturer and supervisor for graduate and postgraduate CBT-psychotherapy programs across Germany. He recently received further professional development in CBASP and systemic therapy.

P. Neudeck (✉)
Praxis für Verhaltenstherapie, Follerstr. 64, D-50676 Köln/Cologne, Germany
e-mail: peterneudeck@gmx.de

H. Walter
Division of Mind and Brain Research, Department of Psychiatry and Psychotherapy, CCM, Charité—Universitätsmedizin Berlin, Charitéplatz 1, Berlin 10117, Germany
e-mail: henrik.walter@charite.de

D. Schoepf
Department of Psychiatry and Psychotherapy, CBASP Centre of Competence, Universitätsklinikum Bonn Sigmund-Freud-Straße 25, Bonn 53105, Germany
e-mail: dieter.schoepf@ukb.uni-bonn.de

P. Neudeck and H.-U. Wittchen (eds.), *Exposure Therapy: Rethinking the Model – Refining the Method*, DOI 10.1007/978-1-4614-3342-2_9,

His main research activities include psychobiology and psychotherapy of anxiety disorders in exposure based treatments, He has released numerous publications on exposure techniques in mental disorders.

Prof. Henrik Walter, M.D., Ph.D. studied Medicine, Philosophy and Psychology and is board certified in Neurology as well as in Psychiatry and Psychotherapy. After holding professorships in Frankfurt and Bonn, he took the newly established Chair of Psychiatry, Psychiatric Neuroscience and Neurophilosophy at the Charité in Berlin in 2010. His main research interest are systemic neuroscience using cognitive neuroscience methods to study and understand psychiatric disorders focusing on emotions, motivation, volition and social cognition. Currently he is leading two multicentric neuroimaging studies on neuropsychotherapy investigating neurobiological mechanisms in chronic depression and the impact of CBASP on their dysfunctions. Furthermore, he works on subjects in philosophy of mind and neuroethics.

Dr. Dieter Schoepf works at Bonn University in leading position. His main research interest is dedicated to affective and developmental disorders and neural mechanisms of change during treatment as well as co-morbidity research in mental disorders. He is a personal trainee of Prof. James P. McCullough and since 2007 the second US certified CBASP-therapist and supervisor in Germany. He is also founder-member of CBASP-Network.org and its first vice president from 2008-2012. He established the CBASP Centre of Competence in University Bonn since 2006, where he is principle site investigator of bi-centric and multi-centric CBASP studies. In psychotherapy, his special subjects are classical, cognitive, and modern behavioral psychotherapies.

9.1 Introduction

The cognitive behavioral analysis system of psychotherapy (CBASP) manual for treating chronic depression (McCullough, 2000, 2003, 2006) is strongly disorder orientated and includes techniques for changing the patient's perception as well as his or her behavior. Based on Skinner's (1953) model of operant learning, Piaget's (1963) model of cognitive development and the person x environment model by A. Bandura (1967), the CBASP is a theory-driven psychotherapy from the third generation of behavior therapy models. Due to the weight that McCullough's multidimensional approach puts on the disturbed person–environment relationship and the resulting deficient ability to act, the patient's core deficit, i.e., the maladjusted way of experiencing the world and the maladjustment with respect to social interaction, becomes the focus of therapy. CBASP's therapeutic strategies can be divided into interventions which have "bottom-up" or "top–down" effects that help the patient to learn in a systematic way to apply proactive, goal-directed, and socially acceptable behavior on his or her social and material environment (Schoepf, Konradt, & Walter, 2007; Schoepf & Neudeck, 2011). As Hofmann and Asmundson (2008) have pointed out, new psychotherapeutic approaches ("third wave therapies"), such as "Acceptance and Commitment Therapy" (Hayes, Strosahl, & Wilson, 1999) and the "CBASP" have to demonstrate a strong link between their theoretical model and how the therapy is applied in practice. In other words, it is imperative that the specific mechanisms underlying the therapeutic methods of new psychotherapies are clearly elucidated.

The deficit in cognitive–emotional development of the chronically depressed patient with early-onset is thought to result from a multidirectional combination of the following factors (Schoepf & Penberthy, 2010): genetically caused dispositions and personality factors like negative affect, (early) experiences of loss and/or chronic neglect in combination with later adverse life events, and intrapersonal and interactional effects of recurrent experiences of helplessness when interacting with the significant others during childhood (for an in-depth discussion of the role of recurrent experiences of helplessness in childhood and adolescence see Schoepf & Neudeck, 2011). According to a biologically predetermined person–environment vicious circle, the patient lacks the experience of a sufficient quantity of reinforcing social events in the appropriate motivational state. In consequence, the patient fails to develop his cognitive–emotional organization. Instead, stimulus learning of stressful encounters with the significant other's has dominated about social adaptive action–outcome learning. A disturbance of the dynamic person–environment interaction is associated. As a consequence, social interaction is experienced as subjectively dissatisfying and is therefore avoided. Required adaptation and the adversities of life cannot be dealt with in adequate ways.

9.2 Theoretical Foundation of CBASP: Learning Model

Perception is the processing of information that is acquired through one of the senses (sight, hearing, smell, taste, touch), in order to use this information about the structure of the physical world for the adaptive control of behavior. Thus, perception and behavior are closely connected. According to a simplified, but useful conception of the psychology of perception, there are two different types of processes of stimulus recognition: bottom-up and top-down. In the case of *bottom-up processing*, a specific property of the stimulus is detected. Specific stimulus properties are then combined into more complex forms until final stimulus recognition takes place. This explains why bottom-up processing is sometimes referred to as "passive" (perception). By contrast, the term *top-down processing* describes the opposite direction. In top-down processing, (perceptual) hypotheses about the stimulus as a entity are formed (expectations and prior knowledge), then specific properties are selected and tested and finally stimulus recognition takes place. Top-down processing is referred to as "active" (behavior). Anatomical correlates of bottom-up processes include the brain stem and the basal forebrain (affect-driven attention). Top-down processes are mediated by the dorsolateral or the prefrontal regions as well as the anterior cingulate gyrus given sufficient sensorial stimulation or individually developed goals.

The CBASP manual for treating chronic depression comprises bottom-up as well as top-down techniques. Generally speaking, top-down techniques guide the therapeutic work from the patient's general descriptions to concrete individual situations. They are used in order to encourage formal operational thinking and behavior. Bottom-up techniques are designed to lead the patient from the concrete therapeutic situation to interpersonal situations which resemble the therapeutic situation. The goal of these techniques is to help the patient modifying adverse interactions or relationship patterns with the help of the therapist's use of disciplined personal involvement (Schoepf et al., 2007). One important bottom-up technique is the interpersonal discrimination exercise (IDE). The IDE is used to address, train, and thereby "repair" developmental trauma arising from negative experiences with abusive significant others. The therapist demonstrates how the therapist's behavior in "hot spot" interpersonal situations stands in contrast to the behavior of significant others, similar to the patients' experiences earlier in his life. Thereby, the therapist puts the deeply personal nature of the therapist–patient relationship "into the foreground of therapeutic efficacy". Here we have both: a "moderator variable of in-session acquisition learning" as well as a therapist who creates a situational context where the patient is exposed to avoided emotions and thoughts (Schoepf & McCullough, 2009). In contrast, the situational analysis (SA) is a top–down technique which enables the patient to learn how his behavior leads to outcomes he can in fact obtain. Illustrating how the patients' concrete behavior affects the behavioral responses of others (emotionally and interpersonal) is the essential motive of the CBASP method. The SA procedure also assists the therapist in identifying and addressing the specific cognitive and behavioral problems that interfere with the patient's effective social management. The SA contains an elicitation phase and a remediation phase. In the elicitation phase the patient usually describes a recent stressful social situation, his interpretations, his verbal and nonverbal responses, the actual situational outcome and the desired outcome in a formal-operative sequence. Usually, the obtained and the desired outcome will differ. During the remediation phase, the therapist and patient work on behavioral alternatives that would have led to the desired outcome. Further important aspects of this phase are: in the first step, shaping of functional (action) interpretations; in step 2, shaping of missing behavioral aspects of the desired pro-social behavior; in step 3, learning summary; and in step 4, transfer to a future situation. In summary, both intrapersonal and interactional problems are addressed by focussing the patient's attention on his interaction with his environment of the learned helplessness effect in order to help him to identify and change his future behavior and thereby the interpersonal experiences that contribute directly to the chronic depression state.

9.3 Transference Areas and the Transference Hypothesis

To perform an IDE, it is necessary at first to develop a transference hypothesis. Transference hypotheses are deduced using the "Significant Others History" (SOH) procedure in CBASP. McCullough (2000, 2006) assumes four transference areas of interaction that, from the perspective of developmental psychology, play an important role in the patient's relationship with significant others. His considerations refer to the concept of "tacit knowledge" (Polanyi, 1966) and the idea of "reasoning based on implicit causal theories" (Nisbett & Wilson, 1977). In accordance with these assumptions, signal learning processes and instrumentally learned interpersonal rules during toxic experienced developmental conditions may have caused implicit attentional- and expectation shifts that have helped the patient as an "emotional" surviving strategy to decrease the contact with interpersonal events, that are expected to have negative outcomes. Correspondingly, unreflected conditioned patterns of interpersonal behaviors are elicited and executed regularly in "hot spot" situations. This rigidly ruled behavior usually does not correspond to the present situation, arouses stress and provides the patient with a social disadvantage.

Specifically, McCullough (2000) describes working with the construct of transference as an exercise in "focused attention." The transference hypothesis differs from Freud's concept of transference since—qua mental representation—it can be actively carried out in session with the therapist and then processed within the IDE.

The four transference areas in which "hot spots" occur are:

1. Interpersonal intimacy (either felt by the patient or the therapist).
2. Emotional needs of the patient toward the therapist.

3. Mistakes the patient has made (e.g., not doing his or her homework or being unable to solve problems presented during therapy sessions).
4. Negative affects of the patient toward the therapist.

After conducting the SOH, one formal transference hypothesis is developed, taking the form of an "if-then" connection. For this, the transference area most relevant to the patient, a transference hypothesis is deduced by the therapist in the absence of the patient, especially in early-onset patients with a positive history of childhood trauma; for example: "If I make mistakes during therapy, the therapist is going to dislike, punish, or humiliate me". (For further examples, compare McCullough, 2006, p. 130 on). The transference hypothesis then becomes central in the IDE because it defines the starting point or interpersonal hot spot. Careful and correct identification of the transference hypotheses is essential. If an incorrect or irrelevant hypothesis is developed, the IDE will not work effectively.

9.4 Administration of the IDE

Three phases are carried out consecutively during the IDE.

The IDE starts with the "negative phase" which occurs during initiation of the hot spot of interpersonal dysfunction. For example, when the patient forgot to do the homework for the session, the therapist might ask: "What would the significant other have done if you had told her that you've forgotten your homework?" In the "negative phase," the following is likely to happen: The patient starts with recalling a typical past interpersonal interaction with one or two of his maltreating significant other's in a similar situation. Then he has to describe the behavioral consequences on himself caused by the behavior of his significant other.

The second phase of the IDE is called the "positive phase." In this phase, the patient is asked to describe his or her perception of the therapist's reactions. Afterward, he characterizes his feelings evoked by the current incident with the therapist. He is then asked to compare the therapist's behavior to the recalled behavior of his significant others in a similar situation. The felt distress of the patient usually decreases at this moment of the exercise.

Sensitive to the timing and the magnitude of the felt decrease of distress in the last phase of the IDE i.e., "the healing phase" the patient is encouraged by the therapist to identify the contrast between the therapist's behavior and the significant others' behavior. "Automatically," there results a felt increase of the potency of the therapist to specifically reduce interpersonal distress during the experienced "hot spot" situation and a new interpersonal reality of the therapist–patient relationship becomes meaningful to the patient.

During therapy, the patient learns to discriminate between the reactions that he or she was expecting due to negative experiences made in the past ("emotional time warp") and the (therapist's) actual reactions. Over time, the patient is supposed to make new experiences with other people in everyday life, and these experiences may be different than prior experiences of the patient. Instead of punishing the patient for a mistake, the therapist listens carefully and shows understanding and interest. Using questions such as “What made you realize that I was interested in your story?” the intervention necessary for the learning theory perspective of IDE directs the patient’s attention to important and relevant aspects of the therapist’s behavior (properties of the stimulus; see also “bottom-up process”).

What is fascinating about this method, apart from the enormous effect it has on both the therapist and the patient, is the fact that it allows for the possibility of describing interpersonal events using learning theory. In fact, it may be possible to describe the unspecific determinant named “therapist–patient relationship” in terms of learning theory and arrive at a transparent analysis. According to McCullough (2006), the positive phase of IDE already contains the mechanism of negative reinforcement. The patient’ is first exposed at his conditioned feeling of aversion, and with the therapist’s positive reaction the aversive emotion is reduced. For further differentiation between cognitive- and emotional forms of IDE’s and modified clinical applications readers may refer to Schoepf, Neudeck, & Walter, 2011 and Schoepf & Neudeck, 2011.

9.5 What Is Learned During the IDE?

In order to describe the learning theory aspects of IDE it is important to recall M. E. Bouton’s model of a synthetic cognitive–biological perspective on instrumental action (Bouton, 2007). Bouton’s model describes the way in which stimuli control behavior. The following abbreviations are used in his model:

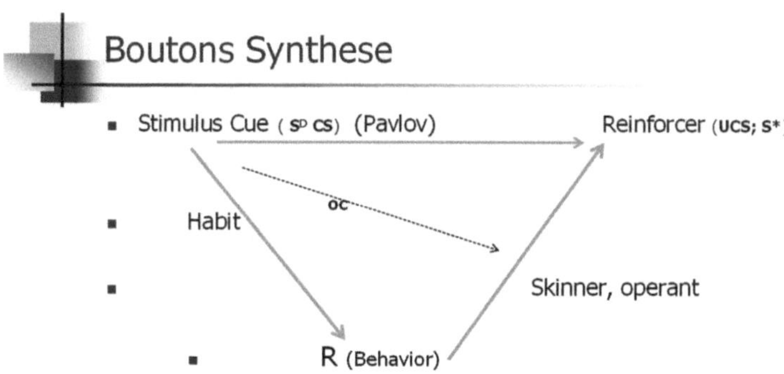

Figure 2 from Bouton, 2007, p. 404

S^D or CS stands for discriminative (S^D signal/cue) stimulus, the conditioned stimulus in the Pavlovian model (CS).

S^* or UCS is the biologically relevant stimulus (reinforcer), the unconditioned stimulus in Pavlov’s model.

The arrow from $R \rightarrow S^*$; UCS designates a theoretical association, i.e., an organism’s knowledge, that a specific behavior leads to a (primary) reinforcer.

OS cue denotes a context cue, informing the individual that, given the presence of a stimulus cue (S^D, CS), a specific behavior (R) leads to a reinforcer (UCS:S^*).

Combining the two models of Pavlov and Skinner results in a twofold learning process:

1. Through the relation S^D:CS → S^*, the organism gains information about the stimulus properties of the system (Pavlov). For example:
   "In the presence of the mother there is safety" OR:
   "In the presence of the mother there is harm".
2. The $R \rightarrow S^*$ relation allows the organism to gain information about the possibilities of attaining reinforcers within the system (Skinner). For example:
   "Getting close to the mother results in safety" OR:
   "Staying away from the mother prevents harm" (Avoidance).

As Bouton (2007) points out, avoidance behavior is always driven by fear. In the case of the chronically depressed patient, it is interpersonal fear that leads to interpersonal avoidance.

As we have summarized, at the beginning of therapy, the therapist defines the transference hypothesis. The following transference hypothesis will serve as an example:

If I make a mistake in front of my therapist, she will punish me.

The variables in Bouton's model are:

S^D, CS: Therapist;

S^*; UCS: Fear;

R: Interpersonal avoidance behavior in order to reduce fear.

In the negative phase of the IDE, cognitive evoked (Pavlovian) fear is evoked in the patient through tacit knowledge. The patient remembers (re-experiences) bad thoughts and associated feelings such as fear, pain, and sadness in the presence of a positive stimulus. Counterconditioning according to the principle of reciprocal inhibition (Schoepf et al., 2007) takes place by the benevolent therapist's reaction. The goal of counterconditioning (Cover Jones, 1924) is the substitution of an existing stimulus–response connection with a new (and better) one. Counterconditioning means that a stimulus–response connection that was established through classical conditioning is unlearned or reconditioned through conditioning with novel stimuli. The underlying mechanism is that of reciprocal inhibition (Hull, 1943; Wolpe, 1958). The feeling of aversion is weakened in the presence of a stimulus-induced positive emotion.

In the positive phase of the IDE, the therapist directs the patient's attention to his or her own behavior and draws a comparison to the behavior of the significant other (i.e., discrimination learning). The focus of the patient's attention is directed outside themselves, and is focused instead on the interpersonal situation and the situational context. Thus, the patient is enabled to perceive interpersonal signals of the other individual in an adequate manner, and the perceptual disconnection barrier has its first cracks. Based on concrete interpersonal in-session situations with the therapist, the patient learns something new about the stimulus properties of the system. The therapist's (S^D) reaction to the patient differs from that of the significant other: Instead of punishing, he or she reacts in a positive (*S**) way. When the patient talks about a mistake (*R*), the therapist (S^D) is interested and open minded. The patient makes a mistake and, instead of being punished, is complimented (*S**) for his or her openness by the therapist. This is the discrimination learning in the IDE. Moreover, through this kind of S–S learning, knowledge about what type of behavior (*R*) leads to reinforcement (*S**;UCS) changes. In order to achieve this, the therapist directs the patient's attention explicitly on the stimuli (cues) that are associated with the behavior in question (e.g., tone of voice, posture, facial expressions, choice of words, exact wording).

In the healing phase of the IDE, both discriminating the behavioral aspects and contrasting the meaningness between S^D;CS = therapist's behavior and significant others, the patient becomes aware of new interpersonal possibilities. The patient learns that he or she no longer needs to behave in a fearful, hostile, submissive, or aggressive way, since his or her behavior is followed by positive consequences (*S**). The mechanism of learning theory potentially underlying discriminative learning in the positive adaptive behavior results from the repeated demonstration and creation of awareness of the eliciting stimulus (behavior of the therapist). It may help the patient to integrate traumatic relationship experiences arising from negative experiences with maltreating significant other's into his self-picture and to experience a new interpersonal reality of liberation.

9.6 Administration of the SA

Two phases are carried out consecutively during the SA. After the patient has identified a stressful situational event that occurred recently (target situation), the SA starts with the *Elicitation phase*. In the first step, the patient is asked to describe the identified situation in a purely observational, descriptive-modus not unlike watching a silent movie. Behavioral actions between interactants are reported until the therapist knows what happened first, then second, etc. Editorial comments by the patient concerning what he thought and felt are discouraged and the patient has to fix the end point of the situation. After the therapist has repeated the sequence of behavioral actions with pinpointing the beginning and the end of the described situation the therapist asks the patient in the second step what the situation meant for him to elicit his cognitive attribution(s). The therapist clarifies the meaning word by word as chronically depressed patients frequently misread situational events. In the third step, the verbal and nonverbal behavioral responses the patient experienced are highlighted. This is important as usually the striking interpersonal skills deficits of chronically depressed patients augment the negative impact they already have on others by being depressed. During the fourth step, the patient describes the situational outcome in behavioral terms; this is labeled the actual outcome (AO). The fifth step is crucial for the analysis. The therapist asks the patient how he wanted the situation to come out in behavioral terms; this is labeled the desired outcome (DO). Usually, in stressful situations there is a clear discrepancy between the AO and the DO. At this point, the therapist has created a negative-reinforcement situation in which the intrapersonal dissonance in the patient can be reduced later by more adaptive strategies. The following two steps are important for the patient in order to become cognitive–emotionally aware of the discrepancy between his actual outcome and the way he wanted to behave in the situation. Therefore in the sixth step, the patient has to judge if he has obtained what he wanted by comparing his AO with his DO. In the seventh step, the patient is gently asked by the therapist to explain why he has not got what he wanted, and to say it in simple words why he did not behave in the way he wanted to behave.

The second phase of the SA is called the *remediation phase*. In the first step, the therapist helps the patient to reduce the dissonance by pinpointing as well as shaping action interpretations and action reads that help the patient to act in favor of his DO. In the second step, missing verbal and nonverbal behaviors of the DO are shaped by the therapist usually in the form of role plays. In the third step the learning results are summarized by the patient in order to recognize what has been missed and to perceive what has helped him to produce his DO. The remediation phase ends with a future SA with the aim to transfer the DO from the therapy session to the daily living arena. Transfer is maximized because the target situations come out of the daily living experiences of the patient.

9.7 What Is Learned During SA

The learning benefits for the patient that result from applying the SA procedure are as follows: (1) the patient starts to think functionally about his relationship with the environment; (2) the patient becomes aware of the stimulus value he has on others and learns how to use it more effectively with respect to the desired outcome; (3) the patient learns to recognize the consequences of his behaviors that are antagonistic to the learned helplessness assumption that it does not matter how he behaves (perceived functionality); (4) the problematic intrapersonal areas of the disorder are addressed by cognitive remediating training through using the SA methodology and behavioral skill training is carried out during the end of the SA; (5) the patient gets a self-evaluate structure to use beyond therapy to assess situational performance. From a learning theory perspective, the SA enables the patient to improve skillful behavior in interpersonal situation. During SA, the patient is confronted with all aspects of his/her reaction: the patient is forced to confront with avoided thoughts, avoided emotions, and avoided physiological reactions. From this point of view, the SA can be seen either as a tool that improves problem-solving behavior as well as an exposure method. With the therapist he/she goes through the activated fear reaction during the elicitation phase, especially at step 5 (DO) and step 7 (patient's explanation why he did not get what he wanted). The fear reaction is diminished when the patient is able to stand it—or in exposure terminology: when the patient habituates to his/her thoughts, emotions, and physiological symptoms. Throughout this phase, a new behavior is learned and can be approved.

9.8 Reducing Interpersonal Avoidance with Interpersonal Confrontation

9.8.1 The Role of Sensitization in the IDE

If the patient expects the therapist to react in a dismissive or devaluating manner to his or her behavior, and if the therapist's behavior repeatedly fails to meet the patient's expectations, it can be assumed that the patient will exhibit enhanced attention and increased readiness to show the behavior in question again. Reflecting upon the therapist's behavior and contrasting it with the significant other's behavior results in the patient focusing on the therapist's behavior. What happens next is this:

The patient realizes that *R* (making mistakes) in the presence of S^D (therapist) doesn't result in punishment (UCS) but, instead, leads to attention and interest (*S**; UCS). The specific stimulus properties of the therapist (therapist's behavior, cues, see above) and the patient's increased willingness to show the relevant behavior again indicate the induction process and trigger sensitization. Through stimulus discrimination and the sensitization that follows, the patient is able to learn a new type of interpersonal behavior.

Sensitization is defined as enhanced perception and increased responsiveness (response readiness) when repeatedly confronted with a certain sensory stimulus. Sensitization is a central nervous mechanism that plays an important physiological role in everyday life. As a result of the repeated presentation of a specific stimulus, an increase in response occurs. A typical increase in response is an increase of attention with respect to the stimulus cue. The better known term of habituation describes the opposite, meaning a decrease in response to a stimulus that is repeatedly presented.

Through sensitization, we learn to pay special attention to important stimuli, rather than ignoring them. Sensitization is largely unspecific to the stimulus, which makes it different from habituation. Both mechanisms are triggered by a specific cognitive stimulus processing and they originate in certain plastic processes in the nervous system. In the literature, sensitization is mostly described as a process that is caused by harmful or noxious stimulus exposure. However, from the neurology of learning we know that positive stimuli can also lead to sensitization (e.g., addiction memory; sensitization is a process contrary to tolerance development and it describes an increase of the potency of a substance given constant dosage, i.e., sensitization of the dopaminergic system). Another example comes from animal training: If, for example, calling a dog becomes meaningful to the dog because the dog gets a reward for coming to the owner, the importance of the stimulus to the dog increases. Therefore, the stimulus will be met with increased attention in the future. Habituation and sensitization are forms of nonassociative learning since no association or combination of stimuli is necessary. They are both stored as knowledge in the part of the memory system called implicit (nondeclarative) memory.

Sensitization is defined as an induction procedure (caused by specific stimulus properties) and the resulting measurable responsivity. If the induction procedure causes an appropriate response, its perpetual repetition leads to a specific learning process that causes hyper-responsivity. The therapist's job is to direct the patient's attention to the new behavior and its consequences. In the Skinnerian sense of the word, the therapist acts as a reinforcer for the patient whereas, within CBASP, the therapist's behavior becomes the discriminative stimulus cue. The patient is able to draw a connection between his or her own behavior and the situational context while the therapist focuses the patient on the relevant new stimuli, thereby starting the process of sensitization. As the patient's way of experiencing changes in the course of sensitization, old physiological patterns and cognitions are altered and a new behavior that is affected by the situation becomes possible.

Similar to exposure therapy where patients learn to omit their avoidance behavior (*R*) and experience a reduction of unpleasant symptoms, resulting in decreased response readiness (habituation), the learning process that is started during the positive phase of the IDE is that of sensitization. Therefore, the IDE can be described as a confrontation with new interpersonal behavior, in which avoidance behavior (interpersonal avoidance) is reduced.

The chronically depressed patient's early learning leads to a pervasive interpersonal avoidance strategy that is generalized to people. The fear of people results in a generalized detached interpersonal style, i.e., keeping distance from others, avoiding showing needs or avoiding making mistakes. Attaining interpersonal felt safety (*S**:UCS) with the clinician (*S*:CS) is the first step. Feeling safe with the therapist enables the patient to work on the *counter-conditioning* (extinction) of interpersonal avoidance by replacing avoidance with interpersonal approach behavior. Shaping new associations is facilitated when patients feel interpersonally safe. Therefore the main condition for the interpersonal confrontation during the IDE is a strong relation between therapist and patient in which the patient experiences the therapist as an SD for primary reinforcement. This is analogue to exposure therapy as described elsewhere. To get in situations or to experience thoughts or emotions which were normally avoided, patients need very good reasons (rationale of the therapy) and a strong relationship with the therapist.

As sensitization is a kind of nonassociative learning, the cerebral regions involved in IDE (bottom-up processing) are the brain stem and the basal forebrain. The internal reactions provoked by the therapist's signals (i.e., the therapist's the behavior) could be instances of so-called basic emotions (information from the environment is translated into internal codes, depending on the degree of attention) that are connected to new behavior and are stored as interoceptive stimuli. The therapist uses the detected basic emotion in the course of the therapy, making it the focus during the healing phase of IDE and using it as an action directive for the remainder of the exercise.

With regards to content, the basic emotions mentioned above are the ones that represent relationships with other people (relational content of emotion) and were triggered during the positive phase of IDE. We know that short-term memory and long-term memory share the same fundamental processes. Short-term and long-term sensitization leads to changes in the strength of synaptic connections between sensory and motor neurons (heterosynaptic reinforcement). In both cases, the increase is due to a heightened release of the corresponding transmitter (serotonin cAMP). This is the reason why IDE should be performed several times in the course of the therapy. The aim is to achieve long-term storage and activation of important cues and emotions.

9.9 Conclusion

IDE and SA are important techniques within the CBASP method for treating chronic depression. The exercises have been described from a learning theory perspective, trying to carve out exposure aspects of IDE and SA. Furthermore, the process of sensitization is assumed to be the mechanism that is started during the positive phase of the IDE. The relationships between bottom-up methods, short-term memory, and long-term memory have been elaborated. In order to develop a rational model of this particular therapeutic tool that goes beyond the present theoretical considerations, empirical data will be needed. By conducting therapy studies and using imaging technologies, more can be learned about the fundamental mechanisms (processes of learning and memory) that take place during an IDE.

Here the working definition of Neuropsychotherapy given by Walter, Berger, and Schnell (2009) fits well. As the authors pointed out, Neuropsychotherapy is about the identification of mediators and functional targets, determination of new therapeutic routes to such targets and the design of psychotherapeutic techniques.

Following this definition, the next step to take is to develop a rational model of the CBASP methods (SA and IDE) that goes beyond the present theoretical considerations. By conducting therapy studies and using imaging technologies, more can be learned about the fundamental mechanisms (what is learned, the role of habituation, sensitization, and memory) that take place during SA and IDE. Therefore, empirical data will be needed to find neural signatures of the psychological mechanisms.

References

Bandura, A. (1967). Behavioral psychotherapy. *Scientific American, 216*, 78–86.

Bouton, M. E. (2007). *Learning and behavior: A contemporary synthesis*. Sunderland: Sinauer Associates.

Cover Jones, M. (1924). A laboratory study of feat: The case of Peter. *Pedagogical Seminary, 31*, 308–315.

Hayes, S. C., Strosahl, K. D., & Wilson, K. G. (1999). *Acceptance and commitment therapy—An experimental approach to behavior change*. New York: Guilford Press.

Hofmann, S. G., & Asmundson, G. J. (2008). Acceptance and mindfulness-based therapy: New wave or old hat? *Clinical Psychology Review, 28*(1), 1–16.

Hull, C. L. (1943). *Principles of behavior*. New York: Appleton-Century-Crofts.

McCullough, J. P., Jr. (2000). *Treatment for chronic depression: Cognitive behavioral analysis system of psychotherapy (CBASP)*. New York: Guilford.

McCullough, J. P., Jr. (2006). *Treating chronic depression with disciplined personal involvement: Cognition behavioral analysis system of psychotherapy (CBASP)*. Berlin: Springer.

McCullough, J. P., Jr. (2003). Treatment for chronic depression: Cognitive behavioral analysis system of psychotherapy (CBASP). *Journal of Psychotherapy Integration, 13*, 241–263.

Nisbett, R., & Wilson, T. (1977). Telling more than we can know: Verbal reports on mental processes. *Psychological Review, 84*, 231–259.

Piaget, J. (1971/original work published in 1963). *Biology and knowledge*. Chicago: The University of Chicago Press (Original work published in 1967).

Polanyi, M. (1966). *The tacit dimension*. New York: Doubleday.

Schoepf, D., Konradt, B., & Walter, H. (2007). Specific psychotherapy of chronic depression with the cognitive behavioral analysis system of psychotherapy. *Nervenheilkunde, 26*(9), 790–802.

Schoepf, D., & McCullough, J. P., Jr. (2009). *CBASP's cutting edges to change the behaviour of the chronically depressed patient*. A 2-Day-CBASP-Workshop, University Bonn.

Schoepf, D., & Penberthy, J. K. (2010). Cognitive behavioral analysis system of psychotherapy (CBASP): New applications and neurobiological mechanisms. Overview of the model. *Symposium 33:KCB 101*. Boston: World Congress of Behavioral and Cognitive Therapies.

Schoepf, D., Neudeck, P., & Walter, H. (2011). *Learning theory aspects of the interpersonal discrimination exercise (IDE) and clinical applications*. Lübeck: Third international CBASP-Network Conference.

Schoepf, D., & Neudeck, P. (2011). Cognitive behavioral analysis system of psychotherapy (CBASP): A disorder oriented, theory-driven psychotherapy method from the "third generation" of behavior therapy models, designed for the treatment of chronic depression. In T. Uehera (Ed.), *Psychiatric disorders-worldwide advances*. ISBN 978-953-833-5.

Skinner, B. F. (1953). *Science and human behavior*. New York: Free Press.

Walter, H., Berger, M., & Schnell, K. (2009). Neuropsychotherapy. Conceptual, empirical and neuroethical issues. *European Archives of Psychiatry and Clinical Neuroscience, 259*(2), 173–182.

Wolpe, J. (1958). *Psychotherapy by reciprocal inhibition*. Stanford: Stanford University Press.

Chapter 10
Emotion-Focused Techniques in Schema Therapy and the Role of Exposure Techniques

Gitta A. Jacob and Arnoud Arntz

Dr. Gitta Jacob is a licensed psychotherapist (CBT) and research fellow with a scholarship of the Margarete von Wrangell Habilitation Programme Baden-Württemberg in the Department of Clinical Psychology and Psychotherapy, Freiburg, Germany. Her main research interests are Borderline Personality Disorder and emotion-focused interventions.

G.A. Jacob (✉)
Clinical Psychology and Psychotherapy, Institute for Psychology, University of Freiburg, Engelbergerstraße 41, D 79085 Freiburg, Germany
e-mail: gitta.jacob@psychologie.uni-freiburg.de

A. Arntz
Clinical Psychology and Experimental Psychopathology, Maastricht University, Maastricht, The Netherlands
e-mail: arnoud.arntz@maastrichtuniversity.nl

P. Neudeck and H.-U. Wittchen (eds.), *Exposure Therapy: Rethinking the Model – Refining the Method*, DOI 10.1007/978-1-4614-3342-2_10,

Professor Dr. Arnoud Arntz is a full Professor of Clinical Psychology and Experimental Psychopathology at Maastricht University, the Netherlands. He is scientific director of the University's Research Institute of Experimental Psychopathology and director of the Postgraduate Clinical Psychology Programme in the south of the Netherlands. He is also associated as a licensed psychotherapist with the Maastricht Community Mental Health Centre.

10.1 Introduction

During the last decade, Schema Therapy (ST), a recent CBT development mainly for the treatment of personality disorders (Arntz & van Genderen, 2009; Young, Klosko & Weishaar, 2003), has become increasingly popular. ST integrates traditional CBT with elements of psychodynamic therapy, experiential therapies, and humanistic therapy. Emotion-focused interventions are extensively used, and systematic emotional work is central to this approach. However, different from standard CBT, ST does not mainly use exposure techniques aiming at habituation and extinction. Instead, the main focus is on changing the implicit and explicit meaning of emotional triggers through emotional restructuring mostly by means of imagery exercises, "chair work," or historical role plays.

This chapter provides, first, a brief overview of the ST approach. Secondly, the model of emotional work in ST is explained. Finally, studies investigating both the effectiveness of ST and emotion-focused interventions (i.e., therapeutic techniques aiming at a direct change of problematic emotions) as used in ST are summarized and open questions are discussed.

10.2 The Schema Therapy Model

The two central concepts in ST are the so-called *early maladaptive schemas* (EMS) and the *schema modes*. EMS as defined by ST are "extremely stable and enduring themes, that develop during childhood and are elaborated upon throughout an individual's lifetime" (Young, 1995). Schema modes, in contrast, represent the

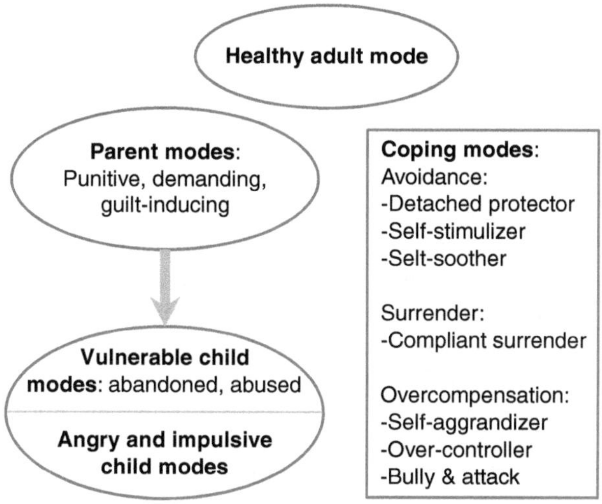

Fig. 10.1 General mode concept

moment-to-moment emotional and cognitive states and coping responses that are active at a given point in time, in which an EMS is triggered. For example, a patient may experience feelings of anxiety or abandonment. At another moment, the same patient may suppress these feelings and feel numb or empty. Both states are conceptualized as different schema modes. The mode model generally describes the rapid shifting in emotion (i.e., shifting between modes) and behavior demonstrated by patients suffering from severe personality disorders (overview in Lobbestael, van Vreeswijk & Arntz, 2007). Schema modes can be triggered by emotional events and an individual may shift from one schema mode into another depending on the situation, the mode constellation, and his individual reactivity.

The concept of schema modes comprises both a general approach and disorder-specific mode conceptualizations. Within the *general approach*, four categories of modes are defined: The first mode category is that of the maladaptive child modes which develop when certain basic emotional needs were not adequately met in childhood. Childhood modes are characterized by strong negative feelings, such as intensive fear of abandonment, helplessness, sadness, rage, or anger. The second category describes dysfunctional parent modes, which reflect internalized problem behaviors of parents, peers, or other significant others toward the patient during childhood. Dysfunctional parent modes are accompanied by self-devaluation, self-hate, or putting extremely high pressure upon oneself. The third category comprises the dysfunctional coping modes that reflect excessive use of maladaptive coping styles of overcompensation, avoidance, or surrender. They occur, for example, when patients suppress their feelings completely or when they cope with threatening situations by exerting overly aggressive behaviors. Finally, there is the healthy adult mode which includes functional cognitions, thoughts, and behaviors (Young et al., 2003). Figure 10.1 gives an overview of the schema mode conceptualization.

Regarding *specific mode concepts*, a particular personality disorder (PD) is characterized by a typical set of modes. The most commonly used specific mode model is the model of borderline personality disorder (BPD; Arntz & van Genderen, 2009), which comprises a strong punitive parent mode, an abandoned, abused child mode, an angry and/or impulsive child mode, and the detached protector coping mode. Pervasive feelings of abandonment and anxiety are connected with the vulnerable child mode, which is assumed to be related to childhood traumatization and abandonment. Problems with rage, such as rage attacks, belong to the angry child mode. The impulsive behavior of BPD is reflected by the impulsive child mode, which fulfills own needs regardless of negative consequences. Self-hate and low self-esteem, which are also typical of BPD, belong to the punitive parent mode, reflecting an internalization of punitive responses of the parents. The detached protector coping mode comprises behaviors that help the patient to suppress the negative emotions connected to dysfunctional child and parent modes; it includes behaviors aimed at numbing unfavorable emotional states such as emptiness or dissociation, for example, by substance abuse or bingeing. Further, the symptoms of identity disturbance and emotional impulsivity are connected to rapid mode switches. Self-harming behaviors such as cutting, are possibly associated with different modes—if the patient uses self-harm as a self-punishment, it belongs to the punitive parent mode, whereas feelings of numbness after self-injury behavior are considered to be part of the detached protector mode.

Case example Maria B

Maria is a 22-year-old woman with BPD. She reports cutting and alcohol abuse during acute emotional crisis, which often occurs in the context of interpersonal conflicts. When she goes clubbing with a new man, she often starts a sexual relationship quite quickly. In the beginning, she typically feels happy to make close contact with somebody, since she mostly feels lonely and abandoned. When a sexual interaction however starts, she is unable to set limits and tolerates sexual intercourse even when she doesn't feel desire. During intercourse, she feels numb and often uses alcohol or drugs. Afterwards she hates herself, feels ashamed and guilty, and often cuts her legs in order to calm down and to punish herself. When she is in this state, her level of functioning declines, i.e., she holes up at home, spends all day with screen activities including impulsive online shopping, and is on sick leaves. Frequent sick leaves often cause conflicts at work, resulting in frequent job changes. Maria usually feels very helpless, but is hardly angry at the same time. However, when a relationship gets closer, she sometimes gets furiously enraged. Maria grew up in an unstable family, her father was an aggressive alcoholic and her mother did not dare leave him. At age 8–10, Maria was sexually abused by a friend of her father, who often served as her babysitter.

Maria's sense of abandonment and her feelings of shame and guilt are conceptualized as vulnerable, abandoned child mode. Rage attacks are related to the angry child mode. Self-hate and self-cutting for the purpose of self-punishment refer to the punitive parent mode, which developed probably due to the

(continued)

(continued)

experiences of aggression by her father, and sexual abuse by one of his friends. Feeling numb and using alcohol to detach from unfavorable emotions belong to the detached protector mode. Her inability to set limits and her pattern of giving in to sexual contact she actually doesn't want may be seen as compliant surrender mode, which was probably also modeled by her mother, who stayed with the father and sustained his aggression instead of leaving him.

The general goal of ST is to help the patient understand how dysfunctional schemas or schema modes have developed, how the patient is handicapped by these schemas and modes today, which needs have not been met during childhood, and how own needs can be adequately met today.

10.3 Treatment

At first, an individual schema mode model is set up together with the patient. In the following, all problems or symptoms are conceptualized and treated in terms of the modes involved. Childhood modes are elicited, vented, soothed, and mitigated. Dysfunctional parent modes are reduced. Patients are empathically confronted with dysfunctional coping modes, their pros and cons are discussed, and they are reduced in the therapy setting and then transferred into the patients' everyday life. Figure 10.2 gives an overview of the treatment.

ST uses emotional, cognitive, behavioral, and therapy relationship techniques to reach these goals. On the *cognitive* level, characteristics and origins of modes are discussed, related cognitive distortions are restructured (for example, "I am worthless" as a cognition related to the punitive parent mode). On the *behavioral* level, usual CBT techniques are applied to reduce symptomatic behaviors, which are often (but not always) part of the dysfunctional coping modes (for example, assertiveness training to teach setting limits or skills training to replace self-injuring behaviors). When patients display persistent avoidance behavior, the therapist may use in-vivo

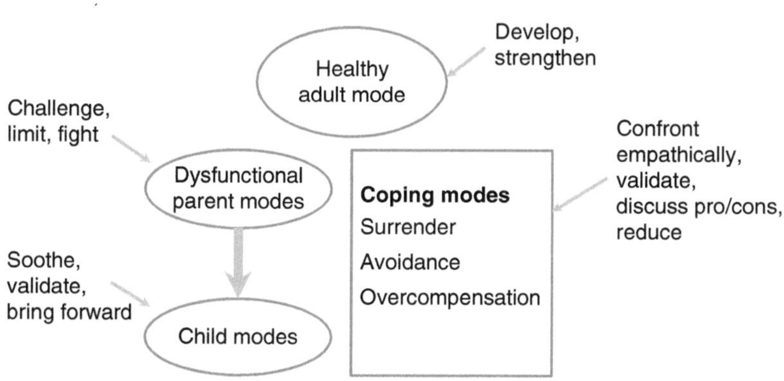

Fig. 10.2 General treatment principles

exposure exercises. Usually, this is done at a later stage in therapy, and often prepared by the use of emotional techniques. On the *emotional* level, the focus is on child and dysfunctional parent modes, since these modes are most strongly associated with intensive unfavorable emotional states such as self-hate, guilt, low self-esteem (dysfunctional parent modes), or abandonment, loneliness, shame, threat, anxiety, sadness, disgust (vulnerable child modes), rage, and anger (angry child mode). In emotional interventions, these emotions are firstly clarified and processed; and then restructured mainly via transformational chair dialogues and imagery techniques (see Sect. 8.3). Concerning the *therapy relationship*, the therapist is empathic, active, self-disclosing, and offers sincere contact as a real person. "Limited reparenting" is used to fulfill needs of the patient which have not been met during childhood, however, to a limited degree. The therapy relationship is also an important vehicle in emotional interventions, since the therapist models functional behaviors and feelings in chair dialogues, comforts the vulnerable child mode, fights the punitive parent mode in imagery exercises, directly supports the transfer to everyday life with the help of transitional objects, etc.

10.4 Emotional Techniques in Schema Therapy

Emotional interventions in ST aim (1) to overcome dysfunctional coping modes and to help the patient to feel emotions which have been avoided so far, (2) to clarify and process problematic negative emotions, (3) to change implicit and explicit meaning, and (4) to strengthen positive emotions and the experience of safe attachment.

10.4.1 Overcome Emotion Avoidance

This is a general goal of all emotional techniques both in ST and in other psychotherapy approaches. Concepts such as defense mechanisms, emotion suppression (Gross & Levenson, 1993), or experiential avoidance (EA), the dysfunctional avoidance of emotions and other private experiences (Hayes, Wilson, Strosahl, Gifford & Follette, 1996) imply that avoiding unfavorable emotions is unhealthy. EA has been investigated in a number of recent studies, and substantially overlaps with dysfunctional coping in ST, in particular with the avoidant coping of avoidant and detached protector modes. Research in EA shows that high EA increases the risk of relapse in substance use disorders, EA moderates the relationship between traumatic experiences and psychological stress, and increases the symptom severity in different psychological disorders (overview in Chawla & Ostafin, 2007; Kashdan, Breen, Afram & Terhar, 2010). High EA is a predictor for negative psychotherapy outcome (Rüsch et al., 2008; Berking, Neacsiu, Comtois & Linehan, 2009) and is associated with lower pleasant activities and less positive emotions (Kashdan, Barrios, Forsyth & Steger, 2006).

Different techniques are used in ST to overcome emotion avoidance or coping modes, respectively. In the therapy relationship, the therapist welcomes emotions, labels them as important, and expresses a clear motivation for emotional work. On the cognitive level, the therapist firstly explains to the patient the disadvantages of emotion avoidance, pros and cons of dysfunctional coping, and avoidance of emotions. When a patient is frightened by the idea of experiencing emotions, therapist and patient discuss how to set up emotional work in small steps. Thereby the patient is pushed into emotional experiences; however, this is within a well-controlled process. This process is very similar to the beginning of exposure therapy. However, different from exposure therapy where emotions are meant to be processed until the patient habituates, during ST emotions are elicited in order to get a starting point for techniques aimed at changing these emotions.

If a dysfunctional coping mode is very strong, cognitive interventions may not be sufficient to motivate the patient to start with emotional interventions. Then two-chair dialogues (coping mode and therapist) with the respective coping mode are used to validate this mode intensively, to explore its functions in more detail, and to find out more about the emotions "behind" it.

10.4.2 Clarify and Process Problematic Negative Emotions

This is also a general goal of all emotional techniques. For example, the mindfulness-oriented "third-wave therapies" (overview in Ost, 2008) aim at decreasing EA by focusing on acceptance instead of control over emotions. As long as they avoid emotions, patients often don't know which emotions they actually feel and what they need. When they start to actually experience emotions, patients get familiar with their feelings and learn to tolerate intensive negative affect, which in turn is an important prerequisite for reducing avoidance. However, in ST "processing" does usually not mean to expose a patient to problematic emotions until habituation. It rather means to process an emotion as long as necessary—until the characteristics of the respective emotion (i.e., shame, sadness), the connected needs (i.e., need for comfort), and/or its biographical background become clear.

Typical emotional interventions with this goal are diagnostic imagery exercises and chair dialogues. Diagnostic imagery exercises are used when a current situation triggers an unexpectedly strong emotional reaction or an unexpectedly strong coping response. The patient closes eyes, relaxes, and re-experiences the current trigger situation as real as possible in imagery. Feelings related to the situation are explored and deepened by focusing on affective and bodily experiences. When the current emotion is clear, the patient is asked to wipe away the inner image and build an affective bridge to earlier biographical images (i.e., "do you remember childhood situations when you felt similar?"). The biographical image is explored, again with an emphasis on (negative) emotions (i.e., "how does the child in the image feel?") and (unmet) needs (i.e., "what does the child need?"). Feelings like loneliness, shame, or sadness are connected with the vulnerable child mode. Self-hate or pressure upon oneself are connected with the punitive parent mode. This exercise often clarifies the biographical origin of problematic emotions and related interactional or behavioral patterns. It helps the patient to understand himself and his reactions on a deeper level. In doing so, the connection between trigger situations and negative emotional reactions becomes weaker, as the emotional reaction is put into perspective.

Case example: Diagnostic imagery with Maria

Maria reports intensive social anxiety combined with self-hate as a central emotional problem, which can be triggered by all kinds of social situations. In a diagnostic imagery exercise, she starts from a party situation in which she felt anxious and threatened. The therapist asks her for a childhood image in which "little Maria" felt similar. Maria recalls a situation in which her drunken father enters the house and starts shouting at her and her mother in a very aggressive way, calling them bad names. Little Maria feels horribly frightened. Anxiety and threat resemble her social anxiety (→ vulnerable child mode), while the negative, aggressive messages of the father can be linked to self-hate (→ punitive parent mode).

Chair dialogues are also a useful tool to clarify inner conflicts or to view a situation from different (inner) perspectives. They can be used when the nature of the emotional experience is ambivalent or unclear, or when an inner conflict seems to be important. Different chairs are used for different perspectives or feelings involved. In ST, different chairs are usually related to different schema modes. The patient alternatingly takes a seat and expresses the related perspective or feeling on each chair. When another emotion pops up during the exercise, the patients changes the seat back to the chair connected to the pop-up emotion, or another chair is added. Note that patients with strong avoidance of emotions often devaluate their own emotions ("emotions are ridiculous and stupid"). This position is connected with the punitive parent mode and biographical experiences concerning the devaluation of emotions are explored. The tasks of the therapist are to detect different emotions and perspectives, to help the patient differentiate between them, and to model those emotions or perspectives the patients finds hard to express. This exercise clarifies ambivalent emotions and inner conflicts. Often the solution for an emotional problem becomes clear by exploring the nature of the problem in this way.

10.4.3 Change of Felt Meaning

In general, emotional interventions are necessary when a distorted cognition cannot be changed by means of cognitive interventions. When a patient responds to the therapist "I know that you're right, but I don't feel it," he relates to the emotional meaning of the respective cognition. Emotional interventions trigger and change the emotional meaning. In ST, negative meaning is related to dysfunctional parent or child modes, and the desired (healthy) meaning is connected to the healthy adult mode. Within emotional interventions, the healthy adult mode either fights the dysfunctional parent mode and/or defends the vulnerable child mode and cares for it. Thus, the healthy meaning is intensified. Both imagery exercises and chair dialogues can be used to set up this process.

With respect to imagery techniques, the technique of *im*agery *res*cripting (ImRS; Arntz & Weertman, 1999) is most useful. In an ImRS exercise, the patient is asked to enter a traumatic biographic (for example, abuse or bullying) situation in imagery. The patient may enter the traumatic situation either directly or via an affective bridge as in a diagnostic imagery exercise. The patient has to stay in the traumatic situation until he clearly feels the related emotions and needs. Note that from an ST-perspective, it is not necessary to relive the whole trauma. In the following "rescripting" part of the exercise, the needs of the patient are fulfilled in the image. Usually a helping person enters the imagery, since in his imagination, the patient is typically either a child or in a helpless position. The helping person may be the patient himself as a strong adult, or the therapist, or any other helping person. In a typical ImRS exercise, the patient recalls a traumatic childhood situation of sexual, physical, or emotional abuse. The therapist enters the image, stops the perpetrator, and protects and cares for the child. Often the therapist then takes the child to a better, i.e. safe place. During the rescripting part, negative emotions such as threat, anxiety, or shame are reduced, and safety is induced. By this, the therapist actively brings about a change in the meaning of the original trauma. As compared to trauma exposition, a patient also relives part of the trauma during an ImRS exercise. However, the trauma is not necessarily fully processed, and the general goal of the exercise is not habituation, but an active change of the meaning of the trauma, including its implications.

Case example: Imagery rescripting with Maria

Since Maria is deeply frightened in the diagnostic imagery (see above), the therapists suggest to rescript the memory. The therapist enters the image of the shouting father and the frightened little girl and offers "little Maria" to hind behind her while she is talking with her father. She then harshly asks the father to stop shouting. As the father gets even more aggressive and threatens to hit the therapist, two police men enter the scene and arrest the father. Then the therapist asks little Maria what she'd like to do and she wishes to go to the playground together. On the playground, the therapist asks Maria about her feelings. She says that it feels good to know that the father has been arrested; however, she's scared what will happen when he returns. The therapist offers her to take her to the therapist's home and stay there in the future. Maria feels much safer with this solution and they leave together to get to the therapist's home.

Chair dialogues can be used for the change of felt meaning as well. Emotional meaning can be changed by chair dialogues in which the healthy adult mode cares for the vulnerable child mode and fights the punitive parent mode—thus, the patient experiences in a highly emotional way that his needs are important and that self-deprecation can be reduced. As long as the patient himself does not feel strong enough to fight the dysfunctional parent mode or care for the vulnerable child mode, the therapists models the healthy adult mode or guides the patient to express it.

Another chair work format is so-called "historical role plays." In this exercise, the therapist and the patient play a traumatic biographical memory together as a role play, in which the patient takes not only the own role (usually as a child) but also the role of the perpetrator. This is particularly helpful, when a patients feels that he is bad or guilty because somebody treated him badly as a child; however, the respective parent figures did not intentionally harm him, but were too weak to protect him against abuse, or too emotional to offer stability and safety. By switching both into the perspective of himself as a child and of the parent figure, the patient experiences another meaning of the situation.

10.4.4 Intensify the Experience of Positive Emotions and Safe Attachment

Patients with mental disorders typically suffer from a high load of unfavorable emotions and often lack positive emotions. In reverse, positive emotions buffer against distress and are related high psychological well-being and self-esteem (Tugade, Fredrickson & Feldman, 2004). Many CBT interventions aim at increasing positive experiences, such as the training of positive activities. Patients with severe PDs, however, often find it hard to experience the respective positive emotions, as they feel mainly threatened, anxious, ashamed, or "odd" in social situations. However, social situations are most relevant to positive emotions, since positive emotions such as safety, love, or joy are usually connected to positive attachment experiences, and most positively evaluated situations are social in nature as well (Jacob et al., 2011).

Thus, ImRS exercises and chair dialogues are also used to intensify positive emotional experiences. The most effective technique is probably the reparenting part of ImRS exercises, after the parent mode has been battered. In the final phase of an ImRS exercise, the helping person/healthy adult mode offers support and positive attachment experiences, such as spending time together playing, talking, eating, etc. This is particular helpful for patients with very unsafe attachment and high anxiety in social situations, since they have the opportunity to engage in safe attachment-related emotions.

10.5 Current State of Research

Studies investigating the effectiveness of ST in patients with BPD according to the manual of Arntz and van Genderen (2009) demonstrated high effectiveness of ST as individual therapy in all BPD symptoms, with respect to functional impairment and secondary outcome measures such as measures of psychopathology (Giesen-Bloo et al., 2006; Nadort et al., 2009). Farrell, Shaw and Webber (2009) found high effectiveness of ST in BPD patients also in a group therapy setting. Since high negative affect and high emotional dysregulation are prominent features of BPD (Lieb, Zanarini, Schmahl, Linehan & Bohus, 2004), emotion-focused interventions were evaluated as extremely helpful. For example, patients' ratings of the therapy relationship were significantly more positive in ST as compared to transference-focused therapy (Spinhoven, Giesen-Bloo, van Dyck, Kooiman & Arntz, 2007).

A range of studies also investigated different facets of imagery and ImRS in other mental disorders than BDP. For example, negative trauma-related images are a central diagnostic criterion of posttraumatic stress disorder (PTSD). However, a growing number of studies show high presence of negative inner biographical images in many other psychological disorders, including obsessive–compulsive disorder (Rachman, 2007), agoraphobia (Day, Holmes & Hackmann, 2004), social phobia (Hackmann, Clark & McManus, 2000), and eating disorders (Somerville, Cooper & Hackmann, 2007). For social phobia, it has been shown that negative self-imagery has a causal role in the development and maintenance of social anxiety (Hirsch, Mathews, Clark, Williams & Morrison, 2006), and that negative images contaminate interpersonal interactions in various ways (Hirsch, Meynen & Clark, 2004). Inner images are clearly different from intrusive thoughts (Hagenaars, Brewin, van Minnen, Holmes & Hoogduin, 2010) and their relationship with emotion is closer than the connection between language and emotion (review in Holmes & Mathews, 2010).

Correspondingly, therapeutic techniques using imagery instead of verbalization probably have a greater impact on emotions (Holmes, Lang & Shah, 2009). Several studies showed surprisingly positive effects of ImRS on different disorders. It is successful in PTSD (Arntz, Tiesema & Kindt, 2007), even when prior exposure therapy had failed (Grunert, Weis, Smucker & Christianson, 2007), in social phobia (Wild, Hackmann & Clark, 2007, 2008), and in depression (Wheatley et al., 2007; Brewin et al., 2009). ImRS reduces also nonfear emotions, which are hardly treatable by exposure techniques, such as guilt, disgust, or anger (Arntz et al., 2007; Grunert et al., 2007; Mason & Richardson, 2010). In patients with personality disorders, ImRS can be effectively conducted both with present and past biographical situations (Weertman & Arntz, 2007).

A few experimental studies provide further evidence for ImRS. Results indicate that ImRS may indeed rather change the meaning of a conditioned stimulus than extinguish the association between conditioned and unconditioned stimulus ("new learning instead of extinction learning"). Hagenaars and Arntz (2010) used a trauma film paradigm, in which study participants watched a movie to induce intrusive imagery, and afterward got different experimental "treatments" including an ImRS condition. As compared to unrelated positive imagery and mere exposure, ImRS was followed by significantly less intrusions in the following week. Dibbets, Poort and Arntz (2010) showed in a conditioning study less fear renewal after ImRS as compared to normal extinction, when the conditioned stimulus was again presented in a new context after the extinction phase. Two studies showed stronger induction particularly of positive emotions with imagery strategies as compared with cognitive strategies (Holmes et al., 2009; Jacob et al., 2011). Positive self-related imagery also seems to enhance the processing of positive self-representations (Stopa, 2010).

10.6 Discussion

This chapter summarizes the central ideas of emotion-focused work in schema therapy. Emotion-focused interventions in ST aim at clarifying, processing, and restructuring emotions. Different from exposure techniques, the rationale behind emotional change is not habituation, but rather to actively change the quality of emotions and thereby to change the meaning of the traumatic memories. Similar to exposure techniques, however, emotional interventions are discussed between therapist and patient and stepwise introduced into therapy. When emotional interventions are hindered by specific modes (e.g., a punitive parent mode forbidding the patient to engage), the function of the mode is discussed first and the mode is reduced step by step.

Schema therapists use interventions which have been developed by different experiential therapy approaches, such as psychodrama or Gestalt therapy. Different from some of these approaches, however, emotional processes are actively guided by the therapist in ST, who takes care that the patient feels safe. The therapy relationship is an important facilitator of social emotional learning. Thus, these emotion-focused techniques can also be used in the treatment of patients with severe PD who are at high risk of decompensation when emotional processes are stimulated. Although ST uses many emotional techniques, classical exposure exercises are seldom used. Only later in treatment, when the focus is more on the present, classical exposure in vivo can be used to address rigid situational avoidance. But even then, this will be supported by emotion-focused exercises to prepare the patient. One of the main reasons why ST doesn't often use exposure techniques is the developmental perspective that ST takes. For example, in processing childhood traumas, ST doesn't use prolonged imageary exposure to trauma memories, as one wouldn't send a child alone, without support, into highly threatening situations. Rather, one would first build a safe attachment relationship, bring safety into threatening situations, prevent trauma, and correct dysfunctional conclusions the child made.

Empirical studies indicate high effectiveness of ST in the treatment of BPD. A first RCT investigating ST for BPD in groups (Farrell et al., 2009) showed excellent results. This may be due to the focus on positive attachment experiences with therapists and peers in the therapy group. A large international RCT testing effectiveness and cost-effectiveness of ST for BPD in groups[1] with a special focus on the therapy relationship is under way.

In other PDs, ST is also highly effective, albeit the effects do not reach the results of BPD treatment (Arntz, 2010). Building upon these positive experiences, clinical developments of ST for different disorders are under way (for example, obsessive–compulsive disorder; Gross, Stelzer & Jacob, 2012). Further clinical trials are necessary to test the effects of ST in other disorders.

With respect to imagery exercises, many further questions warrant for discussion. Is the use of revenge fantasies helpful or dangerous? Does fully processing a traumatic memory increase the effect of ImRS as compared to ImRS after partial processing of the trauma? How important is the induction of positive emotions during an ImRS, and how can it best be achieved?

ImRS is a widely used emotion-focussed technique which has already been subject to a number of empirical studies. Other techniques which are used in ST, such as chair dialogues or historical role plays remain understudied and call for further investigation, i.e. comparison to ImRS and classical imaginary exposure.

With respect to coping modes, we mostly referred to studies investigating experiential avoidance. The overlap between EA and coping modes has to be clarified. Last but not least, the general concept that emotion-focused interventions help to reduce coping modes over the course of therapy, is currently being tested in longitudinal studies).

References

Arntz, A. (2010). Schema therapy for cluster-C personality disorders. *Keynote at the third meeting of the international society of schema therapy ISST*. July 2010, Berlin.

Arntz, A., Tiesema, M., & Kindt, M. (2007). Treatment of PTSD: A comparison of imaginal exposure with and without imagery rescripting. *Journal of Behavior Therapy and Experimental Psychiatry, 38*, 345–370.

Arntz, A., & van Genderen, H. (2009). *Schema therapy for borderline personality disorder*. Sussex: Wiley.

Arntz, A., & Weertman, A. (1999). Treatment of childhood memories: Theory and practice. *Behaviour Research and Therapy, 37*, 715–740.

Berking, M., Neacsiu, A., Comtois, K. A., & Linehan, M. M. (2009). The impact of experiential avoidance on the reduction of depression in treatment for borderline personality disorder. *Behaviour Research and Therapy, 47*, 663–670.

Brewin, C. R., Wheatley, J., Patel, T., Fearon, P., Hackmann, A., Wells, A., et al. (2009). Imagery rescripting as a brief stand-alone treatment for depressed patients with intrusive memories. *Behaviour Research and Therapy, 47*, 569–576.

[1] Funding for German centers (Freiburg, Hamburg, Lübeck) by the Else Kröner-Fresenius-Stiftung; funding in the Netherlands by grant 171-20-2009 from ZonMW, the Netherlands Organisation for Health Research and Development.

Chawla, N., & Ostafin, B. (2007). Experiential avoidance as a functional dimensional approach to psychopathology: An empirical review. *Journal of Clinical Psychology, 63*, 871–890.

Day, S. J., Holmes, E. A., & Hackmann, A. (2004). Occurrence of imagery and its link with early memories in agoraphobia. *Memory, 12*, 416–427.

Dibbets, P., Poort, H., & Arntz, A. (2010). Preventing relapse: the additive effect of imagery rescripting to mere exposure. *Presentation at the third meeting of the international society of schema therapy ISST*. July 2010, Berlin.

Farrell, J., Shaw, I., & Webber, M. (2009). A schema-focused approach to group psychotherapy for outpatients with borderline personality disorder: A randomized controlled trial. *Journal of Behavior Therapy and Experiential Psychology, 40*, 317–328.

Giesen-Bloo, J., van Dyck, R., Spinhoven, P., van Tilburg, W., Dirksen, C., van Asselt, T., et al. (2006). Outpatient psychotherapy for borderline personality disorder: Randomized trial of schema-focused therapy vs. transference-focused psychotherapy. *Archives of General Psychiatry, 63*, 649–658.

Gross, J. J., & Levenson, R. W. (1993). Emotional suppression: Physiology, self-report, and expressive behavior. *Journal of Personality and Social Psychology, 64*, 970–986.

Grunert, B. K., Weis, J. M., Smucker, M. R., & Christianson, H. F. (2007). Imagery rescripting and reprocessing therapy after failed prolonged exposure for post-traumatic stress disorder following industrial injury. *Journal of Behavior Therapy and Experimental Psychiatry, 38*, 317–328.

Hackmann, A., Clark, D. M., & McManus, F. (2000). Recurrent images and early memories in social phobia. *Behaviour Research and Therapy, 38*, 601–610.

Hagenaars, M. A., & Arntz, A. (2010). The effect of post-trauma imagery rescripting on intrusion development and negative appraisal: An analogue experimental study. *Presentation at the third meeting of the international society of schema therapy ISST*. July 2010, Berlin.

Hagenaars, M. A., Brewin, C. R., van Minnen, A., Holmes, E. A., & Hoogduin, K. A. (2010). Intrusive images and intrusive thoughts as different phenomena: Two experimental studies. *Memory, 18*, 76–84.

Hayes, S. C., Wilson, K. G., Strosahl, K., Gifford, E. V., & Follette, V. M. (1996). Experiential avoidance and behavioral disorders: A functional dimensional approach to diagnosis and treatment. *Journal of Consulting and Clinical Psychology, 64*, 1152–1168.

Hirsch, C. R., Mathews, A., Clark, D. M., Williams, R., & Morrison, J. A. (2006). The causal role of negative imagery in social anxiety: A test in confident public speakers. *Journal of Behavior Therapy and Experimental Psychiatry, 37*, 159–170.

Hirsch, C. R., Meynen, T., & Clark, D. M. (2004). Negative self-imagery in social anxiety contaminates social interactions. *Memory, 12*, 496–506.

Holmes, E. A., Lang, T. J., & Shah, D. M. (2009). Developing interpretation bias modification as a "cognitive vaccine" for depressed mood: Imagining positive events makes you feel better than thinking about them verbally. *Journal of Abnormal Psychology, 118*, 76–88.

Holmes, E. A., & Mathews, A. (2010). Mental imagery in emotion and emotional disorders. *Clinical Psychology Review, 30*, 349–362.

Jacob, G. A., Arendt, J., Kolley, L., Scheel, C. N., Bader, K., Lieb, K., et al. (2011). Comparison of different strategies to decrease negative affect and increase positive affect in women with borderline personality disorder. *Behaviour Research and Therapy, 49*, 68–73.

Kashdan, T. B., Barrios, V., Forsyth, J. P., & Steger, M. F. (2006). Experiential avoidance as a generalized psychological vulnerability: Comparisons with coping and emotion regulation strategies. *Behaviour Research and Therapy, 44*, 1301–1320.

Kashdan, T. B., Breen, W. E., Afram, A., & Terhar, D. (2010). Experiential avoidance in idiographic, autobiographical memories: Construct validity and links to social anxiety, depressive, and anger symptoms. *Journal of Anxiety Disorders, 24*, 528–534.

Gross, E. N., Stelzer, N., & Jacob, G. A. (2012). Treating obsessive-compulsive disorder with the schema mode model. In: van Vreeswijk, M., Broersen, J. & Nadort, M. (Ed.), *Handbook of Schema Therapy: Theory, Research and Practice*, pp. 173–185. Sussex: Wiley.

Lieb, K., Zanarini, M. C., Schmahl, C., Linehan, M. M., & Bohus, M. (2004). Borderline personality disorder. *Lancet, 364*, 453–461.

Lobbestael, J., van Vreeswijk, M., & Arntz, A. (2007). Shedding light on schema modes: A clarification of the mode concept and its current research status. *Netherlands Journal of Psychology, 63*, 76–85.
Mason, E. C., & Richardson, R. (2010). Looking beyond fear: The extinction of other emotions implicated in anxiety disorders. *Journal of Anxiety Disorders, 24*, 63–70.
Nadort, M., Arntz, A., Smit, J. H., Giesen-Bloo, J., Eikelenboom, M., Spinhoven, P., et al. (2009). Implementation of outpatient schema therapy for borderline personality disorder with versus without crisis support by the therapist outside office hours: A randomized trial. *Behaviour Research and Therapy, 47*, 961–973.
Ost, L. G. (2008). Efficacy of the third wave of behavioral therapies: A systematic review and meta-analysis. *Behaviour Research and Therapy, 46*, 296–321.
Rachman, S. (2007). Unwanted intrusive images in obsessive-compulsive disorders. *Journal of Behavior Therapy and Experimental Psychiatry, 38*, 402–410.
Rüsch, N., Schiel, S., Corrigan, P. W., Leihener, F., Jacob, G. A., Olschewski, M., et al. (2008). Predictors of dropout from inpatient dialectical behavior therapy among women with borderline personality disorder. *Journal of Behavior Therapy and Experimental Psychiatry, 39*, 497–503.
Somerville, K., Cooper, M., & Hackmann, A. (2007). Spontaneous imagery in women with bulimia nervosa: An investigation into content, characteristics and links to childhood memories. *Journal of Behavior Therapy and Experimental Psychiatry, 38*, 435–446.
Spinhoven, P., Giesen-Bloo, J., van Dyck, R., Kooiman, K., & Arntz, A. (2007). The therapeutic alliance in schema-focused therapy and transference-focused psychotherapy for borderline personality disorder. *Journal of Consulting and Clinical Psychology, 75*, 104–115.
Stopa, L. (2010). Imagery and the self: does imagery rescripting work by making adaptive self-representations more available and accessible? *Presentation at the third meeting of the International Society of Schema Therapy ISST*. July 2010, Berlin.
Tugade, M. M., Fredrickson, B. L., & Feldman, B. L. (2004). Psychological resilience and positive emotional granularity: Examining the benefits of positive emotions on coping and health. *Journal of Personality, 72*, 1161–1190.
Weertman, A., & Arntz, A. (2007). Effectiveness of treatment of childhood memories in cognitivetherapy for personality disorders: A controlled study contrasting methods focusing on the present and methods focusing on childhood memories. *Behaviour Research and Therapy, 45*, 2133–2143.
Wheatley, J., Brewin, C. R., Patel, T., Hackmann, A., Wells, A., Fisher, P., et al. (2007). "I'll believe it when I can see it": Imagery rescripting of intrusive sensory memories in depression. *Journal of Behavior Therapy and Experimental Psychiatry, 38*, 371–385.
Wild, J., Hackmann, A., & Clark, D. M. (2008). Rescripting early memories linked to negative images in social phobia: A pilot study. *Behavior Therapy, 39*, 47–56.
Wild, J., Hackmann, A., & Clark, D. M. (2007). When the present visits the past: Updating traumatic memories in social phobia. *Journal of Behavior Therapy and Experimental Psychiatry, 38*, 386–401.
Young, J. E. (1995). *Cognitive therapy for personality disorders: A schema-focused approach*. Sarasota: Professional Resource Exchange.
Young, J. E., Klosko, J., & Weishaar, M. E. (2003). *Schema therapy: A practitioner's guide*. New York: Guilford.

Chapter 11
Interoceptive Exposure

Alexander L. Gerlach and Peter Neudeck

Alexander L. Gerlach is Professor for Clinical Psychology and Psychotherapy at the University of Cologne. His research specialties are the relevance of bodily symptoms in anxiety and somatoform disorders and research looking at mechanisms responsible for the link between substance abuse disorders and anxiety disorders. He is a licensed psychotherapist and heads an outpatient treatment center specialized in treating anxiety disorder patients.

A.L. Gerlach (✉)
Institute of Clinical Psychology and Psychotherapy, University of Cologne,
Höningerweg 115, Cologne 50969, Germany
e-mail: alexander.gerlach@uni-koeln.de

P. Neudeck
Praxis für Verhaltenstherapie,
Follerstr. 64, D-50676 Köln/Cologne, Germany
e-mail: peterneudeck@gmx.de

P. Neudeck and H.-U. Wittchen (eds.), *Exposure Therapy: Rethinking the Model – Refining the Method*, DOI 10.1007/978-1-4614-3342-2_11,

Dr. Peter Neudeck is a licensed psychotherapist specialized in cognitive behavioral therapy. He worked both in clinical and research positions and has established private practices for psychotherapy in Berlin and Cologne. He is also a lecturer and supervisor for graduate and postgraduate CBT-psychotherapy programs across Germany. He recently received further professional development in CBASP and systemic therapy. His main research activities include psychobiology and psychotherapy of anxiety disorders in exposure based treatments. He has released and numerous publications on exposure techniques in mental disorders.

11.1 Introduction: A Brief History of Interoceptive Exposure

The term "interoceptive exposure" was first introduced by Barlow (1988) in the context of the treatment of panic disorder. Interoceptive exposure was described as a method to expose an individual suffering from panic disorder to the bodily sensations typically experienced shortly before and during a panic attack (rather than to a feared object or situation; this fine-grades difference is often misunderstood in both research and clinical practice).

Arguably, the rationale for this approach partially originated in an understanding of agoraphobia based on learning principles, as eloquently described by Goldstein and Chambless (1978). In their landmark review, they combined the concept of interoceptive conditioning (Razran, 1961) with their clinical observation that sufferers from panic and agoraphobia usually interpret the perception of bodily changes as a sign of an upcoming panic attack. Most importantly, the authors concluded that symptoms of sympathetic arousal act as a conditioned stimulus to trigger a thus conditioned panic attack. Furthermore, Goldstein and Chambless highlighted the concept of "fear of the fear" as constituting the most central phobic element in agoraphobia, and that this specific fear is best understood by conditioning mechanisms involving bodily symptoms (interoceptive conditioning).

The relevance of interoceptive conditioning was first discussed in the beginning of the 1970s. For example, Evans (1972) explained a variety of phenomena with his version of the conditioning theory of "fear of fear." In his understanding, bodily symptoms of arousal may constitute conditioned stimuli which in turn elicit phobic anxiety (i.e., dry mouth when giving a speech as a conditioned stimulus signaling oncoming problems with the competent deliverance of a speech, or the sensation of food intake as conditioned stimulus for psychogenic vomiting). Interestingly, Evan's account does not exclusively focus on panic or agoraphobia, but also holds for specific phobias as well as social anxiety disorder. Bonn, Harrison, and Rees (1973, 1971) were the first to use interoceptive exposure as a treatment method. The authors exposed 33 patients suffering from "free floating anxiety" to "psychological flooding, with the rapid arousal of maximal anxiety" (p. 41; Bonn et al., 1973). Remarkably, to this date their pioneer work has not been recognized well, although there are some exceptions (e.g., Barlow, 1988; Otto, Safren, & Pollack, 2004). Bonn et al. (1973, 1971) treated their patients over the course of 3 weeks with an interoceptive exposure paradigm by employing 6 infusions of sodium lactate in order to produce intense physical discomfort and anxiety. The authors did not explicitly argue that their method was intended to extinguish the conditioned fear reaction to bodily symptoms. Nonetheless, the description of their approach can easily be interpreted in this way. They observed remarkable improvements in their patients with previously intractable anxiety, and also observed these improvements to sustain at the follow-up assessment 6 weeks after treatment. Thus, the first use of interoceptive exposure was based on learning theory and was found to be effective in a group of patients who were considered to be difficult to treat at that time. About a decade later, Griez and van den Hout (1983) explicitly argued that bodily symptoms should be considered as conditioned stimuli, leading to an increase of anxiety. Based on this conceptualization, they reported a case study in which they treated a panic disorder patient with additional agoraphobia. Again, they used a rather technical approach to induce bodily symptoms by asking their patient to repeatedly inhale a gas mixture of 35% CO_2 and 65% O_2. This case study demonstrated also remarkable therapeutic benefits for the repeated exposure to aversive bodily symptoms.

In parallel, starting 1983, Barlow and Czerny experimented with a variety of more easily applicable techniques to induce physical symptoms. These included hyperventilating, holding one's breath, breathing through a straw, various forms of physical exercise, prolonged head shaking, and spinning (Barlow & Czerny, 1988). Arguably due to its mere feasibility, Barlow and Czerny increased the spread of interoceptive exposure methods in a way that these were much more likely to be implemented outside of research facilities and therefore turned into useful techniques for clinical practice. In consequence, interoceptive exposure is nowadays considered to be one of the core techniques used in treating anxiety disorder patients, particularly those suffering from panic disorder.

11.2 Common Rationales for Interoceptive Exposure and Their Consequences in Treatment Protocols

Based on the historical development of this technique, one can argue that the focus of interoceptive exposure is the reduction or elimination of a conditioned reaction (e.g., anxiety) to a conditioned stimulus (e.g., change in heart rate or another bodily symptom). The rationale behind is that by repeated and prolonged exposure to the feared bodily symptoms and omitting any avoidance or safety behaviors, a reduction of the anxiety response will inevitably follow. Within the framework of learning theories, learning-based mechanisms have been proposed to explain the reduction or elimination of the learned anxiety reaction. For example, habituation, extinction, reciprocal inhibition, or counterconditioning have been discussed (Tryon, 2005). Arguably, extinction yielded the best empirical support among the mechanisms based on learning theories potentially behind the effective reduction of anxiety through exposure therapy. Note that extinction learning is not unlearning but rather constitutes new learning. That is, based on the experiences during exposure to a feared stimulus, an individual learns that the respective stimulus (e.g., an increase in heart rate) may have additional meanings other than the originally learned idea that the symptom signals an impending anxiety attack (Bouton, 2002). This extinction-based rationale implies that exposure should be repeated under various circumstances to broaden the basis for the newly learned nonanxious response, namely, exposure to feared bodily symptoms in various situations (Mystkowski, Craske, & Echiverri, 2002) and under various internal conditions as well (e.g., with or without prior coffee consumption; Hermans, Craske, Mineka, & Lovibond, 2006). Also, when situational characteristics are relevant, interoceptive exposure should not exclusively take place at home or at the therapist's office but preferably also in everyday situations, particularly in those where the first anxiety responses were experienced. This kind of interoceptive exposure may also involve exposure techniques that are sometimes described as "secondary interoceptive exposure" (Abramowitz, Deacon, & Whiteside, 2010). At first glance, secondary interoceptive exposure appears to be quite similar to in-vivo exposure; however, the difference between the techniques is the specific purpose: oftentimes, patients develop avoidance behavior in order to prevent the occurrence of aversive physical symptoms such as avoidance of physical exercise or drinking coffee because these might elicit the feared bodily sensations (Asmundson & Stein, 1994). The goal of secondary interoceptive exposure is consequently to reduce such avoidance behaviors and to expose the patient to the physical symptoms provoked by formerly avoided activities. The notion concerning situational characteristics being relevant is supported, however, by very little empirical evidence so far (e.g., Culver, Stoyanova, & Craske, 2011).

Extinction learning can also be conceptualized within an information-processing framework. The landmark publication in this respect is an article by Foa and Kozak (1986) in which the two authors outlined that exposure leads to a modification of the memory structures that underlie emotions (e.g., fear). However, these modifications are only possible if exposure is set up in a way that allows the fear structure to be activated as completely as possible. In consequence, this again suggests that interoceptive exposure will be more effective if it does not exclusively involve the physical symptoms per se but also incorporates situations that are closely associated with these feared symptoms. Additionally, directly addressing fear-related cognitions such as the fear of having a heart attack might be beneficial.

A third common rationale trying to explain the effectiveness of interoceptive exposure is based on cognitive theories. Mainly two mechanisms have been suggested: first, changes in self-efficacy and second, changes in terms of cognitive restructuring. Changes in self-efficacy imply that by exposing oneself to strong bodily symptoms and by dealing with the anxiety these symptoms provoke, patients learn to cope more effectively with aversive symptoms and in consequence increase their self-efficacy in dealing with symptoms of anxiety. In turn, anxiety should be reduced in future encounters since the confidence to be able to cope with strong bodily symptoms should be increased and anticipatory anxiety decreased. Whereas this rationale appears convincing at first sight, data supporting the necessary sequence of effects (first an increase in self-efficacy and consecutively a reduction in anxiety) is missing so far (Tryon, 2005).

Interoceptive exposure can further be introduced to the patient as a behavioral experiment. In this case, the patient is explicitly asked to predict what will happen, when he or she is, for example, hyperventilating. Interestingly, Melzig and colleagues (2008) recently demonstrated that highly anxiety sensitive students report more state anxiety, have higher heart rates, and show more startle potentiation in anticipation of hyperventilation than less anxiety sensitive students. Thus, although subjects in this study had never experienced hyperventilation within the laboratory setting, the mere information that hyperventilation is usually accompanied by physical symptoms lead to substantial anticipatory anxiety measurable in both self-reported and psychophysiological reactivity. In other words, individuals with high anxiety sensitivity (e.g. individuals suffering from panic disorder or other anxiety disorders) react with increased anxiety to the prospect of the experience of bodily symptoms. Arguably, catastrophic cognitions such as the idea, that a heart rate increase signals an impending heart attack build the basis of this anxiety. To explicitly experience to which level this anxiety will actually get, whether or not the patient will be able to cope with these high levels of anxiety, whether his heart will indeed suffer a heart attack are different forms of a behavioral experiments including interoceptive exposure. Behavioral experiments are one of the most potent cognitive therapy techniques and have been comprehensively described by Bennett-Levy et al. (2004). The relevant goals of behavioral experiments are to change catastrophic cognitions concerning the experience of bodily symptoms, to increase the ability of a person to tolerate these symptoms, and to reduce the impact that these symptoms have on state anxiety. This approach may be additionally helpful in cases where biological processes work against habituation processes. Imagine, for example, a case of gastrointestinal panic: the patient may fear bodily symptoms associated with the need to use the restroom. In this special case, the goal of an interoceptive exposure cannot be habituation since the actual biological need to defecate will increase with time as will the level of associated anxiety therefore preventing habituation from taking place. In this case, the focus of interoceptive exposure is different, i.e., not oriented toward habituation: First, the patient estimates how long he or she will be able to tolerate the symptoms without using the restroom. Second, the therapist adds, e.g., 5 min, then 10 min, and so forth to the expected time frame. The patient will learn to get accustomed with these symptoms and gain confidence that he or she is indeed able to tolerate the symptoms without using the restroom over a longer timespan. The focus here lies particularly on the experience of self-efficacy in coping with the feared bodily symptoms beyond the previously assumed abilities of the individual.

Extinction of anxiety when being exposed for prolonged periods of time to interoceptive stimuli can again also be conceptualized within the cognitive framework in form of a behavioral experiment. Specifically, in this case, the patient is asked to predict how long his anxiety will last if he does not do anything against it. The behavioral experiment is then to test whether this prediction is correct (or if habituation occurs). However, note that some pilot work suggests that a therapeutic approach which does not exclusively focus on habituation mechanisms may have stronger effects (Salkovskis, Hackmann, Wells, Gelder, & Clark, 2007). Another aspect that can be tested easily in behavioral experiments is whether safety behavior is helpful. Note that whereas it seems therapeutically sensible to prevent patients from using safety behaviors, findings supporting the need for this precaution are preliminary. The only study examining effects of safety information and safety cues within the context of interoceptive exposure found effects of removing a safety cue within repeated exposures but not an initial effect of safety cues or safety information on initial reactivity to a 35% CO_2 challenge (Schmidt, Richey, Maner, & Woolaway-Bickel, 2006).

Interestingly, when Barlow and Czerny included interoceptive exposure in their treatment package for panic disorder, they too did not exclusively focus on habituation or extinction of the conditioned anxiety response. In fact, an integral part of their introduction to the interoceptive exposure tasks was that patients were asked to compare their initial reaction to each challenge with symptoms usually experienced during panic attacks (Barlow & Czerny, 1988). This aspect has been included in all versions of the panic control treatment in sensu Barlow. Note that this approach is obviously also a variant of a behavioral experiment that allows the patient to explore harmless reasons for his or her bodily symptoms.

Finally, distress intolerance has also been suggested as a mechanism relevant for the reduction of anxiety in response to interoceptive exposure (cf. Leyro, Zvolensky, & Bernstein, 2010). Reactions to common forms of biological challenges such as hyperventilation, inhalation of carbon dioxide-enriched air, and holding one's breath have been used as a measure of distress tolerance for aversive bodily symptoms. In consequence, it has been suggested that interoceptive exposure may aid in correcting the patient's hypersensitivity to bodily sensations (e.g., Schmidt et al., 2000). This notion generally does not emphasize cognitive factors but rather claims that individuals may differ in their ability to tolerate aversive physical symptoms. Consequently, treatment should enable an individual to better tolerate aversive symptoms without engaging in counterproductive control efforts of either a cognitive or a behavioral nature (Eifert & Heffner, 2003). Treatment packages that highlight the need to increase distress tolerance are variants of standard CBT (e.g., Craske & Barlow, 2008) as well as versions of the so-called "third wave" of behavior therapies in form of, for example, acceptance and commitment-based psychotherapies (e.g., Eifert & Forsyth, 2005) (also see Gloster et al. in this book). The latter variants highlight the additional goals of interoceptive exposure to stop experiential avoidance of fear and anxiety and "to assist clients in mastering their ability to experience a full range of emotional responses, fully and without defense, for what they are and not for what their mind tells them they are (i.e., something dangerous and harmful)" (Eifert & Forsyth, 2005, p. 202).

We have described in some detail the diverse explanations usually given by researchers and therapists regarding the reasons for the effectiveness of interoceptive exposure. It is our conviction that neither of these theories possesses the empirical basis to claim the prize for the best explanation or even for the explanation with the best empirical evidence. However, in our clinical work we have repeatedly made the experience that it is important to always be aware of the rationale based on which, in every situation, interoceptive exposure is applied. In fact, this is true for all other forms of exposure as well. We strongly encourage therapists to use this powerful analysis technique as well. In our experience, having a clear rationale is especially helpful if the treatment does not work the way we hoped for. Analyzing the responsible mechanisms behind the treatment failures will then regularly stimulate a change in treatment strategy that hopefully will help the patient to get better after the necessary adjustment.

11.3 How to Provoke Physical Symptoms

To our knowledge, only two studies to date have systematically looked at the effects of various symptom provocation experiments (Antony, Ledley, Liss, & Winson, 2006; Schmidt & Trakowski, 2004). Schmidt and Trakowski (2004) reported on the use of symptom provocation experiments in a sample of 50 individuals suffering from panic disorder with or without agoraphobia who were treated in their treatment facilities. Notably, patients were allocated to different symptom provocation experiments. Whereas this limits the generalizability of the findings concerning specific symptom provocation techniques, the following results can be summarized according to the authors: approximately 90% of the patients reacted with anxiety to at least one of the provocation techniques used by Schmidt and Trakowski (2004). In general, when symptoms were provoked, these symptoms tended to also be associated with anxiety. The most intense symptoms were provoked by spinning, hyperventilation, breathing through a straw, and running in place. Not surprisingly, the symptoms most commonly experienced were dizziness (e.g., while spinning and during hyperventilation) and shortness of breath (while breathing through straw and during and directly after running in place). Schmidt and Trakowski (2004) furthermore report that whereas a wide variety of exercises was used in the initial diagnostic phase, only two of them were regularly employed during treatment, namely hyperventilation and breathing through a straw.

Antony et al. (2006) compared the response of 27 individuals suffering from panic disorder to 25 unaffected individuals. Their results were quite similar to the findings of Schmidt and Trakowski: Breathing through a straw, hyperventilation, and spinning around were found to be the three most anxiety provoking exercises for the panic disorder group. However, running on the spot was not particularly effective in provoking anxiety and physical symptoms in the sample of Antony and colleagues. An additional technique, namely using a tongue depressor, was found to be another strong inducer of anxiety and, more specifically, of feelings of choking and breathlessness. A general finding of both studies is that most symptom provocation techniques result in more than one bodily symptom, and are correlated with self-reported anxiety.

11.3.1 Special Case: Hyperventilation

Hyperventilation is probably the most commonly used symptom induction exercise and is an especially powerful one. It has been used extensively as means to induce bodily symptoms in laboratory research (Meuret, Ritz, Wilhelm, & Roth, 2005) and has served as treatment component in the first attempts to systematically test the benefit of interoceptive exposure (e.g., Beck & Shipherd, 1997). One reason for the popularity of hyperventilation as a treatment and research tool is the simplicity and effectiveness of its use. Breathlessness, dizziness, derealization, and other symptoms can readily and reliably be evoked using hyperventilation (Antony et al., 2006; Schmidt & Trakowski, 2004). Additionally, this result can be achieved with a wide variety of simple instructions (Meuret et al., 2005). Given the regular use of this approach, surprisingly many therapists have only little knowledge concerning the mechanisms behind the symptom provocation of hyperventilation. Consequently, the physiological mechanisms responsible for symptom induction by hyperventilation are described briefly: when a person hyperventilates, excessive amounts of O_2 are absorbed and excessive amounts of CO_2 are expulsed through the lungs. The resulting hypocapnia (low levels of CO_2 in the blood) results in alkalosis of the blood and in turn leads to cerebral vasoconstriction. Additionally, the "Bohr effect" (CO_2-dependent respiratory alkalosis leads to higher affinity of O_2 to blood hemoglobin and reduces in consequence the transport of O_2 to the surrounding tissue) leads to secondary hypoxia. This secondary hypoxia is the main reason why individuals experience breathlessness despite excessive levels of O_2 in the blood during hyperventilation (e.g., Smoller, Pollack, Otto, Rosenbaum, & Kradin, 1996). In addition, respiratory alkalosis also reduces the levels of ionized calcium (hypocalcemia) and in consequence lowers the threshold for the excitation of muscle and nerve potentials. The latter leads to paresthesia and in extreme cases to transient tetany which can be quite frightening for patients.

Clinically, three distinct aspects need to be considered carefully when applying this interoceptive exposure technique. First, albeit rarely, patients may have difficulties stopping hyperventilation because the induced sensation of breathlessness may trigger an intense hunger for air, so individuals continue to breath fast and deep and find themselves unable to stop doing so. Usually, these patients can be identified beforehand by inquiring about hyperventilation episodes (situations in which they could not stop breathing fast and deep and still felt air hunger). The most effective intervention in this case is to ask the individual to breath into a paper bag. If such paper bag is not readily available, it is usually possible to motivate the individuals to slow down their breathing by asking them to breath against their hand, thus increasing the respiratory resistance and slowing down the respiratory rate. Whereas this reaction may be frightening for the patient and also for the inexperienced therapist, hyperventilation attacks are usually not dangerous. A second, but also rare complication can be that an individual faints after hyperventilation. This is mainly the case, if, for some reason, the intracorporal pressure suddenly increases after hyperventilation (e.g., because a person's ribcage is compressed when standing in a crowd). Given that the person does not receive any hurt by a faint-induced fall, this aversive event usually has no long-term consequences. We, however, discourage the reader to provoke the fainting reaction voluntarily. Finally, a number of medical conditions may be contraindications for hyperventilation, specifically asthma. See Feldman, Giardino, and Lehrer (2000) for suggestions on when and how interoceptive exposure can be applied if a patient should suffer from such conditions.

11.3.2 Other Symptom Provocation Methods

The two studies reported above (Antony et al., 2006; Schmidt & Trakowski, 2004) reported on commonly used methods to induce bodily symptoms. However, since these interoceptive exposure exercises focused on individuals suffering from panic disorder, the focus of symptomatology are panic symptoms, and in consequence their focus is rather narrow. In the following, we will describe and suggest a number of additional symptom provocation techniques that have been helpful in the treatment of various disorders by inducing a wider range of physical symptoms.

Fear of nausea can be quite debilitating and is, for example, a core symptom of emetophobia, the fear of emesis. Nausea can be induced fairly easily by asking individuals to spin around. In fact, in susceptible individuals, spinning can even lead to vomiting and it is sensible to have a bucket readily available. Similarly, head mounted displays showing films that are shot with a moving camera can also be used to induce nausea. Alternatively, low doses of Ipecac Syrup can be applied (Dattilio, 2003). Lastly, in order to induce nausea, olfactory stimuli can be used. From our clinical perspective, fear of emesis is commonly accompanied by a fear of nausea, and interoceptive exposure treating this fear is a potent technique in an effective therapy of this disorder (also compare Hunter & Antony, 2009).

Related to nausea is the fear of choking. Here, the use of a tongue depressor, or wearing a tie or a scarf tied tightly around the neck can be useful. This technique is also helpful in patients presenting with globus sensations. The latter is an example of an anxiety symptom that nonetheless may also present as a functional disorder which, in our clinical experience, may nonetheless respond to interoceptive exposure.

Nicotinic acid (niacin) is one of the essential nutrients that humans need. When ingested in large amounts, a strong vasodilatation in the skin is induced, leading to feelings of heat, tingling, prickly, or itching sensations and sometimes to the feeling of having unusually dry and tensed skin. These sensations start approximately 30 min after ingestion and last for approximately another 30 min. Niacin can be especially helpful if used as an additional trigger when confronting socially anxious individuals with feared situations for whom fear of blushing is a core problem. In addition, use of nicotinic acid is beneficial when strong physical sensations are needed that are beyond or only partially under control of the individual (but certainly require the patient's informed consent).

Depersonalization and derealization are also common symptoms of anxiety syndromes which are generally considered to be difficult to induce. As pointed out above, hyperventilation may be of help in this respect. In addition, staring at a dot on the wall, staring into a mirror, wearing a blindfold, and listening to loud twelve-tone music in a dark room have been suggested. In a recent study, Mckay and Moretz (2008) used 3D glasses in the natural environment to successfully induce depersonalization with beneficial effects on symptomatology in three patients suffering from panic disorder with severe depersonalization during panic attacks.

Fear of suffocation is not only a common problem in panic disorder but may also complicate the course and treatment of specific phobias such as dental fears or, more commonly, claustrophobia. Next to breathing through a straw, holding one's breath, hyperventilation, or similar exercises, the use of a snorkel attached to a face mask or putting a paper towel and a piece of wood in the mouth may be helpful when patients need to learn to tolerate the fear of suffocation and the feeling of large objects or instruments in their mouth. Again, it cannot be stressed enough that using such procedures must always be based on the consent of the individual treated with the respective form of interoceptive exposure.

Finally, within the context of the treatment of chronic pain, a variant of interoceptive exposure has recently been suggested. Therein, pain is not directly induced but rather requires individuals to focus their attention on already existing pain symptoms. In consequence, conscious perception and experience of pain in patients are increased (Flink, Nicholas, Boersma, & Linton, 2009). The aim of such interventions is that the acceptance of pain will increase and that debilitating avoidance behavior can be reduced so individuals may have a better chance of participating in their respective social and private lives despite their pain.

11.3.3 Additional Technical Aspects with the Potential to Improve the Use of Interoceptive Exposure

Huppert and Baker-Morissette (2003) have published a comprehensive "insider's guide" to the treatment of panic disorder. They outline a few technical aspects to improve the use of interoceptive exposure in the field. First, it is important to tailor the interoceptive exposure exercises to the specific symptoms experienced by the patient. This can only be accomplished if the therapist always ensures that the feared symptom is provoked. Consequently, patients should be asked by standard whether the feared symptom is experienced (and not to simply expect this since a technique usually provokes certain symptoms). Secondly, they highlight that motivating the patient to excess the point where provoked symptoms can be tolerated. This will help the patient to experience that the patient's ability to tolerate symptoms is in fact much better than previously expected. Finally, they highlight that a panic attack that occurs during interoceptive exposure is an opportunity for the therapist to model an alternative and more relaxed way of dealing with anxiety. In consequence, Huppert and Baker-Morissette stress that a therapist should not try to calm down the patient during these in-session panic attacks but rather to demonstrate a lack of concern for the panic attack. This will additionally help the patient to learn about the harmlessness of anxiety attacks.

11.4 Use of Interoceptive Exposure During In-Vivo Exposure

Sometimes in the course of in vivo exposure, a patient experiences surprisingly little or even no anxiety. The reason for this may be that a patient is using cognitive avoidance strategies such as not focusing on the situation or using the therapist as a safety signal. Sometimes this can also be the result of massive avoidance on part of the patient after the first or only the first few panic attacks. Complete avoidance sometimes may also prevent situations from becoming conditioned stimuli. In these situations, it is often helpful to induce anxiety by asking the patients to additionally engage in interoceptive exposure. This will allow the patient to experience that he or she is able to cope with the situations despite being anxious or having a panic attack. We also regularly use interoceptive exposure once that anxiety has successfully habituated in an in-vivo exposure again in order to provide the patient an additional chance to experience habituation.

11.5 Efficacy and Effectiveness

In a recent review, Lang, Helbig-Lang, and Petermann (2009) reported the evidence for interoceptive exposure as a stand-alone treatment as well as an add-on to other CBT treatment components such as in vivo exposure or cognitive restructuring (also cf. Lang & Helbig-Lang in this book). Generally, evidence points toward the effectiveness of interoceptive exposure in panic disorder. However, evidence using dismantling techniques trying to isolate the effects of interoceptive exposure is relatively scarce. Panic control treatment and its variants (e.g., Barlow & Craske, 1989; Barlow & Czerny, 1988; Margraf, Barlow, Clark, & Telch, 1993) and the treatment for panic disorder as developed by David Clark and colleagues (Clark & Salkovskis, 1989) are nonetheless among the most often and most thoroughly tested therapy manuals.

Both include interoceptive exposure techniques at their core. Studies on the efficacy of these treatments consistently show large and positive effect sizes in the treatment of panic disorder with and without agoraphobia (e.g., Sanchez-Meca, Rosa-Alcazar, Marin-Martinez, & Gomez-Conesa, 2010). Whereas panic disorder was the disorder for which interoceptive exposure originally was developed, in the meantime a number of additional disorders have been proven to respond well to this versatile intervention technique such as specific phobias (e.g., Hunter & Antony, 2009), substance disorders (Otto et al., 2004; Zvolensky, Lejuez, Kahler, & Brown, 2003), but also somatoform disorders such as chronic pain disorder (e.g. Flink et al., 2009) or hypochondriasis (Greeven et al., 2007). Thus, it can be concluded that interoceptive exposure is an established and valuable tool in treating fear of bodily symptoms and should therefore be considered as the treatment of choice whenever fear of bodily symptoms is a relevant aspect of a psychological disorder.

References

Abramowitz, J., Deacon, B., & Whiteside, S. P. (2010). *Exposure therapy for anxiety: Principles and practice*. New York: Guilford Publications.

Antony, M. M., Ledley, D. R., Liss, A., & Winson, R. P. (2006). Responses to symptom induction exercises in panic disorder. *Behavior Research and Therapy, 44*(1), 85–98.

Asmundson, G. J. G., & Stein, M. B. (1994). Resting cardiovascular measures in patients with panic disorder and social phobia and health control subjects: Relationship to habitual exercise frequency. *Anxiety, 1*(1), 26–30.

Barlow, D. H. (1988). *Anxiety and its disorders*. New York: The Guilford Press.

Barlow, D. H., & Craske, M. (1989). *Mastery of your anxiety and panic*. Albany: Greywind.

Barlow, D. H., & Czerny, J. A. (1988). *Psychological treatment of panic*. New York: The Guilford Press.

Beck, J. G., & Shipherd, J. C. (1997). Repeated exposure to interoceptive cues: Does habituation of fear occur in panic disorder patients? A preliminary report. *Behaviour Research and Therapy, 35*(6), 551–557.

Bennett-Levy, J., Butler, G., Fennell, M. J., Hackmann, A., Müller, M., & Westbrook, D. (2004). *Oxford guide to behavioural experiments in cognitive therapy*. Oxford: Oxford University Press.

Bonn, J. A., Harrison, J., & Rees, L. (1973). Lactate infusion in the treatment of "free-floating" anxiety. *Canadian Psychiatric Association Journal, 18*(1), 41–46.

Bonn, J. A., Harrison, J., & Rees, W. L. (1971). Lactate-induced anxiety: Therapeutic application. *The British Journal of Psychiatry, 119*(551), 468–470.

Bouton, M. E. (2002). Context, ambiguity, and unlearning: Sources of relapse after behavioral extinction. *Biological Psychiatry, 52*(10), 976–986.

Clark, D. M., & Salkovskis, P. (1989). *Cognitive therapy for panic and hypochondriasis*. Oxford: Pergamon Press.

Craske, M., & Barlow, D. H. (2008). Panic disorder and agoraphobia. In D. H. Barlow (Ed.), *Clinical handbook of psychological disorders: A step-by-step treatment manual* (4th ed., pp. 1–64). New York: Guilford Press.

Culver, N. C., Stoyanova, M., & Craske, M. G. (2011). Clinical relevance of retrieval cues for attenuating context renewal of fear. *Journal of Anxiety Disorders, 25*(2), 284–292.

Dattilio, F. M. (2003). Emetic exposure and desensitization procedures in the reduction of nausea and a fear of emesis. *Clinical Case Studies, 2*(3), 199–210.

Eifert, G. H., & Forsyth, J. P. (2005). *Acceptance & commitment therapy for anxiety disorders*. Oakland: New Harpinger Publications.

Eifert, G. H., & Heffner, M. (2003). The effects of acceptance versus control contexts on avoidance of panic-related symptoms. *Journal of Behavior Therapy and Experimental Psychiatry, 34*(3–4), 293–312.

Evans, I. M. (1972). Conditioning model of a common neurotic pattern—Fear of fear. *Psychotherapy-Theory Research and Practice, 9*(3), 238–241.

Feldman, J. M., Giardino, N. D., & Lehrer, P. M. (2000). Asthma and panic disorder. In D. I. Mostofsky & D. H. Barlow (Eds.), *The management of stress and anxiety disorders*. Boston: Allyn & Bacon.

Flink, I. K., Nicholas, M. K., Boersma, K., & Linton, S. J. (2009). Reducing the threat value of chronic pain: A preliminary replicated single-case study of interoceptive exposure versus distraction in six individuals with chronic back pain. *Behaviour Research and Therapy, 47*(8), 721–728.

Foa, E. B., & Kozak, M. J. (1986). Emotional processing of fear: Exposure to corrective information. [Research Support, U.S. Gov't, P.H.S.]. *Psychological Bulletin, 99*(1), 20–35.

Goldstein, A. J., & Chambless, D. L. (1978). Reanalysis of agoraphobia. *Behavior Therapy, 9*(1), 47–59.

Greeven, A., van Balkom, A. J. L. M., Visser, S., Merkelbach, J. W., van Rood, Y. R., van Dyck, R., et al. (2007). Cognitive behavior therapy and paroxetine in the treatment of hypochondriasis: A randomized controlled trial. *American Journal of Psychiatry, 164*(1), 91–99.

Griez, E., & van den Hout, M. A. (1983). Treatment of phobophobia by exposure to CO_2-induced anxiety symptoms [Case Reports]. *The Journal of Nervous and Mental Disease, 171*(8), 506–508.

Hermans, D., Craske, M. G., Mineka, S., & Lovibond, P. F. (2006). Extinction in human fear conditioning. *Biological Psychiatry, 60*(4), 361–368.

Hunter, P. V., & Antony, M. M. (2009). Cognitive-behavioral treatment of emetophobia: The role of interoceptive exposure. *Cognitive and Behavioral Practice, 16*(1), 84–91.

Huppert, J. D., & Baker-Morissette, S. L. (2003). Beyond the manual: The insider's guide to panic control treatment. *Cognitive and Behavioral Practice, 10*(1), 2–13.

Lang, T., Helbig-Lang, S., & Petermann, F. (2009). Was wirkt in der Kognitiven Verhaltenstherapie der Panikstörung mit Agoraphobie? Ein systematischer Review. *Zeitschrift für Psychiatrie, Psychologie und Psychotherapie, 57*(3), 161–175.

Leyro, T. M., Zvolensky, M. J., & Bernstein, A. (2010). Distress tolerance and psychopathological symptoms and disorders: A review of the empirical literature among adults. *Psychological Bulletin, 136*(4), 576–600.

Margraf, J., Barlow, D. H., Clark, D. M., & Telch, M. J. (1993). Psychological treatment of panic—Work in progress on outcome, active ingredients, and follow-up. *Behaviour Research and Therapy, 31*(1), 1–8.

Mckay, D., & Moretz, M. W. (2008). Interoceptive cue exposure for depersonalization: A case series. *Cognitive and Behavioral Practice, 15*(4), 435–439.

Melzig, C. A., Michalowski, J. M., Holtz, K., & Hamm, A. O. (2008). Anticipation of interoceptive threat in highly anxiety sensitive persons. *Behaviour Research and Therapy, 46*(10), 1126–1134.

Meuret, A. E., Ritz, T., Wilhelm, F. H., & Roth, W. T. (2005). Voluntary hyperventilation in the treatment of panic disorder-functions of hyperventilation, their implications for breathing training, and recommendations for standardization. *Clinical Psychology Review, 25*(3), 285–306.

Mystkowski, J. L., Craske, M. G., & Echiverri, A. M. (2002). Treatment context and return of fear in spider phobia. *Behavior Therapy, 33*(3), 399–416.

Otto, M. W., Safren, S. A., & Pollack, M. H. (2004). Internal cue exposure and the treatment of substance use disorders: Lessons from the treatment of panic disorder. *Journal of Anxiety Disorders, 18*(1), 69–87.

Razran, G. (1961). The observable unconscious and the inferable conscious in current soviet psychophysiology. *Psychological Review, 68*(2), 81–147.

Salkovskis, P. M., Hackmann, A., Wells, A., Gelder, M. G., & Clark, D. M. (2007). Belief disconfirmation versus habituation approaches to situational exposure in panic disorder with agoraphobia: A pilot study. *Behaviour Research and Therapy, 45*(5), 877–885.

Sanchez-Meca, J., Rosa-Alcazar, A. I., Marin-Martinez, F., & Gomez-Conesa, A. (2010). Psychological treatment of panic disorder with or without agoraphobia: A meta-analysis. *Clinical Psychology Review, 30*(1), 37–50.

Schmidt, N. B., Richey, J. A., Maner, J. K., & Woolaway-Bickel, K. (2006). Differential effects of safety in extinction of anxious responding to a CO_2 challenge in patients with panic disorder. *Journal of Abnormal Psychology, 115*(2), 341–350.

Schmidt, N. B., & Trakowski, J. (2004). Interoceptive assessment and exposure in panic disorder: A descriptive study. *Cognitive and Behavioral Practice, 11*(1), 81–92.

Schmidt, N. B., Woolaway-Bickel, K., Trakowski, J., Santiago, H., Storey, J., Koselka, M., et al. (2000). Dismantling cognitive-behavioral treatment for panic disorder: Questioning the utility of breathing retraining. *Journal of Consulting and Clinical Psychology, 68*(3), 417–424.

Smoller, J. W., Pollack, M. H., Otto, M. W., Rosenbaum, J. F., & Kradin, R. L. (1996). Panic anxiety, dyspnea, and respiratory disease—Theoretical and clinical considerations. *American Journal of Respiratory and Critical Care Medicine, 154*(1), 6–17.

Tryon, W. W. (2005). Possible mechanisms for why desensitization and exposure therapy work. *Clinical Psychology Review, 25*(1), 67–95.

Zvolensky, M. J., Lejuez, C. W., Kahler, C. W., & Brown, R. A. (2003). Integrating an interoceptive exposure-based smoking cessation program into the cognitive-behavioral treatment of panic disorder: Theoretical relevance and case demonstration. *Cognitive and Behavioral Practice, 10*(4), 347–357.

Chapter 12
The Role of Anxiety Control Strategies in Imaginal Exposure

Naomi Koerner and Katie Fracalanza

Naomi Koerner received her Ph.D. from Concordia University in 2007. She is an Assistant Professor in the Department of Psychology at Ryerson University in Toronto, where she directs the Cognition and Psychopathology Laboratory. Her research interests are in the area of cognition and psychopathology with a specific focus on the ways in which concepts and methods from cognitive psychology can be used to inform and refine cognitive-behavioural theories and treatments for anxiety disorders.

N. Koerner (✉) • K. Fracalanza
Department of Psychology (JOR 927), Ryerson University,
350 Victoria Street, Toronto, ON M5B 2K3, Canada
e-mail: naomi.koerner@psych.ryerson.ca

P. Neudeck and H.-U. Wittchen (eds.), *Exposure Therapy: Rethinking the Model – Refining the Method*, DOI 10.1007/978-1-4614-3342-2_12,

Katie Fracalanza, MA is a doctoral student in the Clinical Psychology program at Ryerson University, Toronto and is a member of the Cognition and Psychopathology Lab. She has conducted research on written imaginal exposure for GAD and emotional processes in individuals with GAD.

12.1 Introduction

Although much has been written about in vivo exposure procedures and the specific parameters that either optimize or reduce its effectiveness, research on a closely related treatment strategy—imaginal exposure—currently lags behind, which is somewhat paradoxical considering that one of the first clinical applications of exposure was systematic desensitization, an imagery-based procedure (Wolpe, 1958). In this chapter, we review current procedures for imaginal exposure with a specific emphasis on recommendations that are currently in place with regard to the use of *anxiety control strategies*, and discuss whether such recommendations are empirically justified. Of particular interest is the question of whether engagement in anxiety control strategies during mental imagery hinders or facilitates imaginal exposure.

In the first part of the chapter, we will review the theories that underlie exposure procedures: (1) emotional processing theory (Foa & Kozak, 1986; revision, Foa, Huppert, & Cahill, 2006), a theory that suggests that emotional activation and habituation are necessary ingredients in exposure; and (2) the "belief disconfirmation" theory (Salkovskis, Clark, Hackmann, Wells, & Gelder, 1999), a theory that suggests that disconfirmation of erroneous, fear-related beliefs is central to the effectiveness of exposure. Next, we will introduce the notion of anxiety control strategies, after which we will review the ways in which anxiety control strategies are handled in current in vivo exposure protocols, as a prelude to our discussion of imaginal exposure. Importantly, we will review, and evaluate the evidence for, the recommendations that are typically made with regard to anxiety control strategies in in vivo exposure. In the second part of this chapter, we will describe current imaginal exposure procedures for PTSD and GAD and will highlight recommendations that are made with regard to anxiety control strategies. We will discuss whether such recommendations are warranted based on the extant empirical literature.

12.2 Theories of Exposure and Current Position on Anxiety Control Strategies

12.2.1 Foa and Kozak's Emotional Processing Theory

Emotional processing theory (Foa & Kozak, 1986; revision, Foa et al., 2006) was derived from Peter Lang's seminal work on the structure and psychophysiological correlates of mental imagery across the anxiety disorders (Lang, 1977). In his bio-informational model of emotion, Lang (Lang, 1977; Lang & Cuthbert, 1984; Foa & Kozak, 1986; Foa & Kozak, 1998) proposed that emotional imagery plays an important role in fear and anxiety. According to Lang, a fear-evoking mental image is not merely a picture in the mind's eye of a threatening object or situation; but rather, a "cognitive structure" that contains interconnected information about the characteristics of the feared stimulus, as well as cognitive, affective, and behavioural responses to the feared stimulus, and meaning elements (i.e., beliefs about or interpretations of the feared stimulus and beliefs about one's reactions to it). Thus, fear images (or "fear structures"; Foa & Kozak, 1986) are rich networks of information that act as a "program for escape from danger" (Foa et al., 2006). Activation of one component of the fear structure (e.g. by exposing a person to his or her feared stimulus) promotes activation of other components of the fear structure (e.g. meaning elements). Lang proposed that the salience, interconnectedness and specificity of fear images depend on the concreteness of the fear object or situation. Fear of specific, circumscribed objects and situations (e.g. spiders, snakes, heights) is associated with mental imagery that is highly concrete and detailed. At the opposite end of the spectrum, fears that are somewhat vague and future oriented (e.g. getting fired and the consequences that might ensue) are associated with images that are lacking in detail and coherence (Cuthbert et al., 2003). Lang proposed that fear is evoked more readily in cases in which the fear structure is highly interconnected and coherent and he hypothesized that the main mechanism underlying the efficacy of exposure treatments for anxiety disorders is activation and modification of the fear structure. According to Lang, heart rate reactivity is a proxy measure of fear structure activation. Successful activation and modification of the fear structure is reflected in a rise, followed by a progressive decline, in heart rate reactivity (Foa et al., 2006). Lang proposed that this particular pattern of psychophysiological activity is important for what he termed, "emotional processing."

Foa and Kozak's emotional processing theory was constructed to provide a framework for Lang's findings and to explain phenomena that had been observed in individuals reporting clinically significant levels of anxiety. Their theory (and its revision) expands upon Lang's observations in several important ways. Emotional processing theory distinguishes between an adaptive and maladaptive fear structure. Adaptive fear structures contain information that "reflects reality faithfully" (Foa et al., 2006, p. 5), whereas, maladaptive fear structures do not, as biases in attention, interpretation, and memory produce mental representations that are distorted and inflated. According to Foa et al. (2006), chronic behavioural and cognitive avoidance prevent fear structures from being challenged and in this way maintain pathological fear. Foa and Kozak (1985) also proposed that although there are commonalities in fear structures across the anxiety disorders, there are also distinguishing elements. For example, safe external and internal reminders (stimulus elements) of trauma are associated with danger-related interpretations (meaning elements) in the fear structures of individuals with PTSD; whereas heart palpitations, shortness of breath and dizziness (response elements) are associated with representations of the physical and mental health repercussions of experiencing such sensations (meaning elements) in the fear structures of individuals with panic disorder (Foa et al., 2006).

Foa and Kozak's original and revised theories propose that exposure treatment is effective because it provides an opportunity for new learning to occur and for adjustment of distorted or biased information in the fear structure. Central to the theory is the notion that successful modification of a fear structure via exposure treatment requires that the structure first be accessed or activated. Activation of the fear structure occurs when an individual confronts a stimulus that closely matches one or more elements of a fear structure. For example, spider-related stimuli would activate the fear structure of an individual with spider phobia; whereas exposure to an unrelated or a peripherally related animal would likely not. Although activation is a necessary condition for emotional processing, it is not sufficient (Foa et al., 2006); "corrective" information that is incompatible with the existing fear structure must be introduced. Importantly, the theory states that learning occurs when individuals pay attention to, and do not engage in efforts to avoid, the new, disconfirming information.

Foa and Kozak's theory also makes predictions with regard to the pattern of physiological (i.e., heart rate) reactivity that is likely to be observed if a fear structure has been successfully activated and modified. The original theory stipulated that an optimal level of emotional activation was required for learning to occur; however, as Foa et al. (2006) later noted, "optimal" was not operationalized in the original version of the theory. In the absence of a definition, "optimal levels of activation" came to be understood as "moderate levels of anxiety," perhaps due to the Yerkes–Dodson law that grew out of research demonstrating that performance (in general) is optimized under conditions of moderate arousal. In the revised theory, Foa et al. (2006) acknowledged that the term "optimal" was never defined but that neurobiological evidence suggested that "some level of activation" is required, as long as the activation is not so extreme as to inhibit new learning. The original theory also stated that emotional processing occurs when levels of activation reduce over the course of an exposure session (within-session habituation) and peak intensity of arousal reduces *across* sessions of exposure (between-session habituation). Of note, Foa et al. (2006) revised this aspect of the theory to reflect the fact that most studies have found that the extent of within-session habituation does not predict exposure outcomes. They noted that within-session reductions in arousal may not be a sound indicator of emotional processing, as such reductions may be the product of distraction. Thus, according to Foa and Kozak's theory, a reduction in fear and avoidance comes about when people's existing fear structures are activated and challenged and information that runs contrary to existing maladaptive beliefs becomes integrated into the fear structure. Importantly, some degree of emotional arousal is needed for learning to occur and the peak intensity of arousal should attenuate across sessions of exposure.

12.2.2 Salkovskis's Belief Disconfirmation Theory

Salkovskis et al. (1999) argued that people with anxiety disorders typically engage in strategies to avoid feared consequences that may arise from coming into contact with a feared object or situation. For example, a person with a fear of spiders might avoid going into basements so as not to be "attacked" by a spider. Likewise, a person with social phobia might develop a list of conversation points before going to a party so as not to appear dull when meeting new people. Salkovskis termed these behaviours "safety-seeking behaviours" (also known as "safety behaviours"; Thwaites & Freeston, 2005). Several types of safety behaviours have been identified (Parrish, Radomsky, & Dugas, 2008; Salkovskis et al., 1999; Thwaites & Freeston, 2005): direct avoidance of situations, escape, and subtle behaviours that allow a person to remain in limited contact with his or her feared situation. Subtle safety behaviours are of particular interest to researchers and clinicians as they can become so engrained in a pattern of behaviour that people may not even notice themselves engaging in the behaviour (e.g. gripping a wine glass to stabilize a shaky hand). People may even "convince" themselves that the behaviour is normative (e.g. people who are high in social anxiety may convince themselves that interacting via social networking sites and text messaging is not problematic as these have become normative means of communication). Salkovskis et al. (1999) note that safety behaviours may be observable or non-observable. Although safety behaviours are designed to avert a "feared catastrophe" (Clark, 1999), "they have the secondary effect of preventing the disconfirmation that would otherwise take place" (Salkovskis et al., 1999, p. 573). In other words, although safety behaviours are designed to prevent a feared consequence of some sort, they are ultimately counterproductive as they prevent disconfirmation of erroneous fear-related beliefs. Salkovskis posited that safety behaviours are a maintenance factor in anxiety disorders. He also suggested that safety behaviours may be an interfering factor in exposure, as they may prevent the disconfirmation of maladaptive beliefs.

12.2.3 Current Position on Anxiety Control Strategies in In Vivo Exposure

At the heart of Foa and colleagues' theory and Salkovskis's theory is the notion that exposure is likely to be most effective if people are not engaging in actions that may detract from their ability to process information that has the potential to disconfirm erroneous underlying beliefs about a feared stimulus or situation. We will refer to these potentially counter-therapeutic strategies collectively as *anxiety control strategies*. In practice, most in vivo exposure treatment protocols suggest eliminating anxiety control strategies during exposure (e.g. Barlow, 2008; Craske, Antony, & Barlow, 2006; Zinbarg, Craske, & Barlow, 2006). Several treatment protocols recommend removing anxiety control strategies at the outset of exposure if possible, and gradually, if necessary (i.e., if the client is unwilling or unable to refrain from engaging in safety behaviours; Barlow, 2008; Craske et al., 2006; Zinbarg et al., 2006). These practice guidelines have numerous theoretical underpinnings. One is emotional processing theory (Foa & Kozak, 1986), as described earlier, which suggests that all aspects of a mental representation of a feared stimulus, including responses (e.g. sweating, escaping), and meanings (e.g. threat, danger), should be activated during exposure. Emotional processing theory proposes that after a fear is fully activated, information learned during exposure can be incorporated in the mental representation of the fear, correcting excessive fear responses and modifying meaning elements. From an emotional processing standpoint, anxiety control strategies reduce the effectiveness of exposure by interfering with the full activation of a fear, or by reducing the cognitive resources available to process corrective information. Another relevant theory is Mowrer's two-factor theory of fear and avoidance, which suggests that escape and avoidance reduce fear, and are therefore reinforcing (Mowrer, 1960). The reinforcing nature of escape and avoidance make these responses likely to occur again in similar situations, ultimately serving to maintain fear. A related point has been made by Barlow (2008) in his discussion of the importance of learning during exposure for panic disorder and agoraphobia. Barlow (2008) highlights that two pieces of new learning are considered to be essential components of exposure therapy, namely, learning that: (1) the worst case scenario does not come true, and (2) feelings of anxiety are tolerable. Several safety behaviours, such as leaving a situation prematurely, may interfere with both types of learning during exposure. Another reason to eliminate anxiety control strategies is, as Salkovskis and Westbrook (1987) noted, that positive outcomes are often misattributed to the use of safety aids, as opposed to the remote likelihood of feared catastrophic outcomes. Despite the largely unanimous clinical guidelines recommending that use of safety behaviours be minimized (or even eliminated) during exposure, the empirical evidence behind these recommendations is far from conclusive (see Hood, Antony, Koerner, & Monson, 2010; Parrish et al., 2008; Rachman, Radomsky, & Shafran, 2008 for reviews).

According to recently published papers (Hood et al., 2010; Parrish et al., 2008; Rachman et al., 2008) and our own survey of the literature, several experiments have demonstrated in various anxiety disorder populations (1) that engaging in anxiety control strategies during in vivo exposure attenuates the efficacy of exposure by interfering with extinction of the anxiety response and limiting behavioural approach; and (2) that explicit instruction to refrain from using anxiety control strategies during in vivo exposure appears to lead to better outcomes (e.g. Craske, Street, & Barlow, 1989; Grayson, Foa, & Steketee, 1982; Kamphuis & Telch; 2000; Kim, 2005; Rodriguez & Craske, 1995; Salkovskis et al., 1999; Salkovskis, Thorpe, Wahl, Wroe, & Forrester, 2003; Salkovskis, Westbrook, Davis, Jeavons, & Gledhill, 1997;

Sloan, & Telch, 2002; Wells, Clark, Salkovskis, & Ludgate, 1995). Interestingly, the mere knowledge that safety aids are available if needed has been shown to limit the efficacy of exposure, even if people do not actually use them (Powers, Smits, & Telch, 2004), which speaks to the subtle influence that anxiety control strategies can have on behaviour. However, it should be noted that a more recent investigation produced results suggesting that the perceived availability of safety aids may not interfere with in vivo exposure (Sy, Dixon, Lickel, Nelson, & Deacon, 2011); more research is needed.

In contrast to the aforementioned investigations, there are studies that indicate that even when people do use anxiety control strategies during exposure, their symptoms may still improve (Hood et al., 2010; Parrish et al., 2008). For example, a number of experiments with individuals with animal fears have demonstrated that use of safety aids does not impede reductions in fear and cognitive change; outcomes for people who are instructed to use safety aids and people who are instructed to refrain from their use are in fact comparable (Hood et al., 2010; Milosevic & Radomsky, 2008). If anything, there appears to be an advantage for individuals who use safety aids—they are able to approach their feared animal more rapidly relative to people who do not use safety aids during exposure (Hood et al., 2010; Milosevic & Radomsky, 2008). Authors (Hood et al., 2010; Parrish et al., 2008) have proposed that an increase in self-efficacy (Bandura, Jeffery, & Wright, 1974) may be one mechanism by which safety aids facilitate progress.

Earlier, we referred to one of the guiding principles of exposure—that exposure is most effective when one does not leave the exposure situation prematurely. This popular guideline has been examined in at least two studies. de Silva and Rachman (1984) compared individuals with agoraphobia in three conditions: endurance, escape and waitlist control. Participants in the endurance condition were instructed to remain in an exposure situation until their anxiety reduced by at least half relative to the peak, whereas those in the escape condition were instructed to leave the exposure situation if their anxiety became excessive. Individuals in the endurance and escape conditions reported equivalent improvement in symptoms at posttreatment, whereas people in the waitlist control condition did not improve. Rachman, Craske, Tallman, and Solyom (1986) replicated these findings and extended them as well by demonstrating that gains were maintained at 3-month follow-up. These results are compelling as they call into question a guideline that is commonly followed in practice.

With regard to distraction, research suggests that not all distractors prevent fear reduction during exposure, and certain types can even *facilitate* progress. There is a set of studies suggesting that verbal distraction (i.e., fear-irrelevant conversation) has facilitative effects in exposure for blood-injection fears (Oliver & Page, 2003; Penfold & Page, 1999) and spider fear (Johnstone & Page, 2004). The impact of nonconversation distraction has also been examined in individuals with specific phobias, with findings indicating no detrimental effect on fear reduction (Antony, McCabe, Leeuw, Sano, & Swinson, 2001; Schmid-Leuz, Elsesser, Lohrmann, Jöhren, & Sartory, 2007).

Taken together, the research to date suggests that the use of anxiety control strategies can interfere with optimal exposure outcomes; however, such strategies are less likely to hinder treatment under certain conditions (Hood et al., 2010; Parrish et al., 2008; Rachman et al., 2008). Circumstances in which the use of safety strategies may be appropriate were recently fleshed out in a critical analysis by Parrish et al. (2008): (1) when they boost self-efficacy, (2) when they are not cognitively taxing, (3) when they encourage the client to come closer to a feared stimulus and promote "corrective" learning and (4) when they do not lead to "misattributions of safety." Anxiety control strategies under these conditions may be useful in facilitating engagement in exposures that would otherwise be too challenging or overwhelming for the client (Rachman et al., 2008), particularly at the beginning of treatment. Moreover, the "judicious use" (Rachman et al., 2008) of anxiety control strategies may decrease the high rates of refusal or attrition (see Foa et al., 2005) that are observed in exposure treatment.

12.3 Current Approach to Anxiety Control Strategies in Imaginal Exposure

The main goal of this chapter is to review what is currently known about the role of anxiety control strategies in *imaginal exposure*. We began the chapter with a review of the literature on anxiety control strategies in in vivo exposure to provide some context for this discussion. Whereas in vivo exposure is the systematic and repeated confrontation of fear-evoking "external" objects or situations, imaginal exposure is the systematic and repeated confrontation of *mental images* of threatening events or scenarios and the anxiety that accompanies these images. In this portion of the chapter, we will outline current imaginal exposure procedures for posttraumatic stress disorder (PTSD) and generalized anxiety disorder (GAD), two anxiety disorders that have in common the avoidance of anxiety-provoking mental images of threatening scenarios. We will also discuss the current position on anxiety control strategies in imaginal exposure protocols. We will advance the argument that more empirical work is needed on the impact of anxiety control strategies on the effectiveness of imaginal exposure before any definitive guidelines or recommendations can be made about the way such strategies should be handled in treatment.

12.3.1 Implications of Emotional Processing Theory for Imaginal Exposure Procedures

According to emotional processing theory, fear stimuli can be objects, external situations, bodily sensations, memories or mental images. In their writings, Foa and Kozak did not make a distinction between exposure to concrete, observable stimuli and exposure to mental stimuli; suggesting that mechanisms of action are hypothesized to be similar, irrespective of the "target" stimulus for exposure. As such, procedures for in vivo exposure and imaginal exposure are very similar, except that imaginal exposure is somewhat more challenging to carry out than is in vivo exposure owing to the fact that the feared stimulus is an internal "event" that is not tangible and cannot be observed. In the following paragraphs, we will describe current imaginal exposure procedures for PTSD and GAD. In the case of PTSD, the avoided cognitive activity is a sensory-perceptual trauma memory. In GAD, the avoided cognition is a mental image of one's hypothetical "worst case scenario" coming true. After we describe the essential elements of the exposure procedures for PTSD and GAD, we will discuss how anxiety control strategies are addressed in current imaginal exposure protocols for these anxiety disorders.

12.3.2 Imaginal Exposure for PTSD

Avoidance and emotional numbing are key symptoms of DSM-IV-defined PTSD. Imaginal exposure, in particular prolonged exposure, is employed to reduce avoidance of the trauma memory and may also lead to reductions in re-experiencing symptoms (Ehlers & Clark, 2000; Foa, Hembree, & Rothbaum, 2007). Ehlers and Clark (2000) proposed that the "current sense of threat" that people with PTSD experience is due in part to the way a person processes the trauma. Research suggests that the trauma memories of people with PTSD are disorganized, fragmented, and low on conceptual elaboration. Imaginal exposure is purported to promote conceptual processing (i.e., processing of the meaning associated with the trauma), increases the organization and coherence of the trauma memory, and reduces the distress and anxiety that a person experiences upon recollecting the trauma (Ehlers & Clark, 2000).

The following is an overview of Foa et al.'s (2007) imaginal exposure procedure. The therapist first demonstrates the counterproductive effects of avoiding thoughts of the trauma, using the "white bear" thought suppression exercise. The therapist then asks the client to recount the trauma in the present tense and in as much detail as possible, so as to concretize the image and activate emotion. The therapist is advised not to engage in any conversation during the exposure but he or she may make encouraging statements that promote engagement with the exposure (e.g. "great job, stay with your feelings"; Foa et al., 2007), as long as the comments are not attempts at reassurance. As prolonged exposure progresses, the therapist probes for information to further activate the underlying fear structure (e.g. "What is your body feeling? What do you smell?"; Foa et al., 2007). While the client is recounting the trauma, the therapist regularly asks for anxiety ratings. At the end of the exposure, the therapist and client proceed to the processing phase. During this phase, the client's trauma-related cognitions are explored (e.g. "What does it mean to you that this happened?"; Foa et al., 2007), which promotes activation of "meaning" elements in the fear structure. Foa and colleagues note that in the final sessions of imaginal exposure, anxiety should ideally be in the 10 to 30 range (out of 100).

12.3.3 Recommendations Regarding the Use of Anxiety Control Strategies During Imaginal Exposure for PTSD

According to the emotional engagement hypothesis (Jaycox, Foa, & Morral, 1998), *emotional underengagement*, particularly during the first imaginal exposure session, is a potential barrier to recovery from PTSD. In their treatment manual, Foa et al. (2007) note that an indicator of underengagement is a low level of self-reported anxious arousal during imaginal exposure. Clients may behave in a detached or emotionally disconnected manner during the exposure. For example, they may describe the trauma in a flat tone or the account may come across like a police report (e.g. attackers may be referred to as "perpetrators" or "assailants"). Foa et al. also note that clients may, in an effort to disengage, omit elements that are considered essential to a vivid account of the trauma, such as stimulus elements and response elements.

In a study testing the emotional engagement hypothesis (Jaycox et al., 1998), female victims of assault received 6 to 7 sessions of imaginal exposure, per the standard guidelines. Participants were asked to imagine that the trauma was happening "in the here and now" and to recount the trauma in as much detail as possible, including thoughts and emotions experienced during the trauma. Using a cluster analysis, participants were categorized as high engagers/non-habituators low engagers/non-habituators, and high engagers/habituators based on their subjective units of distress ratings during the exposure. Although gains were observed across all three groups, the people who improved most were those who showed highest emotional activation at Session 1 and extinction of anxiety across sessions of exposure (i.e., high engagers/habituators). To explain the findings, Jaycox and colleagues proposed that the women characterized as high-engagers and habituators showed the greatest gains because they were able to benefit from information that challenged their beliefs about the dangerousness of activating their PTSD symptoms in session. It is important to note, however, that the extent to which the people in this sample held the belief that PTSD symptoms are dangerous is unknown; as such it cannot be ascertained that access to and disconfirmation of this particular belief was in fact the mechanism by which improvement occurred.

Foa et al. (2007) note that attempts to limit engagement in the exposure are typical at the beginning of exposure-based therapy, but that therapists should attempt to increase engagement as treatment progresses. For example, the therapist is advised to probe for sensory-affective detail (e.g. "What do you see right now as you are walking into the room?") and to remind the client to use the first person in his or her account of the trauma. Importantly, therapists should explore with the client reasons for underengagement, as the client may very well have concerns about what could happen if he or she were to allow himself or herself to engage (e.g. " I will lose control of my anxiety").

Taken together, there may be room for anxiety control strategies at the beginning stages of imaginal exposure for PTSD, to facilitate engagement. However, according to Foa and colleagues, the therapist and client should work to reduce the use of anxiety-control strategies as early as possible, the assumption being that continual use of anxiety control strategies will interfere with progress in exposure.

12.3.4 Imaginal Exposure for GAD

GAD is characterized by excessive and uncontrollable worry and anxiety about situations that are uncertain and contain the possibility of a negative outcome. In GAD, the focus of the worry is not restricted to one domain; by definition, the worry extends across multiple domains (e.g. finances, work performance, familial relationships, as well as other interpersonal relationships; Dugas et al., 1998). According to Borkovec's Avoidance Theory of GAD (see Sibrava & Borkovec, 2006), people with GAD avoid thinking about potentially catastrophic scenarios in a concrete and vivid way. For example, a person with GAD might avoid thinking about the negative consequences of losing his or her job or might avoid thinking about what could happen if he or she fails to achieve a passing grade in his or her courses. The verbal–linguistic content of worry is hypothesized to dampen mental images of threatening hypothetical scenarios and suppress anxious arousal. Borkovec and colleagues noted that in the long-run, worry prevents full emotional processing, as the individual does not allow himself or herself to come into contact with images of feared scenarios and the anxiety that accompanies these images. As a result of chronic cognitive avoidance, GAD-relevant fear structures remain unchallenged and consequently, unmodified. Put differently, "worrying in words" allows the individual to avoid thinking about feared scenarios in a "clear" way (Dugas & Robichaud, 2007). This ultimately hinders emotional processing, as it does not provide the person with GAD with the opportunity to objectively evaluate his or her feared scenarios.

Because the situations that individuals with GAD worry about are hypothetical and have a remote probability of occurrence, in vivo exposure to these situations is often not possible. Therefore, in situations in which there is not an *actual* problem to confront or solve (as is often the case in GAD), exposure to mental images of catastrophic scenarios is indicated. Imaginal exposure is a component of at least two cognitive behavioural treatment protocols for GAD (see Craske, Barlow, & O'Leary, 1992 and Dugas & Robichaud, 2007). We will describe the protocols in turn and will then compare them, in particular, on their respective recommendations regarding the use of anxiety-control strategies (also cf. chapter by Hoyer & Beesdo-Baum in this book.

12.3.4.1 Worry Exposure

Craske and colleagues (Craske et al., 1992; Craske, 1999) developed their exposure procedure based on Borkovec's work. In the first step of Craske et al.'s exposure procedure, the therapist and client decide on an exposure target. The client selects a feared hypothetical scenario for the exposure and using the downward arrow technique, the therapist helps the client identify the worst possible outcome (e.g. "if my wife and kids leave me (feared scenario), I will end up penniless in the gutter (worst possible consequence)"; van der Heiden, & ten Broeke, 2009). Lang proposed that individual differences exist in the ability to evoke and engage in mental imagery; as such, Craske (1999) suggested that providing training in imaging may optimize imaginal exposure. Before clients are asked to confront their feared scenario, they practice imaging a neutral scenario (e.g. "Bring to mind an image of rain drops coming down a window"; Craske, 1999). Clients are then asked to close their eyes and generate a mental image of their worst-case scenario and to hold the image in mind for a minimum of 25 min. Clients are asked to refrain from engaging in distraction and other anxiety control strategies (e.g. neutralization, insertion of positive or reassuring elements into the scenario) while holding the image in mind, so as to experience any aversive emotions that may arise as a result of imagining the worst-case scenario. After 25 min, clients stop the exposure and are guided in cognitive re-evaluation. For example, clients may be asked to generate and write down alternative outcomes to the imagined scenario or ways in which they would cope if the feared situation did in fact materialize. The client is then asked to evaluate the veracity of the feared scenario (e.g. by estimating the likelihood of occurrence of the scenario). Craske and colleagues also note that anxiety management strategies (e.g. cued relaxation) may be used, as long as they are introduced *after* the actual exposure.

12.3.4.2 Cognitive Exposure

Dugas and Robichaud (2007) have also outlined a procedure for imaginal exposure that is, to a certain extent, similar to the Craske et al. procedure and is based largely on Foa and Kozak's emotional processing theory, Borkovec and colleagues' conceptualization of worry as cognitive avoidance, and standard procedures for in vivo exposure. In their imaginal exposure approach (referred to in their protocol as "cognitive exposure") the therapist first communicates the rationale for exposure, using fear of dogs as an example. As part of the rationale, the therapist explains the ways in which avoidance and neutralization of a feared object or situation, (although "beneficial" in the short-term), are ultimately counterproductive. Once the client grasps the concepts of avoidance and neutralization, the therapist demonstrates via diagrams how repeated and systematic exposure to feared situations extinguishes the anxiety response. The therapist then explains how exposure is applied to reduce chronic avoidance of worrisome situations.

In preparation for exposure, the client and therapist decide on an exposure scenario, using the downward arrow technique. The client is then asked to write a preliminary exposure "script." Specifically, he or she is instructed to construct a narrative of his or her worst fear coming true. In line with Lang's work and consistent with Foa and colleagues' imaginal exposure procedure for PTSD, the client is asked to insert as many sensory and emotional references, reaction elements and meaning elements into the narrative as possible, to invoke a mental image that will activate the underlying "fear structure." The client is also given instructions to describe his or her feared scenario in the present tense and in the first person, so as to orient the person to the here-and-now and to simulate as closely as possible the experience of being in the feared situation, as though it were actually unfolding in the present moment. These writing instructions are thought to be particularly important for clients with GAD because of the "fuzziness" that characterizes their hypothetical scenarios.

After the client has written the narrative and has reviewed it with the therapist, the exposure begins. The client is asked to read the scenario out loud, slowly, and with expression, into an audio recorder. The therapist asks the client to rate his or her anxiety every minute. At the end of the session, the therapist reviews the anxiety ratings with the client to show that although anxiety is high at first, it decreases over time. The client is then encouraged to listen to the recording repeatedly for 30 to 60 consecutive minutes so as to experience the gradual return of anxiety to baseline that follows the initial increase in anxious arousal. Clients are also given instructions to carry out exposure daily until thinking about their feared scenario no longer arouses more than minimal anxiety (Dugas & Robichaud, 2007).

12.3.5 Recommendations Regarding the Use of Anxiety Control Strategies in Imaginal Exposure for GAD

In their imaginal exposure protocols, Craske and colleagues and Dugas and Robichaud suggest that anxiety control strategies *during* exposure may interfere with emotional processing. As noted earlier, in both protocols, clients are asked to refrain from engaging in avoidance or neutralization during the imaging component of the exposure. Dugas and Robichaud take this recommendation a step further by suggesting that therapists attend to attempts on the part of the client to neutralize right at the outset, when they are preparing the exposure script. Dugas and Robichaud note that efforts to neutralize may manifest in a number of ways: minimal use of emotional terms in the script; omitting elements of the script that are important to the formation of emotional imagery (e.g. response elements, sensory elements); writing the scenario with minimal detail so that it remains vague and undefined; and scripting the feared hypothetical scenario so that the outcome is not uncertain and not catastrophic. The Craske et al. procedure varies from the Dugas and Robichaud procedure in at least three ways. First, Craske and colleagues recommend imagery training as an initial step before engaging in actual exposure, whereas Dugas and Robichaud do not include this (at least not explicitly). Second, the Craske and colleagues protocol allows for anxiety management strategies such as relaxation, as long as they are not engaged in during the actual exposure. Third, Dugas and Rochichaud, in keeping with Foa and Kozak's original theory, suggest that clients stay with the exposure until they experience the "exposure curve," defined as a rise in anxiety followed by a decline, until preexposure baseline levels of arousal are attained.

Taken together, in the treatment of GAD, the general recommendations in published protocols are (1) to watch for attempts on the part of the client to limit engagement in the exposure scenario (e.g. avoiding present-moment focus; describing the scenario in superficial terms) and (2) to encourage clients not to engage in behaviour that may interfere with the ability to become immersed in the exposure scenario.

12.3.6 Empirical Basis of Recommendations Regarding Anxiety Control Strategies in Imaginal Exposure

In sum, the current thinking is that therapists should assess, monitor and discourage the use of anxiety control strategies during imaginal exposure for PTSD or GAD, as these strategies may be countertherapeutic. Given that the target stimulus in imaginal exposure is a mental image of a feared scenario, the anxiety control strategies that people are likely to employ are ones that have the effect of dampening the intensity of the mental image, thereby limiting engagement with the feared situation. These might include giving an account of the feared scenario in overly factual or vague terms, depersonalizing the scenario, situating the event in the past or in the future (i.e., not in the present), or speaking quickly when describing the scenario. Generally, the recommendation is that clients reduce engagement in anxiety control strategies as early as possible in the exposure to promote activation of anxious arousal. Therapists are also advised to be attentive to clients' attempts to reduce the intensity of imaginal exposure. There appears to be a consensus that activation of anxious arousal is important for the effectiveness of imaginal exposure. Exploration of the "meaning elements" associated with the feared scenario seems to be particularly important when working with individuals who have PTSD.

It is important to note that imaginal exposure procedures are based largely on in vivo exposure procedures. Our review suggests that there is a gap between science and clinical practice where imaginal exposure is concerned. Although imaginal exposure procedures are documented in detail in several treatment manuals, very little research has been conducted on the guidelines for these procedures, the mechanisms of these procedures, and the impact of these procedures on underlying vulnerability factors that give rise to, and maintain psychopathology. For example, a study by Hoyer et al. (2009) is the only published trial that has tested the impact of worry exposure on symptoms and cognitive processes associated with GAD. Therefore, we wish to close this chapter with a few questions about imaginal exposure that we believe need to be addressed via empirical work before any definitive recommendations can be made with regard to the way anxiety control strategies should be handled in imaginal exposure procedures. In the following paragraphs, we discuss a few assumptions that we believe require further empirical investigation.

1. *People engage in anxiety control strategies during imaginal exposure and engage in these actions to limit their experience of their feared scenario.* Although anxiety

control strategies are discussed in treatment protocols for imaginal exposure, there is a scarcity of descriptive research on their phenomenology and a lack of experimental research on their impact on treatment outcome. Complicating matters further, when invoking mental images of feared scenarios, individuals with PTSD and GAD may use strategies that are largely covert. To our knowledge, there is no empirically derived description of what people actually "do" during imaginal exposure. Related to this, there are no known experiments demonstrating that engagement-limiting behaviours during imaginal exposure in fact suppress emotional arousal and that people engage in such strategies with the express purpose of limiting engagement during exposure.

2. *People employ avoidant strategies during imaginal exposure to dampen the experience of anxiety (versus other emotions).* It is widely assumed that people with PTSD and GAD avoid thinking about feared scenarios (actual or hypothetical) because this will arouse strong feelings of anxiety that may be difficult to tolerate. Although there are data indicating that individuals with PTSD and individuals with GAD are afraid of, and engage in efforts to avoid their anxiety (Ehlers & Clark, 2000; Roemer, Salters, Raffa, & Orsillo, 2005), this may not be the only emotion that they experience as intolerable and to be avoided. For example, Roemer, Litz, Orsillo, and Wagner (2001) found that the tendency to suppress or withhold positive *and* negative emotions were both positively associated with PTSD. Roemer et al. (2005) found a unique association between GAD and fear of depression. Thus, more research is needed to determine what emotions become activated during exposure and what emotions people with PTSD or GAD are attempting to suppress during imaginal exposure.

3. *Activation of fear, particularly during the first session, is important to the success of imaginal exposure.* A central tenet of emotional processing theory is that some degree of physiological activation is critical (but not sufficient) for the success of exposure. To test this hypothesis, Foa, Riggs, Massie, and Yarczower (1995) examined subjective fear ratings and facial expressions of fear during imaginal exposure with 12 female assault victims. The results showed that more pronounced expressions of fear during the first sessions of imaginal exposure were associated with a better outcome following prolonged exposure. An interesting finding was that high levels of anger at the start of imaginal exposure predicted a *negative* outcome. Sloan, Marx, Epstein, and Lexington (2007) examined whether emotional processing theory may explain the benefits that have been observed with written disclosure. Written disclosure, a paradigm developed by Pennebaker and Beall (1986) involves writing about a stressful or traumatic scenario repeatedly over a number of days in succession. A meta-analysis of written disclosure moderators (Frattaroli, 2006) indicates that three 20-min sessions of writing leads to significant physical and psychological health benefits. Some authors (Goldman, Dugas, Sexton, & Gervais, 2007; Sloan et al., 2007) have suggested that written disclosure may operate by the same mechanisms as conventional forms of imaginal exposure.

Sloan et al. randomly assigned traumatized college students to one of three written disclosure conditions: emotional expression, insight and cognitive assimilation, or a neutral writing condition. All participants were asked to write about their trauma for 20 min on three consecutive days. Participants assigned to the emotional expression condition were asked to write about "the most traumatic experience of their lives with as much emotion and feeling as possible." Participants in the insight and cognitive assimilation condition were also asked to write about the most traumatic event of their lives but with a focus on the meaning of the event and to "challenge their dissonant thoughts about the event." Participants in the neutral writing condition wrote about a nonemotional event.

In keeping with Foa and colleagues' theory, participants in the emotional expression condition benefitted the most from writing. Participants in the emotional expression condition displayed the highest heart rate at the first session of written disclosure. In addition, although participants in the emotional expression and insight and cognitive assimilation conditions showed a decline in heart rate activity from the first session to the last session, this decline was more pronounced for people in the emotional expression condition (note, however, that the more pronounced decline may have been a function of initially higher heart rate activity in the emotional expression condition).

Finally, Sloan et al. examined whether emotional arousal was a predictor of severity of psychological symptoms following written disclosure. They found that changes in self-reported arousal mediated the impact of emotionally expressive writing on reductions in posttraumatic stress symptoms. However, other indicators of emotional reactivity *did not* mediate outcome; specifically, heart-rate activity and self-reported arousal during the first writing session, change in heart-rate activity over the course of the 3 days of written disclosure, and inclusion of negative emotion words in the written disclosure scripts were not mediators of outcome.

These findings have several important implications for our understanding of the mechanisms underlying the effectiveness of exposure. First, Sloan and colleagues' findings suggest that initial levels of emotional engagement may not be a necessary condition for improvement. Second, this study suggests that the instructions commonly utilized in imaginal exposure (i.e., to recount the feared scenario in the present tense with inclusion of sensory referents) may not have any bearing on the impact of exposure, as the findings of the above study indicate that simply writing with "as much emotion and feeling as possible" may be sufficient. Finally and perhaps most important, participants in the study were not given any instructions regarding anxiety control strategies. This implies that people may still benefit from imaginal exposure even if they are not explicitly told to refrain from using anxiety control strategies. Taken together, more research is needed to determine the extent to which emotional arousal, in particular objective change in autonomic arousal, is a determinant of improvement following imaginal exposure.

4. *Imaginal exposure sessions must be sufficiently long in duration to allow anxiety or distress to decrease.* As noted earlier, there is some research (albeit limited), indicating that people may benefit from exposure that is interrupted. Research on

the "optimal" duration of imaginal exposure is needed to determine whether longer sessions are in fact better than shorter sessions. A study by van Minnen and Foa (2006) indicated that 60-min imaginal exposure sessions for PTSD led to greater within-session habituation than did 30-min sessions, but that this was not associated with treatment outcome. Clients who received 30 min showed the same degree of improvement in PTSD symptoms as clients who received 60 min. Similar research is needed in GAD.

5. *Anxiety control strategies interfere with the effectiveness of imaginal exposure.* In our survey of the literature, we could not find any experiments that have directly examined the impact of anxiety control strategies on outcomes following imaginal exposure. Therefore, the extent to which the employment of such strategies hinders or facilitates participation in imaginal exposure remains unknown.

12.4 Conclusion

In this chapter, we set out to determine whether anxiety control strategies hinder or facilitate participation in imaginal exposure, a treatment strategy for PTSD and GAD. Taken together, our survey of the literature suggests that there is an important lack of connection between science and practice where imaginal exposure is concerned. Generally, imaginal exposure protocols emphasize the importance of activating emotional arousal, as such activation encourages mental imagery and provides access to underlying maladaptive beliefs that can then be modified. There is a general consensus among clinicians that clients should minimize actions that may inhibit or limit contact with emotional imagery during imaginal exposure. Although there is a considerable body of research on the role of anxiety control strategies in in vivo exposure, we did not find any experimental research on the direct impact of anxiety control strategies on imaginal exposure. Thus, we were unable to evaluate current recommendations for the use of anxiety control strategies in imaginal exposure. A better understanding of the anxiety control strategies that people use to limit engagement with emotional imagery during imaginal exposure and experimental analyses of the impact of such strategies on this form of exposure are sorely needed.

References

Antony, M. M., McCabe, R. E., Leeuw, I., Sano, N., & Swinson, R. P. (2001). Effect of distraction and coping style on in vivo exposure for specific phobia of spiders. *Behaviour Research and Therapy, 39*, 1137–1150.

Bandura, A., Jeffery, R. W., & Wright, C. L. (1974). Efficacy of participant modeling as a function of response induction aids. *Journal of Abnormal Psychology, 83*, 56–64.

Barlow, D. H. (2008). *Clinical handbook of psychological disorders: A step-by-step treatment manual* (4th ed.). New York: Guilford Press.

Clark, D. M. (1999). Anxiety disorders: Why they persist and how to treat them. *Behaviour Research and Therapy, 37*, S5–S27.

Craske, M. G. (1999). *Anxiety disorders: Psychological approaches to theory and treatment.* Boulder: Westview Press.

Craske, M. G., Antony, M. M., & Barlow, D. H. (2006). *Mastering your fears and phobias (2nd ed.): Therapist guide*. New York: Oxford University Press.

Craske, M. G., Barlow, D. H., & O'Leary, T. A. (1992). *Mastery of your anxiety and worry*. San Antonio: Harcourt Brace/Graywind.

Craske, M. G., Street, L., & Barlow, D. H. (1989). Instructions to focus upon or distract from internal cues during exposure treatment of agoraphobic avoidance. *Behaviour Research and Therapy, 27*, 663–672.

Cuthbert, B. N., Lang, P. J., Strauss, C., Drobes, D., Patrick, C. J., & Bradley, M. M. (2003). The psychophysiology of anxiety disorder: Fear memory imagery. *Psychophysiology, 40*, 407–422.

de Silva, P., & Rachman, S. (1984). Does escape behaviour strengthen agoraphobic avoidance? A preliminary study. *Behaviour Research and Therapy, 22*, 87–91.

Dugas, M. J., Freeston, M. H., Ladouceur, R., Rhéaume, J., Provencher, M., & Boisvert, J.-M. (1998). Worry themes in primary GAD, secondary GAD and other anxiety disorders. *Journal of Anxiety Disorders, 12*, 253–261.

Dugas, M. J., & Robichaud, M. J. (2007). *Cognitive-behavioral treatment for generalized anxiety disorder: From science to practice*. New York: Routledge.

Ehlers, A., & Clark, D. M. (2000). A cognitive model of posttraumatic stress disorder. *Behaviour Research and Therapy, 38*, 319–345.

Foa, E. B., Hembree, E. A., & Rothbaum, B. O. (2007). *Prolonged exposure therapy for PTSD: Emotional processing of traumatic experiences (Therapist Guide)*. New York: Oxford University Press.

Foa, E. B., Huppert, J. D., & Cahill, S. P. (2006). Emotional processing theory: An update. In B. O. Rothbaum (Ed.), *Pathological anxiety: Emotional processing in etiology and treatment* (pp. 3–24). New York: Guilford Press.

Foa, E. B., & Kozak, M. J. (1985). Treatment of anxiety disorders: Implications for psychopathology. In A. H. Tuma & J. D. Maser (Eds.), *Anxiety and the anxiety disorders* (pp. 421–452). Hillsdale: Erlbaum.

Foa, E. B., & Kozak, M. J. (1986). Emotional processing of fear: Exposure to corrective information. *Psychological Bulletin, 99*, 20–35.

Foa, E. B., & Kozak, M. J. (1998). Clinical applications of bioinformational theory: Understanding anxiety and its treatment. *Behavior Therapy, 29*, 675–690.

Foa, E. B., Liebowitz, M. R., Kozak, M. J., Davies, S., Campeas, R., Franklin, M. E., et al. (2005). Randomized, placebo-controlled trial of exposure and ritual prevention, clomipramine, and their combination in the treatment of obsessive-compulsive disorder. *The American Journal of Psychiatry, 162*, 151–161.

Foa, E. B., Riggs, D. S., Massie, E. D., & Yarczower, M. (1995). The impact of fear activation and anger on the efficacy of exposure treatment for posttraumatic stress disorder. *Behavior Therapy, 26*, 487–499.

Frattaroli, J. (2006). Experimental disclosure and its moderators: A meta-analysis. *Psychological Bulletin, 132*, 823–865.

Goldman, N., Dugas, M. J., Sexton, K. A., & Gervais, N. J. (2007). The impact of written exposure on worry: A preliminary investigation. *Behavior Modification, 31*, 512–538.

Grayson, J. B., Foa, E. B., & Steketee, G. (1982). Habituation during exposure treatment: Distraction vs. attention-focusing. *Behaviour Research and Therapy, 20*, 323–328.

Hood, H. K., Antony, M. M., Koerner, N., & Monson, C. M. (2010). Effects of safety behaviors on fear reduction during exposure. *Behaviour Research and Therapy, 48*, 1161–1169.

Hoyer, J., Beesdo, K., Gloster, A. T., Runge, J., Höfler, M., & Becker, E. S. (2009). Worry exposure versus applied relaxation in the treatment of generalized anxiety disorder. *Psychotherapy and Psychosomatics, 78*, 106–115.

Jaycox, L. H., Foa, E. B., & Morral, A. R. (1998). Influence of emotional engagement and habituation on exposure therapy for PTSD. *Journal of Consulting and Clinical Psychology, 66*, 185–192.

Johnstone, K. A., & Page, A. C. (2004). Attention to phobic stimuli during exposure: The effect of distraction on anxiety reduction, self-efficacy and perceived control. *Behaviour Research and Therapy, 42*, 249–275.
Kamphuis, J. H., & Telch, M. J. (2000). Effects of distraction and guided threat reappraisal on fear reduction during exposure-based treatments for specific fears. *Behaviour Research and Therapy, 38*, 1163–1181.
Kim, E. (2005). The effect of the decreased safety behaviors on anxiety and negative thoughts in social phobics. *Journal of Anxiety Disorders, 19*, 69–86.
Lang, P. J. (1977). Imagery in therapy: An information processing analysis of fear. *Behavior Therapy, 8*, 862–886.
Lang, P. J., & Cuthbert, B. N. (1984). Affective information processing and the assessment of anxiety. *Journal of Behavioral Assessment, 6*, 369–395.
Milosevic, I., & Radomsky, A. S. (2008). Safety behaviour does not necessarily interfere with exposure therapy. *Behaviour Research and Therapy, 46*, 1111–1118.
Mowrer, O. H. (1960). *Revised two-factor theory and the concept of habit*. Hoboken: Wiley.
Oliver, N. S., & Page, A. C. (2003). Fear reduction during in vivo exposure to blood-injection stimuli: Distraction vs. attentional focus. *British Journal of Clinical Psychology, 42*, 13–25.
Parrish, C. L., Radomsky, A. S., & Dugas, M. J. (2008). Anxiety-control strategies: Is there room for neutralization in successful exposure treatment? *Clinical Psychology Review, 28*, 1400–1412.
Penfold, K., & Page, A. C. (1999). The effect of distraction on within-session anxiety reduction during brief in vivo exposure for mild blood-injection fears. *Behavior Therapy, 30*, 607–621.
Pennebaker, J. W., & Beall, S. K. (1986). Confronting a traumatic event: Toward an understanding of inhibition and disease. *Journal of Abnormal Psychology, 95*, 274–281.
Powers, M. B., Smits, J. A. J., & Telch, M. J. (2004). Disentangling the effects of safety-behavior utilization and safety-behavior availability during exposure-based treatment: A placebo-controlled trial. *Journal of Consulting and Clinical Psychology, 72*, 448–454.
Rachman, S., Craske, M., Tallman, K., & Solyom, C. (1986). Does escape behavior strengthen agoraphobic avoidance? A replication. *Behavior Therapy, 17*, 366–384.
Rachman, S., Radomsky, A. S., & Shafran, R. (2008). Safety behaviour: A reconsideration. *Behaviour Research and Therapy, 46*, 163–173.
Rodriguez, B. I., & Craske, M. G. (1995). Does distraction interfere with fear reduction during exposure? A test among animal-fearful subjects. *Behavior Therapy, 26*, 337–349.
Roemer, L., Litz, B. T., Orsillo, S. M., & Wagner, A. W. (2001). A preliminary investigation of the role of strategic withholding of emotions in PTSD. *Journal of Traumatic Stress, 14*, 149–156.
Roemer, L., Salters, K., Raffa, S. D., & Orsillo, S. M. (2005). Fear and avoidance of internal experiences in GAD: Preliminary tests of a conceptual model. *Cognitive Therapy and Research, 29*, 71–88.
Salkovskis, P. M., Clark, D. M., Hackmann, A., Wells, A., & Gelder, M. G. (1999). An experimental investigation of the role of safety-seeking behaviours in the maintenance of panic disorder with agoraphobia. *Behaviour Research and Therapy, 37*, 559–574.
Salkovskis, P. M., Thorpe, S. J., Wahl, K., Wroe, A. L., & Forrester, E. (2003). Neutralizing increases discomfort associated with obsessional thoughts: An experimental study with obsessional patients. *Journal of Abnormal Psychology, 112*, 709–715.
Salkovskis, P. M., & Westbrook, D. (1987). Obsessive-compulsive disorder: Clinical strategies for improving behavioural treatments. In H. R. Dent (Ed.), *Clinical psychology: Research and development*. London: Croom Helm.
Salkovskis, P., Westbrook, D., Davis, J., Jeavons, A., & Gledhill, A. (1997). Effects of neutralising on intrusive thoughts: An experiment investigating the etiology of obsessive-compulsive disorder. *Behaviour Research and Therapy, 35*, 211–219.
Schmid-Leuz, B., Elsesser, K., Lohrmann, T., Jöhren, P., & Sartory, G. (2007). Attention focusing versus distraction during exposure in dental phobia. *Behaviour Research and Therapy, 45*, 2691–2703.
Sibrava, N., & Borkovec, T. D. (2006). The cognitive avoidance theory of worry. In G. C. L. Davey & A. Wells (Eds.), *Worry and its psychological disorders: Theory, assessment, and treatment* (pp. 239–256). West Sussex: Wiley.

Sloan, D. M., Marx, B. P., Epstein, E. M., & Lexington, J. M. (2007). Does altering the writing instructions influence outcome associated with written disclosure? *Behavior Therapy, 38*, 155–168.

Sloan, T., & Telch, M. J. (2002). The effects of safety-seeking behavior and guided threat reappraisal on fear reduction during exposure: An experimental investigation. *Behaviour Research and Therapy, 40*, 235–251.

Sy, J. T., Dixon, L. J., Lickel, J. J., Nelson, E. A., & Deacon, B. J. (2011). Failure to replicate the deleterious effects of safety behaviors in exposure therapy. *Behaviour Research and Therapy, 49*, 305–314.

Thwaites, R., & Freeston, M. H. (2005). Safety-seeking behaviours: Fact or function? How can we clinically differentiate between safety behaviours and adaptive coping strategies across anxiety disorders? *Behavioural and Cognitive Psychotherapy, 33*, 177–188.

van der Heiden, C., & ten Broeke, E. (2009). The when, why, and how of worry exposure. *Cognitive and Behavioral Practice, 16*, 386–393.

van Minnen, A., & Foa, E. B. (2006). The effect of imaginal exposure length on outcome of treatment for PTSD. *Journal of Traumatic Stress, 19*, 427–438.

Wells, A., Clark, D. M., Salkovskis, P., & Ludgate, J. (1995). Social phobia: The role of in-situation safety behaviors in maintaining anxiety and negative beliefs. *Behavior Therapy, 26*, 153–161.

Wolpe, J. (1958). *Psychotherapy by reciprocal inhibition.* Stanford, Stanford University Press.

Zinbarg, R. E., Craske, M. G., & Barlow, D. H. (2006). *Mastery of your anxiety and worry (2nd ed.): Therapist guide*. New York: Oxford University Press.

Chapter 13
Variants of Exposure in Body Dysmorphic Disorder and Hypochondriasis

Florian Weck, Viktoria Ritter, and Ulrich Stangier

Florian Weck, Ph.D, is a clinical psychologist and assistant professor of the Department of Clinical Psychology and Psychotherapy at the University of Frankfurt (Germany). Dr. Weck has been interested in health anxiety and hypochondriasis for many years and his doctoral dissertation focused on the effectiveness of a cognitive-behavioral group treatment for hypochondriasis. He published several articles and a book on health anxiety and hypochondriasis. Currently he investigates the efficacy of cognitive therapy vs. exposure therapy for patients with hypochondriasis in a randomized trial.

F. Weck (✉) • V. Ritter • U. Stangier
Department of Clinical Psychology and Psychotherapy, University of Frankfurt, Varrentrappstr. 40–42, Frankfurt 60486, Germany
e-mail: Weck@psych.uni-frankfurt.de; Ritter@psych.uni-frankfurt.de; stangier@psych.uni-frankfurt.de

P. Neudeck and H.-U. Wittchen (eds.), *Exposure Therapy: Rethinking the Model – Refining the Method*, DOI 10.1007/978-1-4614-3342-2_13,

Viktoria Ritter, Dipl. Psych., is a clinical psychologist involved in the research and treatment of body dysmorphic disorder and social anxiety disorder at the Department of Clinical Psychology and Psychotherapy, Frankfurt. She is the author of a self-help book for patients with BDD. Currently she is conducting an experimental investigation on face perception in patients with BDD.

Ulrich Stangier, Ph.D, is Professor for Clinical Psychology and Psychotherapy at the University of Frankfurt (Germany). His main research areas are social phobia and recurrent depression. Dr. Stangier has also published various articles and books on health anxiety and body dysmorphic disorder.

13.1 Introduction

Currently, hypochondriasis and body dysmorphic disorder (BDD) are classified as somatoform disorders in DSM-IV-TR (APA, 2000). In ICD-10 (WHO, 1993), BDD is subsumed under hypochondriasis. Hypochondriasis and BDD have some similarities with respect to symptomatology (fear and avoidance), cognitive and emotional processing (selective attention to abnormalities of the body), and behavioral factors (bodily preoccupation, compulsive checking, reassurance, seeking medical treatment). In turn, due to their similarities within the spectrum of somatoform disorders on the one hand, and their shared features and high comorbidity with anxiety disorders on the other hand, the APA is recommending the removal of at least BDD from the current category of somatoform disorders and placing it in the new category of anxiety and obsessive–compulsive spectrum disorders (Phillips et al., 2010). Although less clear, there is some evidence that a reconceptualization of hypochondriasis as illness anxiety disorder might also be reasonable (see below). Besides these similarities, however, there are also differences with regard to the focus of concern, with hypochondriasis relating to physical health concerns and BDD to concerns about appearance. This chapter describes diagnostic and summarizes empirical evidence for psychological treatment approaches. Finally, an outlook is given on future development of transdiagnostic interventions in the treatment of hypochondriasis and BDD.

13.2 Hypochondriasis

13.2.1 Characteristics of Hypochondriasis

Fears regarding one's own death are primary fears in humanity. Certainly everyone has had the experience that the exposure to serious illnesses awakens those fears and demonstrates one's own mortality. If fears of illness and death become an obsessive preoccupation that causes clinically significant distress or psychosocial impairment, the clinical diagnosis of hypochondriasis should be considered. In the current edition of the Diagnostic and Statistical Manual (DSM-IV-TR; APA, 2000) hypochondriasis is classified among the somatoform disorders. However, this classification of hypochondriasis has often been criticized because hypochondriasis shares many phenomenological characteristics and important functional mechanisms with anxiety disorders. Excessive preoccupation, intolerance of uncertainty, and fear of illness are shared features with obsessive–compulsive disorder, whereas intense fear, body vigilance, and avoidance behavior indicate similarities with panic disorder. Therefore, the classification of hypochondriasis as an anxiety disorder has been suggested (Fava, Fabbri, Sirri, & Wise, 2007; Noyes, 1999; Olatunji, Deacon, & Abramowitz, 2009; Salkovskis & Clark, 1993; Schmidt, 1994; Starcevic, 2001). The diagnostic criteria of hypochondriasis according to DSM-IV-TR (APA, 2000) are as follows:

1. Preoccupation with fears of having, or the idea that one has, a serious disease based on the person's misinterpretation of bodily symptoms.
2. The preoccupation persists despite appropriate medical evaluation and reassurance.
3. The belief in Criterion A is not of delusional intensity (as in delusional disorder, somatic type) and is not restricted to a circumscribed concern about appearance (as in body dysmorphic disorder).
4. The preoccupation causes clinically significant distress or impairment in social, occupational, or other important areas of functioning.
5. The duration of the disturbance is at least 6 months.
6. The preoccupation is not better accounted for by generalized anxiety disorder, obsessive–compulsive disorder, panic disorder, a major depressive episode, separation anxiety, or another somatoform disorder.

However, a significant and necessary revision of the diagnostic criteria of hypochondriasis is planned for DSM-5. Hypochondriasis was renamed in "Illness Anxiety Disorder" and the criteria are currently as follows (APA, 2011):

1. Somatic symptoms are not present or, if present, are only mild in intensity.
2. Preoccupation with having or acquiring a serious illness. If a general medical condition or high risk for developing a general medical condition is present, the illness concerns are clearly excessive or disproportionate. The individual's concern is focused not on any physical distress per se, but rather on a suspected, underlying medical diagnosis.
3. High level of anxiety about health or having or acquiring a serious illness. These individuals have a low threshold for considering themselves to be sick and a low threshold for becoming alarmed about their health.
4. The person performs related excessive behaviors (e.g., checking one's body for signs of disease, repeatedly seeking information and reassurance from the internet or other sources), or exhibits maladaptive avoidance (e.g., avoiding doctor's appointments and hospitals, avoiding visiting sick friends or relatives, avoiding triggers of illness fears such as exercise).
5. Although the preoccupation may not be continuously present, the state of being preoccupied is chronic (at least 6 months).
6. The illness-related preoccupation is not better accounted for by the symptoms of another mental disorder such as complex somatic symptom disorder, panic disorder, generalized anxiety disorder, or obsessive–compulsive disorder.

13.2.1.1 Case Report

Georg is 41 years old and works in the public sector. He is worried that he has stomach cancer. The reasons for his worries are occasional pains in the stomach area. He has been to the doctor repeatedly concerning his fears and has also undergone a gastroscopy. Even though he feels relieved for a short time after a visit to the doctor, the thoughts of stomach cancer always come back. Besides spending a lot of time informing himself about stomach cancer and its symptoms on the Internet, Georg feels his stomach up to 20 times a day for changes and looks at it closely in the mirror in order to detect any possible pathological changes. The sudden illness of his uncle 10 years ago triggered his fear of cancer. His uncle fell ill with a brain tumor and died within 6 months. Consequently, Georg was afraid he himself was suffering from a brain tumor. Ever since the death of his uncle new fears of illness occur continually. He is mostly afraid of cancer but he is also afraid of other serious illnesses, such as multiple sclerosis or heart disease.

13.2.2 Epidemiology

In the general population the diagnosis of hypochondriasis is rare. In representative samples of the general population, only 0–0.2% meet the full diagnostic criteria of hypochondriasis (Lieb et al., 2002; Looper & Kirmayer, 2001; Martin & Jacobi, 2006; Noyes, Carney, Hillis, Jones, & Langbehn, 2005). In contrast, in primary care populations, the prevalence of hypochondriasis is significantly higher. In these populations 0.8–6.9% meet the criteria of hypochondriasis (Barsky, Klerman, Wyshak, & Latham, 1990; Escobar et al., 1998; Gureje, Üstün, & Simon, 1997; Noyes et al., 1994).

The diagnostic criteria for hypochondriasis have been criticized (for an overview, see Starcevic, 2001). In particular, the B-criterion was considered to be problematic. For example, in a large cross-national study of Gureje et al. (1997) it was found that the adherence to the B-criterion led to an underdetection of hypochondriasis and a spuriously decreased prevalence of hypochondriasis. The authors could demonstrate that patients with an abridged hypochondriasis (fulfilling the diagnosis of hypochondriasis with the exception of the B-criterion) were identical to patients meeting the full diagnosis of hypochondriasis regarding their psychopathology, but were different from nonhypochondriatic patients. The abridged hypochondriasis was three times higher (0.8 vs. 2.2%) than the full diagnosis of hypochondriasis.

In line with these findings is the fact that the prevalence of health fears or illness worries (which can be seen as related constructs) is much higher. For example, in the general population 6.9% reported intensive illness worries in the last 6 months and 13.1% in the last 1 month (Noyes et al., 2005). Furthermore, high rates of 24–34% for health anxiety were found in psychotherapeutic outpatients (Weck, Harms, Neng, & Stangier, 2011).

13.2.3 The Cognitive-Behavioral Model of Hypochondriasis and Health Anxiety

The cognitive-behavioral model of hypochondriasis and health anxiety is very similar to the one proposed for panic disorder (Salkovskis, 1989; see Fig. 13.1). Ordinary bodily sensations or illness related information are misinterpreted in a catastrophic manner and as a sign of a serious illness. This misinterpretation leads to an increased focus on the body, higher physiological arousal, checking behavior, and reassurance seeking. These illness behaviors and bodily changes strengthen the (irrational)

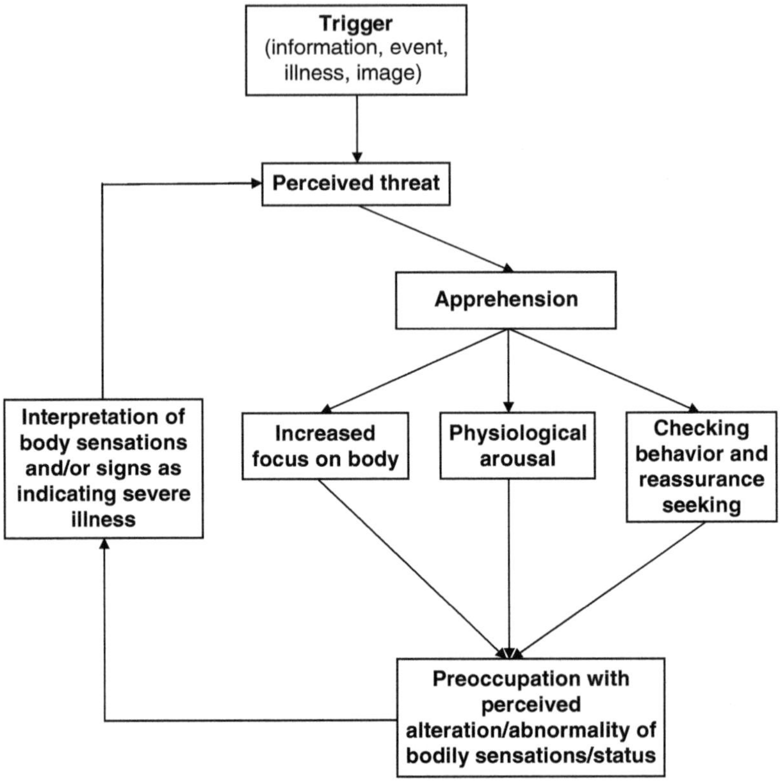

Fig. 13.1 Cognitive-behavioral model of hypochondriasis and health anxiety proposed by Salkovskis (1989, S. 241)

belief that one has a serious illness which in turn produces further physiological arousal and safety behaviors, and so on.

13.2.4 Psychological Treatment for Hypochondriasis and Health Anxiety

Different strategies have been considered for the treatment of hypochondriasis. Psychoeducation, relaxation training, stress-management, exposure, cognitive restructuring, mindfulness-based methods, and biofeedback are frequently used interventions. Only few studies have directly compared different intervention strategies for hypochondriasis. On the basis of these studies, there is no evidence of a superiority of any of the treatment strategies (Thomson & Page, 2007). Further studies with larger samples are also necessary for definitive statements. A recent study found that cognitive-behavioral therapy was superior to short-term psychodynamic therapy (Sørensen, Birket-Smith, Wattar, Buemann, & Salkovskis, 2011). Additionally, cognitive-behavioral treatment seems to also be effective in the routine clinical setting (Wattar et al., 2005).

Because many empirical studies have demonstrated the phenomenological similarities between anxiety disorders and hypochondriasis (Abramowitz, Olatunji, & Deacon, 2007; Barsky, Barnett, & Cleary, 1994; Hiller, Leibbrand, Rief, & Fichter, 2005; Van den Heuvel et al., 2005; Weck, Bleichhardt, Witthöft, & Hiller, 2011), exposure has been considered to be an effective treatment for hypochondriasis. Different types of exposure have been applied in patients with hypochondriasis. Some of them are based on the traditional habituation model, such as exposure in vivo and interoceptive exposure. However, most of the following procedures such as exposure in sensu and behavioral experiments, use exposure to challenge and implicitly or explicitly modify dysfunctional beliefs (Clark et al., 1998).

13.2.5 Description of the Techniques

To begin with, it is important to inform patients about the diagnosis of hypochondriasis (e.g., epidemiology, criteria, characteristics, risk factors). Secondly, it is necessary to identify avoidance and safety behaviors, such as reassurance seeking and body checking.

Usually, safety behaviors aim at reducing anxiety. However, some strategies (e.g., checking illness-related information in the internet for reassurance) increase anxiety. In addition, long-term uncertainty increases and preoccupation with symptoms and the feared illness. Furthermore, and as the most detrimental consequence, safety behaviors prevent the disconfirmation of illness-related beliefs, because the nonoccurrence of the threatening event (e.g., symptom aggravation) can spuriously be reattributed to its preventive effects. Finally, safety behaviors are time consuming and interpersonal problems can result from intensive reassurance.

Thus, even though safety behaviors may sometimes reduce anxiety in the short term, dysfunctional beliefs will be maintained and anxiety will persist or even increase in the long term. Although the dysfunctional role has been proven in a number of anxiety disorders as well, safety behavior may not always have a negative effect, e.g., in animal phobia (cf. Koerner & Fracalanza, this book). However, in contrast to animal phobias related to potentially controllable and immediately observable events (e.g., the snake will bite), the fears in patients with hypochondriasis and BDD focus on rather uncontrollable or covered changes of the body (e.g., the liver spot could develop into a malignant melanoma) and are therefore harder to refute. Thus principal differences in the contingencies of safety behaviors exist which could explain why safety behaviors in hypochondriasis and BDD rather than in animal phobias contribute to retrospective negative attribution of the nonoccurrence of feared events. Therefore, safety behaviors should be reduced by using Socratic questioning to clarify immediate and long-term consequences (see Fig. 13.2). Moreover, the use of behavioral experiments (see below) is indispensable to test the expected consequences of applying and dropping safety behaviors.

Reassurance	Body checking	avoidance
information seeking on the web asking my wife asking a friend asking the therapist consulting a physician	checking the abdomen checking weight	avoiding hospitals avoiding movies about cancer avoiding talking about death avoiding funerals

Direct consequences
reduction of anxiety sometimes increasing anxiety

Long term consequences
Becoming more and more unsure Increasing safety behavior Intolerance of uncertainty getting different information from different sources getting wrong information on the web Addicted to the judgment of others high costs Interpersonal problems with my wife Focus on symptoms and illness Making symptoms worse by body checking Time consuming restrictions on daily life

Fig. 13.2 Safety behaviors

The explanation of the treatment steps and planning of exposure often cause significant distress, because it activates intense anticipatory anxiety (e.g., "I will become crazy if I think too intensely about the feared illness" or "I will be unable to get rid of intrusive images if I see a movie about people suffering"). To encourage the patient, the following arguments may be helpful:

1. It is only by exposure to your fears that you will be able you to learn better ways in coping with them.
2. Intensive fears will decrease after some time. (A chart can be used to make this point clear).
3. Only exposing yourself to the fear will help you to gain further certainty about the facts (e.g., the feared illness is very rare) and overcome anxiety.

Table 13.1 Exercises for interoceptive exposure

Exercise	Description	Produced symptoms
Hyperventilation	Fast and deep breaths, in and out (1 min)	Shortness of breath, formication, dizziness, drowsiness, head pressure, heart palpitations
Running	1 min running in place	Tachycardia, shortness of breath, sweating
Consciously swallowing	Swallow 5× consecutively	Throat feels swollen, feeling of not being able to swallow
Stretching the chest	Breathe deeply into the chest without breathing out completely, until no more air can be taken in	Pain in the chest area
Shifting position	While standing, bend the upper body downward, then stand up straight	Feeling of wanting to pass out, drowsiness, dizziness

4. Avoidance tends to extend to more and more situations, thus spreading over one's entire life.
5. Several studies have demonstrated that exposure is effective in overcoming fears.

13.2.5.1 Interoceptive Exposure

Bodily symptoms are most often the origin of hypochondriac beliefs and fears. Patients with hypochondriasis tend toward catastrophic interpretations of abnormal somatic sensations, since they have a very narrow concept of good health. Good health is seen as the total absence of any somatic symptom (see Rief & Hiller, 1998). Interoceptive exposure is an effective way to activate and modify dysfunctional beliefs (see also Walker & Furer, 2008; Table 13.1).

Depending on the theoretical basis of exposure, interoceptive exposure may be conducted in accordance with the habituation model; or as part of behavioral experiments testing dysfunctional beliefs about somatic symptoms (Silver, Sanders, Morrison, & Cowey, 2008). In behavioral experiments, the therapist will explore the patient's expectations and compare them with the actual results of the experiment. For instance, the therapist may encourage the patient to do exercises associated with somatic symptoms. After the experiment, the therapist will ask the patient for any evidence for and against the belief that the sensations are threatening. In contrast, when using the habituation model, the therapist will continuously monitor his level of anxiety in order to ensure a high initial level and a significant reduction of anxiety throughout the exposure session. In addition, the patient is asked to continue these exercises as homework.

13.2.5.2 Exposure In vivo

Patients with hypochondriasis often avoid situations in which they are confronted with illness or death. Funerals, hospitals, movies about people suffering, documentaries about illness, visiting a sick friend, talking about illness or even using the word "cancer" are all situations which are avoided. For example, some patients believe that watching a movie about a sick person will result in an increased preoccupation with the mentioned symptoms and illness. As a consequence, these patients avoid any movies, reports, or even conversations about the illness. Otherwise they think that they will be plagued by intrusive images about the illness and its consequences. Even though most patients with hypochondriasis demonstrate excessive reassurance behavior by visiting medical doctors, some avoid this confrontation. They fear that the doctor only confirms their worst apprehension.

Exposure involves gradually confronting the real-life situations and bodily sensations that are avoided because of the fear of illness. These situations are listed in a hierarchy ranging from less anxiety-provoking situations to the most anxiety-provoking situation.

An important prerequisite of exposure is response prevention. It involves resisting the urge to seek information or reassurance about health and illness. Instead of calling doctors or running to the web, the patient is instructed to use healthy coping strategies, such as examining the evidence for and against illness.

Georg avoided watching reports about serious illnesses on television. Georg's fear was that the report would cause him to worry even more about a possible illness and that he would not be able to watch how the effected person was suffering. A television report about a person with stomach cancer was chosen as exposure. Georg's anxiety was rated at 10 (scale range from 0 to 10) *before exposure. During the 10-min report, however, there was a reduction in his anxiety. His anxiety was rated at 3 after exposure. Georg's fear of worrying more about the illness did not occur. On the contrary, Georg recognized marked differences between his own sensations and the patient's symptoms and consequently he determined that his fears in terms of stomach cancer were excessive.*

Georg was prone to feeling his stomach in order to be sure that it was not becoming deformed due to a tumor. The advantages and disadvantages of this safety behavior and its long-term maintenance function were discussed with Georg (compare Fig. 13.2). Because of the problems this behavior brings with it, Georg was asked to refrain from carrying out this checking behavior. This resulted in a considerable increase in Georg's fear and nervousness. However, he managed to largely reduce this behavior and noticed that the urge to feel his stomach subsided. The reduction of the checking behavior also resulted in a significantly lower cognitive preoccupation with the topic stomach cancer.

13.2.5.3 Exposure In Sensu

Distressing intrusive images (e.g., seeing oneself dying in a hospital bed) are very common in patients with hypochondriasis (Muse, McManus, Hackmann, Williams, & Williams, 2010). Patients want to escape from their images and try to distract themselves. But this strategy often fails and even enhances intrusive images and fears (like trying not to think of a white bear). In contrast, exposure in sensu is an effective strategy to manage fearful images (Furer & Walker, 2005; Furer, Walker, & Stein, 2007).

Therapist: Georg, you have told me that you often have particular images in your mind that are associated with stomach cancer and that scare you. Today we are going to concentrate on these images. An effective method to encounter these images is direct exposure to them. This method is more effective the more intense the exposure with the scary images is. Through the exposure, it is possible to experience that one can cope emotionally with these bad images. The goal is not to let illness-related thoughts and images influence your life, but rather to face them. It is important during the exposure to imagine different situations very vividly. Could you imagine confronting your illness-related images and fears?

In general, exposure begins with the patient imagining the attending physician making the feared diagnosis (e.g., stomach cancer). The patient is instructed to imagine vividly the worst possible outcome (e.g., persistent pain, sorrow, and the relatives' despair, one's own grief about dying, the funeral). When images or scenes activate strong emotions, it is important to take time until habituation takes place.

13.2.5.4 Imagery Rescripting

Another effective method of changing intrusive images is imagery rescripting. In contrast to exposure in sensu, this approach follows the rationale of cognitive restructuring. Imagery restructuring comprises the identification of fear-related images and their meaning by interview, diaries, or guided imagery; the elaboration of alternative meanings of the images in Socratic questioning; and its implementation in a new script by guided imagery (Holmes, Arntz, & Smucker, 2007).

The worst moment in Georg's scene was when the doctor pronounced the diagnosis: "The doctor looks at me with a sad expression and says that it is serious this time. He says: It is stomach cancer. The cancer is at a very advanced stage and an operation would be pointless. You only have a few more months to live".

In a Socratic dialogue, Georg was asked for possible alternative outcomes. Hence, the scene was rescripted: "The doctor looks at me and says: It is a cyst. It must be removed. It is an uncomplicated procedure, which can be performed on an outpatient basis. Don't worry about it, we do this kind of operation every day".

Patients also often report earlier negative memories related to illness, which are associated with intrusive negative images (cf. Muse et al., 2010). Imagery rescripting can also be effectively applied to these early negative experiences.

13.2.5.5 Behavioral Experiments

Exposure to threatening situations is also an important component of behavioral experiments (e.g., Salkovskis, Warwick, & Deal, 2003; Silver et al., 2008). However, whereas traditional exposure aims at enabling the patient to habituate to fear, fear-related situations are approached in behavioral experiments in order to

problematic belief
If I don't check my abdomen all the time I could overlook the development of a serious illness. The checking behavior helps to control the risk and therefore the fears.
alternative belief
The checking behavior induces abdominal pain. My attention always falls back on my abdomen and the possible Illness, therefore, the fear increases. Additionally, I am not able to evaluate the symptom adequately.
behavioral experiment
I will check my abdomen intensely in the next three days, after three days I will stop checking and will document what influence this behavior has on my fears with the use of an anxiety diary.
result of the behavioral experiment
The checking behavior lead me to worry more. When I checked less I was less preoccupied with the possibility of suffering from cancer and I had fewer fears.
Conclusion
Constant checking of the stomach is not reasonable. It is highly unlikely that I will detect an illness earlier on by doing this. It only reinforces my fears. In the future I will try to refrain from carrying out these safety behaviors.

Fig. 13.3 Behavioral experiment protocol

test dysfunctional expectations and beliefs. Thus, although the setting may be similar to those used in habituation-focused exposure (as described above), the procedure is different; before approaching the situation, predictions are formulated on the basis of the dysfunctional beliefs and recorded in a protocol. This prediction is then tested in a planned experiment by showing critical behavior in a real-life situation and recording the results. Thus, the crucial component is not the full activation of fear, but a planned experiential activity that enables the patient to obtain new information. Some of the beliefs typical for hypochondriasis are presented in Box 1.

Box 1 Behavioral Experiments for Hypochondriasis (Silver et al., 2008, p. 86): Testing Dysfunctional Beliefs

1. About the need to be responsible which maintain preoccupation and worry: e.g., fear of missing warning signs, visiting the medical practitioner, benefits of symptom focusing/seeking medical information/safety behaviors.
2. About health, illness, and death: e.g., abnormality/normality and causes of symptoms and sensations.
3. About the effects of anxiety and worry: controlling worrying thoughts, effects of imagination of illness on physical state.

Figure 13.3 gives an example of a behavioral experiment protocol. The aim of behavioral experiments is not to experience intensive fears and to see that these decrease within the framework of exposure, but to collect evidence against the patient's fears.

13.3 Body Dysmorphic Disorder

13.3.1 Clinical Characteristics of Body Dysmorphic Disorder

BDD is characterized by excessive preoccupation with either an imagined or a real but slight defect in appearance (APA, 2000). Individuals with BDD believe that specific features of their body or face are disfigured and ugly. They focus on several details in the appearance of their body (e.g., shape or size of the breasts, legs, hips, genitals) and most commonly of their face (e.g., shape or size of the nose, eyes, lips, jaw, or chin), skin (e.g., wrinkles, scars, vascular markings, pores, acne), and hair (e.g., hair thinning or excessive body hair). Many individuals report that the defect is on their mind for many hours of the day. Over time, the location of the main defect may change. The diagnostic criteria for BDD (DSM-IV-TR) are defined as follows:

1. Preoccupation with an imagined defect in appearance. If a slight physical anomaly is present, the person's concern is markedly excessive.
2. The preoccupation causes clinically significant distress or impairment in social, occupational, or other important areas of functioning.
3. The preoccupation is not better accounted for by another mental disorder (e.g., dissatisfaction with body shape and size in anorexia nervosa).

However, the diagnostic criteria of BDD will be revised in DSM-5. The proposed revision may be relocated to the obsessive–compulsive and related disorders category of DSM-5 and include the following criteria (APA, 2010):

1. Preoccupation with a perceived defect(s) or flaw(s) in physical appearance that is not observable or appears slight to others.
2. At some point during the course of the disorder, the person has performed repetitive behaviors (e.g., mirror checking, excessive grooming, skin picking, or reassurance seeking) or mental acts (e.g., comparing their appearance with that of others) in response to the appearance concerns.
3. The preoccupation causes clinically significant distress (for example, depressed mood, anxiety, shame) or impairment in social, occupational, or other important areas of functioning (for example, school, relationships, household).
4. The appearance preoccupations are not restricted to concerns with body fat or weight in an eating disorder.

Specify if:
Muscle dysmorphia form of body dysmorphic disorder (the belief that one's body build is too small or is insufficiently muscular)

Specify whether BDD beliefs are currently characterized by:
Good or fair insight: Recognizes that BDD beliefs are definitely or probably not true, or that they may or may not be true.
Poor insight: Thinks BDD beliefs are probably true.
Absent insight (i.e., delusional beliefs about appearance*)*: Completely convinced BDD beliefs are true.

Preoccupation with the defect is experienced as uncontrollable and includes recurrent, persistent and often intrusive thoughts, time-consuming ritualistic checking behaviors (e.g., mirror checking, comparing), safety behaviors (e.g., camouflaging: make-up application, attempts to hide the flaws), and avoidance behaviors (e.g., social avoidance, mirror avoidance). BDD is associated with extensive reduction in quality of life, social isolation, and high rates of lifetime suicidal ideation (78%) and suicide attempts (27.5%; Phillips et al., 2005). High rates of current and lifetime comorbidity have been reported, particularly with depression (74%; Phillips, Didie, & Menard, 2007), social phobia (39%; Coles et al., 2006), and obsessive–compulsive disorders (32%; Gunstad & Phillips, 2003).

13.3.1.1 Case Report

Anna is 30 years old. In the first session, Anna tells the therapist that she suffers from anxieties in public situations and fears negative evaluation and observation by others. Later she offers that she is preoccupied with pigmented moles on her skin. She excessively checks mirrors (about 4 h a day) and repeatedly asks friends and colleagues for reassurance—for example, "Do you think these moles will go away? Do they make me look older?" She worries about appearing vain and superficial, and reports that her skin is frequently on her mind. To improve her skin, Anna spends a lot of time applying makeup, self-tanners, and cover sticks, and wears long clothes to cover her skin. She feels ashamed to expose her body in the presence of her partner, and is afraid of intimacy. Anna's concern with her skin started during adolescence. In the past, she was also preoccupied with her "misshapen" nose, wide hips, small breasts and thick calves. At the age of 18 she underwent rhinoplasty, and at the age of 20 she decided to have a breast augmentation. Despite plastic surgery, she is still dissatisfied with the size of her nose.

13.3.2 Epidemiology

The few existing studies about the prevalence suggest that BDD is more frequent than is generally assumed: In the general population, community surveys report prevalence rates of 0.7–2.4% (e.g., Faravelli et al., 1997; Rief, Buhlmann, Wilhelm, Borkenhagen, & Brähler, 2006; Koran, Abujaoude, Large, & Serpe, 2008, Ritter, Gieler, Brähler, & Stangier (in prep.)). Higher rates were found in clinical populations, especially in dermatological outpatients (8–14%; e.g., Phillips, Dufresne, Wilkel, & Vittorio, 2000; Stangier, Janich, Adam-Schwebe, Berger, & Wolter, 2003; Vulink et al., 2006; Bowe, Leyden, Crerand, Sarwer, & Margolis, 2007) and in individuals undergoing cosmetic surgery (5–15%; see a review by Sarwer & Crerand, 2008) indicating that BDD sufferers often seek dermatological or cosmetic treatments instead of psychological treatment. Note that cosmetic surgery is contraindicated (Phillips, Grant, Siniscalchi, & Albertini, 2001).

In primary care, BDD is still underestimated and underdiagnosed. Most sufferers are afraid to disclose their problems due to feelings of shame, fear of disclosure, poor insight, and low motivation for psychological treatment. In addition mental health professionals and physicians (dermatologists, plastic surgeons) are usually not familiar with the diagnosis; furthermore, symptomatic overlaps with other disorders and high comorbidities make the identification of BDD difficult.

13.3.3 From Cognitive-Behavioral Model to Treatment

Several cognitive-behavioral models have been developed to explain the maintenance of BDD (e.g., Neziroglu, Khemlani-Patel, & Veale, 2008; Veale, 2004; Veale & Neziroglu, 2010). According to these models, individuals with BDD exhibit biased information processing of appearance-related stimuli, including selective attention to details of one's face or other body parts, or sensitive perception for aesthetic stimuli. Veale and Neziroglu (2010) emphasized in their model the role of excessive, self-focused attention. Patients focus on an image of how one looks or a "felt" impression of how one appears to others, associated with a negative appraisal of the imagined or slight defect. Further, maladaptive beliefs, negative emotions (e.g., shame or depression), and dysfunctional behavioral strategies (e.g., compulsive rituals, safety-seeking behaviors) are activated. In turn, these processes increase self-consciousness and awareness of certain features, thus leading to a vicious circle (Fig. 13.4).

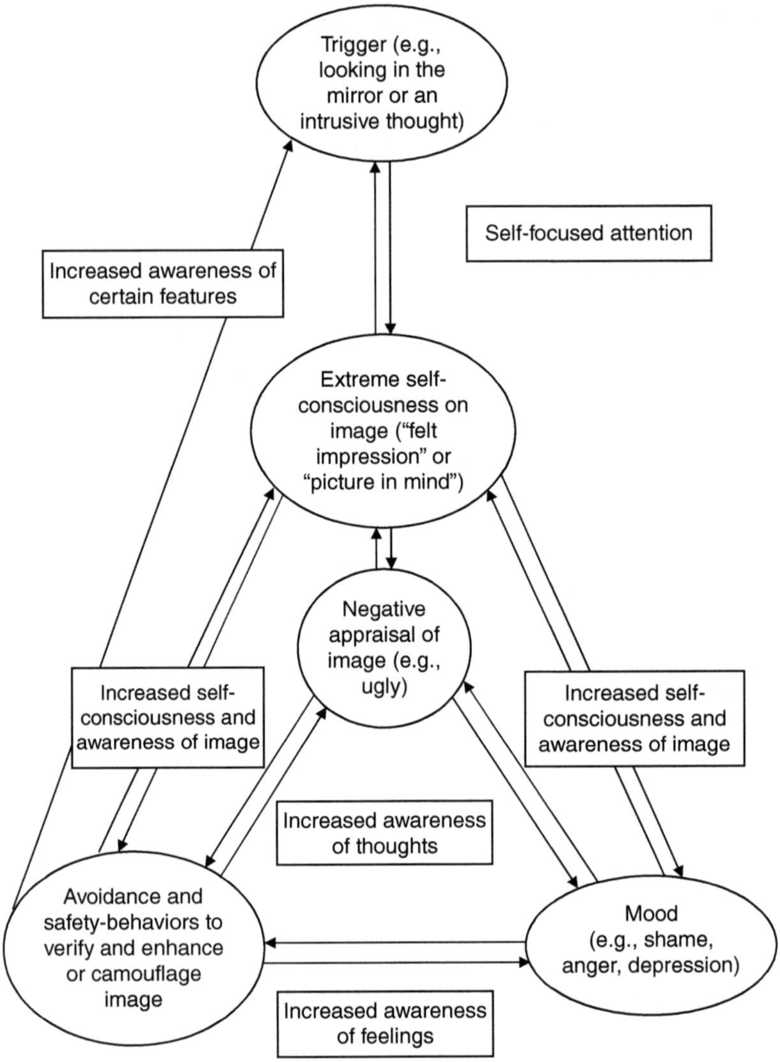

Fig. 13.4 CBT model of BDD (Veale & Neziroglu, 2010, S. 151)

There is growing empirical evidence supporting cognitive-behavioral models of BDD. It has been demonstrated that individuals with BDD have maladaptive thoughts and beliefs about appearance (Veale et al., 1996a) as well as dysfunctional and intrusive mental images (Osman, Cooper, Hackmann, & Veale, 2004). They misinterpret other's facial expressions as threatening (Buhlmann, McNally, Etcoff, Tuschen-Caffier, & Wilhelm, 2004), show an increased accuracy in discrimination of facial stimuli (Stangier, Adam-Schwebe, Müller, & Wolter, 2008). They have an analytic style of perception (Deckersbach et al., 2000), and abnormalities in visual information processing (Feusner, Townsend, Bystritsky, & Bookheimer, 2007). However, these findings have not yet been incorporated in empirically supported treatments. Evidence for psychological treatment and pharmacotherapy is minimal (see meta-analysis by Williams, Hadjistavropoulos, & Sharpe, 2006). Two RCTs have been conducted with CBT (group CBT: Rosen, Reiter, & Orosan, 1995; individual CBT: Veale et al., 1996b), and several case series of CBT or only BT (Exposure plus response prevention: E&RP) in adults (e.g., Gomez-Perez, Marks, & Gutierrez-Fisac, 1994; Neziroglu, McKay, Todaro, & Yaryura-Tobias, 1996). The two RCTs of CBT (including exposure and response prevention as well as cognitive restructuring) have demonstrated that CBT was superior to the waitlist control with regard to reduction of both BDD symptom severity and depressive symptoms. Khemlani-Patel (2001) compared CT plus E&RP and behavioral-only therapy (E&RP) and demonstrated significant improvement on symptom and affective measures and a decrease of overvalued ideation—independent of the treatment condition.

13.3.4 Description of Procedures

Present research suggests that cognitive and emotional processing are important factors in the etiology and maintenance of BDD. Therefore, in most studies exposure has been combined with cognitive restructuring. It is a common principle that maintaining factors have to be modified first, before exposure to critical situations can be applied effectively in reducing anxiety and changing dysfunctional attitudes. Given that BDD shares many features with social phobia (e.g., excessive self-focused attention, mental imagery, fear of negative evaluation), obsessive–compulsive disorders (e.g., recurrent persistent thoughts, ritualistic compulsive behaviors), and health anxiety (e.g., bodily preoccupation, body checking), more recent treatments of BDD draw heavily on the components of cognitive therapy of social phobia (Clark et al., 2006), or OCD (Salkovskis, 1999). The following description will be based on the most updated model and treatment manual by Veale and Neziroglu (2010). Some of the treatment components (e.g., attentional training, imagery rescripting, or video feedback) are not yet empirically evaluated for BDD.

It should be noted that the variability of symptoms, the fluctuations in insight in the psychological nature of the problem, the high comorbidity, and diversity of coexisting problems should be taken into account when planning the treatment. Behavioral activation for depression in BDD, habit-reversal (Azrin & Nunn, 1973) or acceptance and commitment therapy (Hayes, Strohsal, & Wilson, 1999), and other interventions may also be helpful in the treatment—depending on patient's primary worries, symptoms and preoccupations.

In general, an adequate understanding of the problem, commitment to change, and a solid basis for the therapeutic alliance are the most important issues in the initial phase of treatment. In patients with poor insight or overvalued ideas and delusions, it makes little sense to argue about the diagnosis of BDD. It is more helpful to argue that the diagnosis involves a "preoccupation with the way you feel about your appearance, which has become very distressing or handicapping in your life." Deriving an idiosyncratic version of the model by reviewing one or more recent prototypical situations is useful to start therapy and to discover all maintaining factors.

13.3.4.1 Attentional Training

Attentional procedures to modify attentional biases are fundamental and should be introduced to all BDD patients early in therapy and should be practiced regularly/daily (i.e., preparatory work for different variants of exposure in BDD). The goal is to help patients become aware of the difference between self-focused ("picture in mind") and externally focused attention (environment, task), and to be able to shift attention from a self to an external focus in anxiety-provoking situations. Attentional training (Clark et al., 2006; Wells, 2009), task concentration task (Bögels, 2006), or detached mindfulness (Wells, 2005) have been successfully applied in social phobia, health anxiety, or depression and can be adapted for BDD (for a detailed description of all procedures, see Veale & Neziroglu, 2010). One of Anna's first attentional training protocols is shown in Fig. 13.5.

13.3.4.2 Graduated Exposure In Vivo

Graduated exposure aims to overcome all avoidance and safety-seeking behaviors. The goal is to confront feared and avoided situations repeatedly, and to expose the perceived defect until anxiety significantly decreases. Graduated exposure can be conducted along an individualized graduated hierarchy or list of situations that cause BDD-related anxiety, step-by-step, beginning with the least frightening (i.e., minimum score of 30 on the 0–100 scale) and gradually working up to more frightening situations. Anna's graduated hierarchy is shown in Table 13.2.

Anna started with showering with skin exposed in the presence of her partner. Initially she felt very anxious, but the more she did this, the less anxious she became. She also tried repeatedly to shift her attention externally—to the temperature of water or the pleasurable feeling on her skin. She then moved up her hierarchy, frequently being nude in the bathroom. With the help of mirror retraining (as described below) she learnt to use mirrors briefly for functional reasons and to reduce the time taken to look in the mirror. She then felt very anxious walking around without wearing makeup or self-tanners because she feared others would notice her skin, but the more often she did this, the better she felt. She then continued moving up the hierarchy. She overcame her fears and went to swimming and to the sauna again, first, once a week and then twice a week. Gradually, over several months, she put herself in increasingly anxiety-provoking situations, eventually talking with a man at a party. Her fear and avoidance diminished.

The graduated hierarchy should be relevant to patient's real life so that exposure can be repeated as often as possible. Patients should be encouraged to expose themselves without any cognitive or experiential avoidance (i.e., without trying to control or escape the experience), without safety-seeking behaviors, and with an external

Date	Situation	Focusing attention on… (What exactly did you recognize?)	Attention to environment (0-100%)	Attention to self (0-100%)	Preoccupation (Did you think about your appearance?) (0-100%)	Level of Anxiety and Distress (0-10)	Time for practicing
Mon 5/6	*Listening to a music CD. Trying to become aware of different instruments.*	*Different instruments: violin, cello, bass, piano, clarinet, oboe*	*70%*	*30%*	*20%*	*1*	*15 min*
Tue 6/6	*Walking to the park, wearing make-up. Trying to become aware of my surrounding area.*	*Buildings (church..) cars, traffic, plants, trees, people around (smiling faces), colors (green, grey..), shadows*	*40%*	*60%*	*70%*	*5*	*15 min*
	Trying to become aware of myself.	*Body sensations (heat of my face..) thoughts ("I am ugly.") feelings (inner tension..)*	*20%*	*80%*	*80%*	*7*	*5 min*
	Switching my attention between environment & self	*Surrounding area:* *myself:*	*50%* *30%*	*50%* *70%*	*60%* *70%*	*4* *5*	*15 min*

Fig. 13.5 Attentional training protocol

Table 13.2 Example of graduated hierarchy for exposure in vivo

Feared situation	Anxiety rating (0–100)	Avoidance (0–100)	…makes the situation more difficult	…makes the situation easier
Becoming touched by partner, sex	100	90	Candlelight	Dark room
Going to the swimming pool/sauna	90	100	Many people around, no covering clothes (bathrobe)	A few people around, self-tanner/bronzer, waterproof makeup
Meeting a friend face-to-face and wearing no makeup	80	90	Daylight, many people around, no pocket mirror	Dim light, only a few people around, little mirror in pocket
Walking around and wearing no makeup	70	80	Daylight, alone, meeting colleagues	In the evening, in the presence of a friend
Entering a crowded room	60	70	Bright light, small room, shorter distance between the defect and others	Big room, longer distance between the defect and others
Looking in the mirror	50	20	Shorter distance from defect	Alone, longer distance to the defect
Being nude in the bathroom	40	50	Partner is watching me	Alone
Showering	30	20	Partner is watching me, mirror	Alone, mirror is several feet away
Going shopping and wearing makeup	20	10	Meeting a friend	Meeting nobody
Viewing pictures/photos of myself	10	10	Viewing photos of myself with a friend or therapist	Viewing photos of myself alone

focus of attention. It is important to explain that avoidance maintains distress and preoccupation with the defect and prevents their memories from being updated. In the case of strong experiential avoidance or suppression of feelings, images or intrusive thoughts about the defect, which might occur during graduated exposure or between the exposure sessions, detached mindfulness (Wells, 2005) can be helpful to learn how to focus on feelings and thoughts. Patients can be told just to notice or to be aware of them, and to experience them without any control or evaluation (Veale & Neziroglu, 2010).

Exposure in vivo is generally more effective than exposure in sensu, but if the anxiety level is too high, imaginal exposure may be a helpful intermediate step to in-vivo exposure. Both approaches can be combined effectively.

13.3.4.3 Graduated Exposure and Response Prevention

In general, graduated exposure is combined with response prevention. Response prevention aims at stopping the performance of ritualistic compulsive behaviors and at limiting the time spent on these activities to a reasonable amount. Ritualistic compulsive behaviors include mirror checking, skin picking (using hands, tweezers, pins, razor blades, etc.), grooming (make-up application, styling hair, cutting, combing, shaving), asking for and providing reassurance, comparing themselves with others, measuring and weighing, checking the disliked body/ face part, changing clothes, wearing hats, buying beauty products, or seeking frequent surgical or dermatological consultations.

It can be very difficult for patients to control the compulsive behavior completely; therefore, it might be a realistic goal to decrease the frequency or time spent mirror checking. It might be helpful to keep a diary of circumstances or situations that seem to make the behavior more difficult or even easier. To shift attention away from compulsive behaviors, it might also be useful to develop a list of enjoyable activities which can be done instead of ritualistic behavior such as: walking, jogging, listening to one's favorite music, painting, gardening, etc.

13.3.4.4 Behavioral Experiments

Exposure in vivo can be also used as a behavioral experiment to explicitly test patient's dysfunctional beliefs. Attentional training (see Sect. 4.3.1) allows patients to shift their attention to the external situation and to focus on what they see, hear, and experience in a certain situation rather than on how they feel or imagine how they look.

Anna used self-tanners/bronzers daily to cover the pigmentation of her skin, and wore long t-shirts and trousers, even in summer. She was unable to stop using self-tanners/bronzers and wearing long clothes because she believed that people would find her unattractive and would be disgusted by her skin. She predicted that others would react with horror. We encouraged her to use self-tanners/bronzers and cover sticks less and less and asked her to wear short t-shirts, blouses and skirts so that her arms and legs could be exposed. We went with her to a shopping center and exposed her arms to a shop assistant, which was very anxiety provoking for her. Thereby, we applied self-tanner/bronzer and cover stick to only one arm. The task was to ask the shop assistant to look at her skin, to comment on how it looked, to compare both arms and to tell which one had been covered. To her surprise Anna experienced that the assistant did not behave as if he was disgusted by her skin or avoided her, he was friendly, and did not comment her skin as she supposed. Neither occurred, indicating that pigmented moles on the skin had less significance to others than Anna had anticipated.

13.3.4.5 Mirror Retraining

Mirror retraining aims at learning to use mirrors only for functional reasons. In a first step, patients are asked to protocol the frequency and duration of mirror gazing, motivation for mirror checking, and typical beliefs (e.g., "I have to look in the mirror to see if I look normal."). The next step involves encouraging patients to redirect their attention away from their "felt impression" and to focus on the whole face or body rather than on detail. Mirrors should only be used for a specific function (e.g., teeth cleaning) for a limited time period, and the patient should resist the urge to use reflective surfaces.

13.3.4.6 Mirror Feedback

Mirror avoidance also occurs in BDD patients (Veale & Riley, 2001) and has the function of avoiding negative thoughts and feelings that are activated by excessive mirror checking. There are different types of selective mirror avoidance in BDD: avoiding specific mirrors (e.g., distorting or covering mirrors), using only obscured (e.g., dirty) mirrors, avoiding looking at specific "defective" body or face parts, avoiding mirrors only in public or social situations.

Mirror feedback focuses on modifying mirror avoidance and can also be part of graduated exposure with varying degrees of light or the amount of body exposed. Patients are instructed to describe their appearance in an objective manner without any evaluation or rating. Further, they are instructed to focus on the entire body ("the big picture", Wilhelm, 2006) rather than on details of their own face or body and to look at the reflection in the mirror as if it were a stranger.

13.3.4.7 Video and Photo Feedback

Video feedback is an established intervention in the treatment of social phobia (Clark et al., 2006; Harvey, Clark, Ehlers, & Rapee, 2000) and can also be used in BDD. Video feedback, including specific preparation for attentional redirection, allows BDD patients to see movements and behavioral aspects in their observable body/face ("body movie") and to disconfirm the fixed picture in their mind. To maximize perceived discrepancies between patient's mental image and the video, patients are instructed (1) to make a specific prediction of how they look *before* viewing the video, i.e., making objective descriptions (e.g., dark hair, green eyes, three feet tall) rather than evaluations (e.g., ugly, horrible), (2) to watch the video *as if* watching a stranger and only make observations on what they *see* and *hear* while explicitly ignoring their feelings (e.g., rating how ugly they look), (3) to rate the degree to which their observable body/face corresponds to their predictions and to compare both ratings. There should be an objective measure to compare patient's predictions against what he/she actually sees in the video. Video feedback also allows the demonstration of the effects of excessive self-focused attention and safety-seeking behavior in BDD.

Photo feedback can be part of graduated exposure and should be used like video feedback. Both interventions should be seen as exercises to discuss patient's "felt" impression and whether it is helpful to use it as a guide for current behavior.

Anna was also preoccupied with the size of her nose and made the prediction that it was bigger than average. We measured the nose size of about 5 women, photographed them, and printed the photos. We also measured the size of the therapist's nose and then compared both photos of the women and therapist with Anna's nose. Anna discovered that her nose was an average size and that she felt it was overly big.

13.3.4.8 Imagery Rescripting

Imagery rescripting primarily focus on modifying (1) "felt impression" or distressing intrusive imagery of how one appears to others from an observer perspective, and (2) negative early autobiographical memories in BDD (e.g., being teased/bullied/harmed at school, self-consciousness about appearance changes or acne during adolescence, experiences of humiliation or rejection) that are linked to recurrent mental images. The primary goals are to view past experiences as a bad memory rather than an event that is being repeated or has high importance now, and to update the meaning of an event or past memories by using cognitive restructuring. For instance, it could be helpful to introduce an adult-self in the image who cares for the child-self and helps him/her to cope with the situation.

Anne remembered being teased by her peers at the age of 13 who brought up that she was ugly because of her acne and that she would never find a boyfriend looking like that (e.g., "You look like a pizza face.") At the time she felt disfigured, ugly, abnormal, sad, and was excessively preoccupied with her skin. Now she thinks that others are disgusted by her skin and she anticipated that her partner will reject her, especially in intimate situations. The history of being teased for having acne contributed to her belief that she looked ugly, and that others would reject her. Further, the experience of being teased led to her firm conviction that others directed their attention to her "ugly" appearance. We discussed an alternative meaning of the past memories from the adult perspective. During imagery rescripting, Anna protected her younger self from the peers and was able to reassure her younger self that this was a brief time in her life. Her adult-self explained her child-self that now others will have a different perspective of her.

13.4 Conclusion

Although hypochondriasis and body dysmorphic disorder are both frequent disorders in primary care, there is still a big need to develop a better understanding of the mechanisms contributing to the development and maintenance of these disorders, and to design effective psychological treatment methods. So far, there is some empirical evidence that treatment approaches combining exposure with cognitive interventions show promising outcomes. Within the cognitive framework, exposure, in the sense of behavioral experiments, rather aims at testing dysfunctional beliefs than obtaining habituation of anxiety. There is some empirical support for the suggestion that behavioral experiments are superior to traditional exposure (McMillan & Lee, 2010).

In addition, increasing evidence indicates that biased information processing is relevant in the etiology both of hypochondriasis (Marcus, Gurley, Marchi, & Bauer, 2007) and BDD (Neziroglu et al., 2008). In particular, selective attention to disorder-specific threatening stimuli, as well as distorted images, are important factors which are supposed to maintain dysfunctional beliefs. Similar to cognitive therapy for anxiety disorders, these mechanisms have to be modified first before patients should engage in exposure and behavioral experiments. Effective treatments of hypochondriasis and BDD might comprise at least four components:

1. Providing information and deriving an individual model of the problem, which explains the role of cognitive processes such as attention, memories and images, dysfunctional beliefs, and avoidance and safety behaviors in the maintenance of the disorder.
2. The modification of biased attentional processes, memories, and images by using attentional training, guided imagery and video feedback, and imagery rescripting, in an early stage of treatment.
3. Cognitive restructuring including Socratic questioning, diaries, and self-instruction to challenge automatic thoughts and dysfunctional beliefs related to the disorder.
4. Behavioral experiments including exposure to anxiety-provoking situations and processing of corrective information to test dysfunctional beliefs.

As already demonstrated in anxiety disorders such as panic, social phobia, and post-traumatic stress disorder, this combination of modification of cognitive processing, cognitive restructuring, and repeated behavioral experiments is suggested to be the most effective treatment package for hypochondriasis and BDD.

References

Abramowitz, J. S., Olatunji, B. O., & Deacon, B. J. (2007). Health anxiety, hypochondriasis, and the anxiety disorders. *Behavior Therapy, 38*, 86–94. doi:10.1016/j.beth.2006.05.001.

American Psychiatric Association. (2000). *Diagnostic and statistical manual of mental disorders (4th ed., text rev.)*. American Psychiatric Association: Washington.

American Psychiatric Association. (2010). *Obsessive-compulsive and related disorders (DRAFT November 8, 2010)*. Washington: American Psychiatric Association.

American Psychiatric Association. (2011). *Somatic symptom disorders (DRAFT April 18, 2011)*. Washington: American Psychiatric Association.

Azrin, N. H., & Nunn, R. G. (1973). Habit reversal: A method of eliminating nervous habits and tics. *Behavior Research and Therapy, 37*, 715–740. doi:10.1016/0005-7967(73)90119-8.

Barsky, A. J., Barnett, M. C., & Cleary, P. D. (1994). Hypochondriasis and panic disorder-boundary and overlap. *Archives of General Psychiatry, 51*, 918–925.

Barsky, A. J., Klerman, G. L., Wyshak, G., & Latham, K. S. (1990). The prevalence of hypochondriasis in medical outpatients. *Social Psychiatry and Psychiatric Epidemiology, 14*, 89–94.

Bögels, S. M. (2006). Task concentration training versus applied relaxation, in combination with cognitive therapy for social phobia patients with fear of blushing, trembling, and sweating. *Behavior Research and Therapy, 44*, 1199–1210. doi:10.1016/j.brat.2005.08.010.
Bowe, W. P., Leyden, J. J., Crerand, C. E., Sarwer, D. B., & Margolis, D. J. (2007). Body dysmorphic disorder symptoms among patients with acne vulgaris. *Journal of the American Academy of Dermatology, 57*, 222–230. doi:10.1016/j.jaad.2007.03.030.
Buhlmann, U., McNally, R. J., Etcoff, N. L., Tuschen-Caffier, B., & Wilhelm, S. (2004). Emotion recognition deficits in body dysmorphic disorder. *Journal of Psychiatric Research, 38*, 201–206. doi:10.1016/S0022-3956(03)00107-9.
Clark, D. M., Ehlers, A., Hackmann, A., McManus, F., Fennell, M., Grey, N., et al. (2006). Cognitive therapy versus exposure and applied relaxation in social phobia: A randomized control trial. *Journal of Consulting and Clinical Psychology, 74*, 568–578. doi:10.1037/0022-006X.74.3.568.
Clark, D. M., Salkovskis, P. M., Hackmann, A., Wells, A., Fennel, M., Ludgate, J., et al. (1998). Two psychological treatments for hypochondriasis—a randomized controlled trial. *British Journal of Psychiatry, 173*, 218–225. doi:10.1192/bjp.173.3.218.
Coles, M. E., Phillips, K. A., Menard, W., Pagano, M. E., Fay, C., Weisberg, R. B., et al. (2006). Body dysmorphic disorder and social phobia: Cross-sectional and prospective data. *Depression and Anxiety, 23*, 26–33. doi:10.1002/da.20132.
Deckersbach, T., Savage, C. R., Phillips, K. A., Wilhelm, S., Buhlmann, U., Rauch, S. L., et al. (2000). Characteristics of memory dysfunction in body dysmorphic disorder. *Journal of International Neuropsychological Society, 6*, 673–681. doi:10.1017/S1355617700666055.
Escobar, J. I., Gara, M., Waitzkin, H., Silver, R. C., Holman, A., & Compton, W. (1998). DSM-IV hypochondriasis in primary care. *General Hospital Psychiatry, 20*, 155–159. doi:10.1016/S0163-8343(98)00018-8.
Faravelli, C., Salvatori, S., Galassi, F., Aiazzi, L., Drei, C., & Cabras, P. (1997). Epidemiology of somatoform disorder: A community survey in Florence. *Social Psychiatry and Psychiatric Epidemiology, 32*, 24–29. doi:10.1007/BF00800664.
Fava, G. A., Fabbri, S., Sirri, L., & Wise, T. N. (2007). Psychological factors affecting medical condition: A new proposal for DSM-V. *Psychosomatics, 48*, 103–111. doi:10.1176/appi.psy.48.2.103.
Feusner, J., Townsend, J., Bystritsky, A., & Bookheimer, S. (2007). Visual information processing of faces in body dysmorphic disorder. *Archives of General Psychiatry, 64*, 1417–1426. doi:10.1001/archpsyc.64.12.1417.
Furer, P., & Walker, J. R. (2005). Treatment of hypochondriasis with exposure. *Journal of Contemporary Psychotherapy, 35*, 251–267. doi:10.1007/s10879-005-4319-y.
Furer, P., Walker, J. R., & Stein, M. B. (2007). *Treating health anxiety and fear of death: A practitioner's guide*. New York: Springer.
Gomez-Perez, J. C., Marks, I. M., & Gutierrez-Fisac, J. L. (1994). Dysmorphophobia: Clinical features and outcome with behaviour therapy. *European Psychiatry, 9*, 229–235.
Gunstad, J., & Phillips, K. A. (2003). Axis I comorbidity in body dysmorphic disorder. *Comprehensive Psychiatry, 44*, 270–276. doi:10.1016/S0010-440X(03)00088-9.
Gureje, O., Üstün, T. B., & Simon, G. E. (1997). The syndrome of hypochondriasis: A cross-national study in primary care. *Psychological Medicine, 27*, 1001–1010. doi:10.1017/S0033291797005345.
Harvey, A. G., Clark, D. A., Ehlers, A., & Rapee, R. M. (2000). Social anxiety and self-impression: Cognitive preparation enhances the beneficial effects of video feedback following a stressful task. *Behavior Research and Therapy, 38*, 1183–1192. doi:10.1016/S0005-7967(99)00148-5.
Hayes, S. C., Strohsal, K., & Wilson, K. G. (1999). *Acceptance and commitment therapy: An experimental approach to behavior change*. New York: Guilford Press.
Hiller, W., Leibbrand, R., Rief, W., & Fichter, M. M. (2005). Differentiating hypochondriasis from panic disorder. *Journal of Anxiety Disorders, 19*, 29–49. doi:10.1016/j.janxdis.2003.10.006.

Holmes, E. A., Arntz, A., & Smucker, M. R. (2007). Imagery rescripting in cognitive behaviour therapy: Images, treatment techniques and outcomes. *Journal of Behavior Therapy and Experimental Psychiatry, 38*, 297–305. doi:10.1016/j.jbtep.2007.10.007.

Khemlani-Patel, S. (2001). *Cognitive and behavioral therapy for body dysmorphic disorder: A comparative investigation*. PhD Thesis. Hempstead: Hofstra University.

Koran, L., Abujaoude, E., Large, M., & Serpe, R. (2008). The prevalence of Body dysmorphic disorder in the United States adult population. *CNS Spectrums, 13*, 316–322.

Lieb, R., Zimmermann, P., Friis, R. H., Höfler, M., Tholen, S., & Wittchen, H.-U. (2002). The natural course of DSM-IV somatoform disorders and syndromes among adolescents and young adults: A prospective-longitudinal community study. *European Psychiatry, 17*, 321–331. doi:10.1016/S0924-9338(02)00686-7.

Looper, K. J., & Kirmayer, L. J. (2001). Hypochondriacal concerns in a community population. *Psychological Medicine, 31*, 577–584. doi:10.1017/S0033291701003737.

Marcus, D. K., Gurley, J. R., Marchi, M. M., & Bauer, C. (2007). Cognitive and perceptual variables in hypochondriasis and health anxiety: A systematic review. *Clinical Psychology Review, 27*, 127–139. doi:10.1016/j.cpr.2006.09.003.

Martin, A., & Jacobi, F. (2006). Features of hypochondriasis and illness worry in the general population in Germany. *Psychosomatic Medicine, 68*, 770–777. doi:10.1097/01.psy.0000238213.04984.b0.

McMillan, D., & Lee, R. (2010). A systematic review of behavioral experiments vs. exposure alone in the treatment of anxiety disorders: A case of exposure while wearing the emperor's new clothes? *Clinical Psychology Review, 30*, 467–478. doi:10.1016/j.cpr.2010.01.003.

Muse, K., McManus, F., Hackmann, A., Williams, M., & Williams, M. (2010). Intrusive imagery in severe health anxiety: Prevalence, nature and links with memories and maintenance cycles. *Behaviour Research and Therapy, 48*, 792–798. doi:10.1016/j.brat.2010.05.008.

Neziroglu, F., Khemlani-Patel, S., & Veale, D. (2008). Social learning theory and cognitive behavioral models of body dysmorphic disorder. *Body Image, 5*, 28–38. doi:10.1016/j.bodyim.2008.01.002.

Neziroglu, F., McKay, D., Todaro, J., & Yaryura-Tobias, J. A. (1996). Effect of cognitive behaviour therapy on persons with body dysmorphic disorder and comorbid axis II diagnosis. *Behaviour Therapy, 27*, 67–77. doi:10.1016/S0005-7894(96)80036-0.

Noyes, R. (1999). The relationship of hypochondriasis to anxiety disorders. *Psychiatry and Primary Care, 21*, 8–17. doi:10.1016/S0163-8343(98)00063-2.

Noyes, R., Carney, C. P., Hillis, S. L., Jones, L. E., & Langbehn, D. R. (2005). Prevalence and correlates of illness worry in the general population. *Psychosomatics, 46*, 529–539. doi:10.1176/appi.psy.46.6.529.

Noyes, R., Kathol, R. G., Fisher, M., Phillips, B., Suelzer, M., & Woodman, C. (1994). Psychiatric comorbidity among patients with hypochondriasis. *General Hospital Psychiatry, 15*, 78–87. doi:10.1016/0163-8343(94)90049-3.

Olatunji, B. O., Deacon, B. J., & Abramowitz, J. S. (2009). Is hypochondriasis an anxiety disorder? *The British Journal of Psychiatry, 194*, 481–482. doi:10.1192/bjp.194.6.578.

Osman, S., Cooper, M., Hackmann, A., & Veale, D. (2004). Spontaneously occurring images and early memories in people with body dysmorphic disorder. *Memory, 12*, 428–436. doi:10.1080/09658210444000043.

Phillips, K. A., Coles, M. E., Menard, W., Yen, S., Fay, C., & Weisberg, R. B. (2005). Suicidal ideation and suicide attempts in body dysmorphic disorder. *Journal of Clinical Psychiatry, 66*, 717–725.

Phillips, K. A., Didie, E. R., & Menard, W. (2007). Clinical features and correlates of major depressive disorder in individuals with body dysmorphic disorder. *Journal of Affective Disorders, 97*, 129–135. doi:10.1016/j.jad.2006.06.006.

Phillips, K. A., Dufresne, R. G., Jr., Wilkel, C. S., & Vittorio, C. C. (2000). Rate of dysmorphic disorder in dermatology patients. *Journal of the American Academy of Dermatology, 42*, 235–243.

Phillips, K. A., Grant, J., Siniscalchi, J., & Albertini, R. S. (2001). Surgical and nonpsychiatric treatment of patients with body dysmorphic disorder. *Psychosomatics, 42*, 504–510. doi:10.1176/appi.psy.42.6.504.

Phillips, K. A., Stein, D. J., Rauch, S. L., Hollander, E., Fallon, B. A., Barsky, A., et al. (2010). Should an obsessive-compulsive spectrum grouping of disorders be included in DSM-V? *Depression and Anxiety, 27*, 528–555. doi:10.1002/da.20705.

Rief, W., Buhlmann, U., Wilhelm, S., Borkenhagen, A., & Brähler, E. (2006). The prevalence of body dysmorphic disorder: A population-based survey. *Psychological Medicine, 36*, 877–885. doi:10.1017/S0033291706007264.

Rief, W., & Hiller, W. (1998). Cognitive aspects of hypochondriasis and the somatization syndrome. *Journal of Abnormal Psychology, 107*, 587–595. doi:10.1037/0021-843X.107.4.587.

Ritter, V., Gieler, U., Brähler, E., & Stangier, U. (in prep.). Prevalence of body dysmorphic disorder in the German population.

Rosen, J. C., Reiter, J., & Orosan, P. (1995). Cognitive behavioral body image therapy for body dysmorphic disorder. *Journal of Consulting and Clinical Psychology, 63*, 263–269. doi:10.1037/0022-006X.63.2.263.

Salkovskis, P. M. (1989). Somatic problems. In K. Hawton, P. M. Salkovskis, J. Kirk, & D. M. Clark (Eds.), *Cognitive behaviour therapy for psychiatric problems: A practical guide* (pp. 235–276). New York: Oxford University Press.

Salkovskis, P. M. (1999). Understanding and treating obsessive compulsive disorder. *Behaviour Research and Therapy, 19*, 571–583.

Salkovskis, P., & Clark, D. M. (1993). Panic disorder and hypochondriasis. *Advances in Behaviour Research and Therapy, 15*, 23–48. doi:10.1016/0146-6402(93)90002-J.

Salkovskis, P., Warwick, H. M. C., & Deal, A. C. (2003). Cognitive-behavioral treatment for severe and persistent health anxiety (hypochondriasis). *Brief Treatment and Crisis Intervention, 3*, 353–367.

Sarwer, D. B., & Crerand, C. E. (2008). Body dysmorphic disorder and appearance enhancing medical treatments. *Body Image, 5*, 50–58. doi:10.1016/j.bodyim.2007.08.003.

Schmidt, A. T. M. (1994). Bottlenecks in the diagnosis of hypochondriasis. *Comprehensive Psychiatry, 35*, 306–315. doi:10.1016/0010-440X(94)90024-8.

Silver, A., Sanders, D., Morrison, N., & Cowey, C. (2008). Health anxiety. In J. Bennett-Levy, G. Butler, M. Fennell, A. Hackman, M. Mueller, & D. Westbrook (Eds.), *Oxford guide to behavioural experiments in cognitive therapy* (pp. 81–99). New York: Oxford University Press.

Sørensen, P., Birket-Smith, M., Wattar, U., Buemann, I., & Salkovskis, P. (2011). A randomized clinical trial of cognitive behavioural therapy versus short-term psychodynamic psychotherapy versus no intervention for patients with hypochondriasis. *Psychological Medicine, 41*, 431–441. doi:10.1016/0010-440X(94)90024-8.

Stangier, U., Adam-Schwebe, S., Müller, T., & Wolter, M. (2008). Discrimination of facial appearance related stimuli in body dysmorphic disorder. *Journal of Abnormal Psychology, 117*, 435–443. doi:10.1037/0021-843X.117.2.435.

Stangier, U., Janich, C., Adam-Schwebe, S., Berger, P., & Wolter, M. (2003). Screening for body dysmorphic disorder in dermatological outpatients. *Dermatology & Psychosomatics, 4*, 66–71. doi:10.1159/000072194.

Starcevic, V. (2001). Clinical features and diagnosis of hypochondriasis. In V. Starcevic & D. R. Lipsitt (Eds.), *Hypochondriasis: Modern perspectives on an ancient malady* (pp. 21–60). Oxford: Oxford University Press.

Thomson, A. B., & Page, L. A. (2007). Psychotherapies for hypochondriasis. *Cochrane Database of Systematic Reviews, 4*, CD006520. doi: 10.1002/14651858.CD006520.pub2.

Van den Heuvel, O. A., Veltman, D. J., Groenewegen, H. J., Witter, M. P., Merkelbach, J., Cath, D. C., et al. (2005). Disorderspecific neuroanatomical correlates of attentional bias in obsessive-compulsive disorders, panic disorder, and hypochondriasis. *Archives of General Psychiatry, 62*, 922–933. doi:10.1001/archpsyc.62.8.922.

Veale, D. (2004). Advances in a cognitive behavioural model of body dysmorphic disorder. *Body Image, 1*, 113–125. doi:10.1016/S1740-1445(03)00009-3.

Veale, D., Boocock, A., Gournay, L., Dryden, W., Shah, F., Willson, R., et al. (1996a). Body dysmorphic disorder. A survey of fifty cases. *The British Journal of Psychiatry, 169*, 196–201. doi:10.1192/bjp.169.2.196.

Veale, D., Gournay, K., Dryden, W., Boocock, A., Shah, F., Willson, R., et al. (1996b). Body dysmorphic disorder: A cognitive behavioural model and pilot randomised controlled trial. *Behaviour Research and Therapy, 34*, 717–729. doi:10.1192/bjp.169.2.196.

Veale, D., & Neziroglu, F. (2010). *Body dysmorphic disorder. A treatment manual*. Chichester: Wiley.

Veale, D., & Riley, S. (2001). Mirror, mirror on the wall, who is the ugliest of them all? The psychopathology of mirror gazing in body dysmorphic disorder. *Behaviour Research and Therapy, 39*, 1381–1393. doi:10.1016/S0005-7967(00)00102-9.

Vulink, N. C., Sigurdsson, V., Kon, M., Bruijnzeel-Koomen, C. A., Westenberg, H. G., & Denys, D. (2006). Body dysmorphic disorder in 3–8% of patients in outpatient dermatology and plastic surgery clinics [English abstract]. *Nederlands Tijdschrift voor Geneeskunde, 150*, 97–100.

Walker, J. R., & Furer, P. (2008). Interoceptive exposure in the treatment of health anxiety and hypochondriasis. *Journal of Cognitive Psychotherapy: An International Quarterly, 22*, 366–378. doi:10.1891/0889-8391.22.4.366.

Wattar, U., Sorensen, P., Buemann, I., Birket-Smith, M., Salkovskis, P. M., Albertsen, M., et al. (2005). Outcome of cognitive-behavioural treatment for health anxiety (hypochondriasis) in a routine clinical setting. *Behavioural and Cognitive Psychotherapy, 33*, 165–175. doi:10.1017/S1352465804002000.

Weck, F., Bleichhardt, G., Witthöft, M., & Hiller, W. (2011). Explicit and implicit anxiety: Differences between patients with hypochondriasis, patients with anxiety disorders, and healthy controls. *Cognitive Therapy and Research, 35*, 317–325. doi:10.1007/s10608-010-9303-5.

Weck, F., Harms, G., Neng, J. M. B., & Stangier, U. (2011). Hypochondrische Merkmale bei Patienten einer psychotherapeutischen Ambulanz [Hypochondriacal characteristics in psychotherapeutic outpatients. Prevalence and predisposing factors]. *Zeitschrift für Klinische Psychologie und Psychotherapie, 40*, 124–132.

Wells, A. (2005). Detached mindfulness in cognitive therapy: A metacognitive analysis and ten techniques. *Journal of Rational-Emotive & Cognitive-Behavior Therapy, 23*, 337–355. doi:10.1007/s10942-005-0018-6.

Wells, A. (2009). *Meta-cognitive therapy for anxiety and depression*. New York: Guilford Press.

Wilhelm, S. (2006). *Feeling good about the way you look: A program for overcoming body image problems*. New York: Guilford Press.

Williams, J., Hadjistavropoulos, T., & Sharpe, D. (2006). A meta-analysis of psychological and pharmacological treatments for body dysmorphic disorder. *Behaviour Research and Therapy, 44*, 99–111. doi:10.1016/j.brat.2004.12.006.

World Health Organization. (1993). *The ICD-10 classification of mental and behavioural disorders: diagnostic criteria for research*. Geneva: World Health Organization.

Chapter 14
Prolonged Imaginal Exposure Based on Worry Scenarios

Jürgen Hoyer and Katja Beesdo-Baum

Jürgen Hoyer is Professor of Psychology at the University of Dresden. He is director of the outpatient clinic for psychotherapy and of the behavior therapy training program. Among a broad range of interests and experiences in clinical and forensic research, he focuses on generalized anxiety disorder, social phobia, and depression.

J. Hoyer (✉)
Institute of Clinical Psychology and Psychotherapy, Technische Universitaet Dresden, Hohe Str. 53, D-01187 Dresden, Germany
e-mail: hoyer@psychologie.tu-dresden.de

K. Beesdo-Baum
Institute of Clinical Psychology and Psychotherapy, Technische Universitaet Dresden, Chemnitzer Str. 46, D-01187 Dresden, Germany
e-mail: beesdo@psychologie.tu-dresden.de

P. Neudeck and H.-U. Wittchen (eds.), *Exposure Therapy: Rethinking the Model – Refining the Method*, DOI 10.1007/978-1-4614-3342-2_14,

Katja Beesdo-Baum is Professor of Psychology at the University of Dresden, Germany. As a clinician and researcher, she has interests in the phenomenology, epidemiology, etiology, and treatment of anxiety and mood disorders. Her research on Generalized Anxiety Disorder covers clinical, biological, and prospective-longitudinal epidemiological aspects.

14.1 Introduction

Generalized anxiety disorder (GAD) is increasingly recognized as a prevalent anxiety disorder with a chronic course and significant impairment (Wittchen & Hoyer, 2001). Cognitive-behavioral therapy (CBT) is considered the psychological treatment of choice for this disorder (Mitte, 2005). The effects and response rates of CBT in GAD are, however, lower than in other anxiety disorders (Hoyer & Gloster, 2009; Hoyer, van der Heiden, & Portman, 2011; Hunot et al., 2007).

Generally, the most efficient therapeutic intervention to treat anxiety disorders is exposure (see, e.g., Rubin, Spates, Johnson, & Jouppi, 2009) and there is increasing knowledge about the extinction-learning processes underlying the effects of exposure (e.g., Craske et al., 2008; Treanor, 2011). Notably, the focus on exposure is less pronounced in the treatment of GAD than in other anxiety disorders. Most approaches rather use a variety of interventions with exposure being one among other elements in these multimodal treatment packages (Hoyer & Gloster, 2009; Hoyer et al., 2011). The hesitancy to apply exposure in GAD more intensely and straightforwardly might be attributed to the fact that behavioral avoidance, as the symptom typically targeted by exposure, is less evident in GAD (Beesdo-Baum et al., in press). Nevertheless, the application of exposure in GAD appears to be appropriate, but requires specific refinement. More specifically, the key feature of GAD, chronic and uncontrollable worry, as a subtle and covert form of cognitive-emotional avidance (Borkovec, Alcaine, & Behar, 2004) has to be counteracted in exposure. Thus, exposure needs to be applied in its imaginal or in sensu form.

In the present article, we describe the rationale and practice of imaginal exposure with worry scenarios in a prolonged mode, how the groundwork for this procedure can be provided in therapy, and how it should be performed. We base our proposals on our experiences with a RCT testing the procedure (Beesdo-Baum et al., in press; Hoyer et al., 2009) and on our experiences with many GAD patients in a specialized GAD outpatient centre.

14.2 Prolonged Versus Graded Imaginal Exposure to Worry Scenarios

Systematic exposure to what is behind worrisome thoughts operates on the assumption that worry functions as cognitive avoidant behavior. According to the avoidance theory of worrying (e.g., Borkovec et al., 2004; for a refined version of the theory see Newman & Llera, 2011), worry is believed to prevent deeper, and often more aversive, emotional processing of thoughts and images, thus perpetuating worry via negative reinforcement (see also Borkovec, Ray, & Stöber, 1998). Accordingly, excessive worrisome thinking can be reduced by exposing the patient to the emotions, cognitions, and physiological symptoms which are usually avoided during worrying episodes. This is usually accomplished by first generating a fear hierarchy of worrisome thoughts, then having the client expose themselves to *purposeful* worry and to corresponding images for an extended period (i.e., 20–30 min) (e.g., Craske, Barlow, & O'Leary, 1992; Van der Heiden & ten Broecke, 2009). Conceptually, this procedure is especially obvious regarding the generally strong treatment effects of fear exposure in other disorders (Richard, Lauterbach, & Gloster, 2007). However, in the randomized controlled studies which investigated the effects of CBT in GAD, exposure in sensu has always been combined with—sometimes numerous—other interventions from a CBT background, e.g., problem solving training, breathing relaxation, cognitive restructuring, etc. (Behar, DiMarco, Hekler, Mohlman, & Staples, 2009; Hoyer & Gloster, 2009; Hoyer et al., 2011). As a consequence, it is not clear to what extent exposure contributes to the treatment success and which variants of exposure are most successful.

Recently, Hoyer and colleagues (Hoyer et al., 2009) refined the worry exposure protocol and applied it as a massed or prolonged exposure in sensu to feared images and outcomes. In other words, patients were motivated to confront their worst worry imagery right away and to try to experience the accompanying anxiety symptoms as intensely as possible until habituation occurred. It was demonstrated that this treatment, which directly targets the avoidance described in the avoidance theory of worry and largely follows the logic of emotional processing theory (Foa & Kozak, 1986), could be successfully deployed as a stand-alone treatment of GAD (i.e., without the additional use of cognitive or relaxation interventions). Patients treated with massed worry exposure achieved stable improvement equal to applied relaxation (Hoyer et al., 2009). Furthermore, negative meta-cognitions about worry, i.e., fearful cognitions that worrying could be debilitating (Wells, 1999), were successfully reduced. While worry exposure was used as a singular treatment component in order to demonstrate its efficacy in isolation, overall treatment efficacy could possibly be increased by adding further empirically validated therapeutic interventions. However, it is of theoretical

Table 14.1 Treating GAD with prolonged imaginal exposure: Manualized session structure

Session number	Session contents and goals
Session 1–3	Psycho-education focusing on the behavioral components of anxiety and worry. Patients are trained in investigating the nature of their worries and understanding the vicious circle of worrying and the role of avoidance
4–9	Imaginal exposure: Prolonged in-sensu exposure using worry scenarios addressing the avoidant function of worry 1. Providing the exposure rationale • Day chart of anxiety and worry levels • Exploring strategies and behaviors that decrease anxiety and worry over the short run but maintain the disorder over the long run • Thought experiment "What would happen if I'd think my worry through to the worst end" • Explaining habituation processes • Explaining the therapeutic plan 2. Preparation for imaginal exposure • Collecting worry themes • Generate a worry hierarchy (by use of worksheet Table 14.3) • Choosing the high-priority worry (worry # 1) • Developing a worry scenario for the high-priority worry • Training of imagination (if necessary) 3. Conducting imaginal exposure for worry # 1 • Imaginal exposure exercise in session • Talking about the experience with imaginal exposure • Repeat exposure in session • Decatastrophizing (if necessary) • Homework assignment: daily imaginal exposure exercises 4. Preparing and conducting imaginal exposures for worries # 2 and # 3
10–13	In-vivo exposure: Real-life exposure to feared situations targeting patients' safety behavior, avoidance, and reassurance seeking
14–15	Relapse prevention; identifying and coping with at-risk situations

importance that this treatment did not use explicit cognitive interventions, and focused solely on the imaginations which had been avoided through worry.

The protocol of this study followed the manual by Becker and Margraf (2002) which describes imaginal exposure for GAD applied in 15 sessions: Imaginal exposure treatment begins with psychoeducation, in which the disorder is primarily explained using concepts of avoidance. No specific references are made to the role of automatic thoughts or beliefs. Using the concept of habituation, patients are informed that symptom reduction could be achieved by directly exposing themselves in their imagination to what they fear might happen. Treatment commences with self-monitoring of worry. Imaginal exposure begins in the 3rd session and continues through the 10th session. Concurrently, avoidance and reassurance behaviors are addressed and systematically reduced. The final stage of therapy targets generalization and relapse prevention. Patients are continually assigned to do homework exercises. Diaries on the completion of homework assignments are kept throughout the treatment. In the following, we describe the procedures of this manual (see Table 14.1) in greater detail.

14.3 Foundations for Prolonged Imaginal Exposure

Laying the groundwork for prolonged imaginal exposure mainly consists of three components: (a) a strong therapeutic relationship which is largely immunized to patients' efforts to seek reassurance, (b) raising positive treatment expectations, and (c) familiarizing the patient with the rationale.

14.3.1 A Strong Therapeutic Relationship

Like other (anxiety) patients, patients with GAD expect the therapist to be a person they can trust. This understandable wish gets complicated in some cases, when patients seem to think: Only when I leave the session with fewer worries my therapist is right for me; someone I can really trust and believe. In other words: The patient expects the therapist to *directly* help him reduce worrying. Such a belief will potentially be counterproductive if the therapist becomes a part of the patients' efforts to seek reassurance and to reduce his feelings of uncertainty (see also Dugas & Robichaud, 2007). To prevent confusion with regard to what the patient can expect, we usually explain to the patient that his trust in the therapist is justified but that this cannot mean that the therapist solves the patients' problem. Using previous examples of other persons providing reassurance to the patient, the therapist aims at clarifying that his role should differ from that of lay persons. His or her role would rather emphasize facilitating new learning and pertinent change than just immediate consolidation and reassurance.

14.3.2 Raising Positive Treatment Expectations

What would help to make the patient more optimistic about therapy? Even patients who already have undergone (sometimes several) previous therapies, may not have had experiences with exposure treatment, not only because GAD often remains undiagnosed. When exposure was applied but was unsuccessful, it is mandatory to review whether it was applied properly by the patient and what the patient can do to adhere more strictly to its rationale this time. More generally, positive expectations that the problem can be mastered and that the patient himself is able to do so, need to be established. A review of previous episodes in the life of the patient in which he accomplished new behavior patterns and/or was able to perform new or improved behavior would help to establish a mindset associated with positive change expectations. Such a strategy would be called resource activation by Grawe (2006; see also Beesdo-Baum, 2011).

Table 14.2 Evaluating patients' ways to counteract worrying

How do I counteract worrying?	Effective: In the short run (0–10)	Long run (0–10)
1. By thought suppression	5	0
2. By reassurance seeking	8–9	2
3. By drinking alcohol	6–7	0
4. By diverting attention away	8	1

14.3.3 *Making the Patient Familiar with the Rationale in a Convincing Manner*

Since imaginal exposure to worry scenarios is counterintuitive for many patients, it is crucial for the success of the treatment to present the rationale of the procedure in a consistent, easy to understand, and convincing way. Further, beyond just explaining the treatment procedures the individuals' anxious beliefs about what could possibly happen when engaging in the treatment procedures have to be identified, clarified, and discussed.

The usual way to illustrate the "philosophy" of the treatment is to analyze previous worry episodes, to identify the typical strategies of the patients to deal with worrying, and to demonstrate that these strategies either do not work at all or do only work in the short run (Becker & Margraf, 2002).

Typical strategies to counteract worrying are: Distraction, thought suppression, reassurance seeking (e.g., by phoning up/controlling loved ones who are away or by contacting other persons, e.g., friends or relatives who should help calming down the patient), avoiding situations that trigger or enhance worries, taking medication or drugs including alcohol, and worrying itself (jumping to other worry topics in order to avoid deeper elaboration of the previous worry topic).

Making the rationale familiar usually starts with reviewing a structured diary of the week in which the patient lists up all worry episodes and all efforts he took against worrying. The ultimate goal of this review is to clarify that all these efforts have little or no effect or only work in the short run. The best way the therapist can exemplify this is a behavior experiment to illustrate the effects of thought suppression (see, e.g., Becker & Margraf, 2002; Dugas & Robichaud, 2007). Therein, the patient experiences that efforts to suppress thoughts are to no end. Even if a patient would manage to suppress a given thought for some minutes, the rebound effect—which leads to increased availability of this thought—is certain. Hence, we recommend to this experiment as mandatory! Even if the patient anticipates that he or she cannot really suppress thoughts, a demonstration using this experiment is still more convincing than mere verbal discussion.

At the end of this discussion, the patient may develop a list of his or her efforts to counteract worrying and their effectiveness in the short and in the long run (see Table 14.2).

14.4 Implementing Exposure

14.4.1 Selecting Worry Topics and Scenarios

As everybody can worry about nearly everything, the selection of worry episodes that are optimally suited for prolonged exposure is not trivial. Many patients present with the problem that they "worry about everything." The basic assumption is that in these cases especially those worry episodes have to be identified which are typical for *pathological* (as opposed to everyday) worrying. Worries which are only transient, situation-bound, and deal with rather minor hassles should not be considered relevant: If somebody worries that the next bus is not going to arrive in time, this is not a persistent concern. It may be helpful for the patient to realize that not all worries are similarly pertinent or important. Some worries may rather constitute a type of concern that can be dismissed or can at least be learned to be dismissed by simple interventions such as time projection ("would this worry topic be relevant even in a week—or a month from now?"; see, e.g., Butler & Hope, 2007). Similarly, worry episodes which are or can be part of problem-solving activities should not be selected for imaginal exposure. If somebody worries about not being sufficiently prepared for an examination, this may be a solvable (although potentially persistent) problem, since he or she can increase efforts or try to postpone the examination, etc. A systematic strategy to find out which way would be the best to solve the problem is problem-solving training (as introduced, e.g., by D'Zurilla & Goldfried; see D'Zurilla & Nezu, 2007). These two basic ideas can easily be communicated with patients using simple tables which help to systematically identify relevant worries (see Table 14.3).

Finally, also those persistent and important worries which are relatively unrelated to solvable problems are considered excessive or maladaptive. Worries that are related, e.g., to chronic or even terminal diseases of a loved one may not be part of the worry *syndrome*. Many patients realize easily that these worries are acceptable since they are natural given an extreme and realistically threatening situation. (They may, on the other hand, nevertheless be part of experiential avoidance; an aspect to which we return later.)

A dimensional rating of worry topics as more or less important, as more or less related to a solvable problem, and as more or less excessive and "over the top" is clearly preferable over a categorical (yes/no) decision which would be hard to make in many occasions. In the example of Table 14.3, it becomes clear that although there are a number of worry topics, only one of these is completely unrelated to a solvable problem. This topic should become the focus of treatment because it is a source of repeated emotional disturbance. As in our example, to worry about possible incidents affecting loved ones is a typical problem of patients with GAD. It has to be part of the psycho education for these patients to clarify that incidents may happen at any time and that persistent worrying about incidents does not change anything about their possibility. Application of the schema proposed in Table 14.3

Table 14.3 Self-rating of worry topics: The second problem would be optimally suitable for prolonged imaginal exposure

Worry topic	How important is this topic? (0–100)	How much is this topic related to a solvable problem? (0–100)	How natural and acceptable is my worrying about this topic? (0–100)
1. My dog will catch pneumonia	60	50	50
2. My husband will have an accident	100	0	20
3. I am having problems paying back my credit card debt	80	80	100
4. (…)			
5. (…)			

not only catalyzes the process of identifying relevant worry topics, it also can help to make underlying distorted assumptions (including negative meta-cognition; Wells, 2009) more clear. Additionally, it also enables the patient to structure his or her worry problems.

14.4.2 Developing Scenarios

Once a typical and persistent worry *topic* is found, a concrete, imaginable worry scenario (or script) has to be developed. The therapist prompts the patient to explore the feared situation in a deeper and more tangible way than before. The aim is to create an imaginable scene around the most feared outcome. To facilitate imagination, the script should contain all the stimulus qualities (including visual, auditory, tactile, gustatory, and olfactory information) that characterize the scene. To be sufficiently anxiety/experience provoking, the scene should also contain information about the (imagined) response of the patient: how he feels, thinks, and behaves. In other words: The worry "screenplay" should not only be based on a "stimulus script" but also on a "response script" (Vaitl & Petermann, 2004). While asking the relevant questions to gather these kinds of information, the therapist has to be aware: Exploring such a scenario already means to confront the patient with what he or she fears. Typical questions to be asked are:

- What would happen exactly?
- How would it go on?
- What do you exactly fear?
- What would be the worst?
- What do you see (hear, feel, smell, taste) in that situation?
- Which symptoms do you experience?
- Which thoughts cross your mind?

Box 1 Example of a worry scenario

My husband will have an accident

I am at home in my living room. It is comfortably warm. The TV is on. My husband is at our weekend house to clear out the trees in the yard. He wanted to be back by 5pm. I look at the clock—it is shortly after 6pm. I get nervous. I can't concentrate on the TV program. I walk around the room feeling pressure on my chest. My heart beats faster. I walk to the window and look out for him. It is wet and cold outside. I sit down back at the couch. I think "Hopefully nothing happened to him." My heart beats faster. I feel my tension rising. My hands tremble. I begin to expect that something bad happened. Suddenly, the bell is ringing. I react with a start. "He would not ring, he has a key!" I walk to the door and feel that I am shaky. I open the door. It is Sophia—our weekend-home neighbour. I feel dizzy. I now know something bad has happened. Sophia looks terribly pale and has tears in her eyes. She hesitates and then says "something terrible happened—your husband fell off a tree." I say to myself "this is more than I can bear" and have difficulties to keep staying upright. Sophia continues "he died before the emergency ambulance arrived." I freeze. I feel dizzy. My heart rushes. I must sit down on the stairs.

An example of a worry scenario is provided in Box 1. To facilitate imagination, the scenario should be short and in present tense. Ideally it does not include any drastic location or time changes. Of note, although worry scenarios are generally anxiety provoking given that the patient is confronted with the most feared outcome of a worry, the scenario frequently culminates in other emotions, most commonly sadness. Thus, imaginal exposure based on worry scenarios creates an "emotional contrast" (Newman & Llera, 2011) from a "normal" or rather relaxed emotional state to an anxiety state and eventually even to another emotional state (that the patient fears to experience in full intensity).

14.4.3 In-Session Imaginal Exposure and Preventing Covert Avoidance Responses

After elaboration of a suitable worry scenario, the next session is used for imaginal exposure. It is important that the patient understands that he has to tolerate considerable levels of discomfort during the exposure exercise but that he does this purposefully ("the more you do it, the easier it gets"; Himle & Franklin, 2009). Prior to imaginal exposure the patient is therefore instructed to (a) fully concentrate on the scenario, (b) try to draw his attention back to the scenario whenever any disturbances occur (noise from the street, paresthesia, distractive thoughts, etc.), and (c) try to *enhance* anxiety whenever possible.

As patients' capabilities to vividly imagine scenarios (of whatever quality) differ individually, it is often recommendable to train the patients' imagination using everyday examples (such as taking a cold shower or watching the neighbor going to work).

Given that the patient is able to imagine an "everyday" scenario intensely enough we would start with a scenario that elicits a sufficiently high amount of anxiety and tension to challenge the patients' anxious assumptions. In general, the amount of experienced anxiety and tension should be higher than what the patient normally experiences during worry. Usually, GAD patients assume that they are "unable to stand" this challenge, to "go crazy" or to otherwise be overexerted in trying to fully imagine the feared scene. In other words, they think imagining or experiencing the aversive scene would be unbearable for them and that the level of arousal and negative emotionality would rise beyond any point where they had been before. However, the aim of exposure is to enable the patient to experience that also these strongly aversive emotions habituate and/or at least will not be harmful for their mind or body.

Therapists can often prevent possible overt avoidance behaviors which would interfere with the success of exposure treatment through response prevention (e.g., Himle & Franklin, 2009). Covert anxiety-control strategies are more problematic. The patient may resort to distracting his attention from the feared scenario, especially when confrontation with the worry scenario is prolonged and excessive. The therapist has to be able to identify these tendencies, to guide the patient back to the scenario and help him to keep his imagination on a fear-eliciting level. However, as Koerner and Fracalanza (this book) point out, no study ever analyzed the role of anxiety-control strategies during worry exposure. It may well be that some extent of anxiety-control strategies may be helpful to some extent in order to reach full emotional engagement (which is considered a prerequisite for the "contrast experience" exposure tries to provide).

In order to identify whether the patient is actually able to enter the scenario in his imagination, therapist and patient stipulate a sign, e.g., raising the forefinger which signals that the patient is having difficulties to imagine and "feel" the scenario. The therapist can then reread the instruction and also reread the part of the scenario for which the imagination could not be maintained. However, even if the imagination can be fully kept, some patients do not experience the amount of anxiety they originally expected to experience. To ensure that a sufficient anxiety level has been reached, the therapist therefore asks continuously how much anxiety the patient is experiencing. The use of subjective units of distress (ranging from 0 to 100) is particularly relevant here as an easy way to communicate in how far the patient manages to create a vivid image to fully experience the scene. Given that they always avoided imagining the respective scenarios, a lower than expected degree of anxiety is not necessarily surprising and may only demonstrate that the feared scenarios have not been elaborated fully enough before. In these cases, we made positive experiences guiding the patient "deeper" into the scenario using questions such as: "Is there anything else in this situation which you did not yet register?," "How does the situation continue?," "Is there any possibility in this situation which you did not think of yet and which would increase your anxiety?" For instance, a 28-year-old student who was imagining that his girlfriend told him she wanted to breakup and who had stated that this was his most important and frightening worry topic, did only experience anxiety of about 20–30 on a 0–100 scale during this scene. In this case, the therapist instructed the patient to stay in the situation and then asked the patient, if there was anything else which would provoke anxiety and what else the girlfriend might say. The patient continued: "She would say that she is with somebody else." The following increase of the anxiety reaction of the patient was even visible in the videotape of that session. His muscles got tense and he strongly grabbed the handrails of his chair. After staying in *this* scenario he could effectively experience habituation, indicating that emotional processing took place. The experiences of the patient during imaginal exposure are carefully analyzed in a mode of guided discovery. "What did you learn/infer from what you experienced during exposure?" Often new and more balanced views of the feared situation and of the emotional engagement in it result. For example, patients experience that confronting the previously avoided scenario (i.e., confronting worry) and the associated strong emotions cannot do any harm. Furthermore, alternative solutions or outcomes of the scenario often come spontaneously to mind.

14.4.4 Homework Assignments, In-Vivo Exposure, and Relapse Prevention

Once the patient has experienced going through imaginal exposure in the therapy session, ideally with some degree of habituation, it should be carefully explored whether there were any covert activities of the patient in order to counteract the feared consequences of undergoing this exposure. In order to do so, therapist asks the patient whether he or she had done anything to arrive at habituation. If necessary, the therapist encourages the patient to realize that full experiencing of anxious feelings and arousal is the best way of coping with extant anxieties and worries, and encourages the patient to continue with this form of treatment via homework exercises. The ultimate goal of repeated exposures to the feared worst-case scenario of the first worry topic is a stable habituation before proceeding to the next worry scenario with more and more enabling the patient to generate the scripts by him- or herself. From our experience, working through two to three worry scenarios in the therapy is sufficient for the patient to experience a significant decrease in overall anxiety and worry levels.

Additionally, patients are instructed to monitor their everyday worry behaviors (safety behavior, avoidance, and reassurance seeking) using structured diaries. They are then asked to prevent themselves from engaging in these behaviors and to confront themselves with feared/avoided situations. The rationale underlying this treatment phase is the same as before: As worry prevents experiencing of more aversive emotions but only at the expense of a rat race of apprehension and nervousness, it will rather help the patient to confront situations that may elicit worry (and the previously avoided emotions) and to experience that any of these confrontations will only transiently cause emotional stress, if at all.

Once the patient has entered this stage, treatment is incomplete unless possible risk situations have been identified. These risk situations can be defined by putative internal and external stressors which will prone the patient to fall back into his old behavior patterns (including reassurance seeking). For each of these situations, it should be discussed how the patient would behave. The list of resulting strategies constitutes the core of relapse prevention.

14.5 Combination with Other Interventions

Beyond worry exposure, Hoyer et al. (2011) name psycho-education, self-monitoring, stimulus-control interventions, relaxation techniques, self-control desensitization, cognitive restructuring, worry-behavior prevention, and problem solving as central components of CBT treatment for GAD. Although most of these other treatment components can be meaningfully combined with worry exposure, we would argue that worry exposure is the intervention which most directly follows from our present understanding of the avoidance mechanisms underlying GAD (see Newman & Llera, 2011, for the most recent account). Furthermore, we would rather prefer a "parsimonious" treatment—which includes only components that are obvious—over an eclectic one which would make it hard to judge which of the components worked for which reason (Höfler, Gloster, & Hoyer, 2010).

However, as explained above, worry exposure is usually combined with worry behavior prevention. Furthermore, worries which are grounded in solvable problems and which would not be targeted by worry exposure can also lead to relevant distress and impairment. Given that the person's problem-solving ability is low in these cases, systematic problem solving (e.g., D'Zurilla & Nezu, 2007) would be recommendable as a treatment addendum.

14.6 Differential Indication

Prolonged imaginal exposure based on worry scenarios, as we described the technique above, was specifically developed and empirically tested for patients with GAD. It might, however, not be indicated in all treatment-seeking individuals suffering from GAD. Some patients with GAD do not experience the worrying as their primary concern. They rather seek help for the bodily consequences of the disorder such as restlessness, difficulties concentrating, sleep problems, and so on. These patients often have difficulties in expressing their specific worries and rather experience "free-floating" anxiety levels, nervousness, and tension.

The rationale of applied relaxation (Öst, 1987; Öst & Breitholtz, 2000) is much easier to understand and accept for these patients. Given the known effectiveness of this treatment for GAD, it is a valuable alternative to exposure in this subgroup of patients.

Since many patients with GAD suffer from comorbid conditions, it must be clear in which constellations of comorbid disorders imaginal exposure would be indicated or not. One advantage of using exposure as a first-line treatment for GAD is that this procedure combines elegantly with the exposure rationale for comorbid anxiety disorders. When depression is the comorbid disorder, we presently only apply imaginal exposure when there is no more than a mild acute status of depression. Contraindications are all conditions in which the ability to build up a stabile relationship with the therapist (e.g., severe personality disorders) or the ability for reality testing (psychoses, borderline personality disorder) are impaired.

14.7 Difficulties and Pitfalls

Treatment progress is probable when the patient complies with exposure exercises and is able to refrain from subtle avoidance (Craske et al., 2008). Typical problems in doing so arise as a result of underlying distorted basic assumptions of patients with GAD. These are, more specifically, related to (a) negative metacognitions about the dangerousness of worrying (as described by Wells, 1999, 2009), (b) extreme levels of intolerance for uncertainty (Dugas & Robichaud, 2007), and (c), the inability to accept that anxiety is a normal and acceptable part of life (Roemer & Orsillo, 2008).

14.8 Conclusions and Future Perspectives

Imaginal exposure works for GAD. In a considerable portion of cases (more than 40%; Hoyer et al., 2009) full remission is accomplished when used as a stand-alone treatment. In a randomized controlled trial, we demonstrated the effect of this specific intervention alone by dismantling it from other ingredients of typical CBT packages. In the present chapter, we described how this procedure can be deployed in practice. Similar procedures have already been described for obsessive–compulsive disorder (Himle & Franklin, 2009), or posttraumatic stress disorder (Hembree, Rauch, & Foa, 2003). The fact that imaginal exposure alone works also in GAD should not mean that it cannot be improved or combined with other methods. In contrast, we do believe that overall treatment efficacy could be increased, and attrition reduced, by adding further empirically validated treatment components (Hoyer & Gloster, 2009).

At the same time, further improvement of the method of worry exposure itself, which has yet not received much attention in research, seems obvious. In this regard, recent proposals to investigate different strategies of exposure in the treatment of fear, specifically dosed exposure as opposed to prolonged exposure are highly inspiring (Rubin et al., 2009) and should be transferred to the study of worry exposure. On the procedural level, the protocol described here, which grounds in Becker and Margraf's conception (2002), is very similar to other more recent manuals of worry/imaginal exposure (Dugas & Robichaud, 2007; Van der Heiden & ten Broecke, 2009). Nevertheless, some differences may still be of importance: While Van der Heiden and ten Broecke (2009) recommend having the patients expose themselves to the worry scenario for at least 25 min, we simply let the course of anxiety decide how long exposure should be. Usually, exposure or the experience that anxiety levels decrease without any active attempts on the person's part takes *less* than 25 min. From our experience, it would be an extremely demanding mental task to fully and continuously engage in an imaginal scenario for 25 min, be it aversive or not; a task which would be overdemanding for some patients. One important difference to the manual of Dugas and Robichaud (2007) is that in our procedure the therapist first reads worry scenarios to the patient rather than that the patient reads and records it. Also for homework assignments, we do not recommend audio recording because this would lead to an inflexible sequence that runs through the mind of the listener independent of his or her associated experience. We rather want the patient to imagine the scenario without the help of external devices so that he or she learns to deliberately engage in the mental scenario as long as necessary.

These are technical or procedural differences which one might consider to be marginally important as the general strategy—exposure in sensu—is the same. However, we agree with Koerner and Fracalanza (this book) that there is only a loose connection between science and practice concerning imaginal exposure. More research into this technique and its procedural variants would probably increase its efficacy and help to proceed to client-friendly and individualized applications. It may also provide deeper insights into how and why worry exposure works.

References

Becker, E., & Margraf, J. (2002). *Generalisierte Angststörung. Ein Therapieprogramm*. Weinheim: Beltz.

Beesdo-Baum, K. (2011). Ressourcenaktivierung. In H. U. Wittchen & J. Hoyer (Eds.), *Klinische Psychologie und Psychotherapie* (2nd ed., pp. 491–502). Heidelberg: Springer.

Beesdo-Baum, K., Jenjahn, E., Höfler, M., Lueken, U., Becker, E. S., & Hoyer, J. (in press). Avoidance, safety behavior, and reassurance seeking in Generalized Anxiety Disorder. *Depression and Anxiety*.

Behar, E., DiMarco, I. D., Hekler, E. B., Mohlman, J., & Staples, A. M. (2009). Current theoretical models of generalized anxiety disorder (GAD): Conceptual review and treatment implications. *Journal of Anxiety Disorders, 23*(8), 1011–1023.

Borkovec, T. D., Alcaine, O. M., & Behar, E. (2004). Avoidance theory of worry and generalized anxiety disorder. In R. G. Heimberg, C. L. Turk, & D. S. Mennin (Eds.), *Generalized anxiety disorder: Advances in research and practice* (pp. 77–108). New York: Guilford Press.

Borkovec, T. D., Ray, W. J., & Stöber, J. (1998). Worry: A cognitive phenomenon intimately linked to affective, physiological, and interpersonal behavioral processes. *Cognitive Therapy and Research, 22*, 561–576.

Butler, G., & Hope, T. (2007). *Manage your mind. The mental fitness guide*. Oxford: Oxford University Press.
Craske, M. G., Barlow, D. H., & O'Leary, T. A. (1992). *Mastery of your anxiety and worry*. Albany: Graywind.
Craske, M. G., Kircanski, K., Zelikowsky, M., Mystkowski, J. L., Chowdhury, N., & Baker, A. (2008). Optimizing inhibitory learning during exposure therapy. *Behavior Research and Therapy, 46*, 5–27.
D'Zurilla, T. J., & Nezu, A. M. (2007). *Problem-solving therapy: A positive approach to clinical intervention* (3rd ed.). New York: Springer.
Dugas, M. J., & Robichaud, M. (2007). *Cognitive-behavioral treatment for generalized anxiety disorder*. New York: Routledge.
Foa, E., & Kozak, M. J. (1986). Emotional processing of fear: Exposure to corrective information. *Psychological Bulletin, 99*, 20–35.
Grawe, K. (2006). *Neuropsychotherapy. How the neurosciences inform effective psychotherapy*. New York: Laurence Erlbaum.
Hembree, E. A., Rauch, S. A. M., & Foa, E. B. (2003). Beyond the manual: The insider's guide to prolonged exposure therapy for PTSD. *Cognitive and Behavioral Practice, 10*, 22–30.
Himle, M. B., & Franklin, M. E. (2009). The more you do it, the easier it gets: Exposure and response prevention for OCD. *Cognitive and Behavioral Practice, 16*, 29–39.
Höfler, M., Gloster, A. T., & Hoyer, J. (2010). Causal effects in psychotherapy: Counterfactuals counteract overgeneralization. *Psychotherapy Research, 20*, 668–679.
Hoyer, J., Beesdo, K., Gloster, A. T., Runge, J., Höfler, M., & Becker, E. S. (2009). Worry exposure versus applied relaxation in the treatment of generalized anxiety disorder. *Psychotherapy and Psychosomatics, 78*, 106–115.
Hoyer, J., & Gloster, A. T. (2009). Psychotherapy for generalized anxiety disorder: Don't worry, it works! *Psychiatric Clinics of North America, 32*, 629–640.
Hoyer, J., van der Heiden, C., & Portman, M. E. (2011). Psychotherapy of generalized anxiety disorder. *Psychiatric Annals, 41*, 87–94.
Hunot, V., Churchill, R., Silva de Lima, M., & Teixeira, V. (2007). Psychological therapies for generalised anxiety disorder (Review). *Cochrane Database of Systematic Reviews, 1*(CD001848).
Koerner, N., & Fracalanza, K. (2012). The role of anxiety control strategies in imaginal exposure. In P. Neudeck & H.-U. Wittchen (Eds.), *Exposure Therapy: Rethinking the Model – Refining the Method*, 197–216.
Mitte, K. (2005). Meta-analysis of cognitive-behavioral treatments for generalized anxiety disorder: A comparison with pharmacotherapy. *Psychological Bulletin, 131*(5), 785–795.
Newman, M. C., & Llera, S. J. (2011). A novel theory of experiential avoidance in generalized anxiety disorder: A review and synthesis of research supporting a contrast avoidance model of worry. *Clinical Psychology Review*. doi:10.1016/j.cpr.2011.1001.1008.
Öst, L. G. (1987). Applied relaxation: Description of a coping technique and review of controlled studies. *Behaviour Research and Therapy, 25*, 397–409.
Öst, L. G., & Breitholtz, E. (2000). Applied relaxation vs. cognitive therapy in the treatment of generalized anxiety disorder. *Behaviour Research and Therapy, 38*, 777–790.
Richard, D. C. S., Lauterbach, D., & Gloster, A. T. (2007). Description, mechanisms of action, and assessment. In D. C. S. Richard & D. Lauterbach (Eds.), *Handbook of Exposure Therapies* (pp. 1–28). Burlington: Academic Press.
Roemer, L., & Orsillo, S. M. (2008). Efficacy of an acceptance-based behaviour therapy for generalized anxiety disorder: Evaluation in a randomized controlled trial. *Journal of Consulting and Clinical Psychology, 76*, 1083–1089.
Rubin, D. B., Spates, C. R., Johnson, D. A., & Jouppi, L. (2009). Dosed versus prolonged exposure in the treatment of fear: An experimental evaluation and review of behavioral mechanisms. *Journal of Anxiety Disorders, 23*, 806–812.
Treanor, W. (2011). The potential impact of mindfulness on exposure and extinction learning in anxiety disorders. *Clinical Psychology Review, 31*, 617–625.

Vaitl, D., & Petermann, F. (Eds.). (2004). *Entspannungsverfahren. Das Praxishandbuch* (3rd ed.). Weinheim: Psychologie Verlags Union.

Van der Heiden, C., & ten Broecke, E. (2009). The when, why, and how of worry exposure. *Cognitive and Behavioral Practice, 16*, 386–393.

Wells, A. (1999). A metacognitive model and therapy for generalized anxiety disorder. *Clinical Psychology and Psychotherapy, 6*(2), 86–95.

Wells, A. (2009). *Metacognitive therapy for anxiety and depression.* New York/London: Guilford.

Wittchen, H.-U., & Hoyer, J. (2001). Generalized anxiety disorder: Nature and course. *Journal of Clinical Psychiatry, 62*(suppl. 11), 15–19.

Chapter 15
Exposure In Vivo with and Without Presence of a Therapist: Does It Matter?

Thomas Lang and Sylvia Helbig-Lang

Thomas Lang. Born in 1972; 1992–2000 studies of Theology and Psychology at the Saarland University and Johannes Gutenberg University, Mainz. 2000 diploma degree in Psychology. 2000–2003 scholarship from the Christoph Dornier Foundation for Clinical Psychology. 2000–2004 postgradual training in CBT. 2003–2007 academic staff member at the outpatient treatment center for psychotherapy at the Technische Universitaet Dresden. Since 2007, head of the outpatient psychotherapy center at the University Bremen and executive director of the Bremen division of the Christoph Dornier Foundation for Clinical Psychology.

T. Lang (✉)
Christoph Dornier Foundation for Clinical Psychology, Bremen, Germany
e-mail: tlang@uni-bremen.de

S. Helbig-Lang
Department of Clinical Psychology and Psychotherapy, University Hamburg, Hamburg, Germany
e-mail: Sylvia.Helbig-Lang@uni-hamburg.de

P. Neudeck and H.-U. Wittchen (eds.), *Exposure Therapy: Rethinking the Model – Refining the Method*, DOI 10.1007/978-1-4614-3342-2_15,

Sylvia Helbig-Lang. Born in 1978; 1997–2002 studies of Psychology at the Technische Universitaet Dresden, 2002 diploma degree. 2003–2007 academic staff member at the Institute of Clinical Psychology and Psychotherapy, Technische Universitaet Dresden. 2003–2009 postgradual training in CBT. 2007–2011 academic staff member at the Center of Clinical Psychology and Rehabilitation, University Bremen, 2009 PhD. Since 2011, staff member at the Department of Clinical Psychology and Psychotherapy, University Hamburg.

15.1 Introduction

Various forms of cognitive-behavioral therapies (CBT) are well established as first-line treatments for anxiety disorders (Olatunji, Cisler, & Deacon, 2010). However, the questions of why they are so effective and by which mechanisms of action CBT works remain unclear. Exposure refers to a group of interventions designed to expose a patient to feared external or internal stimuli, either in vivo (situ) or in sensu. Exposure is often discussed as a crucial intervention for promoting therapeutic change (Woody & Ollendick, 2006). In fact, a large number of studies suggests that exposure alone or in combination with other interventions is highly effective in reducing anxiety and anxiety-related avoidance across different anxiety disorders (e.g., Hofmann & Smits, 2008; Olatunji et al., 2010; Powers, Halpern, Ferenschak, Gillihan, & Foa, 2010; Sánchez-Meca, Rosa-Alcázar, Marín-Martínez, & Gómez-Conesa, 2010).

So, if CBT works and exposure as well, one would expect that there should also be substantial evidence about their most active ingredients. To our knowledge, there is, however, only little research available about the *modalities of effective exposure in general and its implementation* in clinical practice. Thus, we find almost no empirical evidence and guidance regarding such simple questions like: What is the minimal (optimal) number of exposure exercises needed to induce behavior change? What is the minimum (optimal) duration of exposure? What type of feared stimuli must or must not be exposed? The Emotional Processing Theory by Foa and Kozak (1986) suggests that successful exposure is reflected by an initial fear activation, within-session habituation and in-between session habituation between consecutive exposure trials. There is a paucity of studies examining how these features of successful exposure can be promoted: How much fear is sufficient? Which of the feared stimuli should be chosen for exposure? Is the patients subjective self-report sufficient to determine fear activation and habituation? How long does exposure need to be to allow for inferences about habituation etc?. On the one hand, the rich body of clinical wisdom likely assumes that the therapist knows best. On the other hand, there are theoretical assumptions and indirect findings from experimental studies suggesting that the extinction process—as a psychophysiological correlate of exposure—can be stimulated by using different situations, including the situation, in which the anxiety first emerged, as well as by frequent repetition of the exposure exercises (Boschen, Neumann, & Waters, 2009). Interestingly however, further systematic exploration of these issues is rare (Foa, Riggs, Massie, & Yarczower, 1995; Mineka, Mystkowski, Hladek, & Rodriguez, 1999; Van Minnen & Hagenaars, 2002), and there is little empirical data supporting these assumptions or providing guidance.

15.1.1 The Role of the Therapist During Exposure

One issue that is rarely discussed in this context is the role of the therapist during exposure exercises. The role of the therapist is straightforward in interoceptive exposure, where the therapist implements exposure during the session in the treatment room. It is, however, less clear, when it comes to exposure sessions outside the treatment room, i.e., in real-life situations such as in shops, in public transportation etc. Regarding the latter, the core question is: Should the therapist in fact enter the real-life situations with the patient and support and supervise the patient at least initially? Or is it sufficient to simply introduce, explain, and plan the exposure, hoping that the patient will exert exposure then appropriately on its own?

One might argue that appropriate exposure is a complex and difficult task and therefore the therapist's presence is almost inevitably needed to provide encouragement and assistance in promoting fear and anxiety during the initial phase, ensuring that no overt or covert avoidance behavior occurs, and that the length and frequency of exposure is appropriately put in place to finally ensure habituation and relearning. In contrast, one could also speculate that the therapist's presence may lead to an increased dependency of the patient and thus might make generalization outside of the therapeutic process more difficult.

In the following, we will review evidence from studies providing data on the relevance of therapist presence during exposure, focusing on anxiety disorders and panic/agoraphobia in particular.

15.2 Exposure In Vivo Without Presence of the Therapist

The question whether exposure works without presence of the therapist has been frequently dealt with in studies using the terms "self-directed exposure," or "programmed practice." There are several—mostly older—studies (see Table 15.1) that have found robust effects, irrespective of how self-directed exposure was instructed (e.g., Ghosh & Marks, 1987; Ghosh, Marks, & Cart, 1988). Self-directed exposure was superior to several active control groups including relaxation training (McNamee, O'Sullivan, Lelliott, & Marks, 1989), supportive therapy (McDonald et al., 1979) and problem-solving training (Jannoun, Munby, Catalan, & Gelder, 1980). Exposure instructions even without face-to-face contact with a therapist seemed to work as well. Schneider, Mataix-Cols, Marks, and Bachhofen (2005) compared internet-guided CBT for phobic patients with and without self-exposure. Both conditions were equally effective at posttreatment; however, CBT plus self-exposure showed superiority in five out of ten measures at a 1-month follow-up. Edelman and Chambless (1993) compared agoraphobic patients treated with CBT, who either received self-exposure homework as part of their treatment, or received no homework instruction. Although both groups did not differ in overall outcome, patients spending more time doing homework reported greater reductions in anxiety and avoidance. Thus, self-directed exposure without presence of a therapist during the exposure exercises appeared to be effective as compared to treatments with no explicit exposure elements.

15.3 Exposure In Vivo with Therapist-Assisted Exposure

Ito et al. (2001) examined therapist-assisted in-vivo exposure in combination with different forms of self-exposure for patients with panic disorder and agoraphobia (interoceptive self-exposure, in-vivo self-exposure, or both). All three groups of self-exposure were equally effective and yielded impressive results compared to a control group. Interestingly, dropout rates in self-directed exposure conditions varied to a great extent from 0 to about 50%, indicating that self-exposure might not be appropriate for some patients (e.g. McNamee et al., 1989). Findings do not suggest, however, that dropout rates for self-directed exposure are consistently higher than in active control conditions.

In a small pilot study with six severe agoraphobic women, self-directed exposure remained without any effects, whereas a subsequent therapist-assisted exposure yielded moderate effects (Holden, O'Brien, Barlow, Stetson, & Infantino, 1983). Michelson, Mavissakalian, Marchione, Dancu, and Greenwald (1986) similarly examined the effects of programmed practice in combination with either graduated therapist-assisted exposure, paradoxical intention, or relaxation training for patients with agoraphobia. Combinations of programmed practice and graduated exposure as well as relaxation training were superior to paradoxical intention after treatment,

Table 15.1 Overview of studies examining effects of self-directed exposure

Author	Sample	N	Study conditions	Dropout rates	Results
Uncontrolled studies					
Mathews, Teasdale, Munby, Johnston, and Shaw (1977)	Agoraphobia	12	Programmed practice	0	Improvement in all but one cases
Ghosh and Marks (1987)	Agoraphobia	46	(a) Therapist-instructed SE (b) Book-instructed SE (c) Computer-instructed SE	(a) 14.3% (b) 13.3% (c) 11.8%	a=b=c Significant improvement in all groups
Ghosh et al. (1988)	Phobic patients (Agoraphobia, social phobia, specific phobia)	84	(a) Therapist-instructed SE (b) Book-instructed SE (c) Computer-instructed SE	(a) 17.4% (b) 14.3% (c) 15.2%	a=b=c Significant improvement in all groups
Controlled studies					
McDonald et al. (1979)	Agoraphobia	20	(a) SE (b) Supportive therapy	(a) 0% (b) 10%	a>b
Jannoun et al. (1980)	Agoraphobia	28	(a) Programmed practice (b) Problem solving	Overall 3.6%	a>b
McNamee et al. (1989)	Agoraphobia	23	(a) Written SE instructions (b) Relaxation training	(a) 53.8% (b) 20%	a>b
Ito et al. (2001)	Panic disorder with agoraphobia	80	(a) TE+Interoceptive SE (b) TE+SE in vivo (c) TE+Combined SE (d) Wait list control	(a) 4.8% (b) 5% (c) 9.5%	a=b=c d<a/b/c
Schneider, Mataix-Cols, Marks, and Bachofen (2005)	Phobic patients (Agoraphobia, social phobia, specific phobia)	68	(e) Internet CBT plus SE (f) Internet CBT without SE	(d) 22.2% (e) 26.1%	At post: a=b At follow-up: a>b

Note: CBT cognitive-behavioral therapy, *TE* therapist-assisted exposure, *SE* self-directed exposure although outcome of all three groups did not differ anymore at follow-up. Interestingly, frequency of self-directed exposure exercises was found to be higher in the relaxation group than in the condition with therapist-assisted exposure. Further, patients in the latter group were most likely to drop out of treatment. The authors speculate that relaxation training provided patients with a self-control strategy. Patients might, in turn, have perceived self-exposure as less dangerous than patients in other treatment groups. In a subsequent study, Michelson, Marchione, Greenwald, Testa, and Marchione (1996) assigned 92 patients with panic disorder and agoraphobia to therapist-assisted group exposure plus either relaxation training, cognitive therapy, or an active control group, consisting of a programmed practice discussion group. All groups received additional self-exposure instructions. The active control group—despite receiving both therapist-assisted as well as self-directed exposure instruction—showed significantly less improvement than groups with additional active ingredients, casting doubt on the efficacy of self-directed exposure. Taken together, these studies suggest that self-directed exposure is an active therapy ingredient, and that a combination of self-directed and therapist-assisted exposure might be superior to therapist-assisted exposure alone. However, all of these studies are somewhat inconclusive, because direct comparisons of exposure with and without presence of a therapist and also appropriate control groups are lacking.

Only four studies could be identified that directly compared self-directed with therapist-assisted exposure. Mavissakalian and Michelson (1983) randomly assigned agoraphobic patients to one of four treatment groups. All patients were instructed to conduct self-directed exposure exercises (=programmed practice); three treatment groups either received therapist-assisted flooding, psychopharmacological treatment, or a combination of both in addition. Each of these three active treatment groups was superior to the programmed practice group. Number and duration of exposure exercises notably did not differentiate between the groups. The authors concluded that therapist assistance during exposure might enhance emotional processing, and might therefore be superior to self-directed practice only.

Secondly, Al-Kubaisy et al. (1992) compared three conditions: relaxation training only vs. therapist-assisted exposure with and without self-directed exposure vs. self-exposure only in patients with phobic disorders. Both exposure conditions were superior to relaxation. There were few additive effects of therapist-assisted exposure compared to self-exposure: Only 3 of 27 outcome measures indicated superiority of combining both exposure types; it is noteworthy, however, that results are inconclusive due to high dropout rates and limited statistical power (see Table 15.2).

In contrast, a third study by Öst et al. (1991) found clear superiority of therapist-guided exposure for spider phobia compared to written instructions for self-exposure. This finding was confirmed by results pointing out superiority of therapist-guided exposure over several variations of self-exposure instructions (Hellström & Öst, 1995).

As far as the studies cited above allow direct inspection of differential effects of self-exposure vs. therapist-assisted exposure in anxiety, we summarize inconclusive results. Whereas the two studies with patients suffering from specific phobias clearly indicated therapist-guided exposure to be superior to self-exposure, results from studies on agoraphobia were less clear. Further, several limitations need to be

Table 15.2 Overview of studies comparing self-directed and therapist-assisted in-vivo exposure in anxiety disorders

Author	Sample	N	Study conditions	Dropout rates	Results
Uncontrolled studies					
Holden et al. (1986)	Agoraphobia	6	SE followed by TE	0	TE>SE SE without effects
Edelman and Chambless (1993)	Agoraphobia	48	(a) TE only (b) TE+SE homework instruction	n.r.	a=b
Controlled studies examining SE and TE in combination					
Michelson et al. (1986)	Agoraphobia	39	(a) SE+TE (b) SE+paradoxical intention (c) SE+RT	(a) 32% (b) 9% (c) 17%	a=c b<a/c
Michelson et al. (1996)	Panic disorder with agoraphobia	92	(a) TE+CT (b) TE+RT (c) TE+SE discussion group	(a) 17% (b) 29% (c) 11%	a>b/c b=c
Controlled studies directly comparing SE and TE					
Mavissakalian and Michelson (1983)	Agoraphobia	49	(a) TE (group treatment) (b) Imipramine (c) TE+Imipramine (d) Instructions for SE	n.r.	a=b=c d<a/b/c
Al-Kubaisy et al. (1992)	Phobic patients (specific phobia, social phobia and agoraphobia)	99	(a) TE+SE (b) SE only (c) RT only	(a) 20.6 (b) 23.5% (c) 12.9%	a=b; c<a / b
Hellström and Öst (1995)	Spider phobia	52	(a) TE (1 session) (b) SE—specific instructions home based (c) SE—specific instructions in clinic (d) SE—general instructions home based (e) SE—general instructions in clinic	0	a>c c>b,d,e
Öst et al. (1991)	Spider phobia	34	(a) TE (1 session) (b) SE using written materials	0	a>b

Note: *CBT* cognitive-behavioral therapy, *CT* cognitive therapy, *RT* relaxation training, *SE* self-directed exposure, *TE* therapist-assisted exposure, n.r. not reported

highlighted: Studies varied with regard to exposure modalities and outcome measures considered; instructions for self-directed exposure also varied with regard to detail and specificity, therapist contact time varied, and limited sample size might not have allowed to detect potential differences.

15.4 Does Therapist-Assisted Exposure In Vivo Matter? The MAC Randomized Controlled Clinical Trial

The mechanisms of action (MAC) study for panic disorder and agoraphobia is a large multicenter randomized clinical control study to examine the role of therapist-assisted exposure in vivo for patients with panic disorder and agoraphobia (see Gloster et al., 2009, 2011 for further details). The project's clinical trial was explicitly designed to scrutinize effects of two variations of exposure implementation: Exposure with therapist-assistance during exposure (TE) and instructed self-exposure (SE), including rehearsal and encouragement of self-exposure homework within the therapy room, but no therapist-assistance during the exercises. Based on Foa and Kozak's Emotional Processing Theory, it was assumed that therapist guidance during in-vivo exposure would be advantageous compared to self-directed exposure only, as the therapist would be able to directly monitor and advice the patient during the exercise, and thus, guarantee that crucial mechanisms of action such as experiencing an initial fear activation and a subsequent habituation were realized.

As shown in Fig. 15.1, the clinical trial was designed as a randomized controlled trial with two active treatment conditions: Therapist-assisted exposure (TE) and self-directed exposure (SE) were compared to each other as well as to a wait-list control condition. (For more details about the study's design, inclusion criteria, patient flow, and patient characteristics, see Gloster et al., 2009; Gloster et al., 2011). The intervention was based on a specifically developed treatment manual (Lang, Helbig-Lang, Westphal, Gloster, & Wittchen, 2012) that emphasized exposure to feared stimuli as core mechanism of action. Twelve regular treatment sessions were delivered, each of 100 min duration with two sessions per week. After the last session, two additional booster sessions after 8 and 16 weeks as well as a 6-month follow-up were planned.

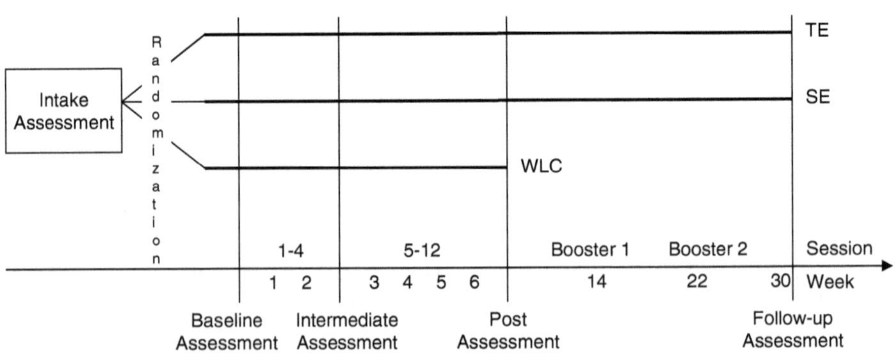

Fig. 15.1 Study design. TE=CBT with therapist-assisted exposure in vivo, SE=CBT without therapist-assisted exposure in vivo (self-directed exposure only via homework assignment), WLC=Wait-list control group

Treatment content, structure, and duration were identical in the SE und TE condition. Treatment included psycho-education about anxiety, panic attacks, and agoraphobia, and behavioral analyses of individual problem behaviors with special attention laid on the role of avoidance and subtle safety behaviors (session 1–3). Sessions 4 and 5 included exposure to interoceptive stimuli in both groups (TE and SE). In session 5, the rationale for in-vivo exposure was explained with a focus on suggested mechanisms of exposure: Patients were instructed to enter feared situations with no safety or avoidance behaviors, to provoke fear (e.g., by using interoceptive exercises) and to stay long enough to experience that the anxiety will subside. Sessions 6–8 and 10 and 11, however, differed between the SE and the TE condition. Sessions 6–8 in TE consisted of therapist-assisted exposure in three standardized agoraphobia relevant exercises: Public transport, shopping mall, and a secluded forest. In contrast, patients in the SE group were instructed to conduct these exercises on their own, without therapist presence. Exercises were then intensively reviewed and discussed. In session 9, progress and problems emerged during the exercises were discussed in both conditions, and changes in anticipatory anxiety were assessed. Sessions 10 and 11 were again reserved for planning or conducting in-vivo exposure with situations from the individual fear hierarchy for the TE group, whereas participants in the SE group were instructed and encouraged to expose themselves as part of homework assignments. In session 12, changes and progress during the therapy were discussed in both conditions.

Thus, it is important to note that in this study the only difference between the two active groups consisted in the implementation of in-vivo exposure: In the TE group, therapists accompanied and guided the patient during the exposure exercises, in the SE group, therapists instructed the patient for exposure but then only extensively discussed and reviewed exposure exercises. In both conditions, the amount of planned exposure exercises was kept equal. Frequency, duration, expected, and actual course of every exposure exercise were assessed using a standardized protocol sheet, providing detailed information about all factors potentially contributing to the effectiveness of exposure.

Outcome evaluation in the study included a wide range of symptom specific and general measures of psychopathology (i.e., HAM-A/SIGH-A; Clinical Global Impression Scale (CGI), Mobility Inventory (MI; Chambless, Caputo, Jasin, Gracely, & Williams, 1985), Panic and Agoraphobia-Scale (PAS, Bandelow, 1997)).

Figure 15.2 shows that both CBT variants were significantly superior to the wait-list control group, yielding large pre-post effect sizes that further increased during the follow-up period in all main outcome measures considered (see Gloster et al., 2011).

It is noteworthy, however, that both the post and the follow-up findings are consistently higher in the TE as compared to the SE group in all measures. Although the differences are clearly not substantial, they are consistent across measures and significant for some measures considered. There were no differences with regard to treatment tolerability; comparable attrition rates in both groups (TE: 20.8%, n = 43; SE: 18.1%, n = 25) were observed and dropout mainly occurred in the second treatment phase (TE: 79.4% vs. SE: 80.0%).

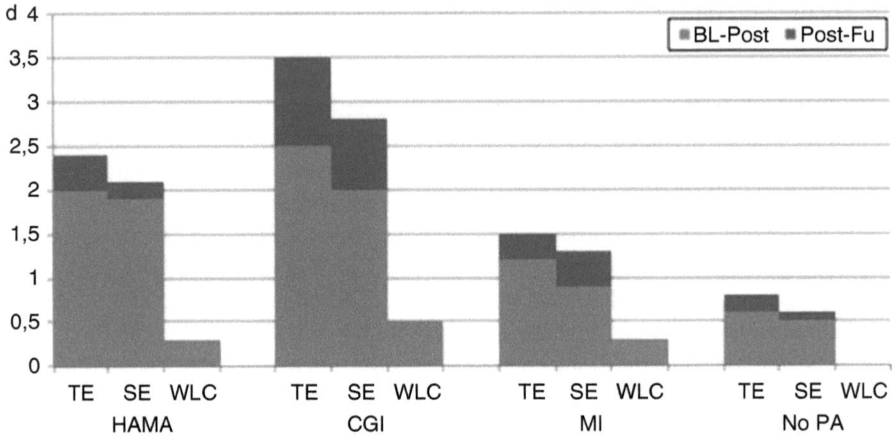

Fig. 15.2 Within-group effect sizes (Cohen d) in the MAC trial for main outcome measures at post-assessment and follow-up. TE=CBT with therapist-assisted exposure, SE=CBT with self-directed exposure, WLC=Wait-list control group; HAMA=Hamilton Anxiety Rating Scale; CGI=Clinical Global Impression Scale; MI=Mobility Inventory, subscale "avoidance unaccompanied"; No PA=Number panic attacks during last week

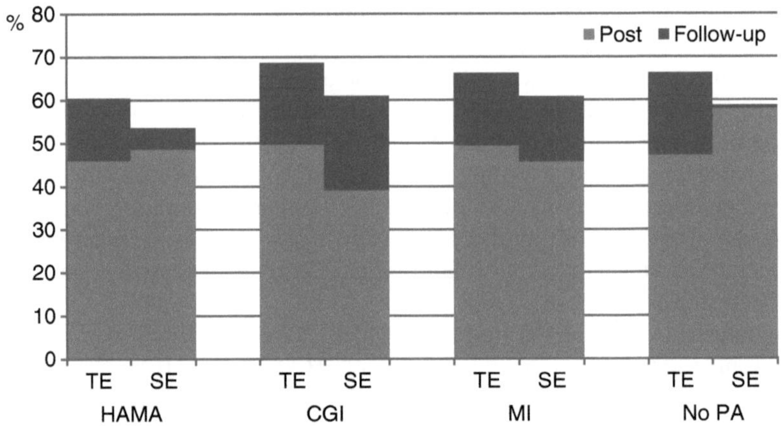

Fig. 15.3 Remission rates (%) at postassessment and 6-month follow-up. Remission is defined as followed: Situational avoidance: MI alone < 1.5; Panic attacks: No panic attacks during last week; Clinical impairment: CGI ≤ 3; Overall anxiety: At least 50% reduction in baseline HAMA scores

Beyond these effect size findings, remission rates were calculated using established cutoff scores for all main outcome measures. Results (Fig. 15.3) showed that patients receiving TE significantly achieved more often remission with regard to agoraphobic avoidance ($p<.05$) and overall clinical severity as measured by the CGI ($p<.01$) (see also Gloster et al., 2011). Within the follow-up period, patients treated with TE also showed significantly more improvement in regard to overall anxiety ($p<.05$) and number of panic attacks experienced ($p<.001$), resulting in superior remission rates for all main outcomes 6 months after treatment.

Taken together, results of this—to our knowledge so far largest and specifically targeted controlled trial—suggest that therapist-assisted exposure might lead to faster and more stable decreases at least with regard to agoraphobic avoidance and clinical severity.

15.5 Conclusion and Clinical Implications

Despite the well-documented efficacy of exposure treatment for panic disorder and agoraphobia, and evident contributions of exposure in vivo to improved outcomes, the empirical data discussed in this chapter do not allow definite answers to the question of whether presence of the therapist matters. Those studies examining this question specifically with appropriate designs and sufficiently powered seem to suggest that it matters indeed. However, up to now, we do not know why, i.e., the mechanisms of action remain unknown and open to speculation.

We are not yet in the position to decide, whether the additional beneficial effects justify the undoubtedly higher logistical demands of therapist assistance during exposure. The effects observed in the MAC study were relatively small and, although significant, do not allow the calculation of substantive cost–benefit ratios.

We are also not able to indicate whether this finding of superior effects in therapy-assisted exposure can be generalized to other anxiety disorders as well as other indications in general. The data available are restricted to patients with panic disorder and agoraphobia.

Taken together, the results show that exposure exercises are crucial elements in the treatment of panic disorder with agoraphobia. All treatment elements were designed to foster exposure, neglecting other interventions such as cognitive restructuring. Hence, exposure is an active treatment ingredient in CBT, powerful enough to produce significant improvements, even when used as the main intervention technique. Therapists' presence during in-vivo exposure yields faster results; however, if carefully prepared, self-directed exposure exercises might gain similar effects in the long run.

References

Al-Kubaisy, T., Marks, I. M., Logsdail, S., Marks, M. P., Lovell, K., Sundry, M., et al. (1992). Role of exposure homework in phobia reduction: a controlled study. *Behavior Therapy, 23*, 599–621.

Bandelow, B. (1997). *Panik und Agoraphobie-Skala (PAS). Handanweisung*. Göttingen: Hogrefe.

Boschen, M. J., Neumann, D. L., & Waters, A. M. (2009). Relapse of successfully treated anxiety and fear: Theoretical issues and recommendations for clinical practice. *Australian and New Zealand Journal of Psychiatry, 43*, 89–100.

Chambless, D. L., Caputo, G. C., Jasin, S. E., Gracely, E. J., & Williams, C. (1985). The mobility inventory for agoraphobia. *Behaviour Research and Therapy, 23*, 35–44.

Edelman, R. E., & Chambless, D. L. (1993). Compliance during sessions and homework in exposure-based treatment of agoraphobia. *Behaviour Research and Therapy, 31*, 767–773.

Foa, E. B., & Kozak, M. J. (1986). Emotional processing of fear: Exposure to corrective information. *Psychological Bulletin, 99*, 20–35.

Foa, E. B., Riggs, D. S., Massie, E. D., & Yarczower, M. (1995). The impact of fear activation and anger on the efficacy of exposure treatment for post-traumatic stress disorder. *Behavior Therapy, 26*, 487–499.

Ghosh, A., & Marks, I. M. (1987). Self-treatment of agoraphobia by exposure. *Behavior Therapy, 18*, 3–16.

Ghosh, A., Marks, I. M., & Cart, A. C. (1988). Therapist contact and outcome of self-exposure treatment for phobias. *British Journal of Psychiatry, 152*, 234–238.

Gloster, A. T., Wittchen, H.-U., Einsle, F., Hofler, M., Lang, T., Helbig-Lang, S., et al. (2009). Mechanism of action in CBT (MAC): Methods of a multi-center randomized controlled trial in 369 patients with panic disorder and agoraphobia. *European Archives of Psychiatry and Clinical Neuroscience, 259*, 155–166.

Gloster, A. T., Wittchen, H.-U., Einsle, F., Lang, T., Helbig-Lang, S., Fydrich, T., et al. (2011). Psychological treatment for panic disorder with agoraphobia: A randomized controlled trial to examine the role of therapist-guided exposure in situ in CBT. *Journal of Consulting and Clinical Psychology, 79*(3), 406–420.

Hellström, K., & Öst, L.-G. (1995). One-session therapist directed exposure vs two forms of manual directed self-exposure in the treatment of spider phobia. *Behaviour Research and Therapy, 33*, 959–965.

Hofmann, S. G., & Smits, A. J. A. (2008). Cognitive-behavioral therapy for adult anxiety disorders: A meta-analysis of randomized placebo-controlled trials. *Journal of Clinical Psychiatry, 69*, 621–632.

Holden, A. E., O'Brien, T., Barlow, D. H., Stetson, D., & Infantino, A. (1983). Self-help manual for agoraphobia: A preliminary report of effectiveness. *Behavior Therapy, 14*, 545–556.

Ito, L. M., De Araujo, L. A., Tess, V. L. C., de Barros-Neto, T. P., Ahsbar, F. R., & Marks, I. (2001). Self-exposure therapy for panic disorder with agoraphobia - Randomised controlled study of external v. interoceptive self-exposure. *British Journal of Psychiatry, 178*, 331–336.

Jannoun, L., Munby, M., Catalan, J., & Gelder, M. (1980). A home-based treatment program for agoraphobia: Replication and controlled evaluation. *Behavior Therapy, 11*, 294–305.

Lang, T., Helbig-Lang, S., Westphal, D., Gloster, A. T., & Wittchen, H.-U. (2012). *Expositionsbasierte, manualisierte Behandlung der Panikstörung und Agoraphobie*. Göttingen: Hogrefe.

Mathews, A. M., Teasdale, J., Munby, M., Johnston, D., & Shaw, P. (1977). A home-based treatment program for agoraphobia. *Behavior Therapy, 8*, 915–924.

Mavissakalian, M., & Michelson, L. (1983). Self-directed in vivo exposure practice in behavioural and pharmacological treatments of agoraphobia. *Behavior Therapy, 14*, 506–519.

McDonald, R., Sartory, 0., Grey, J., Cobb, J. P., Stern, R., & Marks, I. M. (1979). The effect of self-exposure instruction on agoraphobic outpatients. *Behaviour Research and Therapy, 17*, 83–85.

McNamee, G., O'Sullivan, G., Lelliott, P., & Marks, I. M. (1989). Telephone-guided treatment for household agoraphobics with panic disorder: Exposure vs. relaxation. *Behavior Therapy, 20*, 491–497.

Michelson, L. K., Marchione, K. E., Greenwald, M., Testa, S., & Marchione, N. J. (1996). A comparative outcome and follow-up investigation of panic disorder with agoraphobia: The relative and combined efficacy of cognitive therapy, relaxation training, and therapist-assisted exposure. *Journal of Anxiety Disorders, 10*, 297–330.

Michelson, L., Mavissakalian, M., Marchione, K., Dancu, C., & Greenwald, M. (1986). The role fo self-directed in vivo exposure in cognitive, behavioral, and psychophysiological treatments of agoraphobia. *Behavior Therapy, 17*, 91–108.

Mineka, S., Mystkowski, J. L., Hladek, D., & Rodriguez, B. I. (1999). The effects of changing contexts on return of fear following exposure therapy for spider fear. *Journal of Consulting and Clinical Psychology, 67*, 599–604.

Olatunji, B. O., Cisler, J. M., & Deacon, B. J. (2010). Efficacy of cognitive-behavioral therapy for anxiety disorders: A review of meta-analytic findings. *Psychiatric Clinics of North America, 33*, 557–577.

Öst, L.-G., Salkovskis, P. M., & Hellström, K. (1991). One-session therapist-directed exposure vs. self-exposure in the treatment of spider phobia. *Behavior Therapy, 22*, 407–422.

Powers, M. B., Halpern, J. M., Ferenschak, M. P., Gillihan, S. J., & Foa, E. B. (2010). A meta-analytic review of prolonged exposure for posttraumatic stress disorder. *Clinical Psychology Review, 30*, 635–641.

Sánchez-Meca, J., Rosa-Alcázar, A. I., Marín-Martínez, F., & Gómez-Conesa, A. (2010). Psychological treatment of panic disorder with or without agoraphobia: A meta-analysis. *Clinical Psychology Review, 30*, 37–50.

Schneider, A. J., Mataix-Cols, D., Marks, I. M., & Bachofen, M. (2005). Internet-guided self-help with or without exposure therapy for phobic and panic disorders. *Psychotherapy and Psychosomatics, 74*, 154–164.

Van Minnen, A., & Hagenaars, M. (2002). Fear activation and habituation patterns as early process predictors of response to prolonged exposure treatment in PTSD. *Journal of Trauma and Stress, 15*, 359–367.

Woody, S. R., & Ollendick, T. H. (2006). Technique factors in treating anxiety disorders. In L. G. Castonguay & L. E. Beutler (Eds.), *Principles of therapeutic change that work* (pp. 167–186). New York: Oxford University Press.

Chapter 16
Exposure Therapy for Anxiety Disorders: Is There Room for Cognitive Interventions?

Jonas Ramnerö

Jonas Ramnerö is Assistant Professor in Clinical Psychology and Director of Studies for the psychologist programme at the Department of Psychology at Stockholm University. He has extensive experience from clinical work, training and supervision in behavioral treatment of anxiety disorders and is especially interested in the fundamentals of psychology of learning and their application in clinical practice. His clinical research includes a focus on anxiety and depressive disorders, their treatment using exposure techniques, and variables affecting the relationship between patients and therapists.

J. Ramnerö (✉)
Department of Psychology, Stockholm University,
Stockholm, Sweden
e-mail: jramn@psychology.su.se

P. Neudeck and H.-U. Wittchen (eds.), *Exposure Therapy: Rethinking the Model – Refining the Method*, DOI 10.1007/978-1-4614-3342-2_16,

16.1 The Birth of Exposure Treatment

Contemporary psychological treatment protocols for anxiety disorders are usually composed by common elements of which exposure and cognitive interventions play a dominant part. Historically, a cognitive framework has been added to an existing treatment within the behavior therapy tradition. Behavior therapy differed from other therapeutic schools from the time it first saw daylight, in harboring a central conviction to use experimentally verified principles in clinically applied settings (Dougher & Hayes, 1999). As it emerged within the area of anxiety disorders, the classical (respondent) conditioning theories that Watson borrowed from Pavlov in the early days of behaviorism offered an explanation to phobias that became successfully popularized. Methods like "graded retraining" (Meyer & Gelder, 1963) and "systematic desensitization" (Wolpe, 1958) were examples of therapeutic methods that were grounded in these principles, and applied to phobias with some success. But for the common and debilitating condition of agoraphobia, these treatment attempts were both time consuming and rather unsuccessful. A turning point in the treatment of agoraphobia was the landmark study by Agras, Leitenberg, and Barlow (1968), where the therapeutic regime was conceptualized in terms of operant psychology. Three agoraphobic patients were treated by being given the following instruction: "We would like to see how far you can walk by yourself without experiencing undue tension. We find that repeated practice in a structured situation often leads to progress." (p. 424). Praise was provided when the patients strived further in their efforts to walk as far as possible from the safe haven. This turned out to be a very successful regime, especially in comparison to the disappointing results for previous treatment approaches. There were two distinct features of this treatment, above those of using instruction and reinforcement: It was conducted in vivo and no measures were taken trying to minimize anxiety by relaxation in the situations approached, which had been practice in earlier treatments. Gradually a new treatment approach, later known as exposure in vivo, grew from this. Twenty years after the first study, David H. Barlow in his influential book, *Anxiety and its disorders* (1988), labeled the behavioral treatment of agoraphobia as one of the success stories of behavior therapy, or psychotherapy in general. And still in contemporary texts, exposure-based interventions are being described as the core of psychological treatment of anxiety disorders (e.g., Powers, Vervliet, Smits, & Otto, 2010). The two-factor theory of Mowrer (1960) provided a theoretical basis for exposure treatment. One factor is explained in terms of respondent conditioning and the other in terms of operant conditioning. The first factor is constituted when, for example, an aversive event occurs in the presence of a hitherto neutral stimulus, which acquires the property of a conditioned aversive stimulus. It thereby becomes capable of eliciting a fear response. The respondent conditioning of fear also makes it possible for new operant behaviors to be reinforced negatively, when they are instrumental in escaping or reducing this fear. This process constitutes the second factor. Accordingly, the therapeutic agent in behavioral treatments, where the client is systematically exposed to these anxiety-evoking events, has been described in terms of extinction of conditioned fear, which becomes possible when avoidance behavior is eliminated. The theory, in its rather simple form, contained all that seemed necessary to explain the results of this behavioral treatment (Mathews, Gelder, & Johnston, 1981). While the central role of exposure as treatment strategy in behavioral therapies seems undisputable, a definition of the term is more elusive. When searching for a textbook definition it will most often describe a therapeutic regime that involves systematic, repeated contact with the avoided event (e.g., Barlow, 2002). Moreover, it is generally described with certain methodological or technical features, e.g., graded, massed, prolonged, therapist-assisted etc. But when reading these texts it is also revealed that very few firm conclusions can be drawn, whether optimal exposure by necessity should be massed or spaced, graded or intense, performed during high anxiety levels or not, accompanied or self-administered. Hence, a clear definition of the term exposure treatment is not provided.

16.2 Methodological Elaboration

Exposure treatment has often been carried out in a way where different auxiliary interventions have been added with the intent to booster treatment effects. If we stick to the area of panic disorder and agoraphobia, this has been the case with relaxation (Michelson, Marchione, Greenwald, Testa, & Marchione, 1996; Öst, Jerremalm, & Jansson, 1984; Öst, Westling, & Hellström, 1993), assertiveness training (Emmelkamp, van der Hout, & de Vries, 1983; Thorpe, Freedman, & Lazar, 1985), breathing retraining (de Ruiter, Rijken, Garssen, & Kraaimat, 1989; de Beurs, van Balkom, Lange, Koele, & van Dyck, 1995, Schmidt et al., 2000) and even hypnosis (Van Dyck & Spinhoven, 1997). But in the end, with regards to treatment effects, it seems that very little is added by adding further treatment techniques. On the other hand there are some indications that interoceptive exposure does add to the effects of situational exposure (Ito, Noshirvani, Basoglu, & Marks, 1996; Page, 1994). So, a modest proposal in the treatment of agoraphobia would be that little seems to be won by adding complimentary treatment techniques to exposure, but that there is some indication that more exposure (to internal cues) is beneficial. If anything, it seems more promising to add features that involve other parts of the clients' social environment, like forming supportive groups (Hand, Lamontagne, & Marks, 1974; Sinnot, Jones, Scott-Fordham, & Woodward, 1981) and involving spouses (Barlow, O'Brien, & Last, 1984; Arnow, Taylor, Agras, & Telch, 1985).

16.3 Cognitive Therapy for Anxiety Disorders

Given the immense influence of cognitive models and cognitive therapeutic methods have had in the field of psychotherapy, it should come as no surprise that they have had a vast impact on exposure-based treatments. But, here is a difference from what has been said about relaxation, assertiveness training, and other methods. Cognitive therapy came with something more than just auxiliary techniques or methods. It came with an ambition of a better understanding of the core nature of fear and its treatment.

In his early writings on the topic of anxiety, Aaron T. Beck (1976) stated:

> "In essence, a person's fear is a particular *concept*; the content of this concept is oriented to the future and refers to the possibility of personal harm. Anxiety is an unpleasant *emotion*, with familiar subjective and physiological correlates" (p. 139)

Beck pointed to the person's conceptual system, as an area of central importance. While this countered the often antimentalist assertions of behavior therapy, on methodological grounds he clearly acknowledged the kinship between the emerging cognitive therapy and the existing behavior therapy. Even to the point as where he considered behavior therapy a subset of cognitive therapy. But still, the difference between these two approaches was their focal points.

> "The cognitive therapist directs his techniques to modifying the ideational content involved in the symptom, namely the irrational inferences and premises. The behavior therapist concentrates on changing the overt behavior, for example, the maladaptive avoidance response." (Beck, 1976, p. 321)

The cognitive perspective on anxiety disorders was further formulated by Beck, Emery, and Greenberg (1985). They provided more elaborate cognitive formulations of anxiety disorders and their respective treatment. The authors stressed the explanatory power of positing underlying dysfunctional cognitive themes as core processes in the generation of anxiety, and consequently advocating the therapeutic value of correcting these processes.

Three basic methodological approaches were described, when it came to targeting cognitive processes such as fearful thoughts, faulty beliefs, and assumptions.

1. Scrutinizing the evidence, by examining the logic and the evidence.
2. Generating alternative ways of looking at the situation.
3. Questioning the catastrophic nature of the event and the perceived inability to cope if it were to happen.

This will provide the foundation for so-called cognitive interventions for anxiety disorders. But when trying to grasp the nature of cognitive interventions, it is easy to find descriptions (often verbatim) of how they are performed (Beck et al., 1985; Beck, 1995) but a stringent definition of what constitutes a cognitive intervention is elusive. The recent writing by Clark and Beck (2010) echoes the earlier ones when describing the cognitive model of anxiety.

> "…the cognitive model of anxiety is rooted within an information-processing perspective, in which emotional disorders occurs because of an excess or deficient functioning of the cognitive apparatus." (Clark & Beck, 2010, p. 33)

Still, despite this theoretical focus, behavioral interventions are not only acknowledged, they are endorsed on the basis of leading to more fundamental change.

> "Exposure-based treatment strategies are important because they enable a deeper, more generalized or stronger activation of threat schemas and provide opportunities to gather direct disconfirming evidence against high threat value initially assigned by the anxious patient." (Ibid. p. 40)

Clark and Beck also offer a reformulation of the original model with an ambition of encompassing a broad range of cognitive research that goes beyond the traditional concepts of cognitive therapy presented in earlier writings (Beck, 1976; Beck et al., 1985). They clearly regard behavioral change as a critical aspect of cognitive therapy, but behavioral interventions are conceptualized within a cognitive framework. This conceptualization will make a difference on a methodological level when it comes to the rationale for treatment. Methods will be introduced as having a thought or belief as primary target. The therapeutic strategy will differ in that these thoughts should be identified at forehand. Self-monitoring will have the form of thought records and especially the focus at post intervention follow-up will highlight the clients' experience that arises from the intervention, whether it disconfirmed the anxious appraisal and supported alternative interpretations. Questioning will focus on subjective estimates of the probability and severity of harm, as well on estimates of vulnerability and safety. They also state the clients' acceptance of this cognitive model as a prerequisite for treatment.

16.4 Rationale to Adopt Exposure to a Cognitive Framework

The assertion of the cognitive model of anxiety goes beyond methodological elaboration or mere addition of treatment techniques. When it comes to exposure, two different rationales emerge in the literature for the adoption of cognitive verbal interventions to be used in conjunction with exposure or for the adoption of behavioral methods into a cognitive framework.

(a) The patients' difficulties are conceived as expression of underlying cognitive structures and phenomena (e.g., Beck et al., 1985). Enduring behavioral change is regarded as synonymous with or depended upon cognitive change. I will label this *the essential argument.*
(b) The patients' difficulties are conceived as consisting of different features, i.e., negative emotions, anxious thoughts, avoidance behavior, etc (e.g., Michelson & Marchione, 1991). These difficulties are targeted with different techniques in very much the same way as different part of an engine need different tools for repairing. I will label this *the structural argument.*

Reasonably both arguments place the "plain" exposure treatment in a position where it is rendered inconclusive. If these arguments above are supplemented with the assertion that specific methods target specific cognitive dysfunctional patterns, then the reasonable prediction should be increased or more sustained treatment effects when adopting exposure to a cognitive framework. Thus, the established method of exposure has been challenged.

16.5 Empirical Studies of Exposure and Cognitive Interventions for Anxiety Disorders

Despite its clinical appeal, the superiority of the combination of exposure with cognitive interventions, or adoption of exposure to a cognitive framework has not yet been substantiated by empirical evidence. The present chapter concentrates on five diagnostic areas in the anxiety disorders. These will be the diagnostic areas where exposure therapy has a long-standing and firmly established position as a stand-alone treatment of human fears. First, this overview focuses on meta-analyses and reviews predominantly published after the millennia. Meta-analyses are given priority to try to overcome the problem of contradictory findings that often stem from single studies. After these, Individual studies are briefly reviewed when they include a condition of exposure-based treatment that is compared to either exposure with cognitive interventions, exposure that is wrapped up in a cognitive rationale or cognitive therapy contains exposure-like elements (usually in the form of behavioral experiments). The review is, however, limited to group studies that were conducted under clinically representative conditions, present follow-up data, and randomly assigned patients to either treatment condition.

16.5.1 Panic Disorder and Agoraphobia

As mentioned, agoraphobia was the clinical field where exposure first saw daylight. When cognitive therapy made debut in the treatment of agoraphobia, the rationale for including these interventions was often an alleged general beneficial effect (Emmelkamp, Brilman, Kuiper, & Mersch, 1986; Williams & Rappoport, 1983; Emmelkamp & Mersch, 1982). The seminal work of David M. Clark (1988) provided cognitive models that were groundbreaking, not only in regards to treating panic disorder but also in helping to establish cognitive behavior therapy on the clinical arena. Combining exposure in a treatment package with cognitive therapeutic interventions directed at alleviating panic became an apparent treatment-of-choice for behaviorally oriented therapists. The rationale for this seemed obvious in models, where agoraphobic avoidance is considered to be a secondary phenomenon to these attacks. An idea was that cognitive therapy was effective in dealing with panic, and exposure only when it came to avoidance (Van den Hout, Arntz, & Hoekstra, 1994). Exposure was not expected to have panic-alleviating effects. Later studies have refuted this hypothesis and clearly established the effectiveness of exposure when it comes to treating the panic attacks themselves (Arntz, 2002; Bouchard et al., 1995; Öst, Thulin, & Ramnerö, 2004). However, the extra benefit expected of combining the two approached has not been empirically validated.

A meta-analysis of psychological treatment of panic disorder with and without agoraphobia, with the specific focus on different types of interventions (Sanchez-Meca, Rosa-Alcazar, Fulgencio, & Gomez-Conesa, 2010) identified 42 studies, published between 1980 and 2006, yielding a total of 65 comparisons. They concluded that the most efficacious treatment for panic disorder with or without agoraphobia is one that combines exposure (both interoceptive and exteroceptive) with relaxation training, breathing retraining, or anxiety management. Cognitive therapy contributed less than relaxation and breathing-retraining techniques in reducing panic behaviors, and that the application of techniques other than those cited did not seem to contribute further to outcome. Regarding agoraphobia, in vivo exposure seemed to be the most relevant technique, but the difference in efficacy between different techniques seemed less marked than those appearing on panic measures. Additionally, they found support for the hypothesis that home-work and addition of follow-up programs, after treatment has ended, adds beneficial effects to treatment. In a meta-analysis published a few years earlier (Mitte, 2005), 124 studies were included. This meta-analysis used broader inclusion criteria (e.g., range of publication year, use of standardized assessment, and minimum sample size) and identified 47 studies concerning psychological treatments, 24 with combined psychological and pharmacological treatments, and the rest concerned solely pharmacological treatments. In the comparison between behavioral and cognitive-behavioral treatments, both treatments were found to be equally effective in reducing anxiety and improving quality of life. However the cognitive-behavioral treatments, as a group, were found superior to the more purely behavioral ones in reducing associated depressive symptoms and had marginally lower attrition rates.

While most studies on cognitive therapy for panic disorder have been conducted in nonagoraphobic samples (Barlow, 2002), the reverse is the case when investigating the differential effectiveness of adding cognitive interventions to exposure. One exception is a study that compared interoceptive exposure with cognitive therapy for 69 patients with panic disorder without agoraphobia (Arntz, 2002). Both conditions showed essentially equal treatment effects over a range of outcome measures. When moving to samples of panic disorder patients that also fulfill criteria for agoraphobia, a number of relevant studies can be identified. One study compared cognitive therapy with guided mastery therapy (basically a variant of exposure in vivo) when these treatments were integrated with ward activities in an intensive in-patient format (Hoffart, 1995) and found some advantages for the cognitive variant. Williams and Falbo (1996), on the other hand, compared 8 sessions of cognitive therapy, guided mastery therapy, or the combination of both, and found that while all treatments led to significant improvements, on 3 out of 9 measures guided mastery therapy outperformed cognitive therapy. The combination showed no advantages to guided mastery alone. This slight advantage for exposure is echoed in a study of group treatment consisting of either cognitive therapy, or exposure in vivo plus interoceptive exposure (Bouchard et al., 1995). The authors' conclusion mainly stress that the two conditions did equally well on several measures and operated at the same pace. With closer scrutiny is it noted, however, that high end-state functioning, at posttest, was achieved by 86% of the exposure patients, as opposed to 64% of the CT-patients. Further, at follow-up, panic-free status was observed in 71% of the exposure in vivo condition, as compared to 43% of the cognitive therapy condition. In contrast, when Michelson et al. (1996) compared 16 group sessions of exposure alone and in combination with cognitive therapy or relaxation training, for most measures there were no differences between the three conditions, but the cognitive condition outperformed the other conditions in 5 out of 19 measures, at post-treatment. Further, a study of female agoraphobics (Burke, Drummond, & Johnston, 1997) compared individually administered exposure in vivo (10 two-hour sessions) or CBT (10 three-hour sessions), where the amount of in vivo exposure between the two conditions was kept constant. Effects were equal for both groups, except for the behavioral approach test, where the CBT group completed more stages. Overall though, no clear advantage was demonstrated by adding cognitive techniques to exposure. These results are similar to those of Öst et al. (2004) where 73 patients with panic disorder and agoraphobia were treated with a maximum of 16 sessions of individually administered exposure in vivo or CBT. The treatments were found to yield essentially equivalent results. Further, a study that specifically addressed the potentially different impact of a cognitive, versus a desensitization rational for similar exposure treatment yielded equivalent results for both conditions (Söchting et al., 1998).

16.5.2 Social Phobia

Another diagnostic area that received the attention of cognitive therapists early on was social phobia. Dysfunctional thought patterns were explicitly pointed out as critical for maintaining the disorder, thus providing a rationale for incremental effects to be expected from cognitive treatment. But Feske and Chambless (1995) concluded that the results from the early research were rather disappointing in light of the enthusiasm for this approach. This picture that generally prevails in a recent meta-analysis on psychological treatments of social phobia published by Powers, Sigmarsson, and Emmelkamp (2008) identified 34 randomized controlled treatment studies. Of these, 16 studies were relevant for the comparison between exposure and cognitive therapies. They found that, apart from general beneficial effects over a variety of measures that were well maintained at follow-up, the effects of a combination of exposure and cognitive therapy ($d=0.61$) did not differ significantly from that of exposure ($d=0.89$) or cognitive therapy ($d=0.80$) alone. These findings are in unison with a subsequent meta-analysis (Acarturk, Cuipers, van Straten, & de Graaf, 2009). Treatments involving a component of cognitive restructuring (or any other specific techniques for that matter) did not protrude with regard to effect sizes. However, the authors point out that most studies included a variety of different methods in each treatment condition, thereby rendering any firm conclusion of different methods impossible to draw. Both of these meta-analyses essentially echoes the conclusions from the meta-analysis made more than 10 years earlier by Feske and Chambless (1995). They identified eight studies that directly compared exposure treatment to some cognitively oriented variant. Six of these yield equivocal results and two favored the latter. Their general conclusion from the complete meta-analysis, however, was that neither was the cognitive treatment superior on measures on social anxiety, cognitive measures, nor was it superior on measures of depression. Since the Feske and Chambless study a number of further studies with special relevance to the topic at hand have been published, often failing to find differential results (Mersch, 1995; Salaberría & Echeburua, 1998). Two studies comparing Cognitive-Behavioral Group Therapy (GCBT) to exposure have yielded equivocal results. Hope, Heimberg, and Bruch (1995) tested CGBT against group exposure only with 40 patients. While both treatment modalities generally performed better than waitlist control, the subjects in exposure showed broader change, were twice as likely to be classified as responders at posttreatment and attrition was higher in CGBT, but not significantly so. At 6-month follow up, the treatments were equivalent. Another study (Hofmann, 2004) found that exposure group therapy (EGT) and CBGT showed similar results at posttest but only CGBT showed continuing improvement at 6 month follow up. A notable exception from the general equivocality of the field was provided by Clark et al. (2006) were they demonstrated that a comprehensive cognitive therapy program delivered individually clearly outperformed a treatment condition that combined exposure with applied relaxation, and this despite the latter showing rather typical effect sizes for exposure treatments for social phobia. The superiority was shown both at posttreatment and 1 year follow-up.

16.5.3 Specific Phobia

There are few treatment studies on specific phobias relevant for the topic at hand. This diagnostic area is even left out in the Clark and Beck book from 2010, with explicit reference to the scarcity of cognitive models. It is, however, classical territory for exposure therapy and therefore deserves attention in this chapter. Wolitzky-Taylor, Horowitz, Powers, and Telch (2008) published a meta-analysis of 33 randomized psychological treatment studies of specific phobias. Their results gave a clear indication that exposure was the most potent treatment for specific phobias, both regarding immediate and long-term results. This is very much in accordance with the conclusion of a previous qualitative review (Choy, Fyer, & Lipsitz, 2007). However, when comparing the efficacy of exposure plus cognitive interventions versus exposure alone there were only five comparisons, stemming from three studies. These comparisons showed no significant advantage of the combined treatment, neither at posttreatment nor at follow-up. Now, the relevance of two of these studies could be questioned for the present purpose, since the clients were students that received course credit for their participation (Kamphuis & Telch, 2000; Sloan & Telch, 2002). However, as noted by Choy et al, cognitive therapy has been reported efficacious as a solo treatment for claustrophobia in two studies (Booth & Rachman, 1992; Öst, Alm, Brandberg, & Breitholtz, 2001).

16.5.4 Obsessive–Compulsive Disorder

Obsessive compulsive disorder (OCD) represents an area where exposure (with response prevention; ERP) was already established as the treatment of choice, when cognitive therapy made entrance. The alleged success for other anxiety disorders and the fact that even a well-established treatment showed limited success with a substantial portion of the patients offered a rationale for elaborating cognitive models in this area. But, when screening the evidence base, it is difficult to argue that these models have made a substantial contribution to the overall advancement of OCD treatment. Nineteen studies of psychological treatments of OCD, published between 1980 and 2006, were identified in one meta-analysis (Rosa-Alcázar, Sánchez-Meca, Gómez-Conesa, & Marin-Martinez, 2008). These treatments achieved clinically significant improvement on measures of obsessive–compulsive symptoms, as well as general anxiety, depression, social adjustment, and other related measures and the best effect sizes were found for therapist-assisted guided exposure and approaches that combine exposure in vivo with imaginal exposure. The weighted mean effect size indexes calculated over several indices of obsessive–compulsive symptoms were $d_+ = 1.13$ for exposure with response prevention (ERP); $d_+ = 1.09$ for cognitive restructuring (based on only 3 studies) and $d_+ = 1.00$ for the combination of ERP and cognitive restructuring. In a qualitative review, Abramowitz, Taylor, and McKay (2005) conclude that both ERP and cognitive variants of the treatment outperform various credible control therapies, and thus tend to be equally effective. A number of studies contain direct comparison between ERP and cognitively formulated variants of the treatment. In a small study, Emmelkamp and Beens (1991) found no significant difference between ERP alone or in combination with rational emotive therapy. A larger study compared cognitive therapy including behavioral experiments to ERP and found a slight advantage on behalf of the former (van Oppen et al., 1995). Later de Haan et al. (1997) reported the results from 99 patients where the two treatment variants, alone or in combination with fluvoxamine, were found equivalent. It should be noted, though, that in these three studies ERP was conducted solely as homework assignments which could be considered substandard (Rosa-Alcázar et al., 2008). Four studies that compared exposure ERP and a cognitive format, which both involve in-session exposure, have been identified. In a study of 64 patients assigned to 16 weeks of treatment in either of the two formats, Cottraux et al. (2001) found the them equally efficacious on all outcome parameters, apart from depression where an advantage was observed for the CBT approach. On the other hand, an advantage for the results of ERP over those of CBT was found by McLean et al. (2001) when conducting small-group treatment. This tendency, favoring an exposure treatment condition devoid of specific cognitive interventions has also been replicated within the context of individual therapy (Vogel, Stiles, & Götestam, 2004). Two studies favoring conducting OCD treatment within a cognitive framework have been identified. One was published by Whittal, Thordarson, and McLean (2005). Briefly, 83 patients were offered 12 weeks of treatment in either format but no significant differences were found between these treatments. The proportion of patients classified as recovered were larger in the CBT condition (67%) than in the ERP (59%). This difference was also evident at 3-month follow-up, but failed to reach statistical significance at both occasions. The other study (Belloch, Cabedo, & Carrió, 2008) showed slightly superior improvement and recovery rates for the cognitive approach over the traditional ERP, both at posttreatment and at the 1-year follow-up. Perhaps somewhat surprisingly, both treatments were equally effective in modifying dysfunctional beliefs. To conclude this overview of OCD studies, note that Abramowitz et al. (2005) reported higher attrition rates in ERP in two out of four studies.

16.5.5 Post Traumatic Stress Disorder

The last area that is included in this overview of clinical area is post traumatic stress disorder (PTSD), where exposure treatment has been labeled the gold standard of psychological treatments (Foa & Rothbaum, 1998). Exposure procedures heavily focus on phenomena rather placed in an area of private events (e.g., memories and intrusive images). This places the target of exposure in a cognitive domain and could serve as a special invitation to adding cognitive interventions to exposure. But, consistent with the pattern in the diagnostic areas reviewed earlier, this has not shown to add to the treatment effects in any consistent way. In a meta-analysis psychological treatment of PTSD (Bradley, Greene, Russ, Dutra, & Westen, 2005), 26 randomized controlled trials were identified. Exposure-based treatments were included in 13 studies, five studies used cognitive and behavioral strategies other than exposure, and nine studies the combination of exposure and cognitive interventions. Above these treatment conditions, EMDR was the most prevalent treatment condition. They conclude that short-term psychological treatments are generally successful in the task of alleviating post-traumatic stress. Regarding the treatments of interest here, they reported pre- to posteffect sizes of $d=1.57$ for exposure treatments, $d=1.65$ for the cognitive behavioral group and $d=1.66$ for the group where treatment consisted of exposure with the addition of cognitive interventions. The rates of those no longer meeting criteria for PTSD at post-treatment were 52.6%; 46.0% and 53.7%, respectively. The authors did not find support for any significant differential efficacy. Though, perhaps outside the topic of main concern here, a later meta-analysis by Bisson and co-workers (2007) deserves to be mentioned since they did find differential efficacy favoring trauma-focused cognitive behavioral treatments and EMDR over stress management and other psychological treatments, not specifically trauma-focused. It should be noted that both cognitively based and exposure treatments were included in the broader category of trauma focused CBT, so for the present purpose this study is somewhat uninformative. However, it does give an argument that all treatments are not of equivalent effects in the treatment of post-traumatic distress. A later meta-analytic study by Powers, Halpern, Ferenschack, Gillihan, and Foa (2010) focused specifically on prolonged exposure for PTSD and found that this treatment yielded equivalent results to cognitive therapy and cognitive processing therapy (see below).

When moving on to individual studies, the comparison between exposure therapy to a package incorporating exposure, controlled breathing, and cognitive therapy was studied by Paunovic and Öst (2001). Both treatments resulted in significant and durable changes, no significant differences between the treatments were found. Exposure treatment and cognitive therapy has been found to achieve equal clinical benefits (Marks, Lovell, Noshirvani, Livanou, & Thrasher, 1998; Tarrier et al., 1999) and to improve different symptoms in the array of PTSD-symptoms similarly (Lovell, Marks, Noshirvani, Thrasher, & Livanou, 2001). However, in a 5-year follow-up of the Tarrier et al. study, the cognitive therapy condition seemed to produce better long-term results (Tarrier & Sommerfield, 2004). When Bryant, Moulds, Guthrie, Dang, and Nixon (2003) studied imaginal exposure and cognitive restructuring in combination versus imaginal exposure only, the results were interpreted as supporting the idea that the effects of exposure may be enhanced by cognitive restructuring, especially regarding maladaptive cognitions. But, as pointed out by Hassija and Gray (2010), this is a study where the exposure condition deviates from standard prolonged exposure procedures (i.e., Foa & Rothbaum, 1998) and where potentially vital components are left out, thereby making the conclusion somewhat arbitrary. A later study by Foa and co-workers (2005) compared prolonged exposure to prolonged exposure plus cognitive restructuring in a sample of 171 patients with chronic PTSD. In this study, the two treatments were found equivalent. In addition, the two treatments were not found to have different effects on specific cognitive measures (Foa & Rauch, 2004). Cognitive Processing Therapy (CPT; Resick & Schnicke, 1996) is a comprehensive cognitively oriented approach that was compared to prolonged exposure in a study of 121 PTSD-patients (Resick, Nishith, Weaver, Astin, & Feuer, 2002). Both treatments were found to be highly efficacious and producing similar gains over the main outcome measures, but on measures of trauma-related guilt the results favored CPT.

16.5.6 Summary of Overview

We can easily state that the results of individual studies yield equivocal results. That is, none of the meta-analyses gives support for the benefit of adding cognitive interventions to exposure. Here and there, individual findings pop up. One meta-analysis indicated an additional beneficial effect on depression, but not on the primary outcome variables in the treatment of panic disorder. Attrition rates seemed to benefit from presenting treatment within a cognitive package in some studies. One might argue that these are arguments clearly in favor of the cognitive models. But if we consider these models, they are formulated to take a shot at the essence, or at least at vital elements of fear and anxiety. It would be less clear from the theoretical models why the mentioned variables, and not the primary outcome variables, should be affected. The overarching conclusion must be that exposure treatment over a broad range of outcome measures stands well in comparison to other treatment variants, both regarding short-term and long term results. Even the possibility that exposure elements supply the essential ingredient for change in cognitive treatments must be considered (Resolution of this question is, however, beyond the scope of this chapter.) Questioning the utility of cognitive interventions is not a new argument (e.g., Longmore & Worrel, 2007), and it has recently stirred some debate (e.g., Hassija & Gray, 2010). Yet, a convincing overall empirical argument for adding special verbal interventions that are conceptualized as "cognitive" to exposure treatment has not been presented. But, what should the conclusion be from this overview? It would easily seem like trying to settle the score between behaviorism and cognitivism, to the disappointment of the latter. But maybe we should all be discouraged by the fact that different ways of talking in therapy have yet not been found to have a substantial, differential effect on the process of ameliorating fear and anxiety? Discouraged, because we spend so much time and effort to elaborate variants of rhetorical style, when we develop treatment models and when we train therapists.

16.6 Renewed Interest in Learning Theory

Exposure treatment originally stems from a learning account of human fear and since the millennia we have seen a resurgence of the interest in learning theoretical accounts within the field of anxiety research. This will imply a renewed interest both in applying experimentally verified basic principles of learning to clinical problem (Craske, Hermans, & Vanderstegen, 2006), and in theoretical models that de-emphasizes the role of conscious cognitive processes in the etiology of fear-learning (Bouton, Mineka, & Barlow, 2001; Öhman & Wiens, 2004). A central tenet in modern learning theory is that extinction learning does not constitute the erasing of earlier learning, but instead a process of new learning competing with the earlier (Bouton, 2006). This resurgence paves its way into the cognitive literature (Clark & Beck, 2010), where learning theory accounts are acknowledged as important contributions, still stressing the overarching role of a cognitive model. Conversely, in the treatment literature, Powers, Vervliet et al. (2010) provides a recent example that combines theoretical concepts drawn from basic learning theory, with a therapeutic style relying heavily on methods identified within the cognitive domain. The dawning interest in learning theory means that theories used to inspire therapeutic thinking are based upon basic lab-verified principles mainly derived from animal learning. This is, of course very much in line with the basic epistemic tradition of behavior therapy. But, as Dennet reminds us, there is a difference when it comes to studying human subjects, as "(people) are the only subjects of scientific study the preparation of which typically (but not always) involves verbal communication." (Dennet, 1991, p.73). Forsyth and Eifert (1996) point out that the availability and pervasiveness of the ability for language represents a significant difference between animal and human learning. Language provides humans with emotional experiences without exposure to the actual physical stimuli or events that ordinarily elicit those responses. Historically "behavioral therapies" have often been contrasted to "verbal therapies" (e.g. Smith, Glass, & Miller, 1980) and in a curious way sometimes leaves the earlier with an impression to be therapies devoid of talking. If we go back to the study of Agras et al. (1968) what they did study was verbal instructions that oriented patients toward events yet to be experienced. And to be slightly finicky: Verbal praise was provided as reinforcement contingent upon the behavior of reporting advance, rather than upon the actual steps taken in vivo. These are, to use a rather dry experimental language, manipulations in a verbal context. They are also manipulations that would not be used in animal research. Needless to say, behavior therapies are of course "talking cures" very much to the same extent as other therapies in that they rely on verbal communication. So a complete learning theory account of exposure treatment would need to take in the fact that stimulus functions and behavior changes due to verbal influence. Or in the words of Catania (2002): "Words are ways to get people to do things" (p 262). The cognitive literature can be read as a rich source of verbal strategies potentially useful in therapy.

From a behavioral point of view, it could be argued that a cognitive framework would have promise, disregarded the theoretical value of cognitive models of anxiety disorders. We could reasonably argue that since folk psychology tends to be mentalistic and in a cultural context that generally embraces the notion of inner events as causes of behavior, a therapeutic language that profits from these ways of describing should be attractive and credible. This way, the practice of framing exposure treatments in cognitive terms provides a verbal context of discovery and change that, so to speak, works along with the clients' fundamental worldview. Thus, we could label this *the functional argument*, in addition to the earlier given *essential* and *structural arguments*. But it is crucial that this one is not an argument for a cognitive model per se. It is an argument for providing a credible verbal context for the process of change. From clinical experience, many cognitive models do provide a functional language in that sense. But we must not assume that this language mirrors reality in an essential way (Rorty, 1979). If we pursue this argument, we should also call for attention to aspects of the patients' worldview that may hinder a process of change in an agreed direction, i.e., framing strong emotions as dangerous, framing oneself as unable, framing "anxiety disorder" as a disease in front of which you are totally left out to the mercy of others. Forsyth and Eifert (1996) command special interest to the functional properties of such verbal behavior as rules, reasons, and justifications. Scrutinizing the patient's beliefs, from a functional point of view, seems like a viable topic in exposure treatment therapy. Another creative example from the cognitive tradition is when exposure exercises are packaged as "behavioral experiments" (e.g., Clark et al., 2006). In the behavioral tradition, exposure has been presented as "exercises," in many ways reminiscent of the regime of aversive control from your school days. And these exercises are to be repeated often with an overarching aim of experiencing less and less arousal over time. An "experiment", on the other hand, sets the stage for discovery and finding out new things about the feared situation and staying attuned to different aspects of one's ongoing behavior. It sets the stage for functional classes of operant behavior that we would be interested in fostering during exposure.

16.7 Room for Cognitive Interventions

So, is there room for cognitive interventions? I would most definitely say: Yes, there is! But the crucial question is: What kind of room? Given that an empirically supported way of talking does not come along with empirically supported treatments by necessity, and that therapy is largely a verbal enterprise we should draw upon the clinical ingenuity often demonstrated in these verbal strategies. The question must be a matter of priority given in treatment and also in clinical training. If cognitive interventions put special demands on therapists that make long and laborious training necessary to meet highly set standards for these skills, we should put this effort in perspective to cost and the empirical status of these interventions. Various forms of exposure treatment, devoid of auxiliary treatment techniques, have shown broad and reliable effects over a range of areas concerning human fears. It would thus be reasonable to give first priority to address the issue of exposure work both in therapy and training of therapists. This would include providing a plan on how it is to be conducted, what stimuli should be approached, how this can be done as much as possible in vivo, and preferably (at least in some part) assisted by the therapist. The instructions for exposure should be clear, since instructions are not only a prerequisite for treatment. From a learning point of view, instructions should be regarded as a part of the process of change by altering the functions of stimuli (Catania, 2002). For example, this could mean reframing behaviors hitherto immediately aversive and "impossible" as "possible" and opening up for a better life in the long run.

Next, I would suggest so-called "common factors." The support for these ingredients is often correlational (Norcross, 2002). This is naturally problematic, but still outshines the support for a specific rhetorical style and I see no obvious reason to disregard these factors in exposure treatment. These generic skills would include the ability to establish a working alliance with the clients (Horvath & Bedi, 2002), to provide empathy, and to be sensitive to the clients' experience of the therapeutic interaction (Bohart, Elliot, Greenberg, & Watson, 2002). Of special interest for anxiety disorders would be the task of working collaboratively on establishing goal consensus (Tryon & Winograd, 2002). Fear conditioning gets problematic when individuals engage in rigid attempts to control, suppress, escape, or avoid events that have acquired aversive functions through that learning (Forsyth, Eifert, & Barrios, 2006). In this way fear conditioning comes to block access to reinforcers and to interfere with meaningful life. Working to clearly establishing the goals of therapy would imply using language to establish stimulus functions that provide meaning and direction to the often burdensome process of exposure. We are already discussing the verbal framing of the treatment process and drawing a straight demarcation line that separates this from cognitive interventions may neither be possible nor viable. In the following, a learning theory account of exposure treatment will be presumed, but since cognitive interventions contribute with a host of useful verbal strategies they will be discussed as aids in the process of behavior change. The intention here is more to exemplify than attempt to be exhaustive.

From a learning theoretical account two concepts are central for understanding the process of exposure treatment, namely extinction and discrimination learning which are intrinsically linked to each other. When initiating the exposure work, it is advisable to identify solid verbal formulations of what the client fears or what may happen in the anxiety-provoking situation. Apart from the effects of direct respondent and operant learning, persons with anxiety disorders will most likely present verbal and rule-governed behavior capable of eliciting negative affective responses which also motivate escape and avoidance behavior (Forsyth & Eifert, 1996). Formulating these fears should serve the purpose of facilitating discrimination of the patient's own responses taking part in maintaining fear. A clear a priori formulation of what is feared has also been suggested as a means of facilitating the process of extinction by actively drawing the patients' attention to the discrepancies of the predictive value of different conditioned stimuli and the actual experience from exposure (Powers, Vervliet et al., 2010). In cognitive therapy for anxiety disorders, patients are often trained to identify and monitor what has been labeled as "catastrophic thinking."To use a convenient verbal label in therapy may enhance discrimination, distancing, and the process of becoming less entangled with these processes. Verbally governed behavior tends to be insensitive to its consequences and this insensitivity to contingencies generalizes over a wide variety of settings (Catania, 2002). A general purpose of therapy would be training to discriminate our own behavior in the ongoing context—a learning process critical to self-regulation.

During the actual exposure, therapists should work with the client to flexibly attend both what is happening in the outer environment as well as in the inner environment of thoughts and emotions. Again the overarching purpose would be to facilitate discrimination. Questions like "What are you thinking right now?," "Where does your fear take you?" seem ever so relevant from a behavioral perspective. Other kinds of internal events are evaluative statements of anxiety as being "unbearable," "awful," etc. Humans have the capacity to suffer by responding to conditioned responses with evaluative verbal behavior and thinking (Forsyth et al., 2006). The goal for exposure treatment could be stated as a process of creating a more ambiguous meaning of the conditioned stimuli (Bouton 2006) and thus making them accessible to a range of discriminative functions, other than fear and avoidance. The contextual insensitivity of verbal processes may contribute to reduce flexibility and the perception of multiple meanings of an event, when we stick to an overly fearsome and negative evaluation of our experience. Forsyth et al. (2006) stress that enhanced discrimination and less rule-governed behavior, particularly applied to regulating emotional experiences, may serve as a basis for healthy behavior. Emotional regulation will serve functional purposes when it achieves desired outcomes and is flexibly applied in concordance to contextual demands. The overarching aim for working with verbal interventions in order to help the client generate different interpretations and appraisals, provide different foci of attention, evaluating events etc., would probably best be formulated as fostering psychological flexibility given the pervasive role this is ascribed regarding general health and well-being (Kashdan & Rottenberg, 2010). Rigid and indiscriminate behavior in down-regulating emotions (whether applied to processes like attention or moving about in the physical environment) seems to distinguish problematic from functional emotion regulation in many respects. As specific thought content serves as an aversive stimulus or as a part of the fear context, this could be brought into the exposure exercises by suggesting the client to hold on to the thought during exposure (Powers, Vervliet et al., 2010). A general finding is that extinction learning benefits from compound excitors (Bouton, 2006), so rather than trying to reduce the fear-evoking element they would be increased for the sake of the learning experience. But exposure could also benefit from encouraging to flexibly attend to different aspects of the environment, even those that are not associated with fear. This would imply acting in a way that in inconsistent with fear and serve as a counterconditioning approach. This approach of active ambiguation of the feared event could be argued for both from basic lab research (Bouton, 2006), as well as from clinical (Wolitsky & Telch, 2009) and would serve as an active approach of ambiguating the feared event.

Extinction learning in exposure treatment has been described as a process where the new learning of safety competes with the old fear (Powers, Vervliet et al., 2010). To aid this process it would be advisable after the actual exposure, to go through the experience with the client and work to establish the contrast between the event as fearfully anticipated and the actual experience. This should serve a purpose of consolidation and discrimination in one's own behavior, i.e., to strengthen the clients' ability to lean on their actual experience, rather than their capacity for fearful framing of events. The problem of renewal effects or "return of fear" is familiar for every clinician. The process of extinction is largely context dependent (Bouton, 2006), whereas acquisition of fear shows stronger generalization over different contexts. Hence, the challenge for therapeutic work lies in generalization of extinction learning over multiple contexts, especially those outside direct experience in therapy. Since the patient learns that exposure in the presence of the therapist is safe, the therapist may serve as a conditioned inhibitor, thus hindering the further process of extinction. (Vansteenwegen, Dirikx, Hermans, Vervliet, & Eelen, 2006). Powers, Vervliet et al. (2010) advocate exposure over a broad range of stimuli and contexts, plus use of retrieval cues for recall and generalization in order to consolidate learning further. This could imply that clients are encouraged to repeatedly remind themselves of where they were and what they did during exposure therapy as they encounter their phobic stimuli in different daily contexts (Hermans, Vansteenwegen, & Craske, 2006). Verbal descriptions of one's own behavior can have powerful effects on behavior, competing with and sometimes overruling actual reinforcement contingencies (Catania, Matthews, & Shimoff, 1990). Verbal therapy must, at least partly, be considered as a process of shaping a verbal repertoire. The clients should be encouraged to formulate descriptions of their own approach behavior in the face of anxiety-provoking events. Rules should be generated that prepare the patient to approach phobic situations in the future and describe functional approach behaviors (Powers, Vervliet et al., 2010).

This has only been a short attempt to describe verbal strategies to wrap up exposure in a way that, at least theoretically, could serve the interest of enhanced extinction and discrimination learning. It is an attempt to foster a functional language of "the talking cure" inherent in behavior therapy. The current empirical status of different styles of talking in therapy allows no firm recommendation, neither of so-called cognitive interventions nor other specialized verbal techniques to be used within the realms of exposure treatment. Finding room for these interventions is rather a pragmatic search for good ideas for communicating with clients. But there is one critical question: When used within a learning theory framework, can these interventions properly be labeled "cognitive interventions"? From a learning theory account, they would more properly be described as verbal interventions in the service of behavioral change.

Acknowledgments I would like to thank Ph.D. student Rio Cederlund, M.D. Niklas Torneke, and Professor Lars-Goran Ost, for their thoughtful comments on the early draft of the manuscript.

References

Abramowitz, J. S., Taylor, S., & McKay, D. (2005). Potentials and limitations of cognitive treatment of obsessive-compulsive disorder. *Cognitive Behaviour Therapy, 34*, 140–147.

Acarturk, C., Cuipers, P., van Straten, A., & de Graaf, R. (2009). Psychological treatment of social anxiety disorder: A meta-analysis. *Psychological Medicine, 39*, 241–254.

Agras, W. S., Leitenberg, H., & Barlow, D. H. (1968). Social reinforcement in the modification of agoraphobia. *Archives of General Psychiatry, 19*, 423–427.

Arnow, B. A., Taylor, C. B., Agras, W. S., & Telch, M. J. (1985). Enhancing agoraphobia treatment outcome by changing couple communication patterns. *Behavior Therapy, 16*, 452–467.

Arntz, A. (2002). Cognitive therapy versus interoceptive exposure as treatment of panic disorder without agoraphobia. *Behaviour Research and Therapy, 40*, 325–341.

Barlow, D. H. (1988). *Anxiety and its disorders – The nature and treatment of anxiety and panic*. New York: Guilford Press.

Barlow, D. H. (2002). *Anxiety and its disorders – The nature and treatment of anxiety and panic* (2nd ed.). New York: Guilford Press.

Barlow, D. H., O'Brien, G. T., & Last, C. G. (1984). Couples treatment of agoraphobia. *Behavior Therapy, 15*, 41–58.

Beck, A. T. (1976). *Cognitive therapy and the emotional disorders*. New York: Meridian.

Beck, J. (1995). *Cognitive therapy: Basics and beyond*. New York: Guilford.

Beck, A. T., Emery, G., & Greenberg, R. L. (1985). *Anxiety disorders and phobias: A cognitive perspective*. New York: Basic Books.

Belloch, A., Cabedo, E., & Carrió, C. (2008). Empirically grounded clinical interventions: Cognitive versus behaviour therapy in the individual treatment of obsessive-compulsive disorder: Changes in cognitions and clinically significant outcomes at post-treatment and one-year follow-up. *Behavioural and Cognitive Psychotherapy, 36*, 521–540.

Bisson, J. I., Ehlers, A., Mathews, R., Pilling, S., Richards, D., & Turner, S. (2007). Psychological treatments for chronic post-traumatic stress disorder – Systematic review and meta-analysis. *British Journal of Psychiatry, 198*, 97–104.

Bohart, A. C., Elliot, R., Greenberg, L. S., & Watson, J. C. (2002). Empathy. In J. C. Norcross (Ed.), *Psychotherapy relationships that work* (pp. 89–108). Oxford: University Press.

Booth, R., & Rachman, S. (1992). The reduction of claustrophobia: I. *Behaviour Research and Therapy, 30*, 207–221.

Bouchard, S., Gauthier, J. L., Laberge, B., French, D., Pelletier, M.-H., & Godbout, C. (1995). Exposure vs. cognitive restructuring in the treatment of panic disorder with agoraphobia. *Behaviour Research and Therapy, 34*, 213–224.

Bouton, M. E. (2006). *Learning and behavior – A contemporary synthesis*. Sunderland: Sinauer.

Bouton, M. E., Mineka, S., & Barlow, D. H. (2001). A modern learning theory perspective on the etiology of panic disorder. *Psychological Review, 108*, 4–32.

Bradley, R., Greene, J., Russ, E., Dutra, L., & Westen, D. (2005). A multidimensional meta-analysis of psychotherapy for PTSD, *American Journal of Psychiatry, 162*, 214–227. Retrieved from http://ajp.psychiatryonline.org/cgi/reprint/162/2/214.

Bryant, R. A., Moulds, M. L., Guthrie, R. M., Dang, S. T., & Nixon, R. D. (2003). Imaginal exposure alone and imaginal exposure with cognitive restructuring in treatment of posttraumatic stress disorder. *Journal of Consulting and Clinical Psychology, 71*, 706–712.

Burke, M., Drummond, L. M., & Johnston, D. W. (1997). Treatment choice for agoraphobic women: Exposure or cognitive-behaviour therapy? *British Journal of Clinical Psychology, 36*, 409–420.
Catania, A. C. (2002). *Learning* (4th ed.). New Jersey: Prentice.
Catania, A. C., Matthews, B. A., & Shimoff, E. (1990). Properties of rule-governed behavior and their implications. In D. E. Blackman & H. Lejuene (Eds.), *Behavior analysis in theory and practice* (pp. 215–230). Hillsdale, NJ: Erblaum.
Choy, Y., Fyer, A. J., & Lipsitz, J. D. (2007). Treatment of specific phobia in adults. *Clinical Psychology Review, 27*, 266–286.
Clark, D. M. (1988). A cognitive model of panic attacks. In S. Rachman & J. D. Maser (Eds.), *Panic: Psychological perspectives* (pp. 71–89). Hillsdale, NJ: Erblaum.
Clark, D. A., & Beck, A. T. (2010). *Cognitive Therapy of Anxiety Disorders – Science and Practice*. New York: Guilford.
Clark, D. M., Ehlers, A., Hackmann, A., McManus, F., Fennell, M., Grey, N., et al. (2006). Cognitive therapy versus exposure and applied relaxation in social phobia: A randomized controlled trial. *Journal of Consulting and Clinical Psychology, 74*, 568–578.
Cottraux, J., Note, I., Nan Yao, S., Lafont, S., Note, B., Mollard, E., et al. (2001). A randomized controlled trial of cognitive therapy versus intensive behavior therapy in obsessive–compulsive disorder. *Psychotherapy and Psychosomatics, 70*, 288–297.
Craske, M. G., Hermans, D., & Vanderstegen, D. (2006). *Fear and learning – From basic processes to clinical Implications*. Washington DC: APA Books.
de Beurs, E., van Balkom, A.J.L.M., Lange, A., Koele, P., & van Dyck, R. (1995). Treatment of panic disorder of fluvoxamine, placebo, and psychological panic management combined with exposure and of exposure in vivo alone. *American Journal of Psychiatry, 152*, 683–691. Retrieved from http://ajp.psychiatryonline.org/cgi/content/abstract/152/5/683.
de Haan, E., van Oppen, P., van Balkom, A. J. L. M., Spinhoven, P., Hoogduin, K. A. L., & Van Dyck, R. (1997). Prediction of outcome and early vs. late improvement in OCD patients treated with cognitive behaviour therapy and pharmacotherapy. *Acta Psychiatrica Scandinavica, 96*, 354–361.
Dennet, D. (1991). *Consciousness explained*. London: Penguin.
Dougher, M. J., & Hayes, S. C. (1999). Clinical behavior analysis. In M. J. Dougher (Ed.), *Clinical behavior analysis*. Reno: Context Press.
Emmelkamp, P. M. G., & Beens, H. (1991). Cognitive therapy with obsessive–compulsive disorder: A comparative evaluation. *Behaviour Research and Therapy, 29*, 293–300.
Emmelkamp, P. M. G., Brilman, E., Kuiper, H., & Mersch, P. P. (1986). The treatment of agoraphobia: A comparison of self-instructional training, rational emotive therapy and exposure in-vivo. *Behavior Modification, 10*, 37–53.
Emmelkamp, P. M. G., & Mersch, P. P. (1982). Cognition and exposure in vivo in the treatment of agoraphobia: Short-term and delayed effects. *Cognitive Therapy and Research, 6*, 77–88.
Emmelkamp, P. M. G., van der Hout, A., & de Vries, K. (1983). Assertive training for agoraphobics. *Behaviour Research and Therapy, 21*, 63–68.
Feske, U., & Chambless, D. L. (1995). Cognitive behavioral versus exposure only treatment for socialphobia: A meta–analysis. *Behavior Therapy, 26*, 695–720.
Foa, E. B., Hembree, E. A., Cahill, S. P., Rauch, S. A. M., Riggs, D. S., Feeny, N. C., et al. (2005). Randomized trial of prolonged exposure for posttraumatic stress disorder with and without cognitive restructuring: Outcome at academic and community clinics. *Journal of Consulting and Clinical Psychology, 73*, 953–964.
Foa, E. B., & Rauch, S. A. M. (2004). Cognitive changes during prolonged exposure versus prolonged exposure plus cognitive restructuring in female assault survivors with posttraumatic stress disorder. *Journal of Consulting and Clinical Psychology, 72*, 879–884.
Foa, E. B., & Rothbaum, B. O. (1998). *Treating the trauma of rape: Cognitive-behavioral therapy for PTSD*. New York: Guilford Press.

Forsyth, J. P., & Eifert, G. H. (1996). The language of feeling and the feeling of anxiety: Contributions of the behaviorisms toward understanding the function-altering effects of language. *The Psychological Record, 46*, 607–649.
Forsyth, J. P., Eifert, G. H., & Barrios, V. (2006). Fear conditioning in an emotion regulation context: A fresh perspective on the origins of anxiety disorders. In M. G. Craske, D. Hermans, & D. Vanderstegen (Eds.), *Fear and learning – From basic processes to clinical implications* (pp. 133–153). Washington DC: APA Books.
Hand, I., Lamontagne, Y., & Marks, I. M. (1974). Group exposure (flooding) in vivo for agoraphobics. *British Journal of Psychiatry, 124*, 588–602.
Hassija, C. M., & Gray, M. J. (2010). Are cognitive techniques and interventions necessary? A case for the utility of cognitive approaches in the treatment of PTSD. *Clinical Psychology Science and Practice, 17*, 112–127.
Hermans, D., Vansteenwegen, D., & Craske, M. G. (2006). Fear and learning: Debates, future research, and clinical implications. In M. G. Craske, D. Hermans, & D. Vanderstegen (Eds.), *Fear and learning – From basic processes to clinical implications* (pp. 237–244). Washington DC: APA Books.
Hoffart, A. (1995). A comparison of cognitive and guided mastery therapy of agoraphobia. *Behaviour Research and Therapy, 33*, 423–434.
Hofmann, S. G. (2004). Cognitive mediation of treatment change in social phobia. *Journal of Consulting and Clinical Psychology, 72*, 393–399.
Hope, D. A., Heimberg, R. G., & Bruch, M. A. (1995). Dismantling cognitive–behavioral group therapy for social phobia. *Behaviour Research and Therapy, 33*, 637–650.
Horvath, A. O., & Bedi, R. P. (2002). The alliance. In J. C. Norcross (Ed.), *Psychotherapy relationships that work*. Oxford: University Press.
Ito, L. M., Noshirvani, H., Basoglu, M., & Marks, I. M. (1996). Does exposure to internal cues enhance exposure to external cues in agoraphobia with panic? *Psychotherapy and Psychosomatics, 65*, 24–28.
Kamphuis, J. H., & Telch, M. J. (2000). Effects of distraction and guided threat reappraisal on fear reduction during exposure treatments for specific fears. *Behaviour Research and Therapy, 38*, 1163–1181.
Kashdan, T. B., & Rottenberg, J. (2010). Psychological flexibility as a fundamental aspect of health. *Clinical Psychology Review, 30*, 865–878.
Longmore, R. J., & Worrel, M. (2007). Do we need to challenge thought in cognitive behavior therapy? *Clinical Psychology Review, 27*, 173–187.
Lovell, K., Marks, I. M., Noshirvani, H., Thrasher, S., & Livanou, M. (2001). Do cognitive and exposure treatments improve various PTSD symptoms differently? A randomized control trial. *Behavioral and Cognitive Psychotherapy, 29*, 107–112.
Marks, I., Lovell, K., Noshirvani, H., Livanou, M., & Thrasher, S. (1998). Treatment of posttraumatic stress disorder by exposure and/or cognitive restructuring: A controlled study. *Archives of General Psychiatry, 55*, 317–325. Retrieved from http://archpsyc.ama-assn.org/cgi/content/full/55/4/317.
Mathews, A. M., Gelder, M. G., & Johnston, D. W. (1981). *Agoraphobia – nature and treatment*. New York: The Guilford Press.
McLean, P. D., Whittal, M. L., Thordarson, D., Taylor, S., Söchting, I., Koch, W. J., et al. (2001). Cognitive versus behavior therapy in the group treatment of obsessive compulsive disorder. *Journal of Consulting and Clinical Psychology, 69*, 205–214.
Mersch, P. P. (1995). The treatment of social phobia: The differential effectiveness of exposure in vivo and an integration of exposure in vivo, rational emotive therapy and social skills training. *Behaviour Research and Therapy, 33*, 259–269.
Meyer, V., & Gelder, M. G. (1963). Behaviour therapy and phobic disorders. *British Journal of Psychiatry, 109*, 19–28.
Michelson, L. K., & Marchione, K. E. (1991). Behavioral, cognitive, and pharmacological treatments of panic disorder with agoraphobia: Critique and synthesis. *Journal of Clinical and Consulting Therapy, 59*, 100–114.

Michelson, L. K., Marchione, K. E., Greenwald, M., Testa, S., & Marchione, N. J. (1996). A comparative outcome study and follow-up investigation of panic disorder with agoraphobia: The relative and combined efficacy of cognitive therapy, relaxation training, and therapist-assisted exposure. *Journal of Anxiety Disorders, 10*, 297–330.

Mitte, K. (2005). A meta-analysis of the efficacy of psycho- and pharmacotherapy in panic disorder with and without agoraphobia. *Journal of Affective Disorders, 88*, 27–45.

Mowrer, O. H. (1960). *Learning theory and behavior*. New York: Wiley.

Norcross, J. C. (2002). Empirically supported therapy relationships. In J. C. Norcross (Ed.), *Psychotherapy relationships that work*. Oxford: University Press.

Öhman, A., & Wiens, S. (2004). The concept of an evolved fear module and cognitive theories of anxiety. In A. S. R. Manstead, N. Fridja, & A. Fisher (Eds.), *Feelings and emotions: The Amsterdam symposium* (pp. 58–80). Cambridge: University Press.

Öst, L.-G., Alm, T., Brandberg, M., & Breitholtz, E. (2001). One vs five sessions of exposure and five session of cognitive therapy in treatment of claustrophobia. *Behaviour Research and Therapy, 39*, 167–183.

Öst, L.-G., Jerremalm, A., & Jansson, L. (1984). Individual response pattern and the effects of different behavioral methods in the treatment of panic disorder with agoraphobia. *Behaviour Research and Therapy, 22*, 697–202.

Öst, L.-G., Thulin, U., & Ramnerö, J. (2004). Cognitive behaviour therapy vs. exposure *in vivo* in the treatment of panic disorder with agoraphobia. *Behaviour Research and Therapy, 42*, 1105–1127.

Öst, L.-G., Westling, B. E., & Hellström, K. (1993). Applied relaxation, exposure in vivo and cognitive methods in the treatment of panic disorder with agoraphobia. *Behaviour Research and Therapy, 31*, 279–287.

Page, A. C. (1994). Panic provocation in the treatment of agoraphobia: A preliminary investigation. *Australian and New Zealand Journal of Psychiatry, 28*, 82–86.

Paunovic, N., & Öst, L. G. (2001). Cognitive-behavior therapy vs. exposure therapy in the treatment of PTSD in refugees. *Behaviour Research and Therapy, 39*, 1183–1197.

Powers, M. B., Halpern, J. M., Ferenschack, M. P., Gillihan, S. J., & Foa, E. (2010). A meta-analytic review of prolonged exposure for posttraumatic stress disorder. *Clinical Psychology Review, 30*, 365–641.

Powers, M. B., Sigmarsson, S. R., & Emmelkamp, P. M. G. (2008). A meta-analytical review of psychological treatment of social anxiety disorder. *International Journal of Cognitive Therapy, 1*, 94–113.

Powers, M. B., Vervliet, B., Smits, J. A. J., & Otto, M. W. (2010). Helping exposure succeed: Learning theory perspectives on treatment resistance and relapse. In M. W. Otto & S. G. Hofmann (Eds.), *Avoiding treatment failures in the anxiety disorders* (pp. 31–50). New York: Springer.

Resick, P. A., Nishith, P., Weaver, T. L., Astin, M. C., & Feuer, C. A. (2002). A comparison of cognitive-processing therapy with prolonged exposure and a waiting condition for the treatment of chronic posttraumatic stress disorder in female rape victims. *Journal of Consulting and Clinical Psychology, 70*, 867–879.

Resick, P. A., & Schnicke, M. K. (1996). *Cognitive processing therapy for rape victims: A treatment manual*. Thousand Oaks, CA: Sage.

Rorty, R. (1979). *Philosophy and the mirror on nature*. Princeton: University Press.

Rosa-Alcázar, A. I., Sánchez-Meca, J., Gómez-Conesa, A., & Marin-Martinez, F. (2008). Psychological treatment of obsessive–compulsive disorder: A meta-analysis. *Clinical Psychology Review, 28*, 1310–1325.

Ruiter, C., Rijken, H., Garssen, B. B., & Kraaimat, F. (1989). Breathing retraining, exposure and a combination of both, in the treatment of panic disorder with agoraphobia. *Behaviour Research and Therapy, 27*, 647–655.

Salaberría, K., & Echeburua, E. (1998). Long–term outcome of cognitive therapy's contribution to self–exposure in vivo to the treatment of generalized social phobia. *Behavior Modification, 22*, 262–284.

Sanchez-Meca, J., Rosa-Alcazar, A. I., Fulgencio, M. M., & Gomez-Conesa, A. (2010). Psychological treatment of panic disorder with or without agoraphobia: A meta-analysis. *Clinical Psychology Review, 30*, 37–50.

Schmidt, N. B., Woolaway-Bickel, K., Trakowski, J., Santiago, H., Storey, J., Koselka, M., et al. (2000). Dismantling cognitive-behavioral treatment for panic disorder: Questioning the utility of breathing retraining. *Journal of Consulting and Clinical Psychology, 68*, 417–424.

Sinnot, A., Jones, R. B., Scott-Fordham, A., & Woodward, R. (1981). Augmentation of in vivo exposure treatment for agoraphobia by the formation of neighbourhood self-help groups. *Behaviour Research and Therapy, 19*, 339–347.

Sloan, T., & Telch, M. J. (2002). The effects of safety-seeking behavior on and guided threat reappraisal on fear reduction during exposure: An experimental investigation. *Behaviour Research and Therapy, 40*(3), 235–251.

Smith, M. L., Glass, G. V., & Miller, T. I. (1980). *The benefits of psychotherapy*. Baltimore: Johns Hopkins University Press.

Söchting, I., Taylor, S., Freeman, W., de Koning, E., Segerstrom, S., & Thordarson, D. (1998). In vivo exposure for panic disorder and agoraphobia: Does a cognitive rationale enhance treatment efficacy? In E. Sanavio (Ed.), *Behavior and cognitive therapy today: Essays in honor of Hans J. Eysenck* (pp. 279–288). Oxford: Elsevier.

Tarrier, N., Pilgrim, H., Sommerfield, C., Faragher, B., Reynolds, M., Graham, E., et al. (1999). A randomized trial of cognitive therapy and imaginal exposure in the treatment of chronic post-traumatic stress disorder. *Journal of Consulting and Clinical Psychology, 67*, 13–18.

Tarrier, N., & Sommerfield, C. (2004). Treatment of chronic PTSD by cognitive therapy and exposure: 5-Year follow up. *Behavior Therapy, 35*, 231–246.

Thorpe, G. L., Freedman, E. G., & Lazar, J. D. (1985). Assertiveness training and exposure in vivo for agoraphobics. *Behavioural Psychotherapy, 13*, 132–141.

Tryon, G. S., & Winograd, G. (2002). Goal consensus and collaboration. In J. C. Norcross (Ed.), *Psychotherapy relationships that work* (pp. 109–125). Oxford: University Press.

Van den Hout, M., Arntz, A., & Hoekstra, R. (1994). Exposure reduced but not agoraphobia panic, and cognitive therapy reduced panic but not agoraphobia. *Behaviour Research and Therapy, 32*, 447–451.

Van Dyck, R., & Spinhoven, P. (1997). Does preference for treatment matter? A study of exposure in vivo with or without hypnosis in the treatment of panic disorder with agoraphobia. *Behavior Modification, 21*, 172–186.

van Oppen, P., De Haan, E., Van Balkom, A. J. L. M., Spinhoven, P., Hoogduin, K., & Van Dyck, R. (1995). Cognitiv therapy and exposure in vivo in the treatment of obsessive–compulsive disorder. *Behaviour Research and Therapy, 33*, 379–390.

Vansteenwegen, D., Dirikx, T., Hermans, D., Vervliet, B., & Eelen, P. (2006). Renewal and reinstatement of fear: Evidence from human conditioning research. In M. G. Craske, D. Hermans, & D. Vanderstegen (Eds.), *Fear and learning – From basic processes to clinical implications* (pp. 197–215). Washington DC: APA Books.

Vogel, P. A., Stiles, T. C., & Gotestam, K. G. (2004). Adding cognitive therapy elements to exposure therapy for obsessive compulsive disorder: A controlled study. *Behavioural and Cognitive Psychotherapy, 32*, 275–290.

Whittal, M., Thordarson, D., & McLean, P. (2005). Treatment of obsessive-compulsive disorder: Cognitive behavior therapy vs. exposure and response prevention. *Behaviour Research and Therapy, 43*, 1559–1576.

Williams, S. L., & Falbo, J. (1996). Cognitive and performance based treatments for panic attacks in people with varying degrees of agoraphobic disability. *Behaviour Research and Therapy, 32*, 253–264.

Williams, S. L., & Rappoport, A. (1983). Cognitive treatment in the natural environment for agoraphobics. *Behavior Therapy, 14*, 299–313.

Wolitsky, K. B., & Telch, M. J. (2009). Augmenting in vivo exposure with fear antagonistic action strategies: A preliminary test. *Behavior Therapy, 40*, 57–71.

Wolitzky-Taylor, K. B., Horowitz, J. D., Powers, M. B., & Telch, M. J. (2008). Psychological approaches in the treatment of specific phobias: A meta-analysis. *Clinical Psychology Review, 28*, 1021–1037.

Wolpe, J. (1958). *Psychotherapy by reciprocal inhibition*. Stanford: University Press.

Chapter 17
Safety First? Trauma Exposure in PTSD

Frank Neuner

Frank Neuner is Professor of Clinical Psychology and Psychotherapy, and licensed psychotherapist at Bielefeld University, Germany. His main research areas are psychological consequences of violence and treatment of post-traumatic stress disorders after war, torture, and child maltreatment.

F. Neuner (✉)
Clinical Psychology and Psychotherapy, Bielefeld University,
Bielefeld, Germany
e-mail: frank.neuner@uni-bielefeld.de

P. Neudeck and H.-U. Wittchen (eds.), *Exposure Therapy: Rethinking the Model – Refining the Method*, DOI 10.1007/978-1-4614-3342-2_17,

17.1 Dangerous Emotions in Anxiety Treatment and PTSD

Variants of exposure therapy are essential for the treatment of a broad range of anxiety disorders, including phobias, panic disorder, and obsessive–compulsive disorder. Albeit current debates exist about the relative efficacy of graduated and massed exposure approaches, the meaning of additional cognitive treatment elements or the mechanisms of exposure therapy (Richard & Gloster, 2007), confronting the patient with his worst fears has become almost a gold standard in the treatment of anxiety disorders.

Several years of controversy predate the arrival at this current position. Concerns about possible dangers of exposure treatment have been raised during the first attempts of such treatments and have accompanied the development, testing, and dissemination of exposure approaches throughout the years. In particular, the belief that experiencing intense affect during treatment may be harmful for patients has a strong tradition in almost all psychotherapy approaches, including behavior therapy. The most prominent early proponents of behavioral anxiety treatment feared that provoking affect that was too intense during treatment would risk strengthening the conditioned fear through an effect called *incubation* (Eysenck, 1968) or even lead to a shutdown of the organism through *transmarginal inhibition* (Wolpe, 1958). Within the paradigm of counterconditioning, the ground rule for anxiety treatment was that only small and tolerable doses of fear should be provoked in treatment. However, several decades of treatment research including courageous trials have shown that even techniques like flooding and implosive therapy, which aim at provoking maximum fear in patients with anxiety disorders, are both effective and safe (Shipley, 1980). As a consequence, exposure therapies for anxiety disorders have been well established as first-line treatments in guidelines and textbooks, are widely applied in clinical practice and concerns about the dangers of intense fear within well-executed treatments has proven to be unfounded.

However, the case of PTSD seems to be an exception. Still today, concerns are being raised about severe side effects or potential symptom exacerbations through exposure therapy for PTSD (Pitman et al., 1991; Devilly & Foa, 2001; Foa, Zoellner, Feeny, Hembree, & Alvarez-Conrad, 2002). For example the German treatment guidelines caution therapists against a potential "retraumatization" and "affective overflow" that may be caused by techniques that confront the patient with his traumatic memories (Flatten, Gast, & Hofmann, 2004). Such warnings corroborate fears and preoccupations among therapists who are hesitating to employ exposure procedures in the treatment of PTSD (Jaycox & Foa, 1996; Becker, Zayfert, & Anderson, 2004). Many textbooks advise applying variants of so-called stabilization techniques before or instead of exposure therapy to protect patients from negative treatment effects (Herman, 1992; Fischer & Riedesser, 1998; Reddemann, 2007). As the research on side effects and potential harmful effects of therapies has been widely neglected in psychotherapy research, it is reasonable to take clinician's concerns seriously and to weigh the risks and potential benefits of exposure therapy for PTSD.

17.2 Efficacy of Exposure Therapy for PTSD

In the last two decades, more than 40 randomized trials with more than 1,000 participants from different populations of traumatized subjects have enabled the development of a solid evidence base for PTSD treatment. The international guidelines (Foa, Keane, & Friedman, 2004; National Institute for Clinical Excellence, 2005) as well as major reviews and meta-analyses (Bisson et al., 2007) have divided treatment procedures into two principal strategies. Symptom-focused strategies (e.g., stress inoculation therapy or other anxiety management techniques) try to alleviate PTSD symptoms by teaching the patient various techniques (e.g., distraction, thought stop, relaxation) to gain control over their experiences and arousal. Such approaches have sometimes been classified into a category of stabilizing techniques, as they aim to reduce PTSD symptoms without provoking intense emotions in treatment. In contrast, the so-called trauma-focused treatments (see Table 17.1) target the trauma memories rather than the PTSD symptoms. The common idea behind these therapies is that PTSD symptoms are maintained by a pathological memory representation of the traumatic event, which involves an excessive associative connection of stimulus—reaction elements on the one side and a fragmented cognitive and autobiographic memory representation on the other side. Trauma-focused treatments aim at repairing this memory pathology by habituating to the conditioned reminders, reestablishing the autobiographic memory or correcting dysfunctional beliefs related to the trauma (Brewin & Holmes, 2003). Not all trauma-focused treatments explicitly involve elements of exposure and the degree of emotional involvement of the patient differs widely between treatments. Nonetheless, some level of exposure to painful, i.e., traumatic memories is similar across all these approaches. Trauma-focused treatments range from mere exposure approaches such as prolonged exposure that combines exposure *in sensu* to trauma memories and exposure in vivo to avoided situations (Foa & Rothbaum, 1998), to cognitive approaches that aim to modify dysfunctional thinking related to the traumatic experiences (Resick & Schnicke, 1993; Kubany, Hill, & Owens, 2003; Blanchard et al., 2003; Ehlers, Clark, Hackmann, McManus, & Fennell, 2005). A special variant of trauma-focused treatments is the so-called eye movement desensitization and reprocessing (EMDR) method, that combines exposure and reappraisal techniques with concurrent eye movements (Shapiro, 1995). As the additional benefit of the repetitive eye movements during EMDR treatment has not been shown, it is likely that this treatment operates similar to other trauma-focused approaches.

Today, the evidence is quite clear. Across different treatment trials, the variants of trauma-focused treatments have proven to be more efficient than symptom-focused strategies. This stimulated the general recommendation of trauma-focused therapy as the first-line treatment for PTSD in the treatment guidelines of the International Society of Traumatic Stress Studies (Foa et al., 2004) as well as the official guidelines in England (National Institute for Clinical Excellence, 2005). Table 17.1 summarizes the recommended evidence-based treatment approaches for PTSD.

Table 17.1 Variants of trauma-focused treatment approaches with proven efficacy for the therapy of PTSD

Procedure and authors	Patients	Nr. of sessions	Nr. of sessions before exposure	Stabilizing techniques
Prolonged exposure				
(Foa & Rothbaum, 1998)	Rape, sexual abuse, physical abuse, combat, accidents	9–12	2	Breathing exercise
Cognitive Procedures				
Cognitive behavior therapy (Blanchard et al., 2003) Cognitive Therapy (Ehlers et al., 2005) Cognitive Processing Therapy (Resick & Schnicke, 1993) Cognitive Trauma Therapy (Kubany et al., 2003)	Rape, sexual abuse, physical assault, combat, accidents, refugees, inter-partner violence	8–12	1–2	None
Eye movement desensitization and reprocessing (EMDR)				
(Shapiro, 1995)	Rape, sexual abuse, physical abuse, combat, accidents	4–12	1–2	None, breathing exercises, relaxation, imagination of a safe place
Narrative exposure therapy				
(Schauer et al., 2005)	Victims of war and torture	4–10	1	None
Brief eclectic psychotherapy				
(Gersons, Carlier, Lamberts, & van der Kolk, 2000)	Policemen, violence, accidents, natural disaster	16	1	None

17.3 Risks of Exposure Therapy for PTSD

The fact that trauma-focused therapy has been shown to be the most successful therapy for PTSD in most trials does not necessarily prove that it is a safe treatment. The so-called deterioration effect says that the variance of change values of psychopathology scores is larger for patients in psychotherapy than for comparable untreated subjects (Bergin, 1966). This finding suggests that the majority of participants in a trial may profit at the expense of a minority of subjects who may get worse during treatment. As a result, psychotherapy may cause a worsening in single subjects, and a comparison of the treatments on the basis of statistical effect sizes may hide negative trajectories of single individuals.

Clinicians and researchers who highlight potential dangers of exposure therapy most often refer to a classical case study of Pitman who presented a series of treatments of Vietnam veterans with seemingly negative effects during exposure therapy, including a worsening of symptoms or a relapse of substance abuse (Pitman et al., 1991). However, a close inspection of the description of the treatments indicates that in fact it may not have been the exposure therapy itself that caused the problems in treatment, but rather the uncritical application of an untested treatment manual without consideration of basic principles of psychotherapy in the form of an individualized treatment plan. Within this article, Pitman himself does not conclude that exposure therapy itself should be avoided or complemented by stabilization, but that the addition of cognitive treatment elements may be required in the case of severe shame and guilt feelings.

The deterioration effect implies that only studies that count the number of subjects who get worse during therapy can inform about potential risks of therapy approaches in comparison to other approaches or no treatment. Unfortunately, most therapy studies do not provide information about the worsening of single patients, and the definition of worsening differs between treatment studies that do so. Some studies indicate a single subject as having worsened if the symptom scores have increased from pre- to posttest (e.g., Tarrier et al., 1999). Such studies found that some subjects in the control groups who received no treatment or relaxation therapy got worse during the course of the study (e.g., Taylor et al., 2003). This finding implies that not all deterioration that can be detected in case series or in clinical practice can be attributed to treatment, but that worsening may occur spontaneously for some subjects. Across studies, worsening was found for approximately 5–10% of patients in treatment conditions. However, the size of the worsening typically did not reach the criterion for statistically reliable change, which means that the worsening is possibly merely based on the measurement error of the instrument. During the course of exposure therapy for PTSD, about 15% of subjects may present with statistically reliable worsening. However, these negative effects attenuate during the course of treatment and neither imply a negative treatment outcome nor dropout from therapy (Foa et al., 2002). These data show that it can be expected that some single cases get worse during exposure therapy, but that these negative effects are usually temporal and are not more common in exposure for PTSD than in other treatment approaches.

Current research into negative treatment effects does not yet allow for the comparison of the risks of different treatment approaches such as exposure therapies and other procedures. The claim that nonconfronting treatments are generally safer than exposure therapy is therefore unfounded. Some of the most commonly applied symptom-focused treatment approaches have never been studied in randomized trials and there is no information about deterioration that happens in these conditions. Recently, Cottraux and coworkers have found that the careful handling of emotions and collusion with avoidance behavior may not be more protective for patients (Cottraux et al., 2008). In a randomized controlled comparison between cognitive behavioral therapy (including exposure therapy) and client-centered therapy more subjects dropped out or deteriorated in the client-centered condition. This finding indicates that apparently careful treatments may actually be more difficult for anxiety patients and that common beliefs of therapists about the relative danger of different treatment approaches are possibly false.

As there is no evidence that the number of subjects who deteriorate during treatment or who drop out of treatment is larger for exposure therapy than for other approaches that do not use exposure (Hembree et al., 2003), the general warning against exposure therapies is not justified.

17.4 Stabilization Before Exposure

In view of both the undisputed benefit of trauma-focused treatments on the one hand, and the fears of the dangers of trauma confrontation on the other hand, it has been common to recommend a phased-treatment approach, which includes a so-called stabilization phase before confronting the patients with their trauma memory. The aim of the stabilization phase is to reach personal safety and control over symptoms before patients are able to tolerate their trauma memories in exposure. The recommended stabilization procedures differ widely in regard to techniques as well as duration, which ranges from eight sessions (skill training in affect regulation (STAIR) module; Cloitre, Koenen, Cohen, & Han, 2002) to indefinite (Psychodynamic Imaginative Trauma Therapy; PITT; Reddemann, 2003). Table 17.2 presents variants of stabilization as recommended in the literature. The common element of these proposed stabilization techniques is the claim that these procedures increase the patients' abilities to regulate negative emotions such as fear, disgust, or shame.

As noted in Table 17.2, stabilization methods differ widely with regard to their techniques. While all strategies aim to modify skills in regulating negative emotions, some approaches such as the PITT or the stabilizing techniques recommended as an adjunct to EMDR focus on training the imagination of situations that contrast with the trauma memory or symptoms. For example, patients are guided to imagine safe places, where they are protected from hardships and adversities, or to lock their trauma memories into a safe in order to avoid being haunted by unwanted painful

Table 17.2 Stabilization procedures in PTSD

Manual and authors	Procedures	Nr of sessions	Evidence from randomized controlled trials
Psychodynamic imaginative trauma therapy (Reddemann, 2007)	Imagination of mastery and safety situations	Not specified	Not tested
Skill training in affect regulation (STAIR) (Cloitre et al., 2002)	Skills training (DBT), including social competence training	Eight, preceded by exposure	In combination with exposure therapy less dropouts than exposure alone
EMDR/Resource development and installation (Korn & Leeds, 2002)	Imagination of mastery and safety situations combined with bilateral stimulation	Not specified	Not tested
Affect management (Zlotnick et al., 1997)	Skills training (DBT)	15, group format	Moderate effects on PTSD symptom severity

memories. Other treatment approaches include methods derived from therapy for borderline personality disorder. As a substantial proportion of survivors of childhood abuse present with both, symptoms of PTSD and features of borderline disorder, it seems plausible to refer to these well-established techniques. Emotion regulation training is part of Dialectical Behavior Therapy (DBT; Linehan, 1993) and includes techniques such as training in experiencing, labeling, and mindful accepting or reappraising painful emotions. In addition, the skills training component of DBT includes social competence training to modify dysfunctional interpersonal behavior patterns that may originate from early abuse experiences. In programs such as STAIR, these techniques were recently condensed into an eight-session module (Cloitre et al., 2010). DBT-based stabilization approaches such as STAIR focus on two primary aims: First, instead of training avoidance strategies such as the imagination of safe situations, they aim at accepting negative affects. Second, they include a diagnostic assessment and training of interpersonal behavior. Further, they are time restricted and most importantly, they have been successfully tested in randomized trials. As the DBT-based approaches also contain social competence training as well as cognitive strategies to change dysfunctional automatic appraisals of fear-provoking situations, it appears that these are more like a broad cognitive behavioral approach to reduce symptoms other than those of PTSD in complex cases rather than mere trainings in affect regulation. Due to these major differences in primary aims, procedures, and documented efficacy, and because the techniques are not restricted to training affect regulation, it does not seem to be helpful to summarize the imagery-based and the DBT-based strategies into the single category of stabilizing techniques, but to study the potential benefit of single alternatives and additional modules/additions to exposure therapy.

17.5 Stabilization Before Exposure: At Least for the Treatment of "Complex PTSD"?

Trauma-focused psychotherapy approaches that usually contain elements of exposure therapy are definitely the most effective treatments for PTSD. In addition, treatment risks, including dropouts and worsening, do not seem to be more frequent in exposure approaches. As a consequence, it does not seem to be necessary to pontificate on the need for adding stabilizing techniques to increase efficacy or reduce risk. However, some single treatment studies show exceptionally high rates of deteriorations during exposure therapy. In particular, two studies with adult survivors of childhood abuse (McDonagh et al., 2005; Cloitre et al., 2010) found dropout rates of up to 30% and deterioration in up to 40% of the participants in exposure therapy. As survivors of childhood abuse often present with high levels of comorbidity, including personality disorders, these findings seem to corroborate claims that the evidence about the efficacy of PTSD treatment is not valid for patients with a complex presentation of symptoms (Spinazzola, Blaustein, & van der Kolk, 2005). According to this classification, the so-called type-I trauma includes unique and relatively short traumatic experiences such as rape and accidents, whereas the type-II traumas include repeated traumatizations, often in childhood, such as childhood abuse, imprisonment, or torture. Type-II traumas lead to a broader range of symptoms, including dissociative symptoms and difficulties in affect regulation that can only be insufficiently described with the PTSD concept. Some clinicians have suggested alternative or additional categories such as complex PTSD (Herman, 1992; van der Kolk et al., 1996), which has led to the inclusion of disorders of extreme stress not otherwise specified (DESNOS) as a research category in the DSM-IV. Several studies have found high rates of DESNOS symptoms in various populations including abuse survivors and war veterans (Sack, 2004). Although the validity of the DESNOS category is still under debate, some clinicians repeatedly claim that the evidence from PTSD research only refers to the simple, Type I traumas, whereas there is no evidence for any treatment for type-II traumas. So far, DESNOS has not been applied in any treatment study. However, as epidemiological studies have found high rates of DESNOS in veterans and rape victims, there is reason to assume that many DESNOS patients have been included in trials with these patient populations. These studies generally proved to be successful in reducing PTSD and comorbid symptoms. For example, in a post-hoc analysis of a large treatment trial, Resick and colleagues showed that the subgroup of patients with sexual childhood abuse did profit from treatment to the same extent as patients who were raped as adults, although they initially presented with a higher level of symptoms and more comorbidity (Resick, Nishith, & Griffin, 2003).

Another group of patients who are commonly identified as type-II trauma patients are civil victims of war and torture victims. Usually, these patients have undergone a series of traumatic events over an extended period of time (Neuner et al., 2004), which supposedly causes a more complex symptom pattern. So far, seven randomized trials have been published with these populations (for a review, see Crumlish & O'Rourke, 2010). All procedures that have been tested in these studies are variants of trauma-focused therapies. In some studies, these procedures

Table 17.3 Therapy approaches tested in randomized PTSD treatment trials including a substantial rate of subjects with child abuse

Procedure	Elements	Nr. of Sessions	Drop outs	% reduction PTSD symptoms (completer)	Authors
Prolonged exposure	Exposure in sensu and in vivo	14	41%	42.6%	(McDonagh et al., 2005)
Support+prolonged exposure	Supportive counseling, exposure in sensu	8+8	39%	~55%	(Cloitre et al., 2010)
Present centered therapy	Problem solving	14	9%	33.5%	(McDonagh et al., 2005)
Cognitive processing therapy	Exposure in sensu and cognitive therapy	25	22%	86.3%	(Chard, 2005)
STAIR+support	Skills training (DBT), cognitive therapy, supportive counselling and interpersonal skills training	16	29%	55.1%	(Cloitre et al., 2002)
STAIR+Exposure	Skills training (DBT), cognitive therapy, exposure in sensu and interpersonal skills training	16	15%	~72%	(Cloitre et al., 2010)
STAIR+support	Skills training (DBT), cognitive therapy, supportive counseling and interpersonal skills training	8+8	26%	~66%	(Cloitre et al., 2010)
Affect management	Skills training (DBT)	15	29%	31.5%	(Zlotnick et al., 1997)
Cognitive trauma therapy	Exposure in sensu and cognitive therapy	8–11	20%	78.3%	(Kubany et al., 2004)

had been adapted to the symptoms of specific patient groups, like the commonly observed panic attacks in Cambodian refugees (Hinton et al., 2005), which had been successfully treated with an adapted CBT approach. Narrative Exposure Therapy (Schauer, Neuner, & Elbert, 2005) has been specifically developed for survivors of organized violence like war and torture. In contrast to other *in sensu* exposure treatments for PTSD, the focus of therapy is not on a single worst event. Rather, the whole life story of the patient, including all traumatic experiences is being reconstructed during therapy. Albeit there is no explicit stabilizing element within this treatment, the efficacy could be shown for a range of traumatized war victims ranging from Sudanese refugees in Uganda to tortured asylum seekers in Germany (Robjant & Fazel, 2010).

So far, five randomized trials have examined treatment efficacy in adult victims of child abuse, which included child sexual abuse in most cases. Another study was carried out with victims of interpartner violence, most of whom had also experienced sexual abuse in childhood. Table 17.3 summarizes the efficacy and risk indicators of the procedures that were tested in these trials. While the low number of comparative studies precludes valid conclusions, it seems that the exclusive application of exposure techniques leads to comparatively high dropout rates and the efficacy of this treatment appears to be limited. It seems that the additional application of methods that had been developed or adapted specifically for victims of child abuse, in particular, cognitive or DBT-related procedures, increases efficacy and reduces the risk of treatment. Although these findings do not argue for a phased treatment *per se*, they are consistent with the findings that child abuse increases the risk for various psychological symptoms and disorders beyond PTSD (Gilbert et al., 2009), and that an exclusive concentration on treating the conditioned fear response might not meet the needs of the majority of patients. Instead, treatments addressing other emotions than fear, such as shame and disgust, and that also address the often disturbed interpersonal functioning of abuse survivors, appear to be more promising.

17.6 Conclusions

The current state of therapy research in PTSD provides clear recommendations for therapeutic practice. Treatment of PTSD should be trauma- rather than symptom focused, including exposure to trauma memories. Different rationales have been developed for exposure *in sensu* for PTSD, ranging from the prolonged exposure protocol to narrative exposure. These types of trauma-focused procedures are safe and more effective than any known alternative. Treatment research for PTSD indicates that the intention to protect patients from experiencing strong emotions in treatment may actually be more risky than applying well-defined exposure protocols.

However, standard forms of exposure therapy alone do not meet the needs of all trauma survivors. Research has shown that treatment procedures that have been adapted for specific trauma groups, for example, victims of child abuse, torture, or intimate partner violence, can be more promising than the uncritical application of standard manuals of trauma therapy. Although dismantling studies could not show that the combination of exposure therapy with cognitive therapy or other treatment modules is superior to the application of each strategy alone, data from studies with child-abuse survivors indicate that it is more promising to add specifically adapted techniques, in particular, social competence training and cognitive procedures, for patients with a complex presentation of symptoms.

The common recommendation of a stabilization phase for all or specific trauma populations is not helpful, as this term includes different strategies that may have opposite effects. Commonly recommended stabilization procedures, like procedures applied within the PITT or EMDR protocols, often involve training the imagination of safe situations. Such distraction trainings ultimately aim at training patients to use more sophisticated avoidance strategies. As this rationale opposes the logic of all evidence-based PTSD treatments (exposure therapy as well as cognitive therapy), and as there is no evidence for the efficacy and risks of such practices, these techniques should be abandoned until well-designed studies confirm their safety and helpfulness.

Likewise, the suggestion of an obligatory training in emotion regulation training for patients with complex presentations is meaningless, as any psychotherapeutic intervention eventually aims at increasing emotion regulation. Exposure therapy itself is possibly the most typical training in emotion regulation, as it increases the ability to approach and endure fear and reduces avoidance strategies. However, short trainings in labeling, experiencing, and accepting emotions, as practiced in DBT, may be a helpful preparation for trauma exposure for patients with a history of childhood abuse. Some exposure techniques, such as Narrative Exposure Therapy, apply such skills during rather than before trauma exposure as a means of supporting the narrating process. Likewise, strategies to counteract dissociative symptoms, for example, by applying strong sensory stimulations or by applied tension techniques, can also be useful preparations for some patients.

Taken together, there is good (methodologically sound) evidence from treatment trials to suggest individualized treatment plans for the survivors. The key module of treatment will be exposure *in sensu*, and there is good reason not to postpone this element at the expense of unnecessary stabilization. Exposure may be complemented by exposure in vivo, for patients with trauma-related phobic avoidance behavior, as well as cognitive techniques, in particular, for strong issues related to guilt or self-devaluation. Patients with difficulties in experiencing, expressing, and labeling emotions may profit from teaching these skills before or during exposure therapy. Patients with abuse-related deficits in interpersonal functioning may need training in social competence in order to master unwanted emotions. As long as the chosen modules follow the general strategy of exposing the survivor to his traumatic memories, it is likely that the skillful application of such individually tailored treatment modules increases efficacy and reduces risks in clinical practice more than the uncritical application of standardized treatment manuals, be it with or without stabilization module.

References

Becker, C. B., Zayfert, C., & Anderson, E. (2004). A survey of psychologists' attitudes towards and utilization of exposure therapy for PTSD. *Behaviour Research and Therapy, 42*(3), 277–292.

Bergin, A. E. (1966). Some implications of psychotherapy research for therapeutic practice. *Journal of Abnormal Psychology, 71*(4), 235–246.

Bisson, J. I., Ehlers, A., Matthews, R., Pilling, S., Richards, D., & Turner, S. (2007). Psychological treatments for chronic post-traumatic stress disorder. Systematic review and meta-analysis. *British Journal of Psychiatry, 190*, 97–104.

Blanchard, E. B., Hickling, E. J., Devineni, T., Veazey, C. H., Galovski, T. E., Mundy, E., et al. (2003). A controlled evaluation of cognitive behavioural therapy for posttraumatic stress in motor vehicle accident survivors. *Behaviour Research & Therapy, 41*(1), 79–96.

Brewin, C. R., & Holmes, E. A. (2003). Psychological theories of posttraumatic stress disorder. *Clinical Psychology Review, 23*(3), 339–376.

Chard, K. M. (2005). An evaluation of cognitive processing therapy for the treatment of posttraumatic stress disorder related to childhood sexual abuse. *Journal of Consulting & Clinical Psychology, 73*(5), 965–971.

Cloitre, M., Koenen, K. C., Cohen, L. R., & Han, H. (2002). Skills training in affective and interpersonal regulation followed by exposure: A phase-based treatment for PTSD related to childhood abuse. *Journal of Consulting & Clinical Psychology, 70*(5), 1067–1074.

Cloitre, M., Stovall-McClough, K. C., Nooner, K., Zorbas, P., Cherry, S., Jackson, C. L., et al. (2010). Treatment for PTSD Related to Childhood Abuse: A Randomized Controlled Trial. *American Journal of Psychiatry, 167*(8), 915–924.

Cottraux, J., Note, I., Yao, S. N., de Mey-Guillard, C., Bonasse, F., Djamoussian, D., et al. (2008). Randomized controlled comparison of cognitive behavior therapy with Rogerian supportive therapy in chronic post-traumatic stress disorder: A 2-year follow-up. *Psychotherapy & Psychosomatics, 77*(2), 101–110.

Crumlish, N., & O'Rourke, K. (2010). A systematic review of treatments for post-traumatic stress disorder among refugees and asylum-seekers. *Journal of Nervous & Mental Disease, 198*(4), 237–251.

Devilly, G. J., & Foa, E. B. (2001). The investigation of exposure and cognitive therapy: Comment on Tarrier et al (1999). *Journal of Consulting & Clinical Psychology, 69*(1), 114–116.

Ehlers, A., Clark, D. M., Hackmann, A., McManus, F., & Fennell, M. (2005). Cognitive therapy for post-traumatic stress disorder: Development and evaluation. *Behaviour Research & Therapy, 43*(4), 413–431.

Eysenck, H. J. (1968). A theory of the incubation of anxiety-fear responses. *Behaviour Research & Therapy, 6*(3), 309–321.

Fischer, G., & Riedesser, P. (1998). *Lehrbuch der Psychotraumatologie*. München: UTB für Wissenschaft.

Flatten, G., Gast, U., & Hofmann, A. (2004). *Posttraumatische Belastungsstörung. Leitlinie und Quellentext (Leitlinien Psychosomatische Medizin und Psychotherapie)*. Schattauer.

Foa, E. B., Keane, T. M., & Friedman, M. J. (2004). *Effective treatments for PTSD: Practice guidelines from the international society for traumatic stress studies*. New York: The Guilford Press.

Foa, E. B., & Rothbaum, B. O. (1998). *Treating the trauma of rape: Cognitive-behavioral therapy for PTSD*. New York: The Guilford Press.

Foa, E. B., Zoellner, L. A., Feeny, N. C., Hembree, E. A., & Alvarez-Conrad, J. (2002). Does imaginal exposure exacerbate PTSD symptoms? *Journal of Consulting & Clinical Psychology, 70*(4), 1022–1028.

Gersons, B. P., Carlier, I. V., Lamberts, R. D., & van der Kolk, B. A. (2000). Randomized clinical trial of brief eclectic psychotherapy for police officers with posttraumatic stress disorder. *Journal of Traumatic Stress, 13*(2), 333–347.

Gilbert, R., Widom, C. S., Browne, K., Fergusson, D., Webb, E., & Janson, S. (2009). Burden and consequences of child maltreatment in high-income countries. *Lancet, 373*(9657), 68–81.

Hembree, E. A., Foa, E. B., Dorfan, N. M., Street, G. P., Kowalski, J., & Tu, X. (2003). Do patients drop out prematurely from exposure therapy for PTSD? *J Trauma Stress, 16*(6), 555–562.

Herman, J. L. (1992). *Trauma and recovery*. New York: Basic Books.

Hinton, D. E., Chhean, D., Pich, V., Safren, S. A., Hofmann, S. G., & Pollack, M. H. (2005). A randomized controlled trial of cognitive-behavior therapy for Cambodian refugees with treatment-resistant PTSD and panic attacks: A cross-over design. *Journal of Traumatic Stress, 18*(6), 617–629.

Jaycox, L. H., & Foa, E. B. (1996). Obstacles in implementing exposure therapy for PTSD: Case discussions and practical solutions. *Clinical Psychology & Psychotherapy, 3*, 176–184.

Korn, D. L., & Leeds, A. M. (2002). Preliminary evidence of efficacy for EMDR resource development and installation in the stabilization phase of treatment of complex posttraumatic stress disorder. *Journal of Clinical Psychology, 58*(12), 1465–1487.

Kubany, E. S., Hill, E. E., & Owens, J. A. (2003). Cognitive trauma therapy for battered women with PTSD: Preliminary findings. *Journal of Traumatic Stress, 16*(1), 81–91.

Kubany, E. S., Hill, E. E., Owens, J. A., Iannce-Spencer, C., McCaig, M. A., Tremayne, K. J., et al. (2004). Cognitive trauma therapy for battered women with PTSD (CTT-BW). *Journal of Consulting & Clinical Psychology, 72*(1), 3–18.

Linehan, M. M. (1993). *Skills training manual for treating borderline personality disorder*. New York: The Guilford Press.

McDonagh, A., Friedman, M., McHugo, G., Ford, J., Sengupta, A., Mueser, K., et al. (2005). Randomized trial of cognitive-behavioral therapy for chronic posttraumatic stress disorder in adult female survivors of childhood sexual abuse. *Journal of Consulting & Clinical Psychology, 73*(3), 515–524.

National Institute for Clinical Excellence. (2005). *Post-traumatic stress disorder*. London: Gaskell and the British Psychological Society.

Neuner, F., Schauer, M., Karunakara, U., Klaschik, C., Robert, C., & Elbert, T. (2004). Psychological trauma and evidence for enhanced vulnerability for posttraumatic stress disorder through previous trauma among West Nile refugees. *BMC Psychiatry, 4*, 34.

Pitman, R. K., Altman, B., Greenwald, E., Longpre, R. E., Macklin, M. L., Poire, R. E., et al. (1991). Psychiatric complications during flooding therapy for posttraumatic stress disorder. *Journal of Clinical Psychiatry, 52*(1), 17–20.

Reddemann, L. (2003). *Imagination als heilsame Kraft*. Hamburg: Klett-Cotta.

Reddemann, L. (2007). *Psychodynamisch imaginative Traumatherapie*. Klett-Cotta: PITT - das Manual.

Resick, P. A., Nishith, P., & Griffin, M. G. (2003). How well does cognitive-behavioral therapy treat symptoms of complex PTSD? An examination of child sexual abuse survivors within a clinical trial. *CNS Spectrum, 8*(5), 340–355.

Resick, P. A., & Schnicke, M. K. (1993). *Cognitive processing therapy for rape victims*. Newbury Park, CA: Sage.

Richard, D. C. S., & Gloster, A. T. (2007). Exposure therapy has a public relations problem: A dearth of litigation amid a wealth of concern. In D. C. S. Richard & D. Lauterbach (Eds.), *Handbook of exposure therapy* (pp. 409–425). Amsterdam: Academic.

Robjant, K., & Fazel, M. (2010). The emerging evidence for Narrative Exposure Therapy: A review. *Clinical Psychology Review, 30*(8), 1030–1039.

Sack, M. (2004). Diagnostische und klinische Aspekte der komplexen posttraumatischen Belastungsstörung. *Nervenarzt, 75*, 451–459.

Schauer, M., Neuner, F., & Elbert, T. (2005). *Narrative Exposure Therapy - a short term intervention for traumatic stress disorders after war, terror or torture*. Göttingen: Hogrefe & Huber.

Shapiro, F. (1995). *Eye movement desensitization and reprocessing: Basic principles, protocols and procedures*. New York: Guilford Press.

Shipley, R. H. (1980). Flooding and implosive therapy: Are they harmful? *Behavior Therapy, 11*(4), 503–508.

Spinazzola, J., Blaustein, M., & van der Kolk, B. A. (2005). Posttraumatic stress disorder treatment outcome research: The study of unrepresentative samples? *Journal of Traumatic Stress, 18*(5), 425–436.

Tarrier, N., Pilgrim, H., Sommerfield, C., Faragher, B., Reynolds, M., Graham, E., et al. (1999). A randomized trial of cognitive therapy and imaginal exposure in the treatment of chronic posttraumatic stress disorder. *Journal of Consulting & Clinical Psychology, 67*(1), 13–8.

Taylor, S., Thordarson, D. S., Maxfield, L., Fedoroff, I. C., Lovell, K., & Ogrodniczuk, J. (2003). Comparative efficacy, speed, and adverse effects of three PTSD treatments: Exposure therapy, EMDR, and relaxation training. *Journal of Consulting & Clinical Psychology, 71*(2), 330–338.

van der Kolk, B. A., Pelcovitz, D., Roth, S., Mandel, F. S., McFarlane, A., & Herman, J. L. (1996). Dissociation, somatization, and affect dysregulation: The complexity of adaptation of trauma. *American Journal of Psychiatry, 153*(7 Suppl), 83–93.

Wolpe, J. (1958). *Psychotherapy by reciprocal inhibition*. Stanford, CA: Stanford University Press.

Zlotnick, C., Shea, T. M., Rosen, K., Simpson, E., Mulrenin, K., Begin, A., et al. (1997). An affect-management group for women with posttraumatic stress disorder and histories of childhood sexual abuse. *Journal of Traumatic Stress, 10*(3), 425–436.

Chapter 18
Is There Room for Safety Behaviors in Exposure Therapy for Anxiety Disorders?

Michael J. Telch and Cynthia Luethcke Lancaster

Dr. Michael Telch received his Ph.D. from Stanford University. He is currently Professor of Psychology, and Director of the Laboratory for the Study of Anxiety Disorders, and former Director of the Clinical Psychology program at the University of Texas at Austin. He is a fellow of the Association for Psychological Science and the American Association for the Advancement of Preventative Psychology. Dr. Telch is internationally recognized for his scientific research on the nature and treatment of anxiety-related disorders. He has served as a scientific advisor to the National Institute of Mental Health's Anxiety Disorders Education Program and has served on the National Institute of Mental Health's Panic Disorder Education Program. He has published over 130 research articles and book chapters focusing primarily on the nature and treatment of anxiety-related disorders and is the recipient of numerous private, state, and national research grants.

M.J. Telch (✉) • C.L. Lancaster
Laboratory for the Study of Anxiety Disorders,
The University of Texas at Austin, Austin, USA
e-mail: telch@austin.utexas.edu

P. Neudeck and H.-U. Wittchen (eds.), *Exposure Therapy: Rethinking the Model – Refining the Method*, DOI 10.1007/978-1-4614-3342-2_18,

Cynthia Luethcke Lancaster is currently a graduate student working under the direction of Dr. Michael Telch in the Laboratory for the Study of Anxiety Disorders at the University of Texas at Austin. She received her undergraduate degree at Trinity University, and worked as a research assistant at the University of Texas Health Science Center at San Antonio studying the etiology and treatment of combat-related post-traumatic stress disorder. Her current research interests include investigating mechanisms and augmentation strategies for cognitive behavioral treatments for anxiety disorders.

18.1 Introduction

Exposure-based treatments are often regarded as one of the major success stories in the treatment of anxiety disorders (McNally, 2007). Encouraging patients to confront anxiety-provoking cues is a central element in most empirically supported treatments for anxiety disorders. Consequently, it only makes sense for clinical scientists to investigate procedural factors that influence the efficacy of exposure treatments. One procedural issue that has recently become the focus of considerable research and some controversy is whether to make safety behaviors available during exposure treatment (Rachman, Radomsky, & Shafran, 2008). The overarching aim of this chapter is to provide an up-to-date report on the status of safety behavior research in the context of exposure therapy and to provide clinicians specific recommendations for (a) The clinical assessment of safety behaviors; (b) strategies for helping patients withdraw anxiogenic safety behaviors; and (c) strategies for utilizing safety behaviors to enhance exposure treatments.

18.2 Nature of Safety Behaviors Observed in Anxiety Patients

What are safety behaviors? Human beings are hardwired to engage in protective actions when faced with perceived threats. Examples of such actions include wearing seat belts while driving in cars, wearing warm clothing when venturing outside on a winter's day in Chicago, and using condoms with a sexual partner. However, engaging in such protective actions when no real threat exists may actually fuel anxiety disorders and may even play a role in the maintenance of other forms of psychopathology such as insomnia (Harvey, 2002) and pain-related disorders (Tang et al., 2007).

Because this chapter focuses on the role of safety behaviors as they pertain to exposure therapy for anxiety disorders, we focus on a specific subset of safety behaviors—namely those that fulfill no actual safety function. In his seminal paper on safety behaviors in anxiety, Salkovskis (1991) defined safety behaviors as, "overt or covert avoidance of feared outcomes that is carried out within a specific situation." This definition has several limitations. First, it fails to distinguish between safety behaviors that are adaptive such as the wearing of seat belts and those that maintain or even exacerbate anxiety disorder symptoms such as the repeated checking of one's pulse when anxious. Second, it fails to capture a central feature of the safety behaviors observed in anxiety patients—namely the erroneous or exaggerated nature of the threats that the safety behaviors are presumably protecting the individual from.

In their excellent review of safety behaviors in anxiety disorders, Helbig-Lang and Petermann (2010) define safety behaviors as dysfunctional emotion regulation strategies. Borrowing from the early conceptualizations of anxiety-maintaining behaviors in OCD (Rachman and Hodgson, 1980), they subdivide these dysfunctional emotion regulation strategies as either serving a preventive function (preventing future anxiety increases) or a restorative function (impeeding anxiety in a feared situation). One limitation of defining safety behaviors as dysfunctional emotion regulation strategies is that it assumes that the motivation underlying safety behaviors is *always* to reduce or prevent anxiety. While this is often the case, many patients use safety behaviors to prevent, escape from, or lessen the severity of a threat other than anxiety. Examples include the claustrophobic who avoids elevators out of concern that they will be trapped, or the health anxiety patient who avoids caffeine out of concern it will bring on a fatal cardiac event.

In an attempt to address these limitations, we define anxiety-related safety behaviors as *unnecessary actions taken to prevent, escape from, or reduce the severity of a perceived threat.*

18.3 Research on Safety Behaviors

18.3.1 Nature and Phenomenology of Safety Behaviors Observed in Anxiety Patients

Research into the nature of anxiety-related safety behaviors has revealed several important findings deserving of mention. An important finding described by Salkovskis (1991) was that patients tend to engage in safety behaviors that are conceptually linked to their perceived threats. The astute clinician working with anxiety patients has probably observed this phenomenon play out many times. Examples include the cardiac anxiety patient who feels compelled to check his pulse, and avoid exercise, caffeine, and stressful encounters for fear of bringing on a cardiac event; the social phobic who contributes minimally to a group discussion for fear of sounding stupid; and the agoraphobic patient who feels compelled to carry rescue medication in their purse or pocket in the event of a panic attack. Table 18.1 (see below) presents common threats perceived by anxiety patients and the corresponding safety behaviors linked to those threats.

While there is no universally accepted taxonomy for safety behaviors, there have been attempts to use factor-analytic methods to categorize the multitude of anxiety-related safety behaviors. Because safety behaviors are linked to specific perceived threats, and most of the major anxiety disorders can be distinguished on the basis of patient's perceived core threat, it is not surprising that the studies aimed at subtyping

Table 18.1 Examples of safety behaviors and their related threats across anxiety disorders

Anxiety complaint	Perceived threat	Safety behavior(s)
Fear of public speaking	Trembling in front of audience	– Gripping both sides of the podium – Ingest beta blocker before talk
Panic disorder	Losing control of one's vehicle while driving	– Avoid driving – Carrying rescue medication in one's pocket or purse
Post-traumatic stress disorder	Being attacked while walking down the street	– Avoid going out at night – Carrying a weapon in one's pocket or purse
Agoraphobia	Having a panic attack while in the grocery store	– Avoid grocery stores – Have a companion accompany one to the store
Obsessive–compulsive disorder	Slitting husband's throat while he is sleeping	– Locking up all knives and scissors before bed – Avoid arguments with husband
Relationship worry	Rejection from partner	– Reassurance seeking – Checking whereabouts of partner
Acrophobia	Plummet to one's death	– Avoid high places – Tightly grip railing while standing on balcony
Sitophobia	Choke while eating	– Avoid swallowing pills – Pureeing food before eating it

safety behaviors have been conducted separately for several of the major anxiety disorders. Kamphuis and Telch (1998) factor analyzed safety behavior data from 105 panic disorder/agoraphobia patients recruited from the community. Based on their analyses of the 50 Items of the Texas Safety Maneuver Scale (TSMS; Kamphuis & Telch, 1998), five interpretable factors emerged. These five factors were named (a) classic agoraphobic avoidance—such as avoidance of crowded stores, and avoidance of public transportation; (b) relaxation techniques—such as meditation or yoga to relieve anxiety; (c) avoidance of stressful encounters—such as arguments with loved ones or stress at work; (d) avoidance of somatic perturbations—such as avoidance of caffeine or rigorous exercise; and (e) use of distraction techniques—such as listening to music, or staying busy in order to avoid anxiety/panic.

18.3.2 Role of Safety Behaviors in Anxiety Disorders

There is a growing consensus that safety behaviors play a pivotal role in the maintenance of anxiety disorders. For example, in Clark and Wells' (1995) cognitive theory of social anxiety disorder, safety behaviors are assumed to play a causal role in the maintenance of the disorder. Support for this assertion comes from experiments showing that socially anxious people are more likely to experience heightened anxiety, perform more poorly in social situations, and be perceived more poorly by others when they use safety behaviors relative to when they do not (McManus, Sacadura, & Clark, 2008). Use of safety behaviors may paradoxically bring about negative evaluation from others as in the case of the socially anxious person who converses minimally in the group due to fear of saying something stupid only to have others view him as boring or disinterested. Indeed, a recent study demonstrated that socially anxious individuals who were instructed to reduce safety behaviors elicited a more positive evaluation from a conversation partner than controls who were instructed not to reduce safety behaviors; and this effect was mediated by a greater increase in social approach behaviors among those in the safety behavior fading group (Taylor & Alden, 2011).

The anxiety exacerbating effects of safety behaviors are not limited to social anxiety. Deacon and Maack (2008) instructed undergraduates with both low and high levels of contamination fear to begin using contamination-related safety behaviors (e.g., carrying instant hand sanitizer at all times, using disinfecting wipes to clean surfaces at home, and washing hands after touching any object that may be contaminated). Assessment after a full week of performing safety behaviors revealed that both groups experienced comparable increases in contamination obsessions and washing compulsions, estimation of the threat of contaminated objects, and behavioral avoidance and anxiety experienced during contamination-related behavioral approach tests. These findings, although correlational in nature, are consistent with the hypothesis that increased safety behaviors are associated with increased anxiety.

In a recent experiment, Olatunji, Etzel, Tomarken, Ciesielski, and Deacon (2011) had undergraduates either monitor or monitor and perform a series of health-related safety behaviors (e.g., checking body temperature, carrying antibacterial hand sanitizer, checking lymph nodes by palpitation, avoiding touching public door handles, and monitoring pulse rate). After 3 weeks, those assigned to the safety behavior group displayed significantly higher health anxiety questionnaire scores, lower behavioral approach scores on a contamination-related behavioral approach test, and a heightened perceived risk of contracting a cold, the flu, or mononucleosis relative to those in the monitoring-only control group. These findings provide the first experimental demonstration that safety behaviors may play a causal role in health anxiety.

18.3.3 How Might Safety Behaviors Interfere with the Effects of Exposure Therapy?

The processes governing the effects of safety behaviors on the maintenance of pathological anxiety may overlap significantly with the processes governing how safety behaviors impact fear reduction during exposure therapy. First, safety behaviors increase self-focused attention, which has been linked to anxiety maintenance (Wells, 1990). Second, as suggested by Salkovskis (1991), engaging in safety behaviors in the face of phobic threats may prevent the disconfirmation of the perceived threat through a process in which the patient misattributes their safety to the use of the safety behavior thus leaving their perception of threat intact. For example, the flying phobic who repeatedly checks the weather prior to departure might misattribute her safe flight to her diligent weather scanning rather than the inherent safety of air travel. Alternative disconfirmation hypotheses have been put forth by Telch and colleagues who have suggested that safety behaviors may exert an anxiety-maintaining function by reducing one's available cognitive resources to process disconfirming information (Sloan & Telch, 2002). Since the utilization of safety behaviors requires the individual to allocate attention to the availability and execution of safety strategies, less attentional resources are available for processing threat-relevant information. It is also possible that safety-seeking behaviors undermine one's sense of mastery to cope with perceived threats when the safety aids are no longer available. For example, carrying rescue medication to cope with the fear of having a panic attack may inadvertently undermine patients' perceived self-efficacy to manage in situations when the medication is unavailable.

Up to now, our focus on potential pathways through which safety behaviors maintain anxiety disorders has been on cognitive (i.e., appraisal and attentional) processes. However, it is quite possible that safety-seeking behavior maintains pathological anxiety through basic alarm processes independent of higher-level cognitive processes. For instance, Telch and his colleagues (Sloan & Telch, 2002; Telch & Plasencia, 2010) have speculated that through evolution, certain protective actions (e.g., checking for escape routes) may have acquired the capacity to transmit implicit signals of threat thus keeping alarm processes active.

18.4 Research on Safety Behaviors and Exposure Therapy

In the last decade, significant experimental work has emerged on safety behaviors and their potential impact on anxiety disorder patients undergoing exposure therapy. The work described below can be broadly classified as addressing one of the following four central questions: (a) Does making safety behaviors available during exposure therapy reduce its effectiveness? (b) Are the potential negative effects of safety behaviors during exposure therapy a result of their mere availability or their actual use? (c) Does the systematic fading of safety behaviors during exposure therapy improve therapeutic outcome? (d) Under what conditions do safety behaviors interfere with exposure therapy?

18.4.1 Does Making Safety Behaviors Available During Exposure Therapy Reduce Its Effectiveness?

There have been 11 published studies directly investigating this question. In each of the studies listed in Table 18.2, participants were randomly allocated to in vivo exposure treatment with safety aids made available or the same exposure treatment without access to safety aids. Overall, these studies manipulated a wide variety of safety behaviors, which varied according to the presenting anxiety problem being addressed during exposure. For example, in studies of in vivo exposure treatment for agoraphobia (De Silva & Rachman, 1984; Rachman, Craske, Tallman, & Solyom, 1986), participants in the safety behavior group were encouraged to leave the feared situation whenever their anxiety became too high (i.e., escape as a safety behavior). In the case of exposure to enclosure in a small chamber for claustrophobia, safety behaviors included communicating with someone outside the chamber through a two-way radio, and opening a small window in the chamber to let in fresh air (Deacon, Sy, Lickel, & Nelson, 2010; Powers, Smits, & Telch, 2004; Sloan & Telch, 2002; Sy, Dixon, Lickel, Nelson, & Deacon, 2011). Safety behaviors used for a study of social anxiety included avoiding eye contact and pauses in speech during a conversation with a stranger (McManus et al., 2008). For exposure for fear of spiders or snakes, participants were allowed to perform safety behaviors such as confronting the feared animal while wearing gloves (Bandura, Jeffery, & Wright, 1974; Hood, Antony, Koerner, & Monson, 2010; Milosevic & Radomsky, 2008). Finally, in studies investigating exposure for contamination-related fears, participants in the safety behavior group were given hygienic wipes to use after exposure to a contaminate (Rachman, Shafran, Radomsky, & Zysk, 2011; Van den Hout, Engelhard, Toffolo, & van Uijen, 2011).

As seen in Table 18.2, making safety aids available during exposure led to significantly less fear reduction relative to exposure treatment without safety aids in four of the studies (Hood et al., 2010; McManus et al., 2008; Powers et al., 2004; Sloan & Telch, 2002); whereas seven studies showed no differences in fear reduction as a function of the availability of safety aids (Deacon et al., 2010: de Silva &

Table 18.2 Studies experimentally examining the effects of making one or more safety behaviors available during treatment

Study	Anxiety problem	Outcome
De Silva and Rachman (1984)	Agoraphobia	No interference[1]
Rachman et al. (1986)	Agoraphobia	No interference[1]
Sloan and Telch (2002)	Claustrophobia	Interfered with outcome
Powers et al. (2004)	Claustrophobia	Interfered with outcome
McManus et al. (2008)	Social phobia	Interfered with outcome
Milosevic and Radomsky (2008)	Snake phobia	No interference
Deacon et al. (2010)	Claustrophobia	No interference[2]
Hood et al. (2010)	Snake phobia	Interfered with outcome[3]
Rachman et al. (2011)	Contamination fear (OCD)	No interference[4]
Sy et al. (2011)	Claustrophobia	No interference[5]
Van den Hout et al. (2011)	Contamination fear (OCD)	No interference

[1]Low statistical power due to the small sample sizes per group may lack of group differences
[2]Safety behaviors were faded during the last two exposure trials
[3]Interference observed only at follow-up not at posttreatment
[4]Although there were no posttreatment differences in fear, disgust, or danger reduction between groups, exposure with safety behavior use produced greater reduction for feelings of contamination than exposure without safety behaviors
[5]Although there were no differences in fear reduction between groups, exposure with safety behavior use produced more improvement in self-efficacy and claustrophobic cognitions than exposure without safety behaviors

Rachman, 1984; Milosevic & Radomsky, 2008; Rachman et al., 1986; Rachman et al., 2011; Sy et al., 2011; Van den Hout et al., 2011).

Several factors may account for the failure to find exposure interference effects for safety behaviors in some studies. First, one study (Deacon et al., 2010) eliminated participants' use of safety behaviors during the last two trials thus confounding safety behavior availability with safety behavior fading. Second, in the early null-finding studies by Rachman (de Silva & Rachman, 1984; Rachman et al., 1986), small samples (less than 10 per group) may have accounted for the failure to find interference effects for the safety behavior groups. Finally, as noted by Hood et al. (2010), the failure to find exposure interference effects may be a function of the lack of congruence between the safety behaviors selected by the experimenters and those used naturally by anxiety patients.

18.4.2 Are the Potential Negative Effects of Safety Behaviors During Exposure Therapy a Result of Their Mere Availability or Their Actual Use?

We know that not all anxiety patients actually use the safety aids that are available to them. For example, many panic patients carry rescue medication with them but do not actually ingest it and many social phobics who rehearse excuses for leaving a social situation early do not actually enact them. Consequently, disentangling the effects of making safety aids available to patients versus the effects of having patients actually use them has important implications for clinical practice. An experiment to

Table 18.3 Experimental studies examining the effects of fading safety behaviors during exposure treatment

Study	Anxiety problem	Outcome
Wells et al. (1995)	Social phobia	Enhanced outcome
Morgan & Raffle (1999)	Social phobia	Enhanced outcome
Salkovskis, Clark, Hackmann, Wells, and Gelder (1999)	Agoraphobia	Enhanced outcome
Kim (2005)	Social phobia	Enhanced outcome
Salkovskis, Hackmann, Wells, Gelder, and Clark (2006)	Agoraphobia	Enhanced outcome
Okajima and Sakano (2008)	Social phobia	Enhanced outcome
Taylor and Alden (2010)	Social phobia	Enhanced outcome
Taylor and Alden (2011)	Social phobia	Enhanced outcome

address this issue was conducted in our laboratory (Powers et al., 2004). In one condition, threat-relevant safety aids were made available to claustrophobic participants with instructions to try and refrain from using the aids if at all possible. In a second condition, the same aids were made available but subjects were instructed to use at least one of the aids during each of the six exposure trials. In a third control condition, safety aids were not made available. This manipulation provided a direct examination of the effects of the perceived availability of safety aids without the confounding effects of participants' actual use of the safety aids. Results of the study replicated the earlier findings of Sloan and Telch (2002) in showing that making safety aids available during exposure treatment markedly reduced its efficacy (i.e., 94% significantly improved when safety aids were not made available versus 44% significantly improved when safety aids were made available). More importantly, the study also found no significant added disruptive effect in the group that actually utilized the safety aids relative to those that had them available but did not use them. The finding that safety aids do not need to be actually used in order to exert their detrimental effects is consistent with countless clinical observations of anxiety patients carrying rescue medication or other safety aids without actually using them. However, it should be noted that a recent replication study of Powers et al. was not able to reproduce these findings (Sy et al., 2011).

18.4.3 Does the Systematic Fading of Safety Behaviors During Exposure Therapy Improve Therapeutic Outcome?

This question has been addressed in eight separate experiments (see Table 18.3). Note that unlike in the previous group of experiments in which the focus was on the systematic introduction of safety aids (yes versus no), the manipulation in this group of experiments involves the systematic fading of safety behaviors during treatment (yes versus no). In this group of experiments, participants were randomly allocated to receive either exposure treatment with the fading of their safety behaviors or exposure treatment in which they were allowed to continue using their safety behaviors. Results across all nine studies were consistent in showing that fading safety behaviors lead to significantly better outcome than exposure without safety behavior fading (see Table 18.3).

Table 18.4 Differential Predictions of the five proposed hypotheses on how safety behaviors interfere with the effects of exposure treatments

Hypotheses	Prediction of between-group differences
Misattribution	SB-Block, SB-No Block<Exp - No SB
Threat transmission	SB-Block, SB-No Block<Exp - No SB
Context learning	SB-Block, SB-No Block<Exp - No SB
Self-efficacy	SB-Block, SB-No Block<Exp - No SB
Threat disconfirmation	SB-Block<SB-No Block=Exp - No SB

18.4.4 Research Investigating Mechanisms Through Which Safety Behaviors Interfere with the Effects of Exposure Therapy

As discussed earlier, there is much theoretical speculation as to how safety behaviors may interfere with the effects of exposure therapy. Both cognitive (Salkovskis, 1991; Sloan & Telch, 2002; Kim, 2005) and noncognitive (Sloan & Telch, 2002) mechanisms have been suggested. A common feature of several of the theories is that safety behaviors interfere with exposure therapy when the safety behaviors in question block or at least attenuate the central change process of threat disconfirmation, which is believed to be a central mechanism through which exposure therapy exerts its beneficial effects (Foa & Kozak, 1986).

A recent experiment in our laboratory investigated the role of threat disconfirmation in exposure therapy, using a more direct experimental manipulation. Telch and Plasencia (2010) tested whether safety behaviors interfere with exposure therapy by blocking the processing of corrective, threat-disconfirming information. They randomized 99 spider phobic subjects to one of four exposure conditions: (a) exposure therapy allowing subjects to use a safety aid that effectively blocked the movement of the spider (threat disconfirmation blocked); (b) exposure therapy allowing subjects to use a safety aid that did not interfere with the movement of the spider (threat disconfirmation not blocked); (c) exposure therapy without the use of a safety aid; and (d) measurement only control. Subjects in each of the three exposure conditions received six 3-min exposure trials conducted in one session.

The safety aid used in both safety aid groups was identical and consisted of a plastic transparent box secured to the end of a broomstick. During each exposure trial in the threat disconfirmation block condition, subjects stood within 12 in. of the spider while the experimenter positioned the safety aid over the spider so that it trapped the spider within the confines of the small box. The experimenter then handed the subject the safety aid and left the room for the full 3 min duration of the trial. This prevented any significant movement of the spider but allowed the subject to see the spider clearly at all times. Subjects in the threat disconfirmation no-block condition underwent an identical procedure with the exception that the experimenter positioned the safety aid between the subject and the spider, which allowed the spider to move freely in all directions except straight ahead. Subjects in the exposure—no aid condition was provided identical exposure treatment but without the use of the safety aid. Table 18.4 provides differential predictions of five proposed hypotheses for how safety behaviors may interfere with the effects of treatment.

Results of the experiment (see Fig. 18.1) were consistent with predictions from the threat-disconfirmation hypothesis by showing that exposure treatment was only

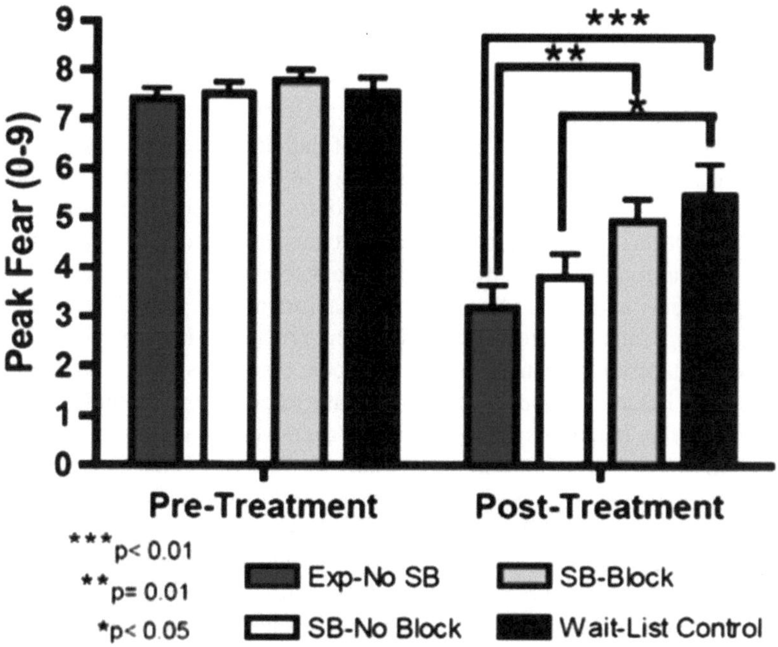

Fig. 18.1 Peak fear during the behavioral approach task at pre- and post-treatment by treatment condition

undermined in the safety aid condition in which the threat-relevant information was blocked. Note that subjects who underwent exposure treatment while using a safety aid that prevented the processing of threat-relevant information (i.e., movement of the spider) were not significantly different at posttreatment relative to subjects who received no treatment! In contrast, subjects who underwent exposure treatment in the SB-No Block condition showed significantly lower fear relative to wait-list controls and comparable levels of fear to those who received exposure treatment without safety aids. These findings are consistent with the hypothesis that safety aids undermine the efficacy of exposure treatment when the safety behavior blocks the processing of threat-disconfirming information. Moreover, the findings are at odds with other proposed mechanisms governing the deleterious effects of safety behaviors in treatment including misattribution, context learning, and threat transmission (see Table 18.4).

18.5 Clinical Issues Relevant to Safety Behaviors and Exposure Therapy

18.5.1 Assessment

Despite the significant interest in safety behaviors and exposure therapy, far less attention has been given to the assessment of safety behaviors. This is unfortunate since the successful fading of safety behaviors during exposure therapy hinges on the clinician being able to identify the range of specific safety behaviors used by each patient. Honing one's skills for assessing safety behaviors is also important because we have found that patients are often unaware of at least some of their safety behaviors.

Prior to performing a formal assessment of patients' safety behaviors, we typically provide education about safety behaviors in the larger context of educating patients about the nature and treatment of anxiety. Safety behaviors are defined as unnecessary actions (either overt or covert) that are performed by the patient in order to avoid, escape from, or lessen the severity of a perceived threat. We have found that providing patients education about safety behaviors and their anxiety–maintaining effects is an important first step in the assessment process. Education takes the forms of didactic instruction and instructional handouts that focus on: (a) the nature and types of safety behaviors displayed; (b) how safety behaviors become strengthened; and (c) how safety behaviors may maintain or even worsen anxiety symptoms.

We often found that patients are more likely to grasp the concept of safety behaviors sooner by first providing examples of safety behaviors that are unrelated to those used by the patient. After the patient has grasped the safety behavior concept, we then turn our attention to helping the patient understand how safety behaviors are strengthened through a process of negative reinforcement (e.g., checking pulse becomes paired with the absence of a heart attack and thus anxiety relief). Next, we focus on helping the patient to see how safety behaviors may contribute to the maintenance of anxiety. Several possible explanations are offered (with examples) to help the patient become more aware of how safety behaviors may fuel anxiety and even interfere with the effects of treatment. One explanation emphasizes how safety behaviors may maintain anxiety by strengthening the patient's belief that they could not have coped with the feared situation without the use of the safety aid. Also, patients learn that engaging in safety behaviors may shift their attention toward the self and their behavior thus preventing or at least interfering with threat disconfirmation—the process of learning that the threat was a false alarm. A third explanation emphasizes how performing a protective action in the absence of any real threat may inadvertently "trick" the brain into keeping the alarm system in danger mode even though there is no actual threat.

We use four primary sources of data to construct the patient's safety behavior profile. These include: (a) data from interviews with patient and significant others; (b) data from psychometric scales; (c) data collected during direct in vivo observation of the patient; and (d) data collected by the patient using daily self-monitoring forms.

18.5.1.1 Interviewing Strategies

The use of interview probes with the patient is one important step for identifying anxiety-maintaining safety behaviors. We recommend starting with open–ended probes such as, "tell me about the things you feel compelled to do in order to feel more safe/reduce your anxiety in this feared situation," or "tell me about any things you feel you need to do mentally (in your head) to feel more safe in this feared situation." In the event that the patient is unable to provide useful information, the clinician should switch over to more specific probes such as: Are there any things you have to carry with you to feel more safe in the situation such as medication, phone numbers, water, etc? Or, *Do you find yourself trying to distract yourself while you're in the feared situation? Do you find yourself avoiding looking people directly in the eyes when you talk to them? Do you repeatedly tell yourself that everything is going to be okay?*

To help confirm that the actions described by the patient are serving as maladaptive safety behaviors, it is useful to probe as to whether the patient forecasts greater anxiety if they were prevented from performing the safety behavior in question. Although it should be noted that patients differ markedly with respect to insight about their safety behaviors. For some, a safety behavior may become so automatic that the patient does not recognize that their actions constitute a safety behavior.

When possible, it is often useful to interview the patient's significant other to obtain data about possible safety behaviors performed outside the therapy session. The probes already described for use with the patient can also be used with their significant others.

18.5.1.2 Assessing Safety Behaviors Using Psychometric Instruments

The administration of established self-report questionnaires can be a useful and cost-effective method for obtaining data regarding patients' use of safety behaviors. Several instruments are currently available for assessing avoidance. Examples include the Mobility Inventory for use with panic disorder/agoraphobia patients (Chambless, Caputo, Jasin, Gracely, & Williams, 1985), the Liebowitz Social Anxiety Scale (Liebowitz, 1987) or the Social Phobia and Anxiety Inventory (Turner, Beidel, Dancu, & Stanley, 1989) for use with patients presenting with social anxiety, and the Yale–Brown Obsessive Compulsive Scale (Goodman et al., 1989) for use with patients presenting with OCD. Unfortunately, these instruments are limited in large part to the avoidance domain and do not assess other classes of safety behaviors (e.g., carrying of rescue medication, reassurance seeking, checking, etc.).

There are several self-report questionnaires currently available that assess the full range of safety behaviors for several major anxiety disorders. Our group at the University of Texas developed the TSMS (Kamphuis & Telch, 1998). This 50-item scale originally developed and validated for patients presenting with panic disorder with or without agoraphobia provides a comprehensive listing of possible safety behaviors typically exhibited in panic disorder with and without agoraphobia. Items were inductively generated based on the following a priori domains: (a) use of companions, (b) use of distraction, (c) use of checking and scanning, (d) avoidance of stress and emotions, (e) avoidance of activities, and (f) focus on escape. Each item is rated on a five-point scale ranging from "never" to "always." Psychometric data on the scale revealed high internal consistency for each of the five interpretable factors and preliminary evidence to support the construct validity of the scale, namely higher scores on the TSMS were inversely correlated with patients' perceived self-efficacy to cope with panic episodes (Kamphuis & Telch, 1998).

Several self-report instruments are available for assessing safety behaviors typically observed in social anxiety disorder. The Safety Behaviors Questionnaire (SBQ; Taylor & Alden, 2010) is a list of 20 items taken from the Social Behaviour Questionnaire developed by Clark, Wells, Hackman, Butler, & Fennell, 1994. The patient rates each safety behavior on a 9-point scale ranging from not at all to all the time. Preliminary psychometric evaluation of the scale indicated acceptable levels of internal consistency; no information on test–retest reliability or discriminant validity were reported (Taylor & Alden, 2010). The Social Phobia safety Behaviors Scale (Pinto-Gouveia, Cunha, & do Céu Salvador, 2003) consists of 15 items each rated on a four-point scale ranging from never to usually. The scale also includes two items in which the patient has the opportunity to add other safety behaviors not included in the list of 15. Preliminary psychometric data indicates that the SPSBS possesses good internal consistency, acceptable test–retest reliability, and distinguishes general social anxiety disorder patients from other anxiety disorders and normal controls (Pinto-Gouveia et al., 2003).

Fear of contamination is a commonly reported threat in OCD. A 27-item self-report checklist for assessing safety behaviors among a sample of participants displaying contamination fear was developed by Deacon and Maack (2008). Sample items included carrying antibacterial sanitizer at all times, avoiding public restrooms, and disinfecting telephone receivers at home. No psychometric data were reported for the scale.

Although not specifically described as a safety behavior scale, the Cardiac Anxiety Questionnaire (CAQ; Eifert et al., 2000) is an 18-item scale for assessing heart-focused anxiety. All items are rated on a 5-point scale ranging from never to always. Close inspection of the scale reveals that many of the items (9 of 18) describe overt safety behaviors (e.g., I avoid physical exertion, I check my pulse) or covert safety behaviors (e.g., I pay attention to my heart). Psychometric data from the CAQ are quite promising and suggest that the scale has high internal consistency, assesses three primary factors (fear, avoidance, and threat-focused attention), and possesses good discriminant validity.

18.5.1.3 In Vivo Assessment of Safety Behaviors

The fact that many safety behaviors are observable makes it possible to assess safety behaviors using in vivo assessment methods. Direct assessment of safety behaviors as they occur has several advantages, most important of which are the increased fidelity associated with the use of direct behavioral measures, as well as the increased ecological validity associated with assessments that are obtained in the actual contexts that trigger the behavior in question. These advantages must be weighed against the increased costs and logistical challenges associated with in vivo assessments. Examples of in vivo assessments include behavioral challenges (sometimes referred to as behavioral approach tests). These can sometimes be conducted in the clinic as in the example of having a panic patient perform a 2-min hyperventilation challenge while the therapist carefully looks for evidence of safety behaviors before, during, and immediately after the challenge. In vivo assessment of safety behaviors can and should be routinely assessed during exposure therapy. In addition to recording the presence of any observable safety behaviors performed during exposure treatment, the therapist should also query the patient as to what if any covert safety behaviors are being used. In our experience, in vivo assessment often reveals safety behaviors that are missed by self-report scales or clinical interview methods.

18.5.1.4 Assessing Safety Behaviors Using Daily Self-monitoring

One additional method for assessing safety behaviors involves the daily self-recording of safety behaviors during the course of treatment. This method has the advantage of allowing the self-monitoring form to be individually tailored to the patient's safety behavior profile. It also has the advantage of providing both the patient and therapist with ongoing feedback related to the patient's use of safety behaviors throughout the course of treatment. We typically will use data collected from the other three safety behavior assessment methods to design each patient's safety behavior self-monitoring form.

18.5.2 Clinical Strategies for Effectively Fading Safety Behaviors During Exposure Therapy

Based on the compelling evidence presented earlier in this chapter (see also Helbig-Lang & Petermann, 2010 for an excellent review of the current status of research on anxiety-related safety behaviors), we can safely say that fading the use of safety behaviors over the course of exposure-based treatments is an important augmentation strategy for enhancing the efficacy of both exposure treatment and cognitive therapy. Although these findings are relatively potent (large effect size) and very robust (perfect agreement across studies), they fail to provide the specific procedural prescriptions for fading anxiety-related safety behaviors. In this section, we offer specific procedural guidelines to assist clinicians in integrating safety behavior fading as an important component of exposure therapy for anxiety disorders.

18.5.2.1 Step 1: Conduct a Thorough Assessment of the Patient's Core Threats

Because safety behaviors are *threat-driven*, and conceptually linked to the specific core threats as perceived by the patient (Salkovskis, 1991;1996), it is critically important that the therapist conduct a thorough assessment of the patients' core threats prior to proceeding with exposure-based treatment. Clinicians often assume incorrectly that patients with the same anxiety diagnosis share similar threat-appraisal profiles. This is just not the case! Although some useful hypotheses might be entertained as a result of knowing the patient's diagnosis, further assessment is needed to fully understand the idiosyncratic threat profile of each anxiety patient. For example, a social anxiety patient who fears blushing in front of his peers and supervisors during a work presentation is a far cry from the social anxiety patient who is concerned about appearing stupid in the same situation. There are now a host of cognitive appraisal scales that can be helpful in assisting the clinician in obtaining an accurate case conceptualization of patients' core threats. Examples include the Panic Appraisal Inventory for panic patients (Telch, Brouillard, Telch, Agras, & Taylor, 1989), the Appraisal of Social Concerns Scale for patients with social anxiety (Telch et al., 2004); the Post-Traumatic Cognitions Questionnaire for patients with PTSD (Foa, Ehlers, Clark, Tolin, & Orsillo, 1999); the Obsessional Beliefs Questionnaire (Woods, Tolin, & Abramowitz, 2004), and Thought–Action Fusion Scale (Rassin, Merckelbach, Muris, & Schmidt, 2001) for patients with OCD; and the Meta-worry Questionnaire (Wells, 2005) for patients presenting with generalized anxiety disorder.

18.5.2.2 Step 2: Provide a Compelling Rationale for the Importance of Fading Safety Behaviors

Most patients become quite apprehensive when the topic of fading safety behaviors is first broached. This is not surprising, since patients often perceived safety behaviors as being instrumental in preventing or managing their feared threats. Consequently, we recommend that the therapist revisit the educational module focusing on the role of safety behaviors in maintaining pathological anxiety and review some of the possible ways in which safety behaviors might slow down their progress. Next, the therapist reviews—at a level appropriate for the patient—the current scientific evidence showing that exposure therapy leads to greater improvement when the patient is encouraged to eliminate safety behaviors during treatment. At this point, patients often respond positively to therapists' probes such as, "*can you take a stab at telling me why treatment works better when one fades out their safety behaviors as part of the treatment?*" Most patients find it quite easy to grasp the idea of "*using a crutch*" and how that might undermine their sense of self-confidence. To further bolster the credibility of the safety behavior-fading procedure, we will often have the patient conduct a behavioral experiment in which they perform a fear-inducing activity such as a voluntary hyperventilation challenge while performing one or more safety behaviors e.g., clutching a chair. Then we have the patient alternate between exposure trials while performing one or more of their safety behaviors and exposure trials without performing their safety behaviors.

18.5.2.3 Step 3: Conduct a Thorough Assessment of the Patient's Safety Behavior Profile

Although obvious, it is hard to proceed effectively in the fading of safety behaviors without completing a through evaluation of the patient's profile of safety behaviors. Earlier in this chapter, we reviewed the four major assessment strategies for obtaining an accurate profile of the patient's safety behavior profile. Using these strategies in combination with a thorough assessment of the patient's core threat (see Step 1) will likely increase your success in helping your patients eliminate anxiety-maintaining safety behaviors.

18.5.2.4 Step 4: Construct a Safety Behavior Fading Hierarchy

Most clinicians working with anxiety disorders—particularly those using behavioral or cognitive behavioral techniques, utilize fear hierarchies as part of their treatment. Constructing a fear hierarchy for fading safety behaviors bears a striking resemblance to the fear hierarchies that are often constructed during exposure-based treatments. However, instead of grading the patient's feared situations, the clinician and patient work together to construct a hierarchy of the patient's current safety behaviors from data collected earlier during the safety behavior profile assessment. During this step, we have found it helpful to have the patient record each of their safety behaviors on separate index cards and then have them place the cards in order from "*least difficult to eliminate*" to "*most difficult to eliminate.*" For those patients who have difficulty with the concept of rating "fading difficulty," we ask them instead to rate separately how anxious they would become if they could not perform each safety behavior.

18.5.2.5 Step 5: Make Sure the Patient Understands that the Elimination of a Safety Aid May Produce a "Temporary" Increase in Their Anxiety When They First Confront Their Fear Without the Safety Behavior

Because it is common for patients to experience heightened anxiety when first attempting to jettison their safety behaviors, the therapist should prepare the patient for this common reaction. However, be sure to inform the patient that their initial increase in anxiety upon eliminating one of their safety aids will soon be followed by an increase in their confidence to handle fear-provoking situations and a significant reduction in their anxiety symptoms.

18.5.2.6 Step 6. The Selection of Safety Behavior Fading Targets Should Be Done Collaboratively

Where to start on the safety behavior hierarchy is guided by the therapist with significant input from the patient. Several factors should be considered in the selection of safety behavior targets. These include the patient's level of anxiety and distress tolerance, as well as the types of safety behaviors used by the patient. In cases where patients are using both overt and covert safety behaviors, we usually begin fading the overt safety behaviors before tackling the patient's mental (covert) ones.

18.5.2.7 Step 7. Practice Safety Behavior Fading in Session Prior to Assigning Safety Behavior Fading Homework

Having the patient practice safety behavior fading in session provides the therapist an opportunity to observe the patient and offer modeling and guided practice in the execution of the exposure trial without the use of the safety behavior. It also helps insure that the patient has not substituted some other aid or safety behavior for the one targeted for fading.

18.5.2.8 Step 8. Monitor the Patient's Anticipated and Actual Fear During Each Exposure Trial

During these in-session exposure trials, it is useful to collect data on the patient's pre-trial anticipated fear and peak fear experienced during the trial. These data help in the threat disconfirmation process by providing the patient evidence that their fear is actually declining despite eliminating the safety behavior. If feasible, monitoring the patient's heart rate during each exposure trial and providing them feedback that their physiologic fear reactions are extinguishing has also been shown to enhance the efficacy of exposure treatments (Telch, Valentiner, Ilai, Petruzzi, & Hehmsoth, 2000). In our experience, we have found this technique helpful across the broad spectrum of anxiety disorders.

18.5.2.9 Step 9. Assist the Patient in Reevaluating Their Core Threats During the Exposure Therapy Session

Our group (Kamphuis & Telch, 2000; Sloan & Telch, 2002) has shown that exposure therapy can be enhanced by using a technique we call guided threat focus and reappraisal. The technique consists of having the patient focus on their core threats during each exposure trial (e.g., I am going to lose control) and examining evidence pertaining to their core threats between trials (e.g., what evidence did you gather that time about the threat(s) you were concerned about?). When done in the context of safety behavior fading, the threat focus and reappraisal technique centers on the patient's perceived threats connected to eliminating their safety behaviors (e.g., what are you worried might happen if you don't carry that inhaler with you?). The strategic goal in using this technique is to structure the exposure session so as to provide maximum threat-disconfirming information to the patient.

18.5.2.10 Step 10. Assign Specific Home Practice in Safety Behavior Fading

Finally, to capitalize on the learning that has taken place during in-session exposure therapy, the patient is strongly encouraged to practice the same exposure with safety behavior fading exercise at home. Potential obstacles for complying with the home practice are elicited from the patient and possible solutions for overcoming these obstacles are discussed. Patients should be provided a monitoring form to track their progress in carrying out their safety behavior fading home practice.

18.5.3 Intentional Use of Safety Behaviors to Enhance Exposure Treatment

Up to now, this chapter has focused primarily on the detrimental effects of safety behaviors and how to eliminate them. However, as reviewed earlier in this chapter as well as the chapter by Koerner & Fracalanza, the patient's use of safety behaviors does not always interfere with treatment. In fact, Rachman and colleagues (Rachman et al., 2008) have argued that safety behaviors can sometimes be helpful in the treatment of anxiety patients. They describe what they refer to as the "*judicious use*" of safety behaviors during treatment and suggest that when used judiciously, safety behaviors may offer several advantages including: (a) increasing the acceptability and tolerability of the treatment thus leading to fewer treatment refusers and fewer treatment dropouts; (b) increasing patients' sense of control during treatment; (c) increasing patients' cooperation with the treatment; (d) facilitating the pacing of treatment; (e) extending the duration of exposure treatment; and (f) assisting the patient to absorb threat-disconfirming information.

18.5.3.1 What Constitutes Judicious Use?

What constitutes judicious use of safety behaviors remains somewhat speculative, although Rachman et al. (2008) offer several guidelines. With respect to dose and timing of use, they suggest that safety behaviors should be used sparingly, and introduced early in the treatment in order to reduce dropouts and increase the patient's sense of control and confidence. Safety behaviors can also be introduced later in therapy as a way to assist the patient in overcoming specific obstacles encountered during the course of treatment. Based on the consistent evidence reported earlier in this chapter, it is suggested that clinicians pay careful attention to the fading of safety behaviors over the course of treatment. The fading of safety behaviors not only enhances the patient's sense of mastery but also reduces the chance that patients will misattribute their success to the aid rather than their own efforts (Bandura et al., 1974). Finally, based on the recent findings of Telch and Plasencia (2010), clinicians should be careful not to allow the patient to use safety behaviors that might block or attenuate the processing of threat-disconfirming information during treatment. Instead, cognitive techniques such as guided threat focus and reappraisal (Kamphuis & Telch; 2000; Sloan & Telch, 2002) have been shown to facilitate fear reduction by enhancing the processing of threat-disconfirming information during exposure treatments.

We still have much to learn about safety behaviors and their effects on treatments for anxiety disorders. Future research will hopefully yield more effective strategies for the optimal use and fading of safety behaviors, as well as a deeper understanding of the underlying mechanisms governing the reduction of pathological fear.

References

Bandura, A., Jeffery, R. W., & Wright, C. L. (1974). Efficacy of participant modeling as a function of response induction aids. *Journal of Abnormal Psychology, 83*(1), 56–64.

Chambless, D. L., Caputo, G. C., Jasin, S. E., Gracely, E. J., & Williams, C. (1985). The mobility inventory for agoraphobia. *Behaviour Research and Therapy, 23*(1), 35–44.

Clark, D. M., & Wells, A. (1995). A cognitive model of social phobia. In R. G. Heimberg, M. Liebowitz, D. A. Hope, & F. R. Schneier (Eds.), *Social phobia: Diagnosis, assessment, and treatment* (pp. 69–93). New York: Guilford.

Clark, D. M., Wells, A., Hackman, A., Butler, G., & Fennell, M. J. U. (1994). *Social behaviour questionnaire*. Unpublished. Department of Psychiatry, University of Oxford, Warneford Hospital, Oxford, England.

Deacon, B., & Maack, D. J. (2008). The effects of safety behaviors on the fear of contamination: An experimental investigation. *Behaviour Research and Therapy, 46*(4), 537–547.

Deacon, B. J., Sy, J. T., Lickel, J. J., & Nelson, E. A. (2010). Does judicious use of safety behaviors improve the efficacy and acceptability of exposure therapy for claustrophobic fear? *Journal of Behavior Therapy and Experimental Psychiatry, 41*, 71–80.

De Silva, P., & Rachman, S. (1984). Does escape behavior strengthen agoraphobic avoidance? A preliminary study. *Behaviour Research and Therapy, 22*(1), 87–91.

Eifert, G. H., Thompson, R. N., Zvolensky, M. J., Edwards, K., Frazer, N. L., Haddad, J. W., et al. (2000). The cardiac anxiety questionnaire: Development and preliminary validity. *Behaviour Research and Therapy, 38*(10), 1039–1053.

Foa, E. B., Ehlers, A., Clark, D. M., Tolin, D. F., & Orsillo, S. M. (1999). The posttraumatic cognitions inventory (PTCI): Development and validation. *Psychological Assessment, 11*(3), 303.

Foa, E. B., & Kozak, M. J. (1986). Emotional processing of fear: Exposure to corrective information. *Psychological Bulletin, 99*(1), 20–35.

Goodman, W. K., Price, L. H., Rasmussen, S. A., Mazure, C., Fleischmann, R. L., Hill, C. L., & Charney, D. S. (1989). The Yale-Brown obsessive compulsive scale. *Archives of General Psychiatry, 46*(11), 1006–1011.

Harvey, A. G. (2002). Identifying safety behaviors in insomnia. *The Journal of nervous and mental disease, 190*(1), 16.

Helbig-Lang, S., & Petermann, F. (2010). Tolerate or eliminate? A systematic review on the effects of safety behavior across anxiety disorders. *Clinical Psychology Science and Practice, 17*, 218–233.

Hood, H. K., Antony, M. M., Koerner, N., & Monson, C. M. (2010). Effects of safety behaviors on fear reduction during exposure. *Behaviour Research and Therapy, 48*, 1161–1169.

Kamphuis, J. H., & Telch, M. J. (1998). Assessment of strategies to manage or avoid perceived threats among panic disorder patients: The Texas safety maneuver scale (TSMS). *Clinical Psychology & Psychotherapy, 5*(3), 177–186.

Kamphuis, J., & Telch, M. J. (2000). Effects of distraction and guided threat reappraisal on the reduction of claustrophobic fear. *Behaviour Research and Therapy, 38*(12), 1163–1181.

Kim, E. J. (2005). The effect of the decreased safety behaviors on anxiety and negative thoughts in social phobics. *Journal of Anxiety Disorders, 19*(1), 69–86.

Liebowitz, M. R. (1987). *Social phobia. Modern problems in pharmacopsychiatry* (Vol. 22, pp. 141–173). Basel, Switzerland: Published by S. Karger AG.

McManus, F., Sacadura, C., & Clark, D. M. (2008). Why social anxiety persists: An experimental investigation of the role of safety behaviours as a maintaining factor. *Journal of Behavior Therapy and Experimental Psychiatry, 39*(2), 147–161.

McNally, R. J. (2007). Mechanisms of exposure therapy: How neuroscience can improve psychological treatments for anxiety disorders. *Clinical Psychology Review, 27*(6), 750–759.

Milosevic, I., & Radomsky, A. S. (2008). Safety behaviour does not necessarily interfere with exposure therapy. *Behaviour Research and Therapy, 46*(10), 1111–1118.

Morgan, H., & Raffle, C. (1999). Does reducing safety behaviours improve treatment response in patients with social phobia? *Australian and New Zealand Journal of Psychiatry, 33*, 503–510.

Okajima, I., & Sakano, Y. (2008). Effect of modification of safety behavior on social anxiety symptoms. *Seishin Igaku, 50*(8), 801–808.

Olatunji, B. O., Etzel, E. N., Tomarken, A. J., Ciesielski, B. G., & Deacon, B. (2011). The effects of safety behaviors on health anxiety: An experimental investigation. *Behaviour Research and Therapy, 49*(11), 719–728.

Pinto-Gouveia, J., Cunha, M. I., & do Céu Salvador, M. (2003). Assessment of social phobia by self-report questionnaires: The social interaction and performance anxiety and avoidance scale and the social phobia safety behaviours scale. *Behavioural and Cognitive Psychotherapy, 31*(3), 291–311.

Powers, M. B., Smits, J. A., & Telch, M. J. (2004). Disentangling the effects of safety-behavior utilization and safety-behavior availability during exposure-based treatment: A placebo-controlled trial. *Journal of Consulting and Clinical Psychology, 72*(3), 448–454.

Rachman, S., Craske, M. G., Tallman, K., & Solyom, C. (1986). Does escape behavior strengthen agoraphobic avoidance? A replication. *Behavior Therapy, 17*, 366–384.

Rachman, S. J., & Hodgson, R. J. (1980). *Obsessions and compulsions*. Englewood Cliffs, NJ: Prentice-Hall.

Rachman, S., Radomsky, A. S., & Shafran, R. (2008). Safety behaviour: A reconsideration. *Behaviour Research and Therapy, 46*(2), 163–173.

Rassin, E., Merckelbach, H., Muris, P., & Schmidt, H. (2001). The thought-action fusion scale: Further evidence for its reliability and validity. *Behaviour Research and Therapy, 39*(5), 537–544.

Rachman, S., Shafran, R., Radomsky, A. S., & Zysk, E. (2011). Reducing contamination by exposure plus safety behaviour. *Journal of Behavior Therapy and Experimental Psychiatry, 42*, 397–404.

Salkovskis, P. M. (1991). The importance of behaviour in the maintenance of anxiety and panic: A cognitive account. *Behavioural Psychotherapy, 19*(01), 6–19.

Salkovskis, P. M. (1996). *The cognitive approach to anxiety: Threat beliefs, safety-seeking behavior, and the special case of health anxiety and obsessions. Frontiers of cognitive therapy* (pp. 48–74). Guilford Press: New York.

Salkovskis, P. M., Clark, D. M., Hackmann, A., Wells, A., & Gelder, M. G. (1999). An experimental investigation of the role of safety-seeking behaviours in the maintenance of panic disorder with agoraphobia. *Behaviour Research and Therapy, 37*(6), 559–574.

Salkovskis, P. M., Hackmann, A., Wells, A., Gelder, M. G., & Clark, D. M. (2006). Belief disconfirmation versus habituation approaches to situational exposure in panic disorder with agoraphobia: A pilot study. *Behaviour Research and Therapy, 45*, 877–885.

Sloan, T., & Telch, M. J. (2002). The effects of safety-seeking behavior and guided threat reappraisal on fear reduction during exposure: An experimental investigation. *Behaviour Research and Therapy, 40*(3), 235–251.

Sy, J. T., Dixon, L. J., Lickel, J. J., Nelson, E. A., & Deacon, B. J. (2011). Failure to replicate the deleterious effects of safety behaviors in exposure therapy. *Behaviour Research and Therapy, 49*, 305–314.

Tang, N. K. Y., Salkovskis, P. M., Poplavskaya, E., Wright, K. J., Hanna, M., & Hester, J. (2007). Increased use of safety-seeking behaviors in chronic back pain patients with high health anxiety. *Behaviour Research and Therapy, 45*(12), 2821–2835.

Taylor, C. T., & Alden, L. E. (2011). To see ourselves as others see us: An experimental integration of the intra and interpersonal consequences of self-protection in social anxiety disorder. *Journal of Abnormal Psychology, 120*(1), 129–141.

Taylor, C. T., & Alden, L. E. (2010). Safety behaviors and judgmental biases in social anxiety disorder. *Behaviour Research and Therapy, 48*, 226–237.

Telch, M. J., Brouillard, M., Telch, C. F., Agras, W. S., & Taylor, C. B. (1989). Role of cognitive appraisal in panic-related avoidance. *Behaviour Research and Therapy, 27*(4), 373–383.

Telch, M. J., Lucas, R. A., Smits, J. A., Powers, M. B., Heimberg, R., & Hart, T. (2004). Appraisal of social concerns: A cognitive assessment instrument for social phobia. *Depression and Anxiety, 19*(4), 217–224.

Telch, M. J., & Plasencia, L. (2010) When are safety behaviors contraindicated in the treatment of anxiety disorders? A test of the threat disconfirmation model. Talk presented at the world congress of behavioral and cognitive therapies, Boston, MA, June 4th 2010.

Telch, M. J., Valentiner, D. P., Ilai, D., Petruzzi, D., & Hehmsoth, M. (2000). The facilitative effects of heart-rate feedback in the emotional processing of claustrophobic fear. *Behaviour Research and Therapy, 38*(4), 373–387.

Turner, S. M., Beidel, D. C., Dancu, C. V., & Stanley, M. A. (1989). An empirically derived inventory to measure social fears and anxiety: The social phobia and anxiety inventory. *Psychological Assessment: A Journal of Consulting and Clinical Psychology, 1*(1), 35–40.

Van den Hout, M. A., Engelhard, I. M., Toffolo, M. B. J., & van Uijen, S. L. (2011). Exposure plus response prevention versus exposure plus safety behaviours in reducing feelings of contamination, fear, danger, and disgust. An extended replication of Rachman, Shafran, Radomsky, & Zysk (2011). *Journal of Behavior Therapy and Experimental Psychiatry, 42*, 364–370.

Wells, A. (1990). Panic disorder in association with relaxation induced anxiety: An attentional training approach to treatment. *Behavior Therapy, 21*(3), 273–280.

Wells, A. (2005). The metacognitive model of GAD: Assessment of meta-worry and relationship with DSM-IV generalized anxiety disorder. *Cognitive Therapy and Research, 29*(1), 107–121.

Wells, A., Clark, D. M., Salkovskis, P., Ludgate, J., Hackmann, A., & Gelder, M. (1995). Social phobia: The role of in-situation safety behaviors in maintaining anxiety and negative beliefs. *Behavior Therapy, 26*(1), 153–161.

Woods, C. M., Tolin, D. F., & Abramowitz, J. S. (2004). Dimensionality of the obsessive beliefs questionnaire (OBQ). *Journal of Psychopathology and Behavioral Assessment, 26*(2), 113–125.

Chapter 19
Exposure Therapy in OCD: Is There a Need for Adding Cognitive Elements?

Susan Daflos and Maureen L. Whittal

Susan Daflos is a doctoral student at the University of Nevada, Reno. She has been conducting behavioral therapies including CBT, DBT, ACT, and ERP with adults for 5 years. She has been involved in randomized controlled trials of CT, DBT, and ACT for 7 years. Her research interests focus on the relationship between anxiety, emotion regulation, and self-injury.

S. Daflos (✉)
University of Nevada, Reno,
Reno, NV, USA
e-mail: sdaflos@unr.edu

M.L. Whittal
Department of Psychiatry, University of British Columbia,
Vancouver, Canada

P. Neudeck and H.-U. Wittchen (eds.), *Exposure Therapy: Rethinking the Model – Refining the Method*, DOI 10.1007/978-1-4614-3342-2_19,

Dr. Maureen L. Whittal received her Ph.D in Clinical Psychology in 1995 from West Virginia University. She is currently Clinical Associate Professor in the Psychiatry Department at the University of British Columbia. For the past 15 years, her research has focused on developing and testing novel treatments for obsessive–compulsive disorder.

19.1 Introduction

Obsessive–compulsive disorder (OCD) has been the subject of a flurry of research over the past several decades, leading to a shift in view of the disorder from highly treatment resistant to responsive to a number of empirically supported psychotherapies (Abramowitz, 1997; Abramowitz, Franklin, & Foa, 2002). Exposure-based therapy, in particular, exposure and response prevention (ERP), is the most widely studied treatment for OCD and is considered the gold standard. However, significant refusal, dropout, and nonresponse rates, as well as inadequate success with specific OCD subtypes such as hoarding and obsessional rumination, have led to a shift toward cognitively based models and treatments of OCD. Many of these models still include significant behavioral components such as exposure, although the exposure exercises are presented as behavioral experiments conducted to aid in the examination of cognitions. This overlap has caused debate about whether the addition of cognitive elements to exposure therapy has resulted in more acceptable and effective treatment, or if such elements are unnecessary, potentially weakening the potency of effective exposure therapies (Kozak, 1999). In this chapter, we review the theoretical models of OCD that support the use of exposure, as well as models that suggest that the addition of cognitive elements may be of benefit. We also review research that supports the efficacy of ERP while highlighting some problem areas that have emerged within this research. Finally, research examining the efficacy of adding cognitive elements to ERP will be discussed, concluding with suggestions for specific applications where exposure alone or with added cognitive elements may be more effective.

OCD is characterized by the presence of obsessions and/or compulsions. Obsessions are intrusive and persistent thoughts, images, or urges that are senseless and spontaneous, resulting in feelings of marked distress and anxiety. The content of obsessions varies widely, although common obsessions may include religious/blasphemous or sexual intrusions, impulses to harm one's self or others, fears of being harmed or contaminated by dirt or germs, and persistent thoughts of doubt. It is important to note that obsessions are not worries about real-life problems, regardless of how excessive such worries may be. Alternately, compulsions involve repetitive behavioral or mental rituals that are conducted either to decrease feelings of distress and anxiety, or to prevent the occurrence of a feared event. These rituals are performed either according to rigid rules or in response to obsessions. Most compulsions are overt (e.g., physical checking when leaving the house), others are also covert (e.g., being away from the house and "rerunning the film" of leaving the house). Like obsessions, there are countless numbers of compulsions, the most common of which range from mental rituals to counting, touching and tapping rituals, excessive checking, cleaning, or washing of the self and/or inanimate objects, ordering and arranging, and hoarding behaviors. Individuals often present with multiple obsessional themes (Rasmussen & Tsuang, 1986) and compulsions are often combined in idiosyncratic ways, such as washing one's hands a certain number of times. These obsessive fears and rituals are significantly distressing, often resulting in interference in a variety of domains of daily functioning, such as work and interpersonal relationships.

19.2 Behavioral Models of OCD

For many years, OCD was believed to be nonresponsive to treatment. The application of psychoanalytic theories of the disorder yielded disappointing results, and it was believed that sufferers would have no respite from their haunting thoughts and the rituals they were compelled to perform (Esman, 1989; Gabbard, 1994). This view began to change with the development of Mowrer's (1960) two-stage theory of the acquisition and maintenance of fear and avoidance behaviors. According to Mowrer, fear is acquired when a previously neutral stimulus (e.g., a grocery cart) is paired with another naturally fear-evoking stimulus (e.g., the idea that the grocery cart is coated with deadly germs), resulting in the previously neutral stimulus (the grocery cart) evoking obsessional fear. This newly acquired fear is then maintained when the anxiety or discomfort is reduced through the use of an avoidance behavior (e.g., using hand sanitizer and washing one's hands for 10 minutes after touching the grocery cart). Operant conditioning is achieved through the negative reinforcement of the avoidance behavior through the immediate reduction in anxiety, resulting in habitual avoidance.

Dollard and Miller (1950) expanded on this two-stage theory by explaining the development of compulsive rituals. Due either to their form (e.g., intrusive images of stabbing one's spouse) or omnipresent nature (e.g., light switches), many stimuli are simply unavoidable. Since the source of anxiety cannot itself be avoided, compulsive rituals (e.g., repeating prayers or turning the light switch on and off a certain number of times) may be developed as active avoidance strategies, and maintained by their ability to reduce feared fear caused by obsessions. Although anxiety is reduced when a ritual or compulsion is completed, this reduction is only temporary, and does not permit the natural extinction of anxiety to occur. Since the fear response is not permitted to gradually decrease and naturally come to an end, a fear response continues to be triggered every time the obsession occurs, perpetuating the obsessional anxiety.

Research on the applicability of the two-stage model to OCD has been mixed (Clark, 2004a). Although there has been little empirical support that anxiety evoked by obsessions is created through the processes of classical conditioning, there is strong support that compulsive rituals maintain obsessional fear through negative reinforcement (operant conditioning). As a result of such findings, Meyer (1966) hypothesized that if individuals with OCD confront their obsessional fears without engaging in compulsive rituals and behaviors, the processes maintaining these fears should be weakened and possibly eliminated. By engaging in situations or with stimuli that would usually be avoided due to obsessional fears, habituation occurs and individuals are able to correct faulty appraisals of the dangerousness of the situation, leading to reductions in both fear and obsessive–compulsive symptoms (Foa & Kozak, 1986). ERP for OCD was created around the use of such procedures.

19.2.1 Efficacy of ERP

In 1966, Meyer published his first report on the effects of ERP applied to an OCD sample. Treatment of the 15 inpatients was largely successful, with 10 patients responding extremely well and the remaining 5 achieving partial symptom reduction. Only 2 of the successfully treated patients had relapsed at follow-up (Meyer, Levy, & Schnurer, 1974). These results triggered a wave of interest in exposure therapy for OCD that has continued for over 30 years. Researchers around the globe in countries such as the United States (Foa, Steketee, & Ozarow, 1985), the United Kingdom (Rachman, Hodgson, & Marks, 1971), Greece (Rabavilas, Boulougouris, & Stefanis, 1976), and Holland (Boersma, den Hengst, Dekker, & Emmelkamp, 1976) have found ERP to be beneficial in the treatment of OCD, and by the end of the 1980s ERP was considered to be the gold standard treatment for those suffering from mild to moderate intrusive thoughts and rituals.

The 1990s ushered in additional controlled trials in an attempt to examine (1) how effective ERP is compared to alternative treatments for OCD, (2) if this effectiveness is maintained across delivery formats, as well as (3) how long these treatment gains are maintained after the completion of therapy. To determine if the success of ERP was due to therapist contact or the passage of time, a number of studies were conducted in which ERP was compared to alternative anxiety interventions. Randomized controlled trials have shown that ERP for OCD provides greater symptom reduction than typical anxiety treatments such as anxiety management training (Lindsay, Crino, & Andrews, 1997) and progressive muscle relaxation

(Fals-Stewart, Marks, & Schafer, 1993). Even more impressive is Foa et al.'s (2005) finding that intensive ERP provides greater reduction in OCD symptoms than clomipramine, a medication that had previously been considered one of the only effective treatments for severe OCD. These treatment gains appear to continue even when ERP is administered in group settings, where ERP has been found to perform slightly better than cognitively focused therapy (McLean et al., 2001). Furthermore, reduction of OCD symptoms appears to be maintained over long periods of time, with one study finding that almost 80% of participants were rated as improved or much improved when assessed 1–6 years posttreatment, and over half the sample rated as much improved to symptom free (O'Sullivan & Marks, 1991). As well, a more recent study by Whittal, Robichaud, Thordarson, and McLean (2008) found that only 10% of participants who completed either group or individual ERP relapsed 2 years posttreatment.

O'Sullivan and Marks' findings highlight the efficaciousness of ERP in achieving significant symptom reduction in a majority of participants who engage in treatment. For example, Foa et al. (1985), who reviewed outcome studies of ERP for OCD that were completed in the 1980s, found that only 10% of participants across studies reported no benefit from ERP, while over half reported being symptom free or very much improved. Over a decade later, Foa and Kozak (1995) concluded that 83% of individuals across ERP outcome studies achieved significant symptom reduction, with ERP achieving a mean symptomatic reduction rate of over 50% (Abramowitz et al., 2002). The finding that ERP is successful in reducing OCD symptoms also translates to large treatment effect sizes, which are in the 0.99–1.53 range according to a number of meta-analyses of treatment outcome studies (Abramowitz, 1996; Abramowitz et al., 2002; Eddy, Dutra, Bradley, & Westen, 2004; Kobak, Greist, Jefferson, Katzelnick, & Henk, 1998). It is important to note that individuals who complete ERP do not only achieve *statistically* significant symptom reduction: approximately 40–50% of treated patients either meet strict criteria for *clinically* significant change or are symptom free posttreatment (Abramowitz, 1998; Eddy et al., 2004; Foa et al., 1985), with over 76% of individuals maintaining these treatment gains over a 2-year follow-up period (Foa & Kozak, 1996). This abundant empirical evidence suggests that ERP is as effective, if not superior, to other psychotherapies and pharmacotherapy, producing significant reduction of obsessive–compulsive symptoms. These results are found with the majority of individuals who complete treatment, regardless of whether therapy is conducted individually or in a group, with lasting results.

19.2.2 Limitations of ERP

There is undeniable evidence supporting ERP as an effective psychotherapy for OCD, so why introduce cognitive elements into exposure therapy for OCD? To begin with, there are theoretical issues with behavioral accounts of OCD. Although behavioral models successfully explain the maintenance of obsessions through negative reinforcement that occurs when anxiety-reducing compulsions are performed, there is no way to explain the development of obsessions. There are also significant limitations in the application of ERP that have become apparent over the years.

19.2.2.1 Refusal and Dropout Rates

Evidence suggests that individuals who *complete* ERP benefit from treatment; however, a problem for ERP has been the number of patients who prematurely terminate from treatment, or refuse to initiate treatment. ERP requires individuals to gradually expose themselves to their most feared situations, thoughts, and objects, a requirement that results in a dramatic increase in distress that may continue for weeks before clients notice any long-lasting symptom reduction. This may be one reason why approximately 5–25% of participants randomized into ERP treatment conditions in randomized controlled trials refused to proceed with treatment (Emmelkamp & Foa, 1983; Foa et al., 2005; Kozak, Liebowitz, & Foa, 2000; Whittal, Thordarson, & McLean, 2005). Unwillingness to engage in ERP becomes an even further problem when adding the 19–28% of individuals who drop out after beginning treatment to the already high refusal rates (Foa et al., 2005; Kozak et al., 2000; Van Oppen et al., 1995). A meta-analysis conducted by Kobak et al. (1998) reported an average dropout rate of 17% for ERP, although other factors may contribute to dropout, such as those with strongly held or overvalued ideation (Foa, Abramowitz, Franklin, & Kozak, 1999). Together, it would appear that a quarter to a third of individuals with OCD will not engage in ERP, making refusal and dropout a particularly concerning matter.

19.2.2.2 Nonresponse Rates and Persistence of Residual Symptoms

Although those who complete ERP are likely to show some symptom improvement, 10% will show no benefit from treatment (Foa et al., 1985). In fact, Steketee, Henninger, and Pollard (2000) found 25–33% of individuals will either fail to benefit from therapy or not maintain treatment gains at follow-up, despite completing some very intensive ERP programs. Of those who do benefit from exposure therapy for OCD, Abramowitz (1998) found that the majority of patients continue experiencing some symptoms, with average ERP treatment completers still reporting more obsessive–compulsive symptoms than nonclinical individuals. At the completion of treatment Eddy et al. (2004) found a mean Yale Brown obsessive compulsive scale (YBOCS) score of 12.48 (3.11), while Abramowitz and colleagues (2002) found an average YBOCS decline of only 43.5% following ERP Salkovskis and Kirk (1997) have also found that there are significant levels of social and occupational impairment that remain posttreatment, persisting through long-term follow-up. These findings provide some explanation as to why the number of individuals achieving clinically significant change criteria is nearly half of those who achieve statistically significant change (Van Oppen et al., 1995). It appears that a significant amount of individuals who manage to complete ERP will either be unresponsive to treatment, or continue to have difficulties with obsessive–compulsive symptoms and quality of life issues for years posttreatment.

19.2.2.3 Relapse and Recurrence Rates

Although gains made after completed ERP appear to be generally maintained, Foa and Kozak's (1996) review found that 7% of treatment responders experienced symptom relapse within 2 years posttreatment. Although this rate is relatively low (Emmelkamp, Kloek, & Blaauw, 1992; Hiss, Foa, & Kozak, 1994), psychological services sought posttreatment may provide a more thorough image of the difficulties individuals continue to face after completion of ERP. Many patients continue seeking services after treatment has been completed, with one-third receiving treatment for depression and 10–18% seeking additional exposure therapy (Stanley & Turner, 1995). At 2-year follow-up, Whittal et al. (2008) reported that 40% of treatment completers sought additional treatment for OCD, while 58% continued psychopharmacological treatment. All of the empirical evidence provided has examined the results of standardized clinical trials in which therapists are highly trained in ERP protocols and adherence is closely monitored. Therefore, it is possible that in clinical settings where exposure therapies may not be performed to the same degree there may be higher rates than those reported here.

19.2.2.4 Inadequate Treatment of OCD Subtypes

There have been a number of reports from treatment outcome studies that suggest that ERP may be better suited to treat particular OCD symptom presentations. Although there is sufficient support that patients presenting with washing and checking compulsions will benefit from ERP (Ball, Baer, & Otto, 1996), those with primarily obsessional symptoms such as obsessional rumination, and intrusive unwanted violent, sexual, or blasphemous thoughts and images may not be so fortunate. For many years behavioral interventions for those suffering primarily from obsessions (including thought stopping and habituation training) were largely ineffective, leading to the belief that primarily obsessional OCD was intractable (Rachman, 1983, 2003; van Oppen & Emmelkamp, 2000; Salkovskis & Westbrook, 1989). There has also been some evidence that only using ERP for treatment of hoarding, symmetry/ordering rituals, or obsessional slowness is inadequate (Clark, 2005; Frost & Steketee, 1998; Rachman, 1985). Other subtypes (e.g., those suffering from religious or repugnant obsessions) have symptoms that are under-represented in clinical trials, so it is uncertain how many subtypes this shortcoming applies to.

19.3 Cognitive Models of OCD

Cognitive theories of OCD were developed from the observation that individuals with OCD tend to support dysfunctional expectations and beliefs that seem to be important factors in the creation and maintenance of their psychopathology (Clark, 2004b; Rachman, 1997). In cognitively based models of OCD, it is theorized that individuals have a constant barrage of naturally occurring nonvolitional thoughts and doubts that typically escape our attention but occasionally penetrate into our conscious awareness (Clark & Rhyno, 2005). Individuals with OCD catastrophically evaluate these thoughts as being personally significant and threatening, and believe that if they are not able to control such thoughts they will bring harm to themselves or others. Often times the following cyclical pattern will occur: an unusual or disturbing thought is noticed and deemed important. Due to its perceived importance, the thought is ruminated upon, strengthening its importance. Questions arise as to why the thought occurred in the first place, with the conclusion that it must have meaning if it occurred. The meaning often entails personal significance (e.g., "I had a thought of swearing in church. That means I'm evil and will go to hell") or overestimatation of probability that the content of the thoughts will occur (e.g., "I had the image of my house burning down. I wouldn't have that thought if my house wasn't in danger"). Fear and anxiety provoked by the thought increase reasoning that the thought is important (e.g., "I feel afraid, so my thought is telling me I'm in danger") and must be attended to. This leads to an increase in identifying anxiety-invoking "important" thoughts, and the cycle begins again. Since such thoughts are interpreted as being extremely threatening, they must be avoided or neutralized via a mental or behavioral compulsive ritual from the patients' point of view in order to either escape anxiety or prevent an imagined feared outcome from occurring (Clark, 2004b; Rachman, 1997, 1998; Salkovskis, 1985, 1999). Cognitive models appear to support the creation of obsessions, and they are also able to account for the presence of obsessions without overt compulsions, which were difficult to describe using a strictly behavioral model.

19.4 Similarities Between Behaviorally and Cognitively Based Treatments

Treatment based on a cognitive model of OCD involves identifying and modifying the erroneous beliefs and appraisals that are responsible for the recurrence of the obsessions (for a detailed description of CBT treatment protocols, see Clark, 2004b; Rachman, 2003; Salkovskis, 1999). As with ERP, it is also important in cognitively based therapies that individuals do not engage in avoidant or neutralizing behaviors or rituals, as these acts lend credence to the belief that thoughts are important and threatening. Instead, faulty beliefs, probabilities, and appraisals can be accurately modified, leading to a reduction in anxiety produced by the thoughts and, ultimately, symptom reduction. In this way, cognitive interventions aim to be educational, relying on clients to gather information that will normalize their obsessions and support the cognitive learning they are engaging in through strategies such as Socratic questioning and thought diaries. However, even such cognitively focused interventions often involve significant behavioral components in the form of behavioral experimentation. Unlike ERP which focuses on the habituation of anxiety, behavioral experiments also involve exposure to feared stimuli, but this exposure is done as a test they can use to determine the accuracy of their faulty appraisals. This stance is similar to Meyer's (1966) initial belief that exposure would lead to the correction of faulty appraisals in individuals with OCD. In fact, as Abramowitz, Taylor, and McKay (2005) have pointed out, cognitive treatments contain behavioral elements and vice versa, behavioral treatments contain cognitive elements with both treatments involving exposure and corrective learning. What distinguishes cognitively framed exposure from exposure conducted in ERP is that the aim of conducting behavioral experiments is to test the veracity of cognitions propositionally while simultaneously engaging in experiential learning, while the goal of exposure is to extinguish the fear response without explicitly testing cognition (Teasdale & Barnard, 1993). By targeting cognitions more directly, cognitive theorists hope to eliminate some of the problems with treatment response rates, relapse, and residual symptoms that have plagued ERP. It is possible that framing behavioral experiments with a rationale of testing one's own cognitions rather than extinguishing fear responses may also address treatment refusal and dropout rates that have also troubled ERP.

19.4.1 Evidence Examining the Role of Cognitive Elements in Exposure

The Cognitive model of OCD suggests that faulty cognitions may be maintaining factors that remain unaddressed with ERP, and that targeting these cognitions directly in treatment may lead to increased clinically significant symptom reduction that is maintained over longer periods of time with lower refusal and dropout rates. A recent study examining metacognitive change in exposure therapy found that even though cognitive change is not a goal of ERP, changes in metacognitions (beliefs about the danger and meaning of thoughts) occur in exposure therapy, and these change are associated with better clinical outcomes (Solem, Håland, Vogel, Hansen, & Wells, 2009). Similarly, Mineka and Zinbarg (2006) and Bouton (2004) have found that in exposure trials, extinction occurs after a violation of expectancies. Framing exposure trials as behavioral experiments of faulty appraisals may increase the effects of exposure by maximizing the chances that such violations will occur (Moscovitch, Antony, & Swinson, 2009).

Although cognitive theorists have hypothesized that explicitly targeting cognitions while also engaging in behavioral experimentation should result in treatment effects greater than those achieved through ERP, results have so far been mixed.

Freeston et al. (1997) compared cognitive behavioral therapy (CBT) to ERP and reported that more participants who received CBT reached recovered status than those who received ERP. However, the difference in pretreatment YBOCS scores between the CBT and ERP conditions was greater than is typically seen in studies comparing CBT and ERP, so these results should be cautiously interpreted. A number of other studies comparing individually delivered CBT to ERP have found the two treatments to be comparable, although adding cognitive interventions does not appear to increase the effectiveness of treatment (Cottraux et al., 2001; Cottraux, Bouvard, & Maud, 2005; Whittal et al., 2005). Results comparing CBT and ERP delivered in group format are less clear, with results indicating that ERP resulted in greater symptom reduction than CBT, but that CBT appeared to be better tolerated and had a lower dropout rate than ERP (McLean et al., 2001). Thus far there does not seem to be empirical support for the hypothesis that the addition of cognitive interventions to behavioral protocols will increase the effectiveness of treatment.

Although protocols containing multiple cognitive components have not been shown to provide statistically greater symptom reduction than traditional ERP, it is worth examining whether this may be achieved simply by presenting exposure with a cognitive rationale. A recent meta-analysis conducted by McMillan and Lee (2010) reviewed studies across a number of anxiety disorders examining the effects of behavioral experiments versus exposure alone, and found support that behavioral experiments result in greater reduction in subjective ratings of anxiety, maladaptive cognitions, and specific anxiety symptoms than exposure alone. These findings suggest that the simple act of setting up exposure as a cognitive test may result in greater treatment effects than exposure that is not set up in this way. Fisher and Wells (2005) examined this effect in application to OCD using a single-case experimental design. Results indicated that presenting exposure as a behavioral experiment resulted in decreased anxiety, believability of cognitions, and urges to neutralize obsessions in comparison to the traditional exposure condition. These results hold promise; exposure therapies may be more effective by slightly altering their presentation in such a way as to support cognitive reappraisal.

Since ERP and CBT protocols appear to achieve similar treatment results, it is worth examining whether cognitive interventions enhance engagement in treatment. Five studies examined the effects of ERP as comparison to CBT or ERP plus cognitive restructuring (Cottraux et al., 2001; McLean et al., 2001; Van Oppen et al., 1995; Vogel, Stiles, & Götestam, 2004; Whittal et al., 2005). McLean et al., Whittal et al., and Vogel et al. all suggested that CBT resulted in fewer treatment dropouts than ERP, while Cottraux et al. and Van Oppen et al. showed no difference between these groups. Abramowitz et al. (2005) conducted an aggregate analysis of the dropout proportions of these four studies and found fewer dropouts in the CBT conditions. Therefore, there is some evidence that the addition of cognitive restructuring may result in lower rates of treatment dropout than ERP alone.

Recent studies indicate that cognitive interventions may be useful in the treatment of some OCD subtypes. Whittal, Woody, McLean, Rachman, and Robichaud (2010) conducted a randomized controlled trial comparing a cognitive therapy (CT) protocol to a stress management condition for the treatment of obsessionals with few to no overt compulsions. Both CT and the stress-management condition provided significant symptom reduction as compared to a waitlist control condition. While CT was not compared to ERP in this study, the fact that clinically significant symptom reduction was achieved while ERP has been unable to produce even statistically significant reduction in obsessional symptoms in this population is encouraging. Similarly, Wilhelm, Steketee, and Yovel (2004) found that patients with washing compulsions noticed symptom improvements when treated with either CT or behavioral therapy. However, in patients without washing compulsions, CT resulted in greater symptom reduction. Thus, it appears that that CT may provide benefit to OCD subtypes that have previously received little relief from strictly behavioral interventions.

19.5 Summary and Conclusions

To date, it appears that cognitive interventions are at least equivalent to ERP in symptom reduction when conducted as individual therapy, although ERP is slightly more effective when presented in a group format. However, there are still too few studies comparing ERP with cognitively focused interventions to allow for definitive conclusions about the utility of adding cognitive elements to behavioral interventions (Clark, 2005). Although there are no studies indicating that CT addresses issues of treatment refusal and nonresponse, it does appear to reduce dropout once treatment is initially engaged (Abramowitz et al., 2005). As well, although still in the early stages of research, there is evidence supporting the efficacy of CT as a treatment for certain OCD subtypes, such as individuals who do not engage in washing compulsions or who suffer from a preponderance of obsessional thoughts with limited compulsions.

Since CBT has largely been found to perform as effectively as ERP across a number of treatment factors, it may be less useful to discuss which treatment is superior and more effective to consider which intervention may be better suited to particular symptom presentations or treatment settings. Cognitive interventions may be a better choice of treatment for individuals suffering primarily from obsessional thinking since ERP has had limited success in the absence of overt compulsions. As well, Abramowitz and his colleagues (Abramowitz, Khandker, Nelson, Deacon, & Rygwall, 2006, 2007, Abramowitz, Nelson, Rygwall, & Khandker, 2007) have found that obsessive beliefs in postpartum mothers mediate the development of obsessive–compulsive symptoms, suggesting that cognitive interventions may be preferred interventions for women suffering from postpartum OCD. Similarly to other anxiety disorders, Geffken, Storch, Gelfand, Adkins, and Goodman (2004) have also suggested that pregnant OCD patients, as well as patients with certain medical issues such as cardiac problems, should attempt cognitive interventions before ERP in order to avoid possible health complications due to increased distress.

ERP may be a preferred treatment to perform in group settings, as it may be more difficult to target dysfunctional beliefs in group settings. It is possible that ERP may be more effective for individuals with more severe presentations or who have limited insight into their symptoms as they may be less able to identify faulty beliefs. However, this is an area that still requires further research. Similarly, ERP will likely be a preferred treatment option for individuals who are unable to engage in appraising their beliefs due to cognitive impairments or developmental delays.

19.6 Future Directions

Treatment outcomes appear to have reached a plateau over the past 20 years, with new interventions for OCD achieving similar results to previous therapies. Although it is definitely worthwhile to focus research efforts on mediational studies that may help us increase the efficacy of exposure and cognitive therapies, it may be time to focus more attention on matching treatments to specific OCD populations rather than assuming that one treatment should be effective for everyone. This can include increased research on the effects of ERP and CBT on specific OCD subtypes, as well as further examination of differential treatment effects according to severity or comorbidity.

Researchers must also begin to consider dissemination issues when determining treatment effectiveness. All of the studies that have been discussed reported on findings of randomized controlled trials conducted in university settings. Sessions were closely monitored to ensure clinician compliance to treatment manuals, and clinicians received intensive training and supervision, providing the "gold standard" of cognitive and exposure therapies. This is not what happens in real-world clinics where therapists often receive minimal training and supervision while simultaneously managing funding restrictions that limit the duration and cost of treatment, resulting in an inability to provide intensive treatment (Gunter & Whittal, 2010). It is for such reasons that dissemination must be considered when studying treatment efficacy.

References

Abramowitz, J. S. (1996). Variants of exposure and response prevention in the treatment of obsessive-compulsive disorder: A meta-analysis. *Behavior Therapy, 27*(4), 583–600.

Abramowitz, J. S. (1997). Effectiveness of psychological and pharmacological treatments for obsessive-compulsive disorder: A quantitative Review. *Journal of Consulting and Clinical Psychology, 65*(1), 44–52.

Abramowitz, J. S. (1998). Does cognitive-behavioral therapy cure obsessive-compulsive disorder? A meta-analytic evaluation of clinical significance. *Behavior Therapy, 29*(2), 339–355.

Abramowitz, J. S., Franklin, M. E., & Foa, E. B. (2002). Empirical status of cognitive-behavioral therapy for obsessive-compulsive disorder: A meta-analytic review. *Romanian Journal of Cognitive & Behavioral Psychotherapies, 2*(2), 89–104.

Abramowitz, J. S., Khandker, M., Nelson, C. A., Deacon, B. J., & Rygwall, R. (2006). The role of cognitive factors in the pathogenesis of obsessive-compulsive symptoms: A prospective study. *Behaviour Research and Therapy, 44*(9), 1361–1374.

Abramowitz, J. S., Nelson, C. A., Rygwall, R., & Khandker, M. (2007). The cognitive mediation of obsessive-compulsive symptoms: A longitudinal study. *Journal of Anxiety Disorders, 21*(1), 91–104.
Abramowitz, J. S., Taylor, S., & McKay, D. (2005). Potentials and limitations of cognitive treatments for obsessive-compulsive disorder. *Cognitive Behaviour Therapy, 34*(3), 140–147.
Ball, S. G., Baer, L., & Otto, M. W. (1996). Symptom subtypes of obsessive-compulsive disorder in behavioral treatment studies: A quantitative review. *Behaviour Research and Therapy, 34*(1), 47–51.
Boersma, K., den Hengst, S., Dekker, J., & Emmelkamp, P. (1976). Exposure and response prevention in the natural environment: A comparison with obsessive-compulsive patients. *Behaviour Research and Therapy, 14*(1), 19–24.
Bouton, M. E. (2004). Context and behavioral processes in extinction. *Learning & Memory, 11*(5), 485–494.
Clark, D. A. (2004a). Cognitive-behavioral theory and treatment of obsessive-compulsive disorder: Past contributions and current developments. In R. L. Leahy (Ed.), *Contemporary cognitive therapy: Theory, research, and practice* (pp. 161–183). New York: Guilford Press.
Clark, D. A. (2004b). *Cognitive-behavioral therapy for OCD*. New York: Guilford Press.
Clark, D. A. (2005). Focus on 'cognition' in cognitive behavior therapy for OCD: Is it really necessary? *Cognitive Behaviour Therapy, 34*(3), 131–139.
Clark, D. A., & Rhyno, S. (2005). Unwanted intrusive thoughts in nonclinical individuals: Implications for clinical disorders. In D. A. Clark (Ed.), *Intrusive thoughts in clinical disorders: Theory, research, and treatment* (pp. 1–29). New York: Guilford Press.
Cottraux, J., Bouvard, M. A., & Maud, M. (2005). Combining pharmacotherapy with cognitive-behavioral interventions for obsessive-compulsive disorder. *Cognitive Behaviour Therapy, 34*(3), 185–192.
Cottraux, J., Note, I., Yao, S. N., Lafont, S., Note, B., Mollard, E., et al. (2001). A randomized controlled trial of cognitive therapy versus intensive behavior therapy in obsessive compulsive disorder. *Psychotherapy and Psychosomatics, 70*(6), 288–297.
Dollard, J., & Miller, N. E. (1950). *Personality and psychotherapy: An analysis in terms of learning, thinking, and culture*. New York: McGraw-Hill.
Eddy, K., Dutra, L., Bradley, R., & Westen, D. (2004). A multidimensional meta-analysis of psychotherapy and pharmacotherapy for obsessive-compulsive disorder. *Clinical Psychology Review, 24*(8).
Emmelkamp, P., & Foa, E. B. (1983). Failures are a challenge. In E. B. Foa & P. Emmelkamp (Eds.), *Failures in behavior therapy*. New York: Wiley.
Emmelkamp, P., Kloek, J., & Blaauw, E. (1992). Obsessive-compulsive disorders. In P. H. Wilson (Ed.), *Principles and practice of relapse prevention* (pp. 213–234). New York: Guilford Press.
Esman, A. (1989). Psychoanalysis in general psychiatry. Obsessive-compulsive disorder as a paradigm. *Journal of the American Psychoanalytic Association, 37*, 319–336.
Fals-Stewart, W., Marks, A. P., & Schafer, J. (1993). A comparison of behavioral group therapy and individual behavior therapy in treating obsessive-compulsive disorder. *Journal of Nervous and Mental Disease, 181*(3), 189–193.
Fisher, P. L., & Wells, A. (2005). Experimental modification of beliefs in obsessive-compulsive disorder: A test of the metacognitive model. *Behaviour Research and Therapy, 43*(6), 821–829.
Foa, E. B., Abramowitz, J. S., Franklin, M. E., & Kozak, M. J. (1999). Feared consequences, fixity of belief, and treatment outcome in patients with obsessive-compulsive disorder. *Behavior Therapy, 30*(4), 717–724.
Foa, E. B., & Kozak, M. J. (1986). Emotional processing of fear: Exposure to corrective information. *Psychological Bulletin, 99*(1), 20–35.
Foa, E. B., & Kozak, M. J. (1995). DSM-IV field trial: Obsessive-compulsive disorder. *The American Journal of Psychiatry, 152*(1), 90–96.
Foa, E. B., & Kozak, M. J. (1996). Psychological treatment for obsessive-compulsive disorder. In M. R. Mavissakalian & R. F. Prien (Eds.), *Long-term treatments of anxiety disorders* (pp. 285–309). Washington, DC: American Psychiatric Association.

Foa, E. B., Liebowitz, M. R., Kozak, M. J., Davies, S., Campeas, R., Franklin, M. E., et al. (2005). Randomized, placebo-controlled trial of exposure and ritual prevention, clomipramine, and their combination in the treatment of obsessive-compulsive disorder. *The American Journal of Psychiatry, 162*(1), 151–161.

Foa, E. B., Steketee, G., & Ozarow, B. (1985). Behavior therapy with obsessive-compulsives: From theory to treatment. In M. Mavissakalian, S. Turner, & L. Michelson (Eds.), *Obsessive-compulsive disorder: Psychological and pharmacological treatment* (pp. 49–129). New York: Plenum Press.

Freeston, M. H., Ladouceur, R., Gagnon, F., Thibodeau, N., Rhéaume, J., & Letarte, H. (1997). Cognitive—behavioral treatment of obsessive thoughts: A controlled study. *Journal of Consulting and Clinical Psychology, 65*(3), 405–413.

Frost, R. O., & Steketee, G. (1998). Hoarding: Clinical aspects and treatment strategies. In M. A. Jenike, L. Baer, & W. E. Minichiello (Eds.), *Obsessive-compulsive disorder: Practical management* (3rd ed., pp. 533–554). St. Louis, MO: Mosby Yearbook Medical.

Gabbard, G. O. (1994). *Psychodynamic psychiatry in clinical practice: The DSM-IV edition.* Washington, DC: American Psychiatric Press.

Geffken, G. R., Storch, E. A., Gelfand, K. M., Adkins, J. W., & Goodman, W. K. (2004). Cognitive-behavioral therapy for obsessive-compulsive disorder: Review of treatment techniques. *Journal of Psychosocial Nursing and Mental Health Services, 42*(12), 44–51.

Gunter, R. W., & Whittal, M. L. (2010). Dissemination of cognitive-behavioral treatments for anxiety disorders: Overcoming barriers and improving patient access. *Clinical Psychology Review, 30*(2), 194–202.

Hiss, H., Foa, E. B., & Kozak, M. J. (1994). Relapse prevention program for treatment of obsessive-compulsive disorder. *Journal of Consulting and Clinical Psychology, 62*(4), 801–808.

Kobak, K. A., Greist, J. H., Jefferson, J. W., Katzelnick, D. J., & Henk, H. J. (1998). Behavioral versus pharmacological treatments of obsessive compulsive disorder: A meta-analysis. *Psychopharmacology, 136*(3), 205–216.

Kozak, M. J. (1999). Evaluating treatment efficacy for obsessive-compulsive disorder: Caveat practitioner. *Cognitive and Behavioral Practice, 6*(4), 422–426. doi:10.1016/S1077-7229(99)80061-3.

Kozak, M. J., Liebowitz, M. R., & Foa, E. B. (2000). Cognitive behavior therapy and pharmacotherapy for obsessive-compulsive disorder: The NIMH-sponsored collaborative study. In W. K. Goodman, M. V. Rudorfer, & J. D. Maser (Eds.), *Obsessive-compulsive disorder: Contemporary issues in treatment. Personality and clinical psychology series* (pp. 501–530). Mahwah: Lawrence Erlbaum Associates Publishers.

Lindsay, M., Crino, R., & Andrews, G. (1997). Controlled trial of exposure and response prevention in obsessive-compulsive disorder. *British Journal of Psychiatry, 171*, 135–139.

McLean, P. D., Whittal, M. L., Thordarson, D. S., Taylor, S., Söchting, I., Koch, W. J., et al. (2001). Cognitive versus behavior therapy in the group treatment of obsessive-compulsive disorder. *Journal of Consulting and Clinical Psychology, 69*(2), 205–214.

McMillan, D., & Lee, R. (2010). A systematic review of behavioral experiments vs. exposure alone in the treatment of anxiety disorders: A case of exposure while wearing the emperor's new clothes? *Clinical Psychology Review, 30*(5), 467–478.

Meyer, V. (1966). Modification of expectations in cases with obsessional rituals. *Behaviour Research and Therapy, 4*(4), 273–280.

Meyer, V., Levy, R., & Schnurer, A. (1974). The behavioural treatment of obsessive-compulsive disorders. In H. R. Beech (Ed.), *Obsessional states.* Methuen & Co: Oxford England.

Mineka, S., & Zinbarg, R. (2006). A contemporary learning theory perspective on the etiology of anxiety disorders: It's not what you thought it was. *American Psychologist, 61*(1), 10–26.

Moscovitch, D. A., Antony, M. M., & Swinson, R. P. (2009). Exposure-based treatments for anxiety disorders: Theory and process. In M. M. Antony & M. B. Stein (Eds.), *Oxford handbook of anxiety and related disorders. Oxford library of psychology* (pp. 461–475). New York: Oxford University Press.

Mowrer, O. H. (1960). *Learning theory and behavior.* Hoboken: John Wiley & Sons Inc.

O'Sullivan, G., & Marks, I. (1991). Follow-up studies of behavioral treatment of phobic and obsessive compulsive neuroses. *Psychiatric Annals, 21*(6), 368–373.

Rabavilas, A. D., Boulougouris, J. C., & Stefanis, C. (1976). Duration of flooding sessions in the treatment of obsessive-compulsive patients. *Behaviour Research and Therapy, 14*(5), 349–355.

Rachman, S. J. (1983). Obstacles in the successful treatment of obsessions. In E. B. Foa & P. Emmelkamp (Eds.), *Failures in behavior therapy* (pp. 35–57). New York: Wiley.

Rachman, S. J. (1985). An overview of clinical and research issues in obsessional-compulsive disorders. In M. Mavissakalian, S. Turner, & L. Michelson (Eds.), *Obsessive-compulsive disorder: Psychological and pharmacological treatment*. New York: Plenum.

Rachman, S. J. (1997). A cognitive theory of obsessions. *Behaviour Research and Therapy, 35*(9), 793–802.

Rachman, S. J. (1998). A cognitive theory of obsessions. In E. Sanavio (Ed.), *Behavior and cognitive therapy today: Essays in honor of Hans J. Eysenck* (pp. 209–222). Oxford England: Elsevier Science Ltd.

Rachman, S. J. (2003). *The treatment of obsessions*. New York: Oxford University Press.

Rachman, S. J., Hodgson, R., & Marks, I. M. (1971). The treatment of chronic obsessive-compulsive neurosis. *Behaviour Research and Therapy, 9*(3), 237–247.

Rasmussen, S. A., & Tsuang, M. T. (1986). Clinical characteristics and family history in DSM-III obsessive-compulsive disorder. *The American Journal of Psychiatry, 143*(3), 317–322.

Salkovskis, P. M. (1985). Obsessional-compulsive problems: A cognitive-behavioural analysis. *Behaviour Research and Therapy, 23*(5), 571–583.

Salkovskis, P. M. (1999). Understanding and treating obsessive–compulsive disorder. Behaviour research and therapy, cognitive behaviour therapy: Evolution and prospects. *A festschrift in honour of Dr S. Rachman Editor of Behavior Research and Therapy, 37*(Suppl 1), S29–S52.

Salkovskis, P. M., & Kirk, J. (1997). Obsessive-compulsive disorder. In D. M. Clark & C. G. Fairburn (Eds.), *Science and practice of cognitive behaviour therapy. Oxford medical publications* (pp. 179–208). New York: Oxford University Press.

Salkovskis, P. M., & Westbrook, D. (1989). Behaviour therapy and obsessional ruminations: Can failure be turned into success? *Behaviour Research and Therapy, 27*(2), 149–160.

Solem, S., Håland, Å. T., Vogel, P. A., Hansen, B., & Wells, A. (2009). Change in metacognitions predicts outcome in obsessive–compulsive disorder patients undergoing treatment with exposure and response prevention. *Behaviour Research and Therapy, 47*(4), 301–307.

Stanley, M. A., & Turner, S. M. (1995). Current status of pharmacological and behavioral treatment of obsessive-compulsive disorder. *Behavior Therapy, 26*(1), 163–186.

Steketee, G., Henninger, N. J., & Pollard, C. A. (2000). Predicting treatment outcomes for obsessive-compulsive disorder: Effects of comorbidity. In W. K. Goodman, M. V. Rudorfer, & J. D. Maser (Eds.), *Obsessive-compulsive disorder: Contemporary issues in treatment. Personality and clinical psychology series* (pp. 257–274). Mahwah: Lawrence Erlbaum Associates Publishers.

Teasdale, J. D., & Barnard, P. J. (1993). *Affect, cognition, and change: Re-modelling depressive thought. Essays in cognitive psychology; 0959-4779*. Hillsdale, England: Lawrence Erlbaum Associates, Inc.

Van Oppen, P., De Haan, E., Van Balkom, A. J. L. M., Spinhoven, P., Hoogduin, K., & Van Dyck, R. (1995). Cognitive therapy and exposure in vivo in the treatment of obsessive compulsive disorder. *Behaviour Research and Therapy, 33*(4), 379–390.

van Oppen, P., & Emmelkamp, P. (2000). Issues in cognitive treatment of obsessive-compulsive disorder. In W. K. Goodman, M. V. Rudorfer, & J. D. Maser (Eds.), *Obsessive-compulsive disorder: Contemporary issues in treatment. Personality and clinical psychology series* (pp. 117–132). Mahwah: Lawrence Erlbaum Associates Publishers.

Vogel, P. A., Stiles, T. C., & Götestam, K. G. (2004). Adding cognitive therapy elements to exposure therapy for obsessive compulsive disorder: A controlled study. *Behavioural and Cognitive Psychotherapy, 32*(3), 275–290.

Whittal, M. L., Robichaud, M., Thordarson, D. S., & McLean, P. D. (2008). Group and individual treatment of obsessive-compulsive disorder using cognitive therapy and exposure plus response prevention: A 2-year follow-up of two randomized trials. *Journal of Consulting and Clinical Psychology, 76*(6), 1003–1014.

Whittal, M. L., Thordarson, D. S., & McLean, P. D. (2005). Treatment of obsessive-compulsive disorder: Cognitive behavior therapy vs. exposure and response prevention. *Behaviour Research and Therapy, 43*(12), 1559–1576.

Whittal, M. L., Woody, S. R., McLean, P. D., Rachman, S. J., & Robichaud, M. (2010). Treatment of obsessions: A randomized controlled trial. *Behaviour Research and Therapy, 48*(4), 295–303.

Wilhelm, S., Steketee, G., & Yovel, I. (2004). *Multi-site study of predictors of treatment outcome for OCD*. Presented at the annual conference of the obsessive compulsive foundation, Chicago, IL.

Index

P. Neudeck and H.-U. Wittchen (eds.), *Exposure Therapy: Rethinking the Model – Refining the Method*, DOI 10.1007/978-1-4614-3342-2,

MIX
Papier aus verantwortungsvollen Quellen
Paper from responsible sources
FSC® C105338

If you have any concerns about our products,
you can contact us on
ProductSafety@springernature.com

In case Publisher is established outside the EU,
the EU authorized representative is:
Springer Nature Customer Service Center GmbH
Europaplatz 3, 69115 Heidelberg, Germany

Printed by Libri Plureos GmbH
in Hamburg, Germany